Internetworking With TCP/IP

Internetworking With TCP/IP

Vol I:

Principles, Protocols, and Architecture

Third Edition

DOUGLAS E. COMER

Department of Computer Sciences
Purdue University
West Lafayette, IN 47907

PRENTICE HALL
Englewood Cliffs, New Jersey 07632

Library of Congress Cataloging-in-Publication Data

Comer, Douglas
    Internetworking with TCP/IP / Douglas E. Comer. -- 3rd ed.
      p.   cm.
    Includes bibliographical references and index.
    Contents: v. 1. Principles, protocols, and architecture
    ISBN 0-13-216987-8 (v. 1)
    1. TCP/IP (Computer network protocol)   2. Client/server computing.
    3. Internetworking (Telecommunication)   I. Title.
TK5105.585.C66   1995
005.2--dc20   95-1830
                                 CIP

Acquisitions editor: ALAN APT
Production editor: IRWIN ZUCKER
Cover designer: WENDY ALLING JUDY
Buyer: LORI BULWIN
Editorial assistant: SHIRLEY MCGUIRE

 ©1995 by Prentice-Hall, Inc.
A Simon & Schuster Company
Englewood Cliffs, New Jersey 07632

UNIX is a registered trademark of UNIX System Laboratories, Incorporated
proNET-10 is a trademark of Proteon Corporation
LSI 11 is a trademark of Digital Equipment Corporation
Microsoft Windows is a trademark of Microsoft Corporation

Printed in the United States of America

10 9 8 7 6 5 4 3 2

ISBN   0-13-216987-8

Prentice-Hall International (UK) Limited, London
Prentice-Hall of Australia Pty. Limited, Sydney
Prentice-Hall Canada Inc., Toronto
Prentice-Hall Hispanoamericana, S.A., Mexico
Prentice-Hall of India Private Limited, New Delhi
Prentice-Hall of Japan, Inc., Tokyo
Simon & Schuster Asia Pte. Ltd., Singapore
Editora Prentice-Hall do Brasil, Ltda., Rio de Janeiro

To Chris

Additional Enthusiastic Comments About
Internetworking With TCP/IP Volume 1

"Unquestionably THE reference for TCP/IP; both informative and easy to read, this book is liked by both novice and experienced."

> – Raj Yavatkar
> University of Kentucky
> US Editor, Computer Communications

"The third edition maintains Comer's Internetworking with TCP/IP as the acknowledged leader in TCP/IP books by adding up-to-the-minute material on ATM, CIDR, firewalls, DHCP and the next version of IP, IPng."

> – Ralph Droms
> Bucknell University
> IFTF Working Group Chair

"Doug Comer remains the first and best voice of Internet technology. Despite the legion of 'Internet carpetbaggers' (the current crop of 'authors' who can barely spell F-T-P) which contributes noise – but no knowledge – on the Internet and its infrastructure, Dr. Comer shines through as the premiere source for lucid explanations and accurate information. He sets a standard for which many strive, but precious few attain."

> – Marshall Rose
> Dover Beach Consulting
> IETF Area Director

"Comer's Volume 1 drastically changed the course of networking history."

> – Dan Lynch
> Interop Company
> IAB Member

"When you need to teach the details of TCP/IP, you need the latest information. Once again, Comer separates the chaff from the wheat with his latest edition of the TCP/IP book that a generation of networkers grew up with."

> – Shawn Ostermann
> Ohio University

Contents

Foreword   **xxi**

Preface   **xxiii**

Chapter 1   Introduction And Overview   **1**

1.1   The Motivation For Internetworking   1
1.2   The TCP/IP Internet   2
1.3   Internet Services   3
1.4   History And Scope Of The Internet   6
1.5   The Internet Architecture Board   8
1.6   The IAB Reorganization   9
1.7   The Internet Society   11
1.8   Internet Request For Comments   11
1.9   Internet Protocols And Standardization   12
1.10   Future Growth And Technology   12
1.11   Organization Of The Text   13
1.12   Summary   14

Chapter 2   Review Of Underlying Network Technologies   **17**

2.1   Introduction   17
2.2   Two Approaches To Network Communication   18
2.3   Wide Area And Local Area Networks   19
2.4   Ethernet Technology   20
2.5   Fiber Distributed Data Interconnect (FDDI)   32
2.6   Asynchronous Transfer Mode   36
2.7   ARPANET Technology   37
2.8   National Science Foundation Networking   39
2.9   ANSNET   44

2.10   A Planned Wide Area Backbone   44
2.11   Other Technologies Over Which TCP/IP Has Been Used   44
2.12   Summary And Conclusion   47

Chapter 3   Internetworking Concept And Architectural Model   49

3.1   Introduction   49
3.2   Application-Level Interconnection   49
3.3   Network-Level Interconnection   50
3.4   Properties Of The Internet   51
3.5   Internet Architecture   52
3.6   Interconnection Through IP Routers   52
3.7   The User's View   54
3.8   All Networks Are Equal   54
3.9   The Unanswered Questions   55
3.10   Summary   56

Chapter 4   Internet Addresses   59

4.1   Introduction   59
4.2   Universal Identifiers   59
4.3   Three Primary Classes Of IP Addresses   60
4.4   Addresses Specify Network Connections   61
4.5   Network And Broadcast Addresses   61
4.6   Limited Broadcast   62
4.7   Interpreting Zero To Mean ''This''   62
4.8   Weaknesses In Internet Addressing   63
4.9   Dotted Decimal Notation   65
4.10   Loopback Address   65
4.11   Summary Of Special Address Conventions   66
4.12   Internet Addressing Authority   66
4.13   An Example   67
4.14   Network Byte Order   69
4.15   Summary   70

Chapter 5   Mapping Internet Addresses To Physical Addresses (ARP)   73

5.1   Introduction   73
5.2   The Address Resolution Problem   73
5.3   Two Types Of Physical Addresses   74
5.4   Resolution Through Direct Mapping   74

5.5   *Resolution Through Dynamic Binding   75*
5.6   *The Address Resolution Cache   76*
5.7   *ARP Refinements   77*
5.8   *Relationship Of ARP To Other Protocols   77*
5.9   *ARP Implementation   77*
5.10   *ARP Encapsulation And Identification   79*
5.11   *ARP Protocol Format   79*
5.12   *Summary   81*

Chapter 6   Determining An Internet Address At Startup (RARP)   83

6.1   *Introduction   83*
6.2   *Reverse Address Resolution Protocol (RARP)   84*
6.3   *Timing RARP Transactions   86*
6.4   *Primary And Backup RARP Servers   86*
6.5   *Summary   87*

Chapter 7   Internet Protocol: Connectionless Datagram Delivery   89

7.1   *Introduction   89*
7.2   *A Virtual Network   89*
7.3   *Internet Architecture And Philosophy   90*
7.4   *The Concept Of Unreliable Delivery   90*
7.5   *Connectionless Delivery System   91*
7.6   *Purpose Of The Internet Protocol   91*
7.7   *The Internet Datagram   91*
7.8   *Internet Datagram Options   100*
7.9   *Summary   106*

Chapter 8   Internet Protocol: Routing IP Datagrams   109

8.1   *Introduction   109*
8.2   *Routing In An Internet   109*
8.3   *Direct And Indirect Delivery   111*
8.4   *Table-Driven IP Routing   113*
8.5   *Next-Hop Routing   113*
8.6   *Default Routes   115*
8.7   *Host-Specific Routes   115*
8.8   *The IP Routing Algorithm   116*
8.9   *Routing With IP Addresses   116*
8.10   *Handling Incoming Datagrams   118*

8.11   *Establishing Routing Tables*   119
8.12   *Summary*   119

Chapter 9   Internet Protocol: Error And Control Messages (ICMP)   123

9.1   *Introduction*   123
9.2   *The Internet Control Message Protocol*   123
9.3   *Error Reporting vs. Error Correction*   124
9.4   *ICMP Message Delivery*   125
9.5   *ICMP Message Format*   126
9.6   *Testing Destination Reachability And Status (Ping)*   127
9.7   *Echo Request And Reply Message Format*   128
9.8   *Reports Of Unreachable Destinations*   128
9.9   *Congestion And Datagram Flow Control*   130
9.10   *Source Quench Format*   130
9.11   *Route Change Requests From Routers*   131
9.12   *Detecting Circular Or Excessively Long Routes*   133
9.13   *Reporting Other Problems*   134
9.14   *Clock Synchronization And Transit Time Estimation*   134
9.15   *Information Request And Reply Messages*   136
9.16   *Obtaining A Subnet Mask*   136
9.17   *Summary*   137

Chapter 10   Subnet And Supernet Address Extensions   139

10.1   *Introduction*   139
10.2   *Review Of Relevant Facts*   139
10.3   *Minimizing Network Numbers*   140
10.4   *Transparent Routers*   141
10.5   *Proxy ARP*   142
10.6   *Subnet Addressing*   143
10.7   *Flexibility In Subnet Address Assignment*   146
10.8   *Implementation Of Subnets With Masks*   147
10.9   *Subnet Mask Representation*   148
10.10   *Routing In The Presence Of Subnets*   149
10.11   *The Subnet Routing Algorithm*   150
10.12   *A Unified Routing Algorithm*   151
10.13   *Maintenance Of Subnet Masks*   152
10.14   *Broadcasting To Subnets*   152
10.15   *Supernet Addressing*   153
10.16   *The Effect Of Supernetting On Routing*   154
10.17   *Summary*   155

Chapter 11 Protocol Layering   159

11.1   Introduction   159
11.2   The Need For Multiple Protocols   159
11.3   The Conceptual Layers Of Protocol Software   160
11.4   Functionality Of The Layers   163
11.5   X.25 And Its Relation To The ISO Model   164
11.6   Differences Between X.25 And Internet Layering   167
11.7   The Protocol Layering Principle   169
11.8   Layering In The Presence Of Network Substructure   171
11.9   Two Important Boundaries In The TCP/IP Model   173
11.10 The Disadvantage Of Layering   174
11.11 The Basic Idea Behind Multiplexing And Demultiplexing   174
11.12 Summary   176

Chapter 12 User Datagram Protocol (UDP)   179

12.1   Introduction   179
12.2   Identifying The Ultimate Destination   179
12.3   The User Datagram Protocol   180
12.4   Format Of UDP Messages   181
12.5   UDP Pseudo-Header   182
12.6   UDP Encapsulation And Protocol Layering   183
12.7   Layering And The UDP Checksum Computation   185
12.8   UDP Multiplexing, Demultiplexing, And Ports   185
12.9   Reserved And Available UDP Port Numbers   186
12.10 Summary   188

Chapter 13 Reliable Stream Transport Service (TCP)   191

13.1   Introduction   191
13.2   The Need For Stream Delivery   191
13.3   Properties Of The Reliable Delivery Service   192
13.4   Providing Reliability   193
13.5   The Idea Behind Sliding Windows   195
13.6   The Transmission Control Protocol   198
13.7   Ports, Connections, And Endpoints   199
13.8   Passive And Active Opens   201
13.9   Segments, Streams, And Sequence Numbers   201
13.10 Variable Window Size And Flow Control   202
13.11 TCP Segment Format   203

13.12 Out Of Band Data   205
13.13 Maximum Segment Size Option   206
13.14 TCP Checksum Computation   207
13.15 Acknowledgements And Retransmission   208
13.16 Timeout And Retransmission   209
13.17 Accurate Measurement Of Round Trip Samples   211
13.18 Karn's Algorithm And Timer Backoff   212
13.19 Responding To High Variance In Delay   213
13.20 Response To Congestion   214
13.21 Establishing A TCP Connection   216
13.22 Initial Sequence Numbers   217
13.23 Closing a TCP Connection   217
13.24 TCP Connection Reset   219
13.25 TCP State Machine   219
13.26 Forcing Data Delivery   221
13.27 Reserved TCP Port Numbers   221
13.28 TCP Performance   221
13.29 Silly Window Syndrome And Small Packets   223
13.30 Avoiding Silly Window Syndrome   224
13.31 Summary   227

Chapter 14   Routing: Cores, Peers, And Algorithms (GGP)   231

14.1   Introduction   231
14.2   The Origin Of Routing Tables   232
14.3   Routing With Partial Information   233
14.4   Original Internet Architecture And Cores   234
14.5   Core Routers   235
14.6   Beyond The Core Architecture To Peer Backbones   238
14.7   Automatic Route Propagation   240
14.8   Vector Distance (Bellman-Ford) Routing   240
14.9   Gateway-To-Gateway Protocol (GGP)   242
14.10   GGP Message Formats   243
14.11   Link-State (SPF) Routing   245
14.12   SPF Protocols   246
14.13   Summary   246

Chapter 15   Routing: Autonomous Systems (EGP)   249

15.1   Introduction   249
15.2   Adding Complexity To The Architectural Model   249
15.3   A Fundamental Idea: Extra Hops   250

15.4   *Autonomous System Concept*   252
15.5   *Exterior Gateway Protocol (EGP)*   254
15.6   *EGP Message Header*   255
15.7   *EGP Neighbor Acquisition Messages*   256
15.8   *EGP Neighbor Reachability Messages*   257
15.9   *EGP Poll Request Messages*   258
15.10   *EGP Routing Update Messages*   259
15.11   *Measuring From The Receiver's Perspective*   261
15.12   *The Key Restriction Of EGP*   262
15.13   *Technical Problems*   264
15.14   *Decentralization Of Internet Architecture*   264
15.15   *Beyond Autonomous Systems*   264
15.16   *Summary*   265

Chapter 16   Routing: In An Autonomous System (RIP, OSPF, HELLO)   267

16.1   *Introduction*   267
16.2   *Static Vs. Dynamic Interior Routes*   267
16.3   *Routing Information Protocol (RIP)*   270
16.4   *The Hello Protocol*   276
16.5   *Combining RIP, Hello, And EGP*   278
16.6   *The Open SPF Protocol (OSPF)*   279
16.7   *Routing With Partial Information*   286
16.8   *Summary*   286

Chapter 17   Internet Multicasting (IGMP)   289

17.1   *Introduction*   289
17.2   *Hardware Broadcast*   289
17.3   *Hardware Multicast*   290
17.4   *IP Multicast*   291
17.5   *IP Multicast Addresses*   291
17.6   *Mapping IP Multicast To Ethernet Multicast*   292
17.7   *Extending IP To Handle Multicasting*   293
17.8   *Internet Group Management Protocol*   294
17.9   *IGMP Implementation*   294
17.10   *Group Membership State Transitions*   295
17.11   *IGMP Message Format*   296
17.12   *Multicast Address Assignment*   297
17.13   *Propagating Routing Information*   297
17.14   *The Mrouted Program*   298
17.15   *Summary*   300

Chapter 18   TCP/IP Over ATM Networks   303

18.1   Introduction   303
18.2   ATM Hardware   304
18.3   Large ATM Networks   304
18.4   The Logical View Of An ATM Network   305
18.5   The Two ATM Connection Paradigms   306
18.6   Paths, Circuits, And Identifiers   307
18.7   ATM Cell Transport   308
18.8   ATM Adaptation Layers   308
18.9   AAL5 Convergence, Segmentation, And Reassembly   311
18.10   Datagram Encapsulation And IP MTU Size   311
18.11   Packet Type And Multiplexing   312
18.12   IP Address Binding In An ATM Network   313
18.13   Logical IP Subnet Concept   314
18.14   Connection Management   315
18.15   Address Binding Within An LIS   316
18.16   ATMARP Packet Format   316
18.17   Using ATMARP Packets To Determine An Address   318
18.18   Obtaining Entries For A Server Database   320
18.19   Timing Out ATMARP Information In A Server   320
18.20   Timing Out ATMARP Information In A Host Or Router   320
18.21   Summary   321

Chapter 19   Client-Server Model Of Interaction   325

19.1   Introduction   325
19.2   The Client-Server Model   325
19.3   A Simple Example: UDP Echo Server   326
19.4   Time And Date Service   328
19.5   The Complexity of Servers   329
19.6   RARP Server   330
19.7   Alternatives To The Client-Server Model   331
19.8   Summary   332

Chapter 20   The Socket Interface   335

20.1   Introduction   335
20.2   The UNIX I/O Paradigm And Network I/O   336
20.3   Adding Network I/O to UNIX   336
20.4   The Socket Abstraction   337

20.5   Creating A Socket   337
20.6   Socket Inheritance And Termination   338
20.7   Specifying A Local Address   339
20.8   Connecting Sockets To Destination Addresses   340
20.9   Sending Data Through A Socket   341
20.10 Receiving Data Through A Socket   343
20.11 Obtaining Local And Remote Socket Addresses   344
20.12 Obtaining And Setting Socket Options   345
20.13 Specifying A Queue Length For A Server   346
20.14 How A Server Accepts Connections   346
20.15 Servers That Handle Multiple Services   347
20.16 Obtaining And Setting Host Names   348
20.17 Obtaining And Setting The Internal Host Domain   349
20.18 BSD UNIX Network Library Calls   349
20.19 Network Byte Order Conversion Routines   350
20.20 IP Address Manipulation Routines   351
20.21 Accessing The Domain Name System   352
20.22 Obtaining Information About Hosts   354
20.23 Obtaining Information About Networks   355
20.24 Obtaining Information About Protocols   355
20.25 Obtaining Information About Network Services   356
20.26 An Example Client   357
20.27 An Example Server   359
20.28 Summary   362

Chapter 21   Bootstrap And Autoconfiguration (BOOTP, DHCP)   365

21.1   Introduction   365
21.2   The Need For An Alternative To RARP   366
21.3   Using IP To Determine An IP Address   366
21.4   The BOOTP Retransmission Policy   367
21.5   The BOOTP Message Format   368
21.6   The Two-Step Bootstrap Procedure   369
21.7   Vendor-Specific Field   370
21.8   The Need For Dynamic Configuration   370
21.9   Dynamic Host Configuration   372
21.10 Dynamic IP Address Assignment   372
21.11 Obtaining Multiple Addresses   373
21.12 Address Acquisition States   374
21.13 Early Lease Termination   374
21.14 Lease Renewal States   376
21.15 DHCP Message Format   377
21.16 DHCP Options And Message Type   378

21.17   *Option Overload*   379
21.18   *DHCP And Domain Names*   379
21.19   *Summary*   380

Chapter 22   The Domain Name System (DNS)   **383**

22.1   *Introduction*   383
22.2   *Names For Machines*   384
22.3   *Flat Namespace*   384
22.4   *Hierarchical Names*   385
22.5   *Delegation Of Authority For Names*   386
22.6   *Subset Authority*   386
22.7   *TCP/IP Internet Domain Names*   387
22.8   *Official And Unofficial Internet Domain Names*   388
22.9   *Items Named And Syntax Of Names*   390
22.10   *Mapping Domain Names To Addresses*   391
22.11   *Domain Name Resolution*   393
22.12   *Efficient Translation*   394
22.13   *Caching: The Key To Efficiency*   395
22.14   *Domain Server Message Format*   396
22.15   *Compressed Name Format*   399
22.16   *Abbreviation Of Domain Names*   399
22.17   *Inverse Mappings*   400
22.18   *Pointer Queries*   401
22.19   *Object Types And Resource Record Contents*   401
22.20   *Obtaining Authority For A Subdomain*   402
22.21   *Summary*   403

Chapter 23   Applications: Remote Login (TELNET, Rlogin)   **407**

23.1   *Introduction*   407
23.2   *Remote Interactive Computing*   407
23.3   *TELNET Protocol*   408
23.4   *Accommodating Heterogeneity*   410
23.5   *Passing Commands That Control The Remote Side*   412
23.6   *Forcing The Server To Read A Control Function*   414
23.7   *TELNET Options*   414
23.8   *TELNET Option Negotiation*   415
23.9   *Rlogin (BSD UNIX)*   416
23.10   *Summary*   417

Chapter 24   Applications: File Transfer And Access (FTP, TFTP, NFS)   419

24.1   *Introduction*   419
24.2   *File Access And Transfer*   419
24.3   *On-line Shared Access*   420
24.4   *Sharing By File Transfer*   421
24.5   *FTP: The Major TCP/IP File Transfer Protocol*   421
24.6   *FTP Features*   422
24.7   *FTP Process Model*   422
24.8   *TCP Port Number Assignment*   424
24.9   *The User's View Of FTP*   424
24.10   *An Example Anonymous FTP Session*   426
24.11   *TFTP*   427
24.12   *NFS*   429
24.13   *NFS Implementation*   429
24.14   *Remote Procedure Call (RPC)*   430
24.15   *Summary*   431

Chapter 25   Applications: Electronic Mail (822, SMTP, MIME)   433

25.1   *Introduction*   433
25.2   *Electronic Mail*   433
25.3   *Mailbox Names And Aliases*   435
25.4   *Alias Expansion And Mail Forwarding*   435
25.5   *The Relationship Of Internetworking And Mail*   436
25.6   *TCP/IP Standards For Electronic Mail Service*   438
25.7   *Electronic Mail Addresses*   438
25.8   *Pseudo Domain Addresses*   440
25.9   *Simple Mail Transfer Protocol (SMTP)*   440
25.10   *The MIME Extension For Non-ASCII Data*   443
25.11   *MIME Multipart Messages*   444
25.12   *Summary*   445

Chapter 26   Applications: Internet Management (SNMP, SNMPv2)   447

26.1   *Introduction*   447
26.2   *The Level Of Management Protocols*   447
26.3   *Architectural Model*   448
26.4   *Protocol Architecture*   450
26.5   *Examples of MIB Variables*   451
26.6   *The Structure Of Management Information*   452

26.7   *Formal Definitions Using ASN.1*   453
26.8   *Structure And Representation Of MIB Object Names*   453
26.9   *Simple Network Management Protocol*   458
26.10   *SNMP Message Format*   460
26.11   *Example Encoded SNMP Message*   462
26.12   *Summary*   463

Chapter 27   Summary Of Protocol Dependencies   465

27.1   *Introduction*   465
27.2   *Protocol Dependencies*   465
27.3   *Application Program Access*   467
27.4   *Summary*   468

Chapter 28   Internet Security And Firewall Design   471

28.1   *Introduction*   471
28.2   *Protecting Resources*   472
28.3   *The Need For An Information Policy*   472
28.4   *Communication, Cooperation, And Mutual Mistrust*   474
28.5   *Mechanisms For Internet Security*   475
28.6   *Firewalls And Internet Access*   476
28.7   *Multiple Connections And Weakest Links*   477
28.8   *Firewall Implementation And High-Speed Hardware*   478
28.9   *Packet-Level Filters*   479
28.10   *Security And Packet Filter Specification*   480
28.11   *The Consequence Of Restricted Access For Clients*   481
28.12   *Accessing Services Through A Firewall*   481
28.13   *The Details Of Firewall Architecture*   483
28.14   *Stub Network*   484
28.15   *An Alternative Firewall Implementation*   484
28.16   *Monitoring And Logging*   485
28.17   *Summary*   486

Chapter 29   The Future Of TCP/IP (IPng, IPv6)   489

29.1   *Introduction*   489
29.2   *Why Change TCP/IP And The Internet?*   490
29.3   *Motivation For Changing IPv4*   491
29.4   *The Road To A New Version Of IP*   492
29.5   *The Name Of The Next IP*   492

29.6   Features Of IPv6   493
29.7   General Form Of An IPv6 Datagram   494
29.8   IPv6 Base Header Format   494
29.9   IPv6 Extension Headers   496
29.10   Parsing An IPv6 Datagram   497
29.11   IPv6 Fragmentation And Reassembly   498
29.12   The Consequence Of End-To-End Fragmentation   498
29.13   IPv6 Source Routing   500
29.14   IPv6 Options   500
29.15   Size Of The IPv6 Address Space   502
29.16   IPv6 Colon Hexadecimal Notation   502
29.17   Three Basic IPv6 Address Types   503
29.18   The Duality Of Broadcast And Multicast   504
29.19   An Engineering Choice And Simulated Broadcast   504
29.20   Proposed IPv6 Address Space Assignment   504
29.21   IPv4 Address Encoding And Transition   506
29.22   Providers, Subscribers, And Address Hierarchy   506
29.23   Additional Hierarchy   507
29.24   Summary   508

Appendix 1   A Guide To RFCs   511

Appendix 2   Glossary Of Internetworking Terms And Abbreviations   557

Bibliography   591

Index   599

Foreword

Professor Douglas Comer's book has become *the* classic text for an introduction to TCP/IP. Writing an introduction to TCP/IP for the uninitiated is a very difficult task. While combining the explanation of the general principles of computer communication with the specific examples from the TCP/IP protocol suite, Doug Comer has provided a very readable book.

While this book is specifically about the TCP/IP protocol suite, it is a good book for learning about computer communications protocols in general. The principles of architecture, layering, multiplexing, encapsulation, addressing and address mapping, routing, and naming are quite similar in any protocol suite, though, of course, different in detail.

Computer communication protocols do not do anything themselves. Like operating systems, they are in the service of application processes. Processes are the active elements that request communication and are the ultimate senders and receivers of the data transmitted. The various layers of protocols are like the various layers in a computer operating system, especially the file system. Understanding protocol architecture is like understanding operating system architecture. In this book Doug Comer has taken the "bottom up" approach – starting with the physical networks and moving up in levels of abstraction to the applications.

Since application processes are the active elements using the communication supported by the protocols, TCP/IP is an "interprocess communication" (IPC) mechanism. While there are several experiments in progress with operating system style message passing and procedure call types of IPC based on IP, the focus in this book is on more traditional applications that use the UDP datagram or TCP logical connection forms of IPC. Typically in operating systems there is a set of functions provided by the operating system to the application processes. This system call interface usually includes calls for opening, reading, writing, and closing files, among other things. In many systems there are similar system calls for IPC functions including network communication. As an example of such an interface Doug Comer presents an overview of the socket interface.

One of the key ideas inherent in TCP/IP and in the title of this book is "internetworking." The power of a communication system is directly related to the number of entities in that system. The telephone network is very useful because (nearly) all the telephones are connected to one network (as it appears to the users). Computer communication systems and networks are currently separated and fragmented. As more users and enterprises adopt TCP/IP as their network communication technology and are joining the Internet this is becoming less of a problem, but there is still a long way to go. The goal of interconnection and internetworking, to have a single powerful computer communication network, is fundamental to the design of TCP/IP.

Essential to internetworking is addressing, and a universal protocol – the Internet Protocol. Of course, the individual networks have their own protocols which are used to carry the IP datagrams, and there must be a mapping between the individual network address and the IP address. Over the lifetime of TCP/IP, the nature of these individual networks have changed from the early days of the ARPANET to the recently developed ATM networks. A new chapter in this edition discusses IP over ATM networks. This book now includes recent developments in Dynamic Host Configuration (DHCP) that will ease the administration of networks and the installation of new computers.

To have an internetwork, the individual networks must be connected. The connecting devices are called routers. Further, these routers must have some procedures for forwarding data from one network to the next. The data is in the form of IP datagrams and the destination is specified by an IP address, but the router must make a routing decision based on the IP address and what it knows about the connectivity of the networks making up the Internet. The procedures for distributing the current connectivity information to the routers are called routing algorithms, and these are currently the subject of much study and development. In particular, the recent development of the Classless InterDomain Routing (CIDR) technique to reduce the amount of routing information exchanged is important.

Like all communication systems, the TCP/IP protocol suite is an unfinished system. It is evolving to meet changing requirements and new opportunities. Thus, this book is, in a sense, a snapshot of TCP/IP. And, as Doug Comer points out, there are many loose ends. With the recent rapid growth of the Internet there is concern about it outgrowing the capabilities of the TCP/IP protocols, particularly the address space. In response the research and engineering community has developed a "next generation" version of the Internet Protocol called IPng. Many of the enterprises now joining the Internet have concerns about security. A new chapter in this edition discusses the security and firewalls.

Most chapters end with a few pointers to material "for further study." Many of these refer to memos of the RFC series of notes. This series of notes is the result of a policy of making the working ideas and the protocol specifications developed by the TCP/IP research and development community widely available. This availability of the basic and detailed information about these protocols, and the availability of the early implementations of them, has had much to do with their current widespread use. This commitment to public documentation at this level of detail is unusual for a research effort, and has had significant benefits for the development of computer communication.

This book brings together information about the various parts of the TCP/IP architecture and protocols and makes it accessible. Its publication is a very significant milestone in the evolution of computer communications.

Jon Postel,
Associate Director for Networking
Information Sciences Institute
University of Southern California

January 1995

Preface

The world has changed dramatically since the second edition of this book was published. It hardly seems possible only four years have elapsed. When I began the second edition in the summer of 1990, the Internet had grown to nearly 300,000 host computers, up from 5,000 hosts when the book was first written. At the time, we marveled at how large an obscure research project had become. Cynics predicted that continued growth would lead to a complete collapse by 1993. Instead of collapsing, the Internet has continued its explosive expansion; the ''large'' Internet of 1990 is only 7% of the current Internet.

TCP/IP and the Internet have accommodated change well. The basic technology has survived over a decade of exponential growth and the associated increases in traffic. The protocols have worked over new high-speed network technologies, and the design has handled applications that could not be imagined a decade ago. Of course, the entire protocol suite has not remained static. New protocols have been deployed, and new techniques have been developed to adapt existing protocols to new network technologies. Changes are documented in RFCs, which have increased by over 50 percent.

This edition contains updated information throughout the text (including use of the commercially popular term *IP router* in place of the traditional scientific term *IP gateway*) as well as new material that describes technical advances and changes. The chapter on subnet addressing now describes supernetting as well as subnetting, and shows how the two techniques are motivated by the same goal. The chapter on bootstrapping explains a significant advance that will eliminate the need for manual configuration of host computers and allow a computer to obtain an IP address automatically: the Dynamic Host Configuration Protocol (DHCP). The chapter on TCP includes a description of Silly Window Syndrome and an explanation of the heuristics TCP uses to prevent the problem. The chapter on electronic mail includes a description of the Multipurpose Internet Mail Extensions (MIME), which permit non-ASCII data to be sent in a standard e-mail message.

Three new chapters contain detailed information about significant developments. Chapter 18 explains how TCP/IP is being used over ATM networks. The chapter discusses the organization of ATM hardware, the purpose of adaptation layer protocols, IP encapsulation, address binding, routing, and virtual circuit management. The chapter illustrates how a connectionless protocol like IP can use the connection-oriented interface that ATM provides. Chapter 28 covers a topic that is crucial to many organizations as they contemplate connecting to the global Internet – security. The chapter describes the internet firewall concept, and shows how a firewall architecture can be used to protect networks and computers inside an organization from unwanted access. The chapter also discusses the principles underlying a two-level firewall design, and considers outside access from a secure computer. Finally, a new chapter is devoted to what may be the most significant change in TCP/IP since its inception: the imminent adoption of a next generation Internet Protocol (IPng). Chapter 29 describes the protocol that the IETF has developed to serve as IPng. Although it has not been thoroughly tested or approved as a permanent standard, the new design appears to be the consensus choice. The chapter presents the proposed design and address assignment scheme.

The third edition retains the same general contents and overall organization as the second edition. The entire text focuses on the concept of internetworking in general and the TCP/IP internet technology in particular. Internetworking is a powerful abstraction that allows us to deal with the complexity of multiple underlying communication technologies. It hides the details of network hardware and provides a high level communication environment. The text reviews both the architecture of network interconnections and the principles underlying protocols that make such interconnected networks function as a single, unified communication system. It also shows how an internet communication system can be used for distributed computation.

After reading this book, you will understand how it is possible to interconnect multiple physical networks into a coordinated system, how internet protocols operate in that environment, and how application programs use the resulting system. As a specific example, you will learn the details of the global TCP/IP Internet, including the architecture of its router system and the application protocols it supports. In addition, you will understand some of the limitations of the internet approach.

Designed as both a college text and as a professional reference, the book is written at an advanced undergraduate or graduate level. For professionals, the book provides a comprehensive introduction to the TCP/IP technology and the architecture of the Internet. Although it is not intended to replace protocol standards, the book is an excellent starting point for learning about internetworking because it provides a uniform overview that emphasizes principles. Moreover, it gives the reader perspective that can be extremely difficult to obtain from individual protocol documents.

When used in the classroom, the text provides more than sufficient material for a single semester network course at either the undergraduate or graduate level. Such a course can be extended to a two-semester sequence if accompanied by programming projects and readings from the literature. For undergraduate courses, many of the details are unnecessary. Students should be expected to grasp the basic concepts described in the text, and they should be able to describe or use them. At the graduate level, students should be expected to use the material here as a basis for further exploration. They should understand the details well enough to answer exercises or solve problems that require them to explore extensions and subtleties. Many of the exercises suggest such subtleties; solving them often requires students to read protocol standards and apply creative energy to comprehend consequences.

At all levels, hands-on experience sharpens the concepts and helps students gain intuition. Thus, I encourage instructors to invent projects that force students to use Internet services and protocols. The semester project in my graduate Internetworking course at Purdue requires students to build an IP router. We supply hardware and the source code for an operating system, including device drivers for network interfaces; students build a working router that interconnects three networks with different MTUs. The course is extremely rigorous, students work in teams, and the results have been impressive (many industries recruit graduates from the course). Although such experimentation is safest when the instructional laboratory network is isolated from production computing facilities, we have found that students exhibit the most enthusiasm, and benefit the most, when they have access to a functional TCP/IP internet.

The book is organized into four main parts. Chapters 1 and 2 form an introduction that provides an overview and discusses existing network technologies. In particular, Chapter 2 reviews physical network hardware. The intention is to provide basic intuition about what is possible, not to spend inordinate time on hardware details. Chapters 3-13 describe the TCP/IP Internet from the viewpoint of a single host, showing the protocols a host contains and how they operate. They cover the basics of Internet addressing and routing as well as the notion of protocol layering. Chapters 14-18 and 28 describe the architecture of an internet when viewed globally. They explore routing architecture and the protocols routers use to exchange routing information. Finally, Chapters 19-27 discuss application level services available in the Internet. They present the client-server model of interaction, and give several examples of client and server software.

The chapters have been organized bottom up. They begin with an overview of hardware and continue to build new functionality on top of it. This view will appeal to anyone who has developed Internet software because it follows the same pattern one uses in implementation. The concept of layering does not appear until Chapter 11. The discussion of layering emphasizes the distinction between conceptual layers of functionality and the reality of layered protocol software in which multiple objects appear at each layer.

A modest background is required to understand the material. The reader is expected to have a basic understanding of computer systems, and to be familiar with data structures like stacks, queues, and trees. Readers need basic intuition about the organization of computer software into an operating system that supports concurrent programming and application programs that users invoke to perform computation. Readers do not need sophisticated mathematics, nor do they need to know information theory or theorems from data communications; the book describes the physical network as a black box around which an internetwork can be built. It states design principles in English and discusses motivations and consequences.

I thank all the people who have contributed to versions of this book. John Lin provided extensive assistance with this edition, including classifying RFCs. Ralph Droms reviewed the chapter on bootstrapping, and Sandeep Kumar, Steve Lodin, and Christoph Schuba, from the COAST security project at Purdue, commented on the security chapter. Special thanks go to my wife, Chris, whose careful editing made many improvements in wording.

1

Introduction And Overview

1.1 The Motivation For Internetworking

Data communication has become a fundamental part of computing. World-wide networks gather data about such diverse subjects as atmospheric conditions, crop production, and airline traffic. Groups establish electronic mailing lists so they can share information of common interest. Hobbyists exchange programs for their home computers. In the scientific world, data networks are essential because they allow scientists to send programs and data to remote supercomputers for processing, to retrieve the results, and to exchange information with colleagues.

Unfortunately, most networks are independent entities, established to serve the needs of a single group. The users choose a hardware technology appropriate to their communication problems. More important, it is impossible to build a universal network from a single hardware technology because no single network suffices for all uses. Some users need a high-speed network to connect machines, but such networks cannot be expanded to span large distances. Others settle for a slower speed network that connects machines thousands of miles apart.

In the past 15 years, a new technology has evolved that makes it possible to interconnect many disparate physical networks and make them function as a coordinated unit. The technology, called *internetworking*, accommodates multiple, diverse underlying hardware technologies by providing a way to interconnect heterogeneous networks and a set of communication conventions. The internet technology hides the details of network hardware and permits computers to communicate independent of their physical network connections.

The internet technology described in this book is an example of *open system interconnection*. It is called an *open system* because, unlike proprietary communication systems available from one specific vendor, the specifications are publicly available. Thus,

1

anyone can build the software needed to communicate across an internet. More important, the entire technology has been designed to foster communication between machines with diverse hardware architectures, to use almost any packet switched network hardware, and to accommodate multiple computer operating systems.

To appreciate internet technology, think of how it affects a professional group. Consider, for example, the effect of interconnecting the computers used by scientists. Any scientist can exchange data resulting from an experiment with any other scientist. National centers can collect data from natural phenomena and make the data available to all scientists. Computer services and programs available at one location can be used by scientists at other locations. As a result, the speed with which scientific investigations proceed increases; the changes are dramatic.

1.2 The TCP/IP Internet

U.S. government agencies have realized the importance and potential of internet technology for many years and have been funding research that has made possible a global internet. This book discusses principles and ideas underlying the internet technology that has resulted from research funded by the *Advanced Research Projects Agency (ARPA)*†. The ARPA technology includes a set of network standards that specify the details of how computers communicate, as well as a set of conventions for interconnecting networks and routing traffic. Officially named the TCP/IP Internet Protocol Suite and commonly referred to as *TCP/IP* (after the names of its two main standards), it can be used to communicate across any set of interconnected networks. For example, some corporations use TCP/IP to interconnect all networks within their corporation, even though the corporation has no connection to outside networks. Other groups use TCP/IP for communication among geographically distant sites.

Although the TCP/IP technology is noteworthy by itself, it is especially interesting because its viability has been demonstrated on a large scale. It forms the base technology for a global internet that connects homes, university campuses and other schools, corporations, and government labs in 61 countries. In the U.S., The *National Science Foundation (NSF)*, the *Department of Energy (DOE)*, the *Department of Defense (DOD)*, the *Health and Human Services Agency, (HHS)* and the *National Aeronautics and Space Administration (NASA)* have all participated in funding the Internet, and use TCP/IP to connect many of their research sites. Known as the *ARPA/NSF Internet*, the *TCP/IP Internet*, the *global Internet*, or just the *Internet*‡, the resulting internet allows researchers at connected institutions to share information with colleagues around the world as easily as they share it with researchers in the next room. An outstanding success, the Internet demonstrates the viability of the TCP/IP technology and shows how it can accommodate a wide variety of underlying network technologies.

Most of the material in this book applies to any internet that uses TCP/IP, but some chapters refer specifically to the global Internet. Readers interested only in the technology should be careful to watch for the distinction between the Internet architecture as it exists and general TCP/IP internets as they might exist. It would be a mis-

---

†ARPA was called the *Defense Advanced Research Projects Agency* for several years during the 1980s.

‡We will follow the usual convention of capitalizing *Internet* when referring specifically to the global Internet, and use lower case to refer to private internets that use TCP/IP.

take, however, to ignore completely sections of the text that describe the global Internet
– many corporate networks are already more complex than the global Internet of ten
years ago, and many of the problems they face have already been solved in the global
Internet.

1.3 Internet Services

One cannot appreciate the technical details underlying TCP/IP without understanding the services it provides. This section reviews internet services briefly, highlighting
the services most users access, and leaves to later chapters the discussion of how computers connect to a TCP/IP internet and how the functionality is implemented.

Much of our discussion of services will focus on standards called *protocols*. Protocols like TCP and IP provide the rules for communication. They contain the details of
message formats, describe how a computer responds when a message arrives, and specify how a computer handles errors or other abnormal conditions. Most important, they
allow us to discuss computer communication independent of any particular vendor's
network hardware. In a sense, protocols are to communication what algorithms are to
computation. An algorithm allows one to specify or understand a computation without
knowing the details of a particular CPU instruction set. Similarly, a communication
protocol allows one to specify or understand data communication without depending on
detailed knowledge of a particular vendor's network hardware.

Hiding the low-level details of communication helps improve productivity in
several ways. First, because programmers deal with higher-level protocol abstractions,
they do not need to learn or remember as many details about a given hardware configuration. They can create new programs quickly. Second, because programs built using higher-level abstractions are not restricted to a particular machine architecture or a
particular network hardware, they do not need to be changed when machines or networks are reconfigured. Third, because application programs built using higher-level
protocols are independent of the underlying hardware, they can provide direct communication for an arbitrary pair of machines. Programmers do not need to build special versions of application software to move and translate data between each possible pair of
machine types.

We will see that all network services are described by protocols. The next sections
refer to protocols used to specify application-level services as well as those used to define network-level services. Later chapters explain each of these protocols in more detail.

1.3.1 Application Level Internet Services

From the user's point of view, a TCP/IP internet appears to be a set of application
programs that use the network to carry out useful communication tasks. We use the
term *interoperability* to refer to the ability of diverse computing systems to cooperate in
solving computational problems. Internet application programs exhibit a high degree of

interoperability. Most users that access the Internet do so merely by running application programs without understanding the TCP/IP technology, the structure of the underlying internet, or even the path the data travels to its destination; they rely on the application programs and the underlying network software to handle such details. Only program- mers who write network application programs need to view the internet as a network and need to understand some of the technology.

The most popular and widespread Internet application services include:

- *Electronic mail.* Electronic mail allows a user to compose memos and send them to individuals or groups. Another part of the mail application allows users to read memos that they have received. Electronic mail has been so successful that many Internet users depend on it for normal business correspondence. Although many electronic mail systems exist, using TCP/IP makes mail delivery more reliable be- cause it does not rely on intermediate computers to relay mail messages. A TCP/IP mail delivery system operates by having the sender's machine contact the receiver's machine directly. Thus, the sender knows that once the message leaves the local machine, it has been successfully received at the destination site.
- *File transfer.* Although users sometimes transfer files using electronic mail, mail is designed primarily for short text messages. The TCP/IP protocols include a file transfer application program that allows users to send or receive arbitrarily large files of programs or data. For example, using the file transfer program, one can copy from one machine to another a large data base containing satellite images, a program written in Pascal or C++, or an English dictionary. The system provides a way to check for authorized users, or even to prevent all access. Like mail, file transfer across a TCP/IP internet is reliable because the two machines involved communicate directly, without relying on intermediate machines to make copies of the file along the way.
- *Remote login.* Remote login allows a user sitting at one computer to connect to a remote machine and establish an interactive login session. The remote login makes it appear that a window on the user's screen connects directly to the remote machine by sending each keystroke from the user's keyboard to the remote machine and displaying each character the remote computer prints in the user's window. When the remote login session terminates, the application returns the user to the local system.

We will return to these and other applications in later chapters to examine them in more detail. We will see exactly how they use the underlying TCP/IP protocols, and why having standards for application protocols has helped ensure that they are widespread.

1.3.2 Network-Level Internet Services

A programmer who writes application programs that use TCP/IP protocols has an entirely different view of an internet than a user who merely executes applications like electronic mail. At the network level, an internet provides two broad types of service that all application programs use. While it is unimportant at this time to understand the details of these services, they cannot be omitted from any overview of TCP/IP:

- *Connectionless Packet Delivery Service.* This service, explained in detail throughout the text, forms the basis for all other internet services. Connectionless delivery is an abstraction of the service that most packet-switching networks offer. It means simply that a TCP/IP internet routes small messages from one machine to another based on address information carried in the message. Because the connectionless service routes each packet separately, it does not guarantee reliable, in-order delivery. Because it usually maps directly onto the underlying hardware, the connectionless service is extremely efficient. More important, having connectionless packet delivery as the basis for all internet services makes the TCP/IP protocols adaptable to a wide range of network hardware.

- *Reliable Stream Transport Service.* Most applications need much more than packet delivery because they require the communication software to recover automatically from transmission errors, lost packets, or failures of intermediate switches along the path between sender and receiver. The reliable transport service handles such problems. It allows an application on one computer to establish a ''connection'' with an application on another computer, and then to send a large volume of data across the connection as if it were a permanent, direct hardware connection. Underneath, of course, the communication protocols divide the stream of data into small messages and send them, one at a time, waiting for the receiver to acknowledge reception.

Many networks provide basic services similar to those outlined above, so one might wonder what distinguishes TCP/IP services from others. The primary distinguishing features are:

- *Network Technology Independence.* While TCP/IP is based on conventional packet switching technology, it is independent of any particular vendor's hardware. The global Internet includes a variety of network technologies ranging from networks designed to operate within a single building to those designed to span large distances. TCP/IP protocols define the unit of data transmission, called a *datagram*, and specify how to transmit datagrams on a particular network.
- *Universal Interconnection.* A TCP/IP internet allows any pair of computers to which it attaches to communicate. Each computer is assigned an *address* that is universally recognized throughout the internet. Every datagram carries the addresses of its source and destination. Intermediate switching computers use the destination address to make routing decisions.
- *End-to-End Acknowledgements.* The TCP/IP internet protocols provide acknowledgements between the source and ultimate destination instead of between successive machines along the path, even when the two machines do not connect to a common physical network.
- *Application Protocol Standards.* In addition to the basic transport-level services (like reliable stream connections), the TCP/IP protocols include standards for

many common applications including electronic mail, file transfer, and remote login. Thus, when designing application programs that use TCP/IP, programmers often find that existing software provides the communication services they need.

Later chapters will discuss the details of the services provided to the programmer as well as many of the application protocol standards.

1.4 History And Scope Of The Internet

Part of what makes the TCP/IP technology so exciting is its almost universal adoption as well as the size and growth rate of the global Internet. ARPA began working toward an internet technology in the mid 1970s, with the architecture and protocols taking their current form around 1977-79. At that time, ARPA was known as the primary funding agency for packet-switched network research and had pioneered many ideas in packet-switching with its well-known *ARPANET*. The ARPANET used conventional point-to-point leased line interconnection, but ARPA had also funded exploration of packet-switching over radio networks and satellite communication channels. Indeed, the growing diversity of network hardware technologies helped force ARPA to study network interconnection, and pushed internetworking forward.

The availability of research funding from ARPA caught the attention and imagination of several research groups, especially those researchers who had previous experience using packet switching on the ARPANET. ARPA scheduled informal meetings of researchers to share ideas and discuss results of experiments. By 1979, so many researchers were involved in the TCP/IP effort that ARPA formed an informal committee to coordinate and guide the design of the protocols and architecture of the emerging Internet. Called the Internet Control and Configuration Board (ICCB), the group met regularly until 1983, when it was reorganized.

The global Internet began around 1980 when ARPA started converting machines attached to its research networks to the new TCP/IP protocols. The ARPANET, already in place, quickly became the backbone of the new Internet and was used for many of the early experiments with TCP/IP. The transition to Internet technology became complete in January 1983 when the Office of the Secretary of Defense mandated that all computers connected to long-haul networks use TCP/IP. At the same time, the *Defense Communication Agency* (DCA) split the ARPANET into two separate networks, one for further research and one for military communication. The research part retained the name ARPANET; the military part, which was somewhat larger, became known as the *military network*, *MILNET*.

To encourage university researchers to adopt and use the new protocols, ARPA made an implementation available at low cost. At that time, most university computer science departments were running a version of the UNIX operating system available in the University of California's *Berkeley Software Distribution*, commonly called *Berkeley UNIX* or *BSD UNIX*. By funding Bolt Beranek and Newman, Inc. (BBN) to implement its TCP/IP protocols for use with UNIX, and funding Berkeley to integrate the protocols with its software distribution, ARPA was able to reach over 90% of the university computer science departments. The new protocol software came at a particularly significant time because many departments were just acquiring second or third computers and connecting them together with local area networks. The departments needed communication protocols and no others were generally available.

The Berkeley software distribution became popular because it offered more than basic TCP/IP protocols. In addition to standard TCP/IP application programs, Berkeley offered a set of utilities for network services that resembled the UNIX services used on a single machine. The chief advantage of the Berkeley utilities lies in their similarity to standard UNIX. For example, an experienced UNIX user can quickly learn how to use Berkeley's remote file copy utility (*rcp*) because it behaves exactly like the UNIX file copy utility except that it allows users to copy files to or from remote machines.

Besides a set of utility programs, Berkeley UNIX provided a new operating system abstraction known as a *socket* that allows application programs to access communication protocols. A generalization of the UNIX mechanism for I/O, the socket has options for several types of network protocols in addition to TCP/IP. Its design has been debated since its introduction, and many operating systems researchers have proposed alternatives. Independent of its overall merits, however, the introduction of the socket abstraction was important because it allowed programmers to use TCP/IP protocols with little effort. Thus, it encouraged researchers to experiment with TCP/IP.

The success of the TCP/IP technology and the Internet among computer science researchers led other groups to adopt it. Realizing that network communication would soon be a crucial part of scientific research, the National Science Foundation took an active role in expanding the TCP/IP Internet to reach as many scientists as possible. Starting in 1985, it began a program to establish access networks centered around its six supercomputer centers. In 1986 it expanded networking efforts by funding a new wide area backbone network, called the *NSFNET*†, that eventually reached all its supercomputer centers and tied them to the ARPANET. Finally, in 1986 NSF provided seed money for many regional networks, each of which now connects major scientific research institutions in a given area. All the NSF-funded networks use TCP/IP protocols, and all are part of the global Internet.

Within seven years of its inception, the Internet had grown to span hundreds of individual networks located throughout the United States and Europe. It connected nearly 20,000 computers at universities, government, and corporate research laboratories. Both the size and the use of the Internet continued to grow much faster than anticipated. By late 1987, it was estimated that the growth had reached 15% per month. By 1994, the global Internet reached over 3 million computers in 61 countries.

Adoption of TCP/IP protocols and growth of the Internet has not been limited to government-funded projects. Major computer corporations connected to the Internet as did many other large corporations including: oil companies, the auto industry, electronics firms, pharmaceutical companies, and telecommunications carriers. Medium and small companies began connecting in the 1990s. In addition, many companies have used the TCP/IP protocols on their internal corporate internets even though they choose not to be part of the global Internet.

---

†The term *NSFNET* is sometimes used loosely to mean all the NSF-funded networking activities, but we will use it to refer to the backbone. The next chapter gives more details about the technology.

Rapid expansion introduced problems of scale unanticipated in the original design and motivated researchers to find techniques for managing large, distributed resources. In the original design, for example, the names and addresses of all computers attached to the Internet were kept in a single file that was edited by hand and then distributed to every site on the Internet. By the mid 1980s, it became apparent that a central database would not suffice. First, requests to update the file would soon exceed the personnel available to process them. Second, even if a correct central file existed, network capacity was insufficient to allow either frequent distribution to every site or on-line access by each site.

New protocols were developed and a naming system was put in place across the global Internet that allows any user to resolve the name of a remote machine automatically. Known as the *Domain Name System*, the mechanism relies on machines called *name servers* to answer queries about names. No single machine contains the entire domain name database. Instead, data is distributed among a set of machines that use TCP/IP protocols to communicate among themselves when answering a query.

1.5 The Internet Architecture Board

Because the TCP/IP internet protocol suite did not arise from a specific vendor or from a recognized professional society, it is natural to ask, "who sets the technical direction and decides when protocols become standard?" The answer is a group known as the *Internet Architecture Board* (*IAB*†). The IAB provides the focus and coordination for much of the research and development underlying the TCP/IP protocols, and guides the evolution of the Internet. It decides which protocols are a required part of the TCP/IP suite and sets official policies.

Formed in 1983 when ARPA reorganized the Internet Control and Configuration Board, the IAB inherited much of its charter from the earlier group. Its initial goals were to encourage the exchange of ideas among the principals involved in research related to TCP/IP and the Internet, and to keep researchers focused on common objectives. Through the first six years, the IAB evolved from an ARPA-specific research group into an autonomous organization. During these years, each member of the IAB chaired an *Internet Task Force* charged with investigating a problem or set of issues deemed to be important. The IAB consisted of approximately ten task forces, with charters ranging from one that investigated how the traffic load from various applications affects the Internet to one that handled short term Internet engineering problems. The IAB met several times each year to hear status reports from each task force, review and revise technical directions, discuss policies, and exchange information with representatives from agencies like ARPA and NSF who funded Internet operations and research.

---

†IAB originally stood for *Internet Activities Board*.

The chairman of the IAB had the title *Internet Architect* and was responsible for suggesting technical directions and coordinating the activities of the various task forces. The IAB chairman established new task forces on the advice of the IAB and also represented the IAB to others.

Newcomers to TCP/IP are sometimes surprised to learn that the IAB did not manage a large budget; although it set direction, it did not fund most of the research and engineering it envisioned. Instead, volunteers performed much of the work. Members of the IAB were each responsible for recruiting volunteers to serve on their task forces, for calling and running task force meetings, and for reporting progress to the IAB. Usually, volunteers came from the research community or from commercial organizations that produced or used TCP/IP. Active researchers participated in Internet task force activities for two reasons. On one hand, serving on a task force provided opportunities to learn about new research problems. On the other hand, because new ideas and problem solutions designed and tested by task forces often became part of the TCP/IP Internet technology, members realized that their work had a direct, positive influence on the field.

1.6 The IAB Reorganization

By the summer of 1989, both the TCP/IP technology and the Internet had grown beyond the initial research project into production facilities on which thousands of people depended for daily business. It was no longer possible to introduce new ideas by changing a few installations overnight. To a large extent, the literally hundreds of commercial companies that offer TCP/IP products determined whether products would interoperate by deciding when to incorporate changes in their software. Researchers who drafted specifications and tested new ideas in laboratories could no longer expect instant acceptance and use of the ideas. It was ironic that the researchers who designed and watched TCP/IP develop found themselves overcome by the commercial success of their brainchild. In short, TCP/IP became a successful, production technology and the market place began to dominate its evolution.

To reflect the political and commercial realities of both TCP/IP and the Internet, the IAB was reorganized in the summer of 1989. The chairmanship changed. Researchers were moved from the IAB itself to a subsidiary group and a new IAB board was constituted to include representatives from the wider community.

Figure 1.1 illustrates the new IAB organization and the relationship of subgroups.

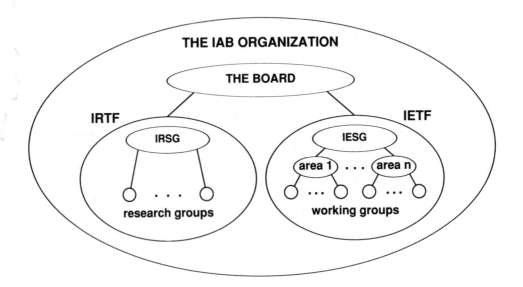

Figure 1.1 The structure of the IAB after the 1989 reorganization.

As Figure 1.1 shows, in addition to the board itself, the IAB organization contains two major groups: the *Internet Research Task Force (IRTF)* and the *Internet Engineering Task Force (IETF)*.

As its name implies, the IETF concentrates on short-term or medium-term engineering problems. The IETF existed in the original IAB structure, and its success provided part of the motivation for reorganization. Unlike most IAB task forces, which were limited to a few individuals who focused on one specific issue, the IETF grew to include dozens of active members who worked on many problems concurrently. Before the reorganization, the IETF was divided into over 20 *working groups*, each focusing on a specific problem. Working groups held individual meetings to formulate problem solutions. In addition, the entire IETF met regularly to hear reports from working groups and discuss proposed changes or additions to the TCP/IP technology. Usually held three times annually, full IETF meetings attracted hundreds of participants and spectators. The IETF had become too large for the chairman to manage.

Because the IETF was known throughout the Internet, and because its meetings were widely recognized and attended, the reorganized IAB structure retains the IETF, but splits it into approximately a dozen areas, each with its own manager. The IETF chairman and the area managers comprise the *Internet Engineering Steering Group (IESG)*, the individuals responsible for coordinating the efforts of IETF working groups. The name "IETF" now refers to the entire body, including the chairman, area managers, and all members of working groups.

Created during the reorganization, the Internet Research Task Force is the research counterpart to the IETF. The IRTF coordinates research activities related to TCP/IP protocols or internet architecture in general. Like the IETF, the IRTF has a small group called the *Internet Research Steering Group* or *IRSG*, that sets priorities and coordinates research activities. Unlike the IETF, the IRTF is currently a much smaller and less active organization. Each member of the IRSG chairs a volunteer *Internet Research Group* analogous to the IETF working groups; the IRTF is not divided into areas.

1.7 The Internet Society

In 1992, as the Internet moved away from its U.S. government roots, a society was formed to encourage participation in the Internet. Called *The Internet Society*, the group is an international organization inspired by the National Geographic Society. The host for the IAB, the Internet Society continues to help people join and use the Internet around the world.

1.8 Internet Request For Comments

We have said that no vendor owns the TCP/IP technology nor does any professional society or standards body. Thus, the documentation of protocols, standards, and policies cannot be obtained from a vendor. Instead, the National Science Foundation funds a group at AT&T to maintain and distribute information about TCP/IP and the global Internet. Known as the *Internet Network Information Center (INTERNIC)*†, the INTERNIC handles many administrative details for the Internet in addition to distributing documentation.

Documentation of work on the Internet, proposals for new or revised protocols, and TCP/IP protocol standards all appear in a series of technical reports called Internet *Requests For Comments*, or *RFCs*. (Preliminary versions of RFCs are known as *Internet drafts*.) RFCs can be short or long, can cover broad concepts or details, and can be standards or merely proposals for new protocols‡. The RFC editor is a member of the IAB. While RFCs are edited, they are not refereed in the same way as academic research papers. Also, some reports pertinent to the Internet were published in an earlier, parallel series of reports called *Internet Engineering Notes*, or *IENs*. Although the IEN series is no longer active, not all IENs appear in the RFC series. There are references to RFCs and a few IENs throughout the text.

The RFC series is numbered sequentially in the chronological order RFCs are written. Each new or revised RFC is assigned a new number, so readers must be careful to obtain the highest numbered version of a document; an index is available to help identify the correct version.

To aid the INTERNIC and make document retrieval quicker, many sites around the world store copies of RFCs and make them available to the community. One can obtain RFCs by postal mail, by electronic mail, or directly across the Internet using a file

---

†Pronounced "Inter-Nick" after its acronym, the organization is a successor to the original Network Information Center (NIC).

‡Appendix *1* contains an introduction to RFCs that examines the diversity of RFCs, including jokes that have appeared.

transfer program. In addition, the INTERNIC and other organizations make available preliminary versions of RFC documents, known as *Internet drafts*. Ask a local network expert how to obtain RFCs or Internet drafts at your site, or refer to Appendix *1* for further instructions on how to retrieve them.

1.9 Internet Protocols And Standardization

Readers familiar with data communication networks realize that many communication protocol standards exist. Many of them precede the Internet, so the question arises, "Why did the Internet designers invent new protocols when so many international standards already existed?" The answer is complex, but follows a simple maxim:

> *Use existing protocol standards whenever such standards apply; invent new protocols only when existing standards are insufficient, and be prepared to use new standards when they become available and provide equivalent functionality.*

So, despite appearances to the contrary, the TCP/IP Internet Protocol Suite was not intended to ignore or avoid extant standards. It came about merely because none of the existing protocols satisfied the need for an interoperable internetworking communication system.

1.10 Future Growth And Technology

Both the TCP/IP technology and the Internet continue to evolve. New protocols are being proposed; old ones are being revised. NSF added considerable complexity to the system by introducing a backbone network, regional networks, and hundreds of campus networks. Other groups around the world continue to connect to the Internet as well. The most significant change comes not from added network connections, however, but from additional traffic. As new users connect to the Internet and new applications appear, traffic patterns change. When physicists, chemists, and biologists began to use the Internet, they exchanged files of data collected from experiments. Such files seemed large compared to electronic mail messages. As the Internet became popular and users began to browse information using services like *gopher* and the *World Wide Web*, traffic increased again.

To accommodate growth in traffic, the capacity of the NSFNET backbone has already been increased three times, making the current capacity approximately 840 times larger than the original; an additional increase by another factor of 3 is scheduled for 1995. At the current time, it is difficult to foresee an end to the need for more capacity.

Growth in demands for networking should not be unexpected. The computer industry has enjoyed a continual demand for increased processing power and larger data
storage for many years. Users have only begun to understand how to use networks. In
the future we can expect continual increases in the demand for communications. Thus,
higher-capacity communication technologies will be needed to accommodate the
growth.

Figure 1.2 summarizes expansion of the Internet and illustrates an important component of growth: the change in complexity arises because multiple autonomous groups
manage parts of the global Internet. The initial designs for many subsystems depended
on centralized management. Much effort is needed to extend those designs to accommodate decentralized management.

	number of networks	number of computers	number of managers
1980	10	10^2	10^0
1990	10^3	10^5	10^1
1997	10^6	10^8	10^2

Figure 1.2 Growth of the connected Internet. In addition to traffic increases
that result from increased size, the Internet faces complexity that
results from decentralized management of both development and
operations.

1.11 Organization Of The Text

The material on TCP/IP has been written in three volumes. This volume presents
the TCP/IP technology, applications that use it, and the architecture of the global Internet in more detail. It discusses the fundamentals of protocols like TCP and IP, and
shows how they fit together in an internet. In addition to giving details, the text
highlights the general principles underlying network protocols and explains why the
TCP/IP protocols adapt easily to so many underlying physical network technologies.
Volume II discusses in depth the internal details of the TCP/IP protocols and shows
how they are implemented. It presents code from a working system to illustrate how
the individual protocols work together, and contains details useful to people responsible
for building a corporate internet. Volume III shows how distributed applications use
TCP/IP for communication. It focuses on the client-server paradigm, the basis for all
distributed programming. It discusses the interface between programs and protocols†,
and shows how clients and server programs are organized. In addition, Volume III
describes the remote procedure concept, and shows how programmers use tools to build
client and server software.

---

†Volume III is available in two versions: one uses the socket interface and the other uses the Transport
Layer Interface.

So far we have talked about the TCP/IP technology and the Internet in general terms, summarizing the services provided and the history of their development. The next chapter provides a brief summary of the type of network hardware used throughout the Internet. Its purpose is not to illuminate nuances of a particular vendor's hardware, but to focus on the features of each technology that are of primary importance to an internet architect. Later chapters delve into the protocols and the Internet, fulfilling three purposes: they explore general concepts and review the Internet architectural model, they examine the details of TCP/IP protocols, and they look at standards for high-level services like electronic mail and electronic file transfer. Chapters *3* through *12* review fundamental principles and describe the network protocol software found in any machine that uses TCP/IP. Later chapters describe services that span multiple machines, including the propagation of routing information, name resolution, and applications like electronic mail.

Two appendices follow the main text. The first appendix contains a guide to RFCs. It expands on the description of RFCs found in this chapter, and gives examples of information that can be found in RFCs. It describes in detail how to obtain RFCs by electronic mail, postal mail, and file transfer. Finally, because the standard RFC index comes in chronological order, the appendix presents a list of RFCs organized by topic to make it easier for beginners to find RFCs pertinent to a given subject.

The second appendix contains an alphabetical list of terms and abbreviations used throughout the literature and the text. Because beginners often find the new terminology overwhelming and difficult to remember, they are encouraged to use the alphabetical list instead of scanning back through the text.

1.12 Summary

An internet consists of a set of connected networks that act as a coordinated whole. The chief advantage of an internet is that it provides universal interconnection while allowing individual groups to use whatever network hardware is best suited to their needs. We will examine principles underlying internet communication in general and the details of one internet protocol suite in particular. We will also discuss how internet protocols are used in an internet. Our example technology, called TCP/IP after its two main protocols, was developed by the Advanced Research Projects Agency. It provides the basis for the global Internet, a large, operational internet that connects universities, corporations, and government departments in many countries around the world. The global Internet is expanding rapidly.

FOR FURTHER STUDY

Cerf's *A History Of The ARPANET* [1989] and *History of the Internet Activities Board* [RFC 1160] provide fascinating reading and point the reader to early research papers on TCP/IP and internetworking. Denning [Nov-Dec 1989] provides a different perspective on the history of the ARPANET. Jennings et. al. [1986] discusses the importance of computer networking for scientists. Denning [Sept-Oct 1989] also points out the importance of internetworking and gives one possible scenario for a world-wide internet. The Federal Coordinating Committee for Science, Engineering and Technology [FCCSET] suggests networking should be a national priority.

The IETF publishes minutes from its regular meetings; these are available from the Corporation for National Research Initiatives in Reston, VA. The *Journal of Internetworking: Research and Experience* reports on internetworking research, with emphasis on experimental validation of ideas. The periodical *Connexions* [Jacobsen 1987-] contains articles about TCP/IP and the Internet as well as official statements of policy from the IAB. Finally, the reader is encouraged to remember that the TCP/IP protocol suite and the Internet continue to change; new information can be found in RFCs and at conferences such as the annual ACM SIGCOMM Symposium and Interop Company's NETWORLD+INTEROP events.

EXERCISES

1.1 Explore application programs at your site that use TCP/IP.

1.2 Find out whether your site connects to the Internet.

1.3 TCP/IP products account for over a billion dollars per year in gross revenue. Read trade publications to find a list of vendors offering such products.

2

Review Of Underlying Network Technologies

2.1 Introduction

It is important to understand that the Internet is not a new kind of physical network. It is, instead, a method of interconnecting physical networks and a set of conventions for using networks that allow the computers they reach to interact. While network hardware plays only a minor role in the overall design, understanding the internet technology requires one to distinguish between the low-level mechanisms provided by the hardware itself and the higher-level facilities that the TCP/IP protocol software provides. It is also important to understand how the facilities supplied by packet-switched technology affect our choice of high-level abstractions.

This chapter introduces basic packet-switching concepts and terminology, and then reviews some of the underlying network hardware technologies that have been used in TCP/IP internets. Later chapters describe how these networks are interconnected and how the TCP/IP protocols accommodate vast differences in the hardware. While the list presented here is certainly not comprehensive, it clearly demonstrates the variety among physical networks over which TCP/IP operates. The reader can safely skip many of the technical details, but should try to grasp the idea of packet switching and try to imagine building a homogeneous communication system using such heterogeneous hardware. Most important, the reader should look closely at the details of the physical address schemes the various technologies use; later chapters will discuss in detail how high-level protocols use physical addresses.

2.2 Two Approaches To Network Communication

Whether they provide connections between one computer and another or between terminals and computers, communication networks can be divided into two basic types: *circuit-switched* (sometimes called *connection oriented*) and *packet-switched*† (sometimes called *connectionless*). Circuit-switched networks operate by forming a dedicated connection (circuit) between two points. The U.S. telephone system uses circuit switching technology – a telephone call establishes a circuit from the originating phone through the local switching office, across trunk lines, to a remote switching office, and finally to the destination telephone. While a circuit is in place, the phone equipment samples the microphone repeatedly, encodes the samples digitally, and transmits them across the circuit to the receiver. The sender is guaranteed that the samples can be delivered and reproduced because the circuit provides a guaranteed data path of 64 Kbps (thousand bits per second), the rate needed to send digitized voice. The advantage of circuit switching lies in its guaranteed capacity: once a circuit is established, no other network activity will decrease the capacity of the circuit. One disadvantage of circuit switching is cost: circuit costs are fixed, independent of traffic. For example, one pays a fixed rate for a phone call, even when the two parties do not talk.

Packet-switched networks, the type usually used to connect computers, take an entirely different approach. In a packet-switched network, data to be transferred across a network is divided into small pieces called *packets* that are multiplexed onto high capacity intermachine connections. A packet, which usually contains only a few hundred bytes of data, carries identification that enables the network hardware to know how to send it to the specified destination. For example, a large file to be transmitted between two machines must be broken into many packets that are sent across the network one at a time. The network hardware delivers the packets to the specified destination, where software reassembles them into a single file again. The chief advantage of packet-switching is that multiple communications among computers can proceed concurrently, with intermachine connections shared by all pairs of machines that are communicating. The disadvantage, of course, is that as activity increases, a given pair of communicating computers receives less of the network capacity. That is, whenever a packet switched network becomes overloaded, computers using the network must wait before they can send additional packets.

Despite the potential drawback of not being able to guarantee network capacity, packet-switched networks have become extremely popular. The motivations for adopting packet switching are cost and performance. Because multiple machines can share the network hardware, fewer connections are required and cost is kept low. Because engineers have been able to build high speed network hardware, capacity is not usually a problem. So many computer interconnections use packet-switching that, throughout the remainder of this text, the term *network* will refer only to packet-switched networks.

---

†In fact, it is possible to build hybrid hardware technologies; for our purposes, only the difference in functionality is important.

2.3 Wide Area And Local Area Networks

Packet-switched networks that span large geographical distances (e.g., the continental U.S.) are fundamentally different from those that span short distances (e.g., a single room). To help characterize the differences in capacity and intended use, packet switched technologies are often divided into two broad categories: *wide area networks* (*WANs*) and *Local Area Networks* (*LANs*). The two categories do not have formal definitions. Instead, vendors apply the terms loosely to help customers distinguish among technologies.

WAN technologies, sometimes called *long haul networks*, provide communication over large distances. Most WAN technologies do not limit the distance spanned; a WAN can allow the endpoints of a communication to be arbitrarily far apart. For example, a WAN can span a continent or can join computers across an ocean. Usually, WANs operate at slower speeds than LANs, and have much greater delay between connections. Typical speeds for a WAN range from 56 Kbps to 155 Mbps (million bits per second). Delays across a WAN can vary from a few milliseconds to several tenths of a second†

LAN technologies provide the highest speed connections among computers, but sacrifice the ability to span large distances. For example, a typical LAN spans a small area like a single building or a small campus and operates between 10 Mbps and 2 Gbps (billion bits per second). Because LAN technologies cover short distances, they offer lower delays than WANs. The delay across a LAN can be as short as a few tenths of a millisecond, or as long as 10 milliseconds.

We have already mentioned the general tradeoff between speed and distance: technologies that provide higher speed communication operate over shorter distances. There are other differences among technologies in the categories as well. In LAN technologies, each computer usually contains a network interface device that connects the machine directly to the network medium (e.g., a copper wire or coaxial cable). Often, the network itself is passive, depending on electronic devices in the attached computers to generate and receive the necessary electrical signals. In WAN technologies, a network usually consists of a series of complex computers called *packet switches* interconnected by communication lines and modems. The size of the network can be extended by adding a new switch and another communication line. Attaching a user's computer to a WAN means connecting it to one of the packet switches. Each switch along a path in the WAN introduces a delay when it receives a packet and forwards it to the next switch. Thus, the larger the WAN becomes the longer it takes to route traffic across it.

This book discusses software that hides the technological differences between networks and makes interconnection independent of the underlying hardware. To appreciate design choices in the software, it is necessary to understand how it relates to network hardware. The next sections present examples of network technologies that have been used in the Internet, showing some of the differences among them. Later chapters show how the TCP/IP software isolates such differences and makes the communication system independent of the underlying hardware technology.

---

†Such long delays result from WANs that communicate by sending signals to a satellite orbiting the earth.

2.3.1 Network Hardware Addresses

Each network hardware technology defines an *addressing mechanism* that computers use to specify the destination for each packet. Every computer attached to a network is assigned a unique address, usually an integer. A packet sent across a network includes a *destination address field* that contains the address of the intended recipient. The destination address appears in the same location in all packets, making it possible for the network hardware to examine the destination address easily. A sender must know the address of the intended recipient, and must place the recipient's address in the destination address field of a packet before transmitting the packet.

Each hardware technology specifies how computers are assigned addresses. The hardware specifies, for example, the number of bits in the address as well as the location of the destination address field in a packet. Although some technologies use compatible addressing schemes, many do not. This chapter contains a few examples of hardware addressing schemes; later chapters explain how TCP/IP accommodates diverse hardware addressing schemes.

2.4 Ethernet Technology

Ethernet is the name given to a popular packet-switched LAN technology invented at Xerox PARC in the early 1970s. Xerox Corporation, Intel Corporation, and Digital Equipment Corporation standardized Ethernet in 1978; IEEE released a compatible version of the standard using the number 802.3. Ethernet has become a popular LAN technology; most medium or large corporations use Ethernets. Because Ethernet is so popular, many variants exist; we will discuss the original design first and then cover variants.

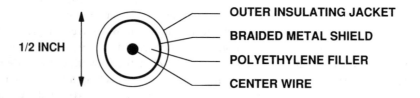

Figure 2.1 A cross-section of the coaxial cable used in the original Ethernet.

Each Ethernet cable is about 1/2 inch in diameter and up to 500 meters long. A resistor is added between the center wire and shield at each end to prevent reflection of electrical signals.

The original Ethernet design used a coaxial cable as Figure 2.1 illustrates. Called the *ether*, the cable itself is completely passive; all the active electronic components that make the network function are associated with computers that are attached to the network.

The connection between a computer and a coaxial Ethernet cable requires a hardware device called a *transceiver*. Physically, the connection between a transceiver and the Ethernet requires a small hole in the outer layers of the cable as Figure 2.2 illustrates. Technicians often use the term *tap* to describe the connection between an Ethernet transceiver and the cable. Usually, small metal pins mounted in the transceiver go through the hole and provide electrical contacts to the center wire and the braided shield. Some manufacturers' connectors require that the cable be cut and a "T" inserted.

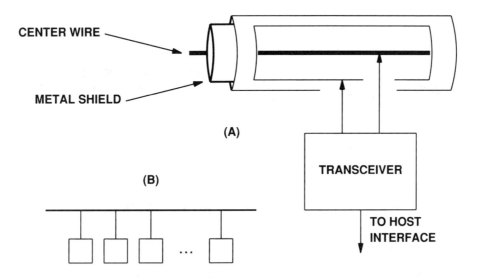

Figure 2.2 (a) A cutaway view of an Ethernet cable showing the details of electrical connections between a transceiver and the cable, and (b) the schematic diagram of an Ethernet with many computers connected.

Each connection to an Ethernet has two major electronic components. A *transceiver* connects to the center wire and braided shield on the cable, sensing and sending signals on the ether. A *host interface* or *host adapter* plugs into the computer's bus (e.g., on a motherboard) and connects to the transceiver.

A transceiver is a small piece of hardware usually found physically adjacent to the ether. In addition to the analog hardware that senses and controls electrical signals on the ether, a transceiver contains digital circuitry that allows it to communicate with a digital computer. The transceiver can sense when the ether is in use and can translate analog electrical signals on the ether to (and from) digital form. A cable called the *Attachment Unit Interface* (AUI) cable connects the transceiver to an adapter board in a host computer. Informally called a *transceiver cable*, the AUI cable contains many wires. The wires carry the electrical power needed to operate the transceiver, the signals that control the transceiver operation, and the contents of the packets being sent or received. Figure 2.3 illustrates how the components form a connection between a bus in a computer system and an Ethernet cable.

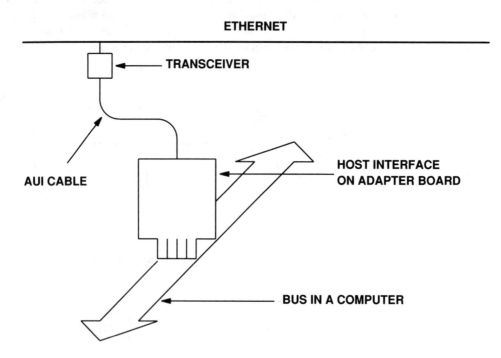

Figure 2.3 The two main electronic components that form a connection between a computer's bus and an Ethernet. The AUI cable that connects the host interface to the transceiver carries power and signals to control transceiver operation as well as packets being transmitted or received.

Each host interface controls the operation of one transceiver according to instructions it receives from the computer software. To the operating system software, the interface appears to be an input/output device that accepts basic data transfer instructions from the computer, controls the transceiver to carry them out, interrupts when the task has been completed, and reports status information. Although the transceiver is a simple hardware device, the host interface can be complex (e.g., it may contain a microprocessor used to control transfers between the computer memory and the ether).

In practice, organizations that use the original Ethernet in a conventional office environment run the Ethernet cable along the ceiling in each hall, and arrange for a connection from each office to attach to the cable. Figure 2.4 illustrates the resulting physical wiring scheme.

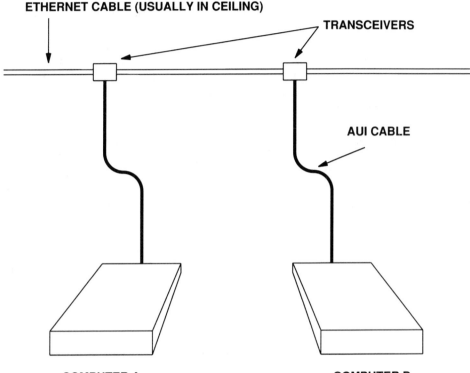

Figure 2.4 The physical connection of two computers to an Ethernet using the original wiring scheme. In an office environment, the Ethernet cable is usually placed in the hallway ceiling; each office has an AUI cable that connects a computer in the office to a transceiver attached to the Ethernet cable.

2.4.1 Thin-Wire Ethernet

Several components of the original Ethernet technology have undesirable properties. For example because a transceiver contains electronic components, it has a nontrivial cost. Furthermore, because transceivers are located with the cable and not with computers, they can be difficult to access or replace. The coaxial cable that forms the ether can also be difficult to install. In particular, to provide maximum protection against electrical interference from devices like electric motors, the cable contains heavy shielding that makes it difficult to bend. Finally, an AUI cable is also thick and difficult to bend.

To reduce costs for environments like offices that do not contain much electrical interference, engineers developed an alternative Ethernet wiring scheme. Called *thin-wire Ethernet* or *thinnet*†, the alternative coaxial cable is thinner, less expensive, and more flexible. However, a thin-wire Ethernet has some disadvantages. Because it does not provide as much protection from electrical interference, thin-wire Ethernet cannot be placed adjacent to powerful electrical equipment like that found in a factory. Furthermore, thin-wire Ethernet covers somewhat shorter distances and supports fewer computer connections per network than thick Ethernet.

To further reduce costs with thin-wire Ethernet, engineers replaced the costly transceiver with special high-speed digital circuits, and provided a direct connection from a computer to the ether. Thus, in a thin-wire scheme, a computer contains both the host interface and the circuitry that connects to the cable. Manufacturers of small computers and workstations find thin-wire Ethernet an especially attractive scheme because they can integrate Ethernet hardware into single board computers and mount connectors directly on the back of the computer.

Because a thin-wire Ethernet connects directly from one computer to another, the wiring scheme works well when many computers occupy a single room. The thin-wire cable runs directly from one computer to the next. To add a new computer, one only needs to link it into the chain. Figure 2.5 illustrates the connections used with thin-wire Ethernet.

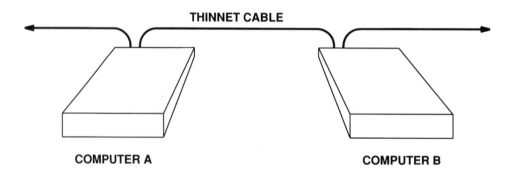

Figure 2.5 The physical connection of two computers using the thinnet wiring scheme. The ether passes directly from one computer to another; no external transceiver hardware is required.

Thin-wire Ethernets are designed to be easy to connect and disconnect. Thin-wire uses *BNC connectors*, which do not require tools to attach a computer to the cable. Thus, a user can connect a computer to a thin-wire Ethernet without the aid of a technician. Of course, allowing users to manipulate the ether has disadvantages: if a user disconnects the ether, it prevents all machines on the ether from communicating. In many situations, however, the advantages outweigh the disadvantages.

---

†To contrast it with thin-wire, the original Ethernet cable is sometimes called *thick Ethernet*, or *thicknet*.

2.4.2 Twisted Pair Ethernet

Advances in technology have made it possible to build Ethernets that do not need the electrical shielding of a coaxial cable. Called *twisted pair Ethernet*, the technology allows a computer to access an Ethernet using a pair of conventional unshielded copper wires similar to the wires used to connect telephones. The advantages of using twisted pair wiring are that it further reduces costs and protects other computers on the network from a user who disconnects a single computer. In some cases, a twisted pair technology can make it possible for an organization to use Ethernet over existing telephone wiring without adding new cables.

Known by the technical name *10Base-T*, the twisted pair wiring scheme connects each computer to an Ethernet *hub* as Figure 2.6 shows.

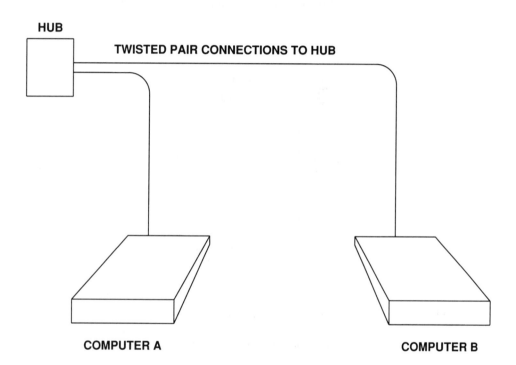

Figure 2.6 An illustration of Ethernet using twisted pair wiring. Each computer connects to a hub over a conventional pair of wires.

The hub is an electronic device that simulates the signals on an Ethernet cable. Physically, a hub consists of a small box that usually resides in a wiring closet; a connection between a hub and a computer must be less than 100 meters long. A hub requires power, and can allow authorized personnel to monitor and control its operation over the network. To the host interface in a computer, a connection to a hub appears to

operate the same way as a connection to a transceiver. That is, an Ethernet hub provides the same communication capability as a thick or thin Ethernet; hubs merely offer
an alternative wiring scheme.

2.4.3 Adapters And Multiple Wiring Schemes

A connection to thick Ethernet requires an AUI connector, a connection to thin-
wire Ethernet requires a BNC connector, and a connection to 10Base-T requires an
RJ45 connector that resembles the modular connectors used with telephones. Many
Ethernet products allow each customer to choose a wiring scheme. For example,
adapter boards for personal computers often come with three connectors as Figure 2.7
illustrates. Although only one connector can be used at any time, a computer that has
such an adapter can be moved from one wiring scheme to another easily.

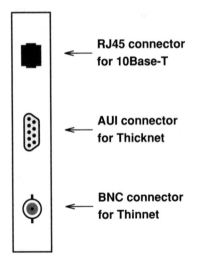

RJ45 connector
for 10Base-T

AUI connector
for Thicknet

BNC connector
for Thinnet

Figure 2.7 A typical Ethernet adapter card with three connectors for the three
Ethernet wiring schemes. Although the adapter contains three
connectors, it can only use one wiring scheme at any time.

2.4.4 Properties of an Ethernet

The Ethernet is a 10 Mbps broadcast bus technology with best-effort delivery semantics and distributed access control. It is a *bus* because all stations share a single
communication channel; it is *broadcast* because all transceivers receive every transmission. The method used to direct packets from one station to just one other station or a
subset of all stations will be discussed later. For now, it is enough to understand that

transceivers do not distinguish among transmissions − a transceiver passes all packets from the cable to the host interface, which chooses packets the computer should receive and filters out all others. Ethernet is called a *best-effort delivery* mechanism because the hardware provides no information to the sender about whether the packet was delivered. For example, if the destination machine happens to be powered down, packets sent to it will be lost, and the sender will not be notified. We will see later how the TCP/IP protocols accommodate best-effort delivery hardware.

Ethernet access control is distributed because, unlike some network technologies, Ethernet has no central authority to grant access. The Ethernet access scheme is called *Carrier Sense Multiple Access* with *Collision Detect* (*CSMA/CD*). It is *CSMA* because multiple machines can access the Ethernet simultaneously and each machine determines whether the ether is idle by sensing whether a carrier wave is present. When a host interface has a packet to transmit, it listens to the ether to see if a message is being transmitted (i.e., performs carrier sensing). When no transmission is sensed, the host interface starts transmitting. Each transmission is limited in duration (because there is a maximum packet size). Furthermore, the hardware must observe a minimum idle time between transmissions, which means that no single pair of communicating machines can use the network without giving other machines an opportunity for access.

2.4.5 Collision Detection And Recovery

When a transceiver begins transmission, the signal does not reach all parts of the network simultaneously. Instead it travels along the cable at approximately 80% of the speed of light. Thus, it is possible for two transceivers to both sense that the network is idle and begin transmission simultaneously. When the two electrical signals cross they become scrambled, such that neither is meaningful. Such incidents are called *collisions*.

The Ethernet handles collisions in an ingenious fashion. Each transceiver monitors the cable while it is transmitting to see if a foreign signal interferes with its transmission. Technically, the monitoring is called *collision detect* (*CD*), making the Ethernet a CSMA/CD network. When a collision is detected, the host interface aborts transmission, waits for activity to subside, and tries again. Care must be taken or the network could wind up with all transceivers busily attempting to transmit and every transmission producing a collision. To help avoid such situations, Ethernet uses a binary exponential backoff policy where a sender delays a random time after the first collision, twice as long if a second attempt to transmit also produces a collision, four times as long if a third attempt results in a collision, and so on. The motivation for exponential backoff is that in the unlikely event many stations attempt to transmit simultaneously, a severe traffic jam could occur. In such a jam, there is a high probability two stations will choose random backoffs that are close together. Thus, the probability of another collision is high. By doubling the random delay, the exponential backoff strategy quickly spreads the stations' attempts to retransmit over a reasonably long period of time, making the probability of further collisions extremely small.

2.4.6 Ethernet Capacity

The standard Ethernet is rated at 10 Mbps, which means that data can be transmitted onto the cable at 10 million bits per second. Although a computer can generate data at Ethernet speed, raw network speed should not be thought of as the rate at which two computers can exchange data. Instead, network speed should be thought of as a measure of network total traffic capacity. Think of a network as a highway connecting multiple cities, and think of packets as cars on the highway. High bandwidth makes it possible to carry heavy traffic loads, while low bandwidth means the highway cannot carry as much traffic. A 10 Mbps Ethernet, for example, can handle a few computers that generate heavy loads, or many computers that generate light loads.

2.4.7 Ethernet Hardware Addresses

Ethernet defines a 48-bit addressing scheme. Each computer attached to an Ethernet network is assigned a unique 48-bit number known as its *Ethernet address*. To assign an address, Ethernet hardware manufacturers purchase blocks of Ethernet addresses† and assign them in sequence as they manufacture Ethernet interface hardware. Thus, no two hardware interfaces have the same Ethernet address.

Usually, the Ethernet address is fixed in machine readable form on the host interface hardware. Because Ethernet addresses belong to hardware devices, they are sometimes called *hardware addresses* or *physical addresses*. Note the following important property of Ethernet physical addresses:

> *Physical addresses are associated with the Ethernet interface hardware; moving the hardware interface to a new machine or replacing a hardware interface that has failed changes the machine's physical address.*

Knowing that Ethernet physical addresses can change will make it clear why higher levels of the network software are designed to accommodate such changes.

The host interface hardware examines packets and determines the packets that should be sent to the host. Recall that each interface receives a copy of every packet – even those addressed to other machines. The host interface uses the destination address field in a packet as a filter. The interface ignores those packets that are addressed to other machines, and passes to the host only those packets addressed to it. The addressing mechanism and hardware filter are needed to prevent a computer from being overwhelmed with incoming data. Although the computer's central processor could perform the check, doing so in the host interface keeps traffic on the Ethernet from slowing down processing on all computers.

A 48-bit Ethernet address can do more than specify a single destination computer. An address can be one of three types:

---

†The Institute for Electrical and Electronic Engineers (IEEE) manages the Ethernet address space and assigns addresses as needed.

- The physical address of one network interface (a *unicast* address)
- The network *broadcast* address
- A *multicast* address

By convention, the broadcast address (all 1s) is reserved for sending to all stations simultaneously. Multicast addresses provide a limited form of broadcast in which a subset of the computers on a network agree to listen to a given multicast address. The set of participating computers is called a *multicast group*. To join a multicast group, a computer must instruct its host interface to accept the group's multicast address. The advantage of multicasting lies in the ability to limit broadcasts: every computer in a multicast group can be reached with a single packet transmission, but computers that choose not to participate in a particular multicast group do not receive packets sent to the group.

To accommodate broadcast and multicast addressing, Ethernet interface hardware must recognize more than its physical address. A host interface usually accepts at least two kinds of packets: those addressed to the interface's physical (i.e., unicast) address and those addressed to the network broadcast address. Some interfaces can be programmed to recognize multicast addresses or even alternate physical addresses. When the operating system starts, it initializes the Ethernet interface, giving it a set of addresses to recognize. The interface then examines the destination address field in each packet, passing on to the host only those transmissions designated for one of the specified addresses.

2.4.8 Ethernet Frame Format

The Ethernet should be thought of as a link-level connection among machines. Thus, it makes sense to view the data transmitted as a *frame*†. Ethernet frames are of variable length, with no frame smaller than 64 octets‡ or larger than 1518 octets (header, data, and CRC). As in all packet-switched networks, each Ethernet frame contains a field that contains the address of its destination. Figure 2.8 shows that the Ethernet frame format contains the physical source address as well as the destination address.

Preamble	Destination Address	Source Address	Frame Type	Frame Data	CRC
8 octets	6 octets	6 octets	2 octets	64–1500 octets	4 octets

Figure 2.8 The format of a frame (packet) as it travels across an Ethernet preceded by a preamble. Fields are not drawn to scale.

In addition to identifying the source and destination, each frame transmitted across the Ethernet contains a *preamble*, *type field*, *data field*, and *Cyclic Redundancy Check* (*CRC*). The preamble consists of 64 bits of alternating *0*s and *1*s to help receiving

---

†The term *frame* derives from communication over serial lines in which the sender "frames" the data by adding special characters before and after the transmitted data.

‡Technically, the term *byte* refers to a hardware-dependent character size; networking professionals use the term *octet*, because it refers to an 8-bit quantity on all computers.

nodes synchronize. The 32-bit CRC helps the interface detect transmission errors: the sender computes the CRC as a function of the data in the frame, and the receiver recomputes the CRC to verify that the packet has been received intact.

The frame type field contains a 16-bit integer that identifies the type of the data being carried in the frame. From the Internet point of view, the frame type field is essential because it means Ethernet frames are *self-identifying*. When a frame arrives at a given machine, the operating system uses the frame type to determine which protocol software module should process the frame. The chief advantages of self-identifying frames are that they allow multiple protocols to be used together on a single machine and they allow multiple protocols to be intermixed on the same physical network without interference. For example, one could have an application program using Internet protocols while another used a local experimental protocol. The operating system uses the type field of an arriving frame to decide how to process the contents. We will see that the TCP/IP protocols use self-identifying Ethernet frames to distinguish among several protocols.

2.4.9 Extending An Ethernet With Repeaters

Although an Ethernet cable has a maximum length, the network can be extended in two ways: using repeaters and bridges. A hardware device called a *repeater* can be used to relay electrical signals from one cable to another. However, at most two repeaters can be placed between any two machines, so the total length of a single Ethernet is still rather short (three segments of 500 meters each). Figure 2.9 shows a typical use of repeaters in an office building. A single cable runs vertically up the building, and a repeater attaches the backbone to an additional cable on each floor. Computers attach to the cables on each floor.

2.4.10 Extending An Ethernet With Bridges

Bridges are superior to repeaters because they do not replicate noise, errors, or malformed frames; a completely valid frame must be received before the bridge will accept and transmit it on the other segment. Furthermore, bridge interfaces follow the Ethernet CSMA/CD rules, so collisions and propagation delays on one wire remain isolated from those on the other. As a result, an (almost) arbitrary number of Ethernets can be connected together with bridges. The important point is:

> *Bridges hide the details of interconnection: a set of bridged segments acts like a single Ethernet.*

A computer uses exactly the same hardware to communicate with a computer across a bridge as it uses to communicate with a computer on the local segment.

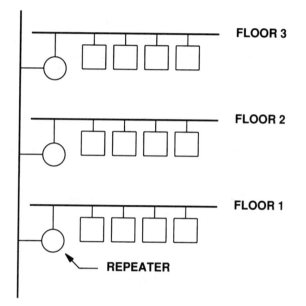

Figure 2.9 Repeaters used to join Ethernet cables in a building. At most two repeaters can be placed between a pair of communicating machines.

Most bridges do much more than replicate frames from one wire to another: they make intelligent decisions about which frames to forward. Such bridges are called *adaptive*, or *learning* bridges. An adaptive bridge consists of a computer with two Ethernet interfaces. The software in an adaptive bridge keeps two address lists, one for each interface. When a frame arrives from Ethernet E_1, the adaptive bridge adds the 48-bit Ethernet *source* address to the list associated with E_1. Similarly, when a frame arrives from Ethernet E_2, the bridge adds the source address to the list associated with E_2. Thus, over time the adaptive bridge will learn which machines lie on E_1 and which lie on E_2.

After recording the source address of a frame, the adaptive bridge uses the destination address to determine whether to forward the frame. If the address list shows that the destination lies on the Ethernet from which the frame arrived, the bridge does not forward the frame. If the destination is not in the address list (i.e., the destination is a broadcast or multicast address or the bridge has not yet learned the location of the destination), the bridge forwards the frame to the other Ethernet.

The advantages of adaptive bridges should be obvious. Because the bridge uses addresses found in normal traffic, it is completely automatic – humans need not configure the bridge with specific addresses. Because it does not forward traffic unnecessarily, a bridge helps improve the performance of an overloaded network by isolating traffic on specific segments. Bridges work exceptionally well if a network can be divided physically into two segments that each contain a set of computers that communicate frequently (e.g., each segment contains a set of workstations along with a server, and the workstations direct most of their traffic to the server). To summarize:

> An adaptive Ethernet bridge connects two Ethernet segments, forwarding frames from one to the other. It uses source addresses to learn which machines lie on which Ethernet segment, and it combines information learned with destination addresses to eliminate forwarding when unnecessary.

From the TCP/IP point of view, bridged Ethernets are merely another form of physical network connection. The important point is:

> Because the connection among physical cables provided by bridges and repeaters is transparent to machines using the Ethernet, we think of multiple Ethernet segments connected by bridges and repeaters as a single physical network system.

Most commercial bridges are much more sophisticated and robust than our description indicates. When first powered up, they check for other bridges and learn the topology of the network. They use a distributed spanning-tree algorithm to decide how to forward frames. In particular, the bridges decide how to propagate broadcast packets so only one copy of a broadcast frame is delivered to each wire. Without such an algorithm, Ethernets and bridges connected in a cycle would produce catastrophic results because they would forward broadcast packets in both directions simultaneously.

2.5 Fiber Distributed Data Interconnect (FDDI)

FDDI is a popular local area networking technology that provides higher bandwidth than Ethernet. Unlike Ethernet and other LAN technologies that use cables to carry electrical signals, FDDI uses glass fibers and transfers data by encoding it in pulses of light†.

Optical fiber has two advantages over copper wire. First, because electrical noise does not interfere with an optical connection, the fiber can lie adjacent to powerful electrical devices. Second, because optical fibers use light, the amount of data that can be sent per unit time is much higher than cables that carry electrical signals.

It might seem that glass fibers would be difficult to install and would break if bent. However, an optical cable is surprisingly flexible. The glass fiber itself has an extremely small diameter, and the cable includes a plastic jacket that protects the fiber from breaking. Such a cable cannot bend at a ninety degree angle, but it can bend in an arc with a diameter of a few inches. Thus, installation is not difficult.

---

†A related technology known as *Copper Distributed Data Interface* (*CDDI*) works like FDDI, but uses copper cables to carry signals.

2.5.1 Properties Of An FDDI Network

An FDDI network is a 100 Mbps token ring technology with a self-healing capability. An FDDI network is a *ring* because the network forms a cycle that starts at one computer, passes through all others computers, and ends back at the source. FDDI is a *token ring* technology because it uses a token to control transmission. When the network is idle, a special, reserved frame called a *token* passes from station to station. When a station has a packet to send, it waits for the token to arrive, sends its packet, and then passes the token to the next station. The circulating token guarantees fairness: it ensures that all stations have an opportunity to send a packet before any station sends a second packet.

Perhaps the most interesting property of an FDDI lies in its ability to detect and correct problems. The network is called *self-healing* because the hardware can automatically accommodate a failure.

2.5.2 Dual Counter-Rotating Rings

To provide automatic recovery from failures, FDDI hardware uses two independent rings that both connect to each computer. Figure 2.10 illustrates the topology.

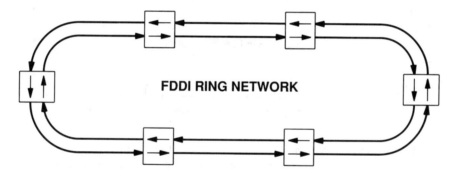

FDDI RING NETWORK

Figure 2.10 An FDDI network with optical fibers interconnecting six computers. Arrows show the direction of traffic on the fibers and through the attached computers.

FDDI rings are called *counter rotating* because traffic passes in the opposite direction on each ring. The reason for using a counter rotating scheme will become clear when we consider how FDDI handles failures.

Unless an error has occurred, an FDDI hardware does not need both rings. In fact, an FDDI interface behaves like any token passing network interface until an error occurs. The interface examines all packets that circulate around the ring, comparing the destination address in each packet to the computer's address. The interface keeps a copy of any packet destined for the local computer, but also forwards the packet around the ring.

When a computer needs to transmit a packet, it waits for the token to arrive, temporarily stops forwarding bits, and sends its packet. After sending one packet, the interface transmits the token, and begins forwarding bits again. If a station has more than one packet ready to be sent when it receives the token, the station only sends one packet before passing the token. Thus, the token-passing scheme guarantees that all stations have fair access to the network.

FDDI hardware becomes more interesting when a hardware error occurs. When an interface detects that it cannot communicate with the adjacent computer, the interface uses the backup ring to bypass the failure. For example, Figure 2.11 shows an FDDI ring in which an interface has failed, and the two adjacent interfaces have eliminated it from the ring.

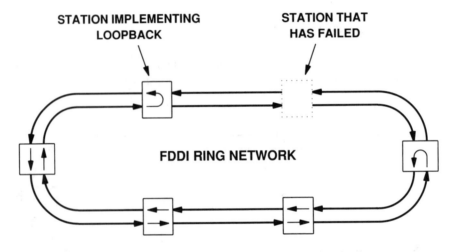

Figure 2.11 An FDDI ring after a failure. When FDDI hardware detects such a failure, it uses the second ring to bypass the failure and allows remaining stations to communicate.

The purpose of the second ring and the reason data flows in the opposite direction should now be clear: a failure can mean that the fiber has been disconnected (e.g., accidentally cut). If the fiber from both rings follows the same physical path, chances are high that the second fiber may have been disconnected as well. FDDI hardware automatically uses the counter rotating ring to form a closed loop in the direction that is still working. Doing so permits the other computers to continue communication despite the failure.

When FDDI hardware detects a failure on the network, it automatically loops data across the backup ring to permit communication among remaining stations.

2.5.3 FDDI Frame Format

FDDI standards specify the exact format of frames used on the network. The table in Figure 2.12 lists fields in an FDDI frame.

Field	Length in 4-bit units	Contents
PA	4 or more	Preamble
SD	2	Start Delimiter
FC	2	Frame Control
DA	4 or 12	Destination Address
SA	4 or 12	Source Address
RI	0 to 60	Routing Information
DATA	0 or more	Data
FCS	8	Frame Check Sequence
ED	1	End Delimiter
FS	3 or more	Frame Status

Figure 2.12 The format of frames used by FDDI, with fields measured in 4-bit units called *symbols*. The maximum frame length is 9000 symbols.

Like other technologies, each computer attached to an FDDI network is assigned an address, and each frame contains a destination address field. However, to make FDDI more flexible and to provide a standard way to interconnect two FDDI rings, the designers allowed more than one frame format. For example, the destination address field is either 4 or 12 symbols long, where a *symbol* is a 4-bit unit. The frame also includes a small field used for routing. The sender can use the routing field to specify that a frame must be sent first to a connection point and then on to a destination on an attached ring.

One of the advantages of FDDI arises from its large frame size. Because a frame can contain 9000 4-bit symbols, the total frame can be 4500 octets long. Because header information occupies at most a few hundred octets, a single frame can carry 4K octets of user data. For applications that transfer large volumes of data (e.g., file transfer), the large frame size means less overhead and consequently high throughput.

2.6 Asynchronous Transfer Mode

Asynchronous Transfer Mode (*ATM*) is the name given to a high-speed, connection-oriented networking technology that has been used in both local area and wide area networks. By current standards, high-speed refers to networks that operate at 100 Mbps and higher; ATM can switch data at gigabit speeds†. Of course, such high speeds require complex, state-of-the-art equipment. As a result, ATM networks are more expensive than other technologies.

To achieve high transfer speeds, an ATM network uses special-purpose hardware and software techniques. First, an ATM network consists of one or more high-speed switches that each connect to host computers and to other ATM switches. Second, ATM uses optical fibers for connections, including connections from a host computer to an ATM switch. Optical fibers provide a higher transfer rate than copper wires; typically, the connection between a host and an ATM switch operates at 100 or 155 Mbps. Third, the lowest layers of an ATM network use fixed-size frames called *cells*. Because each cell is exactly the same size, ATM switch hardware can process cells quickly.

2.6.1 ATM Cell Size

Surprisingly, each ATM cell is only 53 octets long. The cell contains 5 octets of header followed by 48 octets of data. Later chapters will show, however, that when using ATM to send IP traffic, the 53 octet size is irrelevant – an ATM network accepts and delivers much larger packets.

2.6.2 Connection-Oriented Networking

ATM differs from the packet-switching networks described earlier because it offers *connection oriented* service. Before a host computer connected to an ATM can send cells, the host must first interact with the switch to specify a destination. The interaction is analogous to placing a telephone call‡. The host specifies the remote computer's address, and waits for the ATM switch to contact the remote system and establish a path. If the remote computer rejects the request, does not respond, or the ATM switch cannot currently reach the remote computer, the request to establish communication fails.

When a connection succeeds, the local ATM switch chooses an identifier for the connection, and passes the connection identifier to the host along with a message that informs the host of success. The host uses the connection identifier when sending or receiving cells.

When it finishes using a connection, the host again communicates with the ATM switch to request that the connection be broken. The switch disconnects the two computers. Disconnection is equivalent to hanging up a telephone at the end of a telephone call; after a disconnection, the switch can reuse the connection identifier.

---

†One gigabit per second (Gbps) equals 1000 million bits per second. Most computers cannot generate or absorb data at that rate; ATM switches operate at gigabit speed to handle the traffic from many computers.

‡Because ATM was designed to carry voice as well as data, there is a strong relationship between ATM and telephone switching.

2.7 ARPANET Technology

One of the oldest wide area packet-switched networks, the ARPANET, was built by ARPA, the Advanced Research Projects Agency. ARPA awarded a contract for the development of ARPANET software to Bolt, Beranek and Newman of Cambridge, MA in the fall of 1968. By September of 1969, the first pieces of the ARPANET were in place.

The ARPANET served as a testbed for much of the research in packet-switching. In addition to its use for network research, researchers in several universities, military bases, and government labs regularly used the ARPANET to exchange files and electronic mail and to provide remote login among their sites. In 1975, control of the network was transferred from ARPA to the U.S. Defense Communications Agency (DCA). The DCA made the ARPANET part of the Defense Data Network (DDN), a program that provides multiple networks as part of a world-wide communication system for the Department of Defense.

In 1983 the Department of Defense partitioned the ARPANET into two connected networks, leaving the ARPANET for experimental research and forming the *MILNET* for military use. MILNET is restricted to unclassified data. Although under normal circumstances, both ARPANET and MILNET agreed to pass traffic to each other, controls were established that allowed them to be disconnected†. Because the ARPANET and MILNET used the same hardware technology, our description of the technical details apply to both even though we refer mainly to the ARPANET. In fact, the technology was available commercially and was used by several corporations to establish private packet switching networks.

Because the ARPANET was already in place and used daily by many of the researchers who developed the Internet architecture, it had a profound effect on their work. They came to think of the ARPANET as a dependable wide area backbone around which the Internet could be built. The influence of a single, central wide area backbone is still painfully obvious in some of the Internet protocols that we will discuss later, and has prevented the Internet from accommodating additional backbone networks gracefully.

Physically, the ARPANET consisted of approximately 50 BBN Corporation C30 and C300 minicomputers, called *Packet Switching Nodes* or *PSNs*‡ scattered across the continental U.S. and western Europe (the MILNET contained approximately 160 PSNs, including 34 in Europe and 18 in the Pacific and Far East). One PSN resided at each site participating in the network and was dedicated to the task of switching packets; it could not be used for general-purpose computation. Indeed, the PSN was considered to be part of the ARPANET and was owned and controlled by the *Network Operations Center* (*NOC*) located at BBN in Cambridge, Massachusetts.

Point-to-point data circuits leased from common carriers connected the PSNs together to form a network. For example, leased data circuits connected the ARPANET PSN at Purdue University to the ARPANET PSNs at Carnegie Mellon and at the University of Wisconsin. Initially, most of the leased data circuits in the ARPANET operated at 56 Kbps, a speed considered extremely fast in 1968 but slow by current

---

†Perhaps the best known example of disconnection occurred in November, 1988 when a *worm* program attacked the Internet and replicated itself as quickly as possible.

‡PSNs were initially called *Interface Message Processors* or *IMPs*; some publications still use the term IMP as a synonym for packet switch.

standards. Remember to think of the speed as a measure of capacity rather than a measure of the time it takes to deliver packets. As more computers used the ARPANET,
capacity was increased to accommodate the load. For example, during the final year the
ARPANET existed, many of the cross-country links operated over megabit-speed channels.

The idea of having no single point of failure in a system is common in military applications because reliability is important. When building the ARPANET, ARPA decided to follow the military requirements for reliability, so they mandated that each PSN
had to have at least two leased line connections to other PSNs, and the software had to
automatically adapt to failures and choose alternate routes. As a result, the ARPANET
continued to operate even if one of its data circuits failed.

In addition to connections for leased data circuits, each ARPANET PSN had up to
22 *ports* that connected it to user computers, called *hosts*. Originally, all computers that
accessed the ARPANET connected directly to one of the ports on a PSN. Normally,
direct connections were formed with a special-purpose interface board that plugged into
the computer's I/O bus and attached to a PSN host port. When programmed properly,
the interface allowed the computer to contact the PSN to send and receive packets.

The original PSN port hardware used a complex protocol for transferring data
across the ARPANET. Fondly known as 1822, after the number of a technical report
that described it, the protocol permits a host to send a packet across the ARPANET to a
specified destination PSN and a specified port on that PSN. Performing the transfer is
complicated, however, because 1822 offers reliable, flow-controlled delivery. To
prevent a given host from saturating the net, 1822 limits the number of packets that can
be in transit. To guarantee that each packet arrives at its destination, 1822 forces the
sender to await a *Ready For Next Message* (*RFNM*) signal from the PSN before
transmitting each packet. The RFNM acts as an acknowledgement. It includes a buffer
reservation scheme that requires the sender to reserve a buffer at the destination PSN
before sending a packet.

Although there are many aspects of 1822 not discussed here, the key idea to understand is that underneath all the detail, the ARPANET was merely a transfer mechanism.
When a computer connected to one port sent a packet to another port, the data delivered
was exactly the data sent. Because the ARPANET did not provide a network-specific
header, packets sent across it did not have a fixed field to specify packet type. Thus,
unlike some network technologies, the ARPANET did not deliver self-identifying packets.

In summary:

> *Networks such as the ARPANET or an ATM network do not have
> self-identifying frames. The attached computers must agree on the for-
> mat and contents of packets sent or received to a specific destination.*

Unfortunately, 1822 was never an industry standard. Because few vendors
manufacture 1822 interface boards it became difficult to connect new machines to the
ARPANET. To solve the problem, ARPA developed a new PSN interface that uses an

international data communications standard known as *CCITT X.25* (the designator was assigned by the standards committee that developed it). The first version of an X.25 PSN implementation used only the data transfer part of the X.25 standard (known as HDLC/LAPB), but later versions made it possible to use all of X.25 when connecting to a PSN (i.e., ARPANET appeared to be an X.25 network). Many MILNET ports now use X.25.

Internally, of course, the ARPANET used its own set of protocols that are invisible to users. For example, there was a special protocol that allows one PSN to request status from another, another protocol that PSNs used to send packets among themselves, and still another that allowed PSNs to exchange information about link status and optimal routes.

Because the ARPANET was originally built as a single, independent network to be used for research, its protocols and addressing structure were designed without much thought given to expansion. By the mid 1970's, it became apparent no single network would solve all communication problems, and ARPA began to investigate satellite and packet radio network technologies. This experience with a variety of network technologies led to the concept of an internetwork.

Today, the ARPANET has quietly disappeared and been replaced by new technologies. MILNET continues as part of the military side of the connected Internet.

2.7.1 ARPANET Addressing

While the details of ARPANET addressing are unimportant, they illustrate an alternative way in which wide area networks form physical addresses. Unlike local area networks like Ethernet, wide area networks usually embed information in the address that helps the network route packets to their destination efficiently. In the ARPANET technology, each packet switch is assigned a unique integer, P, and each host port on the switch is numbered from 0 to $N-1$. Conceptually, a destination address consists of a pair of small integers, (P,N). In practice, the hardware uses a single, large integer address, with some bits of the address used to represent N and others used to represent P.

2.8 National Science Foundation Networking

Realizing that data communication would soon be crucial to scientific research, in 1987 the National Science Foundation established a *Division of Network and Communications Research and Infrastructure* to help ensure that requisite network communications will be available for U.S. scientists and engineers. Although the division funds basic research in networking, its emphasis so far has been concentrated on providing seed funds to build extensions to the Internet.

NSF's Internet extensions form a three-level hierarchy consisting of a U.S. backbone, a set of "mid-level" or "regional" networks that each span a small geographic area, and a set of "campus" or "access" networks. In the NSF model, mid-level networks attach to the backbone and campus networks attach to the mid-level nets.

Researchers have a connection from their computer to the local campus network. They can use that connection to communicate with local researchers' computers across the local campus net, and they can communicate with researchers further away because their machine will route traffic across the local net and across the mid-level and backbone nets as needed.

2.8.1 The Original NSFNET Backbone

Of all the NSF-funded networks, the NSFNET backbone has the most interesting history and uses the most interesting technology. To date, the backbone has evolved in four major steps; it increased in size and capacity at the time the ARPANET declined until it became the dominant backbone in the Internet. The first version was built quickly, as a temporary measure. One early justification for the backbone was to provide scientists with access to NSF supercomputers. As a result, the first backbone consisted of six Digital Equipment Corporation LSI-11 microcomputers located at the existing NSF supercomputer centers. Geographically, the backbone spanned the continental United States from Princeton, NJ to San Diego, CA, using 56 Kbps leased lines as Figure 2.13 shows.

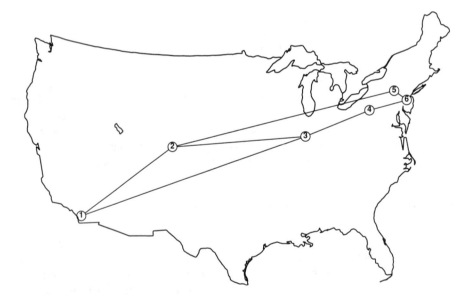

Figure 2.13 Circuits in the original NSFNET backbone with sites in (1) San Diego CA, (2) Boulder CO, (3) Champaign IL, (4) Pittsburgh PA, (5) Ithaca NY, and (6) Princeton NJ.

At each site, the LSI-11 microcomputer ran software affectionately known as *fuzz-ball*† code. Developed by Dave Mills, each fuzzball accessed computers at the local supercomputer center using a conventional Ethernet interface. It accessed leased lines leading to fuzzballs at other supercomputer centers using conventional link-level protocols over leased serial lines. Fuzzballs contained tables with addresses of possible destinations and used those tables to direct each incoming packet toward its destination.

The primary connection between the original NSFNET backbone and the rest of the Internet was located at Carnegie Mellon, which had both an NSFNET backbone node and an ARPANET PSN. When a user, connected to NSFNET, sent traffic to a site on the ARPANET, the packets would travel across the NSFNET to CMU where the fuzzball would route them onto the ARPANET via a local Ethernet. Similarly, the fuzzball understood that packets destined for NSFNET sites should be accepted from the Ethernet and sent across the NSF backbone to the appropriate site.

2.8.2 The Second NSFNET Backbone 1988-1989

Although users were excited about the possibilities of computer communication, the transmission and switching capacities of the original backbone were too small to provide adequate service. Within months after its inception, the backbone became overloaded and its inventor worked to engineer quick solutions for the most pressing problems while NSF began the arduous process of planning for a second backbone.

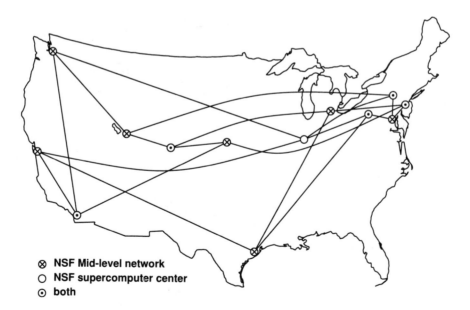

⊗ **NSF Mid-level network**
○ **NSF supercomputer center**
⊙ **both**

Figure 2.14 Logical circuits in the second NSFNET backbone from summer 1988 to summer 1989.

---

†The exact origin of the term ''fuzzball'' is unclear.

In 1987, NSF issued a request for proposals from groups that were interested in establishing and operating a new, higher-speed backbone. Proposals were submitted in August of 1987 and evaluated that fall. On November 24, 1987 NSF announced it had selected a proposal submitted by a partnership of: MERIT Inc., the statewide computer network run out of the University of Michigan in Ann Arbor, IBM Corporation, and MCI Incorporated. The partners proposed to build a second backbone network, establish a network operation and control center in Ann Arbor, and have the system operational by the following summer. Because NSF had funded the creation of several new mid-level networks, the proposed backbone was planned to serve more sites than the original. Each additional site would provide a connection between the backbone and one of the NSF mid-level networks.

The easiest way to envision the division of labor among the three groups is to assume that MERIT was in charge of planning, establishing, and operating the network center. IBM contributed machines and manpower from its research labs to help MERIT develop, configure, and test needed hardware and software. MCI, a long-distance carrier, provided the communication bandwidth using the optical fiber already in place for its voice network. Of course, in practice there was close cooperation between all groups, including joint study projects and representatives from IBM and MCI in the project management.

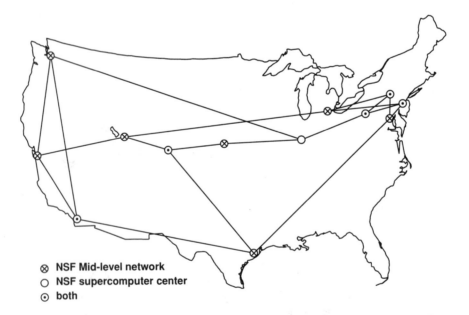

⊗ **NSF Mid-level network**
○ **NSF supercomputer center**
⊙ **both**

Figure 2.15 Circuits in the second NSFNET backbone from summer 1989 to 1990.

By the middle of the summer of 1988, the hardware was in place and NSFNET began to use the second backbone. Shortly thereafter, the original backbone was shut down and disconnected. Figure 2.14 shows the logical topology of the second backbone after it was installed in 1988.

The technology chosen for the second NSFNET backbone was interesting. In essence, the backbone was a wide area network composed of packet routers interconnected by communication lines. As with the original backbone, the packet switch at each site connected to the site's local Ethernet as well as to communication lines leading to other sites.

2.8.3 NSFNET Backbone 1989-1990

After measuring traffic on the second NSFNET backbone for a year, the operations center reconfigured the network by adding some circuits and deleting others. In addition, they increased the speed of circuits to DS-1 (1.544 Mbps). Figure 2.15 shows the revised connection topology, which provided redundant connections to all sites.

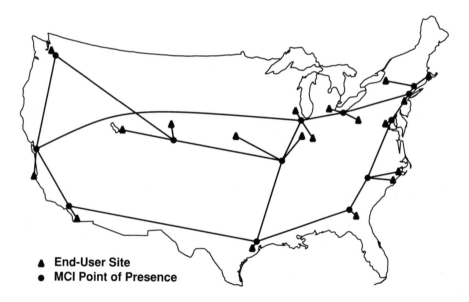

▲ End-User Site
● MCI Point of Presence

Figure 2.16 Circuits in ANSNET, the backbone of the U.S. Internet starting in 1993. Each circuit operates at 45 Mbps.

2.9 ANSNET

By 1991, NSF and other U.S. government agencies began to realize that the Internet was growing beyond its original academic and scientific domain. Companies around the world began to connect to the Internet, and nonresearch uses increased sharply. Traffic on NSFNET had grown to almost one billion packets per day, and the 1.5 Mbps capacity was becoming insufficient for several of the circuits. A higher capacity backbone was needed. As a result, the U.S. government began a policy of commercialization and privatization. NSF decided to move the backbone to a private company and start charging institutions for connections.

Responding to the new government policy in December of 1991, IBM, MERIT, and MCI formed a not-for-profit company named *Advanced Networks and Services* (*ANS*). ANS proposed to build a new, higher speed Internet backbone. Unlike previous wide area networks used in the Internet which had all been owned by the U.S. government, ANS would own the new backbone. By 1993, ANS had installed a new network that replaced NSFNET. Called *ANSNET*, the new backbone operates at 45 Mbps†, giving it approximately 30 times more capacity than the previous NSFNET backbone. Figure 2.16 shows major circuits in ANSNET and a few of the sites connected in 1994. Each point of presence represents a location to which many sites connect.

2.10 A Planned Wide Area Backbone

NSF has awarded MCI a contract to build a 155 Mbps backbone to replace ANSNET. Called the *very high speed Backbone Network Service* (*vBNS*), the new backbone will offer a substantial increase in capacity, and will require higher speed processors to route packets.

2.11 Other Technologies Over Which TCP/IP Has Been Used

One of the major strengths of TCP/IP lies in the variety of physical networking technologies over which it can be used. We have already discussed several widely used technologies, including local area and wide area networks. This section briefly reviews others that help illustrate an important principle:

> *Much of the success of the TCP/IP protocols lies in their ability to accommodate almost any underlying communication technology.*

2.11.1 X25NET

In 1980 NSF formed the CSNET organization to help provide Internet services to industry and small schools. CSNET used several technologies to connect its subscribers to the Internet, including one called *X25NET*. Originally developed at Purdue Universi-

---

†Telecommunication carriers use the term *DS3* to denote a circuit that operates at 45 Mbps; the term is often confused with *T3*, which denotes a specific encoding used over a circuit operating at DS3 speed.

ty, X25NET runs TCP/IP protocols over *Public Data Networks* (*PDN*s). The motivation for building such a network arose from the economics of telecommunications: although leased serial lines were expensive, common carriers had begun to offer public packet-switched services. X25NET was designed to allow a site to use its connection to a public packet-switched service to send and receive Internet traffic.

Readers who know about public packet-switched networks may find X25NET strange because public services use the CCITT† X.25 protocols exclusively while the Internet uses TCP/IP protocols. When used to transport TCP/IP traffic, however, the underlying X.25 network merely provides a path over which Internet traffic can be transferred. We have already stated that many underlying technologies can be used to carry Internet traffic. The technique, sometimes called *tunneling*, simply means that TCP/IP treats a complex network system with its own protocols like any other hardware delivery system. To send TCP/IP traffic through an X.25 *tunnel*, one makes an X.25 connection and then sends TCP/IP packets as if they were data. The X.25 system carries packets along its connection and delivers them to another X.25 endpoint, where they must be picked up and forwarded on to their ultimate destination. Because tunneling treats packets like data, it does not provide for self-identifying frames. Thus, it only works when both ends of the X.25 connection agree *a priori* that they will exchange TCP/IP packets.

What makes the use of X.25 peculiar is its interface. Unlike most network hardware, X.25 protocols provide a reliable transmission stream, sometimes called a *virtual circuit*, between the sender and the receiver, while the Internet protocols have been designed for a packet delivery system, making the two (apparently) incompatible.

Viewing X.25 connections merely as delivery paths produces a strange twist. It turns out that X.25 networks exhibit substantially better throughput with multiple simultaneous connections. Thus, instead of opening a single connection to a given destination, an X25NET sender often opens multiple connections and distributes packets among them to improve performance. The receiver accepts packets from all the X.25 connections and combines them together again.

The addressing scheme used by X.25 networks is given in a related standard known as X.121. X.121 physical addresses each consist of a 14-digit number, with 10 digits assigned by the vendor that supplies the X.25 network service. Resembling telephone numbers, one popular vendor's assignment includes an area code based on geographic location. The addressing scheme is not surprising because it comes from an organization that determines international telephone standards. It is unfortunate, however, because it makes assignment of Internet addresses difficult. Subscribers using X25NET must each maintain a table of mappings between Internet addresses and X.25 addresses. Chapter 5 discusses the address mapping problem in detail and gives an alternative to using fixed tables. Chapter 18 shows how the same problem arises for ATM networks, which use yet another alternative.

Because public X.25 networks operate independently of the Internet, a point of contact must be provided between the two. Both ARPA and CSNET operated dedicated machines that provided the interconnection between X.25 and the ARPANET. The primary interconnection was known as the *VAN gateway*. The VAN agreed to accept X.25

---

†The group in the Consultative Committee for International Telephone and Telegraph responsible for data networking has become the Telecommunication Section of the International Telecommunication Union (ITU-TS).

connections and route each datagram that arrived over such a connection to its destination.

X25NET is significant because it illustrates the flexibility and adaptability of the TCP/IP protocols. In particular, it shows how tunneling makes it possible to use an extremely wide range of complex network technologies in an internet.

2.11.2 Dial-up IP

Another interesting use of TCP/IP pioneered by CSNET involves running TCP/IP protocols over the dial-up voice network (i.e., the telephone system). CSNET member sites that used the Internet infrequently could not justify the cost of a leased line connection. For such sites, CSNET developed a dial-up IP system that worked as expected: whenever a connection was needed, software at the member's site used a modem to form a connection to the CSNET hub over the voice telephone network. A computer at the hub answered the phone call and, after obtaining valid authorization, began to forward traffic between the site and other computers on the Internet. Dialing introduced a delay after the first packet was sent. However, for automated services like electronic mail, the delay was unnoticeable.

2.11.3 Other Token Ring Technologies

FDDI is not the first token ring network technology; token ring products have existed for over a decade. For example, IBM produces a token ring LAN technology used at sites that have IBM computers. The IBM token ring operates at 16 Mbps; early versions operated at 4 Mbps. Like other token ring systems, an IBM token ring network consists of a loop that attaches to all computers. A station must wait for a token before transmitting, and sends the token along after transferring a packet.

An older token ring technology design by Proteon corporation employs a novel hardware addressing scheme that will be used in a later chapter to illustrate one of the ways TCP/IP uses hardware addresses. Called a *proNET* network, the technology permits customers to choose a hardware address for each computer. Unlike an Ethernet, in which each interface board contains a unique address assigned by the manufacturer, a proNET interface board contains eight switches that can be set before the interface is installed in a computer. The switches form a number in binary between 0 and 255, inclusive. A given proNET network can have at most 254 computers attached because address 255 is reserved for broadcast and address 0 is usually not used. When first installing a proNET network, a network administrator chooses a unique address for each computer. Usually, addresses are assigned sequentially, starting with *1*.

A technology that permits customers to assign hardware addresses has advantages and disadvantages. The chief disadvantage arises from the potential for problems that occur if a network administrator accidentally assigns the same address to two machines. The chief advantage arises from ease of maintenance: if an interface board fails, it can be replaced without changing the computer's hardware address.

2.11.4 Packet Radio

One of the most interesting ARPA experiments in packet switching resulted in a technology that used broadcast radio waves to carry packets. Designed for a military environment in which stations might be mobile, packet radio includes hardware and software that allow sites to find other sites, establish point-to-point communication, and then use the point-to-point communication to carry packets. Because sites change geographic location and may move out of communication range, the system must constantly monitor connectivity and recompute routes to reflect changes in topology. An operational packet radio system was built and used to demonstrate TCP/IP communication between a remote packet radio site and other sites on the Internet.

More recently, vendors have begun selling wireless networking equipment that uses spread spectrum techniques such as direct sequencing or frequency hopping to provide wireless network connections. The wireless communication equipment is small and lightweight. It can easily be connected to portable notebook computers, making it convenient to move around an area such as an office building while remaining in communication.

Often, wireless network equipment simulates a conventional packet switching network. For example, one vendor's wireless equipment sends and receives frames using the same format as an Ethernet network. In fact, the hardware has been constructed so it exactly emulates an Ethernet interface. Thus, standard protocol software can be used to communicate across a wireless network as if it were an Ethernet.

2.12 Summary And Conclusion

We have reviewed several network hardware technologies used by the TCP/IP protocols, ranging from high-speed, local area networks like Ethernet to slower-speed, long haul networks like ARPANET and ANSNET. We have also seen that it is possible to run the TCP/IP protocols over other general-purpose network protocols using a technique called tunneling. While the details of specific network technologies are not important, a general idea has emerged:

> *The TCP/IP protocols are extremely flexible in that almost any underlying technology can be used to transfer TCP/IP traffic.*

FOR FURTHER STUDY

Early computer communication systems employed point-to-point interconnection, often using general-purpose serial line hardware that McNamara [1982] describes. Metcalf and Boggs [1976] introduces the Ethernet with a 3 Mbps prototype version. Digital *et. al.* [1980] specifies the 10 Mbps standard adopted by most vendors, with

IEEE standard 802.3 reported in Nelson [1983]. Shoch, Dalal, and Redell [1982] provides an historical perspective of the Ethernet evolution. Related work on the ALOHA network is reported in Abramson [1970], with a survey of technologies given by Cotton [1979].

Token passing ring technology is proposed in Farmer and Newhall [1969]. Miller and Thompson [1982], as well as Andrews and Shultz [1982], give recent summaries. Another alternative, the slotted ring network, is proposed by Pierce [1972]. For a comparison of technologies, see Rosenthal [1982].

Details of the proposal for the second NSFNET backbone can be found in MERIT [November 1987]. For more information on the ARPANET see Cerf [1989] and BBN [1981]. The ideas behind X25NET are summarized in Comer and Korb [1983], Lanzillo and Partridge [January 1989] describes dial-up IP. De Prycker [1993] describes Asynchronous Transfer Mode and its use for wide area services. Partridge [1994] surveys many gigabit technologies, including ATM, and describes the internal structure of high speed switches.

Quarterman [1990] provides a summary of major wide area computer networks. LaQuey [1990] contains a directory of computer networks.

EXERCISES

2.1 Find out which network technologies your site uses.

2.2 What is the maximum size packet that can be sent on a high-speed network like Network System Corporation's Hyperchannel?

2.3 If your site uses Ethernet hub technology, find out how many connections can be attached to a single hub. If your site has multiple hubs (e.g., one on each floor of a building), find out how the hubs communicate.

2.4 What are the advantages and disadvantages of tunneling?

2.5 Read the Ethernet standard to find exact details of the inter-packet gap and preamble size. What is the maximum steady-state rate at which Ethernet can transport data?

2.6 What characteristic of a satellite communication channel is most desirable? Least desirable?

2.7 Find a lower bound on the time it takes to transfer a 5 megabyte file across a network that operates at: 9600 bps, 56 Kbps, 10 Mbps, 100 Mbps, and 2.4 Gbps.

2.8 Does the processor, disk, and internal bus on your computer operate fast enough to send data from a disk file at 2 gigabits per second?

3

Internetworking Concept And Architectural Model

3.1 Introduction

So far we have looked at the low-level details of transmission across individual networks, the foundation on which all computer communication is built. This chapter makes a giant conceptual leap by describing a scheme that allows us to collect the diverse network technologies into a coordinated whole. The primary goal is a scheme that hides the details of underlying network hardware while providing universal communication services. The primary result is a high-level abstraction that provides the framework for all design decisions. Succeeding chapters show how we use this abstraction to build the necessary layers of internet communication software and how the software hides the underlying physical transport mechanisms. Later chapters also show how applications use the resulting communication system.

3.2 Application-Level Interconnection

Designers have taken two different approaches to hiding network details, using application programs to handle heterogeneity or hiding details in the operating system. Early heterogeneous network interconnections provided uniformity through application-level programs. In such systems, an application-level program, executing on each machine in the network, understands the details of the network connections for that machine, and interoperates with the application programs across those connections. For example, some electronic mail systems consist of mailer programs that forward a memo one machine at a time. The path from source to destination may involve many different networks, but that does not matter as long as the mail systems on all the machines cooperate by forwarding each message.

Using application programs to hide network details may seem natural at first, but such an approach results in limited, cumbersome communication. Adding new functionality to the system means building a new application program for each machine. Adding new network hardware means modifying or creating new programs for each possible application. On a given machine, each application program must understand the network connections for that machine, resulting in duplication of code.

Users who are experienced with networking understand that once the interconnections grow to hundreds or thousands of networks, no one can possibly build all the necessary application programs. Furthermore, success of the step-at-a-time communication scheme requires correctness of all application programs executing along the path. When an intermediate program fails, the source and destination remain unable to detect or control the problem. Thus, systems that use intermediate programs cannot guarantee reliable communication.

3.3 Network-Level Interconnection

The alternative to providing interconnection with application-level programs is a system based on network-level interconnection. A network-level interconnection provides a mechanism that delivers packets from their original source to their ultimate destination in real time. Switching small units of data instead of files or large messages has several advantages. First, the scheme maps directly onto the underlying network hardware, making it extremely efficient. Second, network-level interconnection separates data communication activities from application programs, permitting intermediate computers to handle network traffic without understanding the applications that use it. Third, using network connections keeps the entire system flexible, making it possible to build general purpose communication facilities. Fourth, the scheme allows network managers to add new network technologies by modifying or adding a single piece of new network level software, while application programs remain unchanged.

The key to designing universal network-level interconnection can be found in an abstract communication system concept known as *internetworking*. The internetwork, or *internet*, concept is an extremely powerful one. It detaches the notions of communication from the details of network technologies and hides low-level details from the user. More important, it drives all software design decisions and explains how to handle physical addresses and routes. After reviewing basic motivations for internetworking, we will consider the properties of an internet in more detail.

We begin with two fundamental observations about the design of communication systems:

- No single network hardware can satisfy all constraints.
- Users desire universal interconnection.

The first observation is a technical one. Local area networks that provide the highest speed communication are limited in geographic span; wide area networks span large distances but cannot supply high speed connections. No single network technology satisfies all needs, so we are forced to consider multiple underlying hardware technologies.

The second observation is self-evident. Ultimately, we would like to be able to communicate between any two points. In particular, we desire a communication system that is not constrained by the boundaries of physical networks.

The goal is to build a unified, cooperative interconnection of networks that supports a universal communication service. Within each network, computers will use underlying technology-dependent communication facilities like those described in Chapter 2. New software, inserted between the technology-dependent communication mechanisms and application programs, will hide the low-level details and make the collection of networks appear to be a single large network. Such an interconnection scheme is called an *internetwork* or *internet*.

The idea of building an internet follows a standard pattern of system design: researchers imagine a high level computing facility and work from available computing technology, adding layers of software until they have a system that efficiently implements the imagined high-level facility. The next section shows the first step of the design process by defining the goal more precisely.

3.4 Properties Of The Internet

The notion of universal service is important, but it alone does not capture all the ideas we have in mind for a unified internet because there can be many implementations of universal services. In our design, we want to hide the underlying internet architecture from the user. That is, we do not want to require users or application programs to understand the details of hardware interconnections to use the internet. We also do not want to mandate a network interconnection topology. In particular, adding a new network to the internet should not mean connecting to a centralized switching point, nor should it mean adding direct physical connections between the new network and all existing networks. We want to be able to send data across intermediate networks even though they are not directly connected to the source or destination machines. We want all machines in the internet to share a universal set of machine identifiers (which can be thought of as *names* or *addresses*).

Our notion of a unified internet also includes the idea of network independence in the user interface. That is, we want the set of operations used to establish communication or to transfer data to remain independent of the underlying network technologies and the destination machine. Certainly, a user should not have to understand the network interconnection topology when writing application programs that communicate.

3.5 Internet Architecture

We have seen how machines connect to individual networks. The question arises, "How are networks interconnected to form an internetwork?" The answer has two parts. Physically, two networks can only be connected by a computer that attaches to both of them. A physical attachment does not provide the interconnection we have in mind, however, because such a connection does not guarantee that the computer will cooperate with other machines that wish to communicate. To have a viable internet, we need computers that are willing to shuffle packets from one network to another. Computers that interconnect two networks and pass packets from one to the other are called *internet gateways* or *internet routers*†.

Consider an example consisting of two physical networks shown in Figure 3.1. In the figure, router *R* connects to both network *1* and network *2*. For *R* to act as a router, it must capture packets on network *1* that are bound for machines on network *2* and transfer them. Similarly, *R* must capture packets on network *2* that are destined for machines on network *1* and transfer them.

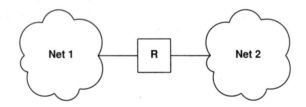

Figure 3.1 Two physical networks interconnected by *R*, a router (IP gateway).

In the figure, clouds are used to denote physical networks because the exact hardware is unimportant. Each network can be a LAN or a WAN, and each may have many hosts attached or a few hosts attached.

3.6 Interconnection Through IP Routers

When internet connections become more complex, routers need to know about the topology of the internet beyond the networks to which they connect. For example, Figure 3.2 shows three networks interconnected by two routers.

---

†The original literature used the term *IP gateway*. However, vendors have adopted the term *IP router* – the two terms are used interchangeably throughout this text.

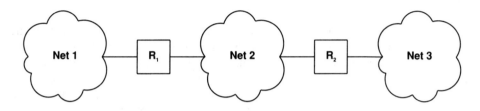

Figure 3.2 Three networks interconnected by two routers.

In this example, router R_1 must transfer from network *1* to network *2* all packets destined for machines on either network *2* or network *3*. For a large internet composed of many networks, the router's task of making decisions about where to send packets becomes more complex.

The idea of a router seems simple, but it is important because it provides a way to interconnect networks, not just machines. In fact, we have already discovered the principle of interconnection used throughout an internet:

> *In a TCP/IP internet, computers called* routers *or* gateways *provide all interconnections among physical networks.*

You might suspect that routers, which must know how to route packets to their destination, are large machines with enough primary or secondary memory to hold information about every machine in the internet to which they attach. However, routers used with TCP/IP internets are usually small computers. They often have little or no disk storage and limited main memories. The trick to building a small internet router lies in the following concept:

> *Routers use the destination network, not the destination host, when routing a packet.*

If routing is based on networks, the amount of information that a router needs to keep is proportional to the number of networks in the internet, not the number of computers.

Because routers play a key role in internet communication, we will return to them in later chapters and discuss the details of how they operate and how they learn about routes. For now, we will assume that it is possible and practical to have correct routes for all networks in each router in the internet. We will also assume that only routers provide connections between physical networks in an internet.

3.7 The User's View

Remember that TCP/IP is designed to provide a universal interconnection among machines independent of the particular networks to which they attach. Thus, we want a user to view an internet as a single, virtual network to which all machines connect despite their physical connections. Figure 3.3a shows how thinking of an internet instead of constituent networks simplifies the details and makes it easy for the user to conceptualize communication. In addition to routers that interconnect physical networks, software is needed on each host to allow application programs to use the internet as if it were a single, real physical network.

The advantage of providing interconnection at the network level now becomes clear. Because application programs that communicate over the internet do not know the details of underlying connections, they can be run without change on any machine. Because the details of each machine's physical network connections are hidden in the internet software, only that software needs to change when new physical connections appear or old ones disappear. In fact, it is possible to optimize the internal structure of the internet by altering physical connections without even recompiling application programs.

A second advantage of having communication at the network level is more subtle: users do not have to understand or remember how networks connect or what traffic they carry. Application programs can be written that communicate independent of underlying physical connectivity. In fact, network managers are free to change interior parts of the underlying internet architecture without changing application software in most of the computers attached to the internet (of course, network software must be reconfigured when a computer moves to a new network).

As Figure 3.3b shows, routers do not provide direct connections among all pairs of networks. It may be necessary for traffic traveling from one machine to another to pass across several intermediate networks. Thus, networks participating in an internet are analogous to highways in the U.S. interstate system: each net agrees to handle transit traffic in exchange for the right to send traffic throughout the internet. Typical users are unaffected and unaware of extra traffic on their local network.

3.8 All Networks Are Equal

Chapter 2 reviewed examples of the network hardware used to build TCP/IP internets, and illustrated the great diversity of technologies. We have described an internet as a collection of cooperative, interconnected networks. It is now important to understand a fundamental concept: from the internet point of view, any communication system capable of transferring packets counts as a single network, independent of its delay and throughput characteristics, maximum packet size, or geographic scale. In particular, Figure 3.3b uses the same small cloud to depict all physical networks because TCP/IP treats them equally despite their differences. The point is:

> *The TCP/IP internet protocols treat all networks equally. A local area network like an Ethernet, a wide area network like the ANSNET backbone, or a point-to-point link between two machines each count as one network.*

Readers unaccustomed to internet architecture may find it difficult to accept such a simplistic view of networks. In essence, TCP/IP defines an abstraction of "network" that hides the details of physical networks; we will learn that such abstractions help make TCP/IP extremely powerful.

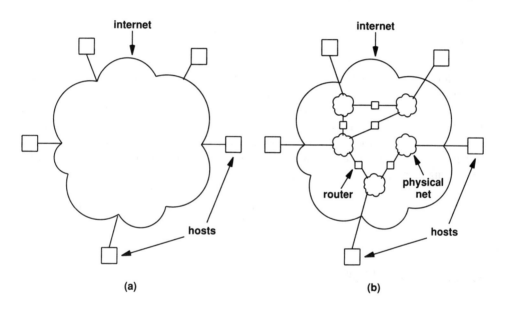

Figure 3.3 (a) The user's view of a TCP/IP internet in which each computer appears to attach to a single large network, and (b) the structure of physical networks and routers that provide interconnection.

3.9 The Unanswered Questions

Our sketch of internets leaves many unanswered questions. For example, you might wonder about the exact form of internet machine addresses or how such addresses relate to the Ethernet, FDDI, or ATM physical hardware addresses described in Chapter 2. The next three chapters confront these questions. They describe the format of IP addresses and illustrate how hosts map between internet addresses and physical addresses. You might also want to know exactly what a packet looks like when it travels through an internet, or what happens when packets arrive too fast for some host or router to handle. Chapter 7 answers these questions. Finally, you might wonder how multiple application programs executing concurrently on a single machine can send and receive packets to multiple destinations without becoming entangled in each other's transmissions or how internet routers learn about routes. All of these questions will be answered as well.

Although it may seem vague now, the direction we are following will let us learn about both the structure and use of internet protocol software. We will examine each part, looking at the concepts and principles as well as technical details. We began by describing the physical communication layer on which an internet is built. Each of the following chapters will explore one part of the internet software, until we understand how all the pieces fit together.

3.10 Summary

An internet is more than a collection of networks interconnected by computers. Internetworking implies that the interconnected systems agree to conventions that allow each computer to communicate with every other computer. In particular, an internet will allow two machines to communicate even if the communication path between them passes across a network to which neither connects directly. Such cooperation is only possible when computers agree on a set of universal identifiers and a set of procedures for moving data to its final destination.

In an internet, interconnections among networks are formed by computers called IP routers, or IP gateways, that attach to two or more networks. A router forwards packets between networks by receiving them from one network and sending them to another.

FOR FURTHER STUDY

Our model of an internetwork comes from Cerf and Cain [1983] and Cerf and Kahn [1974], which describe an internet as a set of networks interconnected by routers and sketch an internet protocol similar to that eventually developed for the TCP/IP protocol suite. More information on the connected Internet architecture can be found in Postel [1980]; Postel, Sunshine, and Chen [1981]; and in Hinden, Haverty, and Sheltzer [1983]. Shoch [1978] presents issues in internetwork naming and addressing. Boggs *et. al.* [1980] describes the internet developed at Xerox PARC, an alternative to the TCP/IP internet we will examine. Cheriton [1983] describes internetworking as it relates to the V-system.

EXERCISES

3.1 Changing the information in a router can be tricky because it is impossible to change all routers simultaneously. Investigate algorithms that guarantee to either install a change on a set of computers or install it on none.

3.2 In an internet, routers periodically exchange information from their routing tables, making it possible for a new router to appear and begin routing packets. Investigate the algorithms used to exchange routing information.

3.3 Compare the organization of a TCP/IP internet to the style of internet designed by Xerox Corporation.

3.4 What processors have been used as routers in the connected Internet? Does the size and speed of early router hardware surprise you? Why?

3.5 Approximately how many networks comprise the internet at your site? Approximately how many routers?

3.6 Consider the internal structure of the example internet shown in Figure 3.3b. Which routers are most crucial? Why?

4

Internet Addresses

4.1 Introduction

The previous chapter defined a TCP/IP internet as a virtual network built by interconnecting physical networks with routers. This chapter discusses addressing, an essential ingredient that helps TCP/IP software hide physical network details and makes the internet appear to be a single, uniform entity.

4.2 Universal Identifiers

A communication system is said to supply *universal communication service* if it allows any host computer to communicate with any other host. To make our communication system universal, it needs a globally accepted method of identifying each computer that attaches to it.

Often, host identifiers are classified as *names*, *addresses*, or *routes*. Shoch [1978] suggests that a name identifies *what* an object is, an address identifies *where* it is, and a route tells *how* to get there. Although these definitions are intuitive, they can be misleading. Names, addresses, and routes really refer to successively lower level representations of host identifiers. In general, people usually prefer pronounceable names to identify machines, while software works more efficiently with compact representations of identifiers that we think of as addresses. Either could have been chosen as the TCP/IP universal host identifiers. The decision was made to standardize on compact, binary addresses that make computations such as the selection of a route efficient. For now, we will discuss only binary addresses, postponing until later the questions of how to map between binary addresses and pronounceable names, and how to use addresses for routing.

4.3 Three Primary Classes Of IP Addresses

Think of an internet as a large network like any other physical network. The difference, of course, is that the internet is a virtual structure, imagined by its designers, and implemented entirely in software. Thus, the designers are free to choose packet formats and sizes, addresses, delivery techniques, and so on; nothing is dictated by hardware. For addresses, the designers of TCP/IP chose a scheme analogous to physical network addressing in which each host on the internet is assigned a 32-bit integer address called its *internet address* or *IP address*. The clever part of internet addressing is that the integers are carefully chosen to make routing efficient. Specifically, an IP address encodes the identification of the network to which a host attaches as well as the identification of a unique host on that network. We can summarize:

Each host on a TCP/IP internet is assigned a unique 32-bit internet
address that is used in all communication with that host.

The details of IP addresses help clarify the abstract ideas. For now, we give a simplified view and expand it later. In the simplest case, each host attached to an internet is assigned a 32-bit universal identifier as its internet address. The bits of IP addresses for all hosts on a given network share a common prefix.

Conceptually, each address is a pair (*netid*, *hostid*), where *netid* identifies a network, and *hostid* identifies a host on that network. In practice, each IP address must have one of the first three forms shown in Figure 4.1†.

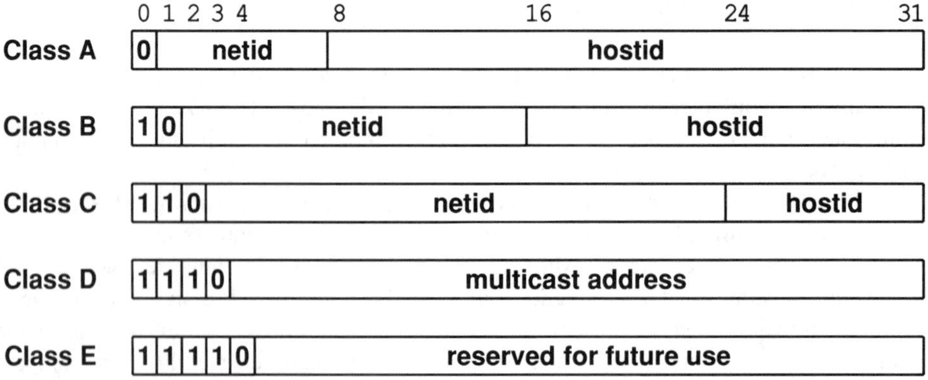

Figure 4.1 The five forms of Internet (IP) addresses. The three primary forms, classes *A*, *B* and *C*, can be distinguished by the first three bits.

---

†The fourth form, reserved for internet multicasting, will be described in a later chapter; for now, we will restrict our comments to the forms that specify addresses of individual objects.

Given an IP address, its class can be determined from the three high-order bits, with two bits being sufficient to distinguish among the three primary classes. Class *A* addresses, which are used for the handful of networks that have more than 2^{16} (i.e., 65,536) hosts, devote 7 bits to netid and 24 bits to hostid. Class *B* addresses, which are used for intermediate size networks that have between 2^8 (i.e., 256) and 2^{16} hosts, allocate 14 bits to the netid and 16 bits to the hostid. Finally, class *C* networks, which have less than 2^8 hosts, allocate 21 bits to the netid and only 8 bits to the hostid. Note that the IP address has been defined in such a way that it is possible to extract the hostid or netid portions quickly. Routers, which use the netid portion of an address when deciding where to send a packet, depend on efficient extraction to achieve high speed.

4.4 Addresses Specify Network Connections

To simplify the discussion, we said that an internet address identifies a host, but that is not strictly accurate. Consider a router that attaches to two physical networks. How can we assign a single IP address if the address encodes a network identifier as well as a host identifier? In fact, we cannot. When conventional computers have two or more physical connections they are called *multi-homed hosts*. Multi-homed hosts and routers require multiple IP addresses. Each address corresponds to one of the machine's network connections. Looking at multi-homed hosts leads to the following important idea:

> *Because IP addresses encode both a network and a host on that network, they do not specify an individual computer, but a connection to a network.*

Thus, a router connecting *n* networks has *n* distinct IP addresses, one for each network connection.

4.5 Network And Broadcast Addresses

We have already cited the major advantage of encoding network information in internet addresses: it makes efficient routing possible. Another advantage is that internet addresses can refer to networks as well as hosts. By convention, hostid *0* is never assigned to an individual host. Instead, an IP address with hostid zero is used to refer to the network itself. In summary:

> *Internet addresses can be used to refer to networks as well as individual hosts. By convention, an address that has all bits of the hostid equal to 0 is reserved to refer to the network.*

Another significant advantage of the internet addressing scheme is that it includes a *broadcast address* that refers to all hosts on the network. According to the standard, any hostid consisting of all *1*s is reserved for broadcast†. On many network technologies (e.g., Ethernet), broadcasting can be as efficient as normal transmission; on others, broadcasting is supported by the network software, but requires substantially more delay than single transmission. Some networks do not support broadcast at all. Thus, having an IP broadcast address does not guarantee the availability or efficiency of broadcast delivery. In summary,

> *IP addresses can be used to specify a broadcast; such addresses map to hardware broadcast, if available. By convention, a broadcast address has hostid with all bits set to 1.*

4.6 Limited Broadcast

Technically, the broadcast address we just described is called a *directed broadcast address* because it contains both a valid network ID and the broadcast hostid. A directed broadcast address can be interpreted unambiguously at any point in an internet because it uniquely identifies the target network in addition to specifying broadcast on that network. Directed broadcast addresses provide a powerful (and somewhat dangerous) mechanism that allows a remote system to send a single packet that will be broadcast on the specified network.

From an addressing point of view, the chief disadvantage of directed broadcast is that it requires knowledge of the network address. Another form of broadcast address, called a *limited broadcast address* or *local network broadcast address*, provides a broadcast address for the local network independent of the assigned IP address. The local broadcast address consists of thirty-two *1*s (hence, it is sometimes called the ''all *1*s'' broadcast address). A host may use the limited broadcast address as part of a start-up procedure before it learns its IP address or the IP address for the local network. Once the host learns the correct IP address for the local network, however, it should use directed broadcast.

As a general rule, TCP/IP protocols restrict broadcasting to the smallest possible set of machines. We will see how this rule affects multiple networks that share addresses in the chapter on subnet addressing.

4.7 Interpreting Zero To Mean "This"

We have seen that a field consisting of *1*s can be interpreted to mean ''all,'' as in ''all hosts'' on a network. In general, internet software interprets fields consisting of *0*s to mean ''this.'' The interpretation appears throughout the literature. Thus, an IP address with hostid *0* refers to ''this'' host, and an internet address with network ID *0* refers to ''this'' network. Of course, it is only meaningful to use such an address in a

---

†Unfortunately, an early release of TCP/IP code that accompanied Berkeley UNIX incorrectly used all zeroes for broadcast. Because the error still survives, TCP/IP software often includes an option that allows a site to use all zeroes for broadcast.

context where it can be interpreted unambiguously. For example, if a machine receives a packet in which the netid portion of the destination address is *0* and the hostid portion of the destination address matches its address, the receiver interprets the netid field to mean "this" network (i.e., the network over which the packet arrived).

Using netid *0* is especially important in those cases where a host wants to communicate over a network but does not yet know the network IP address. The host uses network ID *0* temporarily, and other hosts on the network interpret the address as meaning "this" network. In most cases, replies will have the network address fully specified, allowing the original sender to record it for future use. Chapter 9 will discuss in detail how a host determines the netid of the local network.

4.7.1 Subnet Addressing And Multicasting

The addressing scheme described so far requires a unique network prefix for each physical network. Chapter 10 considers two important extensions to the addressing scheme designed to conserve network addresses: subnet addressing and classless addressing. In addition to broadcasting, the IP address scheme supports a special form of multipoint delivery known as *multicasting*. Multicasting is especially useful for networks where the hardware technology supports multicast delivery. Chapter 17 discusses multicast addressing and delivery in detail.

4.8 Weaknesses In Internet Addressing

Encoding network information in an internet address does have some disadvantages. The most obvious disadvantage is that addresses refer to network connections, not to the host computer:

> *If a host computer moves from one network to another, its IP address must change.*

To understand the consequences, consider travelers who wish to disconnect their personal computers, carry them along on a trip, and reconnect them to the internet after reaching their destination. The personal computer cannot be assigned a permanent IP address because an IP address identifies the network to which the machine attaches.

Another weakness of the internet addressing scheme is that when any class *C* network grows to more than 255 hosts, it must have its address changed to a class *B* address. While this may seem like a minor problem, changing network addresses can be incredibly time-consuming and difficult to debug. Because most software is not designed to handle multiple addresses for the same physical network, administrators cannot plan a smooth transition in which they introduce new addresses slowly. Instead, they must abruptly stop using one network address, change the addresses of all machines, and then resume communication using the new network address.

The most important flaw in the internet addressing scheme will not become fully apparent until we examine routing. However, its importance warrants a brief introduction here. We have suggested that routing will be based on internet addresses, with the netid portion of an address used to make routing decisions. Consider a host with two connections to the internet. We know that such a host must have more than one IP address. The following is true:

> *Because routing uses the network portion of the IP address, the path taken by packets traveling to a host with multiple IP addresses depends on the address used.*

The implications are surprising. Humans think of each host as a single entity and want to use a single name. They are often surprised to find that they must learn more than one name and even more surprised to find that packets sent using multiple names can behave differently.

Another surprising consequence of the internet addressing scheme is that merely knowing one IP address for a destination may not be sufficient; it may be impossible to reach the destination using that address. Consider the example internet shown in Figure 4.2. In the figure, two hosts, A and B, both attach to network *1*, and usually communicate directly using that network. Thus, users on host A should normally refer to host B using IP address I_3. An alternate path from A to B exists through router R, and is used whenever A sends packets to IP address I_5 (B's address on network *2*). Now suppose B's connection to network *1* fails, but the machine itself remains running (e.g., a wire breaks between B and network *1*). Users on A who specify IP address I_3 cannot reach B, although users who specify address I_5 can. These problems with naming and addressing will arise again in later chapters when we consider routing and name binding.

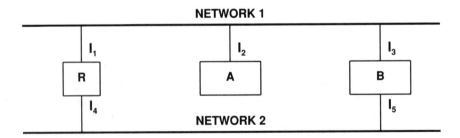

Figure 4.2 An example internet with a multi-homed host, B, that demonstrates a problem with the IP addressing scheme. If interface I_3 becomes disconnected, A must use address I_5 to reach B, sending packets through router R.

4.9 Dotted Decimal Notation

When communicated to humans, either in technical documents or through application programs, IP addresses are written as four decimal integers separated by decimal points, where each integer gives the value of one octet of the IP address†. Thus, the 32-bit internet address

10000000 00001010 00000010 00011110

is written

128.10.2.30

We will use dotted decimal notation when expressing IP addresses throughout the remainder of this text. Indeed, most TCP/IP software that displays or requires a human to enter an IP address uses dotted decimal notation. For example, the UNIX *netstat* command, which displays the current routing, and application programs such as *telnet* and *ftp* all use dotted decimal notation when accepting or displaying IP addresses. Thus, it may be helpful to understand the relationship between IP address classes and dotted decimal numbers. The table in Figure 4.3 summarizes the range of values for each class.

Class	Lowest Address	Highest Address
A	0.1.0.0	126.0.0.0
B	128.0.0.0	191.255.0.0
C	192.0.1.0	223.255.255.0
D	224.0.0.0	239.255.255.255
E	240.0.0.0	247.255.255.255

Figure 4.3 The range of dotted decimal values that correspond to each IP address class. Some values are reserved for special purposes.

4.10 Loopback Address

The table in Figure 4.3 shows that not all possible addresses have been assigned to classes. For example, address 127.0.0.0, a value from the class A range, is reserved for *loopback*; and is intended for use in testing TCP/IP and for inter-process communication on the local machine. When any program uses the loopback address as a destination, the protocol software in the computer returns the data without sending traffic across any network. The literature explicitly states that a packet sent to a network 127 address should never appear on any network. Furthermore, a host or router should never propagate routing or reachability information for network number *127*; it is not a network address.

---

†Dotted decimal notation is sometimes called *dotted quad notation*.

4.11 Summary Of Special Address Conventions

In practice, IP uses only a few combinations of *0*s ("this") or *1*s ("all"). Figure 4.4 lists the possibilities.

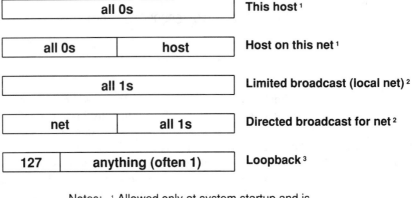

all 0s		This host [1]
all 0s	host	Host on this net [1]
all 1s		Limited broadcast (local net) [2]
net	all 1s	Directed broadcast for net [2]
127	anything (often 1)	Loopback [3]

Notes: [1] Allowed only at system startup and is
never a valid destination address.
[2] Never a valid source address.
[3] Should never appear on a network.

Figure 4.4 Special forms of IP addresses, including valid combinations of *0*s ("this"), *1*s ("all"). The length of the net portion of a directed broadcast depends on the network address class.

As the notes in the figure mention, using all *0*s for the network is only allowed during the bootstrap procedure. It allows a machine to communicate temporarily. Once the machine learns its correct network and IP address, it must not use network *0*.

4.12 Internet Addressing Authority

To ensure that the network portion of an Internet address is unique, all Internet addresses are assigned by a central authority. The *Internet Assigned Number Authority* (*IANA*) has ultimate control over numbers assigned, and sets the policy. However, when an organization joins the Internet, it can obtain network addresses from the *Internet Network Information Center* (*INTERNIC*).

A central authority is only needed to assign the network portion of an address; once an organization obtains a network prefix, it can choose how to assign a unique suffix to each host on its network without contacting the central authority. The Internet authority assigns a class C number to a network with a small number of attached computers (less than 255); it reserves class B numbers for an organization that has a larger network. Finally, an organization must have a network with more than 65535 hosts attached before it can obtain a class A number. The address space is skewed because most networks are small, less are of medium size, and only a few are gigantic.

It is only essential for the central authority to assign IP addresses for networks that are (or will be) attached to the global Internet. An individual corporation could take responsibility for assigning unique network addresses within its TCP/IP internet as long as it never connects that internet to the outside world. Indeed, many corporate groups that use TCP/IP protocols do assign internet addresses on their own. For example, the network address 9.0.0.0 has been assigned to IBM Corporation, and address 12.0.0.0 has been assigned to AT&T. If an organization decides to use TCP/IP protocols on two of their networks with no connections to the global Internet, the organization can choose to assign addresses 9.0.0.0 and 12.0.0.0 to their local networks. Experience has shown, however, that it is unwise to create a private internet using the same network addresses as the global Internet because it prevents future interoperability and may cause problems when trying to exchange software with other sites. Thus, everyone using TCP/IP is strongly encouraged to take the time to obtain official Internet addresses from the INTERNIC.

4.13 An Example

To clarify the IP addressing scheme, consider an example of two networks in the Computer Science Department at Purdue University that were connected to the Internet in the mid-1980s. Figure 4.5 shows the network addresses, and illustrates how routers interconnect the networks.

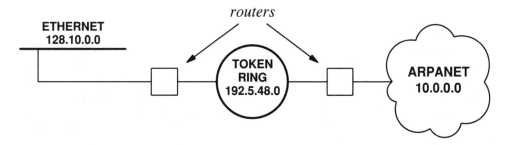

Figure 4.5 The logical connection of two networks to the Internet backbone. Each network has been assigned an IP address.

The example shows three networks and the network numbers they have been assigned: the ARPANET (10.0.0.0), an Ethernet (128.10.0.0), and a token ring network (192.5.48.0). According to the table in Figure 4.3, the addresses have classes A, B, and C, respectively.

Figure 4.6 shows the same networks with host computers attached and Internet addresses assigned to each network connection.

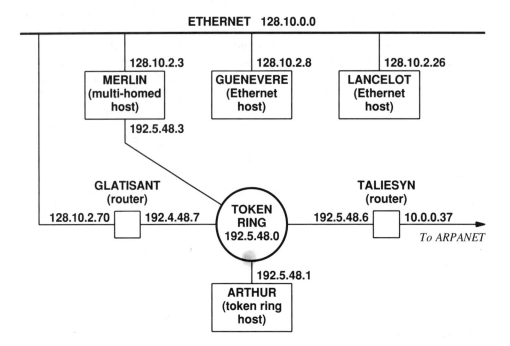

Figure 4.6 Example IP address assignment for routers and hosts attached to the three networks in the previous figure.

In the figure, four hosts labeled *Arthur*, *Merlin*, *Guenevere*, and *Lancelot*, attach to the networks, *Taliesyn* is a router that connects the ARPANET and the token ring network, and *Glatisant* is a router that connects the token ring network to the Ethernet. Host *Merlin* has connections to both the Ethernet and the token ring network, so it can reach destinations on either network directly. Although a multi-homed host like *Merlin* can be configured to route packets between the two nets, most sites use dedicated computers as routers to avoid overloading conventional computer systems with the processing required for routing. In the figure, a dedicated router, *Glatisant*, performs the task of routing traffic between the Ethernet and token ring networks. (Note: actual traffic between these two networks was higher than this configuration suggests because the figure only shows a handful of computers attached to the nets.)

As Figure 4.5 shows, an IP address must be assigned to each network connection. *Lancelot*, which connects only to the Ethernet, has been assigned 128.10.2.26 as its only IP address. *Merlin* has address 128.10.2.3 for its connection to the Ethernet and 192.5.48.3 for its connection to the token ring network. Whoever made the address assignment chose the same value for the low-order byte of each address. The addresses assigned to routers *Glatisant* and *Taliesyn* do not follow the convention. For example, *Taliesyn's* addresses, 10.0.0.37 and 192.5.48.6, are two completely unrelated strings of digits. IP does not care whether any of the bytes in the dotted decimal form of a computer's addresses are the same or different. However, network technicians, managers, and administrators may need to use addresses for maintenance, testing, and debugging. Choosing to make all of a computer's addresses end with the same octet helps makes it easier for humans to remember or guess the address of a particular interface.

4.14 Network Byte Order

To create an internet that is independent of any particular vendor's machine architecture or network hardware, the software must define a standard representation for data. Consider what happens, for example, when software on one computer sends a 32-bit binary integer to another computer. The physical transport hardware moves the sequence of bits from the first machine to the second without changing the order. However, not all machines store 32-bit integers in the same way. On some (called *Little Endian*), the lowest memory address contains the low-order byte of the integer. On others (called *Big Endian*), the lowest memory address holds the high-order byte of the integer. Still others store integers in groups of 16-bit words, with the lowest addresses holding the low-order word, but with bytes swapped. Thus, direct copying of bytes from one machine to another may change the value of the number.

Standardizing byte-order for integers is especially important in an internet because internet packets carry binary numbers that specify information like destination addresses and packet lengths. Such quantities must be understood by both the senders and receivers. The TCP/IP protocols solve the byte-order problem by defining a *network standard byte order* that all machines must use for binary fields in internet packets. Each host or router converts binary items from the local representation to network standard byte order before sending a packet, and converts from network byte order to the host-specific order when a packet arrives. Naturally, the user data field in a packet is exempt from this standard – users are free to format their own data however they choose. Of course, most users rely on standard application programs and do not have to deal with the byte order problem directly.

The internet standard for byte order specifies that integers are sent most significant byte first (i.e., *Big Endian* style). If one considers the successive bytes in a packet as it travels from one machine to another, a binary integer in that packet has its most significant byte nearest the beginning of the packet and its least significant byte nearest the end of the packet. Many arguments have been offered about which data representation should be used, and the internet standard still comes under attack from time to time. However, everyone agrees that having a standard is crucial, and the exact form of the standard is far less important.

4.15 Summary

TCP/IP uses 32-bit binary addresses as universal machine identifiers. Called Internet or IP addresses, the identifiers are divided into three primary classes. Because leading bits define the class of an address, the classes do not have equal size. The IP addressing scheme allows a few hundred networks with over a million hosts each, thousands of networks with thousands of hosts each, and over a million networks with up to 254 hosts each. To make such addresses easier for humans to understand, they are written in dotted decimal notation, with the values of the four octets written in decimal, separated by decimal points.

Because the IP address encodes network identification as well as the identification of a specific host on that network, routing is efficient. An important property of IP addresses is that they refer to network connections. Hosts with multiple connections have multiple addresses. One advantage of the internet addressing scheme is that the form includes an address for a specific host, a network, or all hosts on a network (broadcast). The biggest disadvantage of the IP addressing scheme is that if a machine has multiple addresses, knowing one address may not be sufficient to reach it when no path exists to the specified interface (e.g., because a particular network is unavailable).

To permit the exchange of binary data among machines, TCP/IP protocols enforce a standard byte ordering for integers within protocol fields. A host must convert all binary data from its internal form to network standard byte order before sending a packet, and it must convert from network byte order to internal order upon receipt.

FOR FURTHER STUDY

The internet addressing scheme presented here can be found in Reynolds and Postel [RFC 1700]; further information can be found in Stahl, Romano, and Recker [RFC 1117].

Several important additions have been made to the Internet addressing scheme over the years; later chapters cover them in more detail. Chapter 10 discusses an evolving idea called *classless addressing*, an interim addressing scheme intended to be used during the next few years. In addition, Chapter 10 examines an essential part of the existing Internet address standard called *subnet addressing*. Subnet addressing allows a single network address to be used with multiple physical networks. Chapter 17 continues the exploration of IP addresses by describing how class D addresses are assigned for internet *multicast*.

The INTERNIC can supply information on how to obtain addresses (see Appendix 1 for the INTERNIC's address and telephone number). Cohen [1981] explains bit and byte ordering, and introduces the terms ''Big Endian'' and ''Little Endian.''

EXERCISES

4.1 Exactly how many class *A*, *B*, and *C* networks can exist? Exactly how many hosts can a network in each class have? Be careful to allow for broadcast as well as class *D* and *E* addresses.

4.2 A machine readable list of assigned addresses is sometimes called an internet *host table*. If your site has a host table, find out how many class *A*, *B*, and *C* network numbers have been assigned.

4.3 How many hosts are attached to each of the local area networks at your site? Does your site have any local area networks for which a class *C* address is insufficient?

4.4 What is the chief difference between the IP addressing scheme and the U.S. telephone numbering scheme?

4.5 A single central authority cannot manage to assign Internet addresses fast enough to accommodate the demand. Can you invent a scheme that allows the central authority to divide its task among several groups but still ensure that each assigned address is unique?

4.6 Does network standard byte order differ from your local machine's byte order?

4.7 How many IP addresses would be needed to assign a unique network number to every home in your country? Is the IP address space sufficient?

5

Mapping Internet Addresses
To Physical Addresses
(ARP)

5.1 Introduction

We have described the TCP/IP address scheme in which each host is assigned a 32-bit address and have said that an internet behaves like a virtual network, using only these assigned addresses when sending and receiving packets. We also reviewed several physical network technologies and noted that two machines on a given physical network can communicate *only if they know each other's physical network address*. What we have not mentioned is how a host or a router maps an IP address to the correct physical address when it needs to send a packet across a physical net. This chapter considers that mapping, showing how it is implemented for the two most common physical network address schemes.

5.2 The Address Resolution Problem

Consider two machines A and B that share a physical network. Each has an assigned IP address I_A and I_B and a physical address P_A and P_B. The goal is to devise low-level software that hides physical addresses and allows higher-level programs to work only with internet addresses. Ultimately, however, communication must be carried out by physical networks using whatever physical address scheme the hardware supplies. Suppose machine A wants to send a packet to machine B across a physical network to which they both attach, but A has only B's internet address I_B. The question arises: how does A map that address to B's physical address, P_B?

Address mapping must be performed at each step along a path from the original source to the ultimate destination. In particular, two cases arise. First, at the last step of delivering a packet, the packet must be sent across one physical network to its final destination. The computer sending the packet must map the final destination's Internet address to the destination's physical address. Second, at any point along the path from the source to the destination other than the final step, the packet must be sent to an intermediate router. Thus, the sender must map the intermediate router's Internet address to a physical address.

The problem of mapping high-level addresses to physical addresses is known as the *address resolution problem* and has been solved in several ways. Some protocol suites keep tables in each machine that contain pairs of high-level and physical addresses. Others solve the problem by encoding hardware addresses in high-level addresses. Using either approach exclusively makes high-level addressing awkward at best. This chapter discusses two techniques for address resolution used by TCP/IP protocols and shows when each is appropriate.

5.3 Two Types Of Physical Addresses

There are two basic types of physical addresses, exemplified by the Ethernet, which has large, fixed physical addresses, and proNET, which has small, easily configured physical addresses. Address resolution is difficult for Ethernet-like networks, but easy for networks like proNET. We will consider the easy case first.

5.4 Resolution Through Direct Mapping

Consider a proNET token ring network. Recall from Chapter 2 that proNET uses small integers for physical addresses and allows the user to choose a hardware address when installing an interface board in a computer. The key to making address resolution easy with such network hardware lies in observing that as long as one has the freedom to choose both IP and physical addresses, they can be selected such that parts of them are the same. Typically, one assigns IP addresses with the hostid portion equal to 1, 2, 3, and so on, and then, when installing network interface hardware, selects a physical address that corresponds to the IP address. For example, the system administrator would select physical address 3 for a computer with the IP address 192.5.48.3 because 192.5.48.3 is a class C address with the host portion equal to 3.

For networks like proNET, computing a physical address from an IP address is trivial. The computation consists of extracting the host portion of the IP address. Extraction is computationally efficient because it requires only a few machine instructions. The mapping is easy to maintain because it can be performed without reference to external data. Finally, new machines can be added to the network without changing existing assignments or recompiling code.

Conceptually, choosing a numbering scheme that makes address resolution efficient means selecting a function f that maps IP addresses to physical addresses. The designer may be able to select a physical address numbering scheme as well, depending on the hardware. Resolving IP address I_A means computing

$$P_A = f(I_A)$$

We want the computation of f to be efficient. If the set of physical addresses is constrained, it may be possible to arrange efficient mappings other than the one given in the example above. For instance, when using IP over a connection-oriented network such as ATM, one cannot choose physical addresses. On such networks, one or more computers store pairs of addresses, where each pair contains an Internet address and the corresponding physical address. For example, the values can be stored in a table in memory that must be searched. To make address resolution efficient in such cases, software can use a conventional hash function to search the table. Exercise 5.1 suggests a related alternative.

5.5 Resolution Through Dynamic Binding

To understand why address resolution is difficult for some networks, consider Ethernet technology. Recall from Chapter 2 that each Ethernet interface is assigned a 48-bit physical address when the device is manufactured. As a consequence, when hardware fails and requires that an Ethernet interface be replaced, the machine's physical address changes. Furthermore, because the Ethernet address is 48 bits long, there is no hope it can be encoded in a 32-bit IP address.†

Designers of TCP/IP protocols found a creative solution to the address resolution problem for networks like the Ethernet that have broadcast capability. The solution allows new machines to be added to the network without recompiling code, and does not require maintenance of a centralized database. To avoid maintaining a table of mappings, the designers chose to use a low-level protocol to bind addresses dynamically. Termed the *Address Resolution Protocol* (*ARP*), the protocol provides a mechanism that is both reasonably efficient and easy to maintain.

As Figure 5.1 shows, the idea behind dynamic resolution with ARP is simple: when host A wants to resolve IP address I_B, it broadcasts a special packet that asks the host with IP address I_B to respond with its physical address, P_B. All hosts, including B, receive the request, but only host B recognizes its IP address and sends a reply that contains its physical address. When A receives the reply, it uses the physical address to send the internet packet directly to B. We can summarize:

> *The Address Resolution Protocol, ARP, allows a host to find the physical address of a target host on the same physical network, given only the target's IP address.*

---

†Because direct mapping is more convenient and efficient than dynamic binding, the next generation of IP is being designed to allow 48-bit addresses to be encoded in IP addresses.

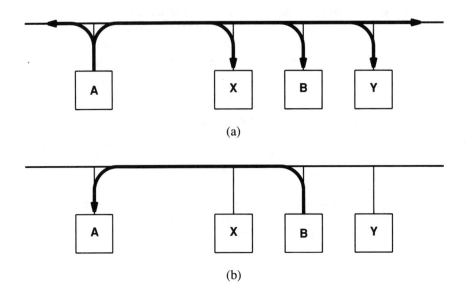

(a)

(b)

Figure 5.1 The ARP protocol. To determine P_B, B's physical address, from I_B, its IP address, (a) host A broadcasts an ARP request containing I_B to all machines on the net, and (b) host B responds with an ARP reply that contains the pair (I_B, P_B).

5.6 The Address Resolution Cache

It may seem silly that for A to send a packet to B it first sends a broadcast that reaches B. Or it may seem even sillier that A broadcasts the question, "how can I reach you?" instead of just broadcasting the packet it wants to deliver. But there is an important reason for the exchange. Broadcasting is far too expensive to be used every time one machine needs to transmit a packet to another because it requires every machine on the network to process the broadcast packet. To reduce communication costs, computers that use ARP maintain a cache of recently acquired IP-to-physical address bindings so they do not have to use ARP repeatedly. Whenever a computer receives an ARP reply, it saves the sender's IP address and corresponding hardware address in its cache for successive lookups. When transmitting a packet, a computer always looks in its cache for a binding before sending an ARP request. If a computer finds the desired binding in its ARP cache, it need not broadcast on the network. Experience shows that because most network communication involves more than one packet transfer, even a small cache is worthwhile.

5.7 ARP Refinements

Several refinements of ARP are possible. First, observe that if host *A* is about to use ARP because it needs to send to *B*, there is a high probability that host *B* will need to send to *A* in the near future. To anticipate *B*'s need and avoid extra network traffic, *A* includes its IP-to-physical address binding when sending a request to *B*. *B* extracts *A*'s binding from the request, saves the binding in its ARP cache, and then sends a reply to *A*. Second, notice that because *A* broadcasts its initial request, all machines on the network receive it and can extract and store in their cache *A*'s IP-to-physical address binding. Third, when a computer has its host interface replaced, (e.g., because the hardware has failed) its physical address changes. Other computers on the net that have stored a binding in their ARP cache need to be informed so they can change the entry. A system can notify others of a new address by sending an ARP broadcast when it boots.

The following rule summarizes refinements:

> *The sender's IP-to-physical address binding is included in every ARP broadcast; receivers update the IP-to-physical address binding information in their cache before processing an ARP packet.*

5.8 Relationship Of ARP To Other Protocols

ARP provides one possible mechanism to map from IP addresses to physical addresses; we have already seen that some network technologies do not need it. The point is that ARP would be completely unnecessary if we could make all network hardware recognize IP addresses. Thus, ARP merely imposes a new address scheme on top of whatever low-level address mechanism the hardware uses. The idea can be summarized:

> *ARP is a low-level protocol that hides the underlying network physical addressing, permitting one to assign an arbitrary IP address to every machine. We think of ARP as part of the physical network system, and not as part of the internet protocols.*

5.9 ARP Implementation

Functionally, ARP is divided into two parts. The first part maps an IP address to a physical address when sending a packet, and the second part answers requests from other machines. Address resolution for outgoing packets seems straightforward, but small details complicate an implementation. Given a destination IP address the software consults its ARP cache to see if it knows the mapping from IP address to physical address.

If it does, the software extracts the physical address, places the data in a frame using that address, and sends the frame. If it does not know the mapping, the software must broadcast an ARP request and wait for a reply.

Broadcasting an ARP request to find an address mapping can become complex. The target machine can be down or just too busy to accept the request. If so, the sender may not receive a reply or the reply may be delayed. Because the Ethernet is a best-effort delivery system, the initial ARP broadcast request can also be lost (in which case the sender should retransmit, at least once). Meanwhile, the host must store the original outgoing packet so it can be sent once the address has been resolved†. In fact, the host must decide whether to allow other application programs to proceed while it processes an ARP request (most do). If so, the software must handle the case where an application generates additional ARP requests for the same address without broadcasting multiple requests for a given target.

Finally, consider the case where machine *A* has obtained a binding for machine *B*, but then *B*'s hardware fails and is replaced. Although *B*'s address has changed, *A*'s cached binding has not, so *A* uses a nonexistent hardware address, making successful reception impossible. This case shows why it is important to have ARP software treat its table of bindings as a cache and remove entries after a fixed period. Of course, the timer for an entry in the cache must be reset whenever an ARP broadcast arrives containing the binding (but it is not reset when the entry is used to send a packet).

The second part of the ARP code handles ARP packets that arrive from the network. When an ARP packet arrives, the software first extracts the sender's IP address and hardware address pair, and examines the local cache to see if it already has an entry for the sender. If a cache entry exists for the given IP address, the handler updates that entry by overwriting the physical address with the physical address obtained from the packet. The receiver then processes the rest of the ARP packet.

A receiver must handle two types of incoming ARP packets. If an ARP request arrives, the receiving machine must see if it is the target of the request (i.e., some other machine has broadcast a request for the receiver's physical address). If so, the ARP software forms a reply by supplying its physical hardware address, and sends the reply directly back to the requester. The receiver also adds the sender's address pair to its cache if the pair is not already present. If the IP address mentioned in the ARP request does not match the local IP address, the packet is requesting a mapping for some other machine on the network and can be ignored.

The other interesting case occurs when an ARP reply arrives. Depending on the implementation, the handler may need to create a cache entry, or the entry may have been created when the request was generated. In any case, once the cache has been updated, the receiver tries to match the reply with a previously issued request. Usually, replies arrive in response to a request, which was generated because the machine has a packet to deliver. Between the time a machine broadcasts its ARP request and receives the reply, application programs or higher-level protocols may generate additional requests for the same address; the software must remember that it has already sent a request and not send more. Usually, ARP software places the additional packets on a queue. Once the reply arrives and the address binding is known, the ARP software re-

---

†If the delay is significant, the host may choose to discard the outgoing packet(s).

moves packets from the queue, places each packet in a frame, and uses the address binding to fill in the physical destination address. If it did not previously issue a request for the IP address in the reply, the machine updates the sender's entry in its cache, and then simply stops processing the packet.

5.10 ARP Encapsulation And Identification

When ARP messages travel from one machine to another, they must be carried in physical frames. Figure 5.2 shows that the ARP message is carried in the data portion of a frame.

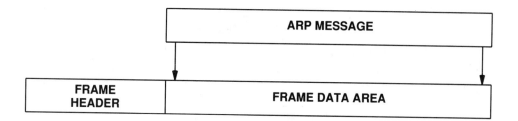

Figure 5.2 An ARP message encapsulated in a physical network frame.

To identify the frame as carrying an ARP message, the sender assigns a special value to the type field in the frame header, and places the ARP message in the frame's data field. When a frame arrives at a computer, the network software uses the frame type to determine its contents. In most technologies, a single type value is used for all frames that carry an ARP message – network software in the receiver must further examine the ARP message to distinguish between ARP requests and ARP replies. For example, on an Ethernet, frames carrying ARP messages have a type field of 0806_{16}. This is a standard value assigned by the authority for Ethernet; other network hardware technologies use other values.

5.11 ARP Protocol Format

Unlike most protocols, the data in ARP packets does not have a fixed-format header. Instead, to make ARP useful for a variety of network technologies, the length of fields that contain addresses depend on the type of network. However, to make it possible to interpret an arbitrary ARP message, the header includes fixed fields near the beginning that specify the lengths of the addresses found in succeeding fields. In fact, the ARP message format is general enough to allow it to be used with arbitrary physical addresses and arbitrary protocol addresses. The example in Figure 5.3 shows the 28-

octet ARP message format used on Ethernet hardware (where physical addresses are 48-bits or 6 octets long), when resolving IP protocol addresses (which are 4 octets long).

Figure 5.3 shows an ARP message with 4 octets per line, a format that is standard throughout this text. Unfortunately, unlike most of the remaining protocols, the variable-length fields in ARP packets do not align neatly on 32-bit boundaries, making the diagram difficult to read. For example, the sender's hardware address, labeled *SENDER HA*, occupies 6 contiguous octets, so it spans two lines in the diagram.

0	8	16	24	31
HARDWARE TYPE		PROTOCOL TYPE		
HLEN	PLEN	OPERATION		
SENDER HA (octets 0-3)				
SENDER HA (octets 4-5)		SENDER IP (octets 0-1)		
SENDER IP (octets 2-3)		TARGET HA (octets 0-1)		
TARGET HA (octets 2-5)				
TARGET IP (octets 0-3)				

Figure 5.3 An example of the ARP/RARP message format when used for IP-to-Ethernet address resolution. The length of fields depends on the hardware and protocol address lengths, which are 6 octets for an Ethernet address and 4 octets for an IP address.

Field *HARDWARE TYPE* specifies a hardware interface type for which the sender seeks an answer; it contains the value *1* for Ethernet. Similarly, field *PROTOCOL TYPE* specifies the type of high-level protocol address the sender has supplied; it contains 0800_{16} for IP addresses. Field *OPERATION* specifies an ARP request (*1*), ARP response (*2*), RARP† request (*3*), or RARP response (*4*). Fields *HLEN* and *PLEN* allow ARP to be used with arbitrary networks because they specify the length of the hardware address and the length of the high-level protocol address. The sender supplies its hardware address and IP address, if known, in fields *SENDER HA* and *SENDER IP*.

When making a request, the sender also supplies the target IP address (ARP), or target hardware address (RARP), using fields *TARGET HA* and *TARGET IP*. Before the target machine responds, it fills in the missing addresses, swaps the target and sender pairs, and changes the operation to a reply. Thus, a reply carries the IP and hardware addresses of the original requester, as well as the IP and hardware addresses of the machine for which a binding was sought.

---

†The next chapter describes RARP, another protocol that uses the same message format.

5.12 Summary

IP addresses are assigned independent of a machine's physical hardware address. To send an internet packet across a physical net from one computer to another, the network software must map the IP address into a physical hardware address and use the hardware address to transmit the frame. If hardware addresses are smaller than IP addresses, a direct mapping can be established by having the machine's physical address encoded in its IP address. Otherwise, the mapping must be performed dynamically. The Address Resolution Protocol (ARP) performs dynamic address resolution, using only the low-level network communication system. ARP permits machines to resolve addresses without keeping a permanent record of bindings.

A machine uses ARP to find the hardware address of another machine by broadcasting an ARP request. The request contains the IP address of the machine for which a hardware address is needed. All machines on a network receive an ARP request. If the request matches a machine's IP address, the machine responds by sending a reply that contains the needed hardware address. Replies are directed to one machine; they are not broadcast.

To make ARP efficient, each machine caches IP-to-physical address bindings. Because internet traffic tends to consist of a sequence of interactions between pairs of machines, the cache eliminates most ARP broadcast requests.

FOR FURTHER STUDY

The address resolution protocol used here is given by Plummer [RFC 826] and has become a TCP/IP internet protocol standard. Dalal and Printis [1981] describes the relationship between Ethernet and IP addresses, and Clark [RFC 814] discusses addresses and bindings in general. Parr [RFC 1029] discusses fault tolerant address resolution. Kirkpatrick and Recker [RFC 1166] specifies values used to identify network frames in the Internet Numbers document. Volume 2 of this text presents an example ARP implementation, and discusses the caching policy.

EXERCISES

5.1   Given a small set of physical addresses (positive integers), can you find a function f and an assignment of IP addresses such that f maps the IP addresses 1-to-1 onto the physical addresses and computing f is efficient? (Hint: look at the literature on perfect hashing).

5.2   In what special cases does a host connected to an Ethernet not need to use ARP or an ARP cache before transmitting an IP datagram?

5.3   One common algorithm for managing the ARP cache replaces the least recently used entry when adding a new one. Under what circumstances can this algorithm produce unnecessary network traffic?

5.4 Read the standard carefully. Should ARP update the cache if an old entry already exists for a given IP address? Why or why not?

5.5 Should ARP software modify the cache even when it receives information without specifically requesting it? Why or why not?

5.6 Any implementation of ARP that uses a fixed-size cache can fail when used on a network that has many hosts and much ARP traffic. Explain how.

5.7 ARP is often cited as a security weakness. Explain why.

5.8 Explain what can happen if the hardware address field in an ARP response becomes corrupted during transmission. Hint: some ARP implementations do not remove cache entries if they are frequently used.

5.9 Suppose machine C receives an ARP request sent from A looking for target B, and suppose C has the binding from I_B to P_B in its cache. Should C answer the request? Explain.

5.10 How can a workstation use ARP when it boots to find out if any other machine on the network is impersonating it? What are the disadvantages of the scheme?

5.11 Explain how sending IP packets to nonexistent addresses on a remote Ethernet can generate excess broadcast traffic on that network.

6

Determining An Internet Address At Startup (RARP)

6.1 Introduction

We now know that physical network addresses are both low-level and hardware dependent, and we understand that each machine using TCP/IP is assigned one or more 32-bit IP addresses that are independent of the machine's hardware addresses. Application programs always use the IP address when specifying a destination. Hosts and routers must use physical addresses to transmit datagrams across underlying networks; they rely on address resolution schemes like ARP to perform the binding.

Usually, a machine's IP address is kept on its secondary storage, where the operating system finds it at startup. The question arises, "How does a machine without a permanently attached disk determine its IP address?" The problem is critical for workstations that store files on a remote server because such machines need an IP address before they can use standard TCP/IP file transfer protocols to obtain their initial boot image. This chapter explores the question of how to obtain an IP address and describes a protocol that many machines use before they boot from a remote file server.

Because an operating system image that has a specific IP address bound into the code cannot be used on multiple computers, designers usually try to avoid compiling a machine's IP address in the operating system code or support software. In particular, the bootstrap code often found in Read Only Memory (ROM) is usually built so the same image can run on many machines. When such code starts execution on a diskless machine, it uses the network to contact a server to obtain the machine's IP address.

The bootstrap procedure sounds paradoxical: a machine communicates with a remote server to obtain an address needed for communication. The paradox is only imagined, however, because the machine *does* know how to communicate. It can use its physical address to communicate over a single network. Thus, the machine must resort to physical network addressing temporarily in the same way that operating systems use physical memory addressing to set up page tables for virtual addressing. Once a machine knows its IP address, it can communicate across an internet.

The idea behind finding an IP address is simple: a machine that needs to know its address sends a request to a *server*† on another machine, and waits until the server sends a response. We assume the server has access to a disk where it keeps a database of internet addresses. In the request, the machine that needs to know its internet address must uniquely identify itself, so the server can look up the correct internet address and send a reply. Both the machine that issues the request and the server that responds use physical network addresses during their brief communication. How does the requester know the physical address of a server? Usually, it does not – it simply broadcasts the request to all machines on the local network. One or more servers respond.

Whenever a machine broadcasts a request for an address, it must uniquely identify itself. What information can be included in its request that will uniquely identify the machine? Any unique hardware identification suffices (e.g., the CPU serial number). However, the identification should be something that an executing program can obtain easily. The objective is to create a single software image that can execute on an arbitrary processor. Furthermore, the length or format of CPU-specific information may vary among processor models, and we would like to devise a server that accepts requests from all machines on the physical network using a single format.

6.2 Reverse Address Resolution Protocol (RARP)

The designers of TCP/IP protocols realized that there is another piece of uniquely identifying information readily available, namely, the machine's physical network address. Using the physical address as a unique identification has two advantages. Because a host obtains its physical addresses from the network interface hardware, such addresses are always available and do not have to be bound into the bootstrap code. Because the identifying information depends on the network and not on the CPU vendor or model, all machines on a given network will supply uniform, unique identifiers. Thus, the problem becomes the reverse of address resolution: given a physical network address, devise a scheme that will allow a server to map it into an internet address.

A diskless machine uses a TCP/IP internet protocol called *RARP* (*Reverse Address Resolution Protocol*) to obtain its IP address from a server. RARP is adapted from the ARP protocol of the previous chapter and uses the same message format shown in Figure 5.3. In practice, the RARP message sent to request an internet address is a little more general than what we have outlined above: it allows a machine to request the IP address of a third party as easily as its own. It also allows for multiple physical network types.

---

†Chapter 19 discusses servers in detail.

Like an ARP message, a RARP message is sent from one machine to another encapsulated in the data portion of a network frame. For example, an Ethernet frame carrying a RARP request has the usual preamble, Ethernet source and destination addresses, and packet type fields in front of the frame. The frame type contains the value 8035_{16} to identify the contents of the frame as a RARP message. The data portion of the frame contains the 28-octet RARP message.

Figure 6.1 illustrates how a host uses RARP. The sender broadcasts a RARP request that specifies itself as both the sender and target machine, and supplies its physical network address in the target hardware address field. All machines on the network receive the request, but only those authorized to supply the RARP service process the request and send a reply; such machines are known informally as *RARP servers*. For RARP to succeed, the network must contain at least one RARP server.

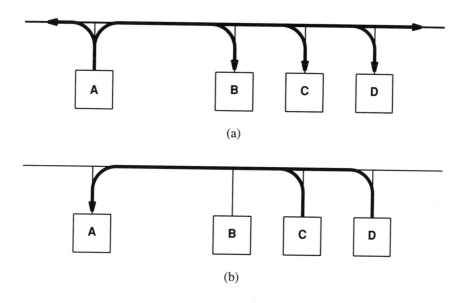

(a)

(b)

Figure 6.1 Example exchange using the RARP protocol. (a) machine *A* broadcasts a RARP request specifying itself as a target, and (b) those machines authorized to supply the RARP service (*C* and *D*) reply directly to *A*.

Servers answer requests by filling in the target protocol address field, changing the message type from *request* to *reply*, and sending the reply back directly to the machine making the request. The original machine receives replies from all RARP servers, even though only the first is needed.

Keep in mind that all communication between the machine seeking its IP address and the server supplying it must be carried out using only the physical network. Furthermore, the protocol allows a host to ask about an arbitrary target. Thus, the sender supplies its hardware address separate from the target hardware address, and the server is careful to send the reply to the sender's hardware address. On an Ethernet, having a field for the sender's hardware address may seem redundant because the information is also contained in the Ethernet frame header. However, not all Ethernet hardware provides the operating system with access to the physical frame header.

6.3 Timing RARP Transactions

Like any communication on a best-effort delivery network, RARP requests are susceptible to loss or corruption. Because RARP uses the physical network directly, no other protocol software will time the response or retransmit the request; RARP software must handle these tasks. In general, RARP is used only on local area networks like the Ethernet, where the probability of failure is low. If a network has only one RARP server, however, that machine may not be able to handle the load, so packets may be dropped.

Some workstations that rely on RARP to boot, choose to retry indefinitely until they receive a response. Other implementations announce failure after only a few tries to avoid flooding the network with unnecessary broadcast traffic (e.g., in case the server is unavailable). On an Ethernet, network failure is less likely than server overload. Making RARP software retransmit quickly may have the unwanted effect of flooding a congested server with more traffic. Using a large delay ensures that servers have ample time to satisfy the request and return an answer.

6.4 Primary And Backup RARP Servers

The chief advantage of having several machines function as RARP servers is that it makes the system more reliable. If one server is down, or too heavily loaded to respond, another answers the request. Thus, it is highly likely that the service will be available. The chief disadvantage of using many servers is that when a machine broadcasts a RARP request, the network becomes overloaded when all servers attempt to respond. On an Ethernet, for example, using multiple RARP servers makes the probability of collision high.

How can the RARP service be arranged to keep it available and reliable without incurring the cost of multiple, simultaneous replies? There are at least two possibilities, and they both involve delaying responses. In the first solution, each machine that makes RARP requests is assigned a *primary server*. Under normal circumstances, only the machine's primary server responds to its RARP request. All nonprimary servers receive the request but merely record its arrival time. If the primary server is unavailable, the original machine will timeout waiting for a response and then rebroadcast the request. Whenever a nonprimary server receives a second copy of a RARP request within a short time of the first, it responds.

The second solution uses a similar scheme but attempts to avoid having all nonprimary servers transmit responses simultaneously. Each nonprimary machine that receives a request computes a random delay and then sends a response. Under normal circumstances, the primary server responds immediately and successive responses are delayed, so there is low probability that they arrive at the same time. When the primary server is unavailable, the requesting machine experiences a small delay before receiving a reply. By choosing delays carefully, the designer can insure that requesting machines do not rebroadcast before they receive an answer.

6.5 Summary

At system startup, a computer that does not have a permanent disk must contact a server to find its IP address before it can communicate using TCP/IP. We examined the RARP protocol that uses physical network addressing to obtain the machine's internet address. The RARP mechanism supplies the target machine's physical hardware address to uniquely identify the processor and broadcasts the RARP request. Servers on the network receive the message, look up the mapping in a table (presumably from secondary storage), and reply to the sender. Once a machine obtains its IP address, it stores the address in memory and does not use RARP again until it reboots.

FOR FURTHER STUDY

The details of RARP are given in Finlayson, *et. al.* [RFC 903]. Finlayson [RFC 906] describes workstation bootstrapping using the TFTP protocol. Bradley and Brown [RFC 1293] specifies a related protocol, *Inverse ARP*. Inverse ARP permits a computer to query the machine at the opposite end of a hardware connection to determine its IP address, and was intended for computers connected via Frame Relay. Volume 2 of this text describes an example implementation of RARP.

Chapter 21 considers alternatives to RARP known as BOOTP and DHCP, a more recent extension. Unlike the low-level address determination scheme RARP supplies, BOOTP and DHCP build on higher level protocols like IP and UDP. Chapter 21 compares the two approaches, discussing the strengths and weaknesses of each.

EXERCISES

6.1   A RARP server can broadcast RARP replies to all machines or transmit each reply directly to the machine that makes the request. Characterize a network technology in which broadcasting replies to all machines is beneficial.

6.2   RARP is a narrowly focused protocol in the sense that replies only contain one piece of information (i.e., the requested IP address). When a computer boots, it usually needs to know its name in addition to its Internet address. Extend RARP to supply the additional information.

6.3   How much larger will Ethernet frames become when information is added to RARP as described in the previous exercise?

6.4   Adding a second RARP server to a network increases reliability. Does it ever make sense to add a third? How about a fourth? Why or Why not?

6.5   The diskless workstations from one vendor use RARP to obtain their IP addresses, but always assume the response comes from the workstation's file server. The diskless machine then tries to obtain a boot image from that server. If it does not receive a response, the workstation enters an infinite loop broadcasting boot requests. Explain how adding a backup RARP server to such a configuration can cause the network to become congested with broadcasts. Hint: think of power failures.

6.6   Monitor a local network while you reboot various computers. Which use RARP?

6.7   The backup RARP servers discussed in the text use the arrival of a second request in a short period of time to trigger a reply. Consider the RARP server scheme that has all servers answer the first request, but avoids congestion by having each server delay a random time before answering. Under what circumstances could such a design yield better results than the design described in the text?

7

Internet Protocol: Connectionless Datagram Delivery

7.1 Introduction

Previous chapters review pieces of network hardware and software that make internet communication possible, explaining the underlying network technologies and address resolution. This chapter explains the fundamental principle of connectionless delivery and discusses how it is provided by the *Internet Protocol* (*IP*), one of the two major protocols used in internetworking. We will study the format of IP datagrams and see how they form the basis for all internet communication. The next two chapters continue our examination of the Internet Protocol by discussing datagram routing and error handling.

7.2 A Virtual Network

Chapter 3 discussed an internet architecture in which routers connect multiple physical networks. Looking at the architecture may be misleading, because the focus should be on the interface that an internet provides to users, not on the interconnection technology.

*A user thinks of an internet as a single virtual network that intercon-
nects all hosts, and through which communication is possible; its
underlying architecture is both hidden and irrelevant.*

In a sense, an internet is an abstraction of physical networks because, at the lowest level, it provides the same functionality: accepting packets and delivering them. Higher
levels of internet software add most of the rich functionality users perceive.

7.3 Internet Architecture And Philosophy

Conceptually, a TCP/IP internet provides three sets of services as shown in Figure
7.1; their arrangement in the figure suggests dependencies among them. At the lowest
level, a connectionless delivery service provides a foundation on which everything rests.
At the next level, a reliable transport service provides a higher level platform on which
applications depend. We will soon explore each of these services, understand what they
provide, and see the protocols associated with them.

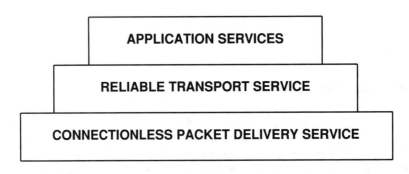

Figure 7.1 The three conceptual layers of internet services.

7.4 The Concept Of Unreliable Delivery

Although we can associate protocol software with each of the services in Figure
7.1, the reason for identifying them as conceptual parts of the internet is that they clearly point out the philosophical underpinnings of the design. The point is:

*Internet software is designed around three conceptual networking ser-
vices arranged in a hierarchy; much of its success has resulted because this architecture is surprisingly robust and adaptable.*

One of the most significant advantages of this conceptual separation is that it becomes possible to replace one service without disturbing others. Thus, research and development can proceed concurrently on all three.

7.5 Connectionless Delivery System

The most fundamental internet service consists of a packet delivery system. Technically, the service is defined as an unreliable, best-effort, connectionless packet delivery system, analogous to the service provided by network hardware that operates on a best-effort delivery paradigm. The service is called *unreliable* because delivery is not guaranteed. The packet may be lost, duplicated, delayed, or delivered out of order, but the service will not detect such conditions, nor will it inform the sender or receiver. The service is called *connectionless* because each packet is treated independently from all others. A sequence of packets sent from one computer to another may travel over different paths, or some may be lost while others are delivered. Finally, the service is said to use *best-effort delivery* because the internet software makes an earnest attempt to deliver packets. That is, the internet does not discard packets capriciously; unreliability arises only when resources are exhausted or underlying networks fail.

7.6 Purpose Of The Internet Protocol

The protocol that defines the unreliable, connectionless delivery mechanism is called the *Internet Protocol* and is usually referred to by its initials, *IP*†. IP provides three important definitions. First, the IP protocol defines the basic unit of data transfer used throughout a TCP/IP internet. Thus, it specifies the exact format of all data as it passes across a TCP/IP internet. Second, IP software performs the *routing* function, choosing a path over which data will be sent. Third, in addition to the precise, formal specification of data formats and routing, IP includes a set of rules that embody the idea of unreliable packet delivery. The rules characterize how hosts and routers should process packets, how and when error messages should be generated, and the conditions under which packets can be discarded. IP is such a fundamental part of the design that a TCP/IP internet is sometimes called an *IP-based technology*.

We begin our consideration of IP in this chapter by looking at the packet format it specifies. We leave until later chapters the topics of routing and error handling.

7.7 The Internet Datagram

The analogy between a physical network and a TCP/IP internet is strong. On a physical network, the unit of transfer is a frame that contains a header and data, where the header gives information such as the (physical) source and destination addresses. The internet calls its basic transfer unit an *Internet datagram*, sometimes referred to as

---

†The abbreviation IP gives rise to the term ''IP address.''

an *IP datagram* or merely a *datagram*. Like a typical physical network frame, a datagram is divided into header and data areas. Also like a frame, the datagram header contains the source and destination addresses and a type field that identifies the contents of the datagram. The difference, of course, is that the datagram header contains IP addresses whereas the frame header contains physical addresses. Figure 7.2 shows the general form of a datagram:

DATAGRAM HEADER	DATAGRAM DATA AREA

Figure 7.2 General form of an IP datagram, the TCP/IP analogy to a network frame. IP specifies the header format including the source and destination IP addresses. IP does not specify the format of the data area; it can be used to transport arbitrary data.

7.7.1 Datagram Format

Now that we have described the general layout of an IP datagram, we can look at the contents in more detail. Figure 7.3 shows the arrangement of fields in a datagram:

0	4	8	16	19	24	31
VERS	HLEN	SERVICE TYPE		TOTAL LENGTH		
IDENTIFICATION			FLAGS	FRAGMENT OFFSET		
TIME TO LIVE		PROTOCOL		HEADER CHECKSUM		
SOURCE IP ADDRESS						
DESTINATION IP ADDRESS						
IP OPTIONS (IF ANY)					PADDING	
DATA						
. . .						

Figure 7.3 Format of an Internet datagram, the basic unit of transfer in a TCP/IP internet.

Because datagram processing occurs in software, the contents and format are not constrained by any hardware. For example, the first 4-bit field in a datagram (*VERS*) contains the version of the IP protocol that was used to create the datagram. It is used to verify that the sender, receiver, and any routers in between them agree on the format of the datagram. All IP software is required to check the version field before processing a datagram to ensure it matches the format the software expects. If standards change, machines will reject datagrams with protocol versions that differ from theirs, preventing them from misinterpreting datagram contents according to an outdated format. The current IP protocol version is *4*.

The header length field (*HLEN*), also 4 bits, gives the datagram header length measured in 32-bit words. As we will see, all fields in the header have fixed length except for the *IP OPTIONS* and corresponding *PADDING* fields. The most common header, which contains no options and no padding, measures 20 octets and has a header length field equal to *5*.

The *TOTAL LENGTH* field gives the length of the IP datagram measured in octets, including octets in the header and data. The size of the data area can be computed by subtracting the length of the header (*HLEN*) from the *TOTAL LENGTH*. Because the *TOTAL LENGTH* field is 16 bits long, the maximum possible size of an IP datagram is 2^{16} or 65,535 octets. In most applications this is not a severe limitation. It may become more important in the future if higher speed networks can carry data packets larger than 65,535 octets.

7.7.2 Datagram Type Of Service And Datagram Precedence

Informally called *Type Of Service* (*TOS*), the 8-bit *SERVICE TYPE* field specifies how the datagram should be handled and is broken down into five subfields as shown in Figure 7.4:

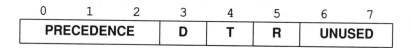

Figure 7.4 The five subfields that comprise the 8-bit *SERVICE TYPE* field.

Three *PRECEDENCE* bits specify datagram precedence, with values ranging from 0 (normal precedence) through 7 (network control), allowing senders to indicate the importance of each datagram. Although most host and router software ignores type of service, it is an important concept because it provides a mechanism that can allow control information to have precedence over data. For example, if all hosts and routers honor precedence, it is possible to implement congestion control algorithms that are not affected by the congestion they are trying to control.

Bits *D*, *T*, and *R* specify the type of transport the datagram desires. When set, the *D* bit requests low delay, the *T* bit requests high throughput, and the *R* bit requests high reliability. Of course, it may not be possible for an internet to guarantee the type of transport requested (i.e., it could be that no path to the destination has the requested property). Thus, we think of the transport request as a hint to the routing algorithms, not as a demand. If a router does know more than one possible route to a given destination, it can use the type of transport field to select one with characteristics closest to those desired. For example, suppose a router can select between a low capacity leased line or a high bandwidth (but high delay) satellite connection. Datagrams carrying keystrokes from a user to a remote computer could have the D bit set requesting that they be delivered as quickly as possible, while datagrams carrying a bulk file transfer could have the T bit set requesting that they travel across the high capacity satellite path.

It is also important to realize that routing algorithms must choose from among underlying physical network technologies that each have characteristics of delay, throughput, and reliability. Often, a given technology trades off one characteristic for another (e.g., higher throughput rates at the expense of longer delay). Thus, the idea is to give the routing algorithm a hint about what is most important; it seldom makes sense to specify all three types of service. To summarize:

> We regard the type of transport specification as a hint to the routing algorithm that helps it choose among various paths to a destination based on its knowledge of the hardware technologies available on those paths. An internet does not guarantee the type of transport requested.

7.7.3 Datagram Encapsulation

Before we can understand the next fields in a datagram, it is important to consider how datagrams relate to physical network frames. We start with a question: "How large can a datagram be?" Unlike physical network frames that must be recognized by hardware, datagrams are handled by software. They can be of any length the protocol designers choose. We have seen that the current datagram format allots only 16 bits to the total length field, limiting the datagram to at most 65,535 octets. However, that limit could be changed in later versions of the protocol.

More fundamental limits on datagram size arise in practice. We know that as datagrams move from one machine to another, they must always be transported by the underlying physical network. To make internet transportation efficient, we would like to guarantee that each datagram travels in a distinct physical frame. That is, we want our abstraction of a physical network packet to map directly onto a real packet if possible.

The idea of carrying one datagram in one network frame is called *encapsulation*. To the underlying network, a datagram is like any other message sent from one machine to another. The hardware does not recognize the datagram format, nor does it understand the IP destination address. Thus, as Figure 7.5 shows, when one machine sends an IP datagram to another, the entire datagram travels in the data portion of the network frame.

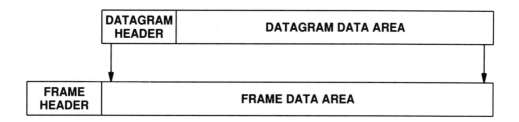

Figure 7.5 The encapsulation of an IP datagram in a frame. The physical network treats the entire datagram, including the header, as data.

7.7.4 Datagram Size, Network MTU, and Fragmentation

In the ideal case, the entire IP datagram fits into one physical frame, making transmission across the physical net efficient.† To achieve such efficiency, the designers of IP might have selected a maximum datagram size such that a datagram would always fit into one frame. But which frame size should be chosen? After all, a datagram may travel across many types of physical networks as it moves across an internet to its final destination.

To understand the problem, we need a fact about network hardware: each packet-switching technology places a fixed upper bound on the amount of data that can be transferred in one physical frame. For example, the Ethernet limits transfers to 1500‡ octets of data, while FDDI permits approximately 4470 octets of data per frame. We refer to these limits as the network's *maximum transfer unit* or *MTU*. MTU sizes can be quite small: some hardware technologies limit transfers to 128 octets or less. Limiting datagrams to fit the smallest possible MTU in the internet makes transfers inefficient when those datagrams pass across a network that can carry larger size frames. However, allowing datagrams to be larger than the minimum network MTU in an internet means that a datagram may not always fit into a single network frame.

The choice should be obvious: the point of the internet design is to hide underlying network technologies and make communication convenient for the user. Thus, instead of designing datagrams that adhere to the constraints of physical networks, TCP/IP software chooses a convenient initial datagram size and arranges a way to divide large datagrams into smaller pieces when the datagram needs to traverse a network that has a small MTU. The small pieces into which a datagram is divided are called *fragments*, and the process of dividing a datagram is known as *fragmentation*.

As Figure 7.6 illustrates, fragmentation usually occurs at a router somewhere along the path between the datagram source and its ultimate destination. The router receives a datagram from a network with a large MTU and must send it over a network for which the MTU is smaller than the datagram size.

---

†A field in the frame header usually identifies the data being carried; Ethernet uses the type value 0800_{16} to specify that the data area contains an encapsulated IP datagram.

‡The limit of 1500 comes from the Ethernet specification; when used with a SNAP header the IEEE 802.3 standard limits data to 1492 octets. Some vendors' implementations allow slightly larger transfers.

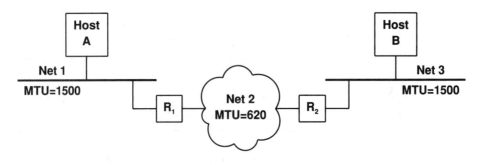

Figure 7.6 An illustration of where fragmentation occurs. Router R_1 fragments large datagrams sent from A to B; R_2 fragments large datagrams sent from B to A.

In the figure, both hosts attach directly to Ethernets which have an MTU of 1500
octets. Thus, both hosts can generate and send datagrams up to 1500 octets long. The
path between them, however, includes a network with an MTU of 620. If host A sends
host B a datagram larger than 620 octets, router R_1 will fragment the datagram. Similarly, if B sends a large datagram to A, router R_2 will fragment the the datagram.

Fragment size is chosen so each fragment can be shipped across the underlying
network in a single frame. In addition, because IP represents the offset of the data in
multiples of eight octets, the fragment size must be chosen to be a multiple of eight. Of
course, choosing the multiple of eight octets nearest to the network MTU does not usually divide the datagram into equal size pieces; the last piece is often shorter than the
others. Fragments must be *reassembled* to produce a complete copy of the original datagram before it can be processed at the destination.

The IP protocol does not limit datagrams to a small size, nor does it guarantee that
large datagrams will be delivered without fragmentation. The source can choose any
datagram size it thinks appropriate; fragmentation and reassembly occur automatically,
without the source taking special action. The IP specification states that routers must
accept datagrams up to the maximum of the MTUs of networks to which they attach.
In addition, a router must always handle datagrams of up to 576 octets. (Hosts are also
required to accept, and reassemble if necessary, datagrams of at least 576 octets.)

Fragmenting a datagram means dividing it into several pieces. It may surprise you
to learn that each piece has the same format as the original datagram. Figure 7.7 illustrates the result of fragmentation.

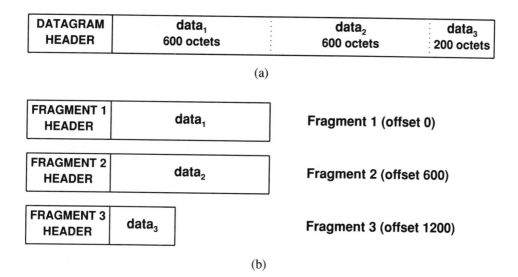

Figure 7.7 (a) An original datagram carrying 1400 octets of data and (b) the
three fragments for network MTU of 620. Headers 1 and 2 have
the *more fragments* bit set. Offsets shown are decimal octets;
they must be divided by 8 to get the value stored in the fragment
headers.

Each fragment contains a datagram header that duplicates most of the original datagram header (except for a bit in the *FLAGS* field that shows it is a fragment), followed by as much data as can be carried in the fragment while keeping the total length
smaller than the MTU of the network over which it must travel.

7.7.5 Reassembly Of Fragments

Should a datagram be reassembled after passing across one network, or should the
fragments be carried to the final host before reassembly? In a TCP/IP internet, once a
datagram has been fragmented, the fragments travel as separate datagrams all the way to
the ultimate destination where they must be reassembled. Preserving fragments all the
way to the ultimate destination has two disadvantages. First, because datagrams are not
reassembled immediately after passing across a network with small MTU, the small
fragments must be carried from the point of fragmentation to the ultimate destination.
Reassembling datagrams at the ultimate destination can lead to inefficiency: even if
some of the physical networks encountered after the point of fragmentation have large
MTU capability, only small fragments traverse them. Second, if any fragments are lost,
the datagram cannot be reassembled. The receiving machine starts a *reassembly timer*
when it receives an initial fragment. If the timer expires before all fragments arrive, the

receiving machine discards the surviving pieces without processing the datagram. Thus, the probability of datagram loss increases when fragmentation occurs because the loss of a single fragment results in loss of the entire datagram.

Despite the minor disadvantages, performing reassembly at the ultimate destination works well. It allows each fragment to be routed independently, and does not require intermediate routers to store or reassemble fragments.

7.7.6 Fragmentation Control

Three fields in the datagram header, *IDENTIFICATION*, *FLAGS*, and *FRAGMENT OFFSET*, control fragmentation and reassembly of datagrams. Field *IDENTIFICATION* contains a unique integer that identifies the datagram. Recall that when a router fragments a datagram, it copies most of the fields in the datagram header into each fragment. The *IDENTIFICATION* field must be copied. Its primary purpose is to allow the destination to know which arriving fragments belong to which datagrams. As a fragment arrives, the destination uses the *IDENTIFICATION* field along with the datagram source address to identify the datagram. Computers sending IP datagrams must generate a unique value for the *IDENTIFICATION* field for each unique datagram†. One technique used by IP software keeps a global counter in memory, increments it each time a new datagram is created, and assigns the result as the datagram's *IDENTIFICATION* field.

Recall that each fragment has exactly the same format as a complete datagram. For a fragment, field *FRAGMENT OFFSET* specifies the offset in the original datagram of the data being carried in the fragment, measured in units of 8 octets‡, starting at offset zero. To reassemble the datagram, the destination must obtain all fragments starting with the fragment that has offset *0* through the fragment with highest offset. Fragments do not necessarily arrive in order, and there is no communication between the router that fragmented the datagram and the destination trying to reassemble it.

The low-order two bits of the 3-bit *FLAGS* field controls fragmentation. Usually, application software using TCP/IP does not care about fragmentation because both fragmentation and reassembly are automatic procedures that occur at a low level in the operating system, invisible to end users. However, to test internet software or debug operational problems, it may be important to test sizes of datagrams for which fragmentation occurs. The first control bit aids in such testing by specifying whether the datagram may be fragmented. It is called the *do not fragment* bit because setting it to *1* specifies that the datagram should not be fragmented. An application may choose to disallow fragmentation when only the entire datagram is useful. For example, consider a computer bootstrap sequence in which a machine begins executing a small program in ROM that uses the internet to request an initial bootstrap, and another machine sends back a memory image. If the software has been designed so it needs the entire image or none of it, the datagram should have the *do not fragment* bit set. Whenever a router needs to fragment a datagram that has the *do not fragment* bit set, the router discards the datagram and sends an error message back to the source.

---

†In theory, retransmissions of a datagram can carry the same *IDENTIFICATION* field as the original; in practice, higher-level protocols usually perform retransmission, resulting in a new datagram with its own *IDENTIFICATION*.

‡To save space in the header, offsets are specified in multiples of 8 octets.

The low order bit in the *FLAGS* field specifies whether the fragment contains data from the middle of the original datagram or from the end. It is called the *more fragments* bit. To see why such a bit is needed, consider the IP software at the ultimate destination attempting to reassemble a datagram. It will receive fragments (possibly out of order) and needs to know when it has received all fragments for a datagram. When a fragment arrives, the *TOTAL LENGTH* field in the header refers to the size of the fragment and not to the size of the original datagram, so the destination cannot use the *TOTAL LENGTH* field to tell whether it has collected all fragments. The *more fragments* bit solves the problem easily: once the destination receives a fragment with the *more fragments* bit turned off, it knows this fragment carries data from the tail of the original datagram. From the *FRAGMENT OFFSET* and *TOTAL LENGTH* fields, it can compute the length of the original datagram. By examining the *FRAGMENT OFFSET* and *TOTAL LENGTH* of all fragments that have arrived, a receiver can tell whether the fragments on hand contain all the data needed to reassemble the entire original datagram.

7.7.7 Time to Live (TTL)

Field *TIME TO LIVE* specifies how long, in seconds, the datagram is allowed to remain in the internet system. The idea is both simple and important: whenever a machine injects a datagram into the internet, it sets a maximum time that the datagram should survive. Routers and hosts that process datagrams must decrement the *TIME TO LIVE* field as time passes and remove the datagram from the internet when its time expires.

Estimating exact times is difficult because routers do not usually know the transit time for physical networks. A few rules simplify processing and make it easy to handle datagrams without synchronized clocks. First, each router along the path from source to destination is required to decrement the *TIME TO LIVE* field by *1* when it processes the datagram header. Furthermore, to handle cases of overloaded routers that introduce long delays, each router records the local time when the datagram arrives, and decrements the *TIME TO LIVE* by the number of seconds the datagram remained inside the router waiting for service.

Whenever a *TIME TO LIVE* field reaches zero, the router discards the datagram and sends an error message back to the source. The idea of keeping a timer for datagrams is interesting because it guarantees that datagrams cannot travel around an internet forever, even if routing tables become corrupt and routers route datagrams in a circle.

7.7.8 Other Datagram Header Fields

Field *PROTOCOL* is analogous to the type field in an network frame. The value in the *PROTOCOL* field specifies which high-level protocol was used to create the message being carried in the *DATA* area of a datagram. In essence, the value of *PROTOCOL* specifies the format of the *DATA* area. The mapping between a high level protocol and the integer value used in the *PROTOCOL* field must be administered by a central authority to guarantee agreement across the entire Internet.

Field *HEADER CHECKSUM* ensures integrity of header values. The IP checksum is formed by treating the header as a sequence of 16-bit integers (in network byte order), adding them together using one's complement arithmetic, and then taking the one's complement of the result. For purposes of computing the checksum, field *HEADER CHECKSUM* is assumed to contain zero.

It is important to note that the checksum only applies to values in the IP header and not to the data. Separating the checksum for headers and data has advantages and disadvantages. Because the header usually occupies fewer octets than the data, having a separate checksum reduces processing time at routers which only need to compute header checksums. The separation also allows higher level protocols to choose their own checksum scheme for the data. The chief disadvantage is that higher level protocols are forced to add their own checksum or risk having corrupted data go undetected.

Fields *SOURCE IP ADDRESS* and *DESTINATION IP ADDRESS* contain the 32-bit IP addresses of the datagram's sender and intended recipient. Although the datagram may be routed through many intermediate routers, the source and destination fields never change; they specify the IP addresses of the original source and ultimate destination†.

The field labeled *DATA* in Figure 7.3 shows the beginning of the data area of the datagram. Its length depends, of course, on what is being sent in the datagram. The *IP OPTIONS* field, discussed below, is variable length. The field labeled *PADDING*, depends on the options selected. It represents bits containing zero that may be needed to ensure the datagram header extends to an exact multiple of 32 bits (recall that the header length field is specified in units of 32-bit words).

7.8 Internet Datagram Options

The *IP OPTIONS* field following the destination address is not required in every datagram; options are included primarily for network testing or debugging. Options processing is an integral part of the IP protocol, however, so all standard implementations must include it.

The length of the *IP OPTIONS* field varies depending on which options are selected. Some options are one octet long; they consist of a single octet *option code*. Other options are variable length. When options are present in a datagram, they appear contiguously, with no special separators between them. Each option consists of a single octet option code, which may be followed by a single octet length and a set of data octets for that option. The option code octet is divided into three fields as Figure 7.8 shows.

---

†An exception is made when the datagram includes the source route options listed below.

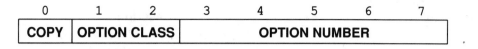

Figure 7.8 The division of the option code octet into three fields of length 1, 2, and 5 bits.

The fields consist of a 1-bit *COPY* flag, a 2-bit *OPTION CLASS*, and the 5-bit *OPTION NUMBER*. The *COPY* flag controls how routers treat options during fragmentation. When the *COPY* bit is set to *1*, it specifies that the option should be copied into all fragments. When set to *0*, the *COPY* bit means that the option should only be copied into the first fragment and not into all fragments.

The *OPTION CLASS* and *OPTION NUMBER* bits specify the general class of the option and give a specific option in that class. The table in Figure 7.9 shows how classes are assigned.

Option Class	Meaning
0	Datagram or network control
1	Reserved for future use
2	Debugging and measurement
3	Reserved for future use

Figure 7.9 Classes of IP options as encoded in the *OPTION CLASS* bits of an option code octet.

The table in Figure 7.10 lists the possible options that can accompany an IP datagram and gives their *OPTION CLASS* and *OPTION NUMBER* values. As the list shows, most options are used for control purposes.

Option Class	Option Number	Length	Description
0	0	-	**End of option list. Used if options do not end at end of header (also see header padding field).**
0	1	-	**No operation (used to align octets in a list of options).**
0	2	11	**Security and handling restrictions (for military applications).**
0	3	var	**Loose source routing. Used to route a datagram along a specified path.**
0	7	var	**Record route. Used to trace a route.**
0	8	4	**Stream identifier. Used to carry a SATNET stream identifier (Obsolete).**
0	9	var	**Strict source routing. Used to route a datagram along a specified path.**
2	4	var	**Internet timestamp. Used to record timestamps along the route.**

Figure 7.10 The eight possible IP options with their numeric class and number codes. The value *var* in the length column stands for *variable*.

7.8.1 Record Route Option

The routing and timestamp options are the most interesting because they provide a way to monitor or control how internet routers route datagrams. The *record route* option allows the source to create an empty list of IP addresses and arrange for each router that handles the datagram to add its IP address to the list. Figure 7.11 shows the format of the record route option.

As described above, the *CODE* field contains the option class and option number (*0* and *7* for record route). The *LENGTH* field specifies the total length of the option as it appears in the IP datagram, including the first three octets. The fields starting with one labeled *FIRST IP ADDRESS* comprise the area reserved for recording internet addresses. The *POINTER* field specifies the offset within the option of the next available slot.

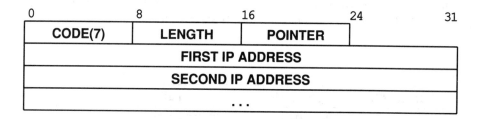

Figure 7.11 The format of the record route option in an IP datagram. The option begins with three octets immediately followed by a list of addresses. Although the diagram shows addresses in 32 bit units, they are not aligned on any octet boundary in a datagram.

Whenever a machine handles a datagram that has the record route option set, the machine adds its address to the record route list (enough space must be allocated in the option by the original source to hold all entries that will be needed). To add itself to the list, a machine first compares the pointer and length fields. If the pointer is greater than the length, the list is full, so the machine forwards the datagram without inserting its entry. If the list is not full, the machine inserts its 4-octet IP address at the position specified by the *POINTER*, and increments the *POINTER* by four.

When the datagram arrives, the destination machine can extract and process the list of IP addresses. Usually, a computer that receives a datagram ignores the recorded route. Using the record route option requires two machines that agree to cooperate; a computer will not automatically receive recorded routes in incoming datagrams after it turns on the record route option in outgoing datagrams. The source must agree to enable the record route option and the destination must agree to process the resultant list.

7.8.2 Source Route Options

Another idea that network builders find interesting is the *source route* option. The idea behind source routing is that it provides a way for the sender to dictate a path through the internet. For example, to test the throughput over a particular physical network, N, system administrators can use source routing to force IP datagrams to traverse network N even if routers would normally choose a path that did not include it. The ability to make such tests is especially important in a production environment, because it gives the network manager freedom to route users' datagrams over networks that are known to operate correctly while simultaneously testing other networks. Of course, such routing is only useful to people who understand the network topology; the average user has no need to know or use it.

IP supports two forms of source routing. One form, called *strict source routing*, specifies a routing path by including a sequence of IP addresses in the option as Figure 7.12 shows.

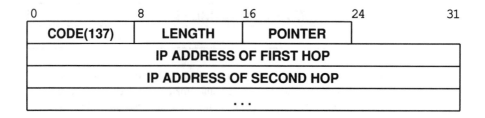

Figure 7.12 The strict source route option specifies an exact route by giving a list of IP addresses the datagram must follow.

Strict source routing means that the addresses specify the exact path the datagram must follow to reach its destination. The path between two successive addresses in the list must consist of a single physical network; an error results if a router cannot follow a strict source route. The other form, called *loose source routing*, also includes a sequence of IP addresses. It specifies that the datagram must follow the sequence of IP addresses, but allows multiple network hops between successive addresses on the list.

Both source route options require routers along the path to overwrite items in the address list with their local network addresses. Thus, when the datagram arrives at its destination, it contains a list of all addresses visited, exactly like the list produced by the record route option.

The format of a source route option resembles that of the record route option shown above. Each router examines the *POINTER* and *LENGTH* fields to see if the list has been exhausted. If it has, the pointer is greater than the length, and the router routes the datagram to its destination as usual. If the list is not exhausted, the router follows the pointer, picks up the IP address, replaces it with the router's address†, and routes the datagram using the address it obtained from the list.

7.8.3 Timestamp Option

The *timestamp option* works like the record route option in that the timestamp option contains an initially empty list, and each router along the path from source to destination fills in one item in the list. Each entry in the list contains two 32-bit items: the IP address of the router that supplied the entry, and a 32-bit integer timestamp. Figure 7.13 shows the format of the timestamp option.

---

†A router has one address for each interface; it records the address that corresponds to the network over which it routes the datagram.

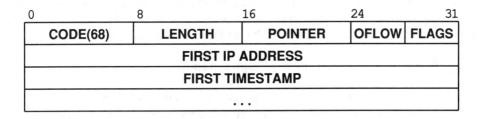

Figure 7.13 The format of the timestamp option. Bits in the FLAGS field
control the exact format and rules routers use to process this option.

In the figure, the *LENGTH* and *POINTER* fields are used to specify the length of
the space reserved for the option and the location of the next unused slot (exactly as in
the record route option). The 4-bit *OFLOW* field contains an integer count of routers
that could not supply a timestamp because the option was too small.

The value in the 4-bit *FLAGS* field controls the exact format of the option and tells
how routers should supply timestamps. The values are:

Flags value	Meaning
0	Record timestamps only; omit IP addresses.
1	Precede each timestamp by an IP address (this is the format shown in Figure 7.13).
3	IP addresses are specified by sender; a router only records a timestamp if the next IP address in the list matches the router's IP address.

Figure 7.14 The interpretation of values in the FLAGS field of a timestamp
option.

Timestamps give the time and date at which a router handles the datagram, expressed as milliseconds since midnight, Universal Time†. If the standard representation
for time is unavailable, the router can use any representation of local time provided it
turns on the high-order bit in the timestamp field. Of course, timestamps issued by independent computers are not always consistent even if represented in universal time;
each machine reports time according to its local clock, and clocks may differ. Thus,
timestamp entries should always be treated as estimates, independent of the representation.

It may seem odd that the timestamp option includes a mechanism to have routers
record their IP addresses along with timestamps because the record route option already

---

† Universal Time was formerly called Greenwich Mean Time; it is the time of day at the prime meridian.

provides that capability. However, recording IP addresses with timestamps eliminates ambiguity. Having the route recorded along with timestamps is also useful because it allows the receiver to know exactly which path the datagram followed.

7.8.4 Processing Options During Fragmentation

The idea behind the *COPY* bit in the option *CODE* field should now be clear. When fragmenting a datagram, a router replicates some IP options in all fragments while it places others in only one fragment. For example, consider the option used to record the datagram route. We said that each fragment will be handled as an independent datagram, so there is no guarantee that all fragments follow the same path to the destination. If all fragments contained the record route option, the destination might receive a different list of routes from each fragment. It could not produce a single, meaningful list of routes for the reassembled datagram. Therefore, the IP standard specifies that the record route option should only be copied into one of the fragments.

Not all IP options can be restricted to one fragment. Consider the source route option, for example, that specifies how a datagram should travel through the internet. Source routing information must be replicated in all fragment headers, or fragments will not follow the specified route. Thus, the code field for source route specifies that the option must be copied into all fragments.

7.9 Summary

The fundamental service provided by TCP/IP internet software is a connectionless, unreliable, best-effort packet delivery system. The Internet Protocol (IP) formally specifies the format of internet packets, called *datagrams*, and informally embodies the ideas of connectionless delivery. This chapter concentrated on datagram formats; later chapters will discuss IP routing and error handling.

Analogous to a physical frame, the IP datagram is divided into header and data areas. Among other information, the datagram header contains the source and destination IP addresses, fragmentation control, precedence, and a checksum used to catch transmission errors. Besides fixed-length fields, each datagram header can contain an options field. The options field is variable length, depending on the number and type of options used as well as the size of the data area allocated for each option. Intended to help monitor and control the internet, options allow one to specify or record routing information, or to gather timestamps as the datagram traverses an internet.

FOR FURTHER STUDY

Postel [1980] discusses possible ways to approach internet protocols, addressing, and routing. In later publications, Postel [RFC 791] gives the standard for the Internet Protocol. Braden [RFC 1122] further refines the standard. Hornig [RFC 894] specifies the standard for the transmission of IP datagrams across an Ethernet. Clark [RFC 815] describes efficient reassembly of fragments. In addition to the packet format, Internet authorities also specify many constants needed in the network protocols. These values can be found in Reynolds and Postel [RFC 1700]. Kent and Mogul [1987] discusses the disadvantages of fragmentation.

An alternative internet protocol suite known as *XNS*, is given in Xerox [1981]. Boggs *et. al.* [1980] describes the PARC Universal Packet (PUP) protocol, an abstraction from *XNS* closely related to the IP datagram.

EXERCISES

7.1 What is the single greatest advantage of having the IP checksum cover only the datagram header and not the data? What is the disadvantage?

7.2 Is it ever necessary to use an IP checksum when sending packets over an Ethernet? Why or why not?

7.3 What is the MTU size for the ANSNET? Hyperchannel? an ATM switch?

7.4 Do you expect a high-speed local area network to have larger or smaller MTU size than a wide area network?

7.5 Argue that fragments should have small, nonstandard headers.

7.6 Find out when the IP protocol version last changed. Is having a protocol version number really useful?

7.7 Can you imagine why a one's complement checksum was chosen for IP instead of a cyclic redundancy check?

7.8 What are the advantages of doing reassembly at the ultimate destination instead of doing it after the datagram travels across one network?

7.9 What is the minimum network MTU required to send an IP datagram that contains at least one octet of data?

7.10 Suppose you are hired to implement IP datagram processing in hardware. Is there any rearrangement of fields in the header that would have made your hardware more efficient? Easier to build?

7.11 If you have access to an implementation of IP, revise it and test your locally available implementations of IP to see if they reject IP datagrams with an out-of-date version number.

7.12 When a minimum-size IP datagram travels across an Ethernet, how large is the frame?

8

Internet Protocol: Routing IP Datagrams

8.1 Introduction

We have seen that all internet services use an underlying, connectionless packet delivery system, and that the basic unit of transfer in a TCP/IP internet is the IP datagram. This chapter adds to the description of connectionless service by describing how routers forward IP datagrams and deliver them to their final destinations. We think of the datagram format from Chapter 7 as characterizing the static aspects of the Internet Protocol. The description of routing in this chapter characterizes the operational aspects. The next chapter concludes our presentation of IP by describing how errors are handled; later chapters show how other protocols use IP to provide higher-level services.

8.2 Routing In An Internet

In a packet switching system, *routing* refers to the process of choosing a path over which to send packets, and *router* refers to a computer making such a choice. Routing occurs at several levels. For example, within a wide area network that has multiple physical connections between packet switches, the network itself is responsible for routing packets from the time they enter until they leave. Such internal routing is completely self-contained inside the wide area network. Machines on the outside cannot participate in decisions; they merely view the network as an entity that delivers packets.

Remember that the goal of IP is to provide a virtual network that encompasses multiple physical networks and offers a connectionless datagram delivery service. Thus, we will focus on *internet routing* or *IP routing*†. Analogous to routing within a physical network, IP routing chooses a path over which a datagram should be sent. The IP routing algorithm must choose how to send a datagram across multiple physical networks.

Routing in an internet can be difficult, especially among computers that have multiple physical network connections. Ideally, the routing software would examine such things as network load, datagram length, or the type of service specified in the datagram header, when selecting the best path. Most internet routing software is much less sophisticated, however, and selects routes based on fixed assumptions about shortest paths.

To understand IP routing completely, we must go back and look at the architecture of a TCP/IP internet. First, recall that an internet is composed of multiple physical networks interconnected by computers called *routers*. Each router has direct connections to two or more networks. By contrast, a host computer usually connects directly to one physical network. We know that it is possible, however, to have a multi-homed host connected directly to multiple networks.

Both hosts and routers participate in routing an IP datagram to its destination. When an application program on a host attempts to communicate, the TCP/IP protocols eventually generate one or more IP datagrams. The host must make a routing decision when it chooses where to send the datagrams. As Figure 8.1 shows, hosts must make routing decisions even if they have only one network connection.

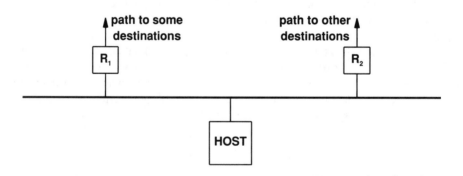

Figure 8.1 An example of a singly-homed host that must route datagrams. The host must choose to send a datagram either to router R₁ or to router R₂, because each router provides the best path to some destinations.

---

†Vendors also use the terms *IP forwarding* and *IP switching* to describe IP routing. Interestingly, most still refer to the needed information as *IP routing information*.

Of course, routers also make IP routing decisions (that is their primary purpose and the motivation for calling them *routers*). What about multi-homed hosts? Any computer with multiple network connections can act as a router, and as we will see, multi-homed hosts running TCP/IP have all the software needed for routing. Furthermore, sites that cannot afford separate routers sometimes use general-purpose timesharing machines as both hosts and routers (the practice is usually limited to university sites). However, the TCP/IP standards draw a sharp distinction between the functions of a host and those of a router, and sites that try to mix host and router functions on a single machine sometimes find that their multi-homed hosts engage in unexpected interactions. For now, we will distinguish hosts from routers and assume that hosts do not perform the router's function of transferring packets from one network to another.

8.3 Direct And Indirect Delivery

Loosely speaking, we can divide routing into two forms: *direct delivery* and *indirect delivery*. Direct delivery, the transmission of a datagram from one machine across a single physical network directly to another, is the basis on which all internet communication rests. Two machines can engage in direct delivery only if they both attach directly to the same underlying physical transmission system (e.g., a single Ethernet). *Indirect delivery* occurs when the destination is not on a directly attached network, forcing the sender to pass the datagram to a router for delivery.

8.3.1 Datagram Delivery Over A Single Network

We know that one machine on a given physical network can send a physical frame directly to another machine on the same network. To transfer an IP datagram, the sender encapsulates the datagram in a physical frame, maps the destination IP address into a physical address, and uses the network hardware to deliver it. Chapter 5 presented two possible mechanisms for address resolution, including using the ARP protocol for dynamic address binding on Ethernet-like networks. Chapter 7 discussed datagram encapsulation. Thus, we have reviewed all the pieces needed to understand direct delivery. To summarize:

> *Transmission of an IP datagram between two machines on a single physical network does not involve routers. The sender encapsulates the datagram in a physical frame, binds the destination IP address to a physical hardware address, and sends the resulting frame directly to the destination.*

How does the sender know whether the destination lies on a directly connected network? The test is straightforward. We know that IP addresses are divided into a network-specific prefix and a host-specific suffix. To see if a destination lies on one of the directly connected networks, the sender extracts the network portion of the destination IP address and compares it to the network portion of its own IP address(es). A match means the datagram can be sent directly. Here we see one of the advantages of the Internet address scheme, namely:

> *Because the internet addresses of all machines on a single network in-*
> *clude a common network prefix, and because extracting that prefix*
> *can be done in a few machine instructions, testing whether a machine*
> *can be reached directly is extremely efficient.*

From an internet perspective, it is easiest to think of direct delivery as the final step in any datagram transmission, even if the datagram traverses many networks and intermediate routers. The final router along the path between the datagram source and its destination will connect directly to the same physical network as the destination. Thus, the final router will deliver the datagram using direct delivery. We can think of direct delivery between the source and destination as a special case of general purpose routing – in a direct route the datagram does not happen to pass through any intervening routers.

8.3.2 Indirect Delivery

Indirect delivery is more difficult than direct delivery because the sender must identify a router to which the datagram can be sent. The router must then forward the datagram on toward its destination network.

To visualize how indirect routing works, imagine a large internet with many networks interconnected by routers but with only two hosts at the far ends. When one host wants to send to the other, it encapsulates the datagram and sends it to the nearest router. We know that it can reach a router because all physical networks are interconnected, so there must be a router attached to each one. Thus, the originating host can reach a router using a single physical network. Once the frame reaches the router, software extracts the encapsulated datagram, and the IP software selects the next router along the path towards the destination. The datagram is again placed in a frame and sent over the next physical network to a second router, and so on, until it can be delivered directly. These ideas can be summarized:

> *Routers in a TCP/IP internet form a cooperative, interconnected*
> *structure. Datagrams pass from router to router until they reach a*
> *router that can deliver the datagram directly.*

How can a router know where to send each datagram? How can a host know which router to use for a given destination? The two questions are related because they both involve IP routing. We will answer them in two stages, considering the basic table-driven routing algorithm in this chapter and postponing a discussion of how routers learn new routes until later.

8.4 Table-Driven IP Routing

The usual IP routing algorithm employs an *Internet routing table* (sometimes called an *IP routing table*) on each machine that stores information about possible destinations and how to reach them. Because both hosts and routers route datagrams, both have IP routing tables. Whenever the IP routing software in a host or router needs to transmit a datagram, it consults the routing table to decide where to send the datagram.

What information should be kept in routing tables? If every routing table contained information about every possible destination address, it would be impossible to keep the tables current. Furthermore, because the number of possible destinations is large, machines would have insufficient space to store the information.

Conceptually, we would like to use the principle of information hiding and allow machines to make routing decisions with minimal information. For example, we would like to isolate information about specific hosts to the local environment in which they exist and arrange for machines that are far away to route packets to them without knowing such details. Fortunately, the IP address scheme helps achieve this goal. Recall that IP addresses are assigned to make all machines connected to a given physical network share a common prefix (the network portion of the address). We have already seen that such an assignment makes the test for direct delivery efficient. It also means that routing tables only need to contain network prefixes and not full IP addresses.

8.5 Next-Hop Routing

Using the network portion of a destination address instead of the complete host address makes routing efficient and keeps routing tables small. More important, it helps hide information, keeping the details of specific hosts confined to the local environment in which those hosts operate. Typically, a routing table contains pairs (N, R), where N is the IP address of a destination *network*, and R is the IP address of the "next" router along the path to network N. Router R is called the *next hop*, and the idea of using a routing table to store a next hop for each destination is called *next-hop routing*. Thus, the routing table in a router R only specifies one step along the path from R to a destination network – the router does not know the complete path to a destination.

It is important to understand that each entry in a routing table points to a router that can be reached across a single network. That is, all routers listed in machine M's routing table must lie on networks to which M connects directly. When a datagram is ready to leave M, IP software locates the destination IP address and extracts the network portion. M then uses the network portion to make a routing decision, selecting a router that can be reached directly.

In practice, we apply the principle of information hiding to hosts as well. We insist that although hosts have IP routing tables, they must keep minimal information in their tables. The idea is to force hosts to rely on routers for most routing.

Figure 8.2 shows a concrete example that helps explain routing tables. The example internet consists of four networks connected by three routers. In the figure, the routing table gives the routes that router R uses. Because R connects directly to networks
20.0.0.0 and 30.0.0.0, it can use direct delivery to send to a host on either of those networks (possibly using ARP to find physical addresses). Given a datagram destined for
a host on network 40.0.0.0, R routes it to address 30.0.0.7, the address of router S. S
will then deliver the datagram directly. R can reach address 30.0.0.7 because both R
and S attach directly to network 30.0.0.0.

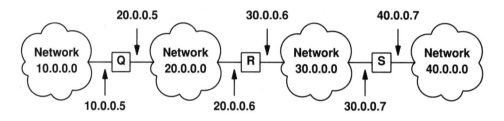

(a)

TO REACH HOSTS ON NETWORK	ROUTE TO THIS ADDRESS
20.0.0.0	DELIVER DIRECTLY
30.0.0.0	DELIVER DIRECTLY
10.0.0.0	20.0.0.5
40.0.0.0	30.0.0.7

(b)

Figure 8.2 (a) An example internet with 4 networks and 3 routers, and (b) the
routing table in R.

As Figure 8.2 demonstrates, the size of the routing table depends on the number of
networks in the internet; it only grows when new networks are added. However, the
table size and contents are independent of the number of individual hosts connected to
the networks. We can summarize the underlying principle:

> *To hide information, keep routing tables small, and make routing de-
> cisions efficient, IP routing software only keeps information about
> destination network addresses, not about individual host addresses.*

Choosing routes based on the destination network ID alone has several consequences. First, in most implementations, it means that all traffic destined for a given network takes the same path. As a result, even when multiple paths exist, they may not be used concurrently. Also, all types of traffic follow the same path without regard to the delay or throughput of physical networks. Second, because only the final router along the path attempts to communicate with the destination host, only it can determine if the host exists or is operational. Thus, we need to arrange a way for that router to send reports of delivery problems back to the original source. Third, because each router routes traffic independently, datagrams traveling from host *A* to host *B* may follow an entirely different path than datagrams traveling from host *B* back to host A. We need to ensure that routers cooperate to guarantee that two-way communication is always possible.

8.6 Default Routes

Another technique used to hide information and keep routing table sizes small consolidates multiple entries into a default case. The idea is to have the IP routing software first look in the routing table for the destination network. If no route appears in the table, the routing routines send the datagram to a *default router*.

Default routing is especially useful when a site has a small set of local addresses and only one connection to the rest of the internet. For example, default routes work well in host machines that attach to a single physical network and reach only one router leading to the remainder of the internet. The entire routing decision consists of two tests: one for the local net, and a default that points to the only possible router. Even if the site contains a few local networks, the routing is simple because it consists of a few tests for the local networks plus a default for all other destinations.

8.7 Host-Specific Routes

Although we said that all routing is based on networks and not on individual hosts, most IP routing software allows per-host routes to be specified as a special case. Having per-host routes gives the local network administrator more control over network use, permits testing, and can also be used to control access for security purposes. When debugging network connections or routing tables, the ability to specify a special route to one individual machine turns out to be especially useful.

8.8 The IP Routing Algorithm

Taking into account everything we have said, the IP routing algorithm becomes:

Algorithm:

RouteDatagram (Datagram , RoutingTable)

Extract destination IP address, D, from the datagram
**   and compute the network prefix, N;**
if N matches any directly connected network address
**   deliver datagram to destination D over that network**
**   (This involves resolving D to a physical address,**
**   encapsulating the datagram, and sending the frame.)**
else if the table contains a host-specific route for D
**   send datagram to next-hop specified in table**
else if the table contains a route for network N
**   send datagram to next-hop specified in table**
else if the table contains a default route
**   send datagram to the default router specified in table**
else declare a routing error;

Figure 8.3 The algorithm IP uses to forward a datagram. Given an IP datagram and a routing table, this algorithm selects the next hop to which the datagram should be sent. All routes must specify a next hop that lies on a directly connected network.

8.9 Routing With IP Addresses

It is important to understand that except for decrementing the time to live and recomputing the checksum, IP routing does not alter the original datagram. In particular, the datagram source and destination addresses remain unaltered; they always specify the IP address of the original source and the IP address of the ultimate destination†. When IP executes the routing algorithm, it selects a new IP address, the IP address of the machine to which the datagram should be sent next. The new address is most likely the address of a router. However, if the datagram can be delivered directly, the new address will be the same as the address of the ultimate destination.

---

†The only exception occurs when the datagram contains a source route option.

We said that the IP address selected by the IP routing algorithm is known as the *next hop* address because it tells where the datagram must be sent next (even though it may not be the ultimate destination). Where does IP store the next hop address? Not in the datagram; no place is reserved for it. In fact, IP does not "store" the next hop address at all. ⏐After executing the routing algorithm, IP passes the datagram and the next hop address to the network interface software responsible for the physical network over which the datagram must be sent. The network interface software binds the next hop address to a physical address, forms a frame using that physical address, places the datagram in the data portion of the frame, and sends the result. After using the next hop address to find a physical address, the network interface software discards the next hop address.

It may seem odd that routing tables store the IP address of a next hop for each destination network when those addresses must be translated into corresponding physical addresses before the datagram can be sent. If we imagine a host sending a sequence of datagrams to the same destination address, the use of IP addresses will appear incredibly inefficient. IP dutifully extracts the destination address in each datagram and uses the routing table to produce a next hop address. It then passes the datagram and next hop address to the network interface, which recomputes the binding to a physical address. If the routing table used physical addresses, the binding between the next hop's IP address and physical address could be performed once, saving unneeded computation.

Why does IP software avoid using physical addresses when storing and computing routes? As Figure 8.4 illustrates, there are two important reasons.

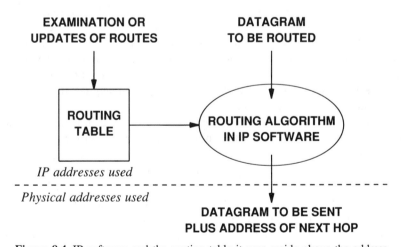

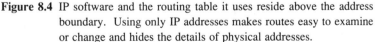

Figure 8.4 IP software and the routing table it uses reside above the address boundary. Using only IP addresses makes routes easy to examine or change and hides the details of physical addresses.

First, the routing table provides an especially clean interface between IP software that routes datagrams and high-level software that manipulates routes. To debug routing problems, network managers often need to examine the routing tables. Using only IP addresses in the routing table makes it easy for managers to understand and easy to see whether software has updated the routes correctly. Second, the whole point of the Internet Protocol is to build an abstraction that hides the details of underlying networks.

Figure 8.4 shows the *address boundary*, the important conceptual division between low-level software that understands physical addresses and internet software that only uses high-level addresses. Above this boundary, all software can be written to communicate using internet addresses; knowledge of physical addresses is relegated to a few small, low-level routines. We will see that observing the boundary also helps keep the implementation of remaining TCP/IP protocols easy to understand, test, and modify.

8.10 Handling Incoming Datagrams

So far, we have discussed IP routing by describing how decisions are made about outgoing packets. It should be clear, however, that IP software must process incoming datagrams as well.

When an IP datagram arrives at a host, the network interface software delivers it to the IP software for processing. If the datagram's destination address matches the host's IP address, IP software on the host accepts the datagram and passes it to the appropriate higher-level protocol software for further processing. If the destination IP address does not match, a host is required to discard the datagram (i.e., hosts are forbidden from attempting to forward datagrams that are accidentally routed to the wrong machine).

Unlike hosts, routers perform forwarding. When an IP datagram arrives at a router, it is delivered to the IP software. Again, two cases arise: the datagram could have reached its final destination, or it may need to travel further. As with hosts, if the datagram destination IP address matches the router's own IP address, the IP software passes the datagram to higher-level protocol software for processing†. If the datagram has not reached its final destination, IP routes the datagram using the standard algorithm and the information in the local routing table.

Determining whether an IP datagram has reached its final destination is not quite as trivial as it seems. Remember that even a host may have multiple physical connections, each with its own IP address. When an IP datagram arrives, the machine must compare the destination internet address to the IP address for each of its network connections. If any match, it keeps the datagram and processes it. A machine must also accept datagrams that were broadcast on the physical network if their destination IP address is the limited IP broadcast address or the directed IP broadcast address for that network. As we will see in Chapters 10 and 17, subnet and multicast addresses make address recognition even more complex. In any case, if the address does not match any of the local machine's addresses, IP decrements the time-to-live field in the datagram header, discarding the datagram if the count reaches zero, or computing a new checksum and routing the datagram if the count remains positive.

---

†Usually, the only datagrams destined for a router are those used to test connectivity or those that carry router management commands.

Should every machine forward the IP datagrams it receives? Obviously, a router must forward incoming datagrams because that is its main function. We have also said that some multi-homed hosts act like routers even though they are really general purpose computing systems. While using a host as a router is not usually a good idea, if one chooses to use that arrangement, the host must be configured to route datagrams just as a router does. But what about other hosts, those that are not intended to be routers? The answer is that hosts not designated to be routers should *not* route datagrams that they receive; they should discard them.

There are four reasons why a host not designated to serve as a router should refrain from performing any router functions. First, when such a host receives a datagram intended for some other machine, something has gone wrong with internet addressing, routing, or delivery. The problem may not be revealed if the host takes corrective action by routing the datagram. Second, routing will cause unnecessary network traffic (and may steal CPU time from legitimate uses of the host). Third, simple errors can cause chaos. Suppose that every host routes traffic and imagine what happens if one machine accidentally broadcasts a datagram that is destined for some host, *H*. Because it has been broadcast, every host on the network receives a copy of the datagram. Every host forwards its copy to *H*, which will be bombarded with many copies. Fourth, as later chapters show, routers do more than merely route traffic. As the next chapter shows, routers use a special protocol to report errors, while hosts do not (again, to avoid having multiple error reports bombard a source). Routers also propagate routing information to ensure that their routing tables are consistent. If hosts route datagrams without participating fully in all router functions, unexpected anomalies may arise.

8.11 Establishing Routing Tables

We have discussed how IP routes datagrams based on the contents of routing tables, without saying how systems initialize their routing tables or update them as the network changes. Later chapters deal with these questions and discuss protocols that allow routers to keep routes consistent. For now, it is only important to understand that IP software uses the routing table whenever it decides how to forward a datagram, so changing routing tables will change the paths datagrams follow.

8.12 Summary

IP routing consists of deciding where to send a datagram based on its destination IP address. Direct delivery is possible if the destination machine lies on a network to which the sending machine attaches; we think of this as the final step in datagram transmission. If the sender cannot reach the destination directly, the sender must forward the datagram to a router. The general paradigm is that hosts send indirectly routed datagrams to the nearest router; the datagrams travel through the internet from router to router until they can be delivered directly across one physical network.

When IP software looks up a route, the algorithm produces the IP address of the next machine (i.e., the address of the next hop) to which the datagram should be sent; IP passes the datagram and next hop address to network interface software. Transmission of a datagram from one machine to the next always involves encapsulating the datagram in a physical frame, mapping the next hop internet address to a physical address, and sending the frame using the underlying hardware.

The internet routing algorithm is table driven and uses only IP addresses. Although it is possible for a routing table to contain a host-specific destination address, most routing tables contain only network addresses, keeping routing tables small. Using a default route can also help keep a routing table small, especially for hosts that can access only one router.

FOR FURTHER STUDY

Routing is an important topic. Frank and Chou [1971] and Schwartz and Stern [1980] discuss routing in general; Postel [1980] discusses internet routing. Braden and Postel [RFC 1009] provides a summary of how Internet routers handle IP datagrams. Almquist [RFC 1716] provides a summary of more recent discussions. Narten [1989] contains a survey of Internet routing. Fultz and Kleinrock [1971] analyzes adaptive routing schemes; and McQuillan, Richer, and Rosen [1980] describes the ARPANET adaptive routing algorithm.

The idea of using policy statements to formulate rules about routing has been considered often. Leiner [RFC 1124] considers policies for interconnected networks. Braun [RFC 1104] discusses models of policy routing for internets, Rekhter [RFC 1092] relates policy routing to the second NSFNET backbone, and Clark [RFC 1102] describes using policy routing with IP.

EXERCISES

8.1 Complete routing tables for all routers in Figure 8.2. Which routers will benefit most from using a default route?

8.2 Examine the routing algorithm used on your local system. Are all the cases mentioned here covered? Does the algorithm allow anything not mentioned?

8.3 What does a router do with the *time to live* value in an IP header?

8.4 Consider a machine with two physical network connections and two IP addresses I_1 and I_2. Is it possible for that machine to receive a datagram destined for I_2 over the network with address I_1? Explain.

8.5 Consider two hosts, A and B, that both attach to a common physical network, N. Is it ever possible, when using our routing algorithm, for A to receive a datagram destined for B? Explain.

8.6   Modify the routing algorithm to accommodate the IP source route options discussed in Chapter 7.

8.7   An IP router must perform a computation that takes time proportional to the length of the datagram header each time it processes a datagram. Explain.

8.8   A network administrator argues that to make monitoring and debugging his local network easier, he wants to rewrite the routing algorithm so it tests host-specific routes *before* it tests for direct delivery. Can you imagine how he could use the revised algorithm to build a network monitor?

8.9   Is it possible to address a datagram to a router's IP address? Does it make sense to do so?

8.10 Consider a modified routing algorithm that examines host-specific routes before testing for delivery on directly connected networks. Under what circumstances might such an algorithm be desirable? undesirable?

8.11 Play detective: after monitoring IP traffic on a local area network for 10 minutes one evening, someone notices that all frames destined for machine *A* carry IP datagrams that have destination equal to *A*'s IP address, while all frames destined for machine *B* carry IP datagrams with destination *not* equal to *B*'s IP address. Users report that both *A* and *B* can communicate. Explain.

8.12 How could you change the IP datagram format to support high-speed packet switching at routers? Hint: a router must recompute a header checksum after decrementing the time-to-live field.

8.13 Compare CLNP, the ISO connectionless delivery protocol (ISO standard 8473) with IP. How well will the ISO protocol support high-speed switching? Hint: variable length fields are expensive.

9

Internet Protocol: Error And Control Messages (ICMP)

9.1 Introduction

The previous chapter shows how the Internet Protocol software provides an unreliable, connectionless datagram delivery service by arranging for each router to forward datagrams. A datagram travels from router to router until it reaches one that can deliver the datagram directly to its final destination. If a router cannot route or deliver a datagram, or if the router detects an unusual condition that affects its ability to forward the datagram (e.g., network congestion), the router needs to inform the original source to take action to avoid or correct the problem. This chapter discusses a mechanism that internet routers and hosts use to communicate such control or error information. We will see that routers use the mechanism to report problems and hosts use it to test whether destinations are reachable.

9.2 The Internet Control Message Protocol

In the connectionless system we have described so far, each router operates autonomously, routing or delivering datagrams that arrive without coordinating with the original sender. The system works well if all machines operate correctly and agree on routes. Unfortunately, no system works correctly all the time. Besides failures of communication lines and processors, IP fails to deliver datagrams when the destination machine is temporarily or permanently disconnected from the network, when the time-to-live counter expires, or when intermediate routers become so congested that they can-

123

not process the incoming traffic. The important difference between having a single net-work implemented with dedicated hardware and an internet implemented with software is that in the former, the designer can add special hardware to inform attached hosts when problems arise. In an internet, which has no such hardware mechanism, a sender cannot tell whether a delivery failure resulted from a local malfunction or a remote one. Debugging becomes extremely difficult. The IP protocol itself contains nothing to help the sender test connectivity or learn about such failures.

To allow routers in an internet to report errors or provide information about unex-pected circumstances, the designers added a special-purpose message mechanism to the TCP/IP protocols. The mechanism, known as the *Internet Control Message Protocol* (*ICMP*), is considered a required part of IP and must be included in every IP implemen-tation.

Like all other traffic, ICMP messages travel across the internet in the data portion of IP datagrams. The ultimate destination of an ICMP message is not an application program or user on the destination machine, however, but the Internet Protocol software on that machine. That is, when an ICMP error message arrives, the ICMP software module handles it. Of course, if ICMP determines that a particular higher-level proto-col or application program has caused a problem, it will inform the appropriate module. We can summarize:

> *The Internet Control Message Protocol allows routers to send error or control messages to other routers or hosts; ICMP provides com-munication between the Internet Protocol software on one machine and the Internet Protocol software on another.*

Initially designed to allow routers to report the cause of delivery errors to hosts, ICMP is not restricted to routers. Although guidelines restrict the use of some ICMP messages, an arbitrary machine can send an ICMP message to any other machine. Thus, a host can use ICMP to correspond with a router or another host. The chief ad-vantage of allowing hosts to use ICMP is that it provides a single mechanism used for all control and information messages.

9.3 Error Reporting vs. Error Correction

Technically, ICMP is an *error reporting mechanism*. It provides a way for routers that encounter an error to report the error to the original source. Although the protocol specification outlines intended uses of ICMP and suggests possible actions to take in response to error reports, ICMP does not fully specify the action to be taken for each possible error. In short,

When a datagram causes an error, ICMP can only report the error condition back to the original source of the datagram; the source must relate the error to an individual application program or take other action to correct the problem.

Most errors stem from the original source, but others do not. Because ICMP reports problems to the original source, however, it cannot be used to inform intermediate routers about problems. For example, suppose a datagram follows a path through a sequence of routers, R_1, R_2, ..., R_k. If R_k has incorrect routing information and mistakenly routes the datagram to router R_E, R_E cannot use ICMP to report the error back to router R_k; ICMP can only send a report back to the original source. Unfortunately, the original source has no responsibility for the problem or control over the misbehaving router. In fact, the source may not be able to determine which router caused the problem.

Why restrict ICMP to communication with the original source? The answer should be clear from our discussion of datagram formats and routing in the previous chapters. A datagram only contains fields that specify the original source and the ultimate destination; it does not contain a complete record of its trip through the internet (except for unusual cases where the record route option is used). Furthermore, because routers can establish and change their own routing tables, there is no global knowledge of routes. Thus, when a datagram reaches a given router, it is impossible to know the path it has taken to arrive there. If the router detects a problem, it cannot know the set of intermediate machines that processed the datagram, so it cannot inform them of the problem. Instead of silently discarding the datagram, the router uses ICMP to inform the original source that a problem has occurred, and trusts that host administrators will cooperate with network administrators to locate and repair the problem.

9.4 ICMP Message Delivery

ICMP messages require two levels of encapsulation as Figure 9.1 shows. Each ICMP message travels across the internet in the data portion of an IP datagram, which itself travels across each physical network in the data portion of a frame. Datagrams carrying ICMP messages are routed exactly like datagrams carrying information for users; there is no additional reliability or priority. Thus, error messages themselves may be lost or discarded. Furthermore, in an already congested network, the error message may cause additional congestion. An exception is made to the error handling procedures if an IP datagram carrying an ICMP message causes an error. The exception, established to avoid the problem of having error messages about error messages, specifies that ICMP messages are not generated for errors that result from datagrams carrying ICMP error messages.

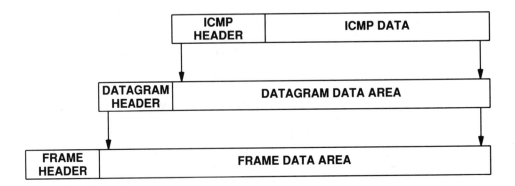

Figure 9.1 Two levels of ICMP encapsulation. The ICMP message is encapsulated in an IP datagram, which is further encapsulated in a frame for transmission. To identify ICMP, the datagram protocol field contains the value *1*.

encapsulated

It is important to keep in mind that even though ICMP messages are encapsulated and sent using IP, ICMP is not considered a higher level protocol – it is a required part of IP. The reason for using IP to deliver ICMP messages is that they may need to travel across several physical networks to reach their final destination. Thus, they cannot be delivered by the physical transport alone.

9.5 ICMP Message Format

Although each ICMP message has its own format, they all begin with the same three fields: an 8-bit integer message *TYPE* field that identifies the message, an 8-bit *CODE* field that provides further information about the message type, and a 16-bit *CHECKSUM* field (ICMP uses the same additive checksum algorithm as IP, but the ICMP checksum only covers the ICMP message). In addition, ICMP messages that report errors always include the header and first 64 data bits of the datagram causing the problem.

The reason for returning more than the datagram header alone is to allow the receiver to determine more precisely which protocol(s) and which application program were responsible for the datagram. As we will see later, higher-level protocols in the TCP/IP suite are designed so that crucial information is encoded in the first 64 bits.

The ICMP *TYPE* field defines the meaning of the message as well as its format. The types include:

Type Field	ICMP Message Type
0	Echo Reply
3	Destination Unreachable
4	Source Quench
5	Redirect (change a route)
8	Echo Request
11	Time Exceeded for a Datagram
12	Parameter Problem on a Datagram
13	Timestamp Request
14	Timestamp Reply
15	Information Request (obsolete)
16	Information Reply (obsolete)
17	Address Mask Request
18	Address Mask Reply

The next sections describe each of these messages, giving details of the message format and its meaning.

9.6 Testing Destination Reachability And Status (Ping)

TCP/IP protocols provide facilities to help network managers or users identify network problems. One of the most frequently used debugging tools invokes the ICMP *echo request* and *echo reply* messages. A host or router sends an ICMP echo request message to a specified destination. Any machine that receives an echo request formulates an echo reply and returns it to the original sender. The request contains an optional data area; the reply contains a copy of the data sent in the request. The echo request and associated reply can be used to test whether a destination is reachable and responding. Because both the request and reply travel in IP datagrams, successful receipt of a reply verifies that major pieces of the transport system work. First, IP software on the source computer must route the datagram. Second, intermediate routers between the source and destination must be operating and must route the datagram correctly. Third, the destination machine must be running (at least it must respond to interrupts), and both ICMP and IP software must be working. Finally, all routers along the return path must have correct routes.

On many systems, the command users invoke to send ICMP echo requests is named *ping*. Sophisticated versions of ping send a series of ICMP echo requests, capture responses, and provide statistics about datagram loss. They allow the user to specify the length of the data being sent and the interval between requests. Less sophisticated versions merely send one ICMP echo request and await a reply.

9.7 Echo Request And Reply Message Format

Figure 9.2 shows the format of echo request and reply messages.

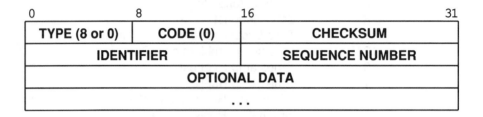

Figure 9.2 ICMP echo request or reply message format.

The field listed as *OPTIONAL DATA* is a variable length field that contains data to be returned to the sender. An echo reply always returns exactly the same data as was received in the request. Fields *IDENTIFIER* and *SEQUENCE NUMBER* are used by the sender to match replies to requests. The value of the *TYPE* field specifies whether the message is a request (*8*) or a reply (*0*).

9.8 Reports Of Unreachable Destinations

When a router cannot forward or deliver an IP datagram, it sends a *destination un-reachable* message back to the original source, using the format shown in Figure 9.3.

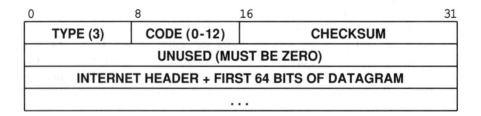

Figure 9.3 ICMP destination unreachable message format.

The *CODE* field in a destination unreachable message contains an integer that further describes the problem. Possible values are:

Code Value	Meaning
0	Network unreachable
1	Host unreachable
2	Protocol unreachable
3	Port unreachable
4	Fragmentation needed and DF set
5	Source route failed
6	Destination network unknown
7	Destination host unknown
8	Source host isolated
9	Communication with destination network administratively prohibited
10	Communication with destination host administratively prohibited
11	Network unreachable for type of service
12	Host unreachable for type of service

Although IP is a best-effort delivery mechanism, discarding datagrams should not be taken lightly. Whenever an error prevents a router from routing or delivering a datagram, the router sends a destination unreachable message back to the source and then *drops* (i.e., discards) the datagram. Network unreachable errors usually imply routing failures; host unreachable errors imply delivery failures†. Because the ICMP error message contains a short prefix of the datagram that caused the problem, the source will know exactly which address is unreachable.

Destinations may be unreachable because hardware is temporarily out of service, because the sender specified a nonexistent destination address, or (in rare circumstances) because the router does not have a route to the destination network. Note that although routers report failures they encounter, they may not know of all delivery failures. For example, if the destination machine connects to an Ethernet network, the network hardware does not provide acknowledgements. Therefore, a router can continue to send packets to a destination after the destination is powered down without receiving any indication that the packets are not being delivered. To summarize:

> *Although a router sends a destination unreachable message when it encounters a datagram that cannot be forwarded or delivered, a router cannot detect all such errors.*

The meaning of protocol and port unreachable messages will become clear when we study how higher level protocols use abstract destination points called *ports*. Most of the remaining messages are self explanatory. If the datagram contains the source route option with an incorrect route, it may trigger a *source route* failure message. If a router needs to fragment a datagram but the ''don't fragment'' bit is set, the router sends a *fragmentation needed* message back to the source.

---

†An exception occurs for routers using the subnet addressing scheme of Chapter 10. They report a subnet routing failure with an ICMP host unreachable message.

9.9 Congestion And Datagram Flow Control

Because IP is connectionless, a router cannot reserve memory or communication resources in advance of receiving datagrams. As a result, routers can be overrun with traffic, a condition known as *congestion*. It is important to understand that congestion can arise for two entirely different reasons. First, a high-speed computer may be able to generate traffic faster than a network can transfer it. For example, imagine a supercomputer generating internet traffic. The datagrams may eventually need to cross a slower-speed wide area network (WAN) even though the supercomputer itself attaches to a high-speed local area net. Congestion will occur in the router that attaches the LAN to the WAN because datagrams arrive faster than they can be sent. Second, if many computers simultaneously need to send datagrams through a single router, the router can experience congestion, even though no single source causes the problem.

When datagrams arrive too quickly for a host or router to process, it enqueues them in memory temporarily. If the datagrams are part of a small burst, such buffering solves the problem. If the traffic continues, the host or router eventually exhausts memory and must discard additional datagrams that arrive. A machine uses ICMP *source quench* messages to report congestion to the original source. A source quench message is a request for the source to reduce its current rate of datagram transmission. Usually, congested routers send one source quench message for every datagram that they discard. Routers may also use more sophisticated congestion control techniques. Some monitor incoming traffic and quench sources that have the highest datagram transmission rates. Others attempt to avoid congestion altogether by arranging to send quench requests as their queues start to become long, but before they overflow.

There is no ICMP message to reverse the effect of a source quench. Instead, a host that receives source quench messages for a destination, *D*, lowers the rate at which it sends datagrams to *D* until it stops receiving source quench messages; it then gradually increases the rate as long as no further source quench requests are received.

9.10 Source Quench Format

In addition to the usual ICMP *TYPE, CODE, CHECKSUM* fields, and an unused 32-bit field, source quench messages have a field that contains a datagram prefix. Figure 9.4 illustrates the format. As with most ICMP messages that report an error, the datagram prefix field contains a prefix of the datagram that triggered the source quench request.

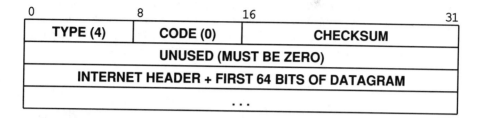

Figure 9.4 ICMP source quench message format. A congested router sends one source quench message each time it discards a datagram; the datagram prefix identifies the datagram that was dropped.

9.11 Route Change Requests From Routers

Internet routing tables usually remain static over long periods of time. Hosts initialize them from a configuration file at system startup, and system administrators seldom make routing changes during normal operations. If the network topology changes, routing tables in a router or host may become incorrect. A change can be temporary (e.g., when hardware needs to be repaired) or permanent (e.g., when a new network is added to the internet). As we will see in later chapters, routers exchange routing information periodically to accommodate network changes and keep their routes up-to-date. Thus, as a general rule:

> *Routers are assumed to know correct routes; hosts begin with minimal routing information and learn new routes from routers.*

To help follow this rule and to avoid duplicating routing information in the configuration file on each host, the initial host route configuration specifies the minimum possible routing information needed to communicate (e.g., the address of a single router). Thus, the host begins with minimal information and relies on routers to update its routing table. In one special case, when a router detects a host using a nonoptimal route, it sends the host an ICMP message, called a *redirect*, requesting that the host change its routes. The router also forwards the original datagram on to its destination.

The advantage of the ICMP redirect scheme is simplicity: it allows a host to boot knowing the address of only one router on the local network. The initial router returns ICMP redirect messages whenever a host sends a datagram for which there is a better route. The host routing table remains small but still contains optimal routes for all destinations in use.

Redirect messages do not solve the problem of propagating routes in a general way, however, because they are limited to interactions between a router and a host on a directly connected network. Figure 9.5 illustrates the limitation. In the figure, assume source S sends a datagram to destination D. Assume that router R_1 incorrectly routes the datagram through router R_2 instead of through router R_4 (i.e., R_1 incorrectly chooses a longer path than necessary). When router R_5 receives the datagram, it cannot send an ICMP redirect message to R_1 because it does not know R_1's address. Later chapters explore the problem of how to propagate routes across multiple networks.

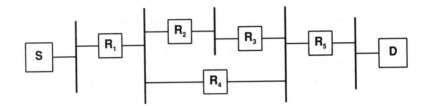

Figure 9.5 ICMP redirect messages do not provide routing among routers. In this example, router R_5 cannot redirect R_1 to use the shorter path for datagrams from S to D.

In addition to the requisite *TYPE*, *CODE*, and *CHECKSUM* fields, each redirect message contains a 32-bit *ROUTER INTERNET ADDRESS* field and an *INTERNET HEADER* field, as Figure 9.6 shows.

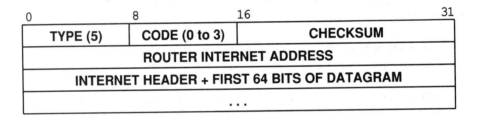

Figure 9.6 ICMP redirect message format.

The *ROUTER INTERNET ADDRESS* field contains the address of a router that the host is to use to reach the destination mentioned in the datagram header. The *INTERNET HEADER* field contains the IP header plus the next 64 bits of the datagram that triggered the message. Thus, a host receiving an ICMP redirect examines the datagram prefix to determine the datagram's destination address. The *CODE* field of an ICMP redirect message further specifies how to interpret the destination address, based on values assigned as follows:

Code Value	Meaning
0	Redirect datagrams for the Net (now obsolete)
1	Redirect datagrams for the Host
2	Redirect datagrams for the Type of Service† and Net
3	Redirect datagrams for the Type of Service and Host

As a general rule, routers only send ICMP redirect requests to hosts and not to other routers. We will see in later chapters that routers use other protocols to exchange routing information.

9.12 Detecting Circular Or Excessively Long Routes

Because internet routers compute a next hop using local tables, errors in routing tables can produce a *routing cycle* for some destination, *D*. A routing cycle can consist of two routers that each route a datagram for destination *D* to the other, or it can consist of several routers. When several routers form a cycle, they each route a datagram for destination *D* to the next router in the cycle. If a datagram enters a routing cycle, it will pass around the cycle endlessly. As mentioned previously, to prevent datagrams from circling forever in a TCP/IP internet, each IP datagram contains a time-to-live counter, sometimes called a *hop count*. A router decrements the time-to-live counter whenever it processes the datagram and discards the datagram when the count reaches zero.

Whenever a router discards a datagram because its hop count has reached zero or because a timeout occurred while waiting for fragments of a datagram, it sends an ICMP *time exceeded* message back to the datagram's source, using the format shown in Figure 9.7.

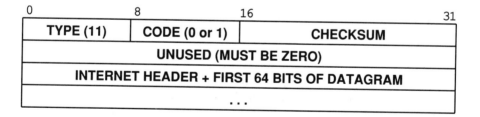

Figure 9.7 ICMP time exceeded message format. A router sends this message whenever a datagram is discarded because the time-to-live field in the datagram header has reached zero or because its reassembly timer expired while waiting for fragments.

The *CODE* field explains the nature of the timeout:

---

†Recall that each IP header specifies a type of service used for routing.

Code Value	Meaning
0	Time-to-live count exceeded
1	Fragment reassembly time exceeded

Fragment reassembly refers to the task of collecting all the fragments from a da-tagram. When the first fragment of a datagram arrives, the receiving host starts a timer and considers it an error if the timer expires before all the pieces of the datagram arrive. Code value *1* is used to report such errors to the sender; one message is sent for each such error.

9.13 Reporting Other Problems

When a router or host finds problems with a datagram not covered by previous ICMP error messages (e.g., an incorrect datagram header), it sends a *parameter problem* message to the original source. One possible cause of such problems occurs when argu-ments to an option are incorrect. The message, formatted as shown in Figure 9.8, is only sent when the problem is so severe that the datagram must be discarded.

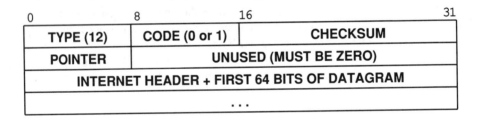

Figure 9.8 ICMP parameter problem message format. Such messages are only sent when the problem causes the datagram to be dropped.

To make the message unambiguous, the sender uses the *POINTER* field in the message header to identify the octet in the datagram that caused the problem. Code *1* is used to report that a required option is missing (e.g., a security option in the military communi-ty); the *POINTER* field is not used for code *1*.

9.14 Clock Synchronization And Transit Time Estimation

Although machines on an internet can communicate, they usually operate indepen-dently, with each machine maintaining its own notion of the current time. Clocks that differ widely can confuse users of distributed systems software. The TCP/IP protocol suite includes several protocols that can be used to synchronize clocks. One of the simplest techniques uses an ICMP message to obtain the time from another machine. A requesting machine sends an ICMP *timestamp request* message to another machine, asking that the second machine return its current value for the time of day. The receiving machine returns a *timestamp reply* back to the machine making the request. Figure 9.9 shows the format of timestamp request and reply messages.

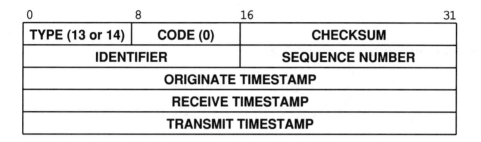

Figure 9.9 ICMP timestamp request or reply message format.

The *TYPE* field identifies the message as a request (*13*) or a reply (*14*); the *IDEN-TIFIER* and *SEQUENCE NUMBER* fields are used by the source to associate replies with requests. Remaining fields specify times, given in milliseconds since midnight, Universal Time†. The *ORIGINATE TIMESTAMP* field is filled in by the original sender just before the packet is transmitted, the *RECEIVE TIMESTAMP* field is filled immediately upon receipt of a request, and the *TRANSMIT TIMESTAMP* field is filled immediately before the reply is transmitted.

Hosts use the three timestamp fields to compute estimates of the delay time between them and to synchronize their clocks. Because the reply includes the *ORIGINATE TIMESTAMP* field, a host can compute the total time required for a request to travel to a destination, be transformed into a reply, and return. Because the reply carries both the time at which the request entered the remote machine, as well as the time at which the reply left, the host can compute the network transit time, and from that, estimate the differences in remote and local clocks.

In practice, accurate estimation of round-trip delay can be difficult and substantially restricts the utility of ICMP timestamp messages. Of course, to obtain an accurate estimate of round trip delay, one must take many measurements and average them. However, the round-trip delay between a pair of machines that connect to a large internet can vary dramatically, even over short periods of time. Furthermore, recall that because IP is a best-effort technology, datagrams can be dropped, delayed, or delivered out of order. Thus, merely taking many measurements may not guarantee consistency; sophisticated statistical analysis may be needed to produce precise estimates.

---

† Universal Time was formerly called Greenwich Mean Time; it is the time of day at the prime meridian.

9.15 Information Request And Reply Messages

The ICMP *information request* and *information reply* messages (types *15* and *16*) are now considered obsolete and should not be used. It was originally intended to allow hosts to discover their internet address at system startup. The current protocols for address determination are RARP, described in Chapter 6, and BOOTP, described in Chapter 21.

9.16 Obtaining A Subnet Mask

Chapter 10 discusses the motivation for subnet addressing as well as the details of how subnets operate. For now, it is only important to understand that when hosts use subnet addressing, some bits in the hostid portion of their IP address identify a physical network. To participate in subnet addressing, a host needs to know which bits of the 32-bit internet address correspond to the physical network and which correspond to host identifiers. The information needed to interpret the address is represented in a 32-bit quantity called the *subnet mask*.

To learn the subnet mask used for the local network, a machine can send an *address mask request* message to a router and receive an *address mask reply*. The machine making the request can either send the message directly, if it knows the router's address, or broadcast the message if it does not. Figure 9.10 shows the format of address mask messages.

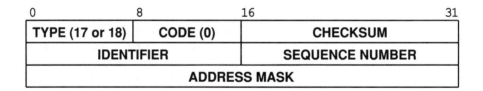

Figure 9.10 ICMP address mask request or reply message format. Usually, hosts broadcast a request without knowing which specific router will respond.

The *TYPE* field in an address mask message specifies whether the message is a request (*17*) or a reply (*18*). A reply contains the network's subnet address mask in the *ADDRESS MASK* field. As usual, the *IDENTIFIER* and *SEQUENCE NUMBER* fields allow a machine to associate replies with requests.

9.17 Summary

Normal communication across an internet involves sending messages from an application on one host to an application on another host. Routers may need to communicate directly with the network software on a particular host to report abnormal conditions or to send the host new routing information.

The Internet Control Message Protocol provides for extranormal communication among routers and hosts; it is an integral, required part of IP. ICMP includes *source quench* messages that retard the rate of transmission, *redirect* messages that request a host to change its routing table, and *echo request/reply* messages that hosts can use to determine whether a destination can be reached. An ICMP message travels in the data area of an IP datagram and has three fixed-length fields at the beginning of the message: an ICMP message *type* field, a *code* field, and an ICMP *checksum* field. The message type determines the format of the rest of the message as well as its meaning.

FOR FURTHER STUDY

Both Tanenbaum [1981] and Stallings [1985] discuss control messages in general and relate them to various network protocols. The central issue is not how to send control messages but when. Grange and Gien [1979], as well as Driver, Hopewell, and Iaquinto [1979], concentrate on a problem for which control messages are essential, namely, flow control. Gerla and Kleinrock [1980] compares flow control strategies analytically.

The Internet Control Message Protocol described here is a TCP/IP standard defined by Postel [RFC 792] and updated by Braden [RFC [1122]. Nagle [RFC 896] discusses ICMP source quench messages and shows how routers should use them to handle congestion control. Prue and Postel [RFC 1016] discusses a more recent technique routers use in response to source quench. Nagle [1987] argues that congestion is always a concern in packet switched networks. Mogul and Postel [RFC 950] discusses subnet mask request and reply messages. Finally, Jain, Ramakrishnan and Chiu [1987] discusses how routers and transport protocols could cooperate to avoid congestion.

For a discussion of clock synchronization protocols see Mills [RFCs 956, 957, and 1305].

EXERCISES

9.1   Devise an experiment to record how many of each ICMP message type appear on your local network during a day.

9.2   Experiment to see if you can send packets through a router fast enough to trigger an ICMP source quench message.

9.3   Devise an algorithm that synchronizes clocks using ICMP timestamp messages.

9.4   See if your local computer system contains a *ping* command. How does the program interface with protocols in the operating system? In particular, does the mechanism allow an arbitrary user to create a *ping* program, or does such a program require special privilege? Explain.

9.5   Assume that all routers send ICMP time-exceeded messages, and that your local TCP/IP software will return such messages to an application program. Use the facility to build a *traceroute* command that reports the list of routers between the source and a particular destination.

9.6   If you connect to the Internet, try to ping host 128.10.2.1 (a machine at Purdue).

9.7   Should a router give ICMP messages priority over normal traffic? Why or why not?

9.8   Consider an Ethernet that has one conventional host, *H*, and 12 routers connected to it. Find a single (slightly illegal) frame carrying an IP packet that, when sent by host *H*, causes *H* to receive exactly 24 packets.

9.9   Compare ICMP source quench packets with Jain's 1-bit scheme used in DECNET. Which is a more effective strategy for dealing with congestion? Why?

9.10   There is no ICMP message that allows a machine to inform the source that transmission errors are causing datagrams to arrive corrupted. Explain why.

9.11   In the previous question, under what circumstances might such a message be useful?

9.12   Should ICMP error messages contain a timestamp that specifies when they are sent? Why or why not?

9.13   Try to reach a server on a nonexistent host on your local network. Also try to communicate with a nonexistent host on a remote network. In which case do you receive an error message? Why?

9.14   Try using *ping* with a network broadcast address. How many computers answer? Read the protocol documents to determine whether answering a broadcast request is required, recommended, not recommended, or prohibited.

10

Subnet And Supernet Address Extensions

10.1 Introduction

Chapter 4 discusses the original Internet addressing scheme and presents the three primary forms of IP addresses. This chapter examines four extensions of the IP address scheme that allow a site to use a single IP network address for multiple physical networks. It considers the motivation for the address extensions and describes the basic mechanisms needed for each. In particular, it presents the details of the subnet scheme that is now part of the TCP/IP standard.

10.2 Review Of Relevant Facts

Chapter 4 discusses addressing in internetworks and presents the fundamentals of the current IP address scheme. We said that the 32-bit addresses are carefully assigned to make the IP addresses of all hosts on a given physical network share a common prefix. In the original IP address scheme, designers thought of the common prefix as defining the network portion of an internet address and the remainder as a host portion. The consequence of importance to us is:

> *In the original IP addressing scheme, each physical network is assigned a unique network address; each host on a network has the network address as a prefix of the host's individual address.*

The chief advantage of dividing an IP address into two parts arises from the size of the routing tables required in routers. Instead of keeping one routing entry per destination host, a router can keep one routing entry per network, and examine only the network portion of a destination address when making routing decisions.

Recall that TCP/IP accommodates widely diverse network sizes by having three classes of primary addresses. Networks assigned class *A* addresses partition the 32 bits into an 8-bit network portion and a 24-bit host portion. Class *B* addresses partition the 32 bits into 16-bit network and host portions, while class *C* partitions the address into a 24-bit network portion and an 8-bit host portion.

To understand the address extensions in this chapter, it will be important to realize that individual sites have the freedom to modify addresses and routes as long as the modifications remain invisible to other sites. That is, a site can choose to assign and use IP addresses in unusual ways internally as long as:

- All hosts and routers at the site agree to honor the site's addressing scheme.
- Other sites on the Internet can treat addresses as in the original scheme.

10.3 Minimizing Network Numbers

The original IP addressing scheme seems to handle all possibilities, but it has a minor weakness. How did the weakness arise? What did the designers fail to envision? The answer is simple: growth. Because they worked in a world of expensive mainframe computers, the designers envisioned an internet with hundreds of networks and thousands of hosts. They did not foresee tens of thousands of small networks of personal computers that would suddenly appear in the decade after TCP/IP was designed.

Growth has been most apparent in the connected Internet, where the size has been doubling every nine months. The large population of networks with trivial size stresses the entire Internet design because it means (1) immense administrative overhead is required merely to manage network addresses, (2) the routing tables in routers are extremely large, and (3) the address space will eventually be exhausted. The second problem is important because it means that when routers exchange information from their routing tables, the load on the internet is high, as is the computational effort required in participating routers. The third problem is crucial because the original address scheme could not accommodate the number of networks currently in the global Internet. In particular, insufficient class B prefixes exist to cover all the medium-size networks in the Internet. So the question is, "How can one minimize the number of assigned network addresses, especially class B, without destroying the original addressing scheme?"

To minimize network addresses, the same IP network prefix must be shared by multiple physical networks. To minimize class B addresses, class C addresses must be used instead. Of course, the routing procedures must be modified, and all machines that connect to the affected networks must understand the conventions used.

The idea of sharing one network address among multiple physical networks is not new and has taken several forms. We will examine three: transparent routers, proxy ARP, and standard IP subnets. We will also consider classless addressing, the idea of assigning multiple class C addresses in place of a class B address.

10.4 Transparent Routers

The *transparent router* scheme is based on the observation that a network assigned a class *A* IP address can be extended through a simple trick illustrated in Figure 10.1.

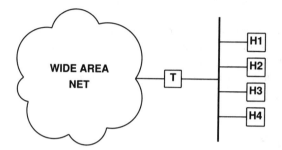

Figure 10.1 Transparent router *T* extending a wide area network to multiple hosts at a site. Each host appears to have an IP address on the WAN.

The trick consists of arranging for a physical network, usually a WAN, to multiplex several host connections through a single host port. As Figure 10.1 shows, a special purpose router, *T*, connects the single host port from the wide area net to a local area network. *T* is called a *transparent router* because other hosts and routers on the WAN do not know it exists.

The local area network does not have its own IP prefix; hosts attached to it are assigned addresses as if they connected directly to the WAN. The transparent router demultiplexes datagrams that arrive from the WAN by sending them to the appropriate host (e.g., by using a table of addresses). The transparent router also accepts datagrams from hosts on the local area network and routes them across the WAN toward their destination.

To make demultiplexing efficient, transparent routers often divide the IP address into multiple parts and encode information in unused parts. For example, the AR-PANET was assigned class *A* network address *10.0.0.0*. Each packet switch node (PSN) on the ARPANET had a unique integer address. Internally, the ARPANET treated any 4-octet IP address of the form *10.p.u.i* as four separate octets that specify a network (*10*), a specific port on the destination PSN (*p*), and a destination PSN (*i*). Octet *u* remained uninterpreted. Thus, the ARPANET addresses *10.2.5.37* and *10.2.9.37* both refer to host 2 on PSN *37*. A transparent router connected to PSN *37* on port *2* can use octet *u* to decide which real host should receive a datagram. The WAN itself need not be aware of the multiple hosts that lie beyond the PSN.

Transparent routers have advantages and disadvantages when compared to conventional routers. The chief advantage is that they require fewer network addresses because

the local area network does not need a separate IP prefix. Another is that they can support load balancing. That is, if two transparent routers connect to the same local area
network, traffic to hosts on that network can be split between them. By comparison,
conventional routers can only advertise one route to a given network.

One disadvantage of transparent routers is that they only work with networks that
have a large address space from which to choose host addresses. Thus, they work best
with class *A* networks, and they do not work well with class *C* networks. Another
disadvantage is that because they are not conventional routers, transparent routers do not
provide all the same services as standard routers. In particular, transparent routers may
not participate fully in ICMP or network management protocols like SNMP. Therefore,
they do not return ICMP echo requests (i.e., one cannot easily ''ping'' a transparent
router to determine if it is operating).

10.5 Proxy ARP

The terms *proxy ARP*, *promiscuous ARP*, and *the ARP hack* refer to a second technique used to map a single IP network prefix into two physical addresses. The technique, which only applies to networks that use ARP to bind internet addresses to physical addresses, can best be explained with an example. Figure 10.2 illustrates the situation.

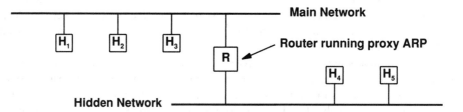

Figure 10.2 Proxy ARP technique (the ARP hack) allows one network ad-
           dress to be shared between two physical nets. Router *R* answers
           ARP requests on each network for hosts on the other network,
           giving its hardware address and then routing datagrams correctly
           when they arrive. In essence, *R* lies about IP-to-physical address
           bindings.

In the figure, two networks share a single IP network address. Imagine that the
network labeled *Main Network* was the original network, and that the second, labeled
Hidden Network, was added later. The router connecting the two networks, *R*, knows
which hosts lie on which physical network and uses ARP to maintain the illusion that
only one network exists. To make the illusion work, *R* keeps the location of hosts completely hidden, allowing all other machines on the network to communicate as if direct-

ly connected. In our example, when host H_1 needs to communicate with host H_4, it first invokes ARP to map H_4's IP address into a physical address. Once it has a physical address, H_1 can send the datagram directly to that physical address.

Because R runs proxy ARP software, it captures the broadcast ARP request from H_1, decides that the machine in question lies on the other physical network, and responds to the ARP request by sending its own physical address. H_1 receives the ARP response, installs the mapping in its ARP table, and then uses the mapping to send datagrams destined for H_4 to R. When R receives a datagram, it searches a special routing table to determine how to route the datagram. R must forward datagrams destined for H_4 over the hidden network. To allow hosts on the hidden network to reach hosts on the main network, R performs the proxy ARP service on that network as well.

Routers using the proxy ARP technique are taking advantage of an important feature of the ARP protocol, namely, trust. ARP is based on the idea that all machines cooperate and that any response is legitimate. Most hosts install mappings obtained through ARP without checking their validity and without maintaining consistency. Thus, it may happen that the ARP table maps several IP addresses to the same physical address, but that does not violate the protocol specification.

Some implementations of ARP are not as lax as others. In particular, ARP implementations designed to alert managers to possible security violations will inform them whenever two distinct IP addresses map to the same physical hardware address. The purpose of alerting the manager is to warn about *spoofing*, a situation in which one machine claims to be another in order to intercept packets. Host implementations of ARP that warn managers of possible spoofing cannot be used on networks that have proxy ARP routers because the software will generate messages frequently.

The chief advantage of proxy ARP is that it can be added to a single router on a network without disturbing the routing tables in other hosts or routers on that network. Thus, proxy ARP completely hides the details of physical connections.

The chief disadvantage of proxy ARP is that it does not work for networks unless they use ARP for address resolution. Furthermore, it does not generalize to more complex network topology (e.g., multiple routers interconnecting two physical networks), nor does it support a reasonable form of routing. In fact, most implementations of proxy ARP rely on managers to maintain tables of machines and addresses manually, making it both time consuming and prone to errors.

10.6 Subnet Addressing

The third technique used to allow a single network address to span multiple physical networks is called *subnet addressing*, *subnet routing*, or *subnetting*. Subnetting is the most widely used of the three techniques because it is the most general and because it has been standardized. In fact, subnetting is a required part of IP addressing.

The easiest way to understand subnet addressing is to imagine that a site has a single class B IP network address assigned to it, but it has two or more physical networks. Only local routers know that there are multiple physical nets and how to route traffic among them; routers in other autonomous systems route all traffic as if there were a single physical network. Figure 10.3 shows an example.

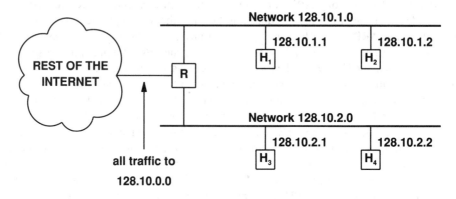

Figure 10.3 A site with two physical networks using subnet addressing to label them with a single class *B* network address. Router *R* accepts all traffic for net 128.10.0.0 and chooses a physical network based on the third octet of the address.

In the example, the site is using the single class *B* network address *128.10.0.0* for two networks. Except for router *R*, all routers in the internet route as if there were a single physical net. Once a packet reaches *R*, it must be sent across the correct physical network to its destination. To make the choice of physical network efficient, the local site has chosen to use the third octet of the address to distinguish between the two networks. The manager assigns machines on one physical net addresses of the form *128.10.1.X*, and machines on the other physical net addresses of the form *128.10.2.X*, where *X* represents a small integer used to identify a specific host. To choose a physical network, *R* examines the third octet of the destination address and routes datagrams with value *1* to the network labeled *128.10.1.0* and those with value *2* to the network labeled *128.10.2.0*.

Conceptually, adding subnets only changes the interpretation of IP addresses slightly. Instead of dividing the 32-bit IP address into a network prefix and a host suffix, subnetting divides the address into a *network portion* and a *local portion*. The interpretation of the network portion remains the same as for networks that do not use subnetting. As before, reachability to the network must be advertised to outside autonomous systems; all traffic destined for the network will follow the advertised route. The interpretation of the local portion of an address is left up to the site (within the constraints of the formal standard for subnet addressing). To summarize:

We think of a 32-bit IP address as having an internet portion and a local portion, where the internet portion identifies a site, possibly with multiple physical networks, and the local portion identifies a physical network and host at that site.

The example of Figure 10.3 showed subnet addressing with a class *B* address that had a 2-octet internet portion and a 2-octet local portion. To make routing among the physical networks efficient, the site administrator in our example chose to use one octet of the local portion to identify a physical network, and the other octet of the local portion to identify a host on that network, as Figure 10.4 shows.

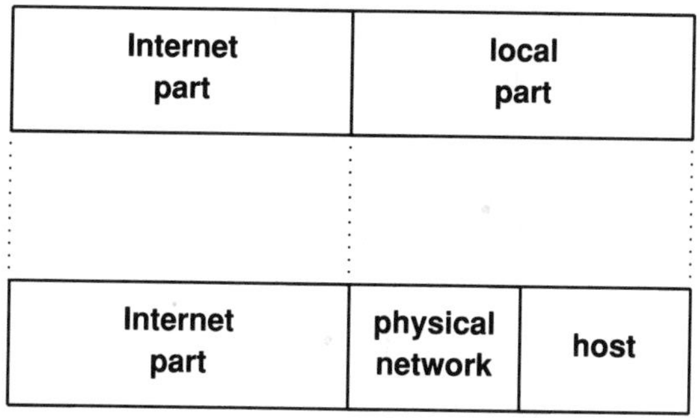

Internet part	local part

Internet part	physical network	host

Figure 10.4 (a) Conceptual interpretation of a 32-bit IP address in the original IP address scheme, and (b) conceptual interpretation of addresses using the subnet scheme shown in Figure 10.3. The local portion is divided into two parts that identify a physical network and a host on that network.

The result is a form of *hierarchical addressing* that leads to corresponding *hierarchical routing*. The top level of the routing hierarchy (i.e., other autonomous systems in the internet) uses the first two octets when routing, and the next level (i.e., the local site) uses an additional octet. Finally, the lowest level (i.e., delivery across one physical network) uses the entire address.

Hierarchical addressing is not new; many systems have used it before. The best example is the U.S. telephone system, where a 10-digit phone number is divided into a 3-digit area code, 3-digit exchange, and 4-digit connection. The advantage of using hierarchical addressing is that it accommodates large growth because it means a given router does not need to know as much detail about distant destinations as it does about local ones. One disadvantage is that choosing a hierarchical structure is difficult, and it often becomes difficult to change a hierarchy once it has been established.

10.7 Flexibility In Subnet Address Assignment

The TCP/IP standard for subnet addressing recognizes that not every site will have the same needs for an address hierarchy; it allows sites flexibility in choosing how to assign them. To understand why such flexibility is desirable, imagine a site with five networks interconnected, as Figure 10.5 shows. Suppose the site has a single class B network address that it wants to use for all physical networks. How should the local part be divided to make routing efficient?

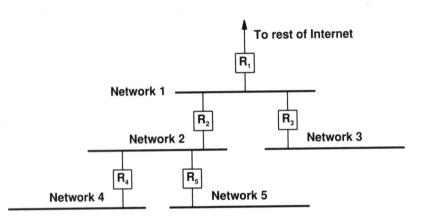

Figure 10.5 A site with five physical networks arranged in three "levels." The simplistic division of addresses into physical net and host parts may not be optimal for such cases.

In our example, the site will choose a partition of the local part of the IP address based on how it expects to grow. Dividing the 16-bit local part into an 8-bit network identifier and an 8-bit host identifier as shown in Figure 10.4 allows up to 256 networks, with up to 256 hosts per network†. Using 3 bits to identify a physical network and 13 bits to identify a host on that network allows up to 8 networks with up to 8192 hosts per network.

No single partition of the local part of the address will work for all sites because some have many networks with few hosts per network, while others have a few networks with many hosts attached to each. More important, it may be that even within one site, some networks may have many hosts while others have few hosts. To allow maximum autonomy, the TCP/IP subnet standard allows the subnet partition to be selected on a per-network basis. Once a partition has been selected for a particular network, all hosts and routers attached to that network must use it. If they do not, datagrams can be lost or misrouted. We can summarize:

---

†In practice, the limit is 254 subnets of 254 hosts per subnet because the all 1s and all 0s host addresses are reserved for broadcast, and the all 1s or all 0s subnet is not recommended.

To allow maximum flexibility in choosing how to partition subnet addresses, the TCP/IP subnet standard permits subnet interpretation to be chosen independently for each physical network. Once a subnet partition has been selected, all machines on that network must honor it.

10.8 Implementation Of Subnets With Masks

We have implied that choosing a subnet addressing scheme is synonymous with choosing how to partition the local portion of an IP address into physical net and host part. Indeed, most sites that use subnet addresses do exactly that, but subnet addressing allows more complex assignments as well. The standard specifies that a site using subnet addressing must choose a 32-bit *subnet mask* for each network. Bits in the subnet mask are set to *1* if the network treats the corresponding bit in the IP address as part of the network address, and *0* if it treats the bit as part of the host identifier. For example, the 32-bit subnet mask:

11111111 11111111 11111111 00000000

specifies that the first three octets identify the network and the fourth octet identifies a host on that network. A subnet mask should have *1*s for all bits that correspond to the network portion of the address (e.g., the subnet mask for a class *B* network will have *1*s for the first two octets plus one or more bits in the last two octets).

The interesting twist in subnet addressing arises because the standard does not restrict subnet masks to select contiguous bits of the address. For example, a network might be assigned the mask:

11111111 11111111 00011000 01000000

which selects the first two octets, two bits from the third octet, and one bit from the fourth. Although such flexibility makes it possible to arrange interesting assignments of addresses to machines, it makes assigning host addresses and understanding routing tables tricky. Thus, it is recommended that sites use contiguous subnet masks and that they use the same mask throughout an entire set of physical nets that share an IP address.

10.9 Subnet Mask Representation

Specifying subnet masks in binary is both awkward and prone to errors. Therefore, most software allows alternative representations. Sometimes, the representation follows whatever conventions the local operating system uses for representation of binary quantities, (e.g., hexadecimal notation).

Dotted decimal representation is also popular for subnet masks; it works best when sites choose to align subnetting on octet boundaries. For example, many sites choose to subnet class *B* addresses by using the third octet to identify the physical net and the fourth octet to identify hosts as on the previous page. In such cases, the subnet mask has dotted decimal representation *255.255.255.0*, making it easy to write and understand.

The literature also contains examples of subnet addresses and subnet masks represented in braces as a 3-tuple:

{ <network number> , <subnet number> , <host number> }

In this representation, the value *-1* means "all ones." For example, if the subnet mask for a class *B* network is *255.255.255.0*, it can be written *{-1, -1, 0}*.

The chief disadvantage of the 3-tuple representation is that it does not accurately specify how many bits are used for each part of the address; the advantage is that it abstracts away from the details of bit fields and emphasizes the values of the three parts of the address. To see why values are sometimes more important than bit fields, consider the 3-tuple:

{ 128.10 , -1, 0 }

which denotes an address with a network number *128.10*, all ones in the subnet field, and all zeroes in the host field. Expressing the same address value using other representations requires a 32-bit IP address and a 32-bit subnet mask, and forces readers to decode bit fields before they can deduce the values of individual fields. Furthermore, the 3-tuple representation is independent of the IP address class or size of the subnet field. Thus, it can be used to represent sets of addresses or abstract ideas. For example, the 3-tuple:

{ <network number>, -1, -1 }

denotes "addresses with a valid network number, a subnet field containing all ones, and a host field containing all ones." We will see additional examples later in this chapter.

10.10 Routing In The Presence Of Subnets

The standard IP routing algorithm must be modified to work with subnet addresses. All hosts and routers attached to a network that uses subnet addressing must use the modified algorithm, which is called *subnet routing*. What may not be obvious is that unless restrictions are added to the use of subnetting, other hosts and routers at the site may also need to use subnet routing. To see why, consider the example set of networks shown in Figure 10.6.

In the figure, physical networks 2 and 3 have been assigned subnet addresses of a single IP network address, N. Although host H does not directly attach to a network that has a subnet address, it must use subnet routing to decide whether to send datagrams destined for network N to router R_1 or router R_2. It could be argued that H can send to either router and let them handle the problem, but that solution means not all traffic will follow a shortest path. In larger examples, the difference between an optimal and nonoptimal path can be significant.

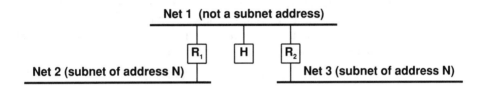

Net 1 (not a subnet address)

R₁   H   R₂

Net 2 (subnet of address N)   **Net 3 (subnet of address N)**

Figure 10.6 An example (illegal) topology with three networks where Nets 2 and 3 are subnets of a single IP network address, N. If such topologies were allowed, host H would need to use subnet routing even though Net 1 does not have a subnet address.

In theory, a simple rule determines when machines need to use subnet routing. The subnet rule is:

> *To achieve optimal routing, a machine* M *must use subnet routing for an IP network address* N, *unless there is a single path* P *such that P is a shortest path between* M *and every physical network that is a subnet of* N.

Unfortunately, understanding the theoretical restriction does not help in assigning subnets. First, shortest paths can change if hardware fails or if routing algorithms redirect traffic around congestion. Such dynamic changes make it difficult to use the subnet rule except in trivial cases. Second, the subnet rule fails to consider the boundaries of sites or the difficulties involved in propagating subnet masks. It is impossible to propagate subnet routes beyond the boundary of a given organization because the routing protocols discussed later do not provide for it. Realistically, it becomes extremely difficult to propagate subnet information beyond a given physical network. Therefore, the designers recommend that if a site uses subnet addressing, that site should keep subnetting as simple as possible. In particular, network administrators should adhere to the following guidelines:

> *All subnets of a given network IP address must be contiguous, the subnet masks should be uniform across all networks, and all machines should participate in subnet routing.*

The guidelines pose special difficulty for a large corporation that has multiple sites each connected to the Internet but not connected directly to one another. Such a corporation cannot use subnets of a single address for all its sites because the physical networks are not contiguous.

10.11 The Subnet Routing Algorithm

Like the standard IP routing algorithm, the subnet routing algorithm bases its decisions on a table of routes. Recall that in the standard algorithm, per-host routes and default routes are special cases that must be checked explicitly; table lookup is used for all others. A conventional routing table contains entries of the form:

(network address, next hop address)

where the *network address* field specifies the IP address of a destination network, N, and the *next hop address* field specifies the address of a router to which datagrams destined for N should be sent. The standard routing algorithm compares the network portion of a destination address to the *network address* field of each entry in the routing table until a match is found. Because the *next hop address* field is constrained to specify a machine that is reachable over a directly connected network, only one table lookup is ever needed.

The standard algorithm knows how an address is partitioned into network portion and local portion because the first three bits encode the address type and format (i.e., class A, B, C, or D). With subnets, it is not possible to decide which bits correspond to the network and which to the host from the address alone. Instead, the modified algorithm used with subnets maintains additional information in the routing table. Each table entry contains one additional field that specifies the subnet mask used with the network in that entry:

(subnet mask, network address, next hop address)

When choosing routes, the modified algorithm uses the *subnet mask* to extract bits of the destination address for comparison with the table entry. That is, it performs a bitwise Boolean *and* of the full 32-bit destination IP address and the *subnet mask* field from an entry, and it then checks to see if the result equals the value in the *network address* field of that entry. If so, it routes the datagram to the address specified in the *next hop address* field† of the entry.

---

†As in the standard routing algorithm, the next hop router must be reachable by a directly connected network.

10.12 A Unified Routing Algorithm

Observant readers may have guessed that if we allow arbitrary masks, the subnet routing algorithm can subsume all the special cases of the standard algorithm. It can handle routes to individual hosts, a default route, and routes to directly connected networks using the same masking technique it uses for subnets. In addition, masks can handle routes to conventional networks (i.e., networks not using subnet addressing). The flexibility comes from the ability to combine arbitrary 32-bit values in a *subnet mask* field and arbitrary 32-bit addresses in a *network address* field. For example, to install a route for a single host, one uses a mask of all *1*s and network address equal to the host's IP address. To install a default route, one uses a subnet mask of all *0*s and a network address of all *0*s (because any destination address *and* zero equals zero). To install a route to a standard, nonsubnet class *B* network, one specifies a mask with two octets of *1*s and two octets of *0*s. Because the table contains more information, the routing algorithm contains fewer special cases as Figure 10.7 shows.

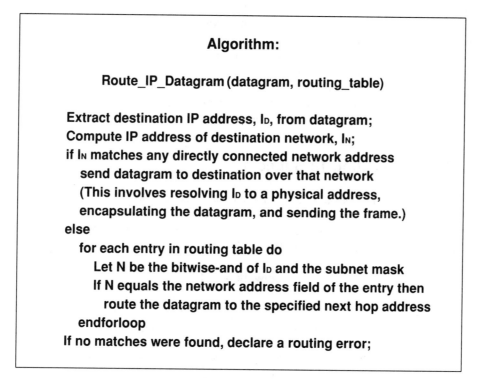

Figure 10.7 The unified IP routing algorithm. Given an IP datagram and a routing table with masks, this algorithm selects a next hop router to which the datagram should be sent. The next hop must lie on a directly connected network.

In fact, clever implementations can eliminate the explicit test for destinations on directly connected networks by adding table entries with appropriate values for the mask and network address.

10.13 Maintenance Of Subnet Masks

How do subnet masks get assigned and propagated? Chapter 9 answered the second part of the question by showing that a host can obtain the subnet mask for a given network by sending an ICMP *subnet mask request* to a router on that network. The request can be broadcast if the host does not know the specific address of a router. However, there is no standard protocol for propagating the information from one router to another.

The first part of the question is more difficult to answer. Each site is free to choose subnet masks for its networks. When making assignments, managers attempt to balance sizes of networks, numbers of physical networks, expected growth, and ease of maintenance. Difficulty arises because nonuniform masks give the most flexibility but make possible assignments that lead to ambiguous routes. Or worse, they allow valid assignments that become invalid if more hosts are added to the networks. There are no easy rules, so most sites make conservative choices. Typically, a site selects contiguous bits from the local portion of an address to identify a network and uses the same partition (i.e., the same mask) for all local physical networks at the site. For example, many sites simply use a single subnet octet when subnetting a class B address.

10.14 Broadcasting To Subnets

Broadcasting is more difficult in a subnet architecture. Recall that in the original IP addressing scheme, an address with a host portion of all 1s denotes broadcast to all hosts on the specified network. From the viewpoint of an observer outside a subnetted site, broadcasting to the network address still makes sense. That is, the address:

$$\{ \text{ network, -1, -1 } \}$$

means ''deliver a copy to all machines that have *network* as their network addresses, even if they lie on separate physical networks.'' Operationally, broadcasting to such an address makes sense only if the routers that interconnect the subnets agree to propagate the datagram to all physical networks. Of course, care must be taken to avoid routing loops. In particular, a router cannot merely propagate a broadcast packet that arrives on one interface to all interfaces that share the subnet prefix. To prevent such loops, routers use *reverse path forwarding*. The router extracts the source of the broadcast datagram, and looks up the source in its routing table. The router then discards the datagram unless it arrived on the interface used to route to the source (i.e., arrived from the shortest path).

Within a set of subnetted networks, it becomes possible to broadcast to a specific subnet (i.e., to broadcast to all hosts on a physical network that has been assigned one of the subnet addresses). The subnet address standard uses a host field of all ones to denote subnet broadcast. That is, a subnet broadcast address becomes:

{ network, subnet, -1 }

Considering subnet broadcast addresses and subnet broadcasting clarifies the recommendation for using a consistent subnet mask across all networks that share a subnetted IP address. As long as the subnet and host fields are identical, subnet broadcast addresses are unambiguous. More complex subnet address assignments may or may not allow broadcasting to selected subsets of the physical networks that comprise a subnet.

10.15 Supernet Addressing

Subnet addressing was invented in the early 1980s to help conserve the IP address space. By 1993, it became apparent that subnet addressing would not prevent Internet growth from eventually exhausting the class B address space. Work had begun on defining an entirely new version of IP with larger addresses. However, to accommodate growth until the new version of IP could be standardized and adopted, a temporary solution was found.

Called *supernetting* or *supernet addressing*, the scheme takes an opposite approach from subnet addressing. Instead of using a single IP network address for multiple physical networks at a given organization, supernetting allows the use of many IP network addresses for a single organization. To understand why supernetting was adopted, one needs to know three facts. First, IP does not divide network addresses into classes equally. Although less than 17 thousand class B numbers can be assigned, more than 2 million class C network numbers exist. Second, class C numbers were being requested slowly; only a small percentage of them had been assigned. Third, studies showed that at the rate class B numbers were being assigned, all numbers would be exhausted in only a few years. The problem became known as the *Running Out of ADdress Space (ROADS)* problem.

To understand how supernetting works, consider a medium-sized organization that joins the Internet. Such an organization would prefer to use a single class B address for two reasons: a class C address cannot accommodate more than 254 hosts and a class B address has sufficient bits to make subnetting convenient. To conserve class B numbers, the supernetting scheme assigns an organization a block of class C addresses instead of a single class B number. The block must be large enough to number all the networks the organization will eventually connect to the Internet. For example, suppose an organization requests a class B address that the organization intends to subnet using the third octet as a subnet field. Instead of a single class B number, supernetting assigns the organization a block of 256 class C numbers that the organization can then assign to physical networks.

Although supernetting is easy to understand when viewed from the point of view of a single site, the proposers intended it to be used in a broader context. They envisioned a hierarchical Internet in which commercial *Network Service Providers* provide Internet connectivity. To connect its networks to the Internet, an organization would contract with one of the Network Service Providers; the service provider handles the details of assigning IP addresses to the organization as well as installing physical connections. The designers of supernetting propose that a Network Service Provider be allowed to obtain a large part of the address space (i.e., a set of addresses that span many class C network numbers). The Network Service Provider can then allocate one or more addresses from the set to each of its subscribers.

10.16 The Effect Of Supernetting On Routing

Allocating many class C addresses in place of a single class B address conserves class B numbers and solves the immediate problem of address space exhaustion. However, it creates a new problem: the information that routers store and exchange increases dramatically. In particular, instead of having one entry per organization, a routing table contains many entries.

A technique known as *Classless Inter-Domain Routing*† (*CIDR*) solves the problem. Conceptually, CIDR collapses a block of contiguous class C addresses into a single entry represented by a pair:

$$(\text{network address}, \text{ count})$$

where *network address* is the smallest network address in the block, and *count* specifies the total number of network addresses in the block. For example, the pair:

$$(192.5.48.0, 3)$$

can be used to specify the three network addresses 192.5.48.0, 192.5.49.0, and 192.5.50.0.

If a few service providers form the core of the Internet and each Network Service Provider owns a large block of contiguous IP network numbers, the benefit of supernetting becomes clear. Consider routing table entries in routers owned by service provider *P*. Of course, the table much have a correct route to each of *P*'s subscribers. The table does not need to contain a route for other provider's subscribers. Instead, the table stores one entry for each other provider. The entry identifies the block of addresses owned by the provider.

In practice, CIDR does not restrict network numbers to class C addresses nor does it use an integer count to specify a block size. Instead, CIDR requires each block of addresses to be a power of two, and uses a bit mask to identify the size of the block. For

---

†The name is a slight misnomer because the scheme specifies addressing as well as routing.

example, suppose an organization was assigned a block of 2048 contiguous addresses starting at address 234.170.168.0. The table in Figure 10.8 shows the binary values of addresses in the range.

	Dotted Decimal	32-bit Binary Equivalent
lowest	234.170.168.0	11101010 10101010 10101000 00000000
highest	234.170.175.255	11101010 10101010 10101111 11111111

Figure 10.8 A block of 2048 addresses. The table shows the lowest and highest addresses in the range expressed as dotted decimal and binary values.

CIDR requires two values to specify the range of values in Figure 10.8: the lowest address and a 32-bit mask. The mask operates like a standard subnet mask by delineating the end of the prefix. For the range shown, the CIDR mask has 21 bits set†:

$$11111111 \quad 11111111 \quad 11111000 \quad 00000000$$

To make use of all possible host addresses in a given range, the routers at a site using classless addressing must be changed. When looking up a route, the routing software does not interpret the destination address class. Instead, each entry in the routing table contains an address and a mask, and the routing software uses a *longest-match* paradigm to select a route. Thus a given block of addresses can be subdivided, and separate routes can be entered for each subdivision. As a result, although the group of computers on a given network will be assigned addresses in a fixed range, the range does not need to correspond to a binary value.

Supernetting treats IP addresses as arbitrary integers, and allows a network administrator to assign a block of contiguous numbers to a given site or a network within a site. Hosts and routers that use supernetting need unconventional routing software that understands ranges of addresses.

10.17 Summary

This chapter examined four techniques that extend the IP address scheme. The original IP address scheme assigns a unique 32-bit internet address to each physical network and requires an IP routing table proportional to the number of networks in the internet. Three of the techniques we examined have been invented to conserve addresses: they allow a site to share one internet address among multiple physical networks. The first uses transparent routers to extend the address space of a single network, usually a WAN, to include hosts on an attached local network. The second, called proxy ARP,

†In dotted decimal, the mask value is *255 . 255 . 248 . 0* .

arranges for a local router to impersonate computers on another physical network by answering ARP messages addressed to them. Proxy ARP is useful only on networks that use ARP for address resolution, and only for ARP implementations that do not complain when multiple internet addresses map to the same hardware address. The third technique, a TCP/IP standard called subnet addressing, allows a site to share a single IP network address among multiple physical networks, as long as all the hosts and routers on those networks cooperate. Subnetting requires hosts to use a modified routing algorithm in which routing table entries contain a subnet mask. The algorithm can be viewed as a generalization of the original routing algorithm because it handles special cases like default routes or host-specific routes.

Finally, we examined the supernetting technique in which a site is assigned an aggregate of many class C numbers. Also known as classless addressing, the supernetting scheme requires changes to the routing software in hosts and routers.

FOR FURTHER STUDY

The standard for subnet addressing comes from Mogul [RFC 950] with updates in Braden [RFC 1122]. Clark [RFC 932], Karels [RFC 936], Gads [RFC 940], and Mogul [RFC 917] all contain early proposals for subnet addressing schemes. Mogul [RFC 922] discusses broadcasting in the presence of subnets. Postel [RFC 925] considers the use of proxy ARP for subnets. Carl-Mitchell and Quarterman [RFC 1027] discusses using proxy ARP to implement transparent subnet routers. Fuller, Li, Yu, and Varadhan [RFC 1519] specifies supernet address extensions and classless inter-domain routing.

EXERCISES

10.1   If routers using proxy ARP use a table of host addresses to decide whether to answer ARP requests, the router table must be changed whenever a new host is added to one of the networks. Explain how to assign IP addresses so hosts can be added without changing tables. Hint: think of subnets.

10.2   Although the standard allows all-0's to be assigned as a subnet number, some vendor's software does not operate correctly. Try to assign a zero subnet at your site and see if the route is propagated correctly.

10.3   Can transparent routers be used with local area networks like the Ethernet? Why or why not?

10.4   Show that proxy ARP can be used with three physical networks that are interconnected by two routers.

10.5   Consider a fixed subnet partition of a class *B* network number that will accommodate at least 76 networks. How many hosts can be on each network?

10.6   Does it ever make sense to subnet a class *C* network address? Why or why not?

10.7   A site that chose to subnet their class *B* address by using the third octet for the physical net was disappointed that they could not accommodate 255 or 256 networks. Explain.

10.8   Design a subnet address scheme for your organization assuming that you have one class *B* address to use.

10.9   Is it reasonable for a single router to use both proxy ARP and subnet addressing? If so, explain how. If not, explain why.

10.10   Argue that any network using proxy ARP is vulnerable to "spoofing" (i.e., an arbitrary machine can impersonate any other machine).

10.11   Can you devise a (nonstandard) implementation of ARP that supports normal use, but prohibits proxy ARP?

10.12   One vendor decided to add subnet addressing to its IP software by allocating a single subnet mask used for all IP network addresses. The vendor modified its standard IP routing software to make the subnet check a special case. Find a simple example in which this implementation cannot work correctly. (Hint: think of a multi-homed host.)

10.13   Characterize the (restricted) situations in which the subnet implementation discussed in the previous exercise will work correctly.

10.14   Read the standard to find out more about broadcasting in the presence of subnets. Can you characterize subnet address assignments that allow one to specify a broadcast address for all possible subnets?

10.15   The standard allows an arbitrary assignment of subnet masks for networks that comprise a subnetted IP address. Should the standard restrict subnet masks to cover contiguous bits in the address? Why or why not?

10.16   Carefully consider default routing in the presence of subnets. What can happen if a packet arrives destined for a nonexistent subnet?

10.17   Compare architectures that use subnet addressing and routers to interconnect multiple Ethernets to an architecture that uses bridges as described in Chapter 2. Under what circumstances is one architecture preferable to the other?

10.18   Consider a site that chooses to subnet a class *B* network address, but decides that some physical nets will use *6* bits of the local portion to identify the physical net while others will use *8*. Find an assignment of host addresses that makes destination addresses ambiguous.

10.19   The subnet routing algorithm in Figure 10.7 uses a sequential scan of entries in the routing table, allowing a manager to place host-specific routes before network-specific or subnet-specific routes. Invent a data structure that achieves the same flexibility but uses hashing to make the lookup efficient. [This exercise was suggested by Dave Mills.]

10.20   If all Internet service providers used supernetting and assign subscribers numbers from their block of addresses, what problem occurs when a subscriber changes from one provider to another?

11

Protocol Layering

11.1 Introduction

Previous chapters review the architectural foundations of internetworking, describe how hosts and routers forward Internet datagrams, and present mechanisms used to map IP addresses to physical network addresses. This chapter considers the structure of the software found in hosts and routers that carries out network communication. It presents the general principle of layering, shows how layering makes Internet Protocol software easier to understand and build, and traces the path of datagrams through the protocol software they encounter when traversing a TCP/IP internet.

11.2 The Need For Multiple Protocols

We have said that protocols allow one to specify or understand communication without knowing the details of a particular vendor's network hardware. They are to computer communication what programming languages are to computation. It should be apparent by now how closely the analogy fits. Like assembly language, some protocols describe communication across a physical network. For example, the details of the Ethernet frame format, network access policy, and frame error handling comprise a protocol that describes communication on an Ethernet. Similarly, the details of IP addresses, the datagram format, and the concept of unreliable, connectionless delivery comprise the Internet Protocol.

Complex data communication systems do not use a single protocol to handle all transmission tasks. Instead, they require a set of cooperative protocols, sometimes called a *protocol family* or *protocol suite*. To understand why, think of the problems that arise when machines communicate over a data network:

- *Hardware failure.* A host or router may fail either because the hardware fails or because the operating system crashes. A network transmission link may fail or accidentally be disconnected. The protocol software needs to detect such failures and recover from them if possible.

- *Network congestion.* Even when all hardware and software operates correctly, networks have finite capacity that can be exceeded. The protocol software needs to arrange ways that a congested machine can suppress further traffic.

- *Packet delay or loss.* Sometimes, packets experience extremely long delays or are lost. The protocol software needs to learn about failures or adapt to long delays.

- *Data corruption.* Electrical or magnetic interference or hardware failures can cause transmission errors that corrupt the contents of transmitted data. Protocol software needs to detect and recover from such errors.

- *Data duplication or sequence errors.* Networks that offer multiple routes may deliver data out of sequence or may deliver duplicates of packets. The protocol software needs to reorder packets and remove any duplicates.

Taken together, all these problems seem overwhelming. It is difficult to understand how to write a single protocol that will handle them all. From the analogy with programming languages, we can see how to conquer the complexity. Program translation has been partitioned into four conceptual subproblems identified with the software that handles each subproblem: compiler, assembler, link editor, and loader. The division makes it possible for the designer to concentrate on one subproblem at a time, and for the implementor to build and test each piece of software independently. We will see that protocol software is partitioned similarly.

Two final observations about our programming language analogy will help clarify the organization of protocols. First, it should be clear that pieces of translation software must agree on the exact format of data passed between them. For example, the data passed from the compiler to the assembler consists of a program defined by the assembly programming language. Thus, we see how the translation process involves multiple programming languages. The analogy will hold for communication software, where we will see that multiple protocols define the interfaces between the modules of communication software. Second, the four parts of the translator form a linear sequence in which output from the compiler becomes input to the assembler, and so on. Protocol software also uses a linear sequence.

11.3 The Conceptual Layers Of Protocol Software

Think of the modules of protocol software on each machine as being stacked vertically into *layers*, as in Figure 11.1. Each layer takes responsibility for handling one part of the problem.

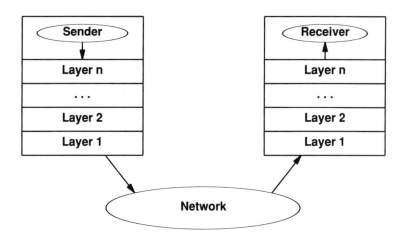

Figure 11.1 The conceptual organization of protocol software in layers.

Conceptually, sending a message from an application program on one machine to an application program on another means transferring the message down through successive layers of protocol software on the sender's machine, transferring the message across the network, and transferring the message up through successive layers of protocol software on the receiver's machine.

In practice, the protocol software is much more complex than the simple model of Figure 11.1 indicates. Each layer makes decisions about the correctness of the message and chooses an appropriate action based on the message type or destination address. For example, one layer on the receiving machine must decide whether to keep the message or forward it to another machine. Another layer must decide which application program should receive the message.

To understand the difference between the conceptual organization of protocol software and the implementation details, consider the comparison shown in Figure 11.2. The conceptual diagram in Figure 11.2a shows an Internet layer between a high level protocol layer and a network interface layer. The realistic diagram in Figure 11.2b shows that the IP software may communicate with multiple high-level protocol modules and with multiple network interfaces.

Although a diagram of conceptual protocol layering does not show all details, it does help explain the general ideas. For example, Figure 11.3 shows the layers of protocol software used by a message that traverses three networks. The diagram shows only the network interface and Internet Protocol layers in routers because only those layers are needed to receive, route, and then send datagrams. We understand that any machine attached to two networks must have two network interface modules, even though the conceptual layering diagram shows only a single network interface layer in each machine.

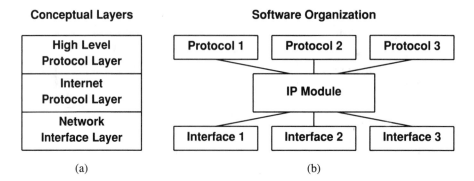

Figure 11.2 A comparison of (a) conceptual protocol layering and (b) a realistic view of software organization showing multiple network interfaces below IP and multiple protocols above it.

As Figure 11.3 shows, a sender on the original machine transmits a message which
the IP layer places in a datagram and sends across network *1*. On intermediate
machines the datagram passes up to the IP layer which routes it back out again (on a
different network). Only when it reaches the final destination machine does IP extract
the message and pass it up to higher layers of protocol software.

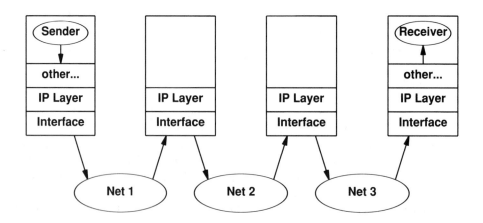

Figure 11.3 The path of a message traversing the Internet from the sender
through two intermediate machines to the receiver. Intermediate
machines only send the datagram to the IP software layer.

11.4 Functionality Of The Layers

Once the decision has been made to partition the communication problem into sub-problems and organize the protocol software into modules that each handle one sub-problem, the question arises: ''what functionality should reside in each module?'' The question is not easy to answer for several reasons. First, given a set of goals and constraints governing a particular communication problem, it is possible to choose an organization that will optimize protocol software for that problem. Second, even when considering general network-level services such as reliable transport, it is possible to choose from among fundamentally distinct approaches to solving the problem. Third, the design of network (or internet) architecture and the organization of the protocol software are interrelated; one cannot be designed without the other.

11.4.1 ISO 7-Layer Reference Model

Two ideas about protocol layering dominate the field. The first, based on work done by the International Organization for Standardization (ISO), is known as ISO's *Reference Model of Open System Interconnection*, often referred to as the *ISO model*. The ISO model contains 7 conceptual layers organized as Figure 11.4 shows.

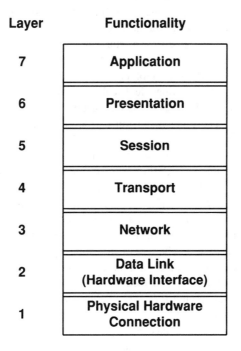

Figure 11.4 The ISO 7-layer reference model for protocol software.

The ISO model, built to describe protocols for a single network, does not contain a specific level for internetwork routing in the same way TCP/IP protocols do.

11.5 X.25 And Its Relation To The ISO Model

Although it was designed to provide a conceptual model and not an implementation guide, the ISO layering scheme has been the basis for several protocol implementations. Among the protocols commonly associated with the ISO model, the set of protocols known as X.25 is probably the best known and most widely used. X.25 was established as a recommendation of the *Telecommunications Section* of the *International Telecommunications Union*† (ITU-TS), an international organization that recommends standards for international telephone services. X.25 has been adopted by public data networks, and is especially popular in Europe. Considering X.25 will help explain the ISO layering.

In the X.25 view, a network operates much like a telephone system. An X.25 network is assumed to consist of complex packet switches that contain the intelligence needed to route packets. Hosts do not attach directly to communication wires of the network. Instead each host attaches to one of the packet switches using a serial communication line. In one sense the connection between a host and an X.25 packet switch is a miniature network consisting of one serial link. The host must follow a complicated procedure to transfer packets onto the network.

• *Physical Layer.* X.25 specifies a standard for the physical interconnection between host computers and network packet switches, as well as the procedures used to transfer packets from one machine to another. In the reference model, level *1* specifies the physical interconnection including electrical characteristics of voltage and current. A corresponding protocol, X.21, gives the details used by public data networks.

• *Data Link Layer.* The level *2* portion of the X.25 protocol specifies how data travels between a host and the packet switch to which it connects. X.25 uses the term *frame* to refer to a unit of data as it passes between a host and a packet switch (it is important to understand that the X.25 definition of *frame* differs slightly from the way we have used it). Because raw hardware delivers only a stream of bits, the level *2* protocol must define the format of frames and specify how the two machines recognize frame boundaries. Because transmission errors can destroy data, the level *2* protocol includes error detection (e.g., a frame checksum). Finally, because transmission is unreliable, the level *2* protocol specifies an exchange of acknowledgements that allows the two machines to know when a frame has been transferred successfully.

One commonly used level *2* protocol, named the *High Level Data Link Communication*, is best known by its acronym, *HDLC*. Several versions of HDLC exist, with the most recent known as *HDLC/LAPB*. It is important to remember that successful transfer at level *2* means a frame has been passed to the network packet switch for delivery; it does not guarantee that the packet switch accepted the packet or was able to route it.

---

†The International Telecommunications Union was formerly named the *Consultative Committee on International Telephony and Telegraphy* (CCITT).

• *Network Layer*. The ISO reference model specifies that the third level contains functionality that completes the definition of the interaction between host and network. Called the *network* or *communication subnet* layer, this level defines the basic unit of transfer across the network and includes the concepts of destination addressing and routing. Remember that in the X.25 world, communication between host and packet switch is conceptually isolated from the traffic that is being passed. Thus, the network might allow packets defined by level 3 protocols to be larger than the size of frames that can be transferred at level 2. The level 3 software assembles a packet in the form the network expects and uses level 2 to transfer it (possibly in pieces) to the packet switch. Level 3 must also respond to network congestion problems.

• *Transport Layer*. Level 4 provides end-to-end reliability by having the destination host communicate with the source host. The idea here is that even though lower layers of protocols provide reliable checks at each transfer, the end-to-end layer double checks to make sure that no machine in the middle failed.

• *Session Layer*. Higher levels of the ISO model describe how protocol software can be organized to handle all the functionality needed by application programs. The ISO committee considered the problem of remote terminal access so fundamental that they assigned layer 5 to handle it. In fact, the central service offered by early public data networks consisted of terminal to host interconnection. The carrier provides a special purpose host computer called a *Packet Assembler And Disassembler* (*PAD*) on the network with dialup access. Subscribers, often travelers who carry their own computer and modem, dial up the local PAD, make a network connection to the host with which they wish to communicate, and log in. Many carriers choose to make using the network for long distance communication less expensive than direct dialup.

• *Presentation Layer*. ISO layer 6 is intended to include functions that many application programs need when using the network. Typical examples include standard routines that compress text or convert graphics images into bit streams for transmission across a network. For example an ISO standard known as *Abstract Syntax Notation 1* (*ASN.1*), provides a representation of data that application programs use. One of the TCP/IP protocols, SNMP, also uses ASN.1 to represent data.

• *Application Layer*. Finally, ISO layer 7 includes application programs that use the network. Examples include electronic mail or file transfer programs. In particular, the ITU-TS has devised a protocol for electronic mail known as the *X.400* standard. In fact, the ITU and ISO worked jointly on message handling systems; the ISO version is called *MOTIS*.

11.5.1 The TCP/IP Internet Layering Model

The second major layering model did not arise from a standards committee, but came instead from research that led to the TCP/IP protocol suite. With a little work, the ISO model can be stretched to describe the TCP/IP layering scheme, but the underlying assumptions are different enough to warrant distinguishing the two.

Broadly speaking, TCP/IP software is organized into four conceptual layers that build on a fifth layer of hardware. Figure 11.5 shows the conceptual layers as well as the form of data as it passes between them.

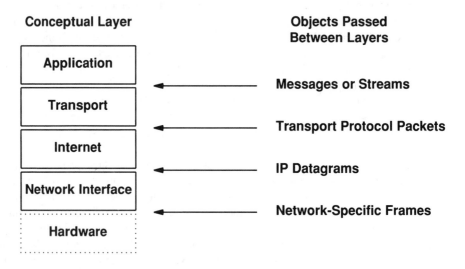

Figure 11.5 The 4 conceptual layers of TCP/IP software and the form of objects passed between layers. The layer labeled *network interface* is sometimes called the *data link* layer.

• *Application Layer.* At the highest level, users invoke application programs that access services available across a TCP/IP internet. An application interacts with one of the transport level protocols to send or receive data. Each application program chooses the style of transport needed, which can be either a sequence of individual messages or a continuous stream of bytes. The application program passes data in the required form to the transport level for delivery.

• *Transport Layer.* The primary duty of the *transport layer* is to provide communication from one application program to another. Such communication is often called *end-to-end*. The transport layer may regulate flow of information. It may also provide reliable transport, ensuring that data arrives without error and in sequence. To do so, transport protocol software arranges to have the receiving side send back acknowledgements and the sending side retransmit lost packets. The transport software divides the stream of data being transmitted into small pieces (sometimes called *packets*) and passes each packet along with a destination address to the next layer for transmission.

Although Figure 11.5 uses a single block to represent the application layer, a general purpose computer can have multiple application programs accessing the internet at one time. The transport layer must accept data from several user programs and send it to the next lower layer. To do so, it adds additional information to each packet, including codes that identify which application program sent it and which application program should receive it, as well as a checksum. The receiving machine uses the checksum to verify that the packet arrived intact, and uses the destination code to identify the application program to which it should be delivered.

• *Internet Layer.* As we have already seen, the Internet layer handles communication from one machine to another. It accepts a request to send a packet from the transport layer along with an identification of the machine to which the packet should be sent. It encapsulates the packet in an IP datagram, fills in the datagram header, uses the routing algorithm to determine whether to deliver the datagram directly or send it to a router, and passes the datagram to the appropriate network interface for transmission. The Internet layer also handles incoming datagrams, checking their validity, and uses the routing algorithm to decide whether the datagram should be processed locally or forwarded. For datagrams addressed to the local machine, software in the internet layer deletes the datagram header, and chooses from among several transport protocols the one that will handle the packet. Finally, the Internet layer sends ICMP error and control messages as needed and handles all incoming ICMP messages.

• *Network Interface Layer.* The lowest level TCP/IP software comprises a network interface layer, responsible for accepting IP datagrams and transmitting them over a specific network. A network interface may consist of a device driver (e.g., when the network is a local area network to which the machine attaches directly) or a complex subsystem that uses its own data link protocol (e.g., when the network consists of packet switches that communicate with hosts using HDLC).

11.6 Differences Between X.25 And Internet Layering

There are two subtle and important differences between the TCP/IP layering scheme and the X.25 scheme. The first difference revolves around the focus of attention on reliability, while the second involves the location of intelligence in the overall system.

11.6.1 Link-Level vs. End-To-End Reliability

One major difference between the TCP/IP protocols and the X.25 protocols lies in their approaches to providing reliable data transfer services. In the X.25 model, protocol software detects and handles errors at all levels. At the link level, complex protocols guarantee that the transfer between a host and the packet switch to which it connects will be correct. Checksums accompany each piece of data transferred, and the receiver acknowledges each piece of data received. The link level protocol includes timeout and retransmission algorithms that prevent data loss and provide automatic recovery after hardware fails and restarts.

Successive levels of X.25 provide reliability of their own. At level *3*, X.25 also provides error detection and recovery for packets transferred onto the network, using checksums as well as timeout and retransmission techniques. Finally, level *4* must provide end-to-end reliability, having the source correspond with the ultimate destination to verify delivery.

In contrast to such a scheme, TCP/IP bases its protocol layering on the idea that reliability is an end-to-end problem. The architectural philosophy is simple: construct the internet so it can handle the expected load, but allow individual links or machines to lose data or corrupt it without trying to repeatedly recover. In fact, there is little or no reliability in most TCP/IP network interface layer software. Instead, the transport layer handles most error detection and recovery problems.

The resulting freedom from interface layer verification makes TCP/IP software much easier to understand and implement correctly. Intermediate routers can discard datagrams that become corrupted because of transmission errors. They can discard datagrams that cannot be delivered. They can discard datagrams when the arrival rate exceeds machine capacity, and can reroute datagrams through paths with shorter or longer delay without informing the source or destination.

Having unreliable links means that some datagrams do not arrive. Detection and recovery of datagram loss is carried out between the source host and the ultimate destination and is, therefore, called *end-to-end* verification. The end-to-end software located in the transport layer uses checksums, acknowledgements, and timeouts to control transmission. Thus, unlike the connection-oriented X.25 protocol layering, the TCP/IP software focuses most of its reliability control in one layer.

11.6.2 Locus of Intelligence and Decision Making

Another difference between the X.25 model and the TCP/IP model emerges when one considers the locus of authority and control. As a general rule, networks using X.25 adhere to the idea that a network is a utility that provides a transport service. The vendor that offers the service controls network access and monitors traffic to keep records for accounting and billing. The network vendor also handles problems like routing, flow control, and acknowledgements internally, making transfers reliable. This view leaves little that the hosts can (or need to) do. In short, the network is a complex, independent system to which one can attach relatively simple host computers; the hosts themselves participate in the network operation very little.

By contrast, TCP/IP requires hosts to participate in almost all of the network protocols. We have already mentioned that hosts actively implement end-to-end error detection and recovery. They also participate in routing because they must choose a router when sending datagrams, and they participate in network control because they must handle ICMP control messages. Thus, when compared to an X.25 network, a TCP/IP internet can be viewed as a relatively simple packet delivery system to which intelligent hosts attach.

11.7 The Protocol Layering Principle

Independent of the particular layering scheme used, or the functions of the layers, the operation of layered protocols is based on a fundamental idea. The idea, called the *layering principle*, can be summarized succinctly:

> *Layered protocols are designed so that layer n at the destination receives exactly the same object sent by layer n at the source.*

The layering principle explains why layering is such a powerful idea. It allows the protocol designer to focus attention on one layer at a time, without worrying about how lower layers perform. For example, when building a file transfer application, the designer thinks only of two copies of the application program executing on two machines and concentrates on the messages they need to exchange for file transfer. The designer assumes that the application on one host receives exactly what the application on the other host sends.

Figure 11.6 illustrates how the layering principle works:

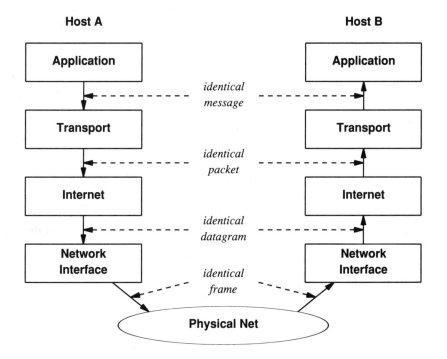

Figure 11.6 The path of a message as it passes from an application on one host to an application on another. Layer *n* on host *B* receives exactly the same object that layer *n* on host *A* sent.

11.7.1 Layering in a TCP/IP Internet Environment

Our statement of the layering principle is somewhat vague, and the illustration in Figure 11.6 skims over an important issue because it fails to distinguish between transfers from source to ultimate destination and transfers across multiple networks. Figure 11.7 illustrates the distinction, showing the path of a message sent from an application program on one host to an application on another through a router.

As the figure shows, message delivery uses two separate network frames, one for the transmission from host *A* to router *R*, and another from router *R* to host *B*. The network layering principle states that the frame delivered to *R* is identical to the frame sent by host *A*. By contrast, the application and transport layers deal with end-to-end issues and are designed so the software at the source communicates with its peer at the ultimate destination. Thus, the layering principle states that the packet received by the transport layer at the ultimate destination is identical to the packet sent by the transport layer at the original source.

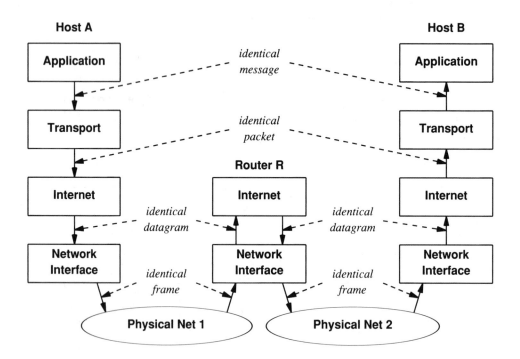

Figure 11.7 The layering principle when a router is used. The frame delivered to router *R* is exactly the frame sent from host *A*, but differs from the frame sent between *R* and *B*.

It is easy to understand that in higher layers, the layering principle applies across end-to-end transfers, and that at the lowest layer it applies to a single machine transfer. It is not as easy to see how the layering principle applies to the Internet layer. On one hand, we have said that hosts attached to an internet should view it as a large, virtual network, with the IP datagram taking the place of a network frame. In this view, datagrams travel from original source to ultimate destination, and the layering principle guarantees that the ultimate destination receives exactly the datagram that the original source sent. On the other hand, we know that the datagram header contains fields, like a *time to live* counter, that change each time the datagram passes through a router. Thus, the ultimate destination will not receive exactly the same datagram as the source sent. We conclude that although most of the datagram stays intact as it passes across an internet, the layering principle only applies to datagrams across single machine transfers. To be accurate, we should not view the Internet layer as providing end-to-end service.

11.8 Layering In The Presence Of Network Substructure

Recall from Chapter 2 that some wide area networks contain multiple packet switches. For example, a WAN can consist of routers that connect to a local network at each site as well as to other routers using leased serial lines. When a router receives a datagram, it either delivers the datagram to its destination on the local network, or transfers the datagram across a serial line to another router. The question arises: ''How do the protocols used on serial lines fit into the TCP/IP layering scheme?'' The answer depends on how the designer views the serial line interconnections.

From the perspective of IP, the set of point-to-point connections among routers can either function like a set of independent physical networks, or they can function collectively like a single physical network. In the first case, each physical link is treated exactly like any other network in the internet. It is assigned a unique (usually class C) network number, and the two hosts that share the link each have a unique IP address assigned for their connection. Routes are added to the IP routing table as they would be for any other network. A new software module is added at the network interface layer to control the new link hardware, but no substantial changes are made to the layering scheme. The main disadvantage of the independent network approach is that it proliferates network numbers (one for each connection between two machines), causing routing tables to be larger than necessary. Both *Serial Line IP* (*SLIP*) and the *Point to Point Protocol* (*PPP*) treat each serial link as a separate network.

The second approach to accommodating point-to-point connections avoids assigning multiple IP addresses to the physical wires. Instead, it treats all the connections collectively as a single, independent IP network with its own frame format, hardware addressing scheme, and data link protocols. Routers that use the second approach need only one IP network number for all point-to-point connections.

Using the single network approach means extending the protocol layering scheme to add a new intranetwork routing layer between the network interface layer and the hardware devices. For machines with only one point-to-point connection, an additional layer seems unnecessary. To see why it is needed, consider a machine with several physical point-to-point connections, and recall from Figure 11.2 how the network interface layer is divided into multiple software modules that each control one network. We need to add one new network interface for the new point-to-point network, but the new interface must control multiple hardware devices. Furthermore, given a datagram to send, the new interface must choose the correct link over which the datagram should be sent. Figure 11.8 shows the organization.

The Internet layer software passes to the network interface all datagrams that should be sent out on any of the point-to-point connections. The interface passes them to the intranet routing module that must further distinguish among multiple physical connections and route the datagram across the correct one.

The programmer who designs the intranet routing software determines exactly how the software chooses a physical link. Usually, the algorithm relies on an intranet routing table. The intranet routing table is analogous to the internet routing table in that it specifies a mapping of destination address to route. The table contains pairs of entries, (D, L), where D is a destination host address and L specifies one of the physical lines used to reach that destination.

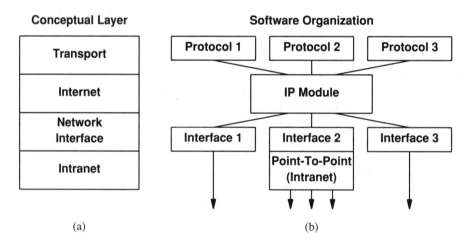

Figure 11.8 (a) conceptual position of an intranet protocol for point-to-point connections when IP treats them as a single IP network, and (b) detailed diagram of corresponding software modules. Each arrow corresponds to one physical device.

The difference between an internet routing table and an intranet routing table is that intranet routing tables are quite small. They only contain routing information for hosts directly attached to the point-to-point network. The reason is simple: the Internet layer maps an arbitrary destination address to a specific router address before passing the datagram to a network interface. Thus, the intranet layer is asked only to distinguish among machines on a single point-to-point network.

11.9 Two Important Boundaries In The TCP/IP Model

The conceptual protocol layering includes two boundaries that may not be obvious: a protocol address boundary that separates high-level and low-level addressing, and an operating system boundary that separates the system from application programs.

11.9.1 High-Level Protocol Address Boundary

Now that we have seen the layering of TCP/IP software, we can be precise about an idea introduced in Chapter 8: a conceptual boundary partitions software that uses low-level (physical) addresses from software that uses high-level (IP) addresses. As Figure 11.9 shows, the boundary occurs between the network interface layer and the Internet layer. That is,

Application programs as well as all protocol software from the Internet layer upward use only IP addresses; the network interface layer handles physical addresses.

Thus, protocols like ARP belong in the network interface layer. They are not part of IP.

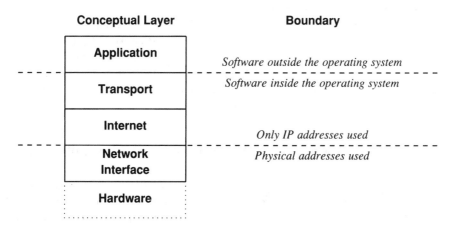

Figure 11.9 The relationship between conceptual layering and the boundaries for operating system and high-level protocol addresses.

11.9.2 Operating System Boundary

Figure 11.9 shows another important boundary as well, the division between software that is generally considered part of the operating system and software that is not. While each implementation of TCP/IP chooses how to make the distinction, many follow the scheme shown. Because they lie inside the operating system, passing data between lower layers of protocol software is much less expensive than passing it between an application program and a transport layer. Chapter 20 discusses the problem in more detail and describes an example of the interface an operating system might provide.

11.10 The Disadvantage Of Layering

We have said that layering is a fundamental idea that provides the basis for protocol design. It allows the designer to divide a complicated problem into subproblems and solve each one independently. Unfortunately, the software that results from strict layering can be extremely inefficient. As an example, consider the job of the transport layer. It must accept a stream of bytes from an application program, divide the stream into packets, and send each packet across the internet. To optimize transfer, the transport layer should choose the largest possible packet size that will allow one packet to travel in one network frame. In particular, if the destination machine attaches directly to one of the same networks as the source, only one physical net will be involved in the transfer, so the sender can optimize packet size for that network. If the software preserves strict layering, however, the transport layer cannot know how the Internet module will route traffic or which networks attach directly. Furthermore, the transport layer will not understand the datagram or frame formats nor will it be able to determine how many octets of header will be added to a packet. Thus, strict layering will prevent the transport layer from optimizing transfers.

Usually, implementors relax the strict layering scheme when building protocol software. They allow information like route selection and network MTU to propagate upward. When allocating buffers, they often leave space for headers that will be added by lower layer protocols and may retain headers on incoming frames when passing them to higher layer protocols. Such optimizations can make dramatic improvements in efficiency while retaining the basic layered structure.

11.11 The Basic Idea Behind Multiplexing And Demultiplexing

Communication protocols uses techniques of *multiplexing* and *demultiplexing* throughout the layered hierarchy. When sending a message, the source computer includes extra bits that encode the message type, originating program, and protocols used.

Eventually, all messages are placed into network frames for transfer and combined into a stream of packets. At the receiving end, the destination machine uses the extra information to guide processing.

Consider an example of demultiplexing shown in Figure 11.10.

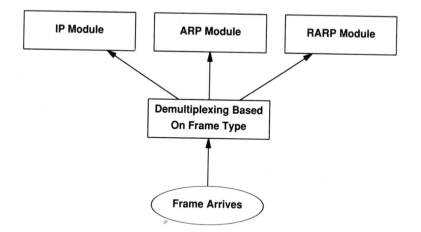

Figure 11.10 Demultiplexing of incoming frames based on the type field found in the frame header.

The figure illustrates how software in the network interface layer uses the frame type to choose a procedure that handles the incoming frame. We say that the network interface *demultiplexes* the frame based on its type. To make such a choice possible, software in the source machine must set the frame type field before transmission. Thus, each software module that sends frames uses the type field to specify frame contents.

Multiplexing and demultiplexing occur at almost every protocol layer. For example, after the network interface demultiplexes frames and passes those frames that contain IP datagrams to the IP module, the IP software extracts the datagram and demultiplexes further based on the transport protocol. Figure 11.11 demonstrates demultiplexing at the Internet layer.

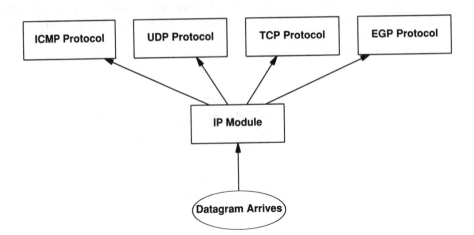

Figure 11.11 Demultiplexing at the Internet layer. IP software chooses an appropriate procedure to handle a datagram based on the protocol type field in the datagram header.

To decide how to handle a datagram, internet software examines the header of a datagram and selects a protocol handler based on the datagram type. In the example, the possible datagram types are: *ICMP*, which we have already examined, and *UDP*, *TCP*, and *EGP*, which we will examine in later chapters.

11.12 Summary

Protocols are the standards that specify how data is represented when being transferred from one machine to another. Protocols specify how the transfer occurs, how errors are detected, and how acknowledgements are passed. To simplify protocol design and implementation, communication problems are segregated into subproblems that can be solved independently. Each subproblem is assigned a separate protocol.

The idea of layering is fundamental because it provides a conceptual framework for protocol design. In a layered model, each layer handles one part of the communication problem and usually corresponds to one protocol. Protocols follow the layering principle, which states that the software implementing layer *n* on the destination machine receives exactly what the software implementing layer *n* on the source machine sends.

We examined the 4-layer Internet reference model as well as the ISO 7-layer reference model. In both cases, the layering model provides only a conceptual framework for protocol software. The ITU-TS X.25 protocols follow the ISO reference model and provide an example of reliable communication service offered by a commercial utility, while the TCP/IP protocols provide an example of a different layering scheme.

In practice, protocol software uses multiplexing and demultiplexing to distinguish among multiple protocols within a given layer, making protocol software more complex than the layering model suggests.

FOR FURTHER STUDY

Postel [RFC 791] provides a sketch of the Internet Protocol layering scheme, and Clark [RFC 817] discusses the effect of layering on implementations. Saltzer, Reed, and Clark [1984] argues that end-to-end verification is important. Chesson [1987] makes the controversial argument that layering produces intolerably bad network throughput. Volume 2 of this text examines layering in detail, and shows an example implementation that achieves efficiency by compromising strict layering and passing pointers between layers.

The ISO protocol documents [1987a] and [1987b] describe ASN.1 in detail. Sun [RFC 1014] describes XDR, an example of what might be called a TCP/IP presentation protocol. Clark discusses passing information upward through layers [Clark 1985].

EXERCISES

11.1   Study the ISO layering model in more detail. How well does the model describe communication on a local area network like an Ethernet?

11.2   Build a case that TCP/IP is moving toward a five-level protocol architecture that includes a presentation layer. (Hint: various programs use the XDR protocol, Courier, and ASN.1.)

11.3   Do you think any single presentation protocol will eventually emerge that replaces all others? Why or why not?

11.4   Compare and contrast the tagged data format used by the ASN.1 presentation scheme with the untagged format used by XDR. Characterize situations in which one is better than the other.

11.5   Find out how UNIX systems uses the *mbuf* structure to make layered protocol software efficient.

11.6   Read about the System V UNIX *streams* mechanism. How does it help make protocol implementation easier? What is its chief disadvantage?

12

User Datagram Protocol
(UDP)

12.1 Introduction

Previous chapters describe a TCP/IP internet capable of transferring IP datagrams among host computers, where each datagram is routed through the internet based on the destination's IP address. At the Internet Protocol layer, a destination address identifies a host computer; no further distinction is made regarding which user or which application program will receive the datagram. This chapter extends the TCP/IP protocol suite by adding a mechanism that distinguishes among multiple destinations within a given host, allowing multiple application programs executing on a given computer to send and receive datagrams independently.

12.2 Identifying The Ultimate Destination

The operating systems in most computers support multiprogramming, which means they permit multiple application programs to execute simultaneously. Using operating system jargon, we refer to each executing program as a *process*, *task*, *application program*, or a *user level process*; the systems are called multitasking systems. It may seem natural to say that a process is the ultimate destination for a message. However, specifying that a particular process on a particular machine is the ultimate destination for a datagram is somewhat misleading. First, because processes are created and destroyed dynamically, senders seldom know enough to identify a process on another machine. Second, we would like to be able to replace processes that receive datagrams without informing all senders (e.g., rebooting a machine can change all the processes, but senders should not be required to know about the new processes). Third, we need to identify destinations from the functions they implement without knowing the process that implements the function (e.g., to allow a sender to contact a file server without knowing which process on the destination machine implements the file server function). More important, in systems that allow a single process to handle two or more functions, it is essential that we arrange a way for a process to decide exactly which function the sender desires.

Instead of thinking of a process as the ultimate destination, we will imagine that each machine contains a set of abstract destination points called *protocol ports*. Each protocol port is identified by a positive integer. The local operating system provides an interface mechanism that processes use to specify a port or access it.

Most operating systems provide synchronous access to ports. From a particular process' point of view, synchronous access means the computation stops during a port access operation. For example, if a process attempts to extract data from a port before any data arrives, the operating system temporarily stops (blocks) the process until data arrives. Once the data arrives, the operating system passes the data to the process and restarts it. In general, ports are *buffered*, so data that arrives before a process is ready to accept it will not be lost. To achieve buffering, the protocol software located inside the operating system places packets that arrive for a particular protocol port in a (finite) queue until a process extracts them.

To communicate with a foreign port, a sender needs to know both the IP address of the destination machine and the protocol port number of the destination within that machine. Each message must carry the number of the *destination port* on the machine to which the message is sent, as well as the *source port* number on the source machine to which replies should be addressed. Thus, it is possible for any process that receives a message to reply to the sender.

12.3 The User Datagram Protocol

In the TCP/IP protocol suite, the *User Datagram Protocol* or *UDP* provides the primary mechanism that application programs use to send datagrams to other application programs. UDP provides protocol ports used to distinguish among multiple programs executing on a single machine. That is, in addition to the data sent, each UDP message contains both a destination port number and a source port number, making it possible for the UDP software at the destination to deliver the message to the correct recipient and for the recipient to send a reply.

UDP uses the underlying Internet Protocol to transport a message from one machine to another, and provides the same unreliable, connectionless datagram delivery semantics as IP. It does not use acknowledgements to make sure messages arrive, it does not order incoming messages, and it does not provide feedback to control the rate at which information flows between the machines. Thus, UDP messages can be lost, duplicated, or arrive out of order. Furthermore, packets can arrive faster than the recipient can process them. We can summarize:

> *The User Datagram Protocol (UDP) provides an unreliable connec-*
> *tionless delivery service using IP to transport messages between*
> *machines. It uses IP to carry messages, but adds the ability to distin-*
> *guish among multiple destinations within a given host computer.*

An application program that uses UDP accepts full responsibility for handling the problem of reliability, including message loss, duplication, delay, out-of-order delivery, and loss of connectivity. Unfortunately, application programmers often ignore these problems when designing software. Furthermore, because programmers often test network software using highly reliable, low-delay local area networks, testing may not expose potential failures. Thus, many application programs that rely on UDP work well in a local environment but fail in dramatic ways when used in a larger TCP/IP internet.

12.4 Format Of UDP Messages

Each UDP message is called a *user datagram*. Conceptually, a user datagram consists of two parts: a UDP header and a UDP data area. As Figure 12.1 shows, the header is divided into four 16-bit fields that specify the port from which the message was sent, the port to which the message is destined, the message length, and a UDP checksum.

```
0                              16                             31
+------------------------------+------------------------------+
|      UDP SOURCE PORT         |    UDP DESTINATION PORT      |
+------------------------------+------------------------------+
|     UDP MESSAGE LENGTH       |       UDP CHECKSUM           |
+------------------------------+------------------------------+
|                          DATA                               |
+-------------------------------------------------------------+
|                          . . .                              |
+-------------------------------------------------------------+
```

Figure 12.1   The format of fields in a UDP datagram.

The *SOURCE PORT* and *DESTINATION PORT* fields contain the 16-bit UDP protocol port numbers used to demultiplex datagrams among the processes waiting to receive them. The *SOURCE PORT* is optional. When used, it specifies the port to which replies should be sent; if not used, it should be zero.

The *LENGTH* field contains a count of octets in the UDP datagram, including the UDP header and the user data. Thus, the minimum value for *LENGTH* is eight, the length of the header alone.

The UDP checksum is optional and need not be used at all; a value of zero in the *CHECKSUM* field means that the checksum has not been computed. The designers chose to make the checksum optional to allow implementations to operate with little computational overhead when using UDP across a highly reliable local area network. Recall, however, that IP does not compute a checksum on the data portion of an IP datagram. Thus, the UDP checksum provides the only way to guarantee that data has arrived intact and should be used.

Beginners often wonder what happens to UDP messages for which the computed checksum is zero. A computed value of zero is possible because UDP uses the same checksum algorithm as IP: it divides the data into 16-bit quantities and computes the one's complement of their one's complement sum. Surprisingly, zero is not a problem because one's complement arithmetic has two representations for zero: all bits set to zero or all bits set to one. When the computed checksum is zero, UDP uses the representation with all bits set to one.

12.5 UDP Pseudo-Header

The UDP checksum covers more information than is present in the UDP datagram alone. To compute the checksum, UDP prepends a *pseudo-header* to the UDP datagram, appends an octet of zeros to pad the datagram to an exact multiple of 16 bits, and computes the checksum over the entire object. The octet used for padding and the pseudo-header are *not* transmitted with the UDP datagram, nor are they included in the length. To compute a checksum, the software first stores zero in the *CHECKSUM* field, then accumulates a 16-bit one's complement sum of the entire object, including the pseudo-header, UDP header, and user data.

The purpose of using a pseudo-header is to verify that the UDP datagram has reached its correct destination. The key to understanding the pseudo-header lies in realizing that the correct destination consists of a specific machine and a specific protocol port within that machine. The UDP header itself specifies only the protocol port number. Thus, to verify the destination, UDP on the sending machine computes a checksum that covers the destination IP address as well as the UDP datagram. At the ultimate destination, UDP software verifies the checksum using the destination IP address obtained from the header of the IP datagram that carried the UDP message. If the checksums agree, then it must be true that the datagram has reached the intended destination host as well as the correct protocol port within that host.

The pseudo-header used in the UDP checksum computation consists of 12 octets of data arranged as Figure 12.2 shows. The fields of the pseudo-header labeled *SOURCE IP ADDRESS* and *DESTINATION IP ADDRESS* contain the source and destination IP addresses that will be used when sending the UDP message. Field *PROTO* contains the IP protocol type code (*17* for UDP), and the field labeled *UDP LENGTH* contains the length of the UDP datagram (not including the pseudo-header). To verify the checksum, the receiver must extract these fields from the IP header, assemble them into the pseudo-header format, and recompute the checksum.

0	8	16	31
SOURCE IP ADDRESS			
DESTINATION IP ADDRESS			
ZERO	PROTO	UDP LENGTH	

Figure 12.2 The 12 octets of the pseudo-header used during UDP checksum computation.

12.6 UDP Encapsulation And Protocol Layering

UDP provides our first example of a transport protocol. In the layering model of Chapter 11, UDP lies in the layer above the Internet Protocol layer. Conceptually, application programs access UDP, which uses IP to send and receive datagrams as Figure 12.3 shows.

Conceptual Layering

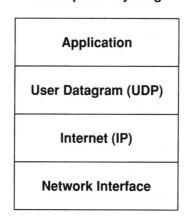

Figure 12.3 The conceptual layering of UDP between application programs and IP.

Layering UDP above IP means that a complete UDP message, including the UDP header and data, is encapsulated in an IP datagram as it travels across an internet as Figure 12.4 shows.

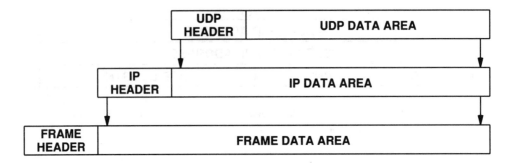

Figure 12.4 A UDP datagram encapsulated in an IP datagram for transmission across an internet. The datagram is further encapsulated in a frame each time it travels across a single network.

For the protocols we have examined, encapsulation means that UDP prepends a header to the data that a user sends and passes it to IP. The IP layer prepends a header to what it receives from UDP. Finally, the network interface layer embeds the datagram in a frame before sending it from one machine to another. The format of the frame depends on the underlying network technology. Usually, network frames include an additional header.

On input, a packet arrives at the lowest layer of network software and begins its ascent through successively higher layers. Each layer removes one header before passing the message on, so that by the time the highest level passes data to the receiving process, all headers have been removed. Thus, the outermost header corresponds to the lowest layer of protocol, while the innermost header corresponds to the highest protocol layer. When considering how headers are inserted and removed, it is important to keep in mind the layering principle. In particular, observe that the layering principle applies to UDP, so the UDP datagram received from IP on the destination machine is identical to the datagram that UDP passed to IP on the source machine. Also, the data that UDP delivers to a user process on the receiving machine will be exactly the data that a user process passed to UDP on the sending machine.

The division of duties among various protocol layers is rigid and clear:

> *The IP layer is responsible only for transferring data between a pair of hosts on an internet, while the UDP layer is responsible only for differentiating among multiple sources or destinations within one host.*

Thus, only the IP header identifies the source and destination hosts; only the UDP layer identifies the source or destination ports within a host.

12.7 Layering And The UDP Checksum Computation

Observant readers will have noticed a seeming contradiction between the layering rules and the UDP checksum computation. Recall that the UDP checksum includes a pseudo-header that has fields for the source and destination IP address. It can be argued that the destination IP address must be known to the user when sending a UDP datagram, and the user must pass it to the UDP layer. Thus, the UDP layer can obtain the destination IP address without interacting with the IP layer. However, the source IP address depends on the route IP chooses for the datagram, because the IP source address identifies the network interface over which the datagram is transmitted. Thus, UDP cannot know a source IP address unless it interacts with the IP layer.

We assume that UDP software asks the IP layer to compute the source and (possibly) destination IP addresses, uses them to construct a pseudo-header, computes the checksum, discards the pseudo-header, and then passes the UDP datagram to IP for transmission. An alternative approach that produces greater efficiency arranges to have the UDP layer encapsulate the UDP datagram in an IP datagram, obtain the source address from IP, store the source and destination addresses in the appropriate fields of the datagram header, compute the UDP checksum, and then pass the IP datagram to the IP layer, which only needs to fill in the remaining IP header fields.

Does the strong interaction between UDP and IP violate our basic premise that layering reflects separation of functionality? Yes. UDP has been tightly integrated with the IP protocol. It is clearly a compromise of the pure separation, made for entirely practical reasons. We are willing to overlook the layering violation because it is impossible to fully identify a destination application program without specifying the destination machine, and we want to make the mapping between addresses used by UDP and those used by IP efficient. One of the exercises examines this issue from a different point of view, asking the reader to consider whether UDP should be separated from IP.

12.8 UDP Multiplexing, Demultiplexing, And Ports

We have seen in Chapter 11 that software throughout the layers of a protocol hierarchy must multiplex or demultiplex among multiple objects at the next layer. UDP software provides another example of multiplexing and demultiplexing. It accepts UDP datagrams from many application programs and passes them to IP for transmission, and it accepts arriving UDP datagrams from IP and passes them to the appropriate application program.

Conceptually, all multiplexing and demultiplexing between UDP software and application programs occur through the port mechanism. In practice, each application program must negotiate with the operating system to obtain a protocol port and an associated port number before it can send a UDP datagram†. Once the port has been assigned, any datagram the application program sends through the port will have that port number in its UDP *SOURCE PORT* field.

---

†For now, we will describe ports abstractly; Chapter 20 provides an example of the operating system primitives used to create and use ports.

While processing input, UDP accepts incoming datagrams from the IP software and demultiplexes based on the UDP destination port, as Figure 12.5 shows.

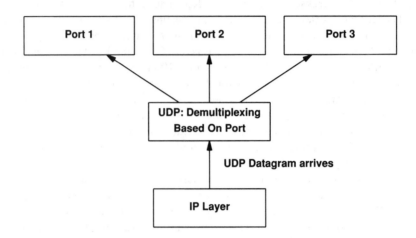

Figure 12.5 Example of demultiplexing one layer above IP. UDP uses the
UDP destination port number to select an appropriate destination
port for incoming datagrams.

The easiest way to think of a UDP port is as a queue. In most implementations, when an application program negotiates with the operating system to use a given port, the operating system creates an internal queue that can hold arriving messages. Often, the application can specify or change the queue size. When UDP receives a datagram, it checks to see that the destination port number matches one of the ports currently in use. If not, it sends an ICMP *port unreachable* error message and discards the datagram. If a match is found, UDP enqueues the new datagram at the port where an application program can access it. Of course, an error occurs if the port is full, and UDP discards the incoming datagram.

12.9 Reserved And Available UDP Port Numbers

How should protocol port numbers be assigned? The problem is important because two computers need to agree on port numbers before they can interoperate. For example, when computer *A* wants to obtain a file from computer *B*, it needs to know what port the file transfer program on computer *B* uses. There are two fundamental approaches to port assignment. The first approach uses a central authority. Everyone agrees to allow a central authority to assign port numbers as needed and to publish the list of all assignments. Then all software is built according to the list. This approach is sometimes called *universal assignment* and the port assignments specified by the authority are called *well-known port assignments*.

The second approach to port assignment uses dynamic binding. In the dynamic binding approach, ports are not globally known. Instead, whenever a program needs a port, the network software assigns one. To learn about the current port assignment on another computer, it is necessary to send a request that asks a question like, "What port is the file transfer service using." The target machine replies by giving the correct port number to use.

The TCP/IP designers adopted a hybrid approach that assigns some port numbers a priori, but leaves many available for local sites or application programs. The assigned port numbers begin at low values and extend upward, leaving large integer values available for dynamic assignment. The table in Figure 12.6 lists some of the currently assigned UDP port numbers. The second column contains Internet standard assigned keywords, while the third contains keywords used on most UNIX systems.

Decimal	Keyword	UNIX Keyword	Description
0	-	-	Reserved
7	ECHO	echo	Echo
9	DISCARD	discard	Discard
11	USERS	systat	Active Users
13	DAYTIME	daytime	Daytime
15	-	netstat	Who is up or NETSTAT
17	QUOTE	qotd	Quote of the Day
19	CHARGEN	chargen	Character Generator
37	TIME	time	Time
42	NAMESERVER	name	Host Name Server
43	NICNAME	whois	Who Is
53	DOMAIN	nameserver	Domain Name Server
67	BOOTPS	bootps	Bootstrap Protocol Server
68	BOOTPC	bootpc	Bootstrap Protocol Client
69	TFTP	tftp	Trivial File Transfer
111	SUNRPC	sunrpc	Sun Microsystems RPC
123	NTP	ntp	Network Time Protocol
161	-	snmp	SNMP net monitor
162	-	snmp-trap	SNMP traps
512	-	biff	UNIX comsat
513	-	who	UNIX rwho daemon
514	-	syslog	system log
525	-	timed	Time daemon

Figure 12.6 An illustrative sample of currently assigned UDP ports showing the standard keyword and the UNIX equivalent; the list is not exhaustive. To the extent possible, other transport protocols that offer identical services use the same port numbers as UDP.

12.10 Summary

Most computer systems permit multiple application programs to execute simultaneously. Using operating system jargon, we refer to each executing program as a *process*.
The User Datagram Protocol, UDP, distinguishes among multiple processes within a
given machine by allowing senders and receivers to add two 16-bit integers called protocol port numbers to each UDP message. The port numbers identify the source and
destination. Some UDP port numbers, called *well known*, are permanently assigned and
honored throughout the Internet (e.g., port *69* is reserved for use by the trivial file
transfer protocol *TFTP* described in Chapter 24). Other port numbers are available for
arbitrary application programs to use.

UDP is a thin protocol in the sense that it does not add significantly to the semantics of IP. It merely provides application programs with the ability to communicate using the unreliable connectionless packet delivery service. Thus, UDP messages can be
lost, duplicated, delayed, or delivered out of order; the application program using UDP
must handle these problems. Many programs that use UDP do not work correctly
across an internet because they fail to accommodate these conditions.

In the protocol layering scheme, UDP lies in the transport layer, above the Internet
Protocol layer and below the application layer. Conceptually, the transport layer is independent of the Internet layer, but in practice they interact strongly. The UDP checksum includes IP source and destination addresses, meaning that UDP software must interact with IP software to find addresses before sending datagrams.

FOR FURTHER STUDY

Tanenbaum [1981] contains a tutorial comparison of the datagram and virtual circuit models of communication. Ball *et. al.* [1979] describes message-based systems
without discussing the message protocol. The UDP protocol described here is a standard for TCP/IP and is defined by Postel [RFC 768].

EXERCISES

12.1   Try UDP in your local environment. Measure the average transfer speed with messages
        of 256, 512, 1024, 2048, 4096, and 8192 bytes. Can you explain the results (hint: what
        is your network MTU)?

12.2   Why is the UDP checksum separate from the IP checksum? Would you object to a pro-
        tocol that used a single checksum for the complete IP datagram including the UDP mes-
        sage?

12.3   Not using checksums can be dangerous. Explain how a single corrupted ARP packet
        broadcast by machine P can make it impossible to reach another machine, Q.

12.4   Should the notion of multiple destinations identified by protocol ports have been built into IP? Why, or why not?

12.5   *Name Registry.* Suppose you want to allow arbitrary pairs of application programs to establish communication with UDP, but you do not wish to assign them fixed UDP port numbers. Instead, you would like potential correspondents to be identified by a character string of 64 or fewer characters. Thus, a program on machine *A* might want to communicate with the "funny-special-long-id" program on machine *B* (you can assume that a process always knows the IP address of the host with which it wants to communicate). Meanwhile, a process on machine *C* wants to communicate with the "comer's-own-program-id" on machine *A*. Show that you only need to assign one UDP port to make such communication possible by designing software on each machine that allows (a) a local process to pick an unused UDP port ID over which it will communicate, (b) a local process to register the 64-character name to which it responds, and (c) a foreign process to use UDP to establish communication using only the 64-character name and destination internet address.

12.6   Implement name registry software from the previous exercise.

12.7   What is the chief advantage of using preassigned UDP port numbers? The chief disadvantage?

12.8   What is the chief advantage of using protocol ports instead of process identifiers to specify the destination within a machine?

12.9   UDP provides unreliable datagram communication because it does not guarantee delivery of the message. Devise a reliable datagram protocol that uses timeouts and acknowledgements to guarantee delivery. How much network overhead and delay does reliability introduce?

12.10 Send UDP datagrams across a wide area network and measure the percentage lost and the percentage reordered. Does the result depend on the time of day? The network load?

13

Reliable Stream Transport Service (TCP)

13.1 Introduction

Previous chapters explore the unreliable connectionless packet delivery service that forms the basis for all internet communication and the IP protocol that defines it. This chapter introduces the second most important and well-known network-level service, reliable stream delivery, and the *Transmission Control Protocol* (*TCP*) that defines it. We will see that TCP adds substantial functionality to the protocols already discussed, but that its implementation is also substantially more complex.

Although TCP is presented here as part of the TCP/IP Internet protocol suite, it is an independent, general purpose protocol that can be adapted for use with other delivery systems. For example, because TCP makes very few assumptions about the underlying network, it is possible to use it over a single network like an Ethernet, as well as over a complex internet. In fact, TCP has been so popular that one of the International Organization for Standardization's open systems protocols, TP-4, has been derived from it.

13.2 The Need For Stream Delivery

At the lowest level, computer communication networks provide unreliable packet delivery. Packets can be lost or destroyed when transmission errors interfere with data, when network hardware fails, or when networks become too heavily loaded to accommodate the load presented. Networks that route packets dynamically can deliver them out of order, deliver them after a substantial delay, or deliver duplicates. Furthermore,

191

underlying network technologies may dictate an optimal packet size or pose other constraints needed to achieve efficient transfer rates.

At the highest level, application programs often need to send large volumes of data from one computer to another. Using an unreliable connectionless delivery system for large volume transfers becomes tedious and annoying, and it requires programmers to build error detection and recovery into each application program. Because it is difficult to design, understand, or modify software that correctly provides reliability, few application programmers have the necessary technical background. As a consequence, one goal of network protocol research has been to find general purpose solutions to the problems of providing reliable stream delivery, making it possible for experts to build a single instance of stream protocol software that all application programs use. Having a single general purpose protocol helps isolate application programs from the details of networking, and makes it possible to define a uniform interface for the stream transfer service.

13.3 Properties Of The Reliable Delivery Service

The interface between application programs and the TCP/IP reliable delivery service can be characterized by 5 features:

• *Stream Orientation*. When two application programs (user processes) transfer large volumes of data, we think of the data as a *stream* of bits, divided into 8-bit *octets*, which are informally called *bytes*. The stream delivery service on the destination machine passes to the receiver exactly the same sequence of octets that the sender passes to it on the source machine.

• *Virtual Circuit Connection*. Making a stream transfer is analogous to placing a telephone call. Before transfer can start, both the sending and receiving application programs interact with their respective operating systems, informing them of the desire for a stream transfer. Conceptually, one application places a "call" which must be accepted by the other. Protocol software modules in the two operating systems communicate by sending messages across an internet, verifying that the transfer is authorized, and that both sides are ready. Once all details have been settled, the protocol modules inform the application programs that a *connection* has been established and that transfer can begin. During transfer, protocol software on the two machines continue to communicate to verify that data is received correctly. If the communication fails for any reason (e.g., because network hardware along the path between the machines fails), both machines detect the failure and report it to the appropriate application programs. We use the term *virtual circuit* to describe such connections because although application programs view the connection as a dedicated hardware circuit, the reliability is an illusion provided by the stream delivery service.

• *Buffered Transfer*. Application programs send a data stream across the virtual circuit by repeatedly passing data octets to the protocol software. When transferring data, each application uses whatever size pieces it finds convenient, which can be as small as a single octet. At the receiving end, the protocol software delivers octets from the data stream in exactly the same order they were sent, making them available to the receiving application program as soon as they have been received and verified. The protocol software is free to divide the stream into packets independent of the pieces the application program transfers. To make transfer more efficient and to minimize network traffic, implementations usually collect enough data from a stream to fill a reasonably large datagram before transmitting it across an internet. Thus, even if the application program generates the stream one octet at a time, transfer across an internet may be quite efficient. Similarly, if the application program chooses to generate extremely large blocks of data, the protocol software can choose to divide each block into smaller pieces for transmission.

For those applications where data should be delivered even though it does not fill a buffer, the stream service provides a *push* mechanism that applications use to force a transfer. At the sending side, a push forces protocol software to transfer all data that has been generated without waiting to fill a buffer. When it reaches the receiving side, the push causes TCP to make the data available to the application without delay. The reader should note, however, that the push function only guarantees that all data will be transferred; it does not provide record boundaries. Thus, even when delivery is forced, the protocol software may choose to divide the stream in unexpected ways.

• *Unstructured Stream.* It is important to understand that the TCP/IP stream service does not honor structured data streams. For example, there is no way for a payroll application to have the stream service mark boundaries between employee records, or to identify the contents of the stream as being payroll data. Application programs using the stream service must understand stream content and agree on stream format before they initiate a connection.

• *Full Duplex Connection.* Connections provided by the TCP/IP stream service allow concurrent transfer in both directions. Such connections are called *full duplex*. From the point of view of an application process, a full duplex connection consists of two independent streams flowing in opposite directions, with no apparent interaction. The stream service allows an application process to terminate flow in one direction while data continues to flow in the other direction, making the connection *half duplex*. The advantage of a full duplex connection is that the underlying protocol software can send control information for one stream back to the source in datagrams carrying data in the opposite direction. Such *piggybacking* reduces network traffic.

13.4 Providing Reliability

We have said that the reliable stream delivery service guarantees to deliver a stream of data sent from one machine to another without duplication or data loss. The question arises: "How can protocol software provide reliable transfer if the underlying communication system offers only unreliable packet delivery?" The answer is complicated, but most reliable protocols use a single fundamental technique known as *positive acknowledgement with retransmission*. The technique requires a recipient to communicate with the source, sending back an *acknowledgement* (*ACK*) message as it receives data. The sender keeps a record of each packet it sends and waits for an acknowledgement before sending the next packet. The sender also starts a timer when it sends a packet and *retransmits* a packet if the timer expires before an acknowledgement arrives.

Figure 13.1 shows how the simplest positive acknowledgement protocol transfers data.

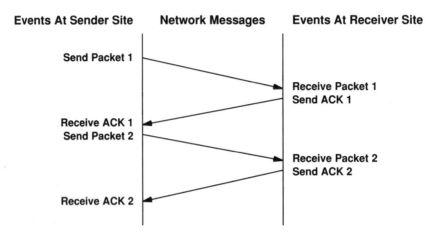

Figure 13.1 A protocol using positive acknowledgement with retransmission in which the sender awaits an acknowledgement for each packet sent. Vertical distance down the figure represents increasing time and diagonal lines across the middle represent network packet transmission.

In the figure, events at the sender and receiver are shown on the left and right. Each diagonal line crossing the middle shows the transfer of one message across the network.

Figure 13.2 uses the same format diagram as Figure 13.1 to show what happens when a packet is lost or corrupted. The sender starts a timer after transmitting a packet. When the timer expires, the sender assumes the packet was lost and retransmits it.

The final reliability problem arises when an underlying packet delivery system duplicates packets. Duplicates can also arise when networks experience high delays that cause premature retransmission. Solving duplication requires careful thought because both packets and acknowledgements can be duplicated. Usually, reliable protocols detect duplicate packets by assigning each packet a sequence number and requiring the receiver to remember which sequence numbers it has received. To avoid confusion caused by delayed or duplicated acknowledgements, positive acknowledgement protocols send sequence numbers back in acknowledgements, so the receiver can correctly associate acknowledgements with packets.

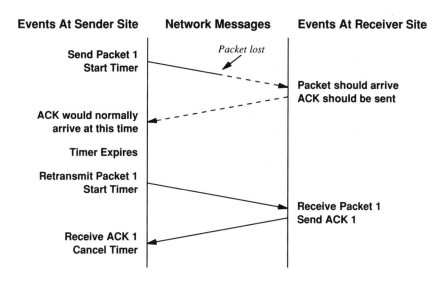

Figure 13.2 Timeout and retransmission that occurs when a packet is lost. The dotted lines show the time that would be taken by the transmission of a packet and its acknowledgement, if the packet was not lost.

13.5 The Idea Behind Sliding Windows

Before examining the TCP stream service, we need to explore an additional concept that underlies stream transmission. The concept, known as a *sliding window*, makes stream transmission efficient. To understand the motivation for sliding windows, recall the sequence of events that Figure 13.1 depicts. To achieve reliability, the sender transmits a packet and then waits for an acknowledgement before transmitting another. As Figure 13.1 shows, data only flows between the machines in one direction at any time, even if the network is capable of simultaneous communication in both directions. The network will be completely idle during times that machines delay responses (e.g., while machines compute routes or checksums). If we imagine a network with high transmission delays, the problem becomes clear:

> *A simple positive acknowledgement protocol wastes a substantial amount of network bandwidth because it must delay sending a new packet until it receives an acknowledgement for the previous packet.*

The sliding window technique is a more complex form of positive acknowledgement and retransmission than the simple method discussed above. Sliding window protocols use network bandwidth better because they allow the sender to transmit multiple packets before waiting for an acknowledgement. The easiest way to envision sliding window operation is to think of a sequence of packets to be transmitted as Figure 13.3 shows. The protocol places a small, fixed-size *window* on the sequence and transmits all packets that lie inside the window.

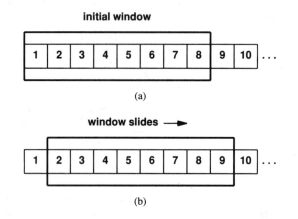

Figure 13.3 (a) A sliding window protocol with eight packets in the window, and (b) The window sliding so that packet *9* can be sent when an acknowledgement has been received for packet *1*. Only unacknowledged packets are retransmitted.

We say that a packet is *unacknowledged* if it has been transmitted but no acknowledgement has been received. Technically, the number of packets that can be unacknowledged at any given time is constrained by the *window size* and is limited to a small, fixed number. For example, in a sliding window protocol with window size *8*, the sender is permitted to transmit *8* packets before it receives an acknowledgement.

As Figure 13.3 shows, once the sender receives an acknowledgement for the first packet inside the window, it ''slides'' the window along and sends the next packet. The window continues to slide as long as acknowledgements are received.

The performance of sliding window protocols depends on the window size and the speed at which the network accepts packets. Figure 13.4 shows an example of the operation of a sliding window protocol when sending three packets. Note that the sender transmits all three packets before receiving any acknowledgements.

With a window size of *1*, a sliding window protocol is exactly the same as our simple positive acknowledgement protocol. By increasing the window size, it is possible to eliminate network idle time completely. That is, in the steady state, the sender can transmit packets as fast as the network can transfer them. The main point is:

*Because a well tuned sliding window protocol keeps the network com-
pletely saturated with packets, it obtains substantially higher
throughput than a simple positive acknowledgement protocol.*

Conceptually, a sliding window protocol always remembers which packets have
been acknowledged and keeps a separate timer for each unacknowledged packet. If a
packet is lost, the timer expires and the sender retransmits that packet. When the sender
slides its window, it moves past all acknowledged packets. At the receiving end, the
protocol software keeps an analogous window, accepting and acknowledging packets as
they arrive. Thus, the window partitions the sequence of packets into three sets: those
packets to the left of the window have been successfully transmitted, received, and acknowledged; those packets to the right have not yet been transmitted; and those packets
that lie in the window are being transmitted. The lowest numbered packet in the window is the first packet in the sequence that has not been acknowledged.

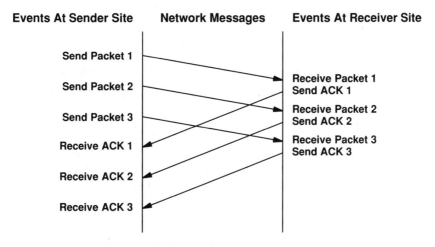

Figure 13.4 An example of three packets transmitted using a sliding window
protocol. The key concept is that the sender can transmit all
packets in the window without waiting for an acknowledgement.

13.6 The Transmission Control Protocol

Now that we understand the principle of sliding windows, we can examine the reliable stream service provided by the TCP/IP Internet protocol suite. The service is defined by the *Transmission Control Protocol*, or *TCP*. The reliable stream service is so important that the entire protocol suite is referred to as TCP/IP. It is important to understand that:

TCP is a communication protocol, not a piece of software.

The difference between a protocol and the software that implements it is analogous to the difference between the definition of a programming language and a compiler. As in the programming language world, the distinction between definition and implementation sometimes becomes blurred. People encounter TCP software much more frequently than they encounter the protocol specification, so it is natural to think of a particular implementation as the standard. Nevertheless, the reader should try to distinguish between the two.

Exactly what does TCP provide? TCP is complex, so there is no simple answer. The protocol specifies the format of the data and acknowledgements that two computers exchange to achieve a reliable transfer, as well as the procedures the computers use to ensure that the data arrives correctly. It specifies how TCP software distinguishes among multiple destinations on a given machine, and how communicating machines recover from errors like lost or duplicated packets. The protocol also specifies how two computers initiate a TCP stream transfer and how they agree when it is complete.

It is also important to understand what the protocol does not include. Although the TCP specification describes how application programs use TCP in general terms, it does not dictate the details of the interface between an application program and TCP. That is, the protocol documentation only discusses the operations TCP supplies; it does not specify the exact procedures application programs invoke to access these operations. The reason for leaving the application program interface unspecified is flexibility. In particular, because programmers usually implement TCP in the computer's operating system, they need to employ whatever interface the operating system supplies. Allowing the implementor flexibility makes it possible to have a single specification for TCP that can be used to build software for a variety of machines.

Because TCP assumes little about the underlying communication system, TCP can be used with a variety of packet delivery systems, including the IP datagram delivery service. For example, TCP can be implemented to use dialup telephone lines, a local area network, a high speed fiber optic network, or a lower speed long haul network. In fact, the large variety of delivery systems TCP can use is one of its strengths.

13.7 Ports, Connections, And Endpoints

Like the User Datagram Protocol (UDP) presented in Chapter 12, TCP resides above IP in the protocol layering scheme. Figure 13.5 shows the conceptual organization. TCP allows multiple application programs on a given machine to communicate concurrently, and it demultiplexes incoming TCP traffic among application programs. Like the User Datagram Protocol, TCP uses *protocol port* numbers to identify the ultimate destination within a machine. Each port is assigned a small integer used to identify it†.

Conceptual Layering

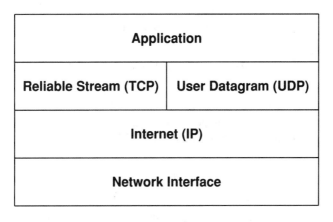

Figure 13.5 The conceptual layering of UDP and TCP above IP. TCP provides a reliable stream service, while UDP provides an unreliable datagram delivery service. Application programs use both.

When we discussed UDP ports, we said to think of each port as a queue into which protocol software places arriving datagrams. TCP ports are much more complex because a given port number does not correspond to a single object. Instead, TCP has been built on the *connection abstraction*, in which the objects to be identified are virtual circuit connections, not individual ports. Understanding that TCP uses the notion of connections is crucial because it helps explain the meaning and use of TCP port numbers:

TCP uses the connection, not the protocol port, as its fundamental abstraction; connections are identified by a pair of endpoints.

---

†Although both TCP and UDP use integer port identifiers starting at *1* to identify ports, there is no confusion between them because an incoming IP datagram identifies the protocol being used as well as the port number.

Exactly what are the "endpoints" of a connection? We have said that a connection consists of a virtual circuit between two application programs, so it might be natural to assume that an application program serves as the connection "endpoint." It is not. Instead, TCP defines an *endpoint* to be a pair of integers (*host, port*), where *host* is the IP address for a host and *port* is a TCP port on that host. For example, the endpoint (*128.10.2.3, 25*) specifies TCP port *25* on the machine with IP address *128.10.2.3*.

Now that we have defined endpoints, it will be easy to understand connections. Recall that a connection is defined by its two endpoints. Thus, if there is a connection from machine (*18.26.0.36*) at MIT to machine (*128.10.2.3*) at Purdue University, it might be defined by the endpoints:

(*18.26.0.36, 1069*) and (*128.10.2.3, 25*).

Meanwhile, another connection might be in progress from machine (*128.9.0.32*) at the Information Sciences Institute to the same machine at Purdue, identified by its endpoints:

(*128.9.0.32, 1184*) and (*128.10.2.3, 53*).

So far, our examples of connections have been straightforward because the ports used at all endpoints have been unique. However, the connection abstraction allows multiple connections to share an endpoint. For example, we could add another connection to the two listed above from machine (*128.2.254.139*) at CMU to the machine at Purdue:

(*128.2.254.139, 1184*) and (*128.10.2.3, 53*).

It might seem strange that two connections can use the TCP port *53* on machine 128.10.2.3 simultaneously, but there is no ambiguity. Because TCP associates incoming messages with a connection instead of a protocol port, it uses both endpoints to identify the appropriate connection. The important idea to remember is:

> *Because TCP identifies a connection by a pair of endpoints, a given TCP port number can be shared by multiple connections on the same machine.*

From a programmer's point of view, the connection abstraction is significant. It means a programmer can devise a program that provides concurrent service to multiple connections simultaneously without needing unique local port numbers for each connection. For example, most systems provide concurrent access to their electronic mail service, allowing multiple computers to send them electronic mail concurrently. Because the program that accepts incoming mail uses TCP to communicate, it only needs to use one local TCP port even though it allows multiple connections to proceed concurrently.

13.8 Passive And Active Opens

Unlike UDP, TCP is a connection oriented protocol that requires both endpoints to agree to participate. That is, before TCP traffic can pass across an internet, application programs at both ends of the connection must agree that the connection is desired. To do so, the application program on one end performs a *passive open* function by contacting its operating system and indicating that it will accept an incoming connection. At that time, the operating system assigns a TCP port number for its end of the connection. The application program at the other end must then contact its operating system using an *active open* request to establish a connection. The two TCP software modules communicate to establish and verify a connection. Once a connection has been created, application programs can begin to pass data; the TCP software modules at each end exchange messages that guarantee reliable delivery. We will return to the details of establishing connections after examining the TCP message format.

13.9 Segments, Streams, And Sequence Numbers

TCP views the data stream as a sequence of octets or bytes that it divides into *segments* for transmission. Usually, each segment travels across an internet in a single IP datagram.

TCP uses a specialized sliding window mechanism to solve two important problems: efficient transmission and flow control. Like the sliding window protocol described earlier, the TCP window mechanism makes it possible to send multiple segments before an acknowledgement arrives. Doing so increases total throughput because it keeps the network busy. The TCP form of a sliding window protocol also solves the end-to-end *flow control* problem, by allowing the receiver to restrict transmission until it has sufficient buffer space to accommodate more data.

The TCP sliding window mechanism operates at the octet level, not at the segment or packet level. Octets of the data stream are numbered sequentially, and a sender keeps three pointers associated with every connection. The pointers define a sliding window as Figure 13.6 illustrates. The first pointer marks the left of the sliding window, separating octets that have been sent and acknowledged from octets yet to be sent. A second pointer marks the right of the sliding window and defines the highest octet in the sequence that can be sent before more acknowledgements are received. The third pointer marks the boundary inside the window that separates those octets that have already been sent from those octets that have not been sent. The protocol software sends all octets in the window without delay, so the boundary inside the window usually moves from left to right quickly.

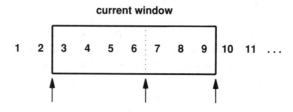

Figure 13.6 An example of the TCP sliding window. Octets through 2 have been sent and acknowledged, octets 3 through 6 have been sent but not acknowledged, octets 7 though 9 have not been sent but will be sent without delay, and octets 10 and higher cannot be sent until the window moves.

We have described how the sender's TCP window slides along and mentioned that the receiver must maintain a similar window to piece the stream together again. It is important to understand, however, that because TCP connections are full duplex, two transfers proceed simultaneously over each connection, one in each direction. We think of the transfers as completely independent because at any time data can flow across the connection in one direction, or in both directions. Thus, TCP software at each end maintains two windows per connection (for a total of four), one slides along the data stream being sent, while the other slides along as data is received.

13.10 Variable Window Size And Flow Control

One difference between the TCP sliding window protocol and the simplified sliding window protocol presented earlier occurs because TCP allows the window size to vary over time. Each acknowledgement, which specifies how many octets have been received, contains a *window advertisement* that specifies how many additional octets of data the receiver is prepared to accept. We think of the window advertisement as specifying the receiver's current buffer size. In response to an increased window advertisement, the sender increases the size of its sliding window and proceeds to send octets that have not been acknowledged. In response to a decreased window advertisement, the sender decreases the size of its window and stops sending octets beyond the boundary. TCP software should not contradict previous advertisements by shrinking the window past previously acceptable positions in the octet stream. Instead, smaller advertisements accompany acknowledgements, so the window size changes at the time it slides forward.

The advantage of using a variable size window is that it provides flow control as well as reliable transfer. If the receiver's buffers begin to become full, it cannot tolerate more packets, so it sends a smaller window advertisement. In the extreme case, the receiver advertises a window size of zero to stop all transmissions. Later, when buffer space becomes available, the receiver advertises a nonzero window size to trigger the flow of data again†.

Having a mechanism for flow control is essential in an internet environment, where machines of various speeds and sizes communicate through networks and routers of various speeds and capacities. There are really two independent flow problems. First, internet protocols need end-to-end flow control between the source and ultimate destination. For example, when a minicomputer communicates with a large mainframe, the minicomputer needs to regulate the influx of data, or protocol software would be overrun quickly. Thus, TCP must implement end-to-end flow control to guarantee reliable delivery. Second, internet protocols need a flow control mechanism that allows intermediate systems (i.e., routers) to control a source that sends more traffic than the machine can tolerate.

When intermediate machines become overloaded, the condition is called *congestion*, and mechanisms to solve the problem are called *congestion control* mechanisms. TCP uses its sliding window scheme to solve the end-to-end flow control problem; it does not have an explicit mechanism for congestion control. We will see later, however, that a carefully programmed TCP implementation can detect and recover from congestion while a poor implementation can make it worse. In particular, although a carefully chosen retransmission scheme can help avoid congestion, a poorly chosen scheme can exacerbate it.

13.11 TCP Segment Format

The unit of transfer between the TCP software on two machines is called a *segment*. Segments are exchanged to establish connections, to transfer data, to send acknowledgements, to advertise window sizes, and to close connections. Because TCP uses piggybacking, an acknowledgement traveling from machine *A* to machine *B* may travel in the same segment as data traveling from machine *A* to machine *B*, even though the acknowledgement refers to data sent from *B* to *A*‡. Figure 13.7 shows the TCP segment format.

---

†There are two exceptions to transmission when the window size is zero. First, a sender is allowed to transmit a segment with the urgent bit set to inform the receiver that urgent data is available. Second, to avoid a potential deadlock that can arise if a nonzero advertisement is lost after the window size reaches zero, the sender probes a zero-sized window periodically.

‡In practice, piggybacking does not usually occur because most applications do not send data in both directions simultaneously.

0 4 10	16 24 31
SOURCE PORT	DESTINATION PORT
SEQUENCE NUMBER	
ACKNOWLEDGEMENT NUMBER	

HLEN	RESERVED	CODE BITS	WINDOW
CHECKSUM			URGENT POINTER
OPTIONS (IF ANY)			PADDING
DATA			
. . .			

Figure 13.7 The format of a TCP segment with a TCP header followed by
data. Segments are used to establish connections as well as to
carry data and acknowledgements.

Each segment is divided into two parts, a header followed by data. The header,
known as the *TCP header*, carries the expected identification and control information.
Fields *SOURCE PORT* and *DESTINATION PORT* contain the TCP port numbers that
identify the application programs at the ends of the connection. The *SEQUENCE
NUMBER* field identifies the position in the sender's byte stream of the data in the segment. The *ACKNOWLEDGEMENT NUMBER* field identifies the number of the octet
that the source expects to receive next. Note that the sequence number refers to the
stream flowing in the same direction as the segment, while the acknowledgement
number refers to the stream flowing in the opposite direction as the segment.

The *HLEN*† field contains an integer that specifies the length of the segment
header measured in 32-bit multiples. It is needed because the *OPTIONS* field varies in
length, depending on which options have been included. Thus, the size of the TCP
header varies depending on the options selected. The 6-bit field marked *RESERVED* is
reserved for future use.

Some segments carry only an acknowledgement while some carry data. Others
carry requests to establish or close a connection. TCP software uses the 6-bit field labeled *CODE BITS* to determine the purpose and contents of the segment. The six bits
tell how to interpret other fields in the header according to the table in Figure 13.8.

---

†The specification says the *HLEN* field is the *offset* of the data area within the segment.

Bit (left to right)	Meaning if bit set to 1
URG	Urgent pointer field is valid
ACK	Acknowledgement field is valid
PSH	This segment requests a push
RST	Reset the connection
SYN	Synchronize sequence numbers
FIN	Sender has reached end of its byte stream

Figure 13.8 Bits of the CODE field in the TCP header.

TCP software advertises how much data it is willing to accept every time it sends a segment by specifying its buffer size in the *WINDOW* field. The field contains a 16-bit unsigned integer in network-standard byte order. Window advertisements provide another example of piggybacking because they accompany all segments, including those carrying data as well as those carrying only an acknowledgement.

13.12 Out Of Band Data

Although TCP is a stream-oriented protocol, it is sometimes important for the program at one end of a connection to send data *out of band*, without waiting for the program at the other end of the connection to consume octets already in the stream. For example, when TCP is used for a remote login session, the user may decide to send a keyboard sequence that *interrupts* or *aborts* the program at the other end. Such signals are most often needed when a program on the remote machine fails to operate correctly. The signals must be sent without waiting for the program to read octets already in the TCP stream (or one would not be able to abort programs that stop reading input).

To accommodate out of band signaling, TCP allows the sender to specify data as *urgent*, meaning that the receiving program should be notified of its arrival as quickly as possible, regardless of its position in the stream. The protocol specifies that when urgent data is found, the receiving TCP should notify whatever application program is associated with the connection to go into ''urgent mode.'' After all urgent data has been consumed, TCP tells the application program to return to normal operation.

The exact details of how TCP informs the application program about urgent data depend on the computer's operating system, of course. The mechanism used to mark urgent data when transmitting it in a segment consists of the URG code bit and the *URGENT POINTER* field. When the URG bit is set, the urgent pointer specifies the position in the segment where urgent data ends.

13.13 Maximum Segment Size Option

Not all segments sent across a connection will be of the same size. However, both ends need to agree on a maximum segment they will transfer. TCP software uses the *OPTIONS* field to negotiate with the TCP software at the other end of the connection; one of the options allows TCP software to specify the *maximum segment size* (*MSS*) that it is willing to receive. For example, when an embedded system that only has a few hundred bytes of buffer space connects to a large supercomputer, it can negotiate an MSS that restricts segments so they fit in the buffer. It is especially important for computers connected by high-speed local area networks to choose a maximum segment size that fills packets or they will not make good use of the bandwidth. Therefore, if the two endpoints lie on the same physical network, TCP usually computes a maximum segment size such that the resulting IP datagrams will match the network MTU. If the endpoints do not lie on the same physical network, they can attempt to discover the minimum MTU along the path between them, or choose a maximum segment size of *536* (the default size of an IP datagram, *576*, minus the standard size of IP and TCP headers).

In a general internet environment, choosing a good maximum segment size can be difficult because performance can be poor for either extremely large segment sizes or extremely small sizes. On one hand, when the segment size is small, network utilization remains low. To see why, recall that TCP segments travel encapsulated in IP datagrams which are encapsulated in physical network frames. Thus, each segment has at least 40 octets of TCP and IP headers in addition to the data. Therefore, datagrams carrying only one octet of data use at most 1/41 of the underlying network bandwidth for user data; in practice, minimum interpacket gaps and network hardware framing bits make the ratio even smaller.

On the other hand, extremely large segment sizes can also produce poor performance. Large segments result in large IP datagrams. When such datagrams travel across a network with small MTU, IP must fragment them. Unlike a TCP segment, a fragment cannot be acknowledged or retransmitted independently; all fragments must arrive or the entire datagram must be retransmitted. Because the probability of losing a given fragment is nonzero, increasing segment size above the fragmentation threshold decreases the probability the datagram will arrive, which decreases throughput.

In theory, the optimum segment size, S, occurs when the IP datagrams carrying the segments are as large as possible without requiring fragmentation anywhere along the path from the source to the destination. In practice, finding S is difficult for several reasons. First, most implementations of TCP do not include a mechanism for doing so. Second, because routers in an internet can change routes dynamically, the path datagrams follow between a pair of communicating computers can change dynamically and so can the size at which datagrams must be fragmented. Third, the optimum size depends on lower-level protocol headers (e.g., the segment size must be reduced to accommodate IP options). Research on the problem of finding an optimal segment size continues.

13.14 TCP Checksum Computation

The *CHECKSUM* field in the TCP header contains a 16-bit integer checksum used to verify the integrity of the data as well as the TCP header. To compute the checksum, TCP software on the sending machine follows a procedure like the one described in Chapter 12 for UDP. It prepends a *pseudo header* to the segment, appends enough zero bits to make the segment a multiple of 16 bits, and computes the 16-bit checksum over the entire result. TCP does not count the pseudo header or padding in the segment length, nor does it transmit them. Also, it assumes the checksum field itself is zero for purposes of the checksum computation. As with other checksums, TCP uses 16-bit arithmetic and takes the one's complement of the one's complement sum. At the receiving site, TCP software performs the same computation to verify that the segment arrived intact.

The purpose of using a pseudo header is exactly the same as in UDP. It allows the receiver to verify that the segment has reached its correct destination, which includes both a host IP address as well as a protocol port number. Both the source and destination IP addresses are important to TCP because it must use them to identify a connection to which the segment belongs. Therefore, whenever a datagram arrives carrying a TCP segment, IP must pass to TCP the source and destination IP addresses from the datagram as well as the segment itself. Figure 13.9 shows the format of the pseudo header used in the checksum computation.

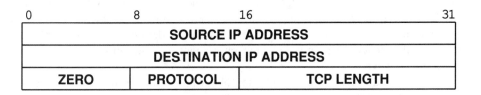

Figure 13.9 The format of the pseudo header used in TCP checksum computations. At the receiving site, this information is extracted from the IP datagram that carried the segment.

The sending TCP assigns field *PROTOCOL* the value that the underlying delivery system will use in its protocol type field. For IP datagrams carrying TCP, the value is 6. The *TCP LENGTH* field specifies the total length of the TCP segment including the TCP header. At the receiving end, information used in the pseudo header is extracted from the IP datagram that carried the segment and included in the checksum computation to verify that the segment arrived at the correct destination intact.

13.15 Acknowledgements And Retransmission

Because TCP sends data in variable length segments, and because retransmitted segments can include more data than the original, acknowledgements cannot easily refer to datagrams or segments. Instead, they refer to a position in the stream using the stream sequence numbers. The receiver collects data octets from arriving segments and reconstructs an exact copy of the stream being sent. Because segments travel in IP datagrams, they can be lost or delivered out of order; the receiver uses the sequence numbers to reorder segments. At any time, the receiver will have reconstructed zero or more octets contiguously from the beginning of the stream, but may have additional pieces of the stream from datagrams that arrived out of order. The receiver always acknowledges the longest contiguous prefix of the stream that has been received correctly. Each acknowledgement specifies a sequence value one greater than the highest octet position in the contiguous prefix it received. Thus, the sender receives continuous feedback from the receiver as it progresses through the stream. We can summarize this important idea:

> *A TCP acknowledgement specifies the sequence number of the next octet that the receiver expects to receive.*

The TCP acknowledgement scheme is called *cumulative* because it reports how much of the stream has accumulated. Cumulative acknowledgements have both advantages and disadvantages. One advantage is that acknowledgements are both easy to generate and unambiguous. Another advantage is that lost acknowledgements do not necessarily force retransmission. A major disadvantage is that the sender does not receive information about all successful transmissions, but only about a single position in the stream that has been received.

To understand why lack of information about all successful transmissions makes cumulative acknowledgements less efficient, think of a window that spans *5000* octets starting at position *101* in the stream, and suppose the sender has transmitted all data in the window by sending five segments. Suppose further that the first segment is lost, but all others arrive intact. As each segment arrives, the receiver sends an acknowledgement, but each acknowledgement specifies octet *101*, the next highest contiguous octet it expects to receive. There is no way for the receiver to tell the sender that most of the data for the current window has arrived.

When a timeout occurs at the sender's side, the sender must choose between two potentially inefficient schemes. It may choose to retransmit one segment or all five segments. In this case retransmitting all five segments is inefficient. When the first segment arrives, the receiver will have all the data in the window, and will acknowledge *5101*. If the sender follows the accepted standard and retransmits only the first unacknowledged segment, it must wait for the acknowledgement before it can decide what and how much to send. Thus, it reverts to a simple positive acknowledgement protocol and may lose the advantages of having a large window.

13.16 Timeout And Retransmission

One of the most important and complex ideas in TCP is embedded in the way it handles timeout and retransmission. Like other reliable protocols, TCP expects the destination to send acknowledgements whenever it successfully receives new octets from the data stream. Every time it sends a segment, TCP starts a timer and waits for an acknowledgement. If the timer expires before data in the segment has been acknowledged, TCP assumes that the segment was lost or corrupted and retransmits it.

To understand why the TCP retransmission algorithm differs from the algorithm used in many network protocols, we need to remember that TCP is intended for use in an internet environment. In an internet, a segment traveling between a pair of machines may traverse a single, low-delay network (e.g., a high-speed LAN), or it may travel across multiple intermediate networks through multiple routers. Thus, it is impossible to know *a priori* how quickly acknowledgements will return to the source. Furthermore, the delay at each router depends on traffic, so the total time required for a segment to travel to the destination and an acknowledgement to return to the source varies dramatically from one instant to another. Figure 13.10, which shows measurements of round trip times across the global Internet for 100 consecutive packets, illustrates the problem. TCP software must accommodate both the vast differences in the time required to reach various destinations and the changes in time required to reach a given destination as traffic load varies.

TCP accommodates varying internet delays by using an *adaptive retransmission algorithm*. In essence, TCP monitors the performance of each connection and deduces reasonable values for timeouts. As the performance of a connection changes, TCP revises its timeout value (i.e., it adapts to the change).

To collect the data needed for an adaptive algorithm, TCP records the time at which each segment is sent, and the time at which an acknowledgement arrives for the data in that segment. From the two times, TCP computes an elapsed time known as a *sample round trip time* or *round trip sample*. Whenever it obtains a new round trip sample, TCP adjusts its notion of the average round trip time for the connection. Usually, TCP software stores the estimated round trip time, *RTT*, as a weighted average and uses new round trip samples to change the average slowly. For example, when computing a new weighted average, one early averaging technique used a constant weighting factor, α, where $0 \le \alpha < 1$, to weight the old average against the latest round trip sample:

$$RTT = (\alpha * Old\_RTT) + ((1-\alpha) * New\_Round\_Trip\_Sample)$$

Choosing a value for α close to *1* makes the weighted average immune to changes that last a short time (e.g., a single segment that encounters long delay). Choosing a value for α close to *0* makes the weighted average respond to changes in delay very quickly.

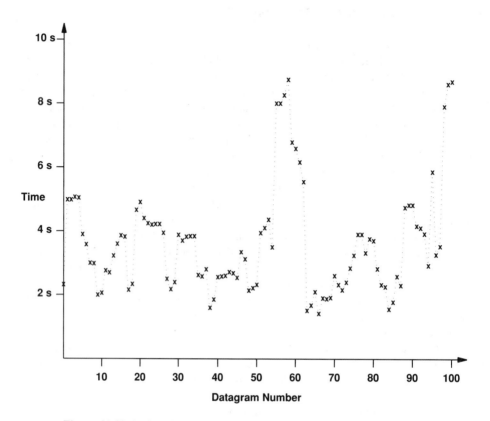

Figure 13.10 A plot of Internet round trip times as measured for 100 successive IP datagrams. Although most parts of the Internet now
operate with much lower delay, delays still vary over time.

When it sends a packet, TCP computes a timeout value as a function of the current
round trip estimate. Early implementations of TCP used a constant weighting factor, β
($\beta > 1$), and made the timeout greater than the current round trip estimate:

$$\text{Timeout} = \beta * \text{RTT}$$

Choosing a value for β can be difficult. On one hand, to detect packet loss quickly, the
timeout value should be close to the current round trip time (i.e., β should be close to
1). Detecting packet loss quickly improves throughput because TCP will not wait an
unnecessarily long time before retransmitting. On the other hand, if $\beta = 1$, TCP is over-
ly eager – any small delay will cause an unnecessary retransmission, which wastes network bandwidth. The original specification recommended setting $\beta = 2$; more recent
work described below has produced better techniques for adjusting timeout.

We can summarize the ideas presented so far:

To accommodate the varying delays encountered in an internet environment, TCP uses an adaptive retransmission algorithm that monitors delays on each connection and adjusts its timeout parameter accordingly.

13.17 Accurate Measurement Of Round Trip Samples

In theory, measuring a round trip sample is trivial – it consists of subtracting the time at which the segment is sent from the time at which the acknowledgement arrives. However, complications arise because TCP uses a cumulative acknowledgement scheme in which an acknowledgement refers to data received, and not to the instance of a specific datagram that carried the data. Consider a retransmission. TCP forms a segment, places it in a datagram and sends it, the timer expires, and TCP sends the segment again in a second datagram. Because both datagrams carry exactly the same data, the sender has no way of knowing whether an acknowledgement corresponds to the original or retransmitted datagram. This phenomenon has been called *acknowledgement ambiguity*, and TCP acknowledgements are said to be *ambiguous*.

Should TCP assume acknowledgements belong with the earliest (i.e., original) transmission or the latest (i.e., the most recent retransmission)? Surprisingly, neither assumption works. Associating the acknowledgement with the original transmission can make the estimated round trip time grow without bound in cases where an internet loses datagrams†. If an acknowledgement arrives after one or more retransmissions, TCP will measure the round trip sample from the original transmission, and compute a new RTT using the excessively long sample. Thus, RTT will grow slightly. The next time TCP sends a segment, the larger RTT will result in slightly longer timeouts, so if an acknowledgement arrives after one or more retransmissions, the next sample round trip time will be even larger, and so on.

Associating the acknowledgement with the most recent retransmission can also fail. Consider what happens when the end-to-end delay suddenly increases. When TCP sends a segment, it uses the old round trip estimate to compute a timeout, which is now too small. The segment arrives and an acknowledgement starts back, but the increase in delay means the timer expires before the acknowledgement arrives, and TCP retransmits the segment. Shortly after TCP retransmits, the first acknowledgement arrives and is associated with the retransmission. The round trip sample will be much too small and will result in a slight decrease of the estimated round trip time, RTT. Unfortunately, lowering the estimated round trip time guarantees that TCP will set the timeout too small for the next segment. Ultimately, the estimated round trip time can stabilize at a value, T, such that the correct round trip time is slightly longer than some multiple of T. Implementations of TCP that associate acknowledgements with the most recent retransmission have been observed in a stable state with RTT slightly less than one-half

---

†The estimate can only grow arbitrarily large if every segment is lost at least once.

of the correct value (i.e., TCP sends each segment exactly twice even though no loss occurs).

13.18 Karn's Algorithm And Timer Backoff

If the original transmission and the most recent transmission both fail to provide accurate round trip times, what should TCP do? The accepted answer is simple: TCP should not update the round trip estimate for retransmitted segments. This idea, known as *Karn's Algorithm*, avoids the problem of ambiguous acknowledgements altogether by only adjusting the estimated round trip for unambiguous acknowledgements (acknowledgements that arrive for segments that have only been transmitted once).

Of course, a simplistic implementation of Karn's algorithm, one that merely ignores times from retransmitted segments, can lead to failure as well. Consider what happens when TCP sends a segment after a sharp increase in delay. TCP computes a timeout using the existing round trip estimate. The timeout will be too small for the new delay and will force retransmission. If TCP ignores acknowledgements from retransmitted segments, it will never update the estimate and the cycle will continue.

To accommodate such failures, Karn's algorithm requires the sender to combine retransmission timeouts with a *timer backoff* strategy. The backoff technique computes an initial timeout using a formula like the one shown above. However, if the timer expires and causes a retransmission, TCP increases the timeout. In fact, each time it must retransmit a segment, TCP increases the timeout (to keep timeouts from becoming ridiculously long, most implementations limit increases to an upper bound that is larger than the delay along any path in the internet).

Implementations use a variety of techniques to compute backoff. Most choose a multiplicative factor, γ, and set the new value to:

$$new\_timeout = \gamma * timeout$$

Typically, γ is 2. (It has been argued that values of γ less than 2 lead to instabilities.) Other implementations use a table of multiplicative factors, allowing arbitrary backoff at each step†.

Karn's algorithm combines the backoff technique with round trip estimation to solve the problem of never increasing round trip estimates:

> *Karn's algorithm: When computing the round trip estimate, ignore samples that correspond to retransmitted segments, but use a backoff strategy, and retain the timeout value from a retransmitted packet for subsequent packets until a valid sample is obtained.*

Generally speaking, when an internet misbehaves, Karn's algorithm separates computation of the timeout value from the current round trip estimate. It uses the round trip estimate to compute an initial timeout value, but then backs off the timeout on each re-

---

†Berkeley UNIX is the most notable system that uses a table of factors, but current values in the table are equivalent to using $\gamma=2$.

transmission until it can successfully transfer a segment. When it sends subsequent segments, it retains the timeout value that results from backoff. Finally, when an acknowledgement arrives corresponding to a segment that did not require retransmission, TCP recomputes the round trip estimate and resets the timeout accordingly. Experience shows that Karn's algorithm works well even in networks with high packet loss†.

13.19 Responding To High Variance In Delay

Research into round trip estimation has shown that the computations described above do not adapt to a wide range of variation in delay. Queueing theory suggests that the variation in round trip time, σ, varies proportional to $1/(1-L)$, where L is the current network load, $0 \le L \le 1$. If an internet is running at 50% of capacity, we expect the round trip delay to vary by a factor of $\pm 2\sigma$, or 4. When the load reaches 80%, we expect a variation of 10. The original TCP standard specified the technique for estimating round trip time that we described earlier. Using that technique and limiting β to the suggested value of 2 means the round trip estimation can adapt to loads of at most 30%.

The 1989 specification for TCP requires implementations to estimate both the average round trip time and the variance, and to use the estimated variance in place of the constant β. As a result, new implementations of TCP can adapt to a wider range of variation in delay and yield substantially higher throughput. Fortunately, the approximations require little computation; extremely efficient programs can be derived from the following simple equations:

$$DIFF = SAMPLE - Old\_RTT$$

$$Smoothed\_RTT = Old\_RTT + \delta * DIFF$$

$$DEV = Old\_DEV + \rho\,(|DIFF| - Old\_DEV)$$

$$Timeout = Smoothed\_RTT + \eta * DEV$$

where DEV is the estimated mean deviation, δ is a fraction between 0 and 1 that controls how quickly the new sample affects the weighted average, ρ is a fraction between 0 and 1 that controls how quickly the new sample affects the mean deviation, and η is a factor that controls how much the deviation affects the round trip timeout. To make the computation efficient, TCP chooses δ and ρ to each be an inverse of a power of 2, scales the computation by 2^n for an appropriate n, and uses integer arithmetic. Research suggests values of $\delta = 1/2^3$, $\rho = 1/2^2$, and $n = 3$ will work well. The original value for η in 4.3BSD UNIX was 2; it was changed to 4 in 4.4 BSD UNIX.

---

†Phil Karn is an amateur radio enthusiast who developed this algorithm to allow TCP communication across a high-loss packet radio connection.

13.20 Response To Congestion

It may seem that TCP software could be designed by considering the interaction between the two endpoints of a connection and the communication delays between those endpoints. In practice, however, TCP must also react to *congestion* in the internet. Congestion is a condition of severe delay caused by an overload of datagrams at one or more switching points (e.g., at routers). When congestion occurs, delays increase and the router begins to enqueue datagrams until it can route them. We must remember that each router has finite storage capacity and that datagrams compete for that storage (i.e., in a datagram based internet, there is no preallocation of resources to individual TCP connections). In the worst case, the total number of datagrams arriving at the congested router grows until the router reaches capacity and starts to drop datagrams.

Endpoints do not usually know the details of where congestion has occurred or why. To them, congestion simply means increased delay. Unfortunately, most transport protocols use timeout and retransmission, so they respond to increased delay by retransmitting datagrams. Retransmissions aggravate congestion instead of alleviating it. If unchecked, the increased traffic will produce increased delay, leading to increased traffic, and so on, until the network becomes useless. The condition is known as *congestion collapse*.

To avoid congestion collapse, TCP must reduce transmission rates when congestion occurs. Routers watch queue lengths and use techniques like ICMP source quench to inform hosts that congestion has occurred†, but transport protocols like TCP can help avoid congestion by reducing transmission rates automatically whenever delays occur. Of course, algorithms to avoid congestion must be constructed carefully because even under normal operating conditions an internet will exhibit wide variation in round trip delays.

To avoid congestion, the TCP standard now recommends using two techniques: *slow-start* and *multiplicative decrease*. They are related and can be implemented easily. We said that for each connection, TCP must remember the size of the receiver's window (i.e., the buffer size advertised in acknowledgements). To control congestion TCP maintains a second limit, called the *congestion window limit* or *congestion window*. At any time, TCP acts as if the window size is:

Allowed_window = min(receiver_advertisement, congestion_window)

In the steady state on a non-congested connection, the congestion window is the same size as the receiver's window. Reducing the congestion window reduces the traffic TCP will inject into the connection. To estimate congestion window size, TCP assumes that most datagram loss comes from congestion and uses the following strategy:

---

†In a congested network, queue lengths grow exponentially for a significant time.

Multiplicative Decrease Congestion Avoidance: Upon loss of a segment, reduce the congestion window by half (down to a minimum of at least one segment). For those segments that remain in the allowed window, backoff the retransmission timer exponentially.

Because TCP reduces the congestion window by half for *every* loss, it decreases the window exponentially if loss continues. In other words, if congestion is likely, TCP reduces the volume of traffic exponentially and the rate of retransmission exponentially. If loss continues, TCP eventually limits transmission to a single datagram and continues to double timeout values before retransmitting. The idea is to provide quick and significant traffic reduction to allow routers enough time to clear the datagrams already in their queues.

How can TCP recover when congestion ends? You might suspect that TCP should reverse the multiplicative decrease and double the congestion window when traffic begins to flow again. However, doing so produces an unstable system that oscillates wildly between no traffic and congestion. Instead, TCP uses a technique called *slow-start*† to scale up transmission:

Slow-Start (Additive) Recovery: Whenever starting traffic on a new connection or increasing traffic after a period of congestion, start the congestion window at the size of a single segment and increase the congestion window by one segment each time an acknowledgement arrives.

Slow-start avoids swamping the internet with additional traffic immediately after congestion clears or when new connections suddenly start.

The term *slow-start* may be a misnomer because under ideal conditions, the start is not very slow. TCP initializes the congestion window to *1*, sends an initial segment, and waits. When the acknowledgement arrives, it increases the congestion window to *2*, sends two segments, and waits. When the two acknowledgements arrive they each increase the congestion window by *1*, so TCP can send *4* segments. Acknowledgements for those will increase the congestion window to *8*. Within four round-trip times, TCP can send *16* segments, often enough to reach the receiver's window limit. Even for extremely large windows, it takes only $\log_2 N$ round trips before TCP can send *N* segments.

To avoid increasing the window size too quickly and causing additional congestion, TCP adds one additional restriction. Once the congestion window reaches one half of its original size before congestion, TCP enters a *congestion avoidance* phase and slows down the rate of increment. During congestion avoidance, it increases the congestion window by *1* only if all segments in the window have been acknowledged.

Taken together, the slow-start increase, multiplicative decrease, congestion avoidance, measurement of variation, and exponential timer backoff improve the performance of TCP dramatically without adding any significant computational overhead to

---

†The term *slow-start* is attributed to John Nagle; the technique was originally called *soft-start*.

the protocol software. Versions of TCP that use these techniques have improved the performance of previous versions by factors of *2* to *10*.

13.21 Establishing A TCP Connection

To establish a connection, TCP uses a three-way handshake. In the simplest case, the handshake proceeds as Figure 13.11 shows.

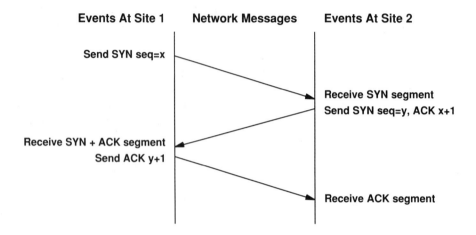

Figure 13.11 The sequence of messages in a three-way handshake. Time proceeds down the page; diagonal lines represent segments sent between sites. SYN segments carry initial sequence number information.

The first segment of a handshake can be identified because it has the SYN† bit set in the code field. The second message has both the SYN bit and ACK bits set, indicating that it acknowledges the first SYN segment as well as continuing the handshake. The final handshake message is only an acknowledgement and is merely used to inform the destination that both sides agree that a connection has been established.

Usually, the TCP software on one machine waits passively for the handshake, and the TCP software on another machine initiates it. However, the handshake is carefully designed to work even if both machines attempt to initiate a connection simultaneously. Thus, a connection can be established from either end or from both ends simultaneously. Once the connection has been established, data can flow in both directions equally well. There is no master or slave.

The three-way handshake is both necessary and sufficient for correct synchronization between the two ends of the connection. To understand why, remember that TCP builds on an unreliable packet delivery service, so messages can be lost, delayed, dupli-

---

†SYN stands for *synchronization*; it is pronounced ``sin''.

cated, or delivered out of order. Thus, the protocol must use a timeout mechanism and retransmit lost requests. Trouble arises if retransmitted and original requests arrive while the connection is being established, or if retransmitted requests are delayed until after a connection has been established, used, and terminated. A three-way handshake (plus the rule that TCP ignores additional requests for connection after a connection has been established) solves these problems.

13.22 Initial Sequence Numbers

The three-way handshake accomplishes two important functions. It guarantees that both sides are ready to transfer data (and that they know they are both ready), and it allows both sides to agree on initial sequence numbers. Sequence numbers are sent and acknowledged during the handshake. Each machine must choose an initial sequence number at random that it will use to identify bytes in the stream it is sending. Sequence numbers cannot always start at the same value. In particular, TCP cannot merely choose sequence *1* every time it creates a connection (one of the exercises examines problems that can arise if it does). Of course, it is important that both sides agree on an initial number, so octet numbers used in acknowledgements agree with those used in data segments.

To see how machines can agree on sequence numbers for two streams after only three messages, recall that each segment contains both a sequence number field and an acknowledgement field. The machine that initiates a handshake, call it *A*, passes its initial sequence number, *x*, in the sequence field of the first SYN segment in the three-way handshake. The second machine, *B*, receives the SYN, records the sequence number, and replies by sending its initial sequence number in the sequence field as well as an acknowledgement that specifies *B* expects octet *x+1*. In the final message of the handshake, *A* "acknowledges" receiving from *B* all octets through *y*. In all cases, acknowledgements follow the convention of using the number of the *next* octet expected.

We have described how TCP usually carries out the three-way handshake by exchanging segments that contain a minimum amount of information. Because of the protocol design, it is possible to send data along with the initial sequence numbers in the handshake segments. In such cases, the TCP software must hold the data until the handshake completes. Once a connection has been established, the TCP software can release data being held and deliver it to a waiting application program quickly. The reader is referred to the protocol specification for the details.

13.23 Closing a TCP Connection

Two programs that use TCP to communicate can terminate the conversation gracefully using the *close* operation. Internally, TCP uses a modified three-way handshake to close connections. Recall that TCP connections are full duplex and that we view them as containing two independent stream transfers, one going in each direction. When an application program tells TCP that it has no more data to send, TCP will close the connection *in one direction*. To close its half of a connection, the sending TCP finishes transmitting the remaining data, waits for the receiver to acknowledge it, and then sends a segment with the FIN bit set. The receiving TCP acknowledges the FIN segment and informs the application program on its end that no more data is available (e.g., using the operating system's end-of-file mechanism).

Once a connection has been closed in a given direction, TCP refuses to accept more data for that direction. Meanwhile, data can continue to flow in the opposite direction until the sender closes it. Of course, acknowledgements continue to flow back to the sender even after a connection has been closed. When both directions have been closed, the TCP software at each endpoint deletes its record of the connection.

The details of closing a connection are even more subtle than suggested above because TCP uses a modified three-way handshake to close a connection. Figure 13.12 illustrates the procedure.

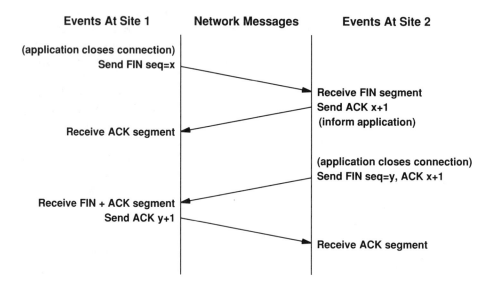

Figure 13.12 The modified three-way handshake used to close connections. The site that receives the first FIN segment acknowledges it immediately and then delays before sending the second FIN segment.

The difference between three-way handshakes used to establish and break connections occurs after a machine receives the initial FIN segment. Instead of generating a second FIN segment immediately, TCP sends an acknowledgement and then informs the application of the request to shut down. Informing the application program of the request and obtaining a response may take considerable time (e.g., it may involve human interaction). The acknowledgement prevents retransmission of the initial FIN segment during the wait. Finally, when the application program instructs TCP to shut down the connection completely, TCP sends the second FIN segment and the original site replies with the third message, an ACK.

13.24 TCP Connection Reset

Normally, an application program uses the close operation to shut down a connection when it finishes using it. Thus, closing connections is considered a normal part of use, analogous to closing files. Sometimes abnormal conditions arise that force an application program or the network software to break a connection. TCP provides a reset facility for such abnormal disconnections.

To reset a connection, one side initiates termination by sending a segment with the RST bit in the *CODE* field set. The other side responds to a reset segment immediately by aborting the connection. TCP also informs the application program that a reset occurred. A reset is an instantaneous abort that means that transfer in both directions ceases immediately, and resources such as buffers are released.

13.25 TCP State Machine

Like most protocols, the operation of TCP can best be explained with a theoretical model called a *finite state machine*. Figure 13.13 shows the TCP finite state machine, with circles representing states and arrows representing transitions between them. The label on each transition shows what TCP receives to cause the transition and what it sends in response. For example, the TCP software at each endpoint begins in the *CLOSED* state. Application programs must issue either a *passive open* command (to wait for a connection from another machine), or an *active open* command (to initiate a connection). An active open command forces a transition from the *CLOSED* state to the *SYN SENT* state. When TCP follows the transition, it emits a SYN segment. When the other end returns a segment that contains a SYN plus ACK, TCP moves to the *ESTABLISHED* state and begins data transfer.

The *TIMED WAIT* state reveals how TCP handles some of the problems incurred with unreliable delivery. TCP keeps a notion of *maximum segment lifetime*, the maximum time an old segment can remain alive in an internet. To avoid having segments from a previous connection interfere with a current one, TCP moves to the *TIMED WAIT* state after closing a connection. It remains in that state for twice the maximum segment lifetime before deleting its record of the connection. If any duplicate segments happen to arrive for the connection during the timeout interval, TCP will reject them. However, to handle cases where the last acknowledgement was lost it acknowledges valid segments and restarts the timer. Because the timer allows TCP to distinguish old connections from new ones, it prevents TCP from responding with a *RST* (reset) if the other end retransmits a *FIN* request.

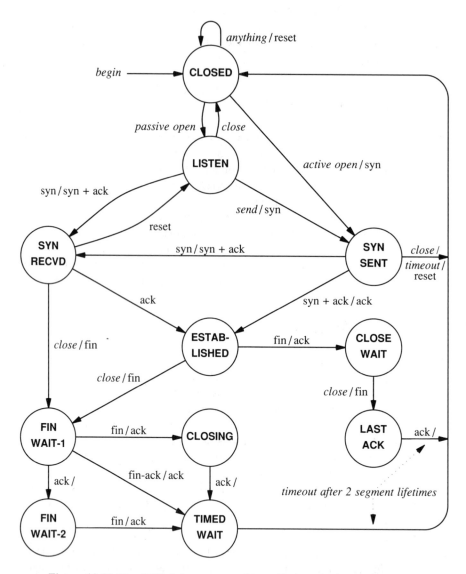

Figure 13.13 The TCP finite state machine. Each endpoint begins in the *closed* state. Labels on transitions show the input that caused the transition followed by the output if any.

13.26 Forcing Data Delivery

We have said that TCP is free to divide the stream of data into segments for transmission without regard to the size of transfer that application programs use. The chief advantage of allowing TCP to choose a division is efficiency. It can accumulate enough octets in a buffer to make segments reasonably long, reducing the high overhead that occurs when segments contain only a few data octets.

Although buffering improves network throughput, it can interfere with some applications. Consider using a TCP connection to pass characters from an interactive terminal to a remote machine. The user expects instant response to each keystroke. If the sending TCP buffers the data, response may be delayed, perhaps for hundreds of keystrokes. Similarly, because the receiving TCP may buffer data before making it available to the application program on its end, forcing the sender to transmit data may not be sufficient to guarantee delivery.

To accommodate interactive users, TCP provides a *push* operation that an application program can use to force delivery of octets currently in the stream without waiting for the buffer to fill. The push operation does more than force TCP to send a segment. It also requests TCP to set the *PSH* bit in the segment code field, so the data will be delivered to the application program on the receiving end. Thus, when sending data from an interactive terminal, the application uses the push function after each keystroke. Similarly, application programs can force output to be sent and displayed on the terminal promptly by calling the push function after writing a character or line.

13.27 Reserved TCP Port Numbers

Like UDP, TCP combines static and dynamic port binding, using a set of *well-known port assignments* for commonly invoked programs (e.g., electronic mail), but leaving most port numbers available for the operating system to allocate as programs need them. Although the standard originally reserved port numbers less than *256* for use as well-known ports, numbers over 1024 have now been assigned. Figure 13.14 lists some of the currently assigned TCP ports. It should be pointed out that although TCP and UDP port numbers are independent, the designers have chosen to use the same integer port numbers for any service that is accessible from both UDP and TCP. For example, a domain name server can be accessed either with TCP or with UDP. In either protocol, port number *53* has been reserved for servers in the domain name system.

13.28 TCP Performance

As we have seen, TCP is a complex protocol that handles communication over a wide variety of underlying network technologies. Many people assume that because TCP tackles a much more complex task than other transport protocols, the code must be cumbersome and inefficient. Surprisingly, the generality we discussed does not seem to hinder TCP performance. Experiments at Berkeley have shown that the same TCP that operates efficiently over the global Internet can deliver 8 Mbps of sustained throughput of user data between two workstations on a 10 Mbps Ethernet†. At Cray Research, Inc., researchers have demonstrated TCP throughput approaching a gigabit per second.

Decimal	Keyword	UNIX Keyword	Description
0			Reserved
1	TCPMUX	-	TCP Multiplexor
5	RJE	-	Remote Job Entry
7	ECHO	echo	Echo
9	DISCARD	discard	Discard
11	USERS	systat	Active Users
13	DAYTIME	daytime	Daytime
15	-	netstat	Network status program
17	QUOTE	qotd	Quote of the Day
19	CHARGEN	chargen	Character Generator
20	FTP-DATA	ftp-data	File Transfer Protocol (data)
21	FTP	ftp	File Transfer Protocol
23	TELNET	telnet	Terminal Connection
25	SMTP	smtp	Simple Mail Transport Protocol
37	TIME	time	Time
42	NAMESERVER	name	Host Name Server
43	NICNAME	whois	Who Is
53	DOMAIN	nameserver	Domain Name Server
77	-	rje	any private RJE service
79	FINGER	finger	Finger
93	DCP	-	Device Control Protocol
95	SUPDUP	supdup	SUPDUP Protocol
101	HOSTNAME	hostnames	NIC Host Name Server
102	ISO-TSAP	iso-tsap	ISO-TSAP
103	X400	x400	X.400 Mail Service
104	X400-SND	x400-snd	X.400 Mail Sending
111	SUNRPC	sunrpc	SUN Remote Procedure Call
113	AUTH	auth	Authentication Service
117	UUCP-PATH	uucp-path	UUCP Path Service
119	NNTP	nntp	USENET News Transfer Protocol
129	PWDGEN	-	Password Generator Protocol
139	NETBIOS-SSN	-	NETBIOS Session Service
160-223	Reserved		

Figure 13.14 Examples of currently assigned TCP port numbers. To the extent possible, protocols like UDP use the same numbers.

---

†Ethernet, IP, and TCP headers and the required inter-packet gap account for the remaining bandwidth.

13.29 Silly Window Syndrome And Small Packets

Researchers who helped developed TCP observed a serious performance problem that can result when the sending and receiving applications operate at different speeds. To understand the problem, remember that TCP buffers incoming data, and consider what can happen if a receiving application chooses to read incoming data one octet at a time. When a connection is first established, the receiving TCP allocates a buffer of K bytes, and uses the *WINDOW* field in acknowledgement segments to advertise the available buffer size to the sender. If the sending application generates data quickly, the sending TCP will transmit segments with data for the entire window. Eventually, the sender will receive an acknowledgement that specifies the entire window has been filled, and no additional space remains in the receiver's buffer.

When the receiving application reads an octet of data from a full buffer, one octet of space becomes available. We said that when space becomes available in its buffer, TCP on the receiving machine generates an acknowledgement that uses the *WINDOW* field to inform the sender. In the example, the receiver will advertise a window of *1* octet. When it learns that space is available, the sending TCP responds by transmitting a segment that contains one octet of data.

Although single-octet window advertisements work correctly to keep the receiver's buffer filled, they result in a series of small data segments. The sending TCP must compose a segment that contains one octet of data, place the segment in an IP datagram, and transmit the result. When the receiving application reads another octet, TCP generates another acknowledgement, which causes the sender to transmit another segment that contains one octet of data. The resulting interaction can reach a steady state in which TCP sends a separate segment for each octet of data.

Transferring small segments consumes unnecessary network bandwidth and introduces unnecessary computational overhead. The transmission of small segments consumes unnecessary network bandwidth because each datagram carries only one octet of data; the ratio of header to data is large. Computational overhead arises because TCP on both the sending and receiving computers must process each segment. The sending TCP software must allocate buffer space, form a segment header, and compute a checksum for the segment. Similarly, IP software on the sending machine must encapsulate the segment in a datagram, compute a header checksum, route the datagram, and transfer it to the appropriate network interface. On the receiving machine, IP must verify the IP header checksum and pass the segment to TCP. TCP must verify the segment checksum, examine the sequence number, extract the data, and place it in a buffer.

Although we have described how small segments result when a receiver advertises a small available window, a sender can also cause each segment to contain a small amount of data. For example, imagine a TCP implementation that aggressively sends data whenever it is available, and consider what happens if a sending application generates data one octet at a time. After the application generates an octet of data, TCP creates and transmits a segment. TCP can also send a small segment if an application generates data in fixed-sized blocks of *B* octets, and the sending TCP extracts data from the buffer in maximum segment sized blocks, *M*, where $M \neq B$, because the last block in a buffer can be small.

Known as *silly window syndrome (SWS)*, the problem plagued early TCP implementations. To summarize,

> *Early TCP implementations exhibited a problem known as* silly window syndrome *in which each acknowledgement advertises a small amount of space available and each segment carries a small amount of data.*

13.30 Avoiding Silly Window Syndrome

TCP specifications now include heuristics that prevent silly window syndrome. A heuristic used on the sending machine avoids transmitting a small amount of data in each segment. Another heuristic used on the receiving machine avoids sending small increments in window advertisements that can trigger small data packets. Although the heuristics work well together, having both the sender and receiver avoid silly window helps ensure good performance in the case that one end of a connection fails to correctly implement silly window avoidance.

In practice, TCP software must contain both sender and receiver silly window avoidance code. To understand why, recall that a TCP connection is full duplex – data can flow in either direction. Thus, an implementation of TCP includes code to send data as well as code to receive it.

13.30.1 Receive-Side Silly Window Avoidance

The heuristic a receiver uses to avoid silly window is straightforward and easiest to understand. In general, a receiver maintains an internal record of the currently available window, but delays advertising an increase in window size to the sender until the window can advance a significant amount. The definition of "significant" depends on the receiver's buffer size and the maximum segment size. TCP defines it to be the minimum of one half of the receiver's buffer or the number of data octets in a maximum-sized segment.

Receive-side silly window prevents small window advertisements in the case where a receiving application extracts data octets slowly. For example, when a receiver's buffer fills completely, it sends an acknowledgement that contains a zero window advertisement. As the receiving application extracts octets from the buffer, the receiving TCP computes the newly available space in the buffer. Instead of sending a window advertisement immediately, however, the receiver waits until the available space reaches one half of the total buffer size or a maximum sized segment. Thus, the sender always receives large increments in the current window, allowing it to transfer large segments. The heuristic can be summarized as follows.

Receive-Side Silly Window Avoidance: Before sending an updated window advertisement after advertising a zero window, wait for space to become available that is either at least 50% of the total buffer size or equal to a maximum sized segment.

13.30.2 Delayed Acknowledgements

Two approaches have been taken to implement silly window avoidance on the receive side. In the first approach, TCP acknowledges each segment that arrives, but does not advertise an increase in its window until the window reaches the limits specified by the silly window avoidance heuristic. In the second approach, TCP delays sending an acknowledgement when silly window avoidance specifies that the window is not sufficiently large to advertise. The standards recommend delaying acknowledgements.

Delayed acknowledgements have both advantages and disadvantages. The chief advantage arises because delayed acknowledgements can decrease traffic and thereby increase throughput. For example, if additional data arrives during the delay period, a single acknowledgement will acknowledge all data received. If the receiving application generates a response immediately after data arrives (e.g., character echo in a remote login session), a short delay may permit the acknowledgement to piggyback on a data segment. Furthermore, TCP cannot move its window until the receiving application extracts data from the buffer. In cases where the receiving application reads data as soon as it arrives, a short delay allows TCP to send a single segment that acknowledges the data and advertises an updated window. Without delayed acknowledgements, TCP will acknowledge the arrival of data immediately, and later send an additional acknowledgement to update the window size.

The disadvantages of delayed acknowledgements should be clear. Most important, if a receiver delays acknowledgements too long, the sending TCP will retransmit the segment. Unnecessary retransmissions lower throughput because they waste network bandwidth. In addition, retransmissions require computational overhead on the sending and receiving machines. Furthermore, TCP uses the arrival of acknowledgements to estimate round trip times; delaying acknowledgements can confuse the estimate and make retransmission times too long.

To avoid potential problems, the TCP standards place a limit on the time TCP delays an acknowledgement. Implementations cannot delay an acknowledgement for more than 500 milliseconds. Furthermore, to guarantee that TCP receives a sufficient number of round trip estimates, the standard recommends that a receiver should acknowledge at least every other data segment.

13.30.3 Send-Side Silly Window Avoidance

The heuristic a sending TCP uses to avoid silly window syndrome is both surprising and elegant. Recall that the goal is to avoid sending small segments. Also recall that a sending application can generate data in arbitrarily small blocks (e.g., one octet at a time). Thus, to achieve the goal, a sending TCP must allow the sending application to make multiple calls to *write*, and must collect the data transferred in each call before transmitting it in a single, large segment. That is, a sending TCP must delay sending a segment until it can accumulate a reasonable amount of data. The technique is known as *clumping*.

The question arises, "How long should TCP wait before transmitting data?" On one hand, if TCP waits too long, the application experiences large delays. More important, TCP cannot know whether to wait because it cannot know whether the application will generate more data in the near future. On the other hand, if TCP does not wait long enough, segments will be small and throughput will be low.

Protocols designed prior to TCP confronted the same problem and used techniques to clump data into larger packets. For example, to achieve efficient transfer across a network, early remote terminal protocols delayed transmitting each keystroke for a few hundred milliseconds to determine whether the user would continue to press keys. Because TCP is designed to be general, however, it can be used by a diverse set of applications. Characters may travel across a TCP connection because a user is typing on a keyboard or because a program is transferring a file. A fixed delay is not optimal for all applications.

Like the algorithm TCP uses for retransmission and the slow start algorithm used to avoid congestion, the technique a sending TCP uses to avoid sending small packets is adaptive – the delay depends on the current performance of the internet. Like slow start, send-side silly window avoidance is called *self clocking* because it does not compute delays. Instead, TCP uses the arrival of an acknowledgement to trigger the transmission of additional packets. The heuristic can be summarized:

> *Send-Side Silly Window Avoidance: When a sending application generates additional data to be sent over a connection for which previous data has been transmitted but not acknowledged, place the new data in the output buffer as usual, but do not send additional segments until there is sufficient data to fill a maximum-sized segment. If still waiting to send when an acknowledgement arrives, send all data that has accumulated in the buffer. Apply the rule even when the user requests a* push *operation.*

If an application generates data one octet at a time, TCP will send the first octet immediately. However, until the ACK arrives, TCP will accumulate additional octets in its buffer. Thus, if the application is reasonably fast compared to the network (i.e., a file transfer), successive segments will each contain many octets. If the application is slow compared to the network (e.g., a user typing on a keyboard), small segments will be sent without long delay.

Known as the *Nagle algorithm* after its inventor, the technique is especially elegant because it requires little computational overhead. A host does not need to keep separate timers for each connection, nor does the host need to examine a clock when an application generates data. More important, although the technique adapts to arbitrary combinations of network delay, maximum segment size, and application speed, it does not lower throughput in conventional cases.

To understand why throughput remains high for conventional communication, observe that applications optimized for high throughput do not generate data one octet at a time (doing so would incur unnecessary operating system overhead). Instead, such applications write large blocks of data with each call. Thus, the outgoing TCP buffer begins with sufficient data for at least one maximum size segment. Furthermore, because the application produces data faster than TCP can transfer data, the sending buffer remains nearly full, and TCP does not delay transmission. As a result, TCP continues to send segments at whatever rate the internet can tolerate, while the application continues to fill the buffer. To summarize:

TCP now requires the sender and receiver to implement heuristics that avoid the silly window syndrome. A receiver avoids advertising a small window, and a sender uses an adaptive scheme to delay transmission so it can clump data into large segments.

13.31 Summary

The Transmission Control Protocol, TCP, defines a key service provided by an internet, namely, reliable stream delivery. TCP provides a full duplex connection between two machines, allowing them to exchange large volumes of data efficiently.

Because it uses a sliding window protocol, TCP can make efficient use of a network. Because it makes few assumptions about the underlying delivery system, TCP is flexible enough to operate over a large variety of delivery systems. Because it provides flow control, TCP allows systems of widely varying speeds to communicate.

The basic unit of transfer used by TCP is a segment. Segments are used to pass data or control information (e.g., to allow TCP software on two machines to establish connections or break them). The segment format permits a machine to piggyback acknowledgements for data flowing in one direction by including them in the segment headers of data flowing in the opposite direction.

TCP implements flow control by having the receiver advertise the amount of data it is willing to accept. It also supports out-of-band messages using an urgent data facility and forces delivery using a push mechanism.

The current TCP standard specifies exponential backoff for retransmission timers and congestion avoidance algorithms like slow-start, multiplicative decrease, and additive increase. In addition, TCP uses heuristics to avoid transferring small packets.

FOR FURTHER STUDY

The standard for TCP can be found in Postel [RFC 793]; Braden [RFC 1122] contains an update that clarifies several points. Clark [RFC 813] describes TCP window management, Clark [RFC 816] describes fault isolation and recovery, and Postel [RFC 879] reports on TCP maximum segment sizes. Nagle [RFC 896] comments on congestion in TCP/IP networks and explains the effect of self clocking for send-side silly window avoidance. Karn and Partridge [1987] discusses estimation of round-trip times, and presents Karn's algorithm. Jacobson [1988] gives the congestion control algorithms that are now a required part of the standard. Tomlinson [1975] considers the three-way handshake in more detail. Mills [RFC 889] reports measurements of Internet round-trip delays. Jain [1986] describes timer-based congestion control in a sliding window environment. Borman [April 1989] summarizes experiments with high-speed TCP on Cray computers.

EXERCISES

13.1   TCP uses a finite field to contain stream sequence numbers. Study the protocol specification to find out how it allows an arbitrary length stream to pass from one machine to another.

13.2   The text notes that one of the TCP options permits a receiver to specify the maximum segment size it is willing to accept. Why does TCP support an option to specify maximum segment size when it also has a window advertisement mechanism?

13.3   Under what conditions of delay, bandwidth, load, and packet loss will TCP retransmit significant volumes of data unnecessarily?

13.4   Lost TCP acknowledgements do not necessarily force retransmissions. Explain why.

13.5   Experiment with local machines to determine how TCP handles machine restart. Establish a connection (e.g., a remote login) and leave it idle. Wait for the destination machine to crash and restart, and then force the local machine to send a TCP segment (e.g., by typing characters to the remote login).

13.6   Imagine an implementation of TCP that discards segments that arrive out of order, even if they fall in the current window. That is, the imagined version only accepts segments that extend the byte stream it has already received. Does it work? How does it compare to a standard TCP implementation?

13.7   Consider computation of a TCP checksum. Assume that although the checksum field in the segment has *not* been set to zero, the result of computing the checksum *is* zero. What can you conclude?

13.8   What are the arguments for and against automatically closing idle connections?

13.9   If two application programs use TCP to send data but only send one character per segment (e.g., by using the PUSH operation), what is the maximum percent of the network bandwidth they will have for their data?

13.10   Suppose an implementation of TCP uses initial sequence number *1* when it creates a connection. Explain how a system crash and restart can confuse a remote system into believing that the old connection remained open.

13.11   Look at the round-trip time estimation algorithm suggested in the ISO TP-4 protocol specification and compare it to the TCP algorithm discussed in this chapter. Which would you prefer to use?

13.12   Find out how implementations of TCP must solve the *overlapping segment problem*. The problem arises because the receiver must receive only one copy of all bytes from the data stream even if the sender transmits two segments that partially overlap one another (e.g., the first segment carries bytes 100 through 200 and the second carries bytes 150 through 250).

13.13   Trace the TCP finite state machine transitions for two sites that execute a passive and active open and step through the three-way handshake.

13.14   Read the TCP specification to find out the exact conditions under which TCP can make the transition from *FIN WAIT-1* to *TIMED WAIT*.

13.15   Trace the TCP state transitions for two machines that agree to close a connection gracefully.

13.16   Assume TCP is sending segments using a maximum window size (64 Kbytes) on a channel that has infinite bandwidth and an average roundtrip time of 20 milliseconds. What is the maximum throughput? How does throughput change if the roundtrip time increases to 40 milliseconds (while bandwidth remains infinite)?

13.17   Can you derive an equation that expresses the maximum possible TCP throughput as a function of the network bandwidth, the network delay, and the time to process a segment and generate an acknowledgement. Hint: consider the previous exercise.

13.18   Describe (abnormal) circumstances that can leave one end of a connection in state *FIN WAIT-2* indefinitely (hint: think of datagram loss and system crashes).

14

Routing: Cores, Peers, And Algorithms (GGP)

14.1 Introduction

Previous chapters concentrate on the network level services TCP/IP offers and the details of the protocols in hosts and routers that provide those services. In the discussion, we assumed that routers always contain correct routes, and we observed that routers can ask directly connected hosts to change routes with the ICMP redirect mechanism.

This chapter considers two broad questions: "What values should routing tables contain?" and "How can those values be obtained?" To answer the first question, we will consider the relationship between internet architecture and routing. In particular, we will discuss internets structured around a backbone and those composed of multiple peer networks, and consider the consequences for routing. While many of our examples are drawn from the global Internet, the ideas apply equally well to smaller corporate internets. To answer the second question, we will consider the two basic types of route propagation algorithms and see how each supplies routing information automatically.

We begin by discussing routing in general. Later sections concentrate on internet architecture and describe the type of protocols routers use to exchange routing information. Chapters 15 and 16 continue to expand our discussion of routing. They explore protocols that routers owned by two independent administrative groups use to exchange information, and protocols that a single group uses among all its routers.

14.2 The Origin Of Routing Tables

Recall from Chapter 3 that IP routers provide active interconnections among networks. Each router attaches to two or more physical networks and forwards IP datagrams among them, accepting datagrams that arrive over one network interface, and routing them out over another interface. Except for destinations on directly attached networks, hosts pass all IP traffic to routers which forward datagrams on toward their final destinations. A datagram travels from router to router until it reaches a router that attaches directly to the same network as the final destination. Thus, the router system forms the architectural basis of an internet and handles all traffic except for direct delivery from one host to another.

Chapter 8 described the IP routing algorithm that hosts and routers follow to forward datagrams, and showed how the algorithm uses a table to make routing decisions. Each entry in the routing table specifies the network portion of a destination address and gives the address of the next machine along a path used to reach that network. Like hosts, routers directly deliver datagrams to destinations on networks to which the router attaches.

Although we have seen the basics of datagram forwarding, we have not said how hosts or routers obtain the information for their routing tables. The issue has two aspects: *what* values should be placed in the tables, and *how* routers obtain those values. Both choices depend on the architectural complexity and size of the internet as well as administrative policies.

In general, establishing routes involves initialization and update. Each router must establish an initial set of routes when it starts, and it must update the table as routes change (e.g., when a network interface fails). Initialization depends on the operating system. In some systems, the router reads an initial routing table from secondary storage at startup, keeping it resident in main memory. In others, the operating system begins with an empty table which must be filled in by executing explicit commands (e.g., commands found in a startup command script). Finally, some operating systems start by deducing an initial set of routes from the set of addresses for the local networks to which the machine attaches and contacting a neighboring machine to ask for additional routes.

Once an initial routing table has been built, a router must accommodate changes in routes. In small, slowly changing internets, managers can establish and modify routes by hand. In large, rapidly changing environments, however, manual update is impossibly slow. Automated methods are needed.

Before we can understand the automatic routing table update protocols used in IP routers, we need to review several underlying ideas. The next sections do so, providing the necessary conceptual foundation for routing. Later sections discuss internet architecture and the protocols routers use to exchange routing information.

14.3 Routing With Partial Information

The principal difference between routers and typical hosts is that hosts usually know little about the structure of the internet to which they connect. Hosts do not have complete knowledge of all possible destination addresses, or even of all possible destination networks. In fact, many hosts have only two routes in their routing table: a route for the local network and a default route for a nearby router. The host sends all nonlocal datagrams to the local router for delivery. The point is that:

> *A host can route datagrams successfully even if it only has partial routing information because it can rely on a router.*

Can routers also route datagrams with only partial information? Yes, but only under certain circumstances. To understand the criteria, imagine an internet to be a foreign country crisscrossed with dirt roads that have directional signs posted at intersections. Imagine that you have no map, cannot ask directions because you cannot speak the local language, have no ideas about visible landmarks, but you need to travel to a village named *Sussex*. You leave on your journey, following the only road out of town and begin to look for directional signs. The first sign reads:

Norfolk to the left; Hammond to the right; others straight ahead.†

Because the destination you seek is not listed explicitly, you continue straight ahead. In routing jargon, we say you follow a *default route*. After several more signs, you finally find one that reads:

Essex to the left; Sussex to the right; others straight ahead.

You turn to the right, follow several more signs, and emerge on a road that leads to Sussex.

Our imagined travel is analogous to a datagram traversing an internet, and the road signs are analogous to routing tables in routers along the path. Without a map or other navigational aids, travel is completely dependent on road signs, just as datagram routing in an internet depends entirely on routing tables. Clearly, it is possible to navigate even though each road sign contains only partial information.

A central question concerns correctness. As a traveler, you might ask, "How can I be sure that following signs will lead to my final destination?" You also might ask, "How can I be sure that following the signs will lead me to my destination along a shortest path?" These questions may seem especially troublesome if you pass many signs without finding your destination listed explicitly. Of course, the answers depend on the topology of the road system and the contents of the signs, but the fundamental idea is that when taken as a whole, the information on the signs should be both consistent and complete. Looking at this another way, we see that it is not necessary for each intersection to have a sign for every destination. The signs can list default paths as

---

†Fortunately, signs are printed in a language you can read.

long as all explicit signs point along a shortest path, and the turns for shortest paths to all destinations are marked. A few examples will explain some ways that consistency can be achieved.

At one extreme, consider a simple star-shaped topology of roads in which each village has exactly one road leading to it, and all those roads meet at a central point. To guarantee consistency, the sign at the central intersection must contain information about all possible destinations. At the other extreme, imagine an arbitrary set of roads with signs at all intersections listing all possible destinations. To guarantee consistency, it must be true that at any intersection if the sign for destination D points to road R, no road other than R leads to a shorter path to D.

Neither of these architectural extremes works well for an internet router system. On one hand, the central intersection approach fails because no machine is fast enough to serve as a central switch through which all traffic passes. On the other hand, having information about all possible destinations in all routers is impractical because it requires propagating large volumes of information whenever a change occurs or whenever administrators need to check consistency. Thus, we seek a solution that allows groups to manage local routers autonomously, adding new network interconnections and routes without changing distant routers.

To help explain some of the architecture described later, consider a third topology in which half the cities lie in the eastern part of the country and half lie in the western part. Suppose a single bridge spans the river that separates east from west. Assume that people living in the eastern part do not like westerners, so they are willing to allow road signs that list destinations in the east but none in the west. Assume that people living in the west do the opposite. Routing will be consistent if every road sign in the east lists all eastern destinations explicitly and points the default path to the bridge, while every road sign in the west lists all western destinations explicitly and points the default path to the bridge.

14.4 Original Internet Architecture And Cores

Much of our knowledge of routing and route propagation protocols has been derived from experience with the global Internet. When TCP/IP was first developed, participating research sites were connected to the ARPANET, which served as the Internet backbone. During initial experiments, each site managed routing tables and installed routes to other destinations by hand. As the fledgling Internet began to grow, it became apparent that manual maintenance of routes was impractical; automated mechanisms were needed.

The Internet designers selected a router architecture that consisted of a small, central set of routers that kept complete information about all possible destinations, and a larger set of outlying routers that kept partial information. In terms of our analogy, it is like designating a small set of centrally located intersections to have signs that list all destinations, and allowing the outlying intersections to list only local destinations. As long as the default route at each outlying intersection points to one of the central intersections, travelers will eventually reach their destination. The advantage of using partial information in outlying routers is that it permits local administrators to manage local structural changes without affecting other parts of the Internet. The disadvantage is that it introduces the potential for inconsistency. In the worst case, an error in an outlying router can make distant routes unreachable.

We can summarize these ideas:

> *The routing table in a given router contains partial information about possible destinations. Routing that uses partial information allows sites autonomy in making local routing changes, but introduces the possibility of inconsistencies that may make some destinations unreachable from some sources.*

Inconsistencies among routing tables usually arise from errors in the algorithms that compute routing tables, incorrect data supplied to those algorithms, or from errors that occur while transmitting the results to other routers. Protocol designers look for ways to limit the impact of errors, with the objective being to keep all routes consistent at all times. If routes become inconsistent for some reason, the routing protocols should be robust enough to detect and correct the errors quickly. Most important, the protocols should be designed to constrain the effect of errors.

14.5 Core Routers

Loosely speaking, early Internet routers could be partitioned into two groups, a small set of *core routers* controlled by the Internet Network Operations Center (INOC), and a larger set of *noncore routers*† controlled by individual groups. The core system was designed to provide reliable, consistent, authoritative routes for all possible destinations; it was the glue that held the Internet together and made universal interconnection possible. By fiat, each site assigned an Internet network address had to arrange to advertise that address to the core system. The core routers communicated among themselves, so they could guarantee that the information they shared was consistent. Because a central authority monitored and controlled the core routers, they were highly reliable.

To fully understand the core router system, it is necessary to recall that the Internet evolved with a wide-area network, the ARPANET, already in place. When the Internet experiments began, designers thought of the ARPANET as a main backbone on which to build. Thus, a large part of the motivation for the core router system came from the desire to connect local networks to the ARPANET. Figure 14.1 illustrates the idea.

---

†The terms *stub router* and *nonrouting router* have also been applied to routers that connected local area networks to the ARPANET.

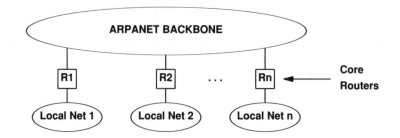

Figure 14.1 The Internet core router system viewed as a set of routers that connect local area networks to the ARPANET. Hosts on the local networks pass all nonlocal traffic to the closest core router.

To understand why such an architecture does not lend itself to routing with partial information, suppose that a large internet consists entirely of local area networks, each attached to a backbone network through a router. Also imagine that some of the routers rely on default routes. Now consider the path a datagram follows. At the source site, the local router checks to see if it has an explicit route to the destination and, if not, sends the datagram along the path specified by its default route. All datagrams for which the router has no route follow the same default path regardless of their ultimate destination. The next router along the path diverts datagrams for which it has an explicit route, and sends the rest along its default route. To insure global consistency, the chain of default routes must reach every router in a giant cycle as Figure 14.2 shows. Thus, the architecture requires all local sites to coordinate their default routes. In addition, depending on default routes can be inefficient even when it is consistent. As Figure 14.2 shows, in the worst case a datagram will pass through all *n* routers as it travels from source to destination instead of going directly across the backbone.

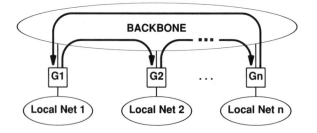

Figure 14.2 A set of routers connected to a backbone network with default routes shown. Routing is inefficient even though it is consistent.

To avoid the inefficiencies default routes cause, Internet designers arranged for all core routers to exchange routing information so that each would have complete information about optimal routes to all possible destinations. Because each core router knew routes to all possible destinations, it did not need a default route. If the destination address on a datagram was not in a core router's routing table, the router would generate an ICMP destination unreachable message and drop the datagram. In essence, the core design avoided inefficiency by eliminating default routes.

Figure 14.3 depicts the conceptual basis of a core routing architecture. The figure shows a central core system consisting of one or more core routers, and a set of outlying routers at local sites. Outlying routers keep information about local destinations and use a default route that sends datagrams destined for other sites to the core.

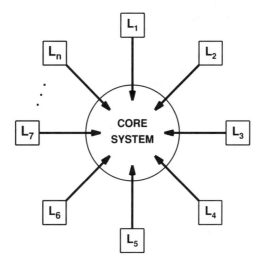

Figure 14.3 The routing architecture of a simplistic core system showing default routes. Core routers do not use default routes; outlying routers, labeled L_i, each have a default route that points to the core.

Although the simplistic core architecture illustrated in Figure 14.3 is easy to understand, it became impractical for three reasons. First, the Internet outgrew a single, centrally managed long-haul backbone. The topology became complex and the protocols needed to maintain consistency among core routers became nontrivial. Second, not every site could have a core router connected to the backbone, so additional routing structure and protocols were needed. Third, because core routers all interacted to ensure consistent routing information, the core architecture did not scale to large size. We will return to this last problem in Chapter 15 after we examine the protocols that the core system used to exchange routing information.

14.6 Beyond The Core Architecture To Peer Backbones

The introduction of the NSFNET backbone into the Internet added new complexity to the routing structure. From the core system point of view, the connection to NSFNET was initially no different than the connection to any other site. NSFNET attached to the ARPANET backbone through a single router in Pittsburgh. The core had explicit routes to all destinations in NSFNET. Routers inside NSFNET knew about local destinations and used a default route to send all non-NSFNET traffic to the core via the Pittsburgh router.

As NSFNET grew to become a major part of the Internet, it became apparent that the core routing architecture would not suffice. The most important conceptual change occurred when multiple connections were added between the ARPANET and NSFNET backbones. We say that the two became *peer backbone networks* or simply *peers*. Figure 14.4 illustrates the resulting peer topology.

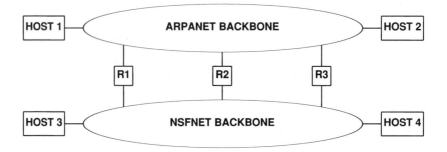

Figure 14.4 An example of peer backbones interconnected through multiple routers. The diagram illustrates the architecture of the Internet in 1989.

To understand the difficulties of IP routing among peer backbones, consider routes from host *3* to host *2* in Figure 14.4. Assume for the moment that the figure shows geographic orientation, so host *3* is on the West Coast attached to the NSFNET backbone while host *2* is on the East Coast attached to the ARPANET backbone. When establishing routes between hosts *3* and *2*, the managers must decide whether to (a) route the traffic from host *3* through the West Coast router, *R1*, and then across the ARPANET backbone, or (b) route the traffic from host *3* across the NSFNET backbone, through the Midwest router, *R2*, and then across the ARPANET backbone to host *2*, or (c) route the traffic across the NSFNET backbone, through the East Coast router, *R3*, and then to host *2*. A more circuitous route is possible as well: traffic could flow from host *3* through the West Coast router, across the ARPANET backbone to the Midwest router, back onto the NSFNET backbone to the East Coast router, and finally across the

ARPANET backbone to host *2*. Such a route may or may not be advisable, depending on the policies for network use and the capacity of various routers and backbones.

For most peer backbone configurations, traffic between a pair of geographically close hosts should take a shortest path, independent of the routes chosen for cross-country traffic. For example, traffic from host *3* to host *1* should flow through the West Coast router because it minimizes distance on both backbones.

All these statements sound simple enough, but they are complex to implement for two reasons. First, although the standard IP routing algorithm uses the network portion of an IP address to choose a route, optimal routing in a peer backbone architecture requires individual routes for individual hosts. For our example above, the routing table in host *3* needs different routes for host *1* and host 2, even though both hosts *1* and *2* attach to the ARPANET backbone. Second, managers of the two backbones must agree to keep routes consistent among all routers or *routing loops* can develop (a routing loop occurs when routes in a set of routers point in a circle).

It is important to distinguish network topology from routing architecture. It is possible, for example, to have a single core system that spans multiple backbone networks. The core machines can be programmed to hide the underlying architectural details and to compute shortest routes among themselves. It is not possible, however, to partition the core system into subsets that each keep partial information without losing functionality. Figure 14.5 illustrates the problem.

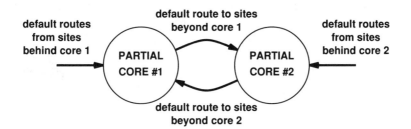

Figure 14.5 An attempt to partition a core routing architecture into two sets of routers that keep partial information and use default routes. Such an architecture results in a routing loop for datagrams that have an illegal (nonexistent) destination.

As the figure shows, outlying routers have default routes to one side of the partitioned core. Each side of the partition has information about destinations on its side of the world and a default route for information on the other side of the world. In such an architecture, any datagram sent to an illegal address will cycle between the two partitions in a routing loop until its time to live counter reaches zero.

We can summarize as follows:

A core routing architecture assumes a centralized set of routers serves as the repository of information about all possible destinations in an internet. Core systems work best for internets that have a single, centrally managed backbone. Expanding the topology to multiple backbones makes routing complex; attempting to partition the core architecture so that all routers use default routes introduces potential routing loops.

14.7 Automatic Route Propagation

We said that the original Internet core system avoided default routes because it propagated complete information about all possible destinations to every core router. Many corporate internets now use a similar scheme – routers in the corporation run programs that communicate routing information. The next sections discuss two basic types of algorithms that compute and propagate routing information, and use the original core routing protocol to illustrate one of the algorithms. A later section describes a protocol that uses the other type of algorithm.

It may seem that automatic route propagation mechanisms are not needed, especially on small internets. However, internets are not static. Connections fail and are later replaced. Networks can become overloaded at one moment and underutilized at the next. The purpose of routing propagation mechanisms is not merely to find a set of routes, but to continually update the information. Humans simply cannot respond to changes fast enough; computer programs must be used. Thus, when we think about route propagation, it is important to consider the dynamic behavior of protocols and algorithms.

14.8 Vector Distance (Bellman-Ford) Routing

The term *vector-distance*† refers to a class of algorithms routers use to propagate routing information. The idea behind vector-distance algorithms is quite simple. The router keeps a list of all known routes in a table. When it boots, a router initializes its routing table to contain an entry for each directly connected network. Each entry in the table identifies a destination network and gives the distance to that network, usually measured in hops (which will be defined more precisely later). For example, Figure 14.6 shows the initial contents of the table on a router that attaches to two networks.

---

†The names *Ford Fulkerson*, *Bellman-Ford*, and *Bellman* are synonymous with *vector-distance*; they are taken from the names of researchers who published the idea.

Destination	Distance	Route
Net 1	0	direct
Net 2	0	direct

Figure 14.6 An initial vector-distance routing table with an entry for each directly connected network. Each entry contains the IP address of a network and an integer distance to that network.

Periodically, each router sends a copy of its routing table to any other router it can reach directly. When a report arrives at router *K* from router *J*, *K* examines the set of destinations reported and the distance to each. If *J* knows a shorter way to reach a destination, or if *J* lists a destination that *K* does not have in its table, or if *K* currently routes to a destination through *J* and *J*'s distance to that destination changes, *K* replaces its table entry. For example, Figure 14.7 shows an existing table in a router, *K*, and an update message from another router, *J*.

Destination	Distance	Route
Net 1	0	direct
Net 2	0	direct
Net 4	8	Router L
Net 17	5	Router M
Net 24	6	Router J
Net 30	2	Router Q
Net 42	2	Router J

(a)

Destination	Distance
Net 1	2
➝ Net 4	3
Net 17	6
➝ Net 21	4
Net 24	5
Net 30	10
➝ Net 42	3

(b)

Figure 14.7 (a) An existing route table for a router *K*, and (b) an incoming routing update message from router *J*. The marked entries will be used to update existing entries or add new entries to *K*'s table.

Note that if *J* reports distance *N*, an updated entry in *K* will have distance *N+1* (the distance to reach the destination from *J* plus the distance to reach *J*). Of course, the routing table entries contain a third column that specifies a route. Initial entries are all marked *direct delivery*. When router *K* adds or updates an entry in response to a message from router *J*, it assigns router *J* as the route for that entry.

The term *vector-distance* comes from the information sent in the periodic messages. A message contains a list of pairs *(V, D)*, where *V* identifies a destination (called the *vector*), and *D* is the distance to that destination. Note that vector-distance algorithms report routes in the first person (i.e., we think of a router advertising, "I can reach destination V at distance D''). In such a design, all routers must participate in the vector-distance exchange for the routes to be efficient and consistent.

Although vector-distance algorithms are easy to implement, they have disadvantages. In a completely static environment, vector-distance algorithms propagate routes to all destinations. When routes change rapidly, however, the computations may not stabilize. When a route changes (i.e, a new connection appears or an old one fails), the information propagates slowly from one router to another. Meanwhile, some routers may have incorrect routing information.

For now, we will examine a protocol that uses the vector-distance algorithm without discussing all the shortcomings. Chapter 16 completes the discussion by showing another vector-distance protocol, the problems that can arise, and the heuristics used to solve the most serious of them.

14.9 Gateway-To-Gateway Protocol (GGP)

The original core routers used a vector-distance protocol known as the *Gateway-to-Gateway Protocol† (GGP)* to exchange routing information. While GGP is no longer a key part of the TCP/IP suite, it does provide a concrete example of vector-distance routing. GGP was designed to travel in IP datagrams similar to UDP datagrams or TCP segments. Each GGP message has a fixed format header that identifies the message type and the format of the remaining fields. Because only core routers participated in GGP, and because core routers were controlled by the INOC, other routers could not interfere with the exchange.

The original core system was arranged to permit new core routers to be added without modifying existing routers. When a new router was added to the core system, it was assigned one or more core *neighbors* with which it communicated. The neighbors, members of the core, already propagated routing information among themselves. Thus, the new router only needed to inform its neighbors about networks it could reach; they updated their routing tables and propagated this new information further.

GGP is a true vector-distance protocol. The information routers exchange with GGP consists of a set of pairs, (N, D), where N is an IP network address, and D is a distance measured in hops. We say that a router using GGP *advertises* the networks it can reach and its cost for reaching them.

GGP measures distance in *router hops*, where a router is defined to be zero hops from directly connected networks, one hop from networks that are reachable through one other router, and so on. Thus, the *number of hops* or the *hop count* along a path from a given source to a given destination refers to the number of routers that a datagram encounters along that path. It should be obvious that using hop counts to calculate shortest paths does not always produce desirable results. For example, a path with hop count *3* that crosses three LANs may be substantially faster than a path with hop count *2* that crosses two slow speed serial lines. Many routers use artificially high hop counts for routes across slow networks.

---

†Recall that although vendors adopted the term *router*, scientists originally used the term *IP gateway*.

14.10 GGP Message Formats

There are four types of GGP messages, each with its own format. The first octet contains a code that identifies the message *type*. Figure 14.8 shows the format of one GGP message type, the message routers exchange to learn about routes. Recall that the information consists of pairs of IP network and distance values. To keep messages small, networks are grouped together by distance, and the message consists of a sequence of sets, where each set contains a distance value followed by a list of all networks at that distance.

The value *12* in the field labeled *TYPE* specifies that this message is a *routing update* message, distinguishing it from other GGP message types. The 16-bit *SEQUENCE NUMBER* is used to validate a GGP message; both sender and receiver must agree on the sequence number before the receiver will accept the message. The field labeled *UPDATE* is a binary value that specifies whether the sender needs an update from the receiver. Because GGP groups networks by distance, the field labeled *NUM DISTANCES* specifies how many distance groups are present in this update.

The last part of a GGP routing update message contains sets of networks grouped by distance. Each set starts with two 8-bit fields that specify a distance value and a count of networks at that distance. If the count specifies *n* networks at a given distance, exactly *n* network IP addresses must occur before the next set header. To conserve space, only the network portion of the IP address is included, so network numbers may be 1, 2, or 3 octets long. The receiver must look at the first bits of the network identifier to determine its length.

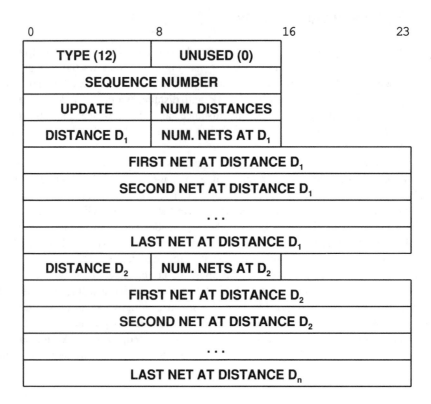

Figure 14.8 The format of a GGP routing update message. A router sends
such a message to advertise destination networks it knows how
to reach. Network numbers contain either 1, 2, or 3 octets,
depending on whether the network is class *A*, *B*, or *C*.

When a router receives a GGP routing update message, it sends a GGP *acknowledgement* message back to the sender, using a positive acknowledgement if the routing update was acceptable, and a negative acknowledgement if an error was detected. Figure 14.9 illustrates the format of GGP acknowledgements:

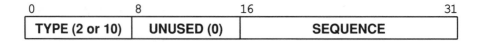

Figure 14.9 The format of a GGP acknowledgement message. Type *2* identifies the message as a positive acknowledgement, while type *10* identifies the message as a negative acknowledgement.

In positive acknowledgement messages, the field labeled *SEQUENCE* specifies a sequence number that the receiver is acknowledging. In negative acknowledgements, the *SEQUENCE* field gives the sequence number that the receiver last received correctly.

In addition to routing update messages, the GGP protocol includes messages that allow one router to test whether another is responding. A router sends an *echo request* message to a neighbor, which requests that the recipient respond by sending back an *echo reply* message. Figure 14.10 shows the echo message formats.

```
0                      8                                              31
 ┌─────────────────────┬───────────────────────────────────────────┐
 │   TYPE (0 or 8)      │              UNUSED (0)                    │
 └─────────────────────┴───────────────────────────────────────────┘
```

Figure 14.10 The format of a GGP echo request or reply message. Type *8* identifies the message as an echo request, while type *0* identifies the message as an echo reply.

14.11 Link-State (SPF) Routing

The main disadvantage of vector-distance algorithms is that they do not scale well. Besides the problem of slow response to change mentioned earlier, the algorithm requires large message exchanges. Because routing update messages contain an entry for every possible network, message size is proportional to the total number of networks in an internet. Furthermore, because a vector-distance protocol requires every router to participate, the volume of information exchanged can be enormous.

The primary alternative to vector-distance algorithms is a class of algorithms known as *link-state*, *Shortest Path First*, or *SPF*†. SPF algorithms require each participating router to have complete topology information. The easiest way to think of the topology information is to imagine that every router has a map that shows all other routers and the networks to which they connect. In abstract terms, the routers correspond to nodes in a graph and networks that connect routers correspond to edges. There is an edge (link) between two nodes if and only if the corresponding routers can communicate directly.

Instead of sending messages that contain lists of destinations, a router participating in an SPF algorithm performs two tasks. First, it actively tests the status of all neighbor routers. In terms of the graph, two routers are neighbors if they share a link; in network terms, two neighbors connect to a common network. Second, it periodically propagates the link status information to all other routers.

To test the status of a directly connected neighbor, a router periodically exchanges short messages that ask whether the neighbor is alive and reachable. If the neighbor replies, the link between them is said to be 'up'. Otherwise, the link is said to be 'down'. (In practice, to prevent oscillations between the up and down states, most protocols use

---

†The name "shortest path first" is an unfortunate misnomer because most route computations choose shortest paths. However, it seems to have gained wide acceptance.

a *k-out-of-n rule* to test liveness, meaning that the link remains up until a significant percentage of requests have no reply, and then it remains down until a significant percentage of messages receive a reply.)

To inform all other routers, each router periodically broadcasts a message that lists the status (state) of each of its links. The status message does not specify routes – it simply reports whether communication is possible between pairs of routers. Protocol software in the routers arranges to deliver a copy of each link status message to all participating routers (if the underlying networks do not support broadcast, delivery is done by forwarding individual copies of the message point-to-point).

Whenever a link status message arrives, a router uses the information to update its map of the internet, by marking links 'up' or 'down'. Whenever link status changes, the router recomputes routes by applying the well-known *Dijkstra shortest path algorithm* to the resulting graph. Dijkstra's algorithm computes the shortest paths to all destinations from a single source.

One of the chief advantages of SPF algorithms is that each router computes routes independently using the same original status data; they do not depend on the computation of intermediate machines. Because link status messages propagate unchanged, it is easy to debug problems. Because routers perform the route computation locally, it is guaranteed to converge. Finally, because link status messages only carry information about the direct connections from a single router, the size does not depend on the number of networks in the internet. Thus, SPF algorithms scale better than vector-distance algorithms.

14.12 SPF Protocols

Besides proprietary protocols offered by vendors, only a few SPF protocols are currently used in the Internet. One of the first examples of SPF comes from the ARPANET, which used an SPF algorithm internally for approximately ten years. At the other extreme, Chapter 16 discusses a general purpose SPF protocol currently used in the Internet.

By 1988, the Internet core system had switched from early Digital Equipment Corporation LSI-11 computers running GGP to Bolt, Beranek, and Newman Computer Corporation *Butterfly* processors that use a Shortest Path First algorithm. The exact protocol, known as *SPREAD* was not documented in the RFC literature.

14.13 Summary

To ensure that all networks remain reachable with high reliability, an internet must provide globally consistent routing. Hosts and most routers contain only partial routing information; they depend on default routes to send datagrams to distant destinations. The global Internet solves the routing problem by using a core router architecture in which a set of core routers contain complete information about all networks. Routers in the original Internet core system exchanged routing information periodically, meaning that once a single core router learned about a route, all core routers learned about it. To prevent routing loops, core routers were forbidden from using default routes.

A single, centrally managed core system works well for an internet architecture built on a single backbone network. However, when an internet has multiple, separately managed peer backbones that interconnect at multiple places, the core architecture does not suffice.

When routers exchange routing information they usually use one of two basic algorithms, vector-distance or SPF. We examined the details of GGP, the vector-distance protocol originally used to propagate routing update information throughout the core. Each GGP routing update can be viewed as an advertisement that lists a set of networks along with the router's cost to reach those network.

The chief disadvantage of vector-distance algorithms is that they perform a distributed shortest path computation that may not converge if the status of network connections changes continually. Another disadvantage is that routing update messages grow large as the number of networks increases.

FOR FURTHER STUDY

The definition of the core router system and GGP protocol in this chapter comes from Hinden and Sheltzer [RFC 823]. Braden and Postel [RFC 1009] contains further specifications for Internet routers. Almquist [RFC 1716] summarizes recent discussions. Braun [RFC 1093] and Rekhter [RFC 1092] discusses routing in the NSFNET backbone. Clark [RFC 1102] and Braun [RFC 1104] both discuss policy-based routing. The next two chapters present protocols used for propagating routing information between separate sites and within a single site.

EXERCISES

14.1 Suppose a router discovers it is about to route an IP datagram back over the same network interface on which the datagram arrived. What should it do? Why?

14.2 After reading RFC 823 and RFC 1009, explain what an Internet core router does in the situation described in the previous question.

14.3 How do routers in a core system use default routes to send all illegal datagrams to a specific machine?

14.4 Imagine students experimenting with a router that attaches a local area network to the Internet. They want to advertise their network to the core router system, but if they accidentally advertise zero length routes to arbitrary networks, real Internet traffic will be diverted to their router. How can the core protect itself from illegal data while still accepting updates from such 'untrusted' routers?

14.5   Which ICMP messages does a router generate?

14.6   How did the original Internet core routers determine whether a designated neighbor was 'up' or 'down'? (Hint: consult RFC 823.)

14.7   Suppose two core routers each advertise the same cost, k, to reach a given network, N. Describe the circumstances under which routing through one of them may take fewer total hops than routing through the other one.

14.8   How does a router know whether an incoming datagram carries a GGP message?

14.9   Consider the vector-distance update shown in Figure 14.7 carefully. Give three reasons why the router will update its table with the three items shown.

15

Routing: Autonomous Systems (EGP)

15.1 Introduction

The previous chapter introduces the idea of route propagation and examines one protocol routers use to exchange routing information. This chapter extends our understanding of internet router architecture. It discusses the concept of autonomous systems and shows a protocol that a group of networks and routers operating under one administrative authority uses to propagate network reachability information to other groups.

15.2 Adding Complexity To The Architectural Model

The original core router system evolved at a time when the Internet had a single backbone. Consequently, part of the motivation for a core architecture was to provide connections between local area networks and the backbone (see Figure 14.1). If an internet consists of only a single backbone plus a set of attached local area networks, no further structure is needed. Each router knows the single local network to which it attaches and learns about all other networks by communicating across the backbone with other routers. Unfortunately, having all routers participate directly in a routing update protocol does not suffice except for trivial internets. First, even if each site attached to the internet has only one local network, a core architecture is inadequate because it cannot grow to accommodate an arbitrary number of sites. Second, most sites have multiple local area networks and multiple routers interconnecting them. Because a core router connects to a single network at each site, the core only knows about one network

249

at that site. Third, a large internet interconnects sets of networks managed by independent groups. A routing architecture must provide a way for each group to independently control routing and access. After examining the consequences of each of these ideas,
we will learn how a single protocol mechanism allows construction of an internet that
spans multiple sites while allowing autonomy at each site.

15.3 A Fundamental Idea: Extra Hops

So far, we have discussed an internet architecture consisting of one or more backbone networks surrounded by a core router system. We have been thinking of the core
system as a central routing mechanism to which noncore routers can send datagrams for
delivery. We also said that it is impossible to expand a single backbone arbitrarily.
Having fewer core routers than networks in the internet means that we must change our
view of core architecture or routing will be suboptimal. To see why, consider the example in Figure 15.1

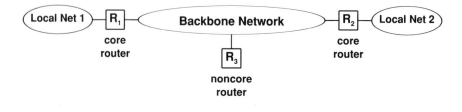

Figure 15.1 The extra hop problem. Noncore routers connected to the backbone must learn routes from core routers to have optimal routing.

In the figure, core routers R_1 and R_2 connect to local area networks *1* and *2*, respectively. Because they exchange routing information, they both know how to reach both networks. Suppose noncore router R_3 thinks of the core as a delivery system and chooses
one of the core routers, say R_1, to deliver all datagrams destined for networks to which
it has no direct connection. R_3 sends datagrams for network *2* across the backbone to
its chosen core router, R_1, which must then send them back across the backbone to
router R_2. The optimal route, of course, requires R_3 to send datagrams destined for network *2* directly to R_2. Notice that the choice of core router makes no difference. Only
destinations that lie beyond the chosen router have optimal routes; all paths that go
through other backbone routers require an extra hop. Also notice that the core routers
cannot use ICMP redirect messages to inform R_3 that it has incorrect routes because
ICMP redirect messages can only be sent to the original source and not to intermediate
routers.

We call the routing anomaly illustrated in Figure 15.1 the *extra hop problem*.
Solving it requires us to change our view of a core architecture:

> *Treating a core system as a central router introduces an extra hop for*
> *most traffic. A mechanism is needed that allows noncore routers to*
> *learn routes from core routers so they can choose optimal backbone*
> *routes.*

Allowing sites to have multiple networks and routers means that the core does not
attach to all networks directly, so an additional mechanism is needed to allow the core
system to learn about them. Consider, for example, the set of networks and routers
shown in Figure 15.2. We might imagine such an interconnection on a corporate or
university campus, where each network corresponds to a single building or to a single
department.

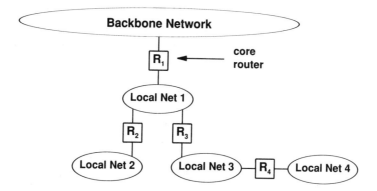

Figure 15.2 An example of multiple networks and routers with a single backbone connection. A mechanism is needed to pass reachability
information about additional local networks to the core system.

Suppose the site has just installed local network *4* and has obtained an internet address
for it. Also assume that the routers R_2, R_3, and R_4 have routes for all four local networks as well as default routes that pass other traffic to the core router, R_1. Hosts
directly attached to local network *4* can communicate with one another, and any
machine on that network can route packets out to other backbone sites. However, because router R_1 attaches only to local network *1*, it does not know about local network
4. We say that, from the point of view of the core system, local network *4* is *hidden*
behind local network *1*. The important point is:

Because individual sites can have an arbitrarily complex structure, a core system will not attach directly to all networks. A mechanism is needed that allows noncore routers to inform the core about hidden networks.

Keep in mind that in addition to providing the core with information about hidden networks, we need a mechanism that allows noncore routers to obtain routing information from the core. Ideally, a single mechanism should solve both problems. Building such a mechanism can be tricky. The subtle issues are responsibility and capability. Exactly where does responsibility for informing the core reside? If we decide that one of the routers should inform the core, which one is capable of doing it? Look again at the example. Router R_4 is the router most closely associated with local network *4*, but it lies *2* hops away from the nearest core router. Thus, R_4 must depend on router R_3 to route packets to network *4*. The point is that R_4 cannot guarantee reachability of local network *4* on its own. Router R_3 lies one hop from the core and can guarantee to pass packets, but it does not directly attach to local network *4*. So, it seems incorrect to grant R_3 responsibility for network *4*. Solving this dilemma will require us to introduce a new concept. The next sections discuss the concept and a protocol built around it.

15.4 Autonomous System Concept

The puzzle over which router should communicate reachability information to the core system arises because we have only considered the mechanics of an internet routing architecture and not the administrative issues. Interconnections, like those in the example of Figure 15.2, that arise when a backbone site has a complex local structure, should not be thought of as multiple independent networks connected to an internet, but as a single organization that has multiple networks under its control. Because the networks and routers fall under a single administrative authority, that authority can guarantee that internal routes remain consistent and viable. Furthermore, the administrative authority can choose one of its machines to serve as the machine that will apprise the outside world of network reachability. In the example from Figure 15.2, because routers R_2, R_3, and R_4 fall under control of one administrative authority, that authority can arrange to have R_3 advertise reachability for networks *2*, *3*, and *4* (we assume the core system already knows about network *1* because a core router attaches directly to it).

For purposes of routing, a group of networks and routers controlled by a single administrative authority is called an *autonomous system*. Routers within an autonomous system are free to choose their own mechanisms for discovering, propagating, validating, and checking the consistency of routes. Note that, under this definition, the core routers themselves form an autonomous system. We said that the original Internet core routers used GGP to communicate among themselves and that a later version used

SPREAD. The change was made without affecting routers in other autonomous systems. The next chapter reviews protocols that autonomous systems now use to propagate routing information.

Conceptually, the autonomous system idea is a straightforward and natural generalization of the architecture, depicted by Figure 15.2, with autonomous systems replacing local area networks. Figure 15.3 illustrates the idea.

To make networks that are hidden inside autonomous systems reachable throughout the Internet, each autonomous system must agree to advertise network reachability information to other autonomous systems. Although advertisements can be sent to any autonomous system, in a core architecture, it is crucial that each autonomous system propagate information to a core router. Usually, one router in an autonomous system takes responsibility for advertising routes and interacts directly with one of the core routers. It is possible, however, to have several routers each advertise a subset of the networks.

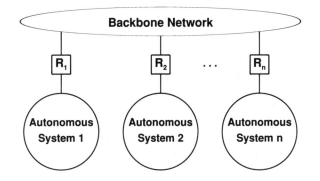

Figure 15.3 Architecture of an internet with autonomous systems at backbone sites. Each autonomous system consists of multiple networks and routers under a single administrative authority.

It may seem that our definition of an autonomous system is vague, but in practice the boundaries between autonomous systems must be precise to allow automated algorithms to make routing decisions. For example, an autonomous system owned by a corporation may choose not to route packets through an autonomous system owned by another even though they connect directly. To make it possible for automated routing algorithms to distinguish among autonomous systems, each is assigned an *autonomous system number* by the same central authority that is charged with assigning all Internet network addresses. When two routers exchange network reachability information, the messages carry the autonomous system identifier that the router represents.

We can summarize these ideas:

*A large TCP/IP internet has additional structure to accommodate ad-
ministrative boundaries: each collection of networks and routers
managed by one administrative authority is considered to be a single
autonomous system. An autonomous system is free to choose an internal routing architecture, but must collect information about all its networks and designate one or more routers that will pass the reachability information to other autonomous systems. Because the connected
Internet uses a core architecture, every autonomous system must pass
reachability information to Internet core routers.*

The next section presents the details of the protocol routers use to advertise network
reachability. Later sections return to architectural questions to discuss an important restriction the protocol imposes on routing. They also show how the Internet model can be
extended.

15.5 Exterior Gateway Protocol (EGP)

Two routers that exchange routing information are said to be *exterior neighbors* if
they belong to two different autonomous systems, and *interior neighbors* if they belong
to the same autonomous system. The protocol that exterior neighbors use to advertise
reachability information to other autonomous systems is called the *Exterior Gateway†
Protocol* or *EGP*, and the routers using it are called *exterior routers*. In the connected
Internet, EGP is especially important because autonomous systems use it to advertise
reachability information to the core system.

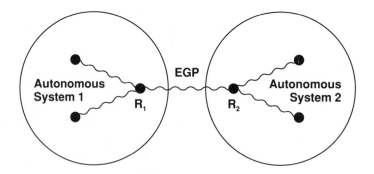

Figure 15.4 Conceptual illustration of two exterior routers, R_1 and R_2, using
EGP to advertise networks in their autonomous systems after
collecting the information. As the name implies, *exterior* routers
are usually close to the outer ''edge'' of an autonomous system.

---

†Remember that scientists originally used the term *IP gateway* instead of *router*.

Figure 15.4 illustrates two exterior neighbors using EGP. Router R_1 gathers information about networks in autonomous system *1* and reports that information to router R_2 using EGP, while router R_2 reports information from autonomous system *2*.

EGP has three main features. First, it supports a *neighbor acquisition* mechanism that allows one router to request another to agree that the two should communicate reachability information. We say that a router *acquires* an *EGP peer* or an *EGP neighbor*. EGP peers are neighbors only in the sense that they will exchange routing information; there is no notion of geographic proximity. Second, a router continually tests whether its EGP neighbors are responding. Third, EGP neighbors periodically exchange network reachability information by passing *routing update messages*.

15.6 EGP Message Header

To accommodate the three basic functions, EGP defines nine message types as the following table shows:

EGP Message Type	Description
Acquisition Request	Requests router become a neighbor (peer)
Acquisition Confirm	Positive response to acquisition request
Acquisition Refuse	Negative response to acquisition request
Cease Request	Requests termination of neighbor relationship
Cease Confirm	Confirmation response to cease request
Hello	Requests neighbor to respond if alive
I Heard You	Response to hello message
Poll Request	Requests network routing update
Routing Update	Network reachability information
Error	Response to incorrect message

All EGP messages begin with a fixed header that identifies the message type. Figure 15.5 shows the EGP header format.

0	8	16	31
VERSION	TYPE	CODE	STATUS
CHECKSUM		AUTONOMOUS SYSTEM NUM.	
SEQUENCE NUMBER			

Figure 15.5 The fixed header that precedes every EGP message.

The header field labeled *VERSION* contains an integer that identifies the version of EGP used to format the message. Receivers check the version number to verify that their software is using the same version of the protocol. Field *TYPE* identifies the type of the message, with the *CODE* field used to distinguish among subtypes. The *STATUS* field contains message-dependent status information.

EGP uses a checksum to verify that the message arrives intact. It uses the same checksum algorithm as IP, treating the entire EGP message as a sequence of 16-bit integers, and taking the one's complement of the one's complement sum. When performing the computation, field *CHECKSUM* is assumed to contain zeros, and the message is padded to a multiple of 16 bits by adding zeros.

The field labeled *AUTONOMOUS SYSTEM NUM.* gives the assigned number of the autonomous system of the router sending the message, and the *SEQUENCE NUMBER* field contains a number that the sender uses to associate replies with messages. A router establishes an initial sequence value when acquiring a neighbor and increments the sequence number each time it sends a message. The neighbor replies with the last sequence number it received, allowing the sender to match responses to transmissions.

15.7 EGP Neighbor Acquisition Messages

A router sends *neighbor acquisition* messages to establish EGP communication with another router. Note that EGP does not specify why or how one router chooses another router as its neighbor. We assume that such choices are made by the organizations responsible for administering the routers and not by the protocol software.

In addition to the standard header with a sequence number, neighbor acquisition messages contain initial values for a time interval to be used for testing whether the neighbor is alive (called a *hello interval*), and a *polling interval* that controls the maximum frequency of routing updates. The sender supplies a polling interval of *n* to specify that the receiver should not poll more often than every *n* seconds†. The original sender can change the polling interval dynamically as time passes. Furthermore, the polling intervals that peers use can be asymmetric, allowing one peer to poll more frequently than another. Figure 15.6 shows the format of acquisition messages and responses.

0	8	16	24	31
VERSION	TYPE (3)	CODE (0 to 4)		STATUS
CHECKSUM		AUTONOMOUS SYSTEMS NUM.		
SEQUENCE NUMBER		HELLO INTERVAL		
POLL INTERVAL				

Figure 15.6 EGP neighbor acquisition message format. Fields beyond the header specify initial parameters used by the protocol.

---

†In practice, most implementations use the polling interval as the exact frequency at which they send poll requests.

The *CODE* field identifies the specific message as the following table shows:

Code	Meaning
0	Acquisition Request
1	Acquisition Confirm
2	Acquisition Refuse
3	Cease Request
4	Cease Confirm

15.8 EGP Neighbor Reachability Messages

EGP permits two forms of testing whether a neighbor is alive. In active mode, routers test neighbors by periodically sending *Hello* messages along with *poll* messages and waiting for responses. In passive mode, a router depends on its neighbor to periodically send *hello* or *poll* messages. A router operating in passive mode uses information from the *status field* of a reachability message (see below) to deduce whether the peer is alive and whether the peer knows it is alive. Usually both routers in a pair operate in active mode.

Separating the calculation of neighbor reachability from routing information exchanges is important because it leads to lower network overhead. Because network routing information does not change as frequently as the status of individual router machines, it need not be passed frequently. Furthermore, neighbor reachability messages are small and require little computational overhead, while routing exchange messages are large and require much computation. Thus, by separating the two tests, neighbors can be tested frequently with minimal computational and communication overhead. Figure 15.7 shows that neighbor reachability requests consist of only the EGP message header.

0	8	16	24	31
VERSION	TYPE (5)	CODE (0 or 1)	STATUS
CHECKSUM		AUTONOMOUS SYSTEMS NUM.	
SEQUENCE NUMBER			

Figure 15.7 EGP neighbor reachability message format. Code *0* specifies a *Hello* request message, while code *1* specifies an *I Heard You* response.

Because it is possible for *Hello* messages or *I Heard You* responses to be lost in transit, EGP uses a form of the *k-out-of-n rule* to determine whether a peer has changed from 'up' to 'down'. The best way to think of the algorithm is to imagine a router sending a continuous sequence of *Hello* messages and receiving *I Heard You* responses, and think of a window spanning the last *n* exchanges. At least *k* of the last *n* exchanges must fail for the router to declare its neighbor down, and at least *j* must succeed for the router to declare that the neighbor is up, once it has been declared down. The protocol standard suggests values for *j* and *k* that imply two successive messages must be lost (received) before EGP will declare the peer down (up).

The hysteresis introduced by *j* and *k* have an important effect on the overall performance of EGP. As with any routing algorithm, EGP should not propagate unnecessary changes. The reason is simple: changes do not stop after a router propagates them to its EGP peer. The peer may propagate them on to other routers as well. Minimizing rapid route changes is especially crucial when an EGP peer uses a vector-distance algorithm to propagate changes because continual changes can make vector-distance algorithms unstable. Thus, if exterior routers report changes of reachability whenever a message is lost, they can cause the routing system to remain in continual transition.

15.9 EGP Poll Request Messages

EGP *poll request* and *poll response* messages allow a router to obtain network reachability information. Figure 15.8 shows the message format. The field labeled *IP SOURCE NETWORK* specifies a network common to the autonomous systems to which both routers attach. The response will contain routes that have distances measured with respect to routers on the specified IP source network.

0	8	16	24	31
VERSION	TYPE (2)	CODE (0 or 1)	STATUS	
CHECKSUM		AUTONOMOUS SYSTEMS NUM.		
SEQUENCE NUMBER		RESERVED		
IP SOURCE NETWORK				

Figure 15.8 EGP poll message format. Code *0* specifies a *Hello* request message, while code *1* specifies an *I Heard You* response.

It may be difficult to understand why EGP chooses to make a polling request specify a source network. There are two reasons. First, recall that a router connects to two or more physical networks. If an application on the router implements EGP, it may not know over which interface EGP requests arrive. Thus, it may not know to which network the request refers. Second, routers that run EGP often collect information for an entire autonomous system. When advertising network reachability, the exterior router sends neighbors a set of pairs that each specify a destination network in the autonomous system and the router used to reach that destination. Of course, the router used to reach a destination depends on where traffic enters the autonomous system. The source network mentioned in the polling request specifies the point at which packets will enter the autonomous system. Figure 15.9 illustrates the idea of a common network used as a base for network reachability information.

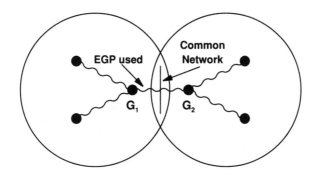

Figure 15.9 Routers in two autonomous systems using EGP to communicate network reachability information. A reachability message specifies routers on a network common to both systems and destinations reachable via those routers.

15.10 EGP Routing Update Messages

An exterior router sends a *routing update* message to convey information about reachable networks to its EGP neighbor. Usually, the router has collected the information and is making that information available to a router in another autonomous system. In principle, a router running EGP could report two types of reachability to a peer. The first type consists of destination networks that are reachable entirely within the router's autonomous system. The second type consists of destination networks that the router has learned about, but which lie beyond the router's autonomous system boundary.

It is important to understand that EGP does not permit an arbitrary router to advertise reachability to an arbitrary destination network. The restriction limits a router to advertising only those destinations for which it is an authority. That is:

> *EGP restricts a (noncore) router to advertise only those networks reachable entirely from within its autonomous system.*

This rule, sometimes called the *EGP third party restriction* is intended to control the propagation of information and allow each autonomous system to choose exactly how it advertises reachability. For example, if each university campus forms an autonomous system, a router on a given university campus might collect information about networks on that campus and advertise them to whoever provides the campus Internet connection, but a campus would not advertise routes to networks on other campuses. Naturally, the third-party restriction does not apply to the core system.

Figure 15.10 illustrates the format of a routing update message. The fields labeled *#INT. GWYS* and *#EXT. GWYS* give the number of interior and exterior routers appearing in the message. Distinguishing between interior and exterior routers allows the recipient to know whether distances are comparable. Unfortunately, it is impossible to make such a distinction from router addresses alone, and the message format contains no other provision. In practice, EGP implementations overcome the problem by sending separate update messages for interior and exterior routers. The field labeled *IP SOURCE NETWORK* gives the network from which all reachability is measured.

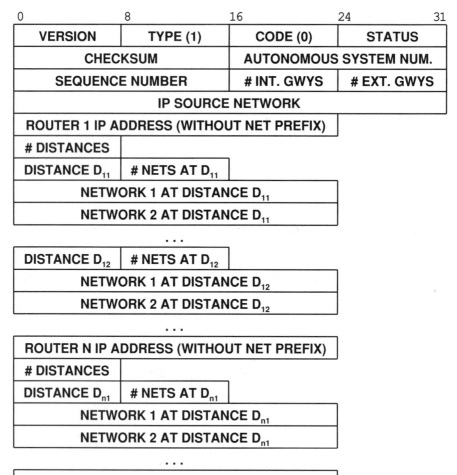

Figure 15.10 EGP routing update message format. All routes are given relative to a specified network. The message lists routers on that network and the distance of destinations through each. A network address contains *1*, *2*, or *3* octets.

In a sense, EGP routing update messages are a generalization of GGP routing update messages because they accommodate multiple routers instead of a single router.
Thus, the fields of the routing update message following the *IP SOURCE NETWORK*
form a sequence of blocks, where each block gives reachability information for one of
the routers on the source network. A block begins with the IP address of a router. The
networks reachable from that router are listed along with their distance. Like GGP,
EGP groups networks into sets based on ''distance.'' For each distance, there is a count
of networks at that distance followed by the list of network addresses. After the list of
all networks at a given distance, the pattern is repeated for all distance values.

15.11 Measuring From The Receiver's Perspective

Unlike most protocols that propagate routing information, EGP does not report its
own costs for reaching destination networks. Instead, it measures distances from the
common source network so all distances are correct from the peer's perspective. Figure
15.11 illustrates the idea.

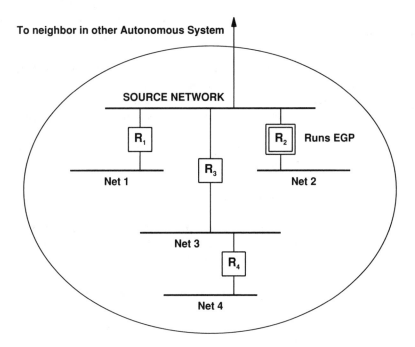

Figure 15.11 Example of an autonomous system. Router R_2 runs EGP and
reports distances to all networks measured from the source network, not from its own routing table.

In the example of Figure 15.11, router R_2 has been designated to run EGP on behalf of the autonomous system. It must report reachability to networks *1* through *4*. It reports network *1* as reachable through router R_1, networks *3* and *4* as reachable through router R_3, and network *2* as reachable through R_2. From R_2's perspective, network *2* lies at distance *0*. However, it reports network *2* at distance *1*, the distance when measured from the source network.

15.12 The Key Restriction Of EGP

We have already seen that EGP restricts routers, allowing them to advertise only those destination networks reachable entirely within the router's autonomous system. However, there is a more fundamental limitation imposed by EGP:

> *EGP does not interpret any of the distance metrics that appear in routing update messages.*

The rules specify that a value of *255* means the network is unreachable, but other values are only comparable if they refer to routers in the same autonomous system. In essence, EGP uses the distance field to specify whether a path exists; the value cannot be used to compute the shorter of two routes unless those routes are both contained within a single autonomous system.

We can see now why a router in one autonomous system should not advertise reachability to networks in another autonomous system (i.e., why the third party rule exists). The essential observation is this: when a router learns of a network in another autonomous system, it does not obtain a universally accepted measure of distance. Therefore, it should not pass that measure on. Advertising reachability with EGP is equivalent to saying, "My autonomous system provides *the* path to this network." There is no way for the router to say, "My autonomous system provides one possible path to this network."

Looking at interpretation of distances another way allows us to realize that EGP cannot be used as a routing algorithm. In particular, even if a router learns about two different routes to the same network, it cannot know which is shorter. Without routing information, we must be careful to advertise only the route we want traffic to follow. As a result, there is only one path from the core to any network. We can summarize:

> *Because EGP only propagates reachability information, it restricts the topology of any internet using EGP to a tree structure in which a core system forms the root; there are no loops among other autonomous systems connected to it.*

The key point here is that any internet that uses EGP to provide routing among autonomous systems forms a tree-shaped topology in which a core autonomous system forms the root.

The restriction on EGP that produces a tree structure results partially from the historical evolution of the Internet centered around a single backbone. Although it may seem innocuous, the restriction has some surprising consequences:

1. Universal connectivity fails if the core router system fails. Of course, it is unlikely the entire Internet core will fail simultaneously, but there have been interesting examples of minor failures. In particular, on several occasions the rapid growth of the Internet resulted in table overflows in core routers, preventing EGP from successfully installing routes to new networks. Those network addresses that could not be installed in the core tables were unreachable from many parts of the Internet.

2. EGP can only advertise one path to a given network. That is, at any given instant, all traffic routed from one autonomous system to a network in another will traverse one path, even if multiple physical connections are present. Also note that an outside autonomous system will only use one return path even if the source system divides outgoing traffic among two or more paths. As a result, delay and throughput between a pair of machines can be asymmetric, making an internet difficult to monitor or debug.

3. EGP does not support load sharing on routers between arbitrary autonomous systems. If two autonomous systems have multiple routers connecting them, one would like to balance the traffic equally between all routers. EGP allows autonomous systems to divide the load by network (e.g., to partition themselves into multiple subsets and have multiple routers advertise partitions), but it does not support more general load sharing.

4. As a special case of point 3, EGP is inadequate for optimal routing in an architecture that has multiple backbone networks interconnected at multiple points. For example, the NSFNET and ARPANET backbone interconnection described in Chapter 14 cannot use EGP alone to exchange routing information if routes are to be optimal. Instead, managers manually divide the set of NSFNET networks and advertise some of them to one exterior router and others to a different router.

5. It is difficult to switch to an alternate physical path if one path fails, especially when the paths cross two or more autonomous systems. Because EGP does not interpret distances, third parties cannot advertise routes and rely on the receiver to switch to an alternate route if one fails. Instead, responsibility for selecting the least cost route falls to the exterior routers that advertise reachability.

15.13 Technical Problems

EGP has several weaknesses, many of which are trivial technicalities. The weaknesses must be repaired before EGP can support the rapidly expanding Internet environment. Attempts to fix some of these problems have concentrated on the most pressing problem: reducing the size of update messages. Recall from Figure 15.10 that update messages contain long lists of networks. For large autonomous systems with many routers and networks, the size of a single EGP routing update message will exceed the MTU of most networks. More important, if any fragments of an IP datagram are lost, the entire datagram must be retransmitted.

Although many technical problems have been identified, several attempts to produce a new version of EGP have failed. The efforts called *EGP2* and *EGP3* were both dropped after participants were unable to agree on approaches and details. While exploring possibilities, the working groups discussed EGP replacements and decided that because so many fundamental changes were needed, simple improvements would be inadequate. Consequently, EGP remains in use, unchanged.

15.14 Decentralization Of Internet Architecture

Two important architecture questions remain unanswered. The first focuses on centralization: how can an internet architecture be modified to further remove dependence on a (centralized) core router system? The second concerns levels of trust: can an internet architecture be expanded to allow closer cooperation (trust) between some autonomous systems than among others?

Removing all dependence on a core system will not be easy. Although TCP/IP architectures continue to evolve, centralized roots are evident in many protocols. As more software is built using existing protocols, inertia increases and change becomes more difficult and expensive. More important, because the connected Internet core system is reliable, supported by a professional staff, and uses automated mechanisms to update routing information, there is little motivation for change. Finally, as the size of an internet grows, so does the volume of routing information that routers must keep. A mechanism must be found to limit the information needed by each node, or the update traffic will inundate the network.

15.15 Beyond Autonomous Systems

Extending the notions of trust between autonomous systems is complex. The easiest step is to group autonomous systems hierarchically. Imagine, for example, three autonomous systems in three separate academic departments on a large university campus. It is natural to group these three together because they share administrative ties. The motivation for hierarchical grouping comes primarily from the notion of trust. Routers within a group trust one another with a high level of confidence.

Grouping autonomous systems requires only minor changes to EGP. New versions of EGP must agree to use an artificial scaling factor when reporting hop counts, allowing counts to be increased when passed across the boundary from one group to another. The technique, loosely called *metric transformation*, partitions distance values into three categories. For example, suppose routers within an autonomous system use distance values less than 128. We could make the rule that when passing distance information across an autonomous system boundary within a single group, the distances must be transformed into the range of 128 to 191. Finally, we could make the rule that when passing distance values across the boundary between two groups, the values must be transformed into the range of 192 to 254†. The effect of such transformations is obvious: for any given destination network, any path that lies entirely within the autonomous system is guaranteed to have lower cost than a path that strays outside the autonomous system. Furthermore, among all paths that stray outside the autonomous system, those that remain within the group have lower cost than those that cross group boundaries. The key advantage of metric transformations is that they use an extant protocol, EGP. Transformations allow an autonomous system manager freedom to choose internal distance metrics, yet make it possible for other systems to compare routing costs.

15.16 Summary

The Internet is composed of a set of autonomous systems, where each autonomous system consists of routers and networks under one administrative authority. An autonomous system uses the Exterior Gateway Protocol (EGP) to advertise routes to other autonomous systems. Specifically, an autonomous system must advertise reachability of its networks to another system before its networks are reachable from sources within that system. We saw that EGP supports three basic functions: neighbor (peer) acquisition, testing neighbor reachability, and advertising reachability to neighbors.

The global Internet architecture consists of a central, connected piece (built around the NSFNET backbone), with autonomous systems connected to the center in a tree structure topology. The NSFNET routing system forms the central core, while the "fringe" consists of local area networks that have only a single connection to the rest of the Internet. Moving from a centralized architecture to a completely distributed one requires substantial changes in protocols like EGP.

FOR FURTHER STUDY

Mills [RFC 904] contains the formal EGP protocol specification. An early version of EGP is given in Rosen [RFC 827], which also discusses the restriction to a tree structured topology. Additional background can be found in the early router documents by Seamonson and Rosen [RFC 888], and Mills [RFC 975]. Braden and Postel [RFC

---

†The term *autonomous confederation* has been used to describe a group of autonomous systems; boundaries of autonomous confederations correspond to transformations beyond 191.

1009] discusses requirements for Internet routers and outlines some of the problems with EGP (also see the predecessor, RFC 985). Lougheed and Rekhter [RFC 1105] describes the Border Gateway Protocol, *BGP*, an EGP-like protocol used within NSFNET. BGP has been through three substantial revisions; later versions appear in [RFCs 1163, 1267, and 1654]. Finally, Kirton [RFC 911] describes the widely used implementation of EGP that runs under Berkeley 4.3 BSD UNIX.

EXERCISES

15.1   If your site connects to NSFNET, find out which routers run EGP. How many routes does NSFNET advertise?

15.2   Implementations of EGP use a "hold down" mechanism that causes the protocol to delay accepting an *acquisition request* from a neighbor for a fixed time following the receipt of a *cease request* message from that neighbor. Read the protocol specification to find out why.

15.3   For the networks in Figure 15.2, which router(s) should run EGP? Why?

15.4   The formal specification of EGP includes a finite state machine that explains how EGP operates. Why does a *confirm* message take the EGP finite state machine from the *acquisition* state to the *down* state, instead of from the *acquisition* state to the *up* state?

15.5   What happens if a router in an autonomous system sends EGP routing update messages to a router in another autonomous system, claiming to have reachability for every possible internet destination?

15.6   Can two autonomous systems establish a routing loop by sending EGP update messages to one another? Explain.

15.7   Should routers treat EGP separately from their own routing tables? For example, should a router ever advertise reachability if it has not installed a route to that network in its routing table? Why or why not?

15.8   Read RFC 1654 and compare BGP4 to EGP. What additional features does BGP4 support?

15.9   If you work for a large corporation, find out whether it includes more than one autonomous system. If so, how do they exchange routing information?

15.10   What is the chief advantage of dividing a large, multinational corporation into multiple autonomous systems? What is the chief disadvantage?

15.11   Corporations *A* and *B* use EGP to exchange routing information. To keep computers in *B* from reaching machines on one of its networks, *N*, the network administrator at corporation *A* configures EGP to omit *N* from advertisements sent to *B*. Is network *N* secure? Why or why not?

16

Routing: In An Autonomous System (RIP, OSPF, HELLO)

16.1 Introduction

The previous chapter introduces the autonomous system concept and examines the Exterior Gateway Protocol that a router uses to advertise networks within its system to other autonomous systems. This chapter completes our overview of internet routing by examining how a router in an autonomous system learns about other networks within its autonomous system.

16.2 Static Vs. Dynamic Interior Routes

Two routers within an autonomous system are said to be *interior* to one another. For example, two Internet core routers are interior to one another because the core forms a single autonomous system. Two routers on a university campus are considered interior to one another as long as machines on the campus are collected into a single autonomous system.

How can routers in an autonomous system learn about networks within the autonomous system? In small, slowly changing internets, managers can establish and modify routes by hand. The administrator keeps a table of networks and updates the table whenever a new network is added to, or deleted from, the autonomous system. For example, consider the small corporate internet shown in Figure 16.1. Routing for such an internet is trivial because only one path exists between any two points. The manager can manually configure routes in all hosts and routers. If the internet changes (e.g., a new network is added), the manager must reconfigure the routes in all machines.

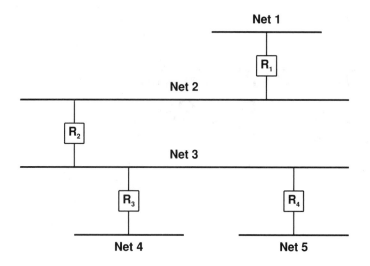

Figure 16.1 An example of a small internet consisting of 5 Ethernets and 4 routers at a single site. Only one possible route exists between any two hosts in this internet.

The disadvantages of a manual system are obvious; manual systems cannot accommodate rapid growth or rapid change. In large, rapidly changing environments like the Internet, humans simply cannot respond to changes fast enough to handle problems; automated methods must be used. Automated methods can also help improve reliability and response to failure in small internets that have alternate routes. To see how, consider what happens if we add one additional router to the internet in Figure 16.1, producing the internet shown in Figure 16.2.

In internet architectures that have multiple physical paths, managers usually choose one to be the primary path. If the routers along the primary path fail, routes must be changed to send traffic along an alternate path. Changing routes manually is both time consuming and error-prone. Thus, even in small internets, an automated system should be used to change routes quickly and reliably.

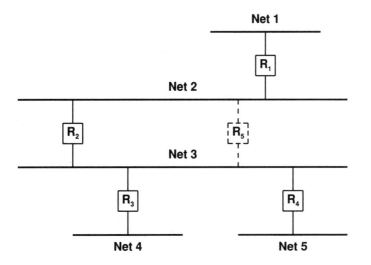

Figure 16.2 The addition of router R_s introduces an alternate path between networks *2* and *3*. Routing software can quickly adapt to a failure and automatically switch routes to the alternate path.

To automate the task of keeping network reachability information accurate, interior routers usually communicate with one another, exchanging either network reachability data or network routing information from which reachability can be deduced. Once the reachability information for an entire autonomous system has been assembled, one of the routers in the system can advertise it to other autonomous systems using EGP.

Unlike exterior router communication, for which EGP provides a widely accepted standard, no single protocol has emerged for use within an autonomous system. Part of the reason for diversity comes from the varied topologies and technologies used in autonomous systems. Another part of the reason stems from the tradeoffs between simplicity and functionality – protocols that are easy to install and configure do not provide sophisticated functionality. As a result, a handful of protocols have become popular; most autonomous systems use one of them exclusively to propagate routing information internally.

Because there is no single standard, we use the term *interior gateway protocol* or *IGP* as a generic description that refers to any algorithm that interior routers use when they exchange network reachability and routing information. For example, the Butterfly core routers form a somewhat specialized autonomous system that uses SPREAD as its Interior Gateway Protocol. Some autonomous systems use EGP as their IGP, although this seldom makes sense for small autonomous systems that span local area networks with broadcast capability.

Figure 16.3 illustrates an autonomous system using an IGP to propagate reachability among interior routers.

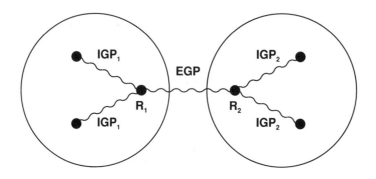

Figure 16.3 Conceptual view of two autonomous systems each using its own
IGP internally, but using EGP to communicate between an exterior router and the other system.

In the figure, *IGP₁* refers to the interior router protocol used within autonomous system *1*, and *IGP₂* refers to the protocol used within autonomous system *2*. The figure also illustrates an important idea:

> *A single router may use two different routing protocols simultaneously, one for communication outside its autonomous system and another for communication within its autonomous system.*

In particular, routers that run EGP to advertise reachability usually also need to run an IGP to obtain information from within their autonomous system.

16.3 Routing Information Protocol (RIP)

One of the most widely used IGPs is the *Routing Information Protocol* (RIP), also known by the name of a program that implements it, *routed*†. The *routed* software was originally designed at the University of California at Berkeley to provide consistent routing and reachability information among machines on their local networks. It relies on physical network broadcast to make routing exchanges quickly. It was not designed to be used on large, wide area networks (although it now is).

Based on earlier internetworking research done at Xerox Corporation's Palo Alto Research Center (PARC), *routed* implements a protocol derived from the Xerox *NS Routing Information Protocol* (*RIP*), but generalizes it to cover multiple families of networks.

Despite minor improvements over its predecessors, the popularity of RIP as an IGP does not arise from its technical merits. Instead, it is the result of Berkeley distributing *routed* software along with their popular 4BSD UNIX systems. Thus, many TCP/IP

---

†The name comes from the UNIX convention of attaching "d" to the names of daemon processes; it is pronounced "route-d".

sites adopted and installed *routed* and started using RIP without even considering its technical merits or limitations. Once installed and running, it became the basis for local routing, and research groups adopted it for larger networks.

Perhaps the most startling fact about RIP is that it was built and widely adopted before a formal standard was written. Most implementations were derived from the Berkeley code, with interoperability among them limited by the programmer's understanding of undocumented details and subtleties. As new versions appeared, more problems arose. An RFC standard appeared in June 1988, and made it possible for vendors to ensure interoperability.

The underlying RIP protocol is a straightforward implementation of vector-distance routing for local networks. It partitions participants into *active* and *passive* (*silent*) machines. Active routers advertise their routes to others; passive machines listen and update their routes based on advertisements, but do not advertise. Only a router can run RIP in active mode; a host must use passive mode.

A router running RIP in active mode broadcasts a message every 30 seconds. The message contains information taken from the router's current routing database. Each message consists of pairs, where each pair contains an IP network address and an integer distance to that network. RIP uses a *hop count metric* to measure the distance to a destination. In the RIP metric, a router is defined to be one hop† from directly connected networks, two hops from networks that are reachable through one other router, and so on. Thus, the *number of hops* or the *hop count* along a path from a given source to a given destination refers to the number of routers that a datagram encounters along that path. It should be obvious that using hop counts to calculate shortest paths does not always produce optimal results. For example, a path with hop count *3* that crosses three Ethernets may be substantially faster than a path with hop count *2* that crosses two slow speed serial lines. To compensate for differences in technologies, many RIP implementations allow managers to configure artificially high hop counts when advertising connections to slow networks.

Both active and passive RIP participants listen to all broadcast messages and update their tables according to the vector-distance algorithm described earlier. For example, in the internet of Figure 16.2, router R_1 will broadcast a message on network *2* that contains the pair (*1,1*), meaning that it can reach network *1* at cost *1*. Routers R_2 and R_5 will receive the broadcast and install a route to network *1* through R_1 (at cost *2*). Later, routers R_2 and R_5 will include the pair (*1,2*) when they broadcast their RIP messages on network *3*. Eventually, all routers and hosts will install a route to network *1*.

RIP specifies a few rules to improve performance and reliability. For example, once a router learns a route from another router, it must keep that route until it learns of a better one. In our example, if routers R_2 and R_5 both advertise network *1* at cost *2*, routers R_3 and R_4 will install a route through the one that happens to advertise first. We can summarize:

> *To prevent routes from oscillating between two or more equal cost paths, RIP specifies that existing routes should be retained until a new route has strictly lower cost.*

---

†Some protocols define direct connections to have cost zero.

What happens if the first router to advertise a route fails (e.g., if it crashes)? RIP specifies that all listeners must timeout routes they learn via RIP. When a router installs a route in its table, it starts a timer for that route. The timer must be restarted whenever the router receives another RIP message advertising the route. The route becomes invalid if 180 seconds pass without the route being advertised again.

RIP must handle three kinds of errors caused by the underlying algorithm. First, because the algorithm does not explicitly detect routing loops, RIP must either assume participants can be trusted or take precautions to prevent such loops. Second, to prevent instabilities RIP must use a low value for the maximum possible distance (RIP uses *16*). Thus, for internets in which legitimate hop counts approach *16*, managers must divide the internet into sections or use an alternative protocol. Third, the vector-distance algorithm used by RIP creates a *slow convergence* or *count to infinity* problem in which inconsistencies arise, because routing update messages propagate slowly across the network. Choosing a small infinity (*16*) helps limit slow convergence, but does not eliminate it.

Routing table inconsistency is not unique to RIP. It is a fundamental problem that occurs with any vector-distance protocol in which update messages carry only pairs of destination network and distance to that network. To understand the problem consider the set of routers shown in Figure 16.4. The figure depicts routes to network *1* for the internet shown in Figure 16.2.

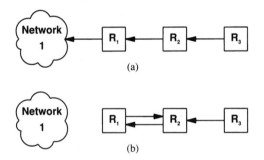

(a)

(b)

Figure 16.4 The slow convergence problem. In (a) three routers each have a
route to network *1*. In (b) the connection to network *1* has van-
ished, but R_2 causes a loop by advertising it.

As Figure 16.4a shows, router R_1 has a direct connection to network *1*, so it has a route in its table with distance *1*; it includes the route in its periodic broadcasts. Router R_2 has learned the route from R_1, installed the route in its routing table, and advertises the route at distance *2*. Finally, R_3 has learned the route from R_2 and advertises it at distance *3*.

Now suppose that R_1's connection to network 1 fails. R_1 will update its routing table immediately to make the distance 16 (infinity). In the next broadcast, R_1 will report the higher cost route. However, unless the protocol includes extra mechanisms to prevent it, some other router could broadcast its routes before R_1. In particular, suppose R_2 happens to advertise routes just after $R_1's$ connection fails. If so, R_1 will receive R_2's message and follow the usual vector-distance algorithm: it notices that R_2 has advertised a route to network 1 at lower cost, calculates that it now takes 3 hops to reach network 1 (2 for R_2 to reach network 1 plus 1 to reach R_2), *and installs a new route through R_2).* Figure 16.4b depicts the result. At this point, if either R_1 or R_2 receives a datagram destined for network 1, they will route the datagram back and forth until its time-to-live counter expires.

Subsequent RIP broadcasts by the two routers do not solve the problem quickly. In the next round of routing exchanges, R_1 broadcasts its routing table entries. When R_2 learns that R_1's route to network 1 has length 3, it calculates a new length for its route, making it 4. In the third round, R_1 receives a report of the increase from R_2 and increases the distance in its table to 5. They continue counting to RIP infinity.

16.3.1 Solving The Slow Convergence Problem

For the example in Figure 16.4, it is possible to solve the slow convergence problem by using a technique known as *split horizon update*. When using split horizons, a router records the interface over which it received a particular route and does not propagate its information about that route back over the same interface. In the example, router R_2 would not advertise its length 2 route to network 1 back to router R_1, so if R_1 loses connectivity to network 1, it would stop advertising a route. After a few rounds of routing updates, all machines would agree that the network is unreachable. However, splitting the horizon does not cover all topologies as one of the exercises suggests.

Another way to think of the slow convergence problem is in terms of information flow. If a router advertises a short route to some network, all receiving routers respond quickly to install that route. If a router stops advertising a route, the protocol must depend on a timeout mechanism before it considers the route unreachable. Once the timeout occurs, the router finds an alternative route and starts propagating that information. Unfortunately, a router cannot know if the alternate route depended on the route that just disappeared. Thus, negative information does not always propagate quickly. A short epigram captures the idea and explains the phenomenon:

Good news travels quickly; bad news travels slowly.

Another technique used to solve the slow convergence problem employs *hold down*. Hold down forces a participating router to ignore information about a network for a fixed period of time following receipt of a message that claims the network is unreachable. Typically, the hold down period is set to 60 seconds. The idea is to wait long enough to ensure that all machines receive the bad news and not mistakenly accept a message that is out of date. It should be noted that all machines participating in a RIP exchange need to use identical notions of hold down, or routing loops can occur. The disadvantage of a hold down technique is that if routing loops occur, they will be preserved for the duration of the hold down period. More important, the hold down technique preserves all incorrect routes during the hold down period, even when alternatives exist.

A final technique for solving the slow convergence problem is called *poison reverse*. Once a connection disappears, the router advertising the connection retains the entry for several update periods, and includes an infinite cost in its broadcasts. To make poison reverse most effective, it must be combined with *triggered updates*. Triggered updates force a router to send an immediate broadcast when receiving bad news, instead of waiting for the next periodic broadcast. By sending an update immediately, a router minimizes the time it is vulnerable to believing good news.

Unfortunately, while triggered updates, poison reverse, hold down, and split horizon techniques all solve some problems, they introduce others. For example, consider what happens with triggered updates when many routers share a common network. A single broadcast may change all their routing tables, triggering a new round of broadcasts. If the second round of broadcasts changes tables, it will trigger even more broadcasts. A broadcast avalanche can result†.

The use of broadcast, potential for routing loops, and use of hold down to prevent slow convergence can make RIP extremely inefficient in a wide area network. Broadcasting always takes substantial bandwidth. Even if no avalanche problems occur, having all machines broadcast periodically means that the traffic increases as the number of routers increases. The potential for routing loops can also be deadly when line capacity is limited. Once lines become saturated by looping packets, it may be difficult or impossible for routers to exchange the routing messages needed to break the loops. Also, in a wide area network, hold down periods are so long that the timers used by higher level protocols can expire and lead to broken connections. Despite these well-known problems, many groups continue to use RIP as an IGP in wide area networks.

16.3.2 RIP Message Format

RIP messages can be broadly classified into two types: routing information messages and messages used to request information. Both use the same format which consists of a fixed header followed by an optional list of network and distance pairs. Figure 16.5 shows the message format:

---

†To help avoid collisions, RIP requires each router to wait a small random time before sending a triggered update.

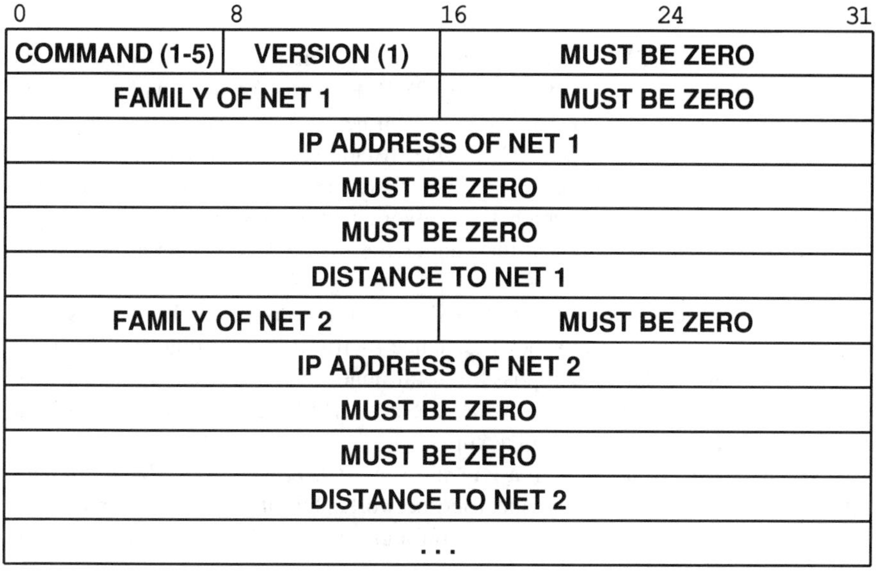

0	8	16	24	31

COMMAND (1-5)	VERSION (1)	MUST BE ZERO		
FAMILY OF NET 1		MUST BE ZERO		
IP ADDRESS OF NET 1				
MUST BE ZERO				
MUST BE ZERO				
DISTANCE TO NET 1				
FAMILY OF NET 2		MUST BE ZERO		
IP ADDRESS OF NET 2				
MUST BE ZERO				
MUST BE ZERO				
DISTANCE TO NET 2				
. . .				

Figure 16.5 The format of a RIP message. After the 32-bit header, the message contains a sequence of pairs, where each pair consists of a network IP address and an integer distance to that network.

In the figure, field *COMMAND* specifies an operation according to the following table:

Command	Meaning
1	Request for partial or full routing information
2	Response containing network-distance pairs from sender's routing table
3	Turn on trace mode (obsolete)
4	Turn off trace mode (obsolete)
5	Reserved for Sun Microsystems internal use

A router or host can ask another router for routing information by sending a *request* command. Routers reply to requests using the *response* command. In most cases, however, routers broadcast unsolicited response messages periodically. Field *VERSION* contains the protocol version number (currently *1*), and is used by the receiver to verify it will interpret the message correctly.

16.3.3 RIP Addressing Conventions

The generality of RIP is also evident in the way it transmits network addresses. The address format is not limited to use by TCP/IP; it can be used with multiple network protocol suites. As Figure 16.5 shows, each network address reported by RIP can have an address of up to 14 octets. Of course, IP addresses need only 4; RIP specifies that the remaining octets must be zero†. The field labeled *FAMILY OF NET i* identifies the protocol family under which the network address should be interpreted. RIP uses values assigned to address families under the 4BSD UNIX operating system (IP addresses are assigned value *2*).

In addition to normal IP addresses, RIP uses the convention that address *0.0.0.0* denotes a *default route*. RIP attaches a distance metric to every route it advertises, including default routes. Thus, it is possible to arrange for two routers to advertise a default route (e.g., a route to the rest of the internet) at different metrics, making one of them a primary path and the other a backup.

The final field of each entry in a RIP message, *DISTANCE TO NET i*, contains an integer count of the distance to the specified network. Distances are measured in router hops, but values are limited to the range *1* through *16*, with distance *16* used to signify infinity (i.e., no route exists).

16.3.4 Transmitting RIP Messages

RIP messages do not contain an explicit length field. Instead, RIP assumes that the underlying delivery mechanism will tell the receiver the length of an incoming message. In particular, when used with TCP/IP, RIP messages rely on UDP to tell the receiver the message length. RIP operates on UDP port *520*. Although a RIP request can originate at other UDP ports, the destination UDP port for requests is always *520*, as is the source port from which RIP broadcast messages originate.

Using RIP as an interior router protocol limits routing to a metric based on hop counts. Often, hop counts provide only a crude measure of network response or capacity that does not produce optimal routes. Furthermore, computing routes on the basis of minimum hop counts has the severe disadvantage that it makes routing relatively static because routes cannot respond to changes in network load.

16.4 The Hello Protocol

The HELLO protocol provides an example of an IGP that uses a routing metric based on network delay instead of hop count. Although HELLO is now obsolete, it was significant in the history of the Internet because it was the IGP used among the original NSFNET backbone ''fuzzball'' routers. HELLO is significant to us because it provides an example of a vector-distance algorithm that does not use hop counts.

---

†The designers chose to locate an IP address in the third through sixth octets of the address field to ensure 32-bit alignment.

HELLO provides two functions: it synchronizes the clocks among a set of machines, and it allows each machine to compute shortest delay paths to destinations. Thus, HELLO messages carry timestamp information as well as routing information. The basic idea behind HELLO is simple: each machine participating in the HELLO exchange maintains a table of its best estimate of the clocks in neighboring machines. Before transmitting a packet, a machine adds its timestamp by copying the current clock value into the packet. When a packet arrives, the receiver computes the current delay on the link. To do so, the receiver subtracts the timestamp on the incoming packet from its estimate for the current clock in the neighbor. Periodically, machines poll their neighbors to reestablish estimates for clocks.

HELLO messages also allow participating machines to compute new routes. The algorithm works much like RIP, but uses delay instead of hop count. Each machine periodically sends its neighbor a table of estimated delays for all other machines. Suppose machine A sends machine B a routing table that specifies destinations and delays. B examines each entry in the table. If B's current delay to reach a given destination, D, is greater than the delay from A to D plus the delay from B to A, B changes its route and sends traffic to D via A. That is, B routes traffic to A as long as taking that path shortens the delay.

As in any routing algorithm, HELLO cannot change routes too rapidly, or it will become unstable. Instabilities in routing algorithms produce a two-stage oscillation effect in which traffic switches back and forth between alternate paths. In the first stage, the machines find a lightly loaded path and abruptly switch their traffic onto it, only to find that it becomes completely overloaded. In the second stage, the machines switch traffic away from the overloaded path, only to find that it becomes the least loaded path, and the cycle continues. Such oscillations do occur. To avoid them, implementations of HELLO choose to change routes only when the difference in delays is large.

Figure 16.6 shows the HELLO message format. The protocol is more complex than the message format indicates because it distinguishes local network connections from those multiple hops away, times out stale entries in its routing tables, and uses local identifiers for hosts instead of full IP addresses.

0	16	24	31
CHECKSUM	DATE		
TIME			
TIMESTAMP	LOCAL ENTRY	# HOSTS	
$DELAY_1$	$OFFSET_1$		
$DELAY_2$	$OFFSET_2$		

. . .

$DELAY_n$	$OFFSET_n$		

Figure 16.6 The format of HELLO messages. Each message carries an entry
for the date and time as well as a timestamp that the protocol
uses to estimate network delays.

Field *CHECKSUM* contains a checksum over the message, field *DATE* contains
the local date of the sender, and field *TIME* contains the local time according to the
sender's clock. The *TIMESTAMP* field is used in round trip computation.

The field labeled *# HOSTS* specifies how many entries follow in the list of hosts
and the field labeled *LOCAL ENTRY* points into the list to mark the block of entries
used for the local network. Each entry contains two fields, *DELAY* and *OFFSET*, that
give the delay to reach a host and the sender's current estimate of the offset between the
host's clock and the sender's clock.

16.5 Combining RIP, Hello, And EGP

We have already observed that a single router may use both an IGP to gather routing information within its autonomous system and EGP to advertise routes to other autonomous systems. In principle, it should be easy to construct a single piece of
software that combines the two protocols, making it possible to gather routes and advertise them without human intervention. In practice, technical and political obstacles
make doing so complex.

Technically, IGP protocols, like RIP and Hello, are routing protocols. A router
uses such protocols to update its routing table based on information it acquires from
other routers inside its autonomous system. Unlike interior router protocols, EGP
works in addition to a router's usual routing table. A router uses EGP to communicate
reachability information to other autonomous systems independent of the router's own
routing table. Thus, *routed*, the UNIX program that implements RIP, advertises information from the local routing table and changes the local routing table when it receives
updates. It trusts those machines that use RIP to pass correct data. In contrast the pro-

gram that implements EGP does not advertise routes from the local routing table; it keeps a separate database of network reachability.

A router using EGP to advertise reachability must take care to propagate only those routes it is authorized to advertise, or it may affect other parts of the internet. For example, if a router in an autonomous system happens to propagate a distance *0* route to a network at Purdue University when it has no such route, RIP will install the route in other machines and start passing Purdue traffic to the router that made the error. As a result, it may be impossible for machines in that autonomous system to reach Purdue. If EGP propagates such errors outside the autonomous system, it may become impossible to reach Purdue from some parts of the internet.

The *gated*† program combines multiple IGPs and EGP according to a set of rules that constrain routes advertised to exterior routers. For example, *gated* can accept RIP messages and modify the local computer's routing table just like the *routed* program. It can advertise routes from within its autonomous system using EGP. The rules allow a system administrator to specify exactly which networks *gated* may and may not advertise and how to report distances to those networks. Thus, although *gated* is not an IGP, it plays an important role in routing because it demonstrates that it is feasible to build an automated mechanism linking an IGP with EGP without sacrificing protection.

Gated performs another useful task by implementing metric transformations. Recall from Chapter 15 that extensions to EGP allow autonomous systems to make intelligent routing decisions as long as all routers using EGP agree to a loose interpretation of distance metrics. In particular, the routers within an autonomous system must agree to use distance values below a fixed threshold, say 128. Whenever an exterior router advertises reachability outside its autonomous system but inside its autonomous confederation, it must transform the distance metrics into a higher range (e.g., 128-191). The transformation tends to keep traffic within an autonomous system by artificially raising the cost to routes outside. Finally, routers transform distances into an even higher range (e.g., 192-254) when passing them across an autonomous confederation boundary to encourage traffic to remain within the autonomous confederation. Because *gated* provides the interface between its autonomous system and other autonomous systems, it can implement such transformations easily.

16.6 The Open SPF Protocol (OSPF)

In Chapter 14, we said that the SPF route propagation algorithm scales better than vector-distance algorithms. A working group of the Internet Engineering Task Force has designed an interior gateway protocol that uses the SPF algorithm. Called *Open SPF (OSPF)*, the new protocol tackles several ambitious goals.

• The specification is available in the published literature, making it an open standard that anyone can implement without paying license fees. The designers hope many vendors will support OSPF and make it a popular replacement for proprietary protocols.

---

†The name *gated* is pronounced "gate d" from "gate daemon".

• OSPF includes *type of service routing*. Managers can install multiple routes to a given destination, one for each type of service (e.g., low delay or high throughput). When routing a datagram, a router running OSPF uses both the destination address and type of service fields in an IP header to choose a route. OSPF is among the first TCP/IP protocols to offer type of service routing.

• OSPF provides *load balancing*. If a manager specifies multiple routes to a given destination at the same cost, OSPF distributes traffic over all routes equally. Again, OSPF is among the first open IGPs to offer load balancing; protocols like RIP compute a single route to each destination.

• To permit growth and make the networks at a site easier to manage, OSPF allows a site to partition its networks and routers into subsets called *areas*. Each area is self-contained; knowledge of an area's topology remains hidden from other areas. Thus, multiple groups within a given site can cooperate in the use of OSPF for routing even though each group retains the ability to change its internal network topology independently.

• The OSPF protocol specifies that all exchanges between routers must be *authenticated*. OSPF allows a variety of authentication schemes, and even allows one area to choose a different scheme than another area. The idea behind authentication is to guarantee that only trusted routers propagate routing information. To understand why this could be a problem, consider what can happen when using RIP, which has no authentication. If a malicious person uses a personal computer to propagate RIP messages advertising low-cost routes, other routers and hosts running RIP will change their routes and start sending datagrams to the personal computer.

• OSPF supports host-specific routes and subnet routes as well as network-specific routes. All three types may be needed in a large internet.

• To accommodate multi-access networks like Ethernet, OSPF extends the SPF algorithm described in Chapter 14. We described the algorithm using a point-to-point graph and said that each router running SPF would periodically broadcast link status messages about each reachable neighbor. If K routers attach to an Ethernet, they will broadcast K^2 reachability messages. OSPF minimizes broadcasts by allowing a more complex graph topology in which each node represents either a router or a network. Consequently, OSPF allows every multi-access network to have a *designated router* (called a *designated gateway* in the standard) that sends link-status messages on behalf of all links from the network to routers attached to the network. OSPF also uses hardware broadcast capabilities, where they exist, to deliver link status messages.

• To permit maximum flexibility, OSPF allows managers to describe a virtual network topology that abstracts away from details of physical connections. For example, a manager can configure a virtual link between two routers in the routing graph even if the physical connection between the two routers requires communication across a transit network.

• OSPF allows routers to exchange routing information learned from other (external) sites. Basically, one or more routers with connections to other sites learn information about those sites and include it when sending update messages. The message format distinguishes between information acquired from external sources and information acquired from routers interior to the site, so there is no ambiguity about the source or reliability of routes.

16.6.1 OSPF Message Format

Each OSPF message begins with a fixed, 24-octet header as Figure 16.7 shows:

0	8	16	24	31
VERSION (1)	**TYPE**	**MESSAGE LENGTH**		
SOURCE ROUTER IP ADDRESS				
AREA ID				
CHECKSUM		**AUTHENTICATION TYPE**		
AUTHENTICATION (octets 0-3)				
AUTHENTICATION (octets 4-7)				

Figure 16.7 The fixed 24-octet OSPF message header.

Field *VERSION* specifies the version of the protocol. Field *TYPE* identifies the message type as one of:

Type	Meaning
1	Hello (used to test reachability)
2	Database description (topology)
3	Link status request
4	Link status update
5	Link status acknowledgement

The field labeled *SOURCE ROUTER IP ADDRESS* gives the address of the sender, and the field labeled *AREA ID* gives the 32-bit identification number for the area.

Because each message can include authentication, field *AUTHENTICATION TYPE* specifies which authentication scheme is used (currently, *0* means no authentication and *1* means a simple password is used).

16.6.2 OSPF Hello Message Format

OSPF sends *hello* messages on each link periodically to establish and test neighbor reachability. Figure 16.8 shows the format.

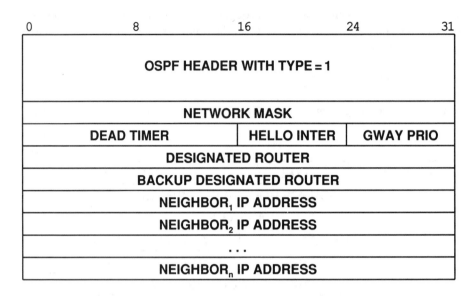

Figure 16.8 OSPF *hello* message format. A pair of neighbor routers exchange these messages periodically to test reachability.

Field *NETWORK MASK* contains a mask for the network over which the message has been sent (see Chapter 10 for details about masks). Field *DEAD TIMER* gives a time in seconds after which a nonresponding neighbor is considered dead. Field *HELLO INTER* is the normal period, in seconds, between hello messages. Field *GWAY PRIO* is the integer priority of this router, and is used in selecting a backup designated router. The fields labeled *DESIGNATED ROUTER* and *BACKUP DESIGNATED ROUTER* contain IP addresses that give the sender's view of the designated router and backup designated router for the network over which the message is sent. Finally, fields labeled *NEIGHBOR$_i$ IP ADDRESS* give the IP addresses of all neighbors from which the sender has recently received hello messages.

16.6.3 OSPF Database Description Message Format

Routers exchange OSPF *database description* messages to initialize their network topology database. In the exchange, one router serves as a master, while the other is a slave. The slave acknowledges each database description message with a response. Figure 16.9 shows the format.

Because it can be large, the topology database may be divided into several messages using the *I* and *M* bits. Bit *I* is set to *1* in the initial message; bit *M* is set to *1* if additional messages follow. Bit *S* indicates whether a message was sent by a master (*1*) or by a slave (*0*). Field *DATABASE SEQUENCE NUMBER* numbers messages sequentially so the receiver can tell if one is missing. The initial message contains a random integer *R*; subsequent messages contain sequential integers starting at *R*.

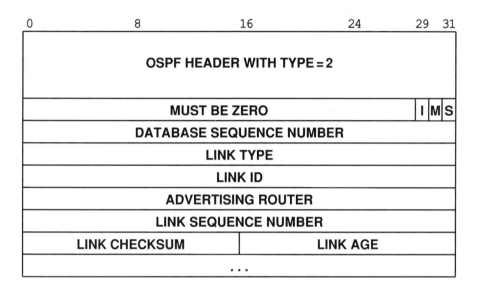

Figure 16.9 OSPF *database description* message format. The fields starting at *LINK TYPE* are repeated for each link being specified.

The fields from *LINK TYPE* through *LINK AGE* describe one link in the network topology; they are repeated for each link. The *LINK TYPE* describes a link according to the following table.

Link Type	Meaning
1	Router link
2	Network link
3	Summary link (IP network)
4	Summary link (link to border router)
5	External link (link to another site)

Field *LINK ID* gives an identification for the link (which can be the IP address of a router or a network, depending on the link type).

Field *ADVERTISING ROUTER* specifies the address of the router advertising this link, and *LINK SEQUENCE NUMBER* contains an integer generated by that router to ensure that messages are not missed or received out of order. Field *LINK CHECKSUM* provides further assurance that the link information has not been corrupted. Finally, field *LINK AGE* also helps order messages – it gives the time in seconds since the link was established.

16.6.4 OSPF Link Status Request Message Format

After exchanging database description messages with a neighbor, a router may discover that parts of its database are out of date. To request that the neighbor supply updated information, the router sends a *link status request* message. The message lists specific links as shown in Figure 16.10. The neighbor responds with the most current information it has about those links. The three fields shown are repeated for each link about which status is requested. More than one request message may be needed if the list of requests is long.

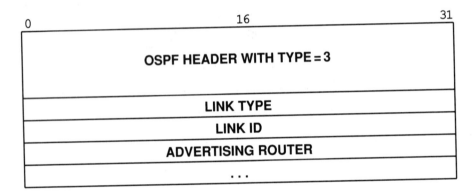

Figure 16.10 OSPF *link status request* message format. A router sends this message to a neighbor to request current information about a specific set of links.

16.6.5 OSPF Link Status Update Message Format

Routers broadcast the status of links with a *link status update* message. Each update consists of a list of advertisements, as Figure 16.11 shows.

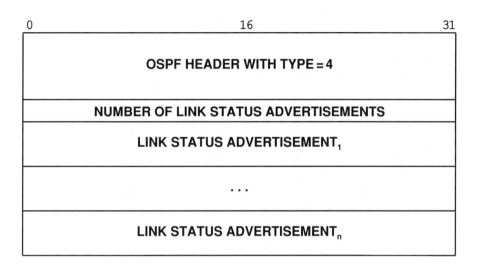

Figure 16.11 OSPF *link status update* message format. A router sends such a message to broadcast information about its directly connected links to all other routers.

Each link status advertisement has a header format as shown in Figure 16.12. The values used in each field are the same as in the database description message.

0	16	31
LINK AGE		LINK TYPE
LINK ID		
ADVERTISING ROUTER		
LINK SEQUENCE NUMBER		
LINK CHECKSUM		LENGTH

Figure 16.12 The format of the header used for all link status advertisements.

Following the link status header comes one of four possible formats to describe the links from a router to a given area, the links from a router to a specific network, the links from a router to the physical networks that comprise a single, subnetted IP network (see Chapter 10), or the links from a router to networks at other sites. In all cases, the *LINK TYPE* field in the link status header specifies which of the formats has been used. Thus, a router that receives a link status update message knows exactly which of the described destinations lie inside the site and which are external.

16.7 Routing With Partial Information

We began our discussion of internet router architecture and routing by discussing the concept of partial information. Hosts can route with only partial information because they rely on routers. It should be clear now that not all routers have complete information. Most autonomous systems have a single router that forms a bridge, connecting the autonomous system to other autonomous systems. If the site connects to the Internet, at least one router must have a connection that leads from the site to a national backbone. Routers within the autonomous system know about destinations within that autonomous system, but they route all other traffic to the bridge.

How to do routing with partial information becomes obvious if we examine a router's routing tables. Routers in a core system have a complete set of routes to all possible destinations; they do not use default routing. In fact, if a destination network address does not appear in the core tables, only two possibilities exist: either the address is not a valid destination IP address, or the address is valid but currently unreachable (e.g., because the only routers leading to that address have failed). Noncore routers do not usually have a complete set of routes; they rely on a default route to handle network addresses they do not understand.

Using default routes for most noncore routers has two consequences. First, it means that local routing errors can go undetected. For example, if a machine in an autonomous system incorrectly routes a packet to an external autonomous system instead of to a local router, the external system will route it back (perhaps sending an ICMP redirect message to the original source). Thus, connectivity may appear to be preserved even if routing is incorrect. The problem may not seem severe for small autonomous systems that have high speed local area networks, but in a wide area network with relatively low speed lines, incorrect routes can be disastrous. Second, on the positive side, having default routes means that the IGP routing update messages will be much smaller than the routing updates a core system uses.

16.8 Summary

Managers must choose how to pass routing information among the local routers within an autonomous system. Manual maintenance of routing information suffices only for small, slowly changing internets that have minimal interconnection; most require automated procedures that discover and update routes automatically. Two routers under the control of a single manager run an Interior Gateway Protocol, IGP, to exchange routing information.

An IGP implements either the vector-distance or SPF algorithm. We examined three specific IGPs: RIP, HELLO, and OSPF. RIP, a vector-distance protocol implemented by the UNIX program *routed*, is the most popular. It uses split horizon, holddown, and poison reverse techniques to help eliminate routing loops and the problem of counting to infinity. Although it is obsolete, Hello is interesting because it illustrates a vector-distance protocol that uses delay instead of hop counts as a distance metric. Finally, OSPF is a protocol that implements the link-status algorithm.

Also, we saw that the *gated* program provides an interface between an interior router protocol like RIP and the Exterior Gateway Protocol, EGP, automating the process of gathering routes from within an autonomous system and advertising them to another autonomous system.

FOR FURTHER STUDY

Hedrick [RFC 1058] discusses algorithms for exchanging routing information in general and contains the standard specification for RIP. The HELLO protocol is documented in Mills [RFC 891]. Mills and Braun [1987] considers the problems of converting between delay and hop-count metrics. Moy [RFC 1583] contains the lengthy specification of OSPF as well as a discussion of the motivation behind it. Fedor [June 1988] describes *gated*.

EXERCISES

16.1   What network families does RIP support? Hint: read the networking section of the 4.3 BSD UNIX Programmer's Manual.

16.2   Consider a large autonomous system using an interior router protocol like HELLO that bases routes on delay. What difficulty does this autonomous system have if a subgroup decides to use RIP on its routers?

16.3   Within a RIP message, each IP address is aligned on a 32-bit boundary. Will such addresses be aligned on a 32-bit boundary if the IP datagram carrying the message starts on a 32-bit boundary?

16.4   An autonomous system can be as small as a single local area network or as large as multiple long haul networks. Why does the variation in size make it difficult to find a standard IGP?

16.5   Characterize the circumstances under which the split horizon technique will prevent slow convergence.

16.6   Consider an internet composed of many local area networks running RIP as an IGP. Find an example that shows how a routing loop can result even if the code uses "hold down" after receiving information that a network is unreachable.

16.7   Should a host ever run RIP in active mode? Why or why not?

16.8   Under what circumstances will a hop count metric produce better routes than a metric that uses delay?

16.9   Can you imagine a situation in which an autonomous system chooses *not* to advertise all its networks? Hint: think of a university.

16.10   In broad terms, we could say that RIP distributes the local routing table, while EGP distributes a table of known networks and routers used to reach them (i.e., a router can send an EGP advertisement for a network without installing a route to that network in its own routing table). What are the advantages of each approach?

16.11   Consider a function used to convert between delay and hop-count metrics. Can you find properties of such functions that are sufficient to prevent routing loops. Are your properties necessary as well? (Hint: look at Mills and Braun [1987].)

16.12   Are there circumstances under which an SPF protocol can form routing loops? Hint: think of best-effort delivery.

16.13   Build an application program that sends a request to a router running RIP and displays the routes returned.

16.14   Read the RIP specification carefully. Can routes reported in a response to a query differ from the routes reported by a routing update message? If so how?

16.15   Read the OSPF specification carefully. How can a manager use the virtual link facility?

16.16   OSPF allows managers to assign many of their own identifiers, possibly leading to duplication of values at multiple sites. Which identifier(s) may need to change if two sites running OSPF decide to merge?

16.17   Compare the version of OSPF available under 4BSD UNIX to the version of RIP for the same system. What are the differences in source code size? Object code size? Data storage size? What can you conclude?

16.18   Can you use ICMP redirect messages to pass routing information among *interior* routers? Why or why not?

16.19   Write a program that takes as input a description of your organization's internet, uses RIP queries to obtain routes from the routers, and reports any inconsistencies.

17

Internet Multicasting (IGMP)

17.1 Introduction

Chapter 4 describes the three primary classes of IP addresses and Chapter 10 presents subnet addressing, an address extension that permits multiple physical networks to share a single IP network address. This chapter explores an addition to the IP addressing scheme that permits efficient multipoint delivery of datagrams. We begin with a brief review of hardware support. Later sections describe the IP address extension that uses multipoint delivery, and present an experimental protocol used to propagate special routing information among routers.

17.2 Hardware Broadcast

Many hardware technologies contain mechanisms to send packets to multiple destinations simultaneously (or nearly simultaneously). Chapter 2 reviews several technologies and discusses the most common form of multipoint delivery: *broadcasting*. Broadcast delivery means that the network delivers one copy of a packet to each destination. On bus technologies like Ethernet, broadcast delivery can be accomplished with a single packet transmission. On networks composed of switches with point-to-point connections, software must implement broadcasting by forwarding copies of the packet across individual connections until all switches have received a copy.

With most hardware, the user specifies broadcast delivery by sending the packet to a special, reserved destination address called the *broadcast address*. For example, Ethernet hardware addresses consist of 48-bit identifiers, with the all ones address used to denote broadcast. Hardware on each machine recognizes the machine's hardware address as well as the broadcast address, and accepts incoming packets that have either address as their destination.

The chief disadvantage of broadcasting is that every broadcast consumes resources on all machines. For example, it would be possible to design an alternative internet protocol suite that used broadcast to deliver datagrams on a local network and relied on IP software to discard datagrams not intended for the local machine. However, such a scheme would be expensive because all computers on the local network would receive and process all datagrams sent on that network, even though most machines would discard most of the datagrams that arrived. Thus, the designers of TCP/IP used address binding mechanisms like ARP to eliminate broadcast delivery.

17.3 Hardware Multicast

Some hardware technologies support a second, less common form of multi-point delivery called *multicasting*. Unlike broadcasting, multicasting allows each machine to choose whether it wants to participate in a multicast. Typically, a hardware technology reserves a large set of addresses for use with multicast. When a group of machines want to communicate, they choose one particular *multicast address* to use for communication. After configuring their network interface hardware to recognize the selected multicast address, all machines in the group will receive a copy of every packet sent to that multicast address.

Multicast addressing can be viewed as a generalization of all other address forms. For example, we can think of a conventional *unicast address* as a form of multicast addressing in which there is exactly one machine in the multicast group. Similarly, we can think of broadcast addressing as a form of multicasting in which every machine is a member of the multicast group. Other multicast addresses can correspond to arbitrary sets of machines.

Ethernet provides the best example of multicasting in hardware. Ethernet uses the low-order bit of the high-order octet to distinguish conventional unicast addresses (*0*) from multicast addresses (*1*). In dotted hexadecimal notation†, the multicast bit is given by:

$$01.00.00.00.00.00_{16}$$

Initially, the network interface hardware is configured to accept packets destined for the Ethernet broadcast address or the machine's hardware address. However, an interface can be reconfigured easily to allow it to recognize a small set of multicast addresses as well.

---

†Dotted hexadecimal notation represents each octet as two hexadecimal digits with octets separated by periods; the subscript *16* can be omitted only when the context is unambiguous.

17.4 IP Multicast

IP multicasting is the internet abstraction of hardware multicasting. It allows transmission of an IP datagram to a set of hosts that form a single multicast group. It is possible for members of the group to be spread across separate physical networks. IP multicasting uses the same best-effort delivery semantics as other IP datagram delivery, meaning that multicast datagrams can be lost, delayed, duplicated, or delivered out of order.

Membership in an IP multicast group is dynamic. A host may join or leave a group at any time. Furthermore, a host may be a member of an arbitrary number of multicast groups. Membership in a group determines whether the host will receive datagrams sent to the multicast group; a host may send datagrams to a multicast group without being a member.

Each multicast group has a unique multicast (class *D*) address. Like protocol ports, some IP multicast addresses are assigned by the Internet authority and correspond to groups that always exist even if they have no current members. Such addresses are said to be *well-known*. Other multicast addresses are available for temporary use. They correspond to *transient multicast groups* that are created when needed and discarded when the count of members reaches zero.

IP multicasting may be used on a single physical network or throughout an internet. In the latter case, special *multicast routers* forward multicast datagrams. However, hosts need not know about multicast routers explicitly. The host transmits multicast datagrams using the local network multicast capability. If a multicast router is present, it will receive the datagram and forward it to other networks as needed. Multicast routers will use the local hardware multicast capability to deliver the datagram on target network(s) that support it. The time-to-live field in a multicast datagram limits propagation through routers exactly like the time to live field in a unicast datagram limits its propagation. Multicast forwarding may be provided by physically independent routers or the capability may be added to conventional routers.

The TCP/IP standard for multicasting defines IP multicast addressing, specifies how hosts send and receive multicast datagrams, and describes the protocol routers use to determine multicast group membership on a network. The next sections examine each aspect in more detail.

17.5 IP Multicast Addresses

Like hardware multicasting, IP multicasting uses the datagram's destination address to specify multicast delivery. IP multicast uses class *D* addresses of the form shown in Figure 17.1.

```
 0 1 2 3 4                                                                  31
┌─┬─┬─┬─┬────────────────────────────────────────────────────────────────┐
│1│1│1│0│                    Group Identification                         │
└─┴─┴─┴─┴────────────────────────────────────────────────────────────────┘
```

Figure 17.1 The format of class D IP addresses used for IP multicasting. Bits *4* through *31* identify a particular multicast group.

The first *4* bits contain *1110* and identify the address as a multicast. The remaining *28* bits specify a particular multicast group. There is no further structure in the group bits. In particular, the group field does not identify the origin of the group, nor does it contain a network address like class *A*, *B*, and *C* addresses.

When expressed in dotted decimal notation, multicast addresses range from

224.0.0.0   through   239.255.255.255

However, address 224.0.0.0 is reserved; it cannot be assigned to any group. Furthermore, address 224.0.0.1 is permanently assigned to the *all hosts group*, which includes all hosts and routers participating in IP multicast. In general, the all hosts group address is used to reach all machines that participate in IP multicast on a local network; there is no IP multicast address that refers to all hosts in the internet.

IP multicast addresses can be used only as destination addresses. They can never appear in the source address field of a datagram, nor can they appear in a source route or record route option. Furthermore, no ICMP error messages can be generated about multicast datagrams (e.g., destination unreachable, source quench, echo reply, or time exceeded).

17.6 Mapping IP Multicast To Ethernet Multicast

Although the standard does not cover all types of network hardware, it does specify how to map IP multicast addresses to Ethernet multicast addresses. The mapping is efficient and easy to understand:

> *To map an IP multicast address to the corresponding Ethernet multicast address, place the low-order 23 bits of the IP multicast address into the low-order 23 bits of the special Ethernet multicast address 01.00.5E.00.00.00$_{16}$.*

For example, IP multicast address 224.0.0.1 becomes Ethernet multicast address 01.00.5E.00.00.01$_{16}$.

Interestingly, the mapping is not unique. Because IP multicast addresses have 28 significant bits that identify the multicast group, more than one group may map onto the same Ethernet multicast address. The designers chose this scheme as a compromise. On one hand, using 23 of the 28 bits for a hardware address means most of the multicast address is included. The set of addresses is large enough so the chances of two groups choosing addresses with all low-order 23 bits identical is small. On the other hand, arranging for IP to use a fixed part of the Ethernet multicast address space makes debugging much easier and eliminates interference between IP and other protocols that share an Ethernet. The consequence of this design is that some multicast datagrams may be received at a host that are not destined for that host. Thus, the IP software must carefully check addresses on all incoming datagrams and discard any unwanted datagrams.

17.7 Extending IP To Handle Multicasting

A host participates in IP multicast at one of three levels as Figure 17.2 shows:

Level	Meaning
0	Host can neither send nor receive IP multicast
1	Host can send but not receive IP multicast
2	Host can both send and receive IP multicast

Figure 17.2 The three levels of participation in IP multicast.

Modifications that allow a machine to send IP multicast are not difficult. The IP software must allow an application program to specify a multicast address as a destination IP address, and the network interface software must be able to map an IP multicast address into the corresponding hardware multicast address (or use broadcast if the hardware does not support multicasting).

Extending host software to receive IP multicast datagrams is more complex. IP software on the host must have an interface that allows an application program to declare that it wants to join or leave a particular multicast group. If multiple application programs join the same group, the IP software must remember to pass each of them a copy of datagrams that arrive destined for that group. If all application programs leave a group, the host must remember that it no longer participates in that group. Furthermore, as we will see in the next section, the host must run a protocol that informs the local multicast routers of its group membership status. Much of the complexity comes from a basic idea:

Hosts join specific IP multicast groups on specific networks.

That is, a host with multiple network connections may join a particular multicast group on one network and not on another. To understand the reason for keeping group membership associated with networks, remember that it is possible to use IP multicasting among local sets of machines. The host may want to use a multicast application to interact with machines on one physical net, but not with machines on another.

Because group membership is associated with particular networks, the software must keep separate lists of multicast addresses for each network to which the machine attaches. Furthermore, an application program must specify a particular network when it asks to join or leave a multicast group.

17.8 Internet Group Management Protocol

To participate in IP multicast on a local network, a host must have software that allows it to send and receive multicast datagrams. To participate in a multicast that spans multiple networks, the host must inform local multicast routers. The local routers contact other multicast routers, passing on the membership information and establishing routes. The idea is quite similar to conventional route propagation among conventional internet routers.

Before a multicast router can propagate multicast membership information, it must determine that one or more hosts on the local network have decided to join a multicast group. To do so, multicast routers and hosts that implement multicast must use the *Internet Group Management Protocol* (*IGMP*) to communicate group membership information.

IGMP is analogous to ICMP†. Like ICMP, it uses IP datagrams to carry messages. Also like ICMP, it provides a service used by IP. Therefore,

> *Although IGMP uses IP datagrams to carry messages, we think of it as an integral part of IP, not a separate protocol.*

Furthermore, IGMP is a standard for TCP/IP; it is required on all machines that participate in IP multicast at level 2.

Conceptually, IGMP has two phases. Phase 1: When a host joins a new multicast group, it sends an IGMP message to the "all hosts" multicast address declaring its membership. Local multicast routers receive the message and establish necessary routing by propagating the group membership information to other multicast routers throughout the internet. Phase 2: Because membership is dynamic, local multicast routers periodically poll hosts on the local network to determine which hosts remain members of which groups. If no host reports membership in a group after several polls, the multicast router assumes that no host on the network remains in that group, and stops advertising group membership to other multicast routers.

17.9 IGMP Implementation

IGMP is carefully designed to avoid congesting a local network. First, all communication between hosts and multicast routers uses IP multicast. That is, when IGMP messages are encapsulated in an IP datagram for transmission, the IP destination address is the all hosts multicast address. Thus, datagrams carrying IGMP messages are

---

†Chapter 9 discusses ICMP, the Internet Control Message Protocol.

transmitted using hardware multicast if it is available. As a result, on networks that support hardware multicast, hosts not participating in IP multicast never receive IGMP messages. Second, a multicast router will not send individual request messages for each multicast group. Instead, it sends a single poll message to request information about membership in all groups. The polling rate is restricted to at most one request per minute. Third, hosts that are members of multiple groups do not send multiple responses at the same time. Instead, after an IGMP request message arrives from a multicast router, the host assigns each group in which it has membership a random delay between *0* and *10* seconds, and sends a response for that group after the delay. Thus, a host spaces its responses randomly over *10* seconds. Fourth, hosts listen to responses from other hosts and suppress any of their responses that are unnecessary.

To understand why a response can be unnecessary, recall why multicast routers send a poll message. Routers do not need to keep an exact record of group membership because all transmissions to the group will be sent using hardware multicast. Instead, multicast routers only need to know whether at least one host on the network remains a member of the group. After the multicast router sends a poll message, all hosts assign a random delay to their response. When the host with smallest delay sends its response (using multicast), other participating hosts receive a copy. Each host assumes that the multicast router also received a copy of the first response and cancels its response. Thus, in practice, only one host from each group responds to a request message from the multicast router.

17.10 Group Membership State Transitions

IGMP must remember the status of each multicast group to which the host belongs. We think of a host as keeping a table in which it records group membership information. Initially, all entries in the table are unused. Whenever an application program on the host joins a new group, IGMP software allocates an entry and fills in information about the group. Among the information, IGMP keeps a group reference counter which it initializes to *1*. If additional applications join the group, IGMP increments the reference counter in the entry. As application programs drop out of the group, IGMP decrements the counter; the host leaves the multicast group when the counter reaches zero.

The actions IGMP software takes in response to IGMP messages can best be explained by the state transition diagram in Figure 17.3.

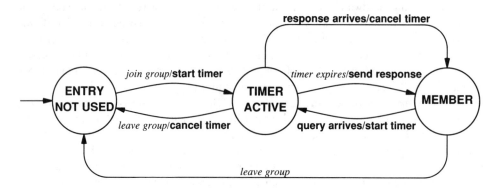

Figure 17.3 The three possible states of an entry in a host's multicast group
table and transitions among them. Transitions are caused by the
arrival of IGMP messages or events at the host (shown in italic).

As Figure 17.3 shows, a single timer mechanism can be used to generate both the
initial response message as well as responses to requests from the multicast router. A
request to join a group places the entry in the *TIMER ACTIVE* state and sets the timer
to a small value. When the timer expires, IGMP generates and sends a response message and moves the entry to the *MEMBER* state.

In the *MEMBER* state, reception of an IGMP query causes the software to choose a
timeout value (at random), start a timer for the entry, and move the entry to the *TIMER
ACTIVE* state. If another host sends a response for the multicast group before the timer
expires, IGMP cancels the timer and moves the entry back to the *MEMBER* state.

17.11 IGMP Message Format

As Figure 17.4 shows, IGMP messages have a simple format.

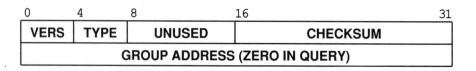

Figure 17.4 The format of an IGMP message.

Field *VERS* gives the protocol version (the current value is *1*). The *TYPE* field identifies the message as a query sent by a multicast router (*1*) or a response sent by a host
(*2*). The *UNUSED* field must contain zero, and the *CHECKSUM* field contains a

checksum for the 8-octet IGMP message. (IGMP checksums are computed with the same algorithm used for TCP and IP checksums.) Finally, hosts use field *GROUP AD-DRESS* to report their membership in a particular multicast group (in a query, the field contains zero, and has no meaning).

17.12 Multicast Address Assignment

The standard does not specify exactly how groups of machines are assigned multicast addresses, but suggests several possibilities. For example, if the local operating system assigns an integer identifier to a set of processes or to a set of applications, that identifier can be used to form an IP multicast address. Of course, it is possible to have a network manager assign addresses manually. Another possibility is to allow a machine to randomly form multicast addresses until it discovers one that is not in use.

17.13 Propagating Routing Information

Although the IP multicasting described in this chapter is a standard for TCP/IP, no standard exists for the propagation of routing information among multicast routers. However, the literature describes an experimental protocol called the *Distance Vector Multicast Routing Protocol (DVMRP)*. Multicast routers use DVMRP to pass group membership information among themselves. They use the information to establish routes so they can deliver a copy of a multicast datagram to every member of the multicast group.

DVMRP resembles the RIP protocol described in Chapter 16, but incorporates ideas that make it more efficient and robust. In essence, the protocol passes information about current multicast group membership and the cost to reach between routers. For each possible multicast group, the routers impose a routing tree on top of the graph of physical interconnections. When a router receives a datagram destined for an IP multicast address, it sends a copy of the datagram out over the network links that correspond to branches in the routing tree.

DVMRP uses IGMP messages to carry information. It defines IGMP message types that allow routers to declare membership in multicast groups, leave a multicast group, and interrogate other routers. The extensions also provide messages that carry routing information including cost metrics. The protocol has been implemented, but more experimentation is needed before conclusions can be drawn about its performance.

17.14 The Mrouted Program

Mrouted is a well-known program that handles multicast routing on UNIX systems. Like *routed†*, *mrouted* cooperates closely with the operating system kernel to install multicast routing information. Unlike *routed*, however, *mrouted* does not use the standard routing table. Instead, it can be used only with a special version of the UNIX system known as a *multicast kernel*. A UNIX multicast kernel contains a special multicast routing table as well as the code needed to forward multicast datagrams. *Mrouted* handles:

- *Route propagation. Mrouted* uses DVMRP to propagate multicast routing information from one router to another. A computer running *mrouted* also interprets multicast routing information, and constructs a multicast routing table using an algorithm known as *Truncated Reverse Path Broadcast* (*TRPB*). *Mrouted* does not replace conventional route propagation protocols; a computer usually runs *mrouted* in addition to standard routing protocol software.

- *Multicast tunneling.* One of the chief problems with internet multicast arises because not all internet routers can forward multicast datagrams. *Mrouted* can arrange to *tunnel* a multicast datagram from one router to another through intermediate routers that do not participate in multicast routing.

Although a single *mrouted* program can perform both tasks, a given computer may not need both functions. To allow a manager to specify exactly how it should operate, *mrouted* uses a configuration file. The configuration file contains entries that specify which multicast groups *mrouted* is permitted to advertise on each interface, and how it should forward datagrams. Furthermore, the configuration file associates a metric and threshold with each route. The metric allows a manager to assign a cost to each path (e.g., to ensure that the cost assigned to a path over a local area network will be lower than the cost of a path across a slow serial link). The threshold gives the minimum IP *time to live* (*TTL*) that a datagram needs to complete the path. If a datagram does not have a sufficient TTL to reach its destination, a multicast kernel does not forward the datagram. Instead, it discards the datagram, which avoids wasting bandwidth.

Multicast tunneling is perhaps the most interesting capability of *mrouted*. A tunnel is needed when (1) two or more computers wish to participate in multicast applications, and (2) one or more routers in the part of the internet that separates the participating computers do not run multicast routing software. Figure 17.5 illustrates the concept.

---

†Recall that *routed* is the UNIX program that implements RIP.

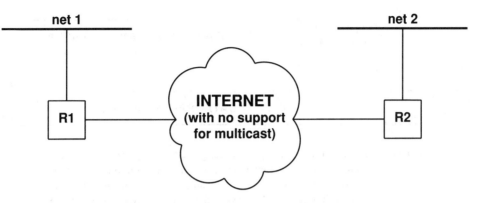

Figure 17.5 An example internet configuration that requires multicast tunneling for computers attached to networks *1* and *2* to participate in
multicast communication. Routers in the internet that separates
the two networks do not propagate multicast routes, and cannot
forward datagrams sent to a multicast address.

To allow computers on separate networks to communicate using multicast,
managers of routers at each site configure *mrouted* to use a *tunnel* for communication
between the two sites. In fact, the tunnel merely consists of an agreement between the
mrouted programs running on the two routers. Each router listens on its local net for
datagrams sent to the multicast group for which the tunnel has been configured. When
a multicast datagram arrives in which the destination address corresponds to that of the
tunnel, *mrouted* sends the datagram to *mrouted* on the other router using a conventional
IP unicast address. When it receives a unicast datagram through the tunnel, *mrouted*
extracts the multicast datagram, and then uses hardware multicast to deliver the datagram to computers on its local net.

How can two programs send a multicast datagram using a unicast address? The
answer is encapsulation. *Mrouted* stores multicast routing information in the kernel,
which causes the kernel to place the entire multicast datagram inside a conventional IP
datagram as Figure 17.6 shows.

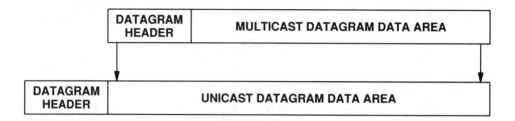

Figure 17.6 A multicast IP datagram encapsulated in a conventional IP datagram; multicast routers use such encapsulation to tunnel multicast traffic across routers that do not understand multicasting.
After it traverses the tunnel, the receiving router extracts the
multicast datagram and uses the multicast destination address to
forward it.

As the figure shows, the multicast datagram, including the header, travels inside
the data area of a conventional unicast datagram. On the receiving machine, the multicast kernel extracts and processes the multicast datagram as if it arrived over a local interface. In particular, the receiving machine decrements the time to live field in the
header by one before forwarding the multicast datagram. Thus, when it creates a tunnel, *mrouted* treats the internet connecting two multicast routers like a single, physical
network. Note that a unicast datagram that carries a multicast datagram has its own
time to live counter, which operates independently from the time to live counter in the
multicast datagram header. Thus, it is possible to limit the number of physical hops
across a given tunnel independent of the number of logical hops a multicast datagram
must visit on its journey from the original source to the ultimate destination.

Multicast tunnels form the basis of the Internet's *Multicast Backbone* (*MBONE*).
The MBONE consists of a set of routers that agree to forward multicast traffic
throughout the Internet. It has been used for services such as audio and video
teleconferences.

17.15 Summary

IP multicasting is an abstraction of hardware multicasting. It allows efficient
delivery of a datagram to multiple destinations. IP uses class *D* addresses to specify
multicast delivery; actual transmission uses hardware multicast if it is available.

IP multicast groups are dynamic: a host can join or leave a group at any time. For
local multicast, hosts only need the ability to send and receive multicast datagrams.
However, IP multicasting is not limited to a single physical network – multicast routers
propagate group membership information and arrange routing so that each member of a
multicast group receives a copy of every datagram sent to that group.

Hosts communicate their group membership to multicast routers using IGMP. IGMP has been designed to be efficient and to avoid using network resources. In most cases, the only traffic IGMP introduces is a periodic message from a multicast router and a single reply for each multicast group to which hosts on that network belong.

Not all routers in the global Internet propagate multicast routes or forward multicast traffic. Groups at two or more sites separated by an internet that does not support multicast routing can use an IP tunnel to transfer multicast datagrams. When using a tunnel, a program encapsulates a multicast datagram in a conventional unicast datagram. The receiver must extract and handle the multicast datagram.

FOR FURTHER STUDY

Deering [RFC 1112] specifies the standard for IP multicasting described in this chapter. Waitzman, Partridge, and Deering [RFC 1075] describes multicast route propagation using a vector-distance protocol similar to RIP. Earlier drafts of these ideas can be found in Deering [RFCs 1054 and 988] and in Deering and Cheriton [RFC 966]. Deering and Cheriton [May 1990] considers modifying various routing algorithms to support wide-area multicasting. Information on *mrouted* can be found in the manual page distributed with the program.

Eriksson [1994] explains the multicast backbone. Casner and Deering [July 1992] reports on the first multicast of an IETF meeting.

EXERCISES

17.1   The standard suggests using 23 bits of an IP multicast address to form a hardware multicast address. In such a scheme, how many IP multicast addresses map to a single hardware multicast address?

17.2   Argue that IP multicast addresses should use only 23 of the 28 possible bits. Hint: what are the practical limits on the number of groups to which a host can belong and the number of hosts on a single network?

17.3   IP must always check the destination addresses on incoming multicast datagrams and discard datagrams if the host is not in the specified multicast group. Explain how the host might receive a multicast destined for a group to which that host is not a member.

17.4   Is there any advantage in having multicast routers know the set of hosts on the local network that belong to a given multicast group?

17.5   Find three applications in your environment that can benefit from IP multicast.

17.6   The standard says that IP software must arrange to deliver a copy of any outgoing multicast datagram to application programs on the host that belong to the specified multicast group. Does this design make programming easier or more difficult?

17.7 When the underlying hardware does not support multicast, IP multicast uses hardware broadcast for delivery. How can doing so cause problems? Is there any advantage to using IP multicast over such networks?

17.8 Read RFC 1075 on DVMRP. What makes DVMRP more complex than RIP?

17.9 The all hosts IP multicast address refers only to the local network, while all other IP multicast addresses refer to internet-wide multicast groups. Argue that it would be advantageous to reserve a set of IP multicast addresses for local use only.

17.10 IGMP does not include a strategy for acknowledgment or retransmission, even when used on networks that use best-effort delivery. What can happen if a query is lost? What can happen if a response is lost?

17.11 Explain why a multihomed host may need to join a multicast group on one network, but not on another. (Hint: consider an audio teleconference.)

18

TCP/IP Over ATM Networks

18.1 Introduction

Previous chapters explain the fundamental parts of TCP/IP and show how components operate over conventional packet-switched LANs and WANs. This chapter explores how TCP/IP, which was designed for connectionless networks, can be used over a connection-oriented technology. We will see that TCP/IP is extremely flexible – although a few of the address binding details change, most protocols remain unchanged.

To make the discussion concrete and relate it to available hardware, we will use *Asynchronous Transfer Mode (ATM)* in all examples. ATM offers high-speed, can be used for both local area and wide area networks, and supports a variety of applications including real-time audio and video as well as conventional data communication. This chapter expands the brief description in Chapter 2, and covers additional details. In particular, the next sections describe the physical topology of an ATM network, the logical connectivity provided, ATM's connection paradigm, and the ATM protocol for data transfer.

Later sections explain the relationship between ATM and TCP/IP. They show how an ATM host address relates to the host's IP address. They describe a modified form of the Address Resolution Protocol (ARP) used to resolve an IP address to an ATM connection, and a modified form of Inverse ARP used to help manage address bindings in a server. Most important, we will see how IP datagrams travel across an ATM network without IP fragmentation.

18.2 ATM Hardware

The basic component of an ATM network is a special-purpose electronic switch designed to transfer data at extremely high speed. A typical small switch can connect between 16 and 32 computers. To permit data communication at high speeds, each connection between a computer and an ATM switch uses a pair of optical fibers†. Figure 18.1 illustrates the connection between a computer and an ATM switch.

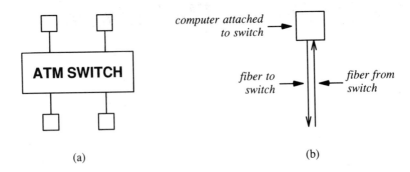

Figure 18.1 (a) The schematic diagram of a single ATM switch with four computers attached, and (b) the details of a single connection. A pair of optical fibers carries data to and from the switch.

Physically, a host interface board plugs into a computer's bus. The interface hardware includes a light emitting diode (LED) or a miniature laser along with the circuitry needed to convert data into pulses of light that travel down the fiber to the switch. The interface also contains the hardware needed to sense pulses of light coming from the switch and convert them back into data bits in electronic form. Because a given fiber can carry light in only one direction, a connection requires a pair of fibers to allow the computer to both send and receive data.

18.3 Large ATM Networks

Although a single ATM switch has finite capacity, multiple switches can be interconnected to form a larger network. In particular, to connect computers at two sites to the same network, a switch can be installed at each site, and the two switches can then be connected. The connection between two switches differs slightly from the connection between a host computer and a switch. For example, interswitch connections can operate at higher speeds, and can use slightly modified protocols. Figure 18.2 illustrates the topology, and shows the difference between a *Network to Network Interface* (*NNI*) and a *User to Network Interface* (*UNI*).

---

†Most installations use the multimode type of fiber.

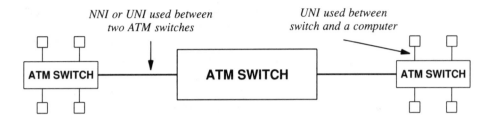

NNI or UNI used between
two ATM switches

UNI used between
switch and a computer

Figure 18.2 Three ATM switches combined to form a large network. Although an NNI interface is designed for use between switches, UNI connections can be used between ATM switches in a private network.

The distinction between UNI and NNI arises because telephone companies designed ATM technology using the same paradigm as they use for the voice network. In general, a phone company that offers ATM data services to customers will also inter-connect with other phone companies. The designers envisioned UNI as the interface between equipment at a customer's site and the switching equipment owned by the common carrier, and NNI as the interface between switches owned and operated by two different phone companies.

18.4 The Logical View Of An ATM Network

To a computer attached to an ATM network, an entire fabric of ATM switches appears to be a homogeneous network. Like the voice telephone system or a bridged Ethernet, ATM hides the details of physical hardware and gives the appearance of a single, physical network with many computers attached. For example, Figure 18.3 illustrates how the ATM switching system in Figure 18.2 appears logically to the eight computers that are attached to it.

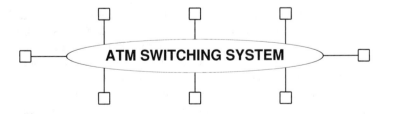

Figure 18.3 The logical view of the ATM switches in Figure 18.2. ATM gives the appearance of a uniform network; any computer can communicate with any other computer.

Thus, ATM provides the same general abstraction across homogeneous ATM hardware that TCP/IP provides for heterogeneous systems:

> *Despite a physical architecture that permits a switching fabric to contain multiple switches, ATM hardware provides attached computers with the appearance of a single, physical network. Any computer on the ATM network can communicate directly with any other; the computers remain unaware of the physical network structure.*

18.5 The Two ATM Connection Paradigms

ATM provides a connection-oriented interface to attached hosts. To reach a remote destination over an ATM network, a host must establish a *connection*, an abstraction that resembles a telephone call. ATM offers two forms of connections. The first is known as a *Switched Virtual Circuit* (*SVC*), and the second is known as a *Permanent Virtual Circuit* (*PVC*).

18.5.1 Switched Virtual Circuits

A switched virtual circuit operates like a conventional voice telephone call. A host communicates with its local ATM switch to request that the switch establish an SVC. The host specifies the complete address of a remote host computer and the quality of service required. The host then waits for the ATM network to create a circuit. The ATM *signaling*† system takes over and establishes a path from the originating host, across the ATM network (possibly through multiple switches), to the remote host computer. The remote computer must agree to accept the virtual circuit.

During signaling, each ATM switch along the path examines the quality of service requested for the circuit. If it agrees to forward data, a switch records information about the circuit and sends the request to the next switch along the path. Such an agreement requires a commitment of hardware and software resources at each switch. When signaling completes, the local ATM switch reports success to both ends of the switched virtual circuit.

The ATM UNI interface uses a 24-bit integer to identify each virtual circuit. When a host creates or accepts a new virtual circuit, the local ATM switch assigns an identifier to the circuit. A packet transmitted across an ATM network contains neither a source nor destination address. Instead, a host labels each outgoing packet and the switch labels each incoming packet with a circuit identifier.

Note that we have skipped over several details of signaling, including the protocol a host uses to request a new circuit and the protocol a switch uses to inform the host that a connection request has arrived from a remote host. Furthermore, we have omitted a few details that are important in practice. For example, two-way communication requires resources to be reserved along the reverse path as well as the forward path.

---

†The term *signaling* derives from telephone jargon; signaling is not yet part of the ATM standard.

18.5.2 Permanent Virtual Circuits

The alternative to a switched virtual circuit is mundane: an administrator interacts with switches in an ATM network to configure virtual circuits by hand. The administrator specifies the source and destination of the circuit, the quality of service the circuit will receive, and the 24-bit identifiers each host uses to access the circuit. Although switched virtual circuits provide more flexibility, permanent virtual circuits are important for three reasons. First, until all vendors agree on a standard signaling mechanism, switches from two vendors must use PVCs to interoperate. Second, PVCs can be used on leased lines. Third, PVCs can be used for network maintenance and debugging.

18.6 Paths, Circuits, And Identifiers

ATM assigns a unique integer identifier to each circuit a host has open; the host uses the identifier when performing I/O operations or when closing the circuit. A circuit identifier is analogous to a descriptor that a program uses to perform I/O. Like an I/O descriptor, a circuit identifier is short compared to the information needed to create a circuit. Also like an I/O descriptor, a circuit identifier only remains valid while the circuit is open. Furthermore, a circuit identifier is meaningful only across a single hop – the circuit identifiers obtained by hosts at the two ends of a given virtual circuit usually differ. For example, the sender may be using identifier *17* while the receiver uses identifier *49*; each ATM switch translates the circuit identifier in a packet as the packet flows from one host to the other.

Technically, a circuit identifier used with the UNI interface consists of a 24-bit integer divided into two fields†. Figure 18.4 shows how ATM partitions the 24 bits into an 8-bit *virtual path identifier (VPI)* and a 16-bit *virtual circuit identifier (VCI)*. Often, the entire identifier is referred to as a *VPI/VCI pair*.

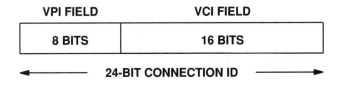

Figure 18.4 The 24-bit connection identifier used with UNI. The identifier is divided into virtual path and virtual circuit parts.

The motivation for dividing a connection identifier into VPI and VCI fields is similar to the reasons for dividing an IP address into network and host fields. If a set of virtual circuits follow the same path, an administrator can arrange for all circuits in the set to use the same VPI. ATM hardware can then use the VPI to route traffic efficient-

---

†The circuit identifier used with NNI has a slightly different format and a different length.

ly. Commercial carriers can also use the VPI for accounting – a carrier can charge a customer for a virtual path, and then allow the customer to decide how to multiplex multiple virtual circuits over the path.

18.7 ATM Cell Transport

At the lowest level, an ATM network uses fixed-size frames called *cells* to carry data. ATM requires all cells to be the same size because doing so makes it possible to build faster switching hardware. Each ATM cell is 53 octets long, and consists of a 5-octet header followed by 48 octets of data. Figure 18.5 shows the format of a cell header.

0	1	2	3	4	5	6	7
FLOW CONTROL				VPI (FIRST 4 BITS)			
VPI (LAST 4 BITS)				VCI (FIRST 4 BITS)			
VCI (MIDDLE 8 BITS)							
VCI (LAST 4 BITS)				PAYLOAD TYPE			PRIO
CYCLIC REDUNDANCY CHECK							

Figure 18.5 The contents of the five octets that comprise the UNI form of an ATM cell header, with one octet shown on each line. Data in the cell immediately follows the header.

18.8 ATM Adaptation Layers

Although ATM switches small cells at the lowest level, application programs that transfer data over an ATM do not read or write cells. Instead, a computer interacts with ATM through an *ATM Adaptation Layer*, which is part of the ATM standard. The adaptation layer performs several functions, including detection and correction of errors such as lost or corrupted cells. Usually, firmware that implements an ATM adaptation layer is located on a host interface along with hardware and firmware that provide cell transmission and reception. Figure 18.6 illustrates the organization of a typical ATM interface, and shows how data passes from the computer's operating system through the interface board and into an ATM network.

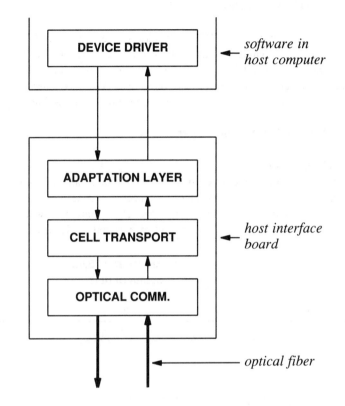

Figure 18.6 The conceptual organization of ATM interface hardware and the
flow of data through it. A host computer interacts with an adaptation layer protocol to send and receive data. The adaptation
layer converts data into outgoing cells and extracts data from incoming cells. The cell transport layer transfers cells to the ATM
switch.

When establishing a connection, a host must specify which adaptation layer protocol to use. Both ends of the connection must agree on the choice, and the adaptation layer cannot be changed once the connection has been established. To summarize:

*Although ATM hardware uses small, fixed-size cells to transport data,
a higher layer protocol called an ATM Adaptation Layer provides
data transfer services for computers that use ATM. When a virtual
circuit is created, both ends of the circuit must agree on which adaptation protocol will be used.*

18.8.1 ATM Adaptation Layer 1

Only two interesting ATM adaptation layer protocols have been defined: one for sending audio or video and another for sending conventional data packets. *ATM Adaptation Layer 1 (AAL1)* accepts and sends data across an ATM network at a fixed bitrate. A connection created to send video uses AAL1 because fixed-rate service is needed to guarantee that video transmission does not cause the image to pause or flicker.

18.8.2 ATM Adaptation Layer 5

Computers use *ATM Adaptation Layer 5 (AAL5)*† to send conventional data packets across an ATM network. Although ATM uses small fixed-size cells at the lowest level, AAL5 presents an interface that accepts and delivers large, variable-length packets. In particular, AAL5 allows each packet to contain between 1 and 65,535 octets of data. Figure 18.7 illustrates the packet format that AAL5 uses.

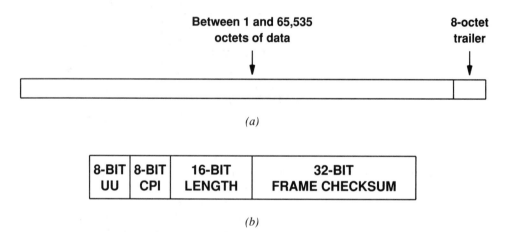

Figure 18.7 (a) The basic packet format that AAL5 accepts and delivers, and (b) the fields in the 8-octet trailer that follows the data.

Unlike most network frames that place control information in a header, AAL5 places control information in an 8-octet trailer at the end of the packet. The AAL5 trailer contains a 16-bit length field, a 32-bit cyclic redundancy check (*CRC*) used as a frame checksum, and two 8-bit fields labeled *UU* and *CPI* that are currently unused‡.

Each AAL5 packet must be divided into cells for transport across an ATM network, and then must be recombined to form a packet before being delivered to the receiving host. If the packet, including the 8-octet trailer, is an exact multiple of 48 octets, the division will produce completely full cells. If the packet is not an exact multiple of 48 octets, the final cell will not be full. To accommodate arbitrary length pack-

---

†Originally, AAL3 and AAL4 were defined for data transmission. They were merged into AAL3/4, and succeeded by AAL5.

‡Field *UU* can contain any value; field *CPI* must be set to zero.

ets, AAL5 allows the final cell to contain between 0 and 40 octets of data, followed by zero padding, followed by the 8-octet trailer. In other words, AAL5 places the trailer in the last 8 octets of the final cell, where it can be found and extracted without knowing the length of the packet.

18.9 AAL5 Convergence, Segmentation, And Reassembly

When an application sends data over an ATM connection using AAL5, the host delivers a block of data to the AAL5 interface. AAL5 generates a trailer, divides the information into 48-octet blocks, and transfers each block across the ATM network in a single cell. On the receiving end of the connection, AAL5 reassembles incoming cells into a packet, checks the CRC to ensure the packet arrived correctly, and passes the result to the host software. The processes of dividing the packet into cells and regrouping them are known as *ATM segmentation and reassembly†* (*SAR*).

How does AAL5 on the receiving side know how many cells comprise a packet? The sending AAL5 uses the low-order bit of the *payload type* field of the ATM cell header to mark the final cell in a packet. We think of it as an *end-of-packet bit*. Thus, the receiving AAL5 collects incoming cells until it finds one with the end-of-packet bit set. ATM standards use the term *convergence* to describe mechanisms that recognize the end of a packet. Although AAL5 uses a single bit in the cell header for convergence, other ATM adaptation layer protocols use other convergence mechanisms.

To summarize:

> *A computer uses ATM Adaptation Layer 5 to transfer a large block of data over an ATM virtual circuit. On the sending host, AAL5 generates a trailer, divides the block of data into cells, and sends each cell over the virtual circuit. On the receiving host, AAL5 reassembles the cells to reproduce the original block of data, strips off the trailer, and delivers the data to the receiving host. AAL5 uses a bit in the cell header to mark the final cell of a given data block.*

18.10 Datagram Encapsulation And IP MTU Size

It should be easy to understand how AAL5 can be used to encapsulate an IP datagram for transfer across an ATM network. In the simplest form, a sender establishes either a switched or permanent virtual circuit through the ATM network to a destination computer, and specifies that the circuit use AAL5. The sender can then pass an entire IP datagram to AAL5 for delivery across the circuit. AAL5 generates a trailer, divides the datagram into cells, and transfers the cells across the network. At the receiver, AAL5 reassembles the datagram, uses information in the trailer to verify that no bits were lost or corrupted, and passes the result to IP.

---

†Use of the term *reassembly* suggests the strong similarity between AAL5 segmentation and IP fragmentation: both mechanisms divide a large block of data into smaller units for transfer.

We said that AAL5 uses a 16-bit length field, making it possible to send 64K octets in a single packet. Despite the capabilities of AAL5, TCP/IP restricts the size of datagrams that can be sent over ATM. The standards impose a limit of 9180 octets† per datagram. That is, IP imposes an MTU of 9180 on ATM networks. As with any network interface, when an outgoing datagram is larger than the network MTU, IP fragments the datagram, and passes each fragment to AAL5. Thus, AAL5 accepts, transfers, and delivers datagrams of 9180 octets or less. To summarize:

> When TCP/IP sends data across an ATM network, it transfers an entire datagram using ATM Adaptation Layer 5. Although AAL5 can accept and transfer packets that contain up to 64K octets, the TCP/IP standards restrict the effective MTU to 9180 octets. IP must fragment any datagram larger than 9180 octets before passing it to AAL5.

18.11 Packet Type And Multiplexing

Observant readers will have noticed that the AAL5 trailer does not include a type field. Thus, an AAL5 frame is not self-identifying. As a result, the simplest form of encapsulation described above does not always suffice. In fact, two possibilities exist:

- The two computers at the ends of a virtual circuit agree *a priori* that the circuit will be used for a specific protocol (e.g., the circuit will only be used to send IP datagrams).
- The two computers at the ends of a virtual circuit agree *a priori* that some octets of the data area will be reserved for use as a type field.

The former scheme, in which the computers agree on the high-level protocol for a given circuit, has the advantage of not requiring additional information in a packet. For example, if the computers agree to transfer IP, a sender can pass each datagram directly to AAL5 to transfer; nothing needs to be sent besides the datagram and the AAL5 trailer. The chief disadvantage of such a scheme lies in duplication of virtual circuits: a computer must create a separate virtual circuit for each high-level protocol. (Because a carrier can charge for each virtual circuit, creating multiple virtual circuits between a pair of computers may add unnecessary cost.)

The latter scheme, in which two computers use a single virtual circuit for multiple protocols, has the advantage of allowing all traffic to travel over the same circuit, but the disadvantage of requiring each packet to contain octets that identify the protocol type. The scheme also has the disadvantage that packets from all protocols travel with the same delay and priority.

The TCP/IP standards specify that computers can choose between the two methods of using AAL5. Both the sender and receiver must agree on how the circuit will be used; the agreement may involve manual configuration. Furthermore, the standards suggest that when computers choose to include type information in the packet, they should use a standard IEEE 802.2 *Logical Link Control* (*LLC*) header followed by a

---

†The size 9180 was chosen to make ATM compatible with an older technology called *Switched Multimegabit Data Service* (*SMDS*).

SubNetwork Attachment Point (*SNAP*) header. Figure 18.8 illustrates the LLC/SNAP information prefixed to a datagram before it is sent over an ATM virtual circuit.

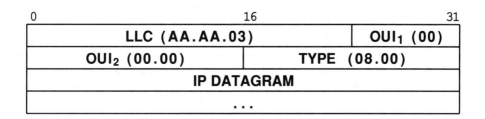

0	16	31
LLC (AA.AA.03)		**OUI₁ (00)**

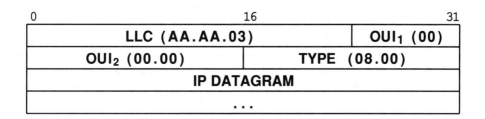

Figure 18.8 The format of packet used to send an IP datagram over AAL5 when multiple protocols are multiplexed on a single virtual circuit. The 8-octet LLC/SNAP header identifies the contents as an IP datagram.

As the figure shows, the LLC field consists of three octets that contain the hexadecimal values *AA.AA.03*†. The SNAP header consists of five octets: three that contain an *Organizationally Unique Identifier* (*OUI*), and two for a type‡. Field *OUI* identifies an organization that administers values in the *TYPE* field, and the *TYPE* field identifies the packet type. For an IP datagram, the *OUI* field contains *00.00.00* to identify the organization responsible for Ethernet standards, and the *TYPE* field contains *08.00*, the value used when encapsulating IP in an Ethernet frame. Software on the sending host must prefix the LLC/SNAP header to each packet before sending it to AAL5, and software on the receiving host must examine the header to determine how to handle the packet.

18.12 IP Address Binding In An ATM Network

We have seen that encapsulating a datagram for transmission across an ATM network is straightforward. By contrast, IP address binding can be difficult. Like other network technologies, ATM assigns each attached computer a physical address that must be used when establishing a virtual circuit. On one hand, because an ATM physical address is larger than an IP address, an ATM physical address cannot be encoded within an IP address. Thus, IP cannot use static address binding for ATM networks. On the other hand, ATM hardware does not support broadcast. Thus, IP cannot use conventional ARP to bind addresses on ATM networks.

ATM permanent virtual circuits further complicate address binding. Because a manager configures each permanent virtual circuit manually, a host only knows the circuit's VPI/VCI pair. Software on the host may not know the IP address nor the ATM hardware address of the remote endpoint. Thus, an IP address binding mechan-

---

†The notation represents each octet as a hexadecimal value separated by decimal points.

‡To accommodate additional octets of header, the MTU of an ATM connection that uses an LLC/SNAP header is 9188.

ism must provide for the identification of a remote computer connected over a PVC as well as the dynamic creation of SVCs to known destinations.

Switched connection-oriented technologies further complicate address binding because they require two levels of binding. First, when creating a virtual circuit over which datagrams will be sent, the IP address of the destination must be mapped to an ATM endpoint address. The endpoint address is used to create a virtual circuit. Second, when sending a datagram to a remote computer over an existing virtual circuit, the destination's IP address must be mapped to the VPI/VCI pair for the circuit. The second binding is used each time a datagram is sent over an ATM network; the first binding is necessary only when a host creates an SVC.

18.13 Logical IP Subnet Concept

Although no protocol has been proposed to solve the general case of address binding for large ATM networks, a protocol has been devised for a restricted form. The restricted form arises when a group of computers uses an ATM network in place of a single (usually local) physical network. The group forms a *Logical IP Subnet* (*LIS*). Multiple logical IP subnets can be defined among a set of computers that all attach to the same ATM hardware network. For example, Figure 18.9 illustrates eight computers attached to an ATM network divided into two LIS.

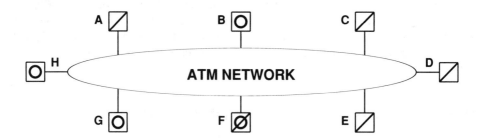

Figure 18.9 Eight computers attached to an ATM network participating in two Logical IP Subnets. Computers marked with a slash participate in one LIS, while computers marked with a circle participate in the other LIS.

As the figure shows, all computers attach to the same physical ATM network. Computers *A*, *C*, *D*, *E*, and *F* participate in one LIS, while computers *B*, *F*, *G*, and *H* participate in another. Each logical IP subnet functions like a separate LAN. The computers participating in an LIS establish virtual circuits among themselves to exchange datagrams†. Because each LIS forms a conceptually separate network, IP applies the standard rules for a physical network to each LIS. For example, all computers in an

---

†Circuits that form the links of an LIS must use LLC/SNAP encapsulation.

LIS share a single IP network prefix, and that prefix differs from the prefixes used by other logical subnets. Furthermore, although the computers in an LIS can choose a non-standard MTU, all computers must use the same MTU on all virtual circuits that comprise the LIS. Finally, despite the ATM hardware that provides potential connectivity, a host in one LIS may not communicate directly with a host in another LIS. Instead, all communication between logical subnets must proceed through a router that participates in multiple logical subnets. In Figure 18.9, for example, machine *F* could be an IP router between the two logical subnets because it participates in both.

To summarize:

> *TCP/IP allows a subset of computers attached to an ATM network to operate like an independent LAN.   Such a group is called a* Logical IP Subnet *(LIS); computers in an LIS share a single IP network address. A computer in an LIS can communicate directly with any other computer in the same LIS, but is required to use a router when communicating with a computer in another LIS.*

18.14 Connection Management

Hosts must manage ATM virtual circuits carefully because creating a circuit takes time and, for commercial ATM services, can incur additional economic cost. Thus, the simplistic approach of creating a virtual circuit, sending one datagram, and then closing the circuit is too expensive. Instead, a host must maintain a record of open circuits so they can be reused.

Circuit management occurs in the network interface software below IP. When a host needs to send a datagram, it uses conventional IP routing to find the appropriate next-hop address, N†, and passes it along with the datagram to the network interface. The network interface examines its table of open virtual circuits. If an open circuit exists to N, the host uses AAL5 to send the datagram. Otherwise, before the host can send the datagram, it must locate a computer with address N, create a circuit, and add the circuit to its table.

The concept of logical IP subnets constrains IP routing. In a properly configured routing table, the next-hop address for each destination must be a computer within the same logical subnet as the sender. To understand the constraint, remember that each LIS is designed to operate like a single LAN. The same constraint holds for a host attached to a LAN, namely, each next-hop address in the routing table must be a router attached to the LAN.

One of the reasons for dividing computers into logical subnets arises from hardware and software constraints. A host cannot maintain an arbitrarily large number of open virtual circuits at the same time because each circuit requires resources in the ATM hardware and in the operating system. Dividing computers into logical subnets limits the maximum number of simultaneously open circuits to the number of computers in the LIS.

---

†As usual, a next-hop address is an IP address.

18.15 Address Binding Within An LIS

When a host creates a virtual circuit to a computer in its LIS, the host must specify an ATM hardware address for the destination. How can a host map a next-hop address into an appropriate ATM hardware address? The host cannot broadcast a request to all computers in the LIS because ATM does not offer hardware broadcast. Instead, it contacts a server to obtain the mapping. Communication between the host and server uses *ATMARP*, a variant of the ARP protocol described in Chapter 5.

As with conventional ARP, a sender forms a request that includes the sender's IP and ATM hardware addresses as well as the IP address of a target for which an ATM hardware address is needed. The sender then transmits the request to the *ATMARP server* for the logical subnet. If the server knows the ATM hardware address, it sends an *ATMARP reply*. Otherwise, the server sends a *negative ATMARP reply*.

18.16 ATMARP Packet Format

Figure 18.10 illustrates the format of an ATMARP packet. As the figure shows, ATMARP modifies the ARP packet format slightly. The major change involves additional address length fields to accommodate ATM addresses. To understand the changes, one must understand that multiple address forms have been proposed for ATM, and that no single form appears to be the emerging standard. Telephone companies that offer public ATM networks use an 8-octet format where each address is an ISDN telephone number defined by ITU-TS standard document *E.164*. By contrast, the ATM Forum† allows each computer attached to a private ATM network to be assigned a 20-octet *Network Service Access Point* (*NSAP*) address. Thus, a two-level hierarchical address may be needed to specify an E.164 address for a remote site and an NSAP address of a host on a local switch at the site.

To accommodate multiple address formats and a two-level hierarchy, an ATMARP packet contains two length fields for each ATM address as well as a length field for each protocol address. As Figure 18.10 shows, an ATMARP packet begins with fixed-size fields that specify address lengths. The first two fields follow the same format as conventional ARP. The field labeled *HARDWARE TYPE* contains the hexadecimal value *0x0013* for ATM, and the field labeled *PROTOCOL TYPE* contains the hexadecimal value *0x0800* for IP.

Because the address format of the sender and target can differ, each ATM address requires a length field. Field *SEND HLEN* specifies the length of the sender's ATM address, and field *SEND HLEN2* specifies the length of the sender's ATM subaddress. Fields *TAR HLEN* and *TAR HLEN2* specify the lengths of the target's ATM address and subaddress. Finally, fields *SEND PLEN* and *TAR PLEN* specify the lengths of the sender's and target's protocol addresses.

Following the length fields in the header, an ATMARP packet contains six addresses. The first three address fields contain the sender's ATM address, ATM subaddress, and protocol address. The last three fields contain the target's ATM address,

---

†The ATM Forum is a consortium of industrial members, including both users and manufacturers, that has agreed on standards for private ATM networks.

ATM subaddress, and protocol address. In the example in Figure 18.10, both the sender and target subaddress length fields contain zero, and the packet does not contain octets for subaddresses.

0	8	16	24	31
HARDWARE TYPE (0x0013)		PROTOCOL TYPE (0x0800)		
SEND. HLEN (20)	SEND. HLEN2 (0)	OPERATION		
SEND. PLEN (4)	TAR. HLEN (20)	TAR. HLEN2 (0)	TAR. PLEN (4)	
SENDER'S ATM ADDRESS (octets 0-3)				
SENDER'S ATM ADDRESS (octets 4-7)				
SENDER'S ATM ADDRESS (octets 8-11)				
SENDER'S ATM ADDRESS (octets 12-15)				
SENDER'S ATM ADDRESS (octets 16-19)				
SENDER'S PROTOCOL ADDRESS				
TARGET'S ATM ADDRESS (octets 0-3)				
TARGET'S ATM ADDRESS (octets 4-7)				
TARGET'S ATM ADDRESS (octets 8-11)				
TARGET'S ATM ADDRESS (octets 12-15)				
TARGET'S ATM ADDRESS (octets 16-19)				
TARGET'S PROTOCOL ADDRESS				

Figure 18.10 The format of an ATMARP packet when used with 20-octet ATM addresses such as those recommended by the ATM Forum.

18.16.1 Format Of ATM Address Length Fields

Because ATMARP is designed for use with either E.164 addresses or 20-octet NSAP addresses, fields that contain an ATM address length include a bit that specifies the address format. Figure 18.11 illustrates how ATMARP encodes the address type and length in an 8-bit field.

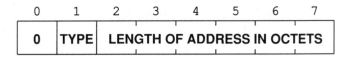

0	1	2	3	4	5	6	7
0	TYPE	LENGTH OF ADDRESS IN OCTETS					

Figure 18.11 The encoding of ATM address type and length in an 8-bit field. Bit *1* distinguishes the two types of ATM addresses.

A single bit encodes the type of an ATM address because only two forms are available. If bit *1* contains zero, the address is in the NSAP format recommended by the ATM Forum. If bit *1* contains one, the address is in the E.164 format recommended by the ITU-TS. Because each ATM address length field in an ATMARP packet has the form shown in Figure 18.11, a single packet can contain multiple types of ATM addresses.

18.16.2 Operation Codes Used With The ATMARP Protocol

The packet format shown in Figure 18.10 is used to request an address binding, reply to a request, or request an inverse address binding. When a computer sends an ATMARP packet, it must set the *OPERATION* field to specify the type of binding. The table in Figure 18.12 shows the values that can be used in the *OPERATION* field of an ATMARP packet, and gives the meaning of each. The remainder of this section explains how the protocol works.

Code	Meaning
1	ATMARP Request
2	ATMARP Reply
8	Inverse ATMARP Request
9	Inverse ATMARP Reply
10	ATMARP Negative Ack

Figure 18.12 The values that can appear in the *OPERATION* field of an ATMARP packet and their meanings. When possible, values have been chosen to agree with the operation codes used in conventional ARP.

18.17 Using ATMARP Packets To Determine An Address

Performing address binding for connection-oriented hardware is slightly more complex than for connectionless hardware. Because ATM hardware supports two types of virtual circuits, two cases arise. First, we will consider the case of permanent virtual circuits. Second, we will consider the case of switched virtual circuits.

18.17.1 Permanent Virtual Circuits

To understand the problems PVCs introduce, recall how ATM hardware operates. A network administrator must configure each PVC; hosts themselves do not participate in PVC setup. In particular, a host begins operation with PVCs in place, and does not receive any information from the hardware about the address of the remote endpoint. Thus, unless address information has been configured into the hosts (e.g., stored on disk), the host does not know the IP address or ATM address of the computer to which a PVC connects.

The *Inverse ATMARP* protocol (*InATMARP*) solves the problem of finding addresses when using PVCs. To use the protocol, a computer must know each of the permanent virtual circuits that have been configured. To determine the IP and ATM addresses of the remote endpoint, a computer sends an Inverse ATMARP request packet with the *OPERATION* field set to *8*. Whenever such a request arrives over a PVC, the receiver generates an Inverse ATMARP reply with the *OPERATION* field set to *9*. Both the request and the reply contain the sender's IP address and ATM address. Thus, a computer at each end of the connection learns the binding for the computer at the other end. In summary,

> *Two computers that communicate over a permanent virtual circuit use Inverse ATMARP to discover each others' IP and ATM addresses. One computer sends an Inverse ATMARP request to which the other sends a reply.*

18.17.2 Switched Virtual Circuits

Within an LIS, computers create switched virtual circuits on demand. When computer *A* needs to send a datagram to computer *B* and no circuit currently exists to *B*, *A* uses ATM signaling to create the necessary circuit. Thus, *A* begins with *B*'s IP address, which must be mapped to an equivalent ATM address. We said that each LIS has an ATMARP server, and all computers in an LIS must be configured so they know how to reach the server (e.g., a computer can have a PVC to the server or can have the server's ATM address stored on disk). A server does not form connections to other computers; the server merely waits for computers in the LIS to contact it. To map address *B* to an ATM address, computer *A* must have a virtual circuit open to the ATMARP server for the LIS. Computer *A* forms an ATMARP request packet and sends it over the connection to the server. The *OPERATION* field in the packet contains *1*, and the target's protocol address field contains *B*.

An ATMARP server maintains a database of mappings from IP address to ATM address. If the server knows *B*'s ATM address, the ATMARP protocol operates similar to Proxy ARP. The server forms an ATMARP reply by setting the *OPERATION* code to *2* and filling in the ATM address that corresponds to the target IP address. As in conventional ARP, the server exchanges sender and target entries before returning the reply to the computer that sent the request.

If the server does not know the ATM address that corresponds to the target IP address in a request, ATMARP differs from conventional ARP. Instead of ignoring the request, the server returns a negative acknowledgement (an ATMARP packet with an *OPERATION* field of *10*). A negative acknowledgement distinguishes between addresses for which a server does not have a binding and a malfunctioning server. Thus, when a host sends a request to an ATMARP server, it determines one of three outcomes unambiguously. The host can learn the ATM address of the target, that the target is not currently available in the LIS, or that the server is not currently responding.

18.18 Obtaining Entries For A Server Database

An ATMARP server builds and maintains its database of bindings automatically. To do so, it uses Inverse ATMARP. Whenever a host or router first opens a virtual circuit to an ATMARP server, the server immediately sends an Inverse ATMARP request packet†. The host or router must answer by sending an Inverse ATMARP reply packet. When it receives an Inverse ATMARP reply, the server extracts the sender's IP and ATM addresses, and stores the binding in its database. Thus, each computer in an LIS must establish a connection to the ATMARP server, even if the computer does not intend to look up bindings.

> *Each host or router in an LIS must register its IP address and corresponding ATM address with the ATMARP server for the LIS. Registration occurs automatically whenever a computer establishes a virtual circuit to an ATMARP server because the server sends an Inverse ATMARP to which the computer must respond.*

18.19 Timing Out ATMARP Information In A Server

Like the bindings in a conventional ARP cache, bindings obtained via ATMARP must be timed out and removed. How long should an entry persist in a server? Once a computer registers its binding with an ATMARP server, the server keeps the entry for a minimum of 20 minutes. After 20 minutes, the server examines the entry. If no circuit exists to the computer that sent the entry, the server deletes the entry‡. If the computer that sent the entry has maintained an open virtual circuit, the server attempts to revalidate the entry. The server sends an Inverse ATMARP request and awaits a response. If the response verifies information in the entry, the server resets the timer and waits another 20 minutes. If the Inverse ATMARP response does not match the information in the entry, the server closes the circuit and deletes the entry.

To help reduce traffic, the ATMARP standard permits an optimization. It allows a host to use a single virtual circuit for all communication with an ATMARP server. When the host sends an ATMARP request, the request contains the host's binding in the *SENDER*'s field. The server can extract the binding and use it to revalidate its stored information. Thus, if a host sends more than one ATMARP request every 20 minutes, the server will not need to send the host an Inverse ATMARP request.

18.20 Timing Out ATMARP Information In A Host Or Router

A host or router must also use timers to invalidate information obtained from an ATMARP server. In particular, the standard specifies that a computer can keep a binding obtained from the ATMARP server for at most 15 minutes. When 15 minutes expire, the entry must be removed or revalidated. If an address binding expires and the

---

†The circuit must use AAL5 with LLC/SNAP type identification.
‡A server does not automatically delete an entry when a circuit is closed; it waits for the timeout period.

host does not have an open virtual circuit to the destination, the host removes the entry from its ARP cache. If a host has an open virtual circuit to the destination, the host attempts to revalidate the address binding. Expiration of an address binding can delay traffic because:

> *A host or router must stop sending data to any destination for which the address binding has expired until the binding can be revalidated.*

The method a host uses to revalidate a binding depends on the type of virtual circuit being used. If the host can reach the destination over a PVC, the host sends an Inverse ATMARP request on the circuit and awaits a reply. If the host has an SVC open to the destination, the host sends an ATMARP request to the ATMARP server.

18.21 Summary

ATM is a high-speed network technology in which a network consists of one or more switches interconnected to form a switching fabric. Logically, an ATM switching fabric operates like a single, large network that allows any host to communicate with any other host.

Because ATM is a connection-oriented technology, two computers must establish a virtual circuit through the network before they can transfer data; a host can choose between the switched or permanent type of virtual circuit. Switched circuits are created on demand; permanent circuits require manual configuration. In either case, ATM assigns each open circuit an integer identifier. Each frame a host sends and each frame the network delivers contains a circuit identifier; a frame does not contain a source or destination address.

Although the lowest levels of ATM use 53-octet cells to transfer information, ATM includes additional mechanisms in its adaptation layer that applications use. In particular, ATM Adaptation Layer 5 (AAL5) is used to send data across an ATM network. AAL5 offers an interface that accepts and delivers variable-size blocks of data, where each block can be up to 64K octets.

To send an IP datagram across an ATM network, the sender must form a virtual circuit connection to the destination that uses AAL5, and send the datagram to AAL5 as a single block of data. AAL5 adds a trailer, divides the datagram and trailer into cells for transmission across the network, and then reassembles the datagram before passing it to the operating system on the destination computer. Thus, when sending datagrams across ATM, IP does not fragment to the ATM cell size. Instead, IP uses an MTU of 9180 and allows AAL5 to segment the datagram into cells.

A Logical IP Subnet (LIS) consists of a set of computers that use ATM in place of a LAN; the computers form virtual circuits among themselves over which they exchange datagrams. Having both permanent and switched virtual circuits in an LIS complicates the address binding problem. A modified ARP protocol known as ATMARP handles address binding for the computers in an LIS connected by a switched virtual circuit. Computers in an LIS rely on an ATMARP server to bind the IP address of another computer in the LIS to an equivalent ATM address. Each computer in the LIS must register with the server by supplying its IP address and ATM address to the server. Other computers can then contact the server to obtain a binding as needed. As with conventional ARP, a binding obtained from ATMARP is aged. After the aging period, the binding must be revalidated or discarded. A related protocol, Inverse ATMARP, is used to discover the ATM and IP addresses of a remote computer connected by a permanent virtual circuit.

FOR FURTHER STUDY

Laubach [RFC 1577] introduces the concept of Logical IP Subnet and defines the ATMARP protocol. Heinanen [RFC 1483] describes the use of LLC/SNAP headers when encapsulating IP in AAL5, and Ackinson [RFC 1626] specifies the default MTU.

Partridge [1994] describes gigabit networking in general, and the importance of cell switching in particular. De Prycker [1993] considers many of the theoretical underpinnings of ATM and discusses its relationship to telephone networks.

EXERCISES

18.1   If your organization has an ATM switch or ATM service, find the technical and economic specifications, and then compare the cost of using ATM with the cost of another technology such as Ethernet.

18.2   Read about the TAXI interface. How did the standard arise?

18.3   Contact an ATM switch vendor to determine the aggregate bandwidth of the switch and the maximum number of computers that can connect to it. How fast does each computer need to generate data to saturate the switch?

18.4   A typical connection between a host and a private ATM switch operates at 155 Mbps. Consider the speed of the bus on your favorite computer. What percentage of the bus is required to keep an ATM interface busy?

18.5   Many operating systems choose TCP buffer sizes to be multiples of 8K octets. If IP fragments datagrams for an MTU of 9180 octets, what size fragments result from a datagram that carries a TCP segment of 16K octets? of 24K octets?

18.6   ATM is a best-effort delivery system in which the hardware can discard cells if the network becomes congested. What is the probability of datagram loss if the probability of loss of a single cell is $1/P$ and the datagram is 576 octets long? 1500 octets? 4500 octets? 9180 octets?

18.7   A typical remote login session using TCP generates datagrams of 41 octets: 20 octets of IP header, 20 octets of TCP header, and 1 octet of data. How many ATM cells are required to send such a datagram using the default IP encapsulation over AAL5?

18.8 How many cells, octets, and bits can be present on a fiber that connects to an ATM switch if the fiber is 3 meters long? 100 meters? 3000 meters? To find out, consider an ATM switch transmitting data at 155 Mbps. Each bit is a pulse of light that lasts $1/(155 \times 10^6)$ second. Assume the pulse travels at the speed of light, calculate its length, and compare to the length of the fiber.

18.9 A host can specify a two-level ATM address when requesting an SVC. What ATM network topologies are appropriate for a two-level addressing scheme? Characterize situations for which additional levels of hierarchy are useful.

18.10 Read about ATM Adaptation Layers 3 and 4, which were originally intended for use with connection-oriented and connectionless transport protocols. What is the chief difference between them?

18.11 An ATM network guarantees to deliver cells in order, but may drop cells if it becomes congested. Is it possible to modify TCP to take advantage of cell ordering to reduce protocol overhead? Why or why not?

18.12 Products exist that add a LAN emulation interface to ATM, making it possible to simulate FDDI or other local area networks. What is the chief advantage of using ATM to emulate other LANs? The chief disadvantage?

18.13 A large organization that uses ATM to interconnect IP hosts must divide hosts into logical IP subnets. Two extremes exist: the organization can place all hosts in one large LIS, or the organization can have many LIS (e.g., each pair of hosts forms an LIS). Explain why neither extreme is desirable.

18.14 How many ATM cells are required to transfer a single ATMARP packet when each ATM address and subaddress is 20 octets and each protocol address is 4 octets?

18.15 ATM allows a host to establish multiple virtual circuits to a given destination. What is the major advantage of doing so?

18.16 Measure the throughput and delay of an ATM switch when using TCP. If your operating system permits, repeat the experiment with the TCP transmit buffer set to various sizes (if your system uses sockets, refer to the manual for details on how to set the buffer size). Do the results surprise you?

18.17 IP does not have a mechanism to associate datagrams traveling across an ATM network with a specific ATM virtual circuit. Under what circumstances would such a mechanism be useful?

18.18 Look at the proposed next generation IP described in Chapter 29. What new mechanism relates directly to ATM?

18.19 A server does not immediately remove an entry from its cache when the host that sent the information closes its connection to the server. What is the chief advantage of such a design? What is the chief disadvantage?

19

Client-Server Model Of Interaction

19.1 Introduction

Early chapters present the details of TCP/IP technology, including the protocols that provide basic services and the router architecture that provides needed routing information. Now that we understand the basic technology, we can examine application programs that profit from the cooperative use of a TCP/IP internet. While the example applications are both practical and interesting, they do not comprise the main emphasis. Instead, focus rests on the patterns of interaction among the communicating application programs. The primary pattern of interaction among cooperating applications is known as the *client-server* paradigm. Client-server interaction forms the basis of most network communication, and is fundamental because it helps us understand the foundation on which distributed algorithms are built. This chapter considers the relationship between client and server; later chapters illustrate the client-server pattern with further examples.

19.2 The Client-Server Model

The term *server* applies to any program that offers a service that can be reached over a network. A server accepts a request over the network, performs its service, and returns the result to the requester. For the simplest services, each request arrives in a single IP datagram and the server returns a response in another datagram.

An executing program becomes a *client* when it sends a request to a server and waits for a response. Because the client-server model is a convenient and natural extension of interprocess communication on a single machine, it is easy to build programs that use the model to interact.

Servers can perform simple or complex tasks. For example, a *time-of-day server* merely returns the current time whenever a client sends the server a packet. A *file server* receives requests to perform operations that store or retrieve data from a file; the server performs the operation and returns the result.

Usually, servers are implemented as application programs†. The advantage of implementing servers as application programs is that they can execute on any computing system that supports TCP/IP communication. Thus, the server for a particular service can execute on a timesharing system along with other programs, or it can execute on a personal computer. Multiple servers can offer the same service, and can execute on the same machine or on multiple machines. In fact, managers commonly replicate copies of a given server onto physically independent machines to increase reliability or improve performance. If a computer's primary purpose is support of a particular server program, the term "server" may be applied to the computer as well as to the server program. Thus, one hears statements such as "machine A is our file server."

19.3 A Simple Example: UDP Echo Server

The simplest form of client-server interaction uses unreliable datagram delivery to convey messages from a client to a server and back. Consider, for example, a *UDP echo server*. The mechanics are straightforward as Figure 19.1 shows. At the server site, a UDP *echo server process* begins by negotiating with its operating system for permission to use the UDP port ID reserved for the *echo* service, the UDP *echo port*. Once it has obtained permission, the echo server process enters an infinite loop that has three steps: (1) wait for a datagram to arrive at the echo port, (2) reverse the source and destination addresses‡ (including source and destination IP addresses as well as UDP port ids), and (3) return the datagram to its original sender. At some other site, a program becomes a UDP *echo client* when it allocates an unused UDP protocol port, sends a UDP message to the UDP echo server, and awaits the reply. The client expects to receive back exactly the same data as it sent.

The UDP echo service illustrates two important points that are generally true about client-server interaction. The first concerns the difference between the lifetime of servers and clients:

> *A server starts execution before interaction begins and (usually) continues to accept requests and send responses without ever terminating. A client is any program that makes a request and awaits a response; it (usually) terminates after using a server a finite number of times.*

---

†Many operating systems refer to a running application program as a *process* or a *user process*.
‡One of the exercises suggests considering this step in more detail.

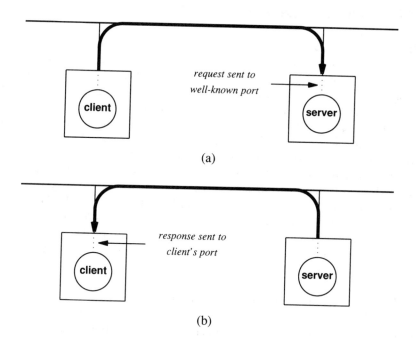

(a)

(b)

Figure 19.1 UDP echo as an example of the client-server model. In (a) the
client sends a request to the server at a known IP address and at
a well-known UDP port, and in (b) the server returns a response.
Clients use any UDP port that is available.

The second point, which is more technical, concerns the use of reserved and non-reserved port identifiers:

> *A server waits for requests at a well-known port that has been*
> *reserved for the service it offers. A client allocates an arbitrary,*
> *unused, nonreserved port for its communication.*

In a client-server interaction, only one of the two ports needs to be reserved. Assigning
a unique port identifier to each service makes it easy to build both clients and servers.

Who would use an echo service? It is not a service that the average user finds interesting. However, programmers who design, implement, measure, or modify network
protocol software, or network managers who test routes and debug communication
problems, often use echo servers in testing. For example, an echo service can also be
used to determine if it is possible to reach a remote machine.

19.4 Time And Date Service

The echo server is extremely simple, and little code is required to implement either the server or client side (provided that the operating system offers a reasonable way to access the underlying UDP/IP protocols). Our second example, a time server, shows that even simple client-server interaction can provide useful services. The problem a time server solves is that of setting a computer's time-of-day clock. The time of day clock is a hardware device that maintains the current date and time, making it available to programs. Once set, the time of day clock keeps time as accurately as a wristwatch.

Many systems solve the problem by asking a programmer to type in the time and date when the system boots. The system increments the clock periodically (e.g., every second). When an application program asks for the date or time, the system consults the internal clock and formats the time of day in human readable form. We can use a client-server interaction to set the system clock automatically when a machine boots. To do so, a manager configures one machine, typically the machine with the most accurate clock, to run a time-of-day server. When other machines boot, they contact the server to obtain the current time.

19.4.1 Representation for the Date and Time

How should an operating system maintain the date and time-of-day? One useful representation stores the time and date as the count of seconds since an epoch date. For example, the UNIX operating system uses the zeroth second of January 1, 1970 as its epoch date. The TCP/IP protocols also define an epoch date and report times as seconds past the epoch. For TCP/IP, the epoch is defined to be the zeroth second of January 1, 1900 and the time is kept in a 32-bit integer, a representation that accommodates all dates in the near future.

Keeping the date as the time in seconds since an epoch makes the representation compact and allows easy comparison. It ties together the date and time of day and makes it possible to measure time by incrementing a single binary integer.

19.4.2 Local and Universal Time

Given an epoch date and representation for the time, to what time zone does the count refer? When two systems communicate across large geographic distances, using the local time zone from one or the other becomes difficult; they must agree on a standard time zone to keep values for date and time comparable. Thus, in addition to defining a representation for the date and choosing an epoch, the TCP/IP time server standard specifies that all values are given with respect to a single time zone. Originally called Greenwich Mean Time, the time zone is now known as *universal coordinated time* or *universal time*.

The interaction between a client and a server that offers time service works much like an echo server. At the server side, the server application obtains permission to use the reserved port assigned to time servers, waits for a UDP message directed to that port, and responds by sending a UDP message that contains the current time in a 32-bit integer. We can summarize:

Sending a datagram to a time server is equivalent to making a request for the current time; the server responds by returning a UDP message that contains the current time.

19.5 The Complexity of Servers

In our examples so far, servers are fairly simple because they are sequential. That is, the server processes one request at a time. After accepting a request, the server forms a reply and sends it before going back to see if another request has arrived. We implicitly assume that the operating system will queue requests that arrive for a server while it is busy, and that the queue will not become too long because the server has only a trivial amount of work to do.

In practice, servers are usually much more difficult to build than clients because they need to accommodate multiple concurrent requests, even if a single request takes considerable time to process. For example, consider a file transfer server responsible for copying a file to another machine on request. Typically, servers have two parts: a single master program that is responsible for accepting new requests, and a set of slaves that are responsible for handling individual requests. The master server performs the following five steps:

Open port
> The master opens the well-known port at which it can be reached.

Wait for client
> The master waits for a new client to send a request.

Choose port
> If necessary, the master allocates a new local protocol port for this request and informs the client (we will see that this step is unnecessary with TCP).

Start Slave
> The master starts an independent, concurrent slave to handle this request (e.g., in UNIX, it forks a copy of the server process). Note that the slave handles one request and then terminates – the slave does not wait for requests from other clients.

Continue
> The master returns to the *wait* step and continues accepting new requests while the newly created slave handles the previous request concurrently.

Because the master starts a slave for each new request, processing proceeds concurrently. Thus, requests that require little time to complete can finish earlier than requests that take longer, independent of the order in which they are started. For example, suppose the first client that contacts a file server requests a large file transfer that takes many minutes. If a second client contacts the server to request a transfer that takes only a few seconds, the second transfer can start and complete while the first transfer proceeds.

In addition to the complexity that results because servers handle concurrent requests, complexity also arises because servers must enforce authorization and protection rules. Server programs usually need to execute with highest privilege because they must read system files, keep logs, and access protected data. The operating system will not restrict a server program if it attempts to access users' files. Thus, servers cannot blindly honor requests from other sites. Instead, each server takes responsibility for enforcing the system access and protection policies.

Finally, servers must protect themselves against malformed requests or against requests that will cause the server program itself to abort. Often, it is difficult to foresee potential problems. For example, one project at Purdue University designed a file server that allowed student operating systems to access files on a UNIX timesharing system. Students discovered that requesting the server to open a file named /dev/tty caused the server to abort because UNIX associates that name with the control terminal to which a program is attached. The server, created at system startup, had no such terminal. Once an abort occurred, no client could access files until a systems programmer restarted the server.

A more serious example of server vulnerability became known in the fall of 1988 when a student at Cornell University built a *worm* program that attacked computers on the global Internet. Once the worm started running on a machine, it searched the Internet for computers with servers that it knew how to exploit, and used the servers to create more copies of itself. In one of the attacks, the worm used a bug in the UNIX *fingerd* server. Because the server did not check incoming requests, the worm was able to send an illegal string of input that caused the server to overwrite parts of its internal data areas. The server, which executed with highest privilege, then misbehaved, allowing the worm to create copies of itself.

We can summarize our discussion of servers:

> *Servers are usually more difficult to build than clients because, although they can be implemented with application programs, servers must enforce all the access and protection policies of the computer system on which they run, and must protect themselves against all possible errors.*

19.6 RARP Server

So far, all our examples of client-server interaction require the client to know the complete server address. The RARP protocol from Chapter 6 provides an example of client-server interaction with a slightly different twist. Recall that when a diskless machine boots, it uses RARP to find its IP address. Instead of having the client communicate directly with a server, RARP clients broadcast their requests. One or more machines executing RARP server processes respond, each returning a packet that answers the query.

There are two significant differences between a RARP server and a UDP echo or time server. First, RARP packets travel across the physical network directly in hardware frames, not in IP datagrams. Thus, unlike the UDP echo server which allows a client to contact a server anywhere on an internet, the RARP server requires the client to be on the same physical network. Second, RARP cannot be implemented by an application program. Echo and time servers can be built as application programs because they use UDP. By contrast, a RARP server needs access to raw hardware packets.

19.7 Alternatives To The Client-Server Model

What are the alternatives to client-server interaction, and when might they be attractive? This section gives at least one answer to these questions.

In the client-server model, programs usually act as clients when they need information, but it is sometimes important to minimize such interactions. The ARP protocol from Chapter 5 gives one example. It uses a modified form of client-server interaction to obtain physical address mappings. Machines that use ARP keep a cache of answers to improve the efficiency of later queries. Caching improves the performance of client-server interaction in cases where the recent history of queries is a good indicator of future use.

Although caching improves performance, it does not change the essence of client-server interaction. The essence lies in our assumption that processing must be driven by demand. We have assumed that a program executes until it needs information and then acts as a client to obtain the needed information. Taking a demand-driven view of the world is natural and arises from experience. Caching helps alleviate the cost of obtaining information by lowering the retrieval cost for all except the first process that makes a request.

How can we lower the cost of information retrieval for the first request? In a distributed system, it may be possible to have concurrent background activities that collect and propagate information *before* any particular program requests it, making retrieval costs low even for the initial request. More important, precollecting information can allow a given system to continue executing even though other machines or the networks connecting them fail.

Precollection is the basis for the 4BSD UNIX *ruptime* command. When invoked, *ruptime* reports the CPU load and time since system startup for each machine on the local network. A background program running on each machine uses UDP to broadcast information about the machine periodically. The same program also collects incoming information and places it in a file. Because machines propagate information continuously, each machine has a copy of the latest information on hand; a client seeking information never needs to access the network. Instead, it reads the information from secondary storage and prints it in a readable form.

The chief advantage of having information collected locally before the client needs it is speed. The *ruptime* command responds immediately when invoked without waiting for messages to traverse the network. A second benefit occurs because the client can find out something about machines that are no longer operating. In particular, if a machine stops broadcasting information, the client can report the time elapsed since the last broadcast (i.e., it can report how long the machine has been off-line).

Precollection has one major disadvantage: it uses processor time and network bandwidth even when no one cares about the data being collected. For example, the ruptime broadcast and collection continues running throughout the night, even if no one is logged in to read the information. If only a few machines connect to a given network, precollection cost is insignificant. It can be thought of as an innocuous background activity. For networks with many hosts, however, the large volume of broadcast traffic generated by precollection makes it too expensive. In particular, the cost of reading and processing broadcast messages becomes high. Thus, precollection is not among the most popular alternatives to client-server.

19.8 Summary

Distributed programs require network communication. Such programs often fall into a pattern of use known as client-server interaction. A server process awaits a request and performs action based on the request. The action usually includes sending a response. A client program formulates a request, sends it to a server, and then awaits a reply.

We have seen examples of clients and servers and found that some clients send requests directly, while others broadcast requests. Broadcast is especially useful on a local network when a machine does not know the address of a server.

We also noted that if servers use internet protocols like UDP, they can accept and respond to requests across an internet. If they communicate using physical frames and physical hardware addresses, they are restricted to a single physical network.

Finally, we considered an alternative to the client-server paradigm that uses precollection of information to avoid delays. An example of precollection came from a machine status service.

FOR FURTHER STUDY

UDP echo service is defined in Postel [RFC 862]. The *UNIX Programmer's Manual* describes the *ruptime* command (also see the related description of *rwho*). Feinler *et. al.* [1985] specifies many standard server protocols not discussed here, including discard, character generation, day and time, active users, and quote of the day. The next chapters consider others.

EXERCISES

19.1   Build a UDP echo client that sends a datagram to a specified echo server, awaits a reply, and compares it to the original message.

19.2   Carefully consider the manipulation of IP addresses in a UDP echo server. Under what conditions is it incorrect to create new IP addresses by reversing the source and destination IP addresses?

19.3   As we have seen, servers can be implemented by separate application programs or by building server code into the protocol software in an operating system. What are the advantages and disadvantages of having an application program (user process) per server?

19.4   Suppose you do not know the IP address of a local machine running a UDP echo server, but you know that it responds to requests sent to port 7. Is there an IP address you can use to reach it?

19.5   Build a client for the UDP time service.

19.6   Characterize situations in which a server can be located on a separate physical network from its client. Can a RARP server ever be located on a separate physical network from it clients? Why or why not?

19.7   What is the chief disadvantage of having all machines broadcast their status periodically?

19.8   Examine the format of data broadcast by the servers that implement the 4BSD UNIX *ruptime* command. What information is available to the client in addition to machine status?

19.9   What servers are running on computers at your site? If you do not have access to system configuration files that list the servers started for a given computer, see if your system has a command that prints a list of open TCP and UDP ports (e.g., the UNIX *netstat* command).

19.10 Some servers allow a manager to gracefully shut them down or restart them. What is the advantage of graceful shutdown?

20

The Socket Interface

20.1 Introduction

So far, we have concentrated on discussing the principles and concepts that underlie the TCP/IP protocols without specifying the interface between the application programs and the protocol software. This chapter reviews one example of an interface between application programs and TCP/IP protocols. There are two reasons for postponing the discussion of interfaces. First, in principle we must distinguish between the interface and TCP/IP protocols because the standards do not specify exactly how application programs interact with protocol software. Thus, the interface architecture is not standardized; its design lies outside the scope of the protocol suite. Second, in practice, it is inappropriate to tie the protocols to a particular interface because no single interface architecture works well on all systems. In particular, because protocol software resides in a computer's operating system, interface details depend on the operating system.

Despite the lack of a standard, reviewing an example will help us understand how programmers use TCP/IP. Although the example we have chosen is from the BSD UNIX operating system, it has become widely accepted and is used in many other systems. In particular, the *Winsock* interface provides socket functionality for Microsoft Windows. The reader should keep in mind that our goal is merely to give one concrete example, not to prescribe how interfaces should be designed. The reader should also remember that the operations listed here do not comprise a standard in any sense.

20.2 The UNIX I/O Paradigm And Network I/O

Developed in the late 1960s and early 1970s, UNIX was originally designed as a timesharing system for single processor computers. It is a process-oriented operating system in which each application program executes as a user level process. An application program interacts with the operating system by making *system calls*. From the programmer's point of view, system calls look and behave exactly like other procedure calls. They take arguments and return one or more results. Arguments can be values (e.g., an integer count) or pointers to objects in the application program (e.g., a buffer to be filled with characters).

Derived from those in Multics and earlier systems, the UNIX input and output (I/O) primitives follow a paradigm sometimes referred to as *open-read-write-close*. Before a user process can perform I/O operations, it calls *open* to specify the file or device to be used and obtains permission. The call to *open* returns a small integer *file descriptor*† that the process uses when performing I/O operations on the opened file or device. Once an object has been opened, the user process makes one or more calls to *read* or *write* to transfer data. *Read* transfers data into the user process; *write* transfers data from the user process to the file or device. Both *read* and *write* take three arguments that specify the file descriptor to use, the address of a buffer, and the number of bytes to transfer. After all transfer operations are complete, the user process calls *close* to inform the operating system that it has finished using the object (the operating system automatically closes all open descriptors if a process terminates without calling *close*).

20.3 Adding Network I/O to UNIX

Originally, UNIX designers cast all I/O operations in the open-read-write-close paradigm described above. The scheme included I/O for character-oriented devices like keyboards and block-oriented devices like disks and data files. An early implementation of TCP/IP under UNIX also used the open-read-write-close paradigm with a special file name, */dev/tcp*.

The group adding network protocols to BSD UNIX decided that because network protocols are more complex than conventional I/O devices, interaction between user processes and network protocols must be more complex than interactions between user processes and conventional I/O facilities. In particular, the protocol interface must allow programmers to create both server code that awaits connections passively as well as client code that forms connections actively. Furthermore, application programs sending datagrams may wish to specify the destination address along with each datagram instead of binding destinations at the time they call *open*. To handle all these cases, the designers chose to abandon the traditional UNIX open-read-write-close paradigm, and added several new operating system calls as well as new library routines. Adding network protocols to UNIX increased the complexity of the I/O interface substantially.

---

†The term "file descriptor" arises because in UNIX all devices are mapped into the file system name space. In most cases, I/O operations on files and devices are indistinguishable.

Further complexity arises in the UNIX protocol interface because designers attempted to build a general mechanism to accommodate many protocols. For example, the generality makes it possible for the operating system to include software for other protocol suites as well as TCP/IP, and to allow an application program to use one or more of them at a time. As a consequence, the application program cannot merely supply a 32-bit address and expect the operating system to interpret it correctly. The application must explicitly specify that the 32-bit number represents an IP address.

20.4 The Socket Abstraction

The basis for network I/O in BSD UNIX centers on an abstraction known as the *socket†*. We think of a socket as a generalization of the UNIX file access mechanism that provides an endpoint for communication. As with file access, application programs request the operating system to create a socket when one is needed. The system returns a small integer that the application program uses to reference the newly created socket. The chief difference between file descriptors and socket descriptors is that the operating system binds a file descriptor to a specific file or device when the application calls *open*, but it can create sockets without binding them to specific destination addresses. The application can choose to supply a destination address each time it uses the socket (e.g., when sending datagrams), or it can choose to bind the destination address to the socket and avoid specifying the destination repeatedly (e.g., when making a TCP connection).

Whenever it makes sense, sockets perform exactly like UNIX files or devices, so they can be used with traditional operations like *read* and *write*. For example, once an application program creates a socket and creates a TCP connection from the socket to a foreign destination, the program can use *write* to send a stream of data across the connection (the application program at the other end can use *read* to receive it). To make it possible to use primitives like *read* and *write* with both files and sockets, the operating system allocates socket descriptors and file descriptors from the same set of integers and makes sure that if a given integer has been allocated as a file descriptor, it will not also be allocated as a socket descriptor.

20.5 Creating A Socket

The *socket* system call creates sockets on demand. It takes three integer arguments and returns an integer result:

$$result = socket(pf, type, protocol)$$

Argument *pf* specifies the protocol family to be used with the socket. That is, it specifies how to interpret addresses when they are supplied. Current families include the TCP/IP internet (PF_INET), Xerox Corporation PUP internet (PF_PUP), Apple Com-

---

†For now, we will describe sockets as part of the operating system because that is the way BSD UNIX provides them; later sections describe how other operating systems use library routines to provide a socket interface.

puter Incorporated Appletalk network (PF_APPLETALK), and UNIX file system (PF_UNIX) as well as many others†.

Argument *type* specifies the type of communication desired. Possible types include reliable stream delivery service (SOCK_STREAM) and connectionless datagram delivery service (SOCK_DGRAM), as well as a raw type (SOCK_RAW) that allows privileged programs to access low-level protocols or network interfaces. Two additional types have been planned but not implemented.

Although the general approach of separating protocol families and types may seem sufficient to handle all cases easily, it does not. First, it may be that a given family of protocols does not support one or more of the possible service types. For example, the UNIX family has an interprocess communication mechanism called a *pipe* that uses a reliable stream delivery service, but has no mechanism for sequenced packet delivery. Thus, not all combinations of protocol family and service type make sense. Second, some protocol families have multiple protocols that support one type of service. For example, it may be that a single protocol family has two connectionless datagram delivery services. To accommodate multiple protocols within a family, the *socket* call has a third argument that can be used to select a specific protocol. To use the third argument, the programmer must understand the protocol family well enough to know the type of service each protocol supplies.

Because the designers tried to capture many of the conventional UNIX operations in their socket design, they needed a way to simulate the UNIX pipe mechanism. It is not necessary to understand the details of pipes; only one salient feature is important: pipes differ from standard network operations because the calling process creates both endpoints for the communication simultaneously. To accommodate pipes, the designers added a *socketpair* system call that takes the form:

$$socketpair(pf, type, protocol, sarray)$$

Socketpair has one more argument than the *socket* procedure, *sarray*. The additional argument gives the address of a two-element integer array. *Socketpair* creates two sockets simultaneously and places the two socket descriptors in the two elements of *sarray*. Readers should understand that *socketpair* is not meaningful when applied to the TCP/IP protocol family (it has been included here merely to make our description of the interface complete).

20.6 Socket Inheritance And Termination

UNIX uses the *fork* and *exec* system calls to start new application programs. It is a two-step procedure. In the first step, *fork* creates a separate copy of the currently executing application program. In the second step, the new copy replaces itself with the desired application program. When a program calls *fork*, the newly created copy inherits access to all open sockets just as it inherits access to all open files. When a program calls *exec*, the new application retains access to all open sockets. We will see that master servers use socket inheritance when they create slave servers to handle a specific

---

†In UNIX, application programs contain symbolic names like *PF_INET*; system files contain the definitions that specify numeric values for each name.

connection. Internally, the operating system keeps a reference count associated with each socket, so it knows how many application programs (processes) have access to it.

Both the old and new processes have the same access rights to existing sockets, and both can access the sockets. Thus, it is the responsibility of the programmer to ensure that the two processes use the shared socket meaningfully.

When a process finishes using a socket it calls *close*. *Close* has the form:

close(socket)

where argument *socket* specifies the descriptor of a socket to close. When a process terminates for any reason, the system closes all sockets that remain open. Internally, a call to *close* decrements the reference count for a socket and destroys the socket if the count reaches zero.

20.7 Specifying A Local Address

Initially, a socket is created without any association to local or destination addresses. For the TCP/IP protocols, this means no local protocol port number has been assigned and no destination port or IP address has been specified. In many cases, application programs do not care about the local address they use and are willing to allow the protocol software to choose one for them. However, server processes that operate at a well-known port must be able to specify that port to the system. Once a socket has been created, a server uses the *bind* system call to establish a local address for it. *Bind* has the following form:

bind(socket, localaddr, addrlen)

Argument *socket* is the integer descriptor of the socket to be bound. Argument *localaddr* is a structure that specifies the local address to which the socket should be bound, and argument *addrlen* is an integer that specifies the length of the address measured in bytes. Instead of giving the address merely as a sequence of bytes, the designers chose to use a structure for addresses as Figure 20.1 illustrates.

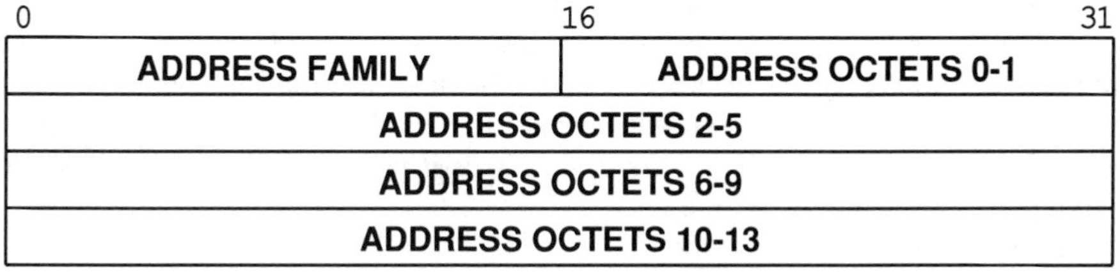

0	16	31
ADDRESS FAMILY	**ADDRESS OCTETS 0-1**	
ADDRESS OCTETS 2-5		
ADDRESS OCTETS 6-9		
ADDRESS OCTETS 10-13		

Figure 20.1 The *sockaddr* structure used when passing a TCP/IP address to the socket interface.

The structure, generically named *sockaddr*, begins with a 16-bit *ADDRESS FAMI-LY* field that identifies the protocol suite to which the address belongs. It is followed by an address of up to *14* octets. When declared in C, the socket address structure is a union of structures for all possible address families.

The value in the *ADDRESS FAMILY* field determines the format of the remaining address octets. For example, the value *2†* in the *ADDRESS FAMILY* field means the remaining address octets contain a TCP/IP address. Each protocol family defines how it will use octets in the address field. For TCP/IP addresses, the socket address is known as *sockaddr_in*. It includes both an IP address and a protocol port number (i.e., an internet socket address structure can contain both an IP address and a protocol port at that address). Figure 20.2 shows the exact format of a TCP/IP socket address.

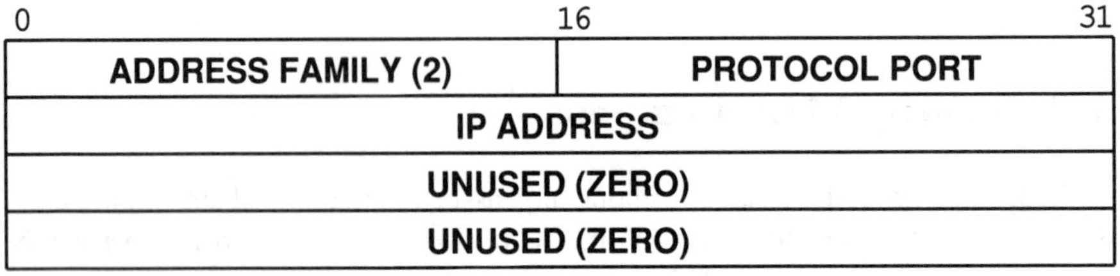

0	16	31
ADDRESS FAMILY (2)		PROTOCOL PORT
IP ADDRESS		
UNUSED (ZERO)		
UNUSED (ZERO)		

Figure 20.2 The format of a socket address structure (*sockaddr_in*) when used with a TCP/IP address. The structure includes both an IP address and a protocol port at that address.

Although it is possible to specify arbitrary values in the address structure when calling *bind*, not all possible bindings are valid. For example, the caller might request a local protocol port that is already in use by another program, or it might request an invalid IP address. In such cases, the *bind* call fails and returns an error code.

20.8 Connecting Sockets To Destination Addresses

Initially, a socket is created in the *unconnected state*, which means that the socket is not associated with any foreign destination. The system call *connect* binds a permanent destination to a socket, placing it in the *connected state*. An application program must call *connect* to establish a connection before it can transfer data through a reliable stream socket. Sockets used with connectionless datagram services need not be connected before they are used, but doing so makes it possible to transfer data without specifying the destination each time.

The *connect* system call has the form:

connect(socket, destaddr, addrlen)

---

†UNIX uses the symbolic name *PF_INET* to denote TCP/IP addresses.

Argument *socket* is the integer descriptor of the socket to connect. Argument *destaddr* is a socket address structure that specifies the destination address to which the socket should be bound. Argument *addrlen* specifies the length of the destination address measured in bytes.

The semantics of *connect* depend on the underlying protocols. Selecting the reliable stream delivery service in the PF_INET family means choosing TCP. In such cases, *connect* builds a TCP connection with the destination and returns an error if it cannot. In the case of connectionless service, *connect* does nothing more than store the destination address locally.

20.9 Sending Data Through A Socket

Once an application program has established a socket, it can use the socket to transmit data. There are five possible operating system calls from which to choose: *send*, *sendto*, *sendmsg*, *write*, and *writev*. *Send*, *write*, and *writev* only work with connected sockets because they do not allow the caller to specify a destination address. The differences between the three are minor. *Write* takes three arguments:

write(socket, buffer, length)

Argument *socket* contains an integer socket descriptor (*write* can also be used with other types of descriptors). Argument *buffer* contains the address of the data to be sent, and argument *length* specifies the number of bytes to send. The call to *write* blocks until the data can be transferred (e.g., it blocks if internal system buffers for the socket are full). Like most system calls in UNIX, *write* returns an error code to the application calling it, allowing the programmer to know if the operation succeeded.

The system call *writev* works like *write* except that it uses a "gather write" form, making it possible for the application program to write a message without copying the message into contiguous bytes of memory. *Writev* has the form:

writev(socket, iovector, vectorlen)

Argument *iovector* gives the address of an array of type *iovec* that contains a sequence of pointers to the blocks of bytes that form the message. As Figure 20.3 shows, a length accompanies each pointer. Argument *vectorlen* specifies the number of entries in *iovector*.

0   31

| POINTER TO BLOCK$_1$ (32-bit address) |
| LENGTH OF BLOCK$_1$ (32-bit integer) |
| POINTER TO BLOCK$_2$ (32-bit address) |
| LENGTH OF BLOCK$_2$ (32-bit integer) |
| . . . |

Figure 20.3 The format of an iovector of type *iovec* used with *writev* and *readv*.

The *send* system call has the form:

    send(socket, message, length, flags)

where argument *socket* specifies the socket to use, argument *message* gives the address of the data to be sent, argument *length* specifies the number of bytes to be sent, and argument *flags* controls the transmission. One value for *flags* allows the sender to specify that the message should be sent out-of-band on sockets that support such a notion. For example, recall from Chapter 13 that out-of-band messages correspond to TCP's notion of urgent data. Another value for *flags* allows the caller to request that the message be sent without using local routing tables. The intention is to allow the caller to take control of routing, making it possible to write network debugging software. Of course, not all sockets support all requests from arbitrary programs. Some requests require the program to have special privileges; others are simply not supported on all sockets.

System calls *sendto* and *sendmsg* allow the caller to send a message through an unconnected socket because they both require the caller to specify a destination. *Sendto*, which takes the destination address as an argument, has the form:

    sendto(socket, message, length, flags, destaddr, addrlen)

The first four arguments are exactly the same as those used with the *send* system call. The final two arguments specify a destination address and give the length of that address. Argument *destaddr* specifies the destination address using the *sockaddr_in* structure as defined in Figure 20.2.

A programmer may choose to use system call *sendmsg* in cases where the long list of arguments required for *sendto* makes the program inefficient or difficult to read. *Sendmsg* has the form:

    sendmsg(socket, messagestruct, flags)

where argument *messagestruct* is a structure of the form illustrated in Figure 20.4. The structure contains information about the message to be sent, its length, the destination address, and the address length. This call is especially useful because there is a corresponding input operation (described below) that produces a message structure in exactly the same format.

```
0                                                                              31
┌──────────────────────────────────────────────────────────────────────────┐
│                      POINTER TO SOCKETADDR                                  │
├──────────────────────────────────────────────────────────────────────────┤
│                       SIZE OF SOCKETADDR                                    │
├──────────────────────────────────────────────────────────────────────────┤
│                      POINTER TO IOVEC LIST                                  │
├──────────────────────────────────────────────────────────────────────────┤
│                      LENGTH OF IOVEC LIST                                   │
├──────────────────────────────────────────────────────────────────────────┤
│                  POINTER TO ACCESS RIGHTS LIST                              │
├──────────────────────────────────────────────────────────────────────────┤
│                  LENGTH OF ACCESS RIGHTS LIST                               │
└──────────────────────────────────────────────────────────────────────────┘
```

Figure 20.4 The format of message structure *messagestruct* used by *sendmsg*.

20.10 Receiving Data Through A Socket

Analogous to the five different output operations, BSD UNIX offers five system calls that a process can use to receive data through a socket: *read*, *readv*, *recv*, *recvfrom*, and *recvmsg*. The conventional UNIX input operation, *read*, can only be used when the socket is connected. It has the form:

read(descriptor, buffer, length)

where *descriptor* gives the integer descriptor of a socket or file descriptor from which to read data, *buffer* specifies the address in memory at which to store the data, and *length* specifies the maximum number of bytes to read.

An alternative form, *readv*, allows the caller to use a "scatter read" style of interface that places the incoming data in noncontiguous locations. *Readv* has the form:

readv(descriptor, iovector, vectorlen)

Argument *iovector* gives the address of a structure of type *iovec* (see Figure 20.3) that contains a sequence of pointers to blocks of memory into which the incoming data should be stored. Argument *vectorlen* specifies the number of entries in *iovector*.

In addition to the conventional input operations, there are three additional system calls for network message input. Processes call *recv* to receive data from a connected socket. It has the form:

recv(socket, buffer, length, flags)

Argument *socket* specifies a socket descriptor from which data should be received. Argument *buffer* specifies the address in memory into which the message should be placed, and argument *length* specifies the length of the buffer area. Finally, argument *flags* allows the caller to control the reception. Among the possible values for the *flags* argument is one that allows the caller to look ahead by extracting a copy of the next incoming message without removing the message from the socket.

The system call *recvfrom* allows the caller to specify input from an unconnected socket. It includes additional arguments that allow the caller to specify where to record the sender's address. The form is:

recvfrom(socket, buffer, length, flags, fromaddr, addrlen)

The two additional arguments, *fromaddr* and *addrlen*, are pointers to a socket address structure and an integer. The operating system uses *fromaddr* to record the address of the message sender and uses *fromlen* to record the length of the sender's address. Notice that the output operation *sendto*, discussed above, takes an address in exactly the same form as *recvfrom* generates. Thus, sending replies is easy.

The final system call used for input, *recvmsg*, is analogous to the *sendmsg* output operation. *Recvmsg* operates like *recvfrom*, but requires fewer arguments. Its form is:

recvmsg(socket, messagestruct, flags)

where argument *messagestruct* gives the address of a structure that holds the address for an incoming message as well as locations for the sender's address. The structure produced by *recvmsg* is exactly the same as the structure used by *sendmsg*, making them operate well as a pair.

20.11 Obtaining Local And Remote Socket Addresses

We said that newly created processes inherit the set of open sockets from the process that created them. Sometimes, a newly created process needs to determine the destination address to which a socket connects. A process may also wish to determine the local address of a socket. Two system calls provide such information: *getpeername* and *getsockname* (despite their names, both deal with what we think of as "addresses").

A process calls *getpeername* to determine the address of the peer (i.e., the remote end) to which a socket connects. It has the form:

getpeername(socket, destaddr, addrlen)

Argument *socket* specifies the socket for which the address is desired. Argument *destaddr* is a pointer to a structure of type *sockaddr* (see Figure 20.1) that will receive the socket address. Finally, argument *addrlen* is a pointer to an integer that will receive the length of the address. *Getpeername* only works with connected sockets.

System call *getsockname* returns the local address associated with a socket. It has the form:

getsockname(socket, localaddr, addrlen)

As expected, argument *socket* specifies the socket for which the local address is desired. Argument *localaddr* is a pointer to a structure of type *sockaddr* that will contain the address, and argument *addrlen* is a pointer to an integer that will contain the length of the address.

20.12 Obtaining And Setting Socket Options

In addition to binding a socket to a local address or connecting it to a destination address, the need arises for a mechanism that permits application programs to control the socket. For example, when using protocols that use timeout and retransmission, the application program may want to obtain or set the timeout parameters. It may also want to control the allocation of buffer space, determine if the socket allows transmission of broadcast, or control processing of out-of-band data. Rather than add new system calls for each new control operation, the designers decided to build a single mechanism. The mechanism has two operations: *getsockopt* and *setsockopt*.

System call *getsockopt* allows the application to request information about the socket. A caller specifies the socket, the option of interest, and a location at which to store the requested information. The operating system examines its internal data structures for the socket and passes the requested information to the caller. The call has the form:

getsockopt(socket, level, optionid, optionval, length)

Argument *socket* specifies the socket for which information is needed. Argument *level* identifies whether the operation applies to the socket itself or to the underlying protocols being used. Argument *optionid* specifies a single option to which the request applies. The pair of arguments *optionval* and *length* specify two pointers. The first gives the address of a buffer into which the system places the requested value, and the second gives the address of an integer into which the system places the length of the option value.

System call *setsockopt* allows an application program to set a socket option using the set of values obtained with *getsockopt*. The caller specifies a socket for which the option should be set, the option to be changed, and a value for the option. The call to *setsockopt* has the form:

setsockopt(socket, level, optionid, optionval, length)

where the arguments are like those for *getsockopt*, except that the *length* argument contains the length of the option being passed to the system. The caller must supply a legal value for the option as well as a correct length for that value. Of course, not all options apply to all sockets. The correctness and semantics of individual requests depend on the current state of the socket and the underlying protocols being used.

20.13 Specifying A Queue Length For A Server

One of the options that applies to sockets is used so frequently, a separate system call has been dedicated to it. To understand how it arises, consider a server. The server creates a socket, binds it to a well-known protocol port, and waits for requests. If the server uses a reliable stream delivery, or if computing a response takes nontrivial amounts of time, it may happen that a new request arrives before the server finishes responding to an old request. To avoid having protocols reject or discard incoming requests, a server must tell the underlying protocol software that it wishes to have such requests enqueued until it has time to process them.

The system call *listen* allows servers to prepare a socket for incoming connections. In terms of the underlying protocols, *listen* puts the socket in a passive mode ready to accept connections. When the server invokes *listen*, it also informs the operating system that the protocol software should enqueue multiple simultaneous requests that arrive at the socket. The form is:

listen(socket, qlength)

Argument *socket* gives the descriptor of a socket that should be prepared for use by a server, and argument *qlength* specifies the length of the request queue for that socket. After the call, the system will enqueue up to *qlength* requests for connections. If the queue is full when a request arrives, the operating system will refuse the connection by discarding the request. *Listen* applies only to sockets that have selected reliable stream delivery service.

20.14 How A Server Accepts Connections

As we have seen, a server process uses the system calls *socket*, *bind*, and *listen* to create a socket, bind it to a well-known protocol port, and specify a queue length for connection requests. Note that the call to *bind* associates the socket with a well-known protocol port, but that the socket is not connected to a specific foreign destination. In fact, the foreign destination must specify a *wildcard*, allowing the socket to receive connection requests from an arbitrary client.

Once a socket has been established, the server needs to wait for a connection. To do so, it uses system call *accept*. A call to *accept* blocks until a connection request arrives. It has the form:

newsock = accept(socket, addr, addrlen)

Argument *socket* specifies the descriptor of the socket on which to wait. Argument *addr* is a pointer to a structure of type *sockaddr*, and *addrlen* is a pointer to an integer. When a request arrives, the system fills in argument *addr* with the address of the client that has placed the request and sets *addrlen* to the length of the address. Finally, the system creates a new socket that has its destination connected to the requesting client, and returns the new socket descriptor to the caller. The original socket still has a wild-card foreign destination, and it still remains open. Thus, the master server can continue to accept additional requests at the original socket.

When a connection request arrives, the call to *accept* returns. The server can either handle requests iteratively or concurrently. In the iterative approach, the server handles the request itself, closes the new socket, and then calls *accept* to obtain the next connection request. In the concurrent approach, after the call to *accept* returns, the master server creates a slave to handle the request (in UNIX terminology, it forks a child process to handle the request). The slave process inherits a copy of the new socket, so it can proceed to service the request. When it finishes, the slave closes the socket and terminates. The original (master) server process closes its copy of the new socket after starting the slave. It then calls *accept* to obtain the next connection request.

The concurrent design for servers may seem confusing because multiple processes will be using the same local protocol port number. The key to understanding the mechanism lies in the way underlying protocols treat protocol ports. Recall that in TCP a pair of endpoints define a connection. Thus, it does not matter how many processes use a given local protocol port number as long as they connect to different destinations. In the case of a concurrent server, there is one process per client and one additional process that accepts connections. The socket the master server process uses has a wildcard for the foreign destination, allowing it to connect with an arbitrary foreign site. Each remaining process has a specific foreign destination. When a TCP segment arrives, it will be sent to the socket connected to the segment's source. If no such socket exists, the segment will be sent to the socket that has a wildcard for its foreign destination. Furthermore, because the socket with a wildcard foreign destination does not have an open connection, it will only honor TCP segments that request a new connection.

20.15 Servers That Handle Multiple Services

The BSD UNIX interface provides another interesting possibility for server design because it allows a single process to wait for connections on multiple sockets. The system call that makes the design possible is called *select*, and it applies to I/O in general, not just to communication over sockets. *Select* has the form:

nready = select(ndesc, indesc, outdesc, excdesc, timeout)

In general, a call to *select* blocks waiting for one of a set of file descriptors to become ready. Argument *ndesc* specifies how many descriptors should be examined (the descriptors checked are always *0* through *ndesc*-1). Argument *indesc* is a pointer to a bit mask that specifies the file descriptors to check for input, argument *outdesc* is a pointer to a bit mask that specifies the file descriptors to check for output, and argument *excdesc* is a pointer to a bit mask that specifies the file descriptors to check for exception conditions. Finally, if argument *timeout* is nonzero, it is the address of an integer that specifies how long to wait for a connection before returning to the caller. A zero value for timeout forces the call to block until a descriptor becomes ready. Because the *timeout* argument contains the address of the timeout integer and not the integer itself, a process can request zero delay by passing the address of an integer that contains zero (i.e., a process can poll to see if I/O is ready).

A call to *select* returns the number of descriptors from the specified set that are ready for I/O. It also changes the bit masks specified by *indesc*, *outdesc*, and *excdesc* to inform the application which of the selected file descriptors are ready. Thus, before calling *select*, the caller must turn on those bits that correspond to descriptors to be checked. Following the call, all bits that remain set to *1* correspond to a ready file descriptor.

To communicate over more than one socket at a time, a process first creates all the sockets it needs and then uses *select* to determine which of them becomes ready for I/O first. Once it finds a socket has become ready, the process uses the input or output procedures defined above to communicate.

20.16 Obtaining And Setting Host Names

The BSD UNIX operating system maintains an internal host name. For machines on the Internet, the internal name is usually chosen to be the domain name for the machine's main network interface. The *gethostname* system call allows user processes to access the host name, and the *sethostname* system call allows privileged processes to set the host name. *Gethostname* has the form:

gethostname(name, length)

Argument *name* gives the address of an array of bytes where the name is to be stored, and argument *length* is an integer that specifies the length of the *name* array. To set the host name, a privileged process makes a call of the form:

sethostname(name, length)

Argument *name* gives the address of an array where the name is stored, and argument *length* is an integer that gives the length of the name array.

20.17 Obtaining And Setting The Internal Host Domain

The operating system maintains a string that specifies the naming domain to which a machine belongs. When a site obtains authority for part of the domain name space, it invents a string that identifies its piece of the space and uses that string as the name of the domain. For example, machines in the domain

cs.purdue.edu

have names taken from the Arthurian legend. Thus, one finds machines named *merlin*, *arthur*, *guenevere*, and *lancelot*. The domain itself has been named *camelot*, so the operating system on each host in the group must be informed that it resides in the *camelot* domain. To do so, a privileged process uses system call *setdomainname*, which has the form:

setdomainname(name, length)

Argument *name* gives the address of an array of bytes that contains the name of a domain, and argument *length* is an integer that gives the length of the name.

User processes call *getdomainname* to retrieve the name of the domain from the system. It has the form:

getdomainname(name, length)

where argument *name* specifies the address of an array where the name should be stored, and argument *length* is an integer that specifies the length of the array.

20.18 BSD UNIX Network Library Calls

In addition to the system calls described above, BSD UNIX offers a set of library routines that perform useful functions related to networking. Figure 20.5 illustrates the difference between system calls and library routines. System calls pass control to the computer's operating system, while library routines are like other procedures that the programmer binds into a program.

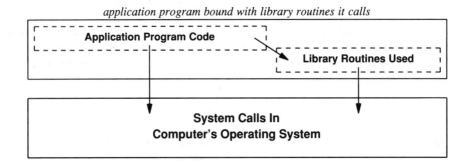

application program bound with library routines it calls

Figure 20.5 The difference between library routines, which are bound into an
application program, and system calls, which are part of the
operating system. A program can call either; library routines
can call other library routines or system calls.

Many of the BSD UNIX library routines provide database services that allow a
process to determine the names of machines and network services, protocol port
numbers, and other related information. For example, one set of library routines provides access to the database of network services. We think of entries in the services database as 3-tuples, where each 3-tuple contains the (human readable) name of a network
service, the protocol that supports the service, and a protocol port number for the service. Library routines exist that allow a process to obtain information from an entry
given any piece.

The next sections examine groups of library routines, explaining their purposes and
providing information about how they can be used. As we will see, the sets of library
routines that provide access to a sequential database follow a pattern. Each set allows
the application to: establish a connection to the database, obtain entries one at a time,
and close the connection. The routines used for these three operations are named *setX-
ent*, *getXent*, and *endXent*, where *X* is the name of the database. For example, the library routines for the host database are named *sethostent*, *gethostent*, and *endhostent*.
The sections that describe these routines summarize the calls without repeating the details of their use.

20.19 Network Byte Order Conversion Routines

Recall that machines differ in the way they store integer quantities and that the
TCP/IP protocols define a machine independent standard for byte order. BSD UNIX
provides four library functions that convert between the local machine byte order and
the network standard byte order. To make programs portable, they must be written to
call the conversion routines every time they copy an integer value from the local
machine to a network packet, or when they copy a value from a network packet to the
local machine.

All four conversion routines are functions that take a value as an argument and return a new value with the bytes rearranged. For example, to convert a short (2-byte) integer from network byte order to the local host byte order, a programmer calls *ntohs*
(network to host short). The format is:

$$localshort = ntohs(netshort)$$

Argument *netshort* is a 2-byte (16-bit) integer in network standard byte order and the
result, *localshort*, is in local host byte order.

UNIX calls 4 byte (32 bit) integers *longs*. Function *ntohl* (network to host long)
converts 4-byte longs from network standard byte order to local host byte order. Programs invoke *ntohl* as a function, supplying a long integer in network byte order as an
argument:

$$locallong = ntohl(netlong)$$

Two analogous functions allow the programmer to convert from local host byte
order to network byte order. Function *htons* converts a 2-byte (short) integer in the
host's local byte order to a 2-byte integer in network standard byte order. Programs invoke *htons* as a function:

$$netshort = htons(localshort)$$

The final conversion routine, *htonl*, converts long integers to network standard byte
order. Like the others, *htonl* is a function:

$$netlong = htonl(locallong)$$

It should be obvious that the conversion routines preserve the following mathematical relationships:

$$netshort = htons(ntohs(netshort))$$

and

$$localshort = ntohs(htons(localshort))$$

Similar relationships hold for the long integer conversion routines.

20.20 IP Address Manipulation Routines

Because many programs translate between 32-bit IP addresses and the corresponding dotted decimal notation, the BSD UNIX library includes utility routines that perform the translation. Procedures *inet_addr* and *inet_network* both translate from dotted
decimal format to a 32-bit IP address in network byte order. *Inet_addr* forms a 32-bit

host IP address; *inet_network* forms the network address with zeroes for the host part. They have the form:

$$address = inet\_addr(string)$$

and

$$address = inet\_network(string)$$

where argument *string* gives the address of an ASCII string that contains the number expressed in dotted decimal format. The dotted decimal form can have 1 to 4 segments of digits separated by periods (dots). If all 4 appear, each corresponds to a single byte of the resulting 32-bit integer. If less than 4 appear, the last segment is expanded to fill remaining bytes.

Procedure *inet_ntoa* performs the inverse of *inet_addr* by mapping a 32-bit integer to an ASCII string in dotted decimal format. It has the form:

$$str = inet\_ntoa(internetaddr)$$

where argument *internetaddr* is a 32-bit IP address in network byte order, and *str* is the address of the resulting ASCII version.

Often programs that manipulate IP addresses must combine a network address with the local address of a host on that network. Procedure *inet_makeaddr* performs such a combination. It has the form:

$$internetaddr = inet\_makeaddr(net, local)$$

Argument *net* is a 32-bit network IP address in host byte order, and argument *local* is the integer representing a local host address on that network, also in local host byte order.

Procedures *inet_netof* and *inet_lnaof* provide the inverse of *inet_makeaddr* by separating the network and local portions of an IP address. They have the form:

$$net = inet\_netof(internetaddr)$$

and

$$local = inet\_lnaof(internetaddr)$$

where argument *internetaddr* is a 32-bit IP address in network byte order, and the results are returned in host byte order.

20.21 Accessing The Domain Name System†

A set of five library procedures comprise the BSD UNIX interface to the TCP/IP domain name system. Application programs that call these routines become clients of one domain name system, sending one or more servers requests and receiving responses.

---

†Chapter 22 considers the Domain Name System in detail.

The general idea is that a program makes a query, sends it to a server, and awaits an answer. Because many options exist, the routines have only a few basic parameters and use a global structure, *res*, to hold others. For example, one field in *res* enables debugging messages while another controls whether the code uses UDP or TCP for queries. Most fields in *res* begin with reasonable defaults, so the routines can be used without changing *res*.

A program calls *res_init* before using other procedures. The call takes no arguments:

res_init()

Res_init reads a file that contains information like the name of the machine that runs the domain name server and stores the results in global structure *res*.

Procedure *res_mkquery* forms a domain name query and places it in a buffer in memory. The form of the call is:

res_mkquery(op, dname, class, type, data, datalen, newrr, buffer, buflen)

The first seven arguments correspond directly to the fields of a domain name query. Argument *op* specifies the requested operation, *dname* gives the address of a character array that contains a domain name, *class* is an integer that gives the class of the query, *type* is an integer that gives the type of the query, *data* gives the address of an array of data to be included in the query, and *datalen* is an integer that gives the length of the data. In addition to the library procedures, UNIX provides application programs with definitions of symbolic constants for important values. Thus, programmers can use the domain name system without understanding the details of the protocol. The last two arguments, *buffer* and *buflen*, specify the address of an area into which the query should be placed and the integer length of the buffer area, respectively. Finally, in the current implementation, argument *newrr* is unused.

Once a program has formed a query, it calls *res_send* to send it to a name server and obtain a response. The form is:

res_send(buffer, buflen, answer, anslen)

Argument *buffer* is a pointer to memory that holds the message to be sent (presumably, the application called procedure *res_mkquery* to form the message). Argument *buflen* is an integer that specifies the length. Argument *answer* gives the address in memory into which a response should be written, and integer argument *anslen* specifies the length of the answer area.

In addition to routines that make and send queries, the BSD UNIX library contains two routines that translate domain names between conventional ASCII and the compressed format used in queries. Procedure *dn_expand* expands a compressed domain name into a full ASCII version. It has the form:

dn_expand(msg, eom, compressed, full, fullen)

Argument *msg* gives the address of a domain name message that contains the name to be expanded, with *eom* specifying the end-of-message limit beyond which the expansion cannot go. Argument *compressed* is a pointer to the first byte of the compressed name. Argument *full* is a pointer to an array into which the expanded name should be written, and argument *fullen* is an integer that specifies the length of the array.

Generating a compressed name is more complex than expanding a compressed name because compression involves eliminating common suffixes. When compressing names, the client must keep a record of suffixes that have appeared previously. Procedure *dn_comp* compresses a full domain name by comparing suffixes to a list of previously used suffixes and eliminating the longest possible suffix. A call has the form:

$$dn\_comp(full, compressed, cmprlen, prevptrs, lastptr)$$

Argument *full* gives the address of a full domain name. Argument *compressed* points to an array of bytes that will hold the compressed name, with argument *cmprlen* specifying the length of the array. The argument *prevptrs* is the address of an array of pointers to previously compressed suffixes, with *lastptr* pointing to the end of the array. Normally, *dn_comp* compresses the name and updates *prevptrs* if a new suffix has been used.

Procedure *dn_comp* can also be used to translate a domain name from ASCII to the internal form without compression (i.e., without removing suffixes). To do so, a process invokes *dn_comp* with the *prevptrs* argument set to *NULL* (i.e., zero).

20.22 Obtaining Information About Hosts

Library procedures exist that allow a process to retrieve information about a host given either its domain name or its IP address. When used on a machine that has access to a domain name server, the library procedures make the process a client of the domain name system by sending a request to a server and waiting for a response. When used on systems that do not have access to the domain name system (e.g., a host not on the Internet), the routines obtain the desired information from a database kept on secondary storage.

Function *gethostbyname* takes a domain name and returns a pointer to a structure of information for that host. A call takes the form:

$$ptr = gethostbyname(namestr)$$

Argument *namestr* is a pointer to a character string that contains a domain name for the host. The value returned, *ptr*, points to a structure that contains the following information: the official host name, a list of aliases that have been registered for the host, the host address type (i.e., whether the address is an IP address), the address length, and a list of one or more addresses for the host. More details can be found in the UNIX Programmer's Manual.

Function *gethostbyaddr* produces the same information as *gethostbyname*. The difference between the two is that *gethostbyaddr* accepts a host address as an argument:

$$ptr = gethostbyaddr(addr, len, type)$$

Argument *addr* is a pointer to a sequence of bytes that contain a host address. Argument *len* is an integer that gives the length of the address, and argument *type* is an integer that specifies the type of the address (e.g., that it is an IP address).

As mentioned earlier, procedures *sethostent*, *gethostent*, and *endhostent* provide sequential access to the host database.

20.23 Obtaining Information About Networks

Hosts running BSD UNIX either use the domain name system or keep a simple database of networks in their internet. The network library routines include five routines that allow a process to access the network database. Procedure *getnetbyname* obtains and formats the contents of an entry from the database given the domain name of a network. A call has the form:

$$ptr = getnetbyname(name)$$

where argument *name* is a pointer to a string that contains the name of the network for which information is desired. The value returned is a pointer to a structure that contains fields for the official name of the network, a list of registered aliases, an integer address type, and a 32-bit network address (i.e., an IP address with the host portion set to zero).

A process calls library routine *getnetbyaddr* when it needs to search for information about a network given its address. The call has the form:

$$ptr = getnetbyaddr(netaddr, addrtype)$$

Argument *netaddr* is a 32-bit network address, and argument *addrtype* is an integer that specifies the type of *netaddr*. Procedures *setnetent*, *getnetent*, and *endnetent* provide sequential access to the network database.

20.24 Obtaining Information About Protocols

Five library routines provide access to the database of protocols available on a machine. Each protocol has an official name, registered aliases, and an official protocol number. Procedure *getprotobyname* allows a caller to obtain information about a protocol given its name:

$$ptr = getprotobyname(name)$$

Argument *name* is a pointer to an ASCII string that contains the name of the protocol for which information is desired. The function returns a pointer to a structure that has fields for the official protocol name, a list of aliases, and a unique integer value assigned to the protocol.

Procedure *getprotobynumber* allows a process to search for protocol information using the protocol number as a key:

$$ptr = getprotobynumber(number)$$

Finally, procedures *getprotoent*, *setprotoent*, and *endprotoent* provide sequential access to the protocol database.

20.25 Obtaining Information About Network Services

Recall from Chapters 12 and 13 that some UDP and TCP protocol port numbers are reserved for well-known services. For example, TCP port *43* is reserved for the *whois* service. *Whois* allows a client on one machine to contact a server on another and obtain information about a user that has an account on the server's machine. The entry for *whois* in the services database specifies the service name, *whois*, the protocol, *TCP*, and the protocol port number *43*. Five library routines exist that obtain information about services and the protocol ports they use.

Procedure *getservbyname* maps a named service onto a port number:

$$ptr = getservbyname(name, proto)$$

Argument *name* specifies the address of a string that contains the name of the desired service, and integer argument *proto* specifies the protocol with which the service is to be used. Typically, protocols are limited to TCP and UDP. The value returned is a pointer to a structure that contains fields for the name of the service, a list of aliases, an identification of the protocol with which the service is used, and an integer protocol port number assigned for that service.

Procedure *getservbyport* allows the caller to obtain an entry from the services database given the port number assigned to it. A call has the form:

$$ptr = getservbyport(port, proto)$$

Argument *port* is the integer protocol port number assigned to the service, and argument *proto* specifies the protocol for which the service is desired. As with other databases, a process can access the services database sequentially using *setservent*, *getservent*, and *endservent*.

20.26 An Example Client

The following example C program illustrates the BSD UNIX operating system interface to TCP/IP. It is a simple implementation of a *whois* client and server. As defined in RFC 954, the *whois* service allows a client on one machine to obtain information about a user on a remote system. In this implementation, the client is an application program that a user invokes with two arguments: the name of a remote machine and the name of a user on that machine about whom information is desired. The client calls *gethostbyname* to map the remote machine name into an IP address and calls *getservbyname* to find the well-known port for the *whois* service. Once it has mapped the host and service names, the client creates a socket, specifying that the socket will use reliable stream delivery (i.e., TCP). The client then binds the socket to the *whois* protocol port on the specified destination machine.

```c
/* whoisclient.c - main */

#include <stdio.h>
#include <sys/types.h>
#include <sys/socket.h>
#include <netinet/in.h>
#include <netdb.h>


/*-------------------------------------------------------------
 * Program:     whoisclient
 *
 * Purpose:     UNIX application program that becomes a client for the
 *              Internet "whois" service.
 *
 * Use:         whois hostname username
 *
 * Author:      Barry Shein, Boston University
 *
 * Date:        January, 1987
 *
 *-------------------------------------------------------------
 */
main(argc, argv)
int argc;                       /* standard UNIX argument declarations  */
char *argv[];
{
    int s;                      /* socket descriptor                    */
    int len;                    /* length of received data              */
    struct sockaddr_in sa;      /* Internet socket addr. structure      */
    struct hostent *hp;         /* result of host name lookup           */
```

```
struct servent *sp;              /* result of service lookup            */
char buf[BUFSIZ+1];              /* buffer to read whois information     */
char *myname;                    /* pointer to name of this program      */
char *host;                      /* pointer to remote host name          */
char *user;                      /* pointer to remote user name          */

myname = argv[0];
/*
 * Check that there are two command line arguments
 */
if(argc != 3) {
        fprintf(stderr, "Usage: %s host username\n", myname);
        exit(1);
}
host = argv[1];
user = argv[2];
/*
 * Look up the specified hostname
 */
if((hp = gethostbyname(host)) == NULL) {
        fprintf(stderr,"%s: %s: no such host?\n", myname, host);
        exit(1);
}
/*
 * Put host's address and address type into socket structure
 */
bcopy((char *)hp->h_addr, (char *)&sa.sin_addr, hp->h_length);
sa.sin_family = hp->h_addrtype;
/*
 * Look up the socket number for the WHOIS service
 */
if((sp = getservbyname("whois","tcp")) == NULL) {
        fprintf(stderr,"%s: No whois service on this host\n", myname);
        exit(1);
}
/*
 * Put the whois socket number into the socket structure.
 */
sa.sin_port = sp->s_port;
/*
 * Allocate an open socket
 */
if((s = socket(hp->h_addrtype, SOCK_STREAM, 0)) < 0) {
        perror("socket");
```

```
        exit(1);
    }
    /*
     * Connect to the remote server
     */
    if(connect(s, &sa, sizeof sa) < 0) {
        perror("connect");
        exit(1);
    }
    /*
     * Send the request
     */
    if(write(s, user, strlen(user)) != strlen(user)) {
        fprintf(stderr, "%s: write error\n", myname);
        exit(1);
    }
    /*
     * Read the reply and put to user's output
     */
    while( (len = read(s, buf, BUFSIZ)) > 0)
        write(1, buf, len);
    close(s);
    exit(0);
}
```

20.27 An Example Server

The example server is only slightly more complex than the client. The server listens on the well-known ''whois'' port and returns the requested information in response to a request from any client. The information is taken from the UNIX password file on the server's machine.

```
/* whoisserver.c - main */

#include <stdio.h>
#include <sys/types.h>
#include <sys/socket.h>
#include <netinet/in.h>
#include <netdb.h>
#include <pwd.h>


/*-----------------------------------------------------------------
 * Program:     whoisserver
```

```
 *
 * Purpose:     UNIX application program that acts as a server for
 *              the "whois" service on the local machine.  It listens
 *              on well-known WHOIS port (43) and answers queries from
 *              clients.  This program requires super-user privilege to
 *              run.
 *
 * Use:         whois hostname username
 *
 * Author:      Barry Shein, Boston University
 *
 * Date:        January, 1987
 *
 *-----------------------------------------------------------------------
 */


#define BACKLOG         5        /* # of requests we're willing to queue */
#define MAXHOSTNAME     32       /* maximum host name length we tolerate */

main(argc, argv)
int argc;                        /* standard UNIX argument declarations  */
char *argv[];
{
  int s, t;                      /* socket descriptors                   */
  int i;                         /* general purpose integer              */
  struct sockaddr_in sa, isa;    /* Internet socket address structure    */
  struct hostent *hp;            /* result of host name lookup           */
  char *myname;                  /* pointer to name of this program      */
  struct servent *sp;            /* result of service lookup             */
  char localhost[MAXHOSTNAME+1]; /* local host name as character string  */

  myname = argv[0];
  /*
   * Look up the WHOIS service entry
   */
  if((sp = getservbyname("whois","tcp")) == NULL) {
       fprintf(stderr, "%s: No whois service on this host\n", myname);
       exit(1);
  }
  /*
   * Get our own host information
   */
  gethostname(localhost, MAXHOSTNAME);
  if((hp = gethostbyname(localhost)) == NULL) {
```

```
            fprintf(stderr, "%s: cannot get local host info?\n", myname);
            exit(1);
    }
    /*
     * Put the WHOIS socket number and our address info
     * into the socket structure
     */
    sa.sin_port = sp->s_port;
    bcopy((char *)hp->h_addr, (char *)&sa.sin_addr, hp->h_length);
    sa.sin_family = hp->h_addrtype;
    /*
     * Allocate an open socket for incoming connections
     */
    if((s = socket(hp->h_addrtype, SOCK_STREAM, 0)) < 0) {
            perror("socket");
            exit(1);
    }
    /*
     * Bind the socket to the service port
     * so we hear incoming connections
     */
    if(bind(s, &sa, sizeof sa) < 0) {
            perror("bind");
            exit(1);
    }
    /*
     * Set maximum connections we will fall behind
     */
    listen(s, BACKLOG);
    /*
     * Go into an infinite loop waiting for new connections
     */
    while(1) {
            i = sizeof isa;
            /*
             * We hang in accept() while waiting for new customers
             */
            if((t = accept(s, &isa, &i)) < 0) {
              perror("accept");
              exit(1);
            }
            whois(t);               /* perform the actual WHOIS service */
            close(t);
    }
}
```

```
}
/*
 * Get the WHOIS request from remote host and format a reply.
 */
whois(sock)
int sock;
{
    struct passwd *p;
    char buf[BUFSIZ+1];
    int i;

    /*
     * Get one line request
     */
    if( (i = read(sock, buf, BUFSIZ)) <= 0)
        return;
    buf[i] = '\0';              /* Null terminate */
    /*
     * Look up the requested user and format reply
     */
    if((p = getpwnam(buf)) == NULL)
        strcpy(buf,"User not found\n");
    else
        sprintf(buf, "%s: %s\n", p->pw_name, p->pw_gecos);
    /*
     * Return reply
     */
    write(sock, buf, strlen(buf));
    return;
}
```

20.28 Summary

Because TCP/IP protocol software resides inside an operating system, the exact interface between an application program and TCP/IP protocols depends on the details of the operating system; it is not specified by the TCP/IP protocol standard. We examined the socket interface originally designed for BSD UNIX, and saw that it adopted the UNIX open-read-write-close paradigm. To use TCP, a program must create a socket, bind addresses to it, accept incoming connections, and then communicate using the *read* or *write* primitives. Finally, when finished using a socket, the program must close it. In addition to the socket abstraction and system calls that operate on sockets, BSD UNIX includes library routines that help programmers create and manipulate IP addresses, convert integers between the local machine format and network standard byte order, and search for information such as network addresses.

The socket interface has become popular and is widely supported by many vendors. Vendors who do not offer socket facilities in their operating systems often provide a socket library that makes it possible for programmers to write applications using socket calls even though the underlying operating system uses a different set of system calls.

FOR FURTHER STUDY

Detailed information on the socket system calls can be found in the *UNIX Programmer's Manual*, where Section 2 contains a description of each UNIX system call and Section 3 contains a description of each library procedure. UNIX also supplies on-line copies of the manual pages via the *man* command. Leffler, McKusick, Karels, and Quarterman [1989] explores the UNIX system in more detail.

Operating system vendors often provide libraries of procedures that emulate sockets on their systems. In addition, Microsoft and other vendors have cooperated to define the *Winsock* interface which permits application programs that make socket calls to run with Microsoft Windows; several vendors offer Winsock compatible products. Consult vendors' programming manuals for details.

The socket version of Volume 3 of this text describes how client and server programs are structured and how they use the socket interface. The TLI version of Volume 3 provides an introduction to the *Transport Layer Interface*, an alternative to sockets used in System V UNIX.

EXERCISES

20.1   Try running the sample *whois* client and server on your local system.

20.2   Build a simple server that accepts multiple concurrent connections (to test it, have the process that handles a connection print a short message, delay a random time, print another message, and exit).

20.3   When is the *listen* call important?

20.4   What procedures does your local system provide to access the domain name system?

20.5   Devise a server that uses a single UNIX process, but handles multiple concurrent TCP connections. Hint: think of *select* (*poll* in SYSTEM V).

20.6   Read about the AT&T System V Transport Library Interface (TLI) and compare it to the socket interface. What are the major conceptual differences?

20.7   Each operating system limits the number of sockets a given program can use at any time. How many sockets can a program create on your local system?

20.8   The socket/file descriptor mechanism and associated *read* and *write* operations can be considered a form of object-oriented design. Explain why.

20.9   Consider an alternative interface design that provides an interface for every layer of protocol software (e.g., the system allows an application program to send and receive raw packets without using IP, or to send and receive IP datagrams without using UDP or TCP). What are the advantages of having such an interface? The disadvantages?

20.10 A client and server can both run on the same computer and use a TCP socket to communicate. Explain how it is possible to build a client and server that can communicate on a single machine without learning the host's IP address.

20.11 Experiment with the sample server in this chapter to see if you can generate TCP connections sufficiently fast to exceed the backlog the server specifies. Do you expect incoming connection requests to exceed the backlog faster if the server operates on a computer that that has *1* processor than on a computer that has *5* processors? Explain.

21

Bootstrap And Autoconfiguration (BOOTP, DHCP)

21.1 Introduction

This chapter shows how the client-server paradigm is used for bootstrapping. Each computer attached to a TCP/IP internet needs to know its IP address before it can send or receive datagrams. In addition, a computer needs other information such as the address of a router, the subnet mask to use, and the address of a name server. Chapter 6 describes how a computer can use the RARP protocol at system startup to determine its IP address. This chapter discusses an alternative: two closely-related bootstrap protocols that each allows a host to determine its IP address without using RARP. Surprisingly, the client and server communicate using UDP, the User Datagram Protocol described in Chapter 12.

What makes the bootstrapping procedure surprising is that UDP relies on IP to transfer messages, and it might seem impossible that a computer could use UDP to find an IP address to use when communicating. Examining the protocols will help us understand how a computer can use the special IP addresses mentioned in Chapter 4 and the flexibility of the UDP/IP transport mechanism. We will also see how a server assigns an IP address to a computer automatically. Such assignment is especially important in environments that permit temporary internet connections or where computers move from one network to another (e.g., an employee with a portable computer moves from one location in a company to another).

21.2 The Need For An Alternative To RARP

Chapter 6 presents the problem diskless computers face during system startup. Such machines usually contain a startup program in nonvolatile storage (e.g., in ROM). To minimize cost and keep parts interchangeable, a vendor places exactly the same program in all machines. Because computers with different IP addresses run the same boot program, the code cannot contain an IP address. Thus, a diskless machine must obtain its IP address from another source. In fact, a diskless computer needs to know much more than its IP address. Usually, the ROM only contains a small startup program, so the diskless computer must also obtain an initial memory image to execute. In addition, each diskless machine must determine the address of a file server on which it can store and retrieve data, and the address of the nearest IP router.

The RARP protocol of Chapter 6 has three drawbacks. First, because RARP operates at a low level, using it requires direct access to the network hardware. Thus, it may be difficult or impossible for an application programmer to build a server. Second, although RARP requires a packet exchange between a client machine and a computer that answers its request, the reply contains only one small piece of information: the client's 4-octet IP address. This drawback is especially annoying on networks like an Ethernet that enforce a minimum packet size because additional information could be sent in the response at no additional cost. Third, because RARP uses a computer's hardware address to identify the machine, it cannot be used on networks that dynamically assign hardware addresses.

To overcome some of the drawbacks of RARP, researchers developed the *BOOTstrap Protocol* (*BOOTP*). More recently, the *Dynamic Host Configuration Protocol* (*DHCP*) has been proposed as a successor to BOOTP. Because the two protocols are closely related, most of the description in this chapter applies to both. To simplify the text, we will describe BOOTP first, and then see how DHCP extends the functionality to provide dynamic address assignment.

Because it uses UDP and IP, BOOTP can be implemented with an application program. Like RARP, BOOTP operates in the client-server paradigm and requires only a single packet exchange. However, BOOTP is more efficient than RARP because a single BOOTP message specifies many items needed at startup, including a computer's IP address, the address of a router, and the address of a server. BOOTP also includes a vendor-specific field in the reply that allows hardware vendors to send additional information used only for their computers†.

21.3 Using IP To Determine An IP Address

We said that BOOTP uses UDP to carry messages and that UDP messages are encapsulated in IP datagrams for delivery. To understand how a computer can send BOOTP in an IP datagram before the computer learns its IP address, recall from Chapter 4 that there are several special-case IP addresses. In particular, when used as a destination address, the IP address consisting of all *1*s (255.255.255.255) specifies limit-

---

†As we will see, the term "vendor-specific" is a misnomer because the current specification also recommends using the vendor-specific area for general purpose information such as subnet masks; DHCP changes the name of the field to *options*.

ed broadcast. IP software can accept and broadcast datagrams that specify the limited broadcast address even before the software has discovered its local IP address information. The point is that:

> *An application program can use the limited broadcast IP address to force IP to broadcast a datagram on the local network before IP has discovered the IP address of the local network or the machine's IP address.*

Suppose client machine *A* wants to use BOOTP to find bootstrap information (including its IP address) and suppose *B* is the server on the same physical net that will answer the request. Because *A* does not know *B*'s IP address or the IP address of the network, it must broadcast its initial BOOTP request using the IP limited broadcast address. What about the reply? Can *B* send a directed reply? No, not usually. Although it may not be obvious, *B* may need to use the limited broadcast address for its reply, even though it knows *A*'s IP address. To see why, consider what will happen if an application program on *B* attempts to send a datagram using *A*'s IP address. After routing the datagram, IP software on *B* will pass the datagram to the network interface software. The interface software must map the next hop IP address to a corresponding hardware address, presumably using ARP as described in Chapter 5. However, because *A* has not yet received the BOOTP reply, it does not recognize its IP address, so it cannot answer *B*'s ARP request. Therefore, *B* has only two alternatives: either broadcast the reply or use information from the request packet to manually add an entry to its ARP cache. On systems that do not allow application programs to modify the ARP cache, broadcasting is the only solution.

21.4 The BOOTP Retransmission Policy

BOOTP places all responsibility for reliable communication on the client. We know that because UDP uses IP for delivery, messages can be delayed, lost, delivered out of order, or duplicated. Furthermore, because IP does not provide a checksum for data, the UDP datagram could arrive with some bits corrupted. To guard against corruption, BOOTP requires that UDP use checksums. It also specifies that requests and replies should be sent with the *do not fragment* bit set to accommodate clients that have too little memory to reassemble datagrams. BOOTP is also constructed to allow multiple replies; it accepts and processes the first.

To handle datagram loss, BOOTP uses the conventional technique of *timeout and retransmission*. When the client transmits a request, it starts a timer. If no reply arrives before the timer expires, the client must retransmit the request. Of course, after a power failure all machines on a network will reboot simultaneously, possibly overrunning the BOOTP server(s) with requests. If all clients use exactly the same retransmission timeout, many or all of them will attempt to retransmit simultaneously. To avoid the resulting collisions, the BOOTP specification recommends using a random delay. In addition, the specification recommends starting with a random timeout value between *0* and *4* seconds, and doubling the timer after each retransmission. After the timer reaches a large value, *60* seconds, the client does not increase the timer, but continues to use randomization. Doubling the timeout after each retransmission keeps BOOTP from adding excessive traffic to a congested network; the randomization helps avoid simultaneous transmissions.

21.5 The BOOTP Message Format

To keep an implementation as simple as possible, BOOTP messages have fixed-length fields, and replies have the same format as requests. Although we said that clients and servers are programs, the BOOTP protocol uses the terms loosely, referring to the machine that sends a BOOTP request as the *client* and any machine that sends a reply as a *server*. Figure 21.1 shows the BOOTP message format.

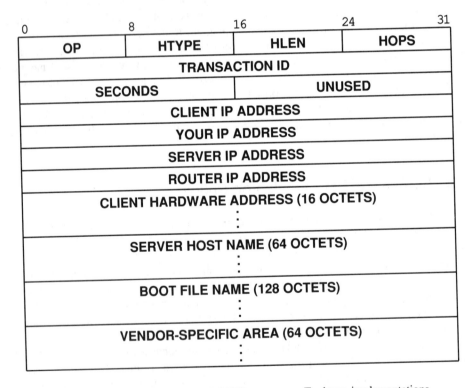

Figure 21.1 The format of a BOOTP message. To keep implementations small enough to fit in ROM, all fields have fixed length.

Field *OP* specifies whether the message is a request (*1*) or a reply (*2*). As in ARP, fields *HTYPE* and *HLEN* specify the network hardware type and length of the hardware address (e.g., Ethernet has type *1* and address length *6*)†. The client places *0* in the *HOPS* field. If it receives the request and decides to pass the request on to another machine (e.g., to allow bootstrapping across multiple routers), the BOOTP server increments the *HOPS* count. The *TRANSACTION ID* field contains an integer that diskless machines use to match responses with requests. The *SECONDS* field reports the number of seconds since the client started to boot.

The *CLIENT IP ADDRESS* field and all fields following it contain the most important information. To allow the greatest flexibility, clients fill in as much information as they know and leave remaining fields set to zero. For example, if a client knows the name or address of a specific server from which it wants information, it can fill in the *SERVER IP ADDRESS* or *SERVER HOST NAME* fields. If these fields are nonzero, only the server with matching name/address will answer the request; if they are zero, any server that receives the request will reply.

BOOTP can be used from a client that already knows its IP address (e.g., to obtain boot file information). A client that knows its IP address places it in the *CLIENT IP ADDRESS* field; other clients use zero. If the client's IP address is zero in the request, a server returns the client's IP address in the *YOUR IP ADDRESS* field.

21.6 The Two-Step Bootstrap Procedure

BOOTP uses a two-step bootstrap procedure. It does not provide clients with a memory image – it only provides the client with information needed to obtain an image. The client then uses a second protocol (e.g., TFTP from Chapter 24) to obtain the memory image. While the two-step procedure many seem unnecessary, it allows a clean separation of configuration and storage. A BOOTP server does not need to run on the same machine that stores memory images. In fact, the BOOTP server operates from a simple database that only knows the names of memory images.

Keeping configuration separate from storage is important because it allows administrators to configure sets of machines so they act identically or independently. The *BOOT FILE NAME* field of a BOOTP message illustrates the concept. Suppose an administrator has several workstations with different hardware architectures, and suppose that when users boot one of the workstations, they either choose to run UNIX or a local operating system. Because the set of workstations includes multiple hardware architectures, no single memory image will operate on all machines. To accommodate such diversity, BOOTP allows the *BOOT FILE NAME* field in a request to contain a generic name like "unix," which means, "I want to boot the UNIX operating system for this machine." The BOOTP server consults its configuration database to map the generic name into a specific file name that contains the UNIX memory image appropriate for the client hardware, and returns the specific (i.e., fully qualified) name in its reply. Of course, the configuration database also allows completely automatic bootstrapping in which the client places zeros in the *BOOT FILE NAME* field, and BOOTP selects a

---

†Values for the *HTYPE* field can be found in the latest Assigned Numbers RFC.

memory image for the machine. The advantage of the automatic approach is that it allows users to specify generic names that work on any machine; they do not need to remember specific file names or hardware architectures.

21.7 Vendor-Specific Field

The *VENDOR-SPECIFIC AREA* contains optional information to be passed from the server to the client. Although the syntax is intricate, it is not difficult. The first four octets of the field are called a *magic cookie* and define the format of remaining items; the standard format described here uses a magic cookie value of 99.130.83.99 (dotted decimal notation). A list of items follows the cookie, where each item contains a one-octet *type*, an optional one-octet *length*, and a multi-octet *value*. The standard defines the following types that have predetermined, fixed length values:

Item Type	Item Code	Value Length	Contents of Value
Padding	0	-	Zero - used only for padding
Subnet Mask	1	4	Subnet mask for local net
Time of Day	2	4	Time of day in universal time
End	255	-	End of item list

Figure 21.2 Items in the vendor information. The length field must exist for types *1* and *2*; it must not exist for types *0* and *255*.

Although a computer can obtain subnet mask information with an ICMP request, the standard now recommends that BOOTP servers supply the subnet mask in each reply to eliminate unnecessary ICMP messages.

Additional items in the *VENDOR-SPECIFIC AREA* all have a *type* octet, *length* octet, and *value*, as Figure 21.3 shows.

21.8 The Need For Dynamic Configuration

Like RARP, BOOTP was designed for a relatively static environment in which each host has a permanent network connection. A manager creates a BOOTP configuration file that specifies a set of BOOTP parameters for each host. The file does not change frequently because the configuration usually remains stable. Typically, a configuration continues unchanged for weeks.

With the advent of wireless networking and portable computers such as laptops and notebooks, it has become possible to move a computer from one location to another quickly and easily. BOOTP does not adapt to such situations because configuration information cannot be changed quickly. BOOTP only provides a static mapping from a host identifier to parameters for the host. Furthermore, a manager must enter a set of

Item Type	Item Code	Length Octet	Contents of Value
Routers	3	N	IP addresses of N/4 routers
Time Server	4	N	IP addresses of N/4 time servers
IEN116 Server	5	N	IP addresses of N/4 IEN116 servers
Domain Server	6	N	IP addresses of N/4 DNS servers
Log Server	7	N	IP addresses of N/4 log servers
Quote Server	8	N	IP addresses of N/4 quote servers
Lpr Servers	9	N	IP addresses of N/4 lpr servers
Impress	10	N	IP addresses of N/4 Impress servers
RLP Server	11	N	IP addresses of N/4 RLP servers
Hostname	12	N	N bytes of client host name
Boot Size	13	2	2-octet integer size of boot file
RESERVED	128-254	-	Reserved for site specific use

Figure 21.3 Types and contents of items in the *VENDOR-SPECIFIC AREA* of a BOOTP reply that have variable lengths.

parameters for each host, and then store the information in a BOOTP server configuration file – BOOTP does not include a way to dynamically assign values to individual machines. In particular, a manager must assign each host an IP address, and must configure the server so it understands the mapping from host identifier to IP address.

Static parameter assignment works well if computers remain at fixed locations and a manager has sufficient IP addresses to assign each computer a unique IP address. However, in cases where computers move frequently or the number of physical computers exceeds the number of available IP host addresses, static assignment incurs excessive overhead.

To understand how the number of computers can exceed the number of available IP addresses, consider a LAN in a college laboratory that has been assigned a class C address or a subnet of a class B address with 255 addresses. Assume that because the laboratory only has seats for 30 students, the college schedules labs at ten different times during the week to accommodate up to 300 students. Further assume that each student carries a personal notebook computer that they use in the lab. At any given time, the net has at most 30 active computers. However, because the network address can accommodate at most 255 hosts, a manager cannot assign a unique address to each computer. Thus, although resources such as physical connections limit the number of simultaneous connections, the number of potential computers that can use the facility is high. Clearly, a system is inadequate if it requires a manager to change the server's configuration file before a new computer can be added to the network and begin to communicate; an automated mechanism is needed.

21.9 Dynamic Host Configuration

To handle automated address assignment, the IETF has designed a new protocol. Known as the *Dynamic Host Configuration Protocol* (*DHCP*), the new protocol extends BOOTP in two ways. First, DHCP allows a computer to acquire all the configuration information it needs in a single message. For example, in addition to an IP address, a DHCP message can contain a subnet mask. Second, DHCP allows a computer to obtain an IP address quickly and dynamically. To use DHCP's dynamic address allocation mechanism, a manager must configure a DHCP server by supplying a set of IP addresses. Whenever a new computer connects to the network, the new computer contacts the server and requests an address. The server chooses one of the addresses the manager specified, and allocates that address to the computer.

To be completely general, DHCP allows three types of address assignment; a manager chooses how DHCP will respond for each network or for each host. Like BOOTP, DHCP allows *manual configuration* in which a manager can configure a specific address for a specific computer. DHCP also permits *automatic configuration* in which a manager allows a DHCP server to assign a permanent address when a computer first attaches to the network. Finally, DHCP permits completely *dynamic configuration* in which a server "loans" an address to a computer for a limited time.

Like BOOTP, DHCP uses the identity of the client to decide how to proceed. When a client contacts a DHCP server, the client sends an identifier, usually the client's hardware address. The server uses the client's identifier and the network to which the client has connected to determine how to assign the client and IP address. Thus, a manager has complete control over how addresses are assigned. A server can be configured to allocate addresses to specific computers statically (like BOOTP), while allowing other computers to obtain permanent or temporary addresses dynamically.

21.10 Dynamic IP Address Assignment

Dynamic address assignment is the most significant and novel aspect of DHCP. Unlike the static address assignment used in BOOTP, dynamic address assignment is not a one-to-one mapping, and the server does not need to know the identity of a client *a priori*. In particular, a DHCP server can be configured to permit an arbitrary computer to obtain an IP address and begin communicating. Thus, DHCP makes it possible to design systems that autoconfigure. After such a computer has been attached to a network, the computer uses DHCP to obtain an IP address, and then configures its TCP/IP software to use the address. Of course, autoconfiguration is subject to administrative restrictions – a manager decides whether each DHCP server allows autoconfiguration. To summarize:

> *Because it allows a host to obtain all the parameters needed for communication without manual intervention, DHCP permits autoconfiguration. Autoconfiguration is, of course, subject to administrative constraints.*

To make autoconfiguration possible, a DHCP server begins with a set of IP addresses that the network administrator gives the server to manage. The administrator specifies the rules by which the server operates. A DHCP client negotiates use of an address by exchanging messages with a server. In the exchange, the server provides an address for the client, and the client verifies that it accepts the address. Once a client has accepted an address, it can begin to use that address for communication.

Unlike static address assignment, which permanently allocates each IP address to a specific host, dynamic address assignment is temporary. We say that a DHCP server *leases* an address to a client for a finite period of time. The server specifies the lease period when it allocates the address. During the lease period, the server will not lease the same address to another client. At the end of the lease period, however, the client must renew the lease or stop using the address.

How long should a DHCP lease last? The optimal time for a lease depends on the particular network and the needs of a particular host. For example, to guarantee that addresses can be recycled quickly, computers on a network used by students in a university laboratory might have a short lease period (e.g., one hour). By contrast, a corporate network might use a lease period of one day or one week. To accommodate all possible environments, DHCP does not specify a fixed constant for the lease period. Instead, the protocol allows a client to request a specific lease period, and allows a server to inform the client of the lease period it grants. Thus, a manager can decide how long each server should allocate an address to a client. In the extreme, DHCP reserves a value for *infinity* to permit a lease to last arbitrarily long like the permanent address assignments used in BOOTP.

21.11 Obtaining Multiple Addresses

A multi-homed computer connects to more than one network. When such a computer boots, it may need to obtain configuration information for each of its interfaces. Like a BOOTP message, a DHCP message only provides information about one interface. A computer with multiple interfaces must handle each interface separately. Thus, although we will describe DHCP as if a computer needs only one address, the reader must remember that each interface of a multi-homed computer may be at a different point in the protocol.

Both BOOTP and DHCP use the notion of *relay agent* to permit a computer to contact a server on a nonlocal network. When a relay agent receives a broadcast request from a client, it forwards the request to a server and then returns the reply from the server to the host. Relay agents can complicate multi-homed configuration because a server may receive multiple requests from the same computer. However, although both BOOTP and DHCP use the term *client identifier*, we assume that a multihomed client sends a value that identifies a particular interface (e.g., a unique hardware address). Thus, a server will always be able to distinguish among requests from a multi-homed host, even when the server receives such requests via a relay agent.

21.12 Address Acquisition States

When it uses DHCP to obtain an IP address, a client is in one of six states. The state transition diagram in Figure 21.4 shows events and messages that cause a client to change state.

When a client first boots, it enters the *INITIALIZE* state. To start acquiring an IP address, the client first contacts all DHCP servers in the local net. To do so, the client broadcasts a *DHCPDISCOVER* message and moves to the state labeled *SELECT*. Because the protocol is an extension of BOOTP, the client sends the *DHCPDISCOVER* message in a UDP datagram with the destination port set to the BOOTP port (i.e., port *67*). All DHCP servers on the local net receive the message, and those servers that have been programmed to respond to the particular client send a *DHCPOFFER* message. Thus, a client may receive zero or more responses.

While in state *SELECT*, the client collects *DHCPOFFER* responses from DHCP servers. Each offer contains configuration information for the client along with an IP address that the server is offering to lease to the client. The client must choose one of the responses (e.g., the first to arrive), and negotiate with the server for a lease. To do so, the client sends the server a *DHCPREQUEST* message, and enters the *REQUEST* state. To acknowledge receipt of the request and start the lease, the server responds by sending a *DHCPACK*. Arrival of the acknowledgement causes the client to move to the *BOUND* state, where the client proceeds to use the address. To summarize:

> *To use DHCP, a host becomes a client by broadcasting a message to all servers on the local network. The host then collects offers from servers, selects one of the offers, and verifies acceptance with the server.*

21.13 Early Lease Termination

We think of the *BOUND* state as the normal state of operation; a client typically remains in the *BOUND* state while it uses the IP address it has acquired. If a client has secondary storage (e.g., a local disk), the client can store the IP address it was assigned, and request the same address when it restarts again. In some cases, however, a client in the *BOUND* state may discover it no longer needs an IP address. For example, suppose a user attaches a portable computer to a network, uses DHCP to acquire an IP address, and then uses TCP/IP to read electronic mail. The user may not know how long reading mail will require, or the portable computer may allow the server to choose a lease period. In any case, DHCP specifies a minimum lease period of one hour. If after obtaining an IP address, the user discovers that no e-mail messages are waiting to be read, the user may choose to shutdown the portable computer and move to another location.

When it no longer needs a lease, DHCP allows a client to terminate a lease without waiting for the lease to expire. Such termination is helpful in cases where neither the client nor the server can determine an appropriate lease duration at the time the lease is

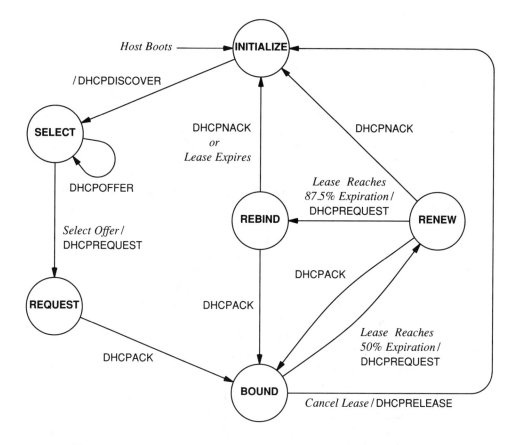

Figure 21.4 The six main states of a DHCP client and transitions among
them. Each label on a transition lists the incoming message or
event that causes the transmission, followed by a slash and the
message the client sends.

granted because it allows a server to choose a reasonably long lease period. Early termination is especially important if the number of IP addresses a server has available is
much smaller than the number of computers that attach to the network. If each client
terminates its lease as soon as the IP address is no longer needed, the server will be able
to assign the address to another client.

   To terminate a lease early, a client sends a *DHCPRELEASE* message to the server.
Releasing an address is a final action that prevents the client from using the address
further. Thus, after transmitting the release message, the client must not send any other
datagrams that use the address. In terms of the state transition diagram of Figure 21.4,
a host that sends a *DHCPRELEASE* leaves the *BOUND* state, and must start at the *INI-
TIALIZE* state again before it can use IP.

21.14 Lease Renewal States

We said that when it acquires an address, a DHCP client moves to the *BOUND* state. Upon entering the *BOUND* state, the client sets three timers that control lease renewal, rebinding, and expiration. A DHCP server can specify explicit values for the timers when it allocates an address to the client; if the server does not specify timer values, the client uses defaults. The default value for the first timer is one-half of the total lease time. When the first timer expires, the client must attempt to renew its lease. To request a renewal, the client sends a *DHCPREQUEST* message to the server form which the lease was obtained. The client then moves to the *RENEW* state to await a response. The *DHCPREQUEST* contains the IP address the client is currently using, and asks the server to extend the lease on the address. As in the initial lease negotiation, a client can request a period for the extension, but the server ultimately controls the renewal. A server can respond to a client's renewal request in one of two ways: it can instruct the client to stop using the address or it can approve continued use. If it approves, the server sends a *DHCPACK*, which causes the client to return to the *BOUND* state and continue using the address. The *DHCPACK* can also contain new values for the client's timers. If a server disapproves of continued use, the server sends a *DHCPNACK* (negative acknowledgement), which causes the client to stop using the address immediately and return to the *INITIALIZE* state.

After sending a *DHCPREQUEST* message that requests an extension on its lease, a client remains in state *RENEW* awaiting a response. If no response arrives, the server that granted the lease is either down or unreachable. To handle the situation, DHCP relies on a second timer, which was set when the client entered the *BOUND* state. The second timer expires after *87.5%* of the lease period, and causes the client to move from state *RENEW* to state *REBIND*. When making the transition, the client assumes the old DHCP server is unavailable, and begins broadcasting a *DHCPREQUEST* message to any server on the local net. Any server configured to provide service to the client can respond positively (i.e., to extend the lease), or negatively (i.e. to deny further use of the IP address). If it receives a positive response, the client returns to the *BOUND* state, and resets the two timers. If it receives a negative response, the client must move to the *INITIALIZE* state, must immediately stop using the IP address, and must acquire a new IP address before it can continue to use IP.

After moving to the *REBIND* state, a client will have asked the original server plus all servers on the local net for a lease extension. In the rare case that a client does not receive a response from any server before its third timer expires, the lease expires. The client must stop using the IP address, must move back to the *INITIALIZE* state, and begin acquiring a new address.

21.15 DHCP Message Format

As Figure 21.5 illustrates, DHCP uses the BOOTP message format, but modifies the contents and meanings of some fields.

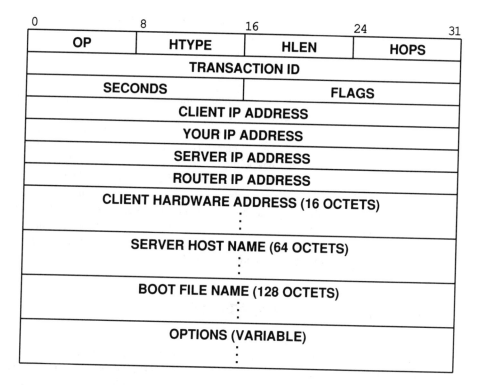

Figure 21.5 The format of a DHCP message, which is an extension of a BOOTP message. The options field is variable length; a client must be prepared to accept at least 312 octets of options.

As the figure shows, most of the fields in a DHCP message are identical to fields in a BOOTP message. In fact, the two protocols are compatible; a DHCP server can be programmed to answer BOOTP requests. However, DHCP changes the meaning of two fields. First, DHCP interprets BOOTP's *UNUSED* field as a 16-bit *FLAGS* field. In fact, Figure 21.6 shows that only the high-order bit of the *FLAGS* field has been assigned a meaning.

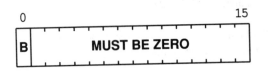

Figure 21.6 The format of the 16-bit *FLAGS* field in a DHCP message. The leftmost bit is interpreted as a broadcast request; all others bits must be set to zero.

Because the DHCP request message contains the client's hardware address, a DHCP server normally sends its responses to the client using hardware unicast. A client sets the high-order bit in the *FLAGS* field to request that the server respond using hardware broadcast instead of hardware unicast. To understand why a client might choose a broadcast response, recall that while a client communicates with a DHCP server, it does not yet have an IP address. If a datagram arrives via hardware unicast and the destination address does not match the computer's address, IP can discard the datagram. However, IP is required to accept and handle any datagram sent to the IP broadcast address. To ensure IP software accepts and delivers DHCP messages that arrive before the machine's IP address has been configured, a DHCP client can request that the server send responses using IP broadcast.

21.16 DHCP Options And Message Type

Surprisingly, DHCP does not add new fixed fields to the BOOTP message format, nor does it change the meaning of most fields. For example, the *OP* field in a DHCP message contains the same values as the *OP* field in a BOOTP message: the message is either a boot request (*1*) or a boot reply (*2*). To encode information such as the lease duration, DHCP uses *options*. In particular, Figure 21.7 illustrates the *DHCP message type* option used to specify which DHCP message is being sent.

The options field has the same format as the *VENDOR SPECIFIC AREA*, and DHCP honors all the vendor specific information items defined for BOOTP. As in BOOTP, each option consists of a 1-octet code field and a 1-octet length field followed by octets of data that comprise the option. As the figure shows, the option used to specify a DHCP message type consists of exactly three octets. The first octet contains the code *53*, the second contains the length *1*, and the third contains a value used to identify one of the possible DHCP messages.

```
0                    8                   16                  23
┌─────────────────┬─────────────────┬─────────────────┐
│    CODE (53)    │   LENGTH (1)    │   TYPE (1 - 7)  │
└─────────────────┴─────────────────┴─────────────────┘
```

TYPE FIELD	Corresponding DHCP Message Type
1	DHCPDISCOVER
2	DHCPOFFER
3	DHCPREQUEST
4	DHCPDECLINE
5	DHCPACK
6	DHCPNACK
7	DHCPRELEASE

Figure 21.7 The format of a DHCP message type option used to specify the DHCP message being sent. The table lists possible values of the third octet and their meaning.

21.17 Option Overload

Fields *SERVER HOST NAME* and *BOOT FILE NAME* in the DHCP message header each occupy many octets. If a given message does not contain information in either of those fields, the space is wasted. To allow a DHCP server to use the two fields for other options, DHCP defines an *Option Overload* option. When present, the overload option tells a receiver to ignore the usual meaning of the *SERVER HOST NAME* and *BOOT FILE NAME* fields, and look for options in the fields instead.

21.18 DHCP And Domain Names†

Although it can allocate an IP address to a computer on demand, DHCP does not completely automate all the procedures required to attach a permanent host to an internet. In particular, DHCP does not interact with the domain name system. Thus, the binding between a host name and the IP address DHCP assigns the host must be managed independently.

What name should a host receive when it obtains an IP address from DHCP? Conceptually, there are three possibilities. First, the host does not receive a name. Although it is possible to run client software on a host without a name, using an unnamed computer can be inconvenient. Second, the host is automatically assigned a name along with an IP address. This method is currently popular because names can be preallocated, and no change is required to the DNS. For example, a system administrator can configure the local domain name server to have a host name for each IP address

---

†Chapter 22 considers the Domain Name System in detail.

DHCP manages. Once it has been installed in DNS, the name-to-address binding remains static. The chief disadvantage of a static binding is that the host receives a new name whenever it receives a new address (e.g., if a host moves from one physical net to another). Third, the host can be assigned a permanent name that remains unchanged. Keeping a permanent host name is convenient because the computer can always be reached via one name, independent of the computer's current location.

Additional mechanisms are needed to support permanent host names. In particular, permanent host names require coordination between DHCP and DNS. A DNS server must change the name-to-address binding whenever a host receives an IP address, and must remove the binding when a lease expires. Although, an IETF working group is currently considering how DHCP should interact with the domain name system, there is currently no protocol for dynamic DNS update. Thus, until a dynamic update mechanism is developed, there is no protocol that maintains permanent host names while allowing DHCP to change IP addresses.

21.19 Summary

The BOOTstrap Protocol, BOOTP, provides an alternative to RARP for a computer that needs to determine its IP address. BOOTP is more general than RARP because it uses UDP, making it possible to extend bootstrapping across a router. BOOTP also allows a machine to determine a router address, a (file) server address, and the name of a program the computer should run. Finally, BOOTP allows administrators to establish a configuration database that maps a generic name, like ''unix,'' into the fully qualified file name that contains a memory image appropriate for the client hardware.

BOOTP is designed to be small and simple enough to reside in a bootstrap ROM. The client uses the limited broadcast address to communicate with the server, and takes responsibility for retransmitting requests if the server does not respond. Retransmission uses an exponential backoff policy similar to Ethernet to avoid congestion.

Designed as a successor to BOOTP, the Dynamic Host Configuration Protocol (DHCP) extends BOOTP in several ways. Most important, DHCP permits a server to allocate IP addresses automatically or dynamically. Dynamic allocation is necessary for environments such as a wireless network where computers can attach and detach quickly. To use DHCP, a computer becomes a client. The computer broadcasts a request for DHCP servers, selects one of the offers it receives, and exchanges messages with the server to obtain a lease on the advertised IP address.

When a client obtains an IP address, the client starts three timers. After the first timer expires, the client attempts to renew its lease. If a second timer expires before renewal completes, the client attempts to rebind its address from any server. If the final timer expires before a lease has been renewed, the client stops using the IP address and returns to the initial state to acquire a new address. A finite state machine explains lease acquisition and renewal.

FOR FURTHER STUDY

BOOTP is a standard protocol in the TCP/IP suite. Further details can be found in Croft and Gilmore [RFC 951], which compares BOOTP to RARP and serves as the official standard. Reynolds [RFC 1084] tells how to interpret the vendor-specific area, and Braden [RFC 1123] recommends using the vendor-specific area to pass the subnet mask.

Droms [RFC 1541] gives the latest specification for DHCP, including a detailed description of state transitions; another revision is expected soon. A related document, Alexander [RFC 1533], specifies the encoding of DHCP options and BOOTP vendor extensions. Finally, Droms [RFC 1534] discusses the interoperability of BOOTP and DHCP.

EXERCISES

21.1 BOOTP does not contain an explicit field for returning the time of day from the server to the client, but makes it part of the (optional) vendor-specific information. Should the time be included in the required fields? Why or why not?

21.2 Argue that separation of configuration and storage of memory images is *not* good. (See RFC 951 for hints.)

21.3 The BOOTP message format is inconsistent because it has two fields for client IP address and one for the name of the boot image. If the client leaves its IP address field empty, the server returns the client's IP address in the second field. If the client leaves the boot file name field empty, the server *replaces* it with an explicit name. Why?

21.4 Read the standard to find out how clients and servers use the *HOPS* field.

21.5 When a BOOTP client receives a reply via hardware broadcast, how does it know whether the reply is intended for another BOOTP client on the same physical net?

21.6 When a machine obtains its subnet mask with BOOTP instead of ICMP, it places less load on *other* host computers. Explain.

21.7 Read the standard to find out how a DHCP client and server can agree on a lease duration without having synchronized clocks.

21.8 Consider a host that has a disk and uses DHCP to obtain an IP address. If the host stores its address on disk along with the date the lease expires, and then reboots within the lease period, can it use the address? Why or why not?

21.9 DHCP mandates a minimum address lease of one hour. Can you imagine a situation in which DHCP's minimum lease causes inconvenience? Explain.

21.10 Read the RFC to find out how DHCP specifies renewal and rebinding timers. Should a server ever set one without the other? Why or why not?

21.11 The state transition diagram does not show retransmission. Read the standard to find out how many times a client should retransmit a request.

21.12 Can DHCP guarantee that a client is not ''spoofing'' (i.e., can DHCP guarantee that it will not send configuration information for host *A* to host *B*)? Does the answer differ for BOOTP? Why or why not?

21.13 DHCP specifies that a client must be prepared to handle at least *312* octets of options. How did the number *312* arise?

21.14 Can a computer that uses DHCP to obtain an IP address operate a server? If so, how does a client reach the server?

22

The Domain Name System (DNS)

22.1 Introduction

The protocols described in earlier chapters use 32-bit integers called Internet Protocol addresses (IP addresses) to identify machines. Although such addresses provide a convenient, compact representation for specifying the source and destination in packets sent across an internet, users prefer to assign machines pronounceable, easily remembered names.

This chapter considers a scheme for assigning meaningful high-level names to a large set of machines, and discusses a mechanism that maps between high-level machine names and IP addresses. It considers both the translation from high-level names to IP addresses and the translation from IP addresses to high-level machine names. The naming scheme is interesting for two reasons. First, it has been used to assign machine names throughout the global Internet. Second, because it uses a geographically distributed set of servers to map names to addresses, the implementation of the name mapping mechanism provides a large scale example of the client–server paradigm described in Chapter 19.

22.2 Names For Machines

The earliest computer systems forced users to understand numeric addresses for objects like system tables and peripheral devices. Timesharing systems advanced computing by allowing users to invent meaningful symbolic names for both physical objects (e.g., peripheral devices) and abstract objects (e.g., files). A similar pattern has emerged in computer networking. Early systems supported point-to-point connections between computers and used low-level hardware addresses to specify machines. Internetworking introduced universal addressing as well as protocol software to map universal addresses into low-level hardware addresses. Because most computing environments contain multiple machines, users need meaningful, symbolic names to identify them.

Early machine names reflected the small environment in which they were chosen. It was quite common for a site with a handful of machines to choose names based on the machines' purposes. For example, machines often had names like *research*, *production*, *accounting*, and *development*. Users find such names preferable to cumbersome hardware addresses.

Although the distinction between *address* and *name* is intuitively appealing, it is artificial. Any *name* is merely an identifier that consists of a sequence of characters chosen from a finite alphabet. Names are only useful if the system can efficiently map them to the object they denote. Thus, we think of an IP address as a *low-level name*, and we say that users prefer *high-level names* for machines.

The form of high-level names is important because it determines how names are translated to lower-level names or bound to objects, as well as how name assignments are authorized. When only a few machines interconnect, choosing names is easy, and any form will suffice. On the Internet, to which over four million machines connect, choosing symbolic names becomes difficult. For example, when its main departmental computer was connected to the Internet in 1980, the Computer Science Department at Purdue University chose the name *purdue* to identify the connected machine. The list of potential conflicts contained only a few dozen names. By mid 1986, the official list of hosts on the Internet contained 3100 officially registered names and 6500 official aliases†. Although the list was growing rapidly in the 1980s, most sites had additional machines (e.g., personal computers) that were not registered.

22.3 Flat Namespace

The original set of machine names used throughout the Internet formed a *flat namespace* in which each name consisted of a sequence of characters without any further structure. In the original scheme, a central site, the Network Information Center (NIC), administered the namespace and determined whether a new name was appropriate (i.e., it prohibited obscene names or new names that conflicted with existing names). Later, the NIC was replaced by the INTERnet Network Information Center (*INTER-NIC*).

---

†By 1990, more than 137,000 Internet hosts had names, and by 1995 the number exceeded 4 million.

The chief advantage of a flat namespace is that names are convenient and short; the chief disadvantage is that a flat namespace cannot generalize to large sets of machines for both technical and administrative reasons. First, because names are drawn from a single set of identifiers, the potential for conflict increases as the number of sites increases. Second, because authority for adding new names must rest at a single site, the administrative workload at that central site also increases with the number of sites. To understand the severity of the problem, imagine a rapidly growing internet with thousands of sites, each of which has hundreds of individual personal computers and workstations. Every time someone acquires and connects a new personal computer, its name must be approved by the central authority. Third, because the name-to-address bindings change frequently, the cost of maintaining correct copies of the entire list at each site is high and increases as the number of sites increases. Alternatively, if the name database resides at a single site, network traffic to that site increases with the number of sites.

22.4 Hierarchical Names

How can a naming system accommodate a large, rapidly expanding set of names without requiring a central site to administer it? The answer lies in decentralizing the naming mechanism by delegating authority for parts of the namespace and distributing responsibility for the mapping between names and addresses. TCP/IP internets use such a scheme. Before examining the details of the TCP/IP scheme, we will consider the motivation and intuition behind it.

The partitioning of a namespace must be defined in a way that supports efficient name mapping and guarantees autonomous control of name assignment. Optimizing only for efficient mapping can lead to solutions that retain a flat namespace and reduce traffic by dividing the names among multiple mapping machines. Optimizing only for administrative ease can lead to solutions that make delegation of authority easy but name mapping expensive or complex.

To understand how the namespace should be divided, consider the internal structure of large organizations. At the top, a chief executive has overall responsibility. Because the chief executive cannot oversee everything, the organization may be partitioned into divisions, with an executive in charge of each division. The chief executive grants each division autonomy within specified limits. More to the point, the executive in charge of a particular division can hire or fire employees, assign offices, and delegate authority, without obtaining direct permission from the chief executive.

Besides making it easy to delegate authority, the hierarchy of a large organization introduces autonomous operation. For example, when an office˙worker needs information like the telephone number of a new employee, he or she begins by asking local clerical workers (who may contact clerical workers in other divisions). The point is that although authority always passes down the corporate hierarchy, information can flow across the hierarchy from one office to another.

22.5 Delegation Of Authority For Names

A hierarchical naming scheme works like the management of a large organization. The namespace is *partitioned* at the top level, and authority for names in subdivisions is passed to designated agents. For example, one might choose to partition the namespace based on *site name* and to delegate to each site responsibility for maintaining names within its partition. The topmost level of the hierarchy divides the namespace and delegates authority for each division; it need not be bothered by changes within a division.

The syntax of hierarchically assigned names often reflects the hierarchical delegation of authority used to assign them. As an example, consider a namespace with names of the form:

$$local.site$$

where *site* is the site name authorized by the central authority, *local* is the part of a name controlled by the site, and the period† ("**.**") is a delimiter used to separate them. When the topmost authority approves adding a new site, X, it adds X to the list of valid sites and delegates to site X authority for all names that end in "*.X*".

22.6 Subset Authority

In a hierarchical namespace, authority may be further subdivided at each level. In our example of partition by sites, the site itself may consist of several administrative groups, and the site authority may choose to subdivide its namespace among the groups. The idea is to keep subdividing the namespace until each subdivision is small enough to be manageable.

Syntactically, subdividing the namespace introduces another partition of the name. For example, adding a *group* subdivision to names already partitioned by site produces the following name syntax:

$$local.group.site$$

Because the topmost level delegates authority, group names do not have to agree among all sites. A university site might choose group names like *engineering*, *science*, and *arts*, while a corporate site might choose group names like *production*, *accounting*, and *personnel*.

The U.S. telephone system provides another example of a hierarchical naming syntax. The 10 digits of a phone number have been partitioned into a 3-digit *area code*, 3-digit *exchange*, and 4-digit *subscriber number* within the exchange. Each exchange has authority for assigning subscriber numbers within its piece of the namespace. Although it is possible to group arbitrary subscribers into exchanges and to group arbitrary exchanges into area codes, the assignment of telephone numbers is not capricious; they are carefully chosen to make it easy to route phone calls across the telephone network.

---

†In domain names, the period delimiter is pronounced "dot."

The telephone example is important because it illustrates a key distinction between the hierarchical naming scheme used in a TCP/IP internet and other hierarchies: partitioning the set of machines owned by an organization along lines of authority does not necessarily imply partitioning by physical location. For example, it could be that at some university, a single building houses the mathematics department as well as the computer science department. It might even turn out that although the machines from these two groups fall under completely separate administrative domains, they connect to the same physical network. It also may happen that a single group owns machines on several physical networks. For these reasons, the TCP/IP naming scheme allows arbitrary delegation of authority for the hierarchical namespace without regard to physical connections. The concept can be summarized:

> *In a TCP/IP internet, hierarchical machine names are assigned according to the structure of organizations that obtain authority for parts of the namespace, not necessarily according to the structure of the physical network interconnections.*

Of course, at many sites the organizational hierarchy corresponds with the structure of physical network interconnections. At a large university, for example, most departments have their own local area network. If the department is assigned part of the naming hierarchy, all machines that have names in its part of the hierarchy will also connect to a single physical network.

22.7 TCP/IP Internet Domain Names

The mechanism that implements a machine name hierarchy for TCP/IP internets is called the *Domain Name System (DNS)*. DNS has two, conceptually independent aspects. The first is abstract: it specifies the name syntax and rules for delegating authority over names. The second is concrete: it specifies the implementation of a distributed computing system that efficiently maps names to addresses. This section considers the name syntax, and later sections examine the implementation.

The domain name system uses a hierarchical naming scheme known as *domain names*. As in our earlier examples, a domain name consists of a sequence of subnames separated by a delimiter character, the period. In our examples we said that individual sections of the name might represent sites or groups, but the domain system simply calls each section a *label*. Thus, the domain name

cs.purdue.edu

contains three *labels*: *cs, purdue*, and *edu*. Any suffix of a label in a domain name is also called a *domain*. In the above example the lowest level domain is *cs.purdue.edu*, (the domain name for the Computer Science Department at Purdue University), the second level domain is *purdue.edu* (the domain name for Purdue University), and the top-level domain is *edu* (the domain name for educational institutions). As the example shows, domain names are written with the local label first and the top domain last. As we will see, writing them in this order makes it possible to compress messages that contain multiple domain names.

22.8 Official And Unofficial Internet Domain Names

In theory, the domain name standard specifies an abstract hierarchical namespace with arbitrary values for labels. Because the domain system dictates only the form of names and not their actual values, it is possible for any group that builds an instance of the domain system to choose labels for all parts of its hierarchy. For example, a private company can establish a domain hierarchy in which the top-level labels specify corporate subsidiaries, the next level labels specify corporate divisions, and the lowest level labels specify departments.

However, most users of the domain technology follow the hierarchical labels used by the official Internet domain system. There are two reasons. First, as we will see, the Internet scheme is both comprehensive and flexible. It can accommodate a wide variety of organizations, and allows each group to choose between geographical or organizational naming hierarchies. Second, most sites follow the Internet scheme so they can attach their TCP/IP installations to the global Internet without changing names. Because the Internet naming scheme dominates almost all uses of the domain name system, examples throughout the remainder of this chapter have labels taken from the Internet naming hierarchy. Readers should remember that, although they are most likely to encounter these particular labels, the domain name system technology can be used with other labels if desired.

The Internet authority has chosen to partition its top level into the domains listed in Figure 22.1.

Domain Name	Meaning
COM	Commercial organizations
EDU	Educational institutions
GOV	Government institutions
MIL	Military groups
NET	Major network support centers
ORG	Organizations other than those above
ARPA	Temporary ARPANET domain (obsolete)
INT	International organizations
country code	Each country (geographic scheme)

Figure 22.1 The top-level Internet domains and their meanings. Although labels are shown in upper case, domain name system comparisons are insensitive to case, so *EDU* is equivalent to *edu*.

Conceptually, the top-level names permit two completely different naming hierarchies: geographic and organizational. The geographic scheme divides the universe of machines by country. Machines in the United States fall under the top-level domain *US*; when a foreign country wants to register machines in the domain name system, the central authority assigns the country a new top-level domain with the country's international standard 2-letter identifier as its label. The authority for the US domain has chosen to divide it into one second-level domain per state. For example, the domain for the state of Virginia is

$$va.us$$

As an alternative to the geographic hierarchy, the top-level domains also allow organizations to be grouped by organizational type. When an organization wants to participate in the domain naming system, it chooses how it wishes to be registered and requests approval. The central authority reviews the application and assigns the organization a subdomain† under one of the existing top-level domains. For example, it is possible for a university to register itself as a second-level domain under *EDU* (the usual practice), or to register itself under the state and country in which it is located. So far, few organizations have chosen the geographic hierarchy; most prefer to register under *COM, EDU, MIL,* or *GOV*. There are two reasons. First, geographic names are longer and therefore more difficult to type. Second, geographic names are much more difficult to discover or guess. For example, Purdue University is located in West Lafayette, Indiana. While a user could easily guess an organizational name, like *purdue.edu*, a geographic name is often difficult to guess because it is usually an abbreviation, like *laf.in.us*.

Another example may help clarify the relationship between the naming hierarchy and authority for names. A machine named *xinu* in the Computer Science Department at Purdue University has the official domain name

$$xinu.cs.purdue.edu$$

The machine name was approved and registered by the local network manager in the Computer Science Department. The department manager had previously obtained authority for the subdomain *cs.purdue.edu* from a university network authority, who had obtained permission to manage the subdomain *purdue.edu* from the Internet authority. The Internet authority retains control of the *edu* domain, so new universities can only be added with its permission. Similarly, the university network manager at Purdue University retains authority for the *purdue.edu* subdomain, so new third-level domains may only be added with the manager's permission.

Figure 22.2 illustrates a small part of the Internet domain name hierarchy. As the figure shows, Digital Equipment Corporation, a commercial organization, registered as *dec.com*, Purdue University registered as *purdue.edu*, and the National Science Foundation, a government agency, registered as *nsf.gov*. In contrast, the Corporation for National Research Initiatives chose to register under the geographic hierarchy as *cnri.reston.va.us‡*.

---

†The standard does not define the term "subdomain." We have chosen to use it because its analogy to "subset" helps clarify the relationship among domains.

‡Interestingly, CNRI also registered using the name *nri.reston.va.us*.

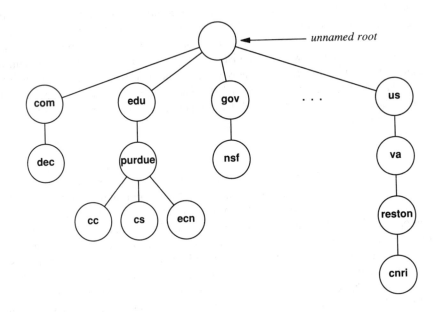

unnamed root

Figure 22.2 A small part of the Internet domain name hierarchy (tree). In practice, the tree is broad and flat; most host entries appear by the fifth level.

22.9 Items Named And Syntax Of Names

The domain name system is quite general because it allows multiple naming hierarchies to be embedded in one system. To allow clients to distinguish among multiple kinds of entries, each named item stored in the system is assigned a *type* that specifies whether it is the address of a machine, a mailbox, a user, and so on. When a client asks the domain system to resolve a name, it must specify the type of answer desired. For example, when an electronic mail application uses the domain system to resolve a name, it specifies that the answer should be the address of a *mail exchanger*. A remote login application specifies that it seeks a machine's IP address. It is important to understand the following:

> *A given name may map to more than one item in the domain system. The client specifies the type of object desired when resolving a name, and the server returns objects of that type.*

In addition to specifying the type of answer sought, the domain system allows the client to specify the protocol family to use. The domain system partitions the entire set of names by *class*, allowing a single database to store mappings for multiple protocol suites†.

_____

†In practice, few domain servers use multiple protocol suites.

The syntax of a name does not determine what type of object it names or the class of protocol suite. In particular, the number of labels in a name does not determine whether the name refers to an individual object (machine) or a domain. Thus, in our example, it is possible to have a machine named

gwen.purdue.edu

even though

cs.purdue.edu

names a subdomain. We can summarize this important point:

One cannot distinguish the names of subdomains from the names of individual objects or the type of an object using only the domain name syntax.

22.10 Mapping Domain Names To Addresses

In addition to the rules for name syntax and delegation of authority, the domain name scheme includes an efficient, reliable, general purpose, distributed system for mapping names to addresses. The system is distributed in the technical sense, meaning that a set of servers operating at multiple sites cooperatively solve the mapping problem. It is efficient in the sense that most names can be mapped locally; only a few require internet traffic. It is general purpose because it is not restricted to machine names (although we will use that example for now). Finally, it is reliable in that no single machine failure will prevent the system from operating correctly.

The domain mechanism for mapping names to addresses consists of independent, cooperative systems called *name servers*. A name server is a server program that supplies name-to-address translation, mapping from domain names to IP addresses. Often, server software executes on a dedicated processor, and the machine itself is called the name server. The client software, called a *name resolver*, uses one or more name servers when translating a name.

The easiest way to understand how domain servers work is to imagine them arranged in a tree structure that corresponds to the naming hierarchy, as Figure 22.3 illustrates. The root of the tree is a server that recognizes the top-level domains and knows which server resolves each domain. Given a name to resolve, the root can choose the correct server for that name. At the next level, a set of name servers each provide answers for one top-level domain (e.g., *edu*). A server at this level knows which servers can resolve each of the subdomains under its domain. At the third level of the tree, name servers provide answers for subdomains (e.g., *purdue* under *edu*). The conceptual tree continues with one server at each level for which a subdomain has been defined.

Links in the conceptual tree do not indicate physical network connections. Instead, they show which other name servers a given server knows and contacts. The servers themselves may be located at arbitrary locations on an internet. Thus, the tree of servers is an abstraction that uses an internet for communication.

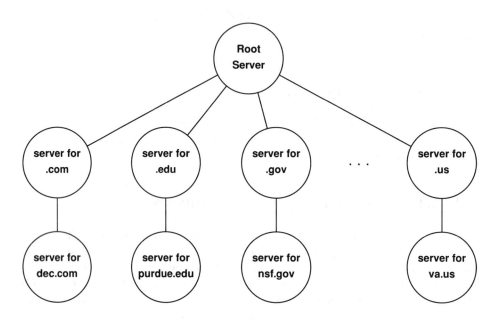

Figure 22.3 The conceptual arrangement of domain name servers in a tree that corresponds to the naming hierarchy. In theory, each server knows the addresses of all lower-level servers for all sub-domains within the domain it handles.

If servers in the domain system worked exactly as our simplistic model suggests, the relationship between connectivity and authorization would be quite simple. When authority was granted for a subdomain, the organization requesting it would need to es-tablish a domain name server for that subdomain and link it into the tree.

In practice, the relationship between the naming hierarchy and the tree of servers is not as simple as our model implies. The tree of servers has few levels because a single physical server can contain all of the information for large parts of the naming hierar-chy. In particular, organizations often collect information from all of their subdomains into a single server. Figure 22.4 shows a more realistic organization of servers for the naming hierarchy of Figure 22.2.

A root server contains information about the root and top-level domains, and each organization uses a single server for its names. Because the tree of servers is shallow, at most two servers need to be contacted to resolve a name like *xinu.cs.purdue.edu*:

the root server and the server for domain *purdue.edu* (i.e., the root server knows which server handles *purdue.edu*, and the entire domain information for Purdue resides in one server).

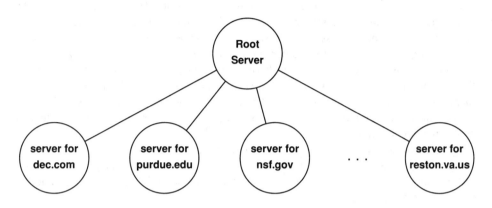

Figure 22.4 A realistic organization of servers for the naming hierarchy of Figure 22.2. Because the tree is broad and flat, few servers need to be contacted when resolving a name.

22.11 Domain Name Resolution

Although the conceptual tree makes understanding the relationship between servers easy, it hides several subtle details. Looking at the name resolution algorithm will help explain them. Conceptually, domain name resolution proceeds top-down, starting with the root name server and proceeding to servers located at the leaves of the tree. There are two ways to use the domain name system: by contacting name servers one at a time or asking the name server system to perform the complete translation. In either case, the client software forms a domain name query that contains the name to be resolved, a declaration of the class of the name, the type of answer desired, and a code that specifies whether the name server should translate the name completely. It sends the query to a name server for resolution.

When a domain name server receives a query, it checks to see if the name lies in the subdomain for which it is an authority. If so, it translates the name to an address according to its database, and appends an answer to the query before sending it back to the client. If the name server cannot resolve the name completely, it checks to see what type of interaction the client specified. If the client requested complete translation (*recursive resolution*, in domain name terminology), the server contacts a domain name server that can resolve the name and returns the answer to the client. If the client requested non-recursive resolution (*iterative resolution*), the name server cannot supply an answer. It generates a reply that specifies the name server the client should contact next to resolve the name.

How does a client find a name server at which to begin the search? How does a name server find other name servers that can answer questions when it cannot? The answers are simple. A client must know how to contact at least one name server. To ensure that a domain name server can reach others, the domain system requires that each server know the address of at least one root server†. In addition, a server may know the address of a server for the domain immediately above it (called the *parent*).

Domain name servers use a well-known protocol port for all communication, so clients know how to communicate with a server once they know the IP address of the machine in which the server executes. There is no standard way for hosts to locate a machine in the local environment on which a name server runs; that is left to whoever designs the client software‡.

In some systems, the address of the machine that supplies domain name service is bound into application programs at compile time, while in others, the address is configured into the operating system at startup. In others, the administrator places the address of a server in a file on secondary storage.

22.12 Efficient Translation

Although it may seem natural to resolve queries by working down the tree of name servers, it can lead to inefficiencies for three reasons. First, most name resolution refers to local names, those found within the same subdivision of the namespace as the machine from which the request originates. Tracing a path through the hierarchy to contact the local authority would be inefficient. Second, if each name resolution always started by contacting the topmost level of the hierarchy, the machine at that point would become overloaded. Third, failure of machines at the topmost levels of the hierarchy would prevent name resolution, even if the local authority could resolve the name. The telephone number hierarchy mentioned earlier helps explain. Although telephone numbers are assigned hierarchically, they are resolved in a bottom-up fashion. Because the majority of telephone calls are local, they can be resolved by the local exchange without searching the hierarchy. Furthermore, calls within a given area code can be resolved without contacting sites outside the area code. When applied to domain names, these ideas lead to a two-step name resolution mechanism that preserves the administrative hierarchy but permits efficient translation.

We have said that most queries to name servers refer to local names. In the two-step name resolution process, resolution begins with the local name server. If the local server cannot resolve a name, the query must then be sent to another server in the domain system.

---

†For reliability, there are multiple servers for each node in the domain server tree; the root server is further replicated to provide load balancing.

‡See BOOTP/DHCP in Chapter 21 for one possible approach.

22.13 Caching: The Key To Efficiency

The cost of lookup for nonlocal names can be extremely high if resolvers send each query to the root server. Even if queries could go directly to the server that has authority for the name, name lookup can present a heavy load to an internet. Thus, to improve the overall performance of a name server system, it is necessary to lower the cost of lookup for nonlocal names.

Internet name servers use *name caching* to optimize search costs. Each server maintains a cache of recently used names as well as a record of where the mapping information for that name was obtained. When a client asks the server to resolve a name, the server first checks to see if it has authority for the name according to the standard procedure. If not, the server checks its cache to see if the name has been resolved recently. Servers report cached information to clients, but mark it as a *nonauthoritative* binding, and give the domain name of the server, S, from which they obtained the binding. The local server also sends along additional information that tells the client the binding between S and an IP address. Therefore, clients receive answers quickly, but the information may be out-of-date. If efficiency is important, the client will choose to accept the nonauthoritative answer and proceed. If accuracy is important, the client will choose to contact the authority and verify that the binding between name and address is still valid.

Caching works well in the domain name system because name to address bindings change infrequently. However, they do change. If servers cached information the first time it was requested and never changed it, entries in the cache could become incorrect. To keep the cache correct, servers time each entry and dispose of entries that exceed a reasonable time. When the server is asked for the information after it has removed the entry from the cache, it must go back to the authoritative source and obtain the binding again. More important, servers do not apply a single fixed timeout to all entries, but allow the authority for an entry to configure its timeout. Whenever an authority responds to a request, it includes a *Time To Live* (TTL) value in the response that specifies how long it guarantees the binding to remain. Thus, authorities can reduce network overhead by specifying long timeouts for entries that they expect to remain unchanged, while improving correctness by specifying short timeouts for entries that they expect to change frequently.

Caching is important in hosts as well as in local domain name servers. Many timesharing systems run a complex form of resolver code that attempts to provide even more efficiency than the server system. The host downloads the complete database of names and addresses from a local domain name server at startup, maintains its own cache of recently used names, and uses the server only when names are not found. Naturally, a host that maintains a copy of the local server database must check with the server periodically to obtain new mappings, and the host must remove entries from its cache after they become invalid. However, most sites have little trouble maintaining consistency because domain names change so infrequently.

Keeping a copy of the local server's database in each host has several advantages. Obviously, it makes name resolution on local hosts extremely fast because it means the host can resolve names without any network activity. It also means that the local site has protection in case the local name server fails. Finally, it reduces the computational load on the name server, and makes it possible for a given server to supply names to more machines.

22.14 Domain Server Message Format

Looking at the details of messages exchanged between clients and domain name servers will help clarify how the system operates from the view of a typical application program. We assume that a user invokes an application program and supplies the name of a machine with which the application must communicate. Before it can use protocols like TCP or UDP to communicate with the specified machine, the application program must find the machine's IP address. It passes the domain name to a local resolver and requests an IP address. The local resolver checks its cache and returns the answer if one is present. If the local resolver does not have an answer, it formats a message and sends it to the server (i.e., it becomes a client). Although our example only involves one name, the message format allows a client to ask multiple questions in a single message. Each question consists of a domain name for which the client seeks an IP address, a specification of the query class (i.e., *internet*), and the type of object desired (e.g., *address*). The server responds by returning a similar message that contains answers to the questions for which the server has bindings. If the server cannot answer all questions, the response will contain information about other name servers that the client can contact to obtain the answers.

Responses also contain information about the servers that are authorities for the replies and the IP addresses of those servers. Figure 22.5 shows the message format. As the figure shows, each message begins with a fixed header. The header contains a unique *IDENTIFICATION* field that the client uses to match responses to queries, and a *PARAMETER* field that specifies the operation requested and a response code. Figure 22.6 gives the interpretation of bits in the *PARAMETER* field.

The fields labeled *NUMBER OF* each give a count of entries in the corresponding sections that occur later in the message. For example, the field labeled *NUMBER OF QUESTIONS* gives the count of entries that appear in the *QUESTION SECTION* of the message.

The *QUESTION SECTION* contains queries for which answers are desired. The client fills in only the question section; the server returns the questions and answers in its response. Each question consists of a *QUERY DOMAIN NAME* followed by *QUERY TYPE* and *QUERY CLASS* fields, as Figure 22.7 shows.

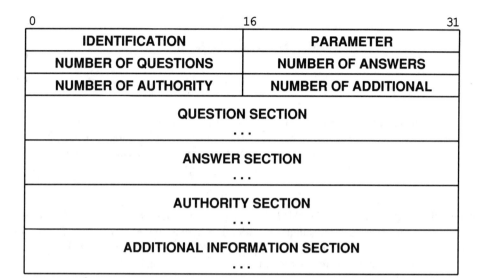

Figure 22.5 Domain name server message format. The question, answer, authority, and additional information sections are variable length.

Bit of PARAMETER field	Meaning
0	Operation: 0 Query 1 Response
1-4	Query Type: 0 Standard 1 Inverse 2 Completion 1 (now obsolete) 3 Completion 2 (now obsolete)
5	Set if answer authoritative
6	Set if message truncated
7	Set if recursion desired
8	Set if recursion available
9-11	Reserved
12-15	Response Type: 0 No error 1 Format error in query 2 Server failure 3 Name does not exist

Figure 22.6 The meaning of bits of the *PARAMETER* field in a domain name server message. Bits are numbered left to right starting at 0.

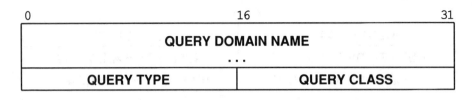

0   16   31

QUERY DOMAIN NAME	
. . .	
QUERY TYPE	QUERY CLASS

Figure 22.7 The format of entries in the *QUESTION SECTION* of a domain
name server message. The domain name is variable length.
Clients fill in the questions; servers return them along with
answers.

Although the *QUERY DOMAIN NAME* field has variable length, we will see in the next
section that the internal representation of domain names makes it possible for the receiver to know the exact length. The *QUERY TYPE* encodes the type of the question
(e.g., whether the question refers to a machine name or a mail address). The *QUERY
CLASS* field allows domain names to be used for arbitrary objects because official Internet names are only one possible class. It should be noted that, although the diagram in
Figure 22.5 follows our convention of showing formats in 32-bit multiples, the *QUERY
DOMAIN NAME* field may contain an arbitrary number of octets. No padding is used.
Therefore, messages to or from domain name servers may contain an odd number of oc-
tets.

In a domain name server message, each of the *ANSWER SECTION*, *AUTHORITY
SECTION*, and *ADDITIONAL INFORMATION SECTION* consists of a set of *resource
records* that describe domain names and mappings. Each resource record describes one
name. Figure 22.8 shows the format.

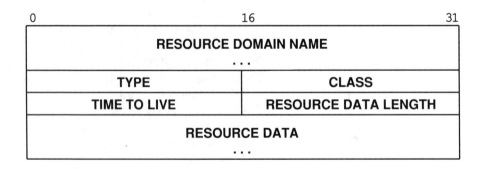

0   16   31

RESOURCE DOMAIN NAME	
. . .	
TYPE	CLASS
TIME TO LIVE	RESOURCE DATA LENGTH
RESOURCE DATA	
. . .	

Figure 22.8 The format of resource records used in later sections of messages
returned by domain name servers.

The *RESOURCE DOMAIN NAME* field contains the domain name to which this resource record refers. It may be an arbitrary length. The *TYPE* field specifies the type of the data included in the resource record; the *CLASS* field specifies the data's class. The *TIME TO LIVE* field contains an integer that specifies the number of seconds information in this resource record can be cached. It is used by clients who have requested a name binding and may want to cache the results. The last two fields contain the results of the binding, with the *RESOURCE DATA LENGTH* field specifying the count of octets in the *RESOURCE DATA* field.

22.15 Compressed Name Format

When represented in a message, domain names are stored as a sequence of labels. Each label begins with an octet that specifies its length. Thus, the receiver reconstructs a domain name by repeatedly reading a 1-octet length, *n*, and then reading a label *n* octets long. A length octet containing zero marks the end of the name.

Domain name servers often return multiple answers to a query and, in many cases, suffixes of the domain overlap. To conserve space in the reply packet, the name servers compress names by storing only one copy of each domain name. When extracting a domain name from a message, the client software must check each segment of the name to see whether it consists of a literal string (in the format of a 1-octet count followed by the characters that make up the name) or a pointer to a literal string. When it encounters a pointer, the client must follow the pointer to a new place in the message to find the remainder of the name.

Pointers always occur at the beginning of segments and are encoded in the count byte. If the top two bits of the 8-bit segment count field are 1s, the client must take the next 14 bits as an integer pointer. If the top two bits are zero, the next 6 bits specify the number of characters in the label that follow the count octet.

22.16 Abbreviation Of Domain Names

The telephone number hierarchy illustrates another useful feature of local resolution, *name abbreviation*. Abbreviation provides a method of shortening names when the resolving process can supply part of the name automatically. Normally, a subscriber omits the area code when dialing a local telephone number. The resulting digits form an abbreviated name assumed to lie within the same area code as the subscriber's phone. Abbreviation also works well for machine names. Given a name like *xyz*, the resolving process can assume it lies in the same local authority as the machine on which it is being resolved. Thus, the resolver can supply missing parts of the name automatically. For example, within the Computer Science Department at Purdue, the abbreviated name

xinu

is equivalent to the full domain name

xinu.cs.purdue.edu

Most client software implements abbreviations with a *domain suffix list*. The local network manager configures a list of possible suffixes to be appended to names during lookup. When a resolver encounters a name, it steps through the list, appending each suffix and trying to look up the resulting name. For example, the suffix list for the Computer Science Department at Purdue includes:

`.cs.purdue.edu`
`.cc.purdue.edu`
`.purdue.edu`
null

Thus, local resolvers first append *cs.purdue.edu* onto the name *xinu*. If that lookup fails, they append *cc.purdue.edu* onto the name and look that up. The last suffix in the example list is the null string, meaning that if all other lookups fail, the resolver will attempt to look up the name with no suffix. Managers can use the suffix list to make abbreviation convenient or to restrict application programs to local names.

We said that the client takes responsibility for the expansion of such abbreviations, but it should be emphasized that such abbreviations are not part of the domain name system itself. The domain system only allows lookup of a fully specified domain name. As a consequence, programs that depend on abbreviations may not work correctly outside the environment in which they were built. We can summarize:

> *The domain name system only maps full domain names into addresses; abbreviations are not part of the domain name system itself, but are introduced by client software to make local names convenient for users.*

22.17 Inverse Mappings

We said that the domain name system can provide mappings other than machine name to IP address. *Inverse queries* allow the client to ask a server to map "backwards" by taking an answer and generating the question that would produce that answer. Of course, not all answers have a unique question. Even when they do, a server may not be able to provide it. Although inverse queries have been part of the domain system since it was first specified, they are generally not used because there is often no way to find the server that can resolve the query without searching the entire set of servers.

22.18 Pointer Queries

One form of inverse mapping is so obviously needed that the domain system supports a special domain and a special form of question called a *pointer query* to answer it. In a pointer query, the question presented to a domain name server specifies an IP address encoded as a printable string in the form of a domain name (i.e., a textual representation of digits separated by periods). A pointer query requests the name server to return the correct domain name for the machine with the specified IP address. Pointer queries are especially useful for diskless machines because they allow the system to obtain a high-level name given only an IP address. (We have already seen in Chapter 6 how a diskless machine can obtain its IP address.)

Pointer queries are not difficult to generate. If we think of an IP address written in dotted-decimal form, it has the following format:

$$aaa.bbb.ccc.ddd$$

To form a pointer query, the client rearranges the dotted decimal representation of the address into a string of the form:

$$ddd.ccc.bbb.aaa.in\text{-}addr.arpa$$

The new form is a name in the special *in-addr.arpa* domain†. Because the local name server may not be the authority for either the *arpa* domain or the *in-addr.arpa* domain, it may need to contact other name servers to complete the resolution. To make the resolution of pointer queries efficient, the Internet root domain servers maintain a database of valid IP addresses along with information about domain name servers that can resolve each address.

22.19 Object Types And Resource Record Contents

We have mentioned that the domain name system can be used for translating a domain name to a mail exchanger address as well as for translating a host name to an IP address. The domain system is quite general in that it can be used for arbitrary hierarchical names. For example, one might decide to store the names of available computational services along with a mapping from each name to the telephone number to call to find out about the corresponding service. Or one might store names of protocol products along with a mapping to the names and addresses of vendors that offer such products.

Recall that the system accommodates a variety of mappings by including a *type* in each resource record. When sending a request, a client must specify the type in its query‡; servers specify the data type in all resource records they return. The type determines the contents of the resource record according to the table in Figure 22.9

---

†The octets of the IP address must be reversed when forming a domain name because IP addresses have the most significant octets first while domain names have the least-significant octets first.

‡Queries can specify a few additional types (e.g., there is a query type that requests all resource records).

Type	Meaning	Contents
A	Host Address	32-bit IP address
CNAME	Canonical Name	Canonical domain name for an alias
HINFO	CPU & OS	Name of CPU and Operating System
MINFO	Mailbox info	Information about a mailbox or mail list
MX	Mail Exchanger	16-bit preference and name of host that acts as mail exchanger for the domain
NS	Name Server	Name of authoritative server for domain
PTR	Pointer	Domain name (like a symbolic link)
SOA	Start of Authority	Multiple fields that specify which parts of the naming hierarchy a server implements
TXT	Arbitrary text	Uninterpreted string of ASCII text

Figure 22.9 Domain name system resource record types.

Most data is of type *A*, meaning that it consists of the name of a host attached to the Internet along with the host's IP address. The second most useful domain type, *MX*, is assigned to names used for electronic mail exchangers. It allows a site to specify multiple hosts that are each capable of accepting mail. When sending electronic mail, the user specifies an electronic mail address in the form *user@domain-part*. The mail system uses the domain name system to resolve *domain-part* with query type *MX*. The domain system returns a set of resource records that each contain a preference field and a host's domain name. The mail system steps through the set from highest preference to lowest (lower numbers mean higher preference). For each *MX* resource record, the mailer extracts the domain name and uses a type *A* query to resolve that name to an IP address. It then tries to contact the host and deliver mail. If the host is unavailable, the mailer will continue trying other hosts on the list.

To make lookup efficient, a server always returns additional bindings that it knows in the *ADDITIONAL INFORMATION SECTION* of a response. In the case of *MX* records, a domain server can use the *ADDITIONAL INFORMATION SECTION* to return type *A* resource records for domain names reported in the *ANSWER SECTION*. Doing so substantially reduces the number of queries a mailer sends to its domain server.

22.20 Obtaining Authority For A Subdomain

Before an institution is granted authority for an official second-level domain, it must agree to operate a domain name server that meets Internet standards. Of course, a domain name server must obey the protocol standards that specify message formats and the rules for responding to requests. The server must also know the addresses of servers that handle each subdomain (if any exist) as well as the address of at least one root server.

In practice, the domain system is much more complex than we have outlined. In most cases, a single physical server can handle more than one part of the naming hierarchy. For example, a single name server at Purdue University handles both the second-level domain *purdue.edu* as well as the geographic domain *laf.in.us*. A subtree of names managed by a given name server forms a *zone of authority*. Another practical complication arises because servers must be able to handle many requests, even though some requests take a long time to resolve. Usually, servers support concurrent activity, allowing work to proceed on later requests while earlier ones are being processed. Handling requests concurrently is especially important when the server receives a recursive request that forces it to send the request on to another server for resolution.

Server implementation is also complicated because the Internet authority requires that the information in every domain name server be replicated. Information must appear in at least two servers that do not operate on the same computer. In practice, the requirements are quite stringent: the servers must have no single common point of failure. Avoiding common points of failure means that the two name servers cannot both attach to the same network; they cannot even obtain electrical power from the same source. Thus, to meet the requirements, a site must find at least one other site that agrees to operate a backup name server. Of course, at any point in the tree of servers, a server must know how to locate both the primary and backup name servers for sub-domains, and it must direct queries to a backup name server if the primary server is unavailable.

22.21 Summary

Hierarchical naming systems allow delegation of authority for names, making it possible to accommodate an arbitrarily large set of names without overwhelming a central site with administrative duties. Although name resolution is separate from delegation of authority, it is possible to create hierarchical naming systems in which resolution is an efficient process that starts at the local server even though delegation of authority always flows from the top of the hierarchy downward.

We examined the Internet domain name system (DNS) and saw that it offers a hierarchical naming scheme. DNS uses distributed lookup in which domain name servers map each domain name to an IP address or mail exchanger address. Clients begin by trying to resolve names locally. When the local server cannot resolve the name, the client must choose to work through the tree of name servers iteratively or request the local name server to do it recursively. Finally, we saw that the domain name system supports a variety of bindings including bindings from IP addresses to high-level names.

FOR FURTHER STUDY

Mockapetris [RFC 1034] discusses Internet domain naming in general, giving the overall philosophy, while Mockapetris [RFC 1035] provides a protocol standard for the domain name system. Mockapetris [RFC 1101] discusses using the domain name system to encode network names and proposes extensions useful for other mappings. Older versions appeared in Mockapetris [RFC 882, 883, and 973]. Postel and Reynolds [RFC 920] states the requirements that an Internet domain name server must meet. Stahl [RFC 1032] gives administrative guidelines for establishing a domain, and Lottor [RFC 1033] provides guidelines for operating a domain name server. Partridge [RFC 974] relates domain naming to electronic mail addressing. Finally, Lottor [RFC 1296] provides an interesting summary of Internet growth obtained by walking the domain name tree.

EXERCISES

22.1   Machine names should not be bound into the operating system at compile time. Explain why.

22.2   Would you prefer to use a machine that obtained its name from a remote file or from a name server? Why?

22.3   Why should each name server know the IP address of its parent instead of the domain name of its parent?

22.4   Devise a naming scheme that tolerates changes to the naming hierarchy. As an example, consider two large companies that each have an independent naming hierarchy, and suppose the companies merge. Can you arrange to have all previous names still work correctly?

22.5   Read the standard and find out how the domain name system uses *SOA* records.

22.6   The Internet domain name system can also accommodate mailbox names. Find out how.

22.7   The standard suggests that when a program needs to find the domain name associated with an IP address, it should send an inverse query to the local server first and use domain *in-addr.arpa* only if that fails. Why?

22.8   How would you accommodate abbreviations in a domain naming scheme? As an example, show two sites that are both registered under *.edu* and a top level server. Explain how each site would treat each type of abbreviation.

22.9   Obtain the official description of the domain name system and build a client program. Look up the name *merlin.cs.purdue.edu*.

22.10 Extend the exercise above to include a pointer query. Try looking up the domain name for address *128.10.2.3*.

22.11 Find a copy of the program *nslookup*, and use it to look up the names in the two previous exercises.

22.12   If we extended the domain name syntax to include a dot after the top-level domain, names and abbreviations would be unambiguous. What are the advantages and disadvantages of the extension?

22.13   Read the RFCs on the domain name system. What are the maximum and minimum possible values a DNS server can store in the *TIME-TO-LIVE* field of a resource record?

22.14   Should the domain name system permit partial match queries (i.e. a wildcard as part of a name)? Why or why not?

22.15   The Computer Science Department at Purdue University chose to place the following type *A* resource record entry in its domain name server:

```
localhost.cs.purdue.edu     127.0.0.1
```

Explain what will happen if a remote site tries to *ping* a machine with domain name *localhost.cs.purdue.edu*.

23

Applications: Remote Login (TELNET, Rlogin)

23.1 Introduction

This chapter and the next four continue our exploration of internetworking by examining high-level internet services and the protocols that support them. These services form an integral part of TCP/IP. They determine how users perceive an internet and demonstrate the power of the technology.

We will learn that high-level services provide increased communication functionality, and allow users and programs to interact with automated services on remote machines and with remote users. We will see that high-level protocols are implemented with application programs, and will learn how they depend on the network level services described in previous chapters. This chapter begins by examining remote login.

23.2 Remote Interactive Computing

We have already seen how the client–server model can provide specific computational services like a time-of-day service to multiple machines. Reliable stream protocols like TCP make possible interactive use of remote machines as well. For example, imagine building a server that provides a remote text editing service. To implement an editing service, we would need a server that accepts requests to edit a file and a client to make such requests. To invoke the remote editor service, a user would execute the client program. The client would establish a TCP connection from the local machine to the server, and would then begin sending keystrokes to the server and reading output that the server sent back.

How can our imagined remote interactive editing service be generalized? The problem with using one server for each computational service is that machines quickly become swamped with server processes. We can eliminate most specialized servers and provide more generality by allowing the user to establish a login session on the remote machine and then execute commands. With a *remote login* facility, users have access to all the commands available on the remote system, and system designers need not provide specialized servers.

Of course, providing remote login may not be simple. Computer systems designed without considering networking expect login sessions only from a directly connected keyboard and display. On such a computer, adding a remote login server requires modifying the machine's operating system. Building interactive client software may also be difficult. Consider, for example, a system that assigns special meaning to some keystrokes. If the local system interprets Control–C to mean "abort the currently executing command process," it may be impossible to pass Control–C to the remote machine. If the client does pass Control-C to the remote site, it may be impossible to abort the local client process.

Despite the technical difficulties, system programmers have managed to build remote login server software for most operating systems and to construct application programs that act as clients. Often, the client software overrides the local interpretation of all keys except one, allowing a user to interact with the remote machine exactly as one would from a locally connected terminal. The single key exception provides a way for a user to escape to the local environment and control the client (e.g., to abort the client). In addition, some remote login protocols recognize a set of *trusted hosts*, permitting remote login from such hosts without verifying passwords.

23.3 TELNET Protocol

The TCP/IP protocol suite includes a simple remote terminal protocol called *TELNET*. TELNET allows a user at one site to establish a TCP connection to a login server at another. TELNET then passes keystrokes from the user's keyboard directly to the remote computer as if they had been typed on a keyboard attached to the remote machine. TELNET also carries output from the remote machine back to the user's screen. The service is called *transparent* because it gives the appearance that the user's keyboard and display attach directly to the remote machine.

Although TELNET is not sophisticated compared to some remote terminal protocols, it is widely available. Usually, TELNET client software allows the user to specify a remote machine either by giving its domain name or IP address. Because it accepts IP addresses, TELNET can be used with hosts even if a name-to-address binding cannot be established (e.g., when domain naming software is being debugged).

TELNET offers three basic services. First, it defines a *network virtual terminal* that provides a standard interface to remote systems. Client programs do not have to understand the details of all possible remote systems; they are built to use the standard interface. Second, TELNET includes a mechanism that allows the client and server to negotiate options, and it provides a set of standard options (e.g., one of the options controls whether data passed across the connection uses the standard 7-bit ASCII character set or an 8-bit character set). Finally, TELNET treats both ends of the connection symmetrically. In particular, TELNET does not force client input to come from a keyboard, nor does it force the client to display output on a screen. Thus, TELNET allows an arbitrary program to become a client. Furthermore, either end can negotiate options.

Figure 23.1 illustrates how application programs implement a TELNET client and server.

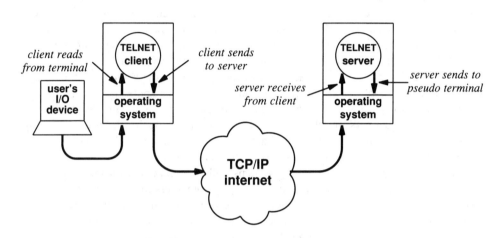

Figure 23.1 The path of data in a TELNET remote terminal session as it travels from the user's keyboard to the remote operating system. Adding a TELNET server to a timesharing system usually requires modifying the operating system.

As the figure shows, when a user invokes TELNET, an application program on the user's machine becomes the client. The client establishes a TCP connection to the server over which they will communicate. Once the connection has been established, the client accepts keystrokes from the user's keyboard and sends them to the server, while it concurrently accepts characters that the server sends back and displays them on the user's screen. The server must accept a TCP connection from the client, and then relay data between the TCP connection and the local operating system.

In practice, the server is more complex than the figure shows because it must handle multiple, concurrent connections. Usually, a master server process waits for new connections and creates a new slave to handle each connection. Thus, the 'TELNET server', shown in Figure 23.1, represents the slave that handles one particular connection. The figure does not show the master server that listens for new requests, nor does it show the slaves handling other connections.

We use the term *pseudo terminal*† to describe the operating system entry point that allows a running program like the TELNET server to transfer characters to the operating system as if they came from a keyboard. It is impossible to build a TELNET server unless the operating system supplies such a facility. If the system supports a pseudo terminal abstraction, the TELNET server can be implemented with application programs. Each slave server connects a TCP stream from one client to a particular pseudo terminal.

Arranging for the TELNET server to be an application level program has advantages and disadvantages. The most obvious advantage is that it makes modification and control of the server easier than if the code were embedded in the operating system. The obvious disadvantage is inefficiency. Each keystroke travels from the user's keyboard through the operating system to the client program, from the client program back through the operating system and across the internet to the server machine. After reaching the destination machine, the data must travel up through the server's operating system to the server application program, and from the server application program back into the server's operating system at a pseudo terminal entry point. Finally, the remote operating system delivers the character to the application program the user is running. Meanwhile, output (including remote character echo if that option has been selected) travels back from the server to the client over the same path.

Readers who understand operating systems will appreciate that for the implementation shown in Figure 23.1, every keystroke requires computers to switch process context several times. In most systems, an additional context switch is required because the operating system on the server's machine must pass characters from the pseudo terminal back to another application program (e.g., a command interpreter). Although context switching is expensive, the scheme is practical because users do not type at high speed.

23.4 Accommodating Heterogeneity

To make TELNET interoperate between as many systems as possible, it must accommodate the details of heterogeneous computers and operating systems. For example, some systems require lines of text to be terminated by the ASCII *carriage control* character (*CR*). Others require the ASCII *linefeed* (*LF*) character. Still others require the two-character sequence of CR-LF. In addition, most interactive systems provide a way for a user to enter a key that interrupts a running program. However, the specific keystroke used to interrupt a program varies from system to system (e.g., some systems use Control–C, while others use ESCAPE).

To accommodate heterogeneity, TELNET defines how data and command sequences are sent across the Internet. The definition is known as the *network virtual terminal* (*NVT*). As Figure 23.2 illustrates, the client software translates keystrokes and command sequences from the user's terminal into NVT format and sends them to the server. Server software translates incoming data and commands from NVT format into the format the remote system requires. For data returning, the remote server translates

---

†UNIX calls the system entry point a *pseudo tty* because character-oriented devices are called *ttys*.

from the remote machine's format to NVT, and the local client translates from NVT format to the local machine's format.

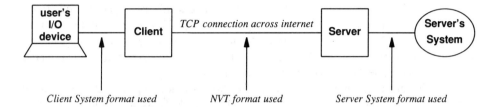

Figure 23.2 Use of the Network Virtual Terminal (NVT) format by TELNET.

The definition of NVT format is fairly straightforward. All communication involves 8-bit bytes. At startup, NVT uses the standard 7-bit USASCII representation for data and reserves bytes with the high order bit set for command sequences. The US-ASCII character set includes 95 characters that have "printable" graphics (e.g., letters, digits, and punctuation marks) as well as 33 "control" codes. All printable characters are assigned the same meaning as in the standard USASCII character set. The NVT standard defines interpretations for control characters as shown in Figure 23.3†.

ASCII Control Code	Decimal Value	Assigned Meaning
NUL	0	No operation (has no effect on output)
BEL	7	Sound audible/visible signal (no motion)
BS	8	Move left one character position
HT	9	Move right to the next horizontal tab stop
LF	10	Move down (vertically) to the next line
VT	11	Move down to the next vertical tab stop
FF	12	Move to the top of the next page
CR	13	Move to the left margin on the current line
other control	–	No operation (has no effect on output)

Figure 23.3 The TELNET NVT interpretation of USASCII control characters.
TELNET does not specify the locations of tab stops.

In addition to the control character interpretation in Figure 23.3, NVT defines the standard line termination to be a two-character sequence *CR-LF*. When a user presses the key that corresponds to end-of-line on the local terminal (e.g., *ENTER* or *RETURN*), the TELNET client must map it into *CR-LF* for transmission. The TELNET server translates *CR-LF* into the appropriate end-of-line character sequence for the remote machine.

---

†The NVT interpretation of control characters follows the usual ASCII interpretation.

23.5 Passing Commands That Control The Remote Side

We said that most systems provide a mechanism that allows users to terminate a running program. Usually, the local operating system binds such mechanisms to a particular key or keystroke sequence. For example, unless the user specifies otherwise, many UNIX systems reserve the character generated by *CONTROL-C* as the interrupt key. Depressing *CONTROL-C* causes UNIX to terminate the executing program; the program does not receive *CONTROL-C* as input. The system may reserve other characters or character sequences for other control functions.

TELNET NVT accommodates control functions by defining how they are passed from the client to the server. Conceptually, we think of NVT as accepting input from a keyboard that can generate more than 128 possible characters. We assume the user's keyboard has virtual (imaginary) keys that correspond to the functions typically used to control processing. For example, NVT defines a conceptual "interrupt" key that requests program termination. Figure 23.4 lists the control functions that NVT allows.

Signal	Meaning
IP	Interrupt Process (terminate running program)
AO	Abort Output (discard any buffered output)
AYT	Are You There (test if server is responding)
EC	Erase Character (delete the previous character)
EL	Erase Line (delete the entire current line)
SYNCH	Synchronize (clear data path until TCP urgent data point, but do interpret commands)
BRK	Break (break key or attention signal)

Figure 23.4 The control functions TELNET NVT recognizes. Conceptually, the client receives these from a user in addition to normal data, and passes them to the server's system where they must be interpreted.

In practice, most keyboards do not provide extra keys for commands. Instead, individual operating systems or command interpreters have a variety of ways to generate them. We already mentioned the most common technique: binding an individual ASCII character to a control function so when the user presses the key, the operating system takes the appropriate action instead of accepting the character as input. The NVT designers chose to keep commands separate from the normal ASCII character set for two reasons. First, defining the control functions separately means TELNET has greater flexibility. It can transfer all possible ASCII character sequences between client and server as well as all possible control functions. Second, by separating signals from normal data, NVT allows the client to specify signals unambiguously – there is never confusion about whether an input character should be treated as data or as a control function.

To pass control functions across the TCP connection, TELNET encodes them using an *escape sequence*. An escape sequence uses a reserved octet to indicate that a control code octet follows. In TELNET, the reserved octet that starts an escape sequence is known as the *interpret as command* (*IAC*) octet. Figure 23.5 lists the possible commands and the decimal encoding used for each.

Command	Decimal Encoding	Meaning
IAC	255	Interpret next octet as command (when the IAC octet appears as data, the sender doubles it and sends the 2-octet sequence IAC-IAC)
DON'T	254	Denial of request to perform specified option
DO	253	Approval to allow specified option
WON'T	252	Refusal to perform specified option
WILL	251	Agreement to perform specified option
SB	250	Start of option subnegotiation
GA	249	The "go ahead" signal
EL	248	The "erase line" signal
EC	247	The "erase character" signal
AYT	246	The "are you there" signal
AO	245	The "abort output" signal
IP	244	The "interrupt process" signal
BRK	243	The "break" signal
DMARK	242	The data stream portion of a SYNCH (always accompanied by TCP Urgent notification)
NOP	241	No operation
SE	240	End of option subnegotiation
EOR	239	End of record

Figure 23.5 Telnet commands and encoding for each. The codes only have meaning if preceded by an *IAC* character. When *IAC* occurs in the data, it is sent twice.

As the figure shows, the signals generated by conceptual keys on an NVT keyboard each have a corresponding command. For example, to request that the server interrupt the executing program, the client must send the 2-octet sequence *IAC IP* (255 followed by 244). Additional commands allow the client and server to negotiate which options they will use and to synchronize communication.

23.6 Forcing The Server To Read A Control Function

Sending control functions along with normal data is not always sufficient to guarantee the desired results. To see why, consider the situation under which a user might send the *interrupt process* control function to the server. Usually, such control is only needed when the program executing on the remote machine is misbehaving and the user wants the server to terminate the program. For example, the program might be executing an endless loop without reading input or generating output. Unfortunately, if the application at the server's site stops reading input, operating system buffers will eventually fill and the server will be unable to write more data to the pseudo terminal. When this happens, the server must stop reading data from the TCP connection, causing its buffers to fill. Eventually, TCP on the server machine will begin advertising a zero window size, preventing data from flowing across the connection.

If the user generates an interrupt control function when buffers are filled, the control function will never reach the server. That is, the client can form the command sequence *IAC IP* and write it to the TCP connection, but because TCP has stopped sending to the server's machine, the server will not read the control sequence. The point is:

> *TELNET cannot rely on the conventional data stream alone to carry control sequences between client and server, because a misbehaving application that needs to be controlled might inadvertently block the data stream.*

To solve the problem, TELNET uses an *out of band* signal. TCP implements out of band signaling with the *urgent data* mechanism. Whenever it places a control function in the data stream, TELNET also sends a *SYNCH* command. TELNET then appends a reserved octet called the *data mark*, and causes TCP to signal the server by sending a segment with the URGENT DATA bit set. Segments carrying urgent data bypass flow control and reach the server immediately. In response to an urgent signal, the server reads and discards all data until it finds the data mark. The server returns to normal processing when it encounters the data mark.

23.7 TELNET Options

Our simple description of TELNET omits one of the most complex aspects: options. In TELNET, options are negotiable, making it possible for the client and server to reconfigure their connection. For example, we said that usually the data stream passes 7-bit data and uses octets with the eighth bit set to pass control information like the *Interrupt Process* command. However, TELNET also provides an option that allows the client and server to pass 8-bit data (when passing 8-bit data, the reserved octet *IAC* must still be doubled if it appears in the data). The client and server must negotiate, and both must agree to pass 8-bit data before such transfers are possible.

The range of TELNET options is wide: some extend the capabilities in major ways while others deal with minor details. For example, the original protocol was designed for a half-duplex environment where it was necessary to tell the other end to ''go ahead'' before it would send more data. One of the options controls whether TELNET operates in half- or full-duplex mode. Another option allows the server on a remote machine to determine the user's terminal type. The terminal type is important for software that generates cursor positioning sequences (e.g., a full screen editor executing on a remote machine).

Figure 23.6 lists several of the most commonly implemented TELNET options.

Name	Code	RFC	Meaning
Transmit Binary	0	856	Change transmission to 8-bit binary
Echo	1	857	Allow one side to echo data it receives
Suppress-GA	3	858	Suppress (no longer send) Go-ahead signal after data
Status	5	859	Request for status of a TELNET option from remote site
Timing-Mark	6	860	Request timing mark be inserted in return stream to synchronize two ends of a connection
Terminal-Type	24	884	Exchange information about the make and model of a terminal being used (allows programs to tailor output like cursor positioning sequences for the user's terminal)
End-of-Record	25	885	Terminate data sent with EOR code
Linemode	34	1116	Use local editing and send complete lines instead of individual characters

Figure 23.6 Commonly used TELNET options.

23.8 TELNET Option Negotiation

The way TELNET negotiates options is interesting. Because it sometimes makes sense for the server to initiate a particular option, the protocol is designed to allow either end to make a request. Thus, the protocol is said to be *symmetric* with respect to option processing. The receiving end either responds to a request with a positive acceptance or a rejection. In TELNET terminology, the request is *WILL X*, meaning *will you agree to let me use option X*; and the response is either *DO X* or *DON'T X*, meaning *I do agree to let you use option X* or *I don't agree to let you use option X*. The symmetry arises because *DO X* requests that the receiving party begin using option X, and *WILL X* or *WON'T X* means *I will start using option X* or *I won't start using it*†.

---

†To eliminate potential loops that arise when two sides each think the other's acknowledgement is a request, the protocol specifies that no acknowledgement be given to a request for an option that is already in use.

Another interesting negotiation concept arises because both ends are required to run an unenhanced NVT implementation (i.e., one without any options turned on). If one side tries to negotiate an option that the other does not understand, the side receiving the request can simply decline. Thus, it is possible to interoperate newer, more sophisticated versions of TELNET clients and servers (i.e., software that understands more options) with older, less sophisticated versions. If both the client and server understand the new options, they may be able to improve interaction. If not, they will revert to a less efficient, but workable style.

We can summarize:

> *TELNET uses a symmetric option negotiation mechanism to allow clients and servers to reconfigure the parameters controlling their interaction. Because all TELNET software understands a basic NVT protocol, clients and servers can interoperate even if one understands options another does not.*

23.9 Rlogin (BSD UNIX)

Operating systems derived from BSD UNIX include a remote login service, *rlogin*, that supports trusted hosts. It allows system administrators to choose a set of machines over which login names and file access protections are shared and to establish equivalences among user logins. Users can control access to their accounts by authorizing remote login based on remote host and remote user name. Thus, it is possible for a user to have login name X on one machine and Y on another, and still be able to remotely login from one of the machines to the other without typing a password each time.

Having automatic authorization makes remote login facilities useful for general purpose programs as well as human interaction. One variant of the *rlogin* command, *rsh*, invokes a command interpreter on the remote UNIX machine and passes the command line arguments to the command interpreter, skipping the login step completely. The format of a command invocation using *rsh* is:

rsh *machine command*

Thus, typing

rsh merlin ps

on any of the machines in the Computer Science Department at Purdue University executes the *ps* command on machine *merlin*, with UNIX's standard input and standard output connected across the network to the user's keyboard and display. The user sees the output as if he or she were logged into machine *merlin*. Because the user can arrange to have *rsh* invoke remote commands without prompting for a password, it can be used in programs as well as from the keyboard.

Because protocols like *rlogin* understand both the local and remote computing environments, they communicate better than general purpose remote login protocols like TELNET. For example, *rlogin* understands the UNIX notions of *standard input*, *standard output*, and *standard error*, and uses TCP to connect them to the remote machine. Thus, it is possible to type

```
rsh merlin ps > filename
```

and have output from the remote command redirected† into file *filename*. *Rlogin* also understands terminal control functions like flow control characters (typically Control–S and Control–Q). It arranges to stop output immediately without waiting for the delay required to send them across the network to the remote host. Finally, rlogin exports part of the user's environment to the remote machine, including information like the user's terminal type (i.e., the *TERM* variable). As a result, a remote login session appears to behave almost exactly like a local login session.

23.10 Summary

Much of the rich functionality associated with TCP/IP results from a variety of high-level services supplied by application programs. The high-level remote login protocols these programs use build on the basic services: unreliable datagram delivery and reliable stream transport. The services usually follow the client-server model in which servers operate at known protocol ports so clients know how to contact them.

We reviewed two remote login systems: TELNET, the TCP/IP internet standard, and rlogin, a popular protocol used with systems derived from BSD UNIX. TELNET provides a basic service. It allows the client to pass commands such as *interrupt process* as well as data to the server. It also permits a client and server to negotiate many options. In contrast to TELNET, *rlogin* allows system managers and users more flexibility in establishing the equivalence of accounts on multiple machines, but it is not as widely available as TELNET.

FOR FURTHER STUDY

Many high-level protocols have been proposed, but only a few are in common use. Edge [1979] compares end-to-end protocols with the hop-by-hop approach. Saltzer, Reed, and Clark [1984] argues for having the highest level protocols perform end-to-end acknowledgement and error detection.

Postel [RFC 854] contains the TELNET remote login protocol specification. It was preceded by over three dozen RFCs that discuss TELNET options, weaknesses, experiments, and proposed changes, including Postel [RFC 764] that contains an earlier standard. Postel and Reynolds [RFC 855] gives a specification for options and considers subnegotiation. A lengthy list of options can be found in RFCs 856, 857, 858, 859,

---

†The "greater than" symbol is the usual UNIX syntax for directing the output of a command into a file.

860, 861, 884, 885, 1041, 1091, 1096, 1097, 1184, 1372, 1416, and 1572. The program
tn3270 uses a TELNET-like mechanism to provide access to IBM computers running
the VM/CMS operating system [RFCs 1576, 1646 and 1647]; Rekhter [RFC 1041] covers the TELNET option that permits communication with IBM 3270 displays.

EXERCISES

23.1   Experiment with both TELNET and *rlogin*. What are the noticeable differences?

23.2   Despite the large volume of notes written about TELNET, it can be argued that the pro-
          tocol is still not well-defined. Experiment with TELNET: use it to reach a machine, *A*,
          and invoke TELNET on *A* to reach a second machine, *B*. Does the combination of two
          TELNET connections handle *line feed* and *carriage control* characters properly?

23.3   What is a remote procedure call?

23.4   Folklore says that operating systems come and go while protocols last forever. Test this
          axiom by surveying your local computing site to see whether operating systems or com-
          munication protocols have changed more frequently.

23.5   Build TELNET client software.

23.6   Use a TELNET client to connect your keyboard and display to the TCP protocol port for
          echo or *chargen* on your local system to see what happens.

23.7   Read the TELNET standard and find out how the SYNCH operation works.

23.8   TELNET uses TCP's *urgent data* mechanism to force the remote operating system to
          respond to control functions quickly. Read the standard to find out which commands the
          remote server honors while scanning the input stream.

23.9   How can the symmetric DO/DON'T – WILL/WON'T option negotiation produce an
          endless loop of responses if the other party *always* acknowledges a request?

23.10   The text file for RFC 854 (the TELNET protocol specification) contains exactly 854
          lines. Do you think there is cosmic significance in this?

24

Applications: File Transfer And Access (FTP, TFTP, NFS)

24.1 Introduction

This chapter continues our exploration of application protocols. It examines the file access and transfer protocols that are part of the TCP/IP protocol suite. It describes their design and shows an example of a typical user interface. We will learn that the most widely used file transfer protocol builds on TCP, covered in Chapter 13, and TEL-NET, described in the previous chapter.

24.2 File Access And Transfer

Many network systems provide computers with the ability to access files on remote machines. Designers have explored a variety of approaches to remote access; each approach optimizes for a particular set of goals. For example, some designs use remote file access to lower overall cost. In such architectures, a single, centralized *file server* provides secondary storage for a set of inexpensive computers that have no local disk storage. For example, the diskless machines can be portable, hand-held devices used for chores such as inventory. Such machines communicate with a file server over a high-speed wireless network.

Some designs use remote storage to archive data. In such designs, users have conventional computers with local storage facilities and operate them as usual. Periodically the conventional computers send copies of files (or copies of entire disks) across a network to an archival facility, where they are stored in case of accidental loss.

Finally, some designs emphasize the ability to share data across multiple programs, multiple users, or multiple sites. For example, an organization might choose to have a single on-line catalog of products shared by all groups in the organization.

24.3 On-line Shared Access

File sharing comes in two distinct forms: *on-line access* and *whole-file copying*. Shared on-line access means allowing multiple programs to access a single file concurrently. Changes to the file take effect immediately and are available to all programs that access the file. Whole-file copying means that whenever a program wants to access a file, it obtains a local copy. Copying is often used for read-only data, but if the file must be modified, the program makes changes to the local copy and transfers the modified file back to the original site.

Many users think that on-line data sharing can only be provided by a database system that operates as a server and allows users (clients) to contact it from remote sites. However, file sharing is usually more sophisticated and easier to use. For example, a file system that provides shared, on-line access for remote users does not necessarily require a user to invoke a special client program as a database system does. Instead, the operating system provides access to remote, shared files exactly the same way it provides access to local files. A user can execute any application program using a remote file as input or output. We say that the remote file is *integrated* with local files, and that the entire file system provides *transparent access* to shared files.

The advantage of transparent access should be obvious: remote file access occurs with no visible changes to application programs. Users can access both local and remote files, allowing them to perform arbitrary computations on shared data. The disadvantages are less obvious. Users may be surprised by the results. For example, consider an application program that uses both local and remote files. If the network or the remote machine is down, the application program may not work even though the user's machine is operating. Even if the remote machine is operating, it may be overloaded or the network may be congested, causing the application program to run slowly, or causing communication protocols to report timeout conditions that the user does not expect. The program seems unreliable.

Despite its advantages, implementing integrated, transparent file access can be difficult. In a heterogeneous environment, file names available on one computer may be impossible to map into the file namespace of another. Similarly, a remote file access mechanism must handle notions of ownership, authorization, and access protection, which do not transcend computer system boundaries. Finally, because file representations and allowed operations vary from machine to machine, it may be difficult or impossible to implement all operations on all files.

24.4 Sharing By File Transfer

The alternative to integrated, transparent on-line access is *file transfer*. Accessing remote data with a transfer mechanism is a two-step process: the user first obtains a local copy of a file and then operates on the copy. Most transfer mechanisms operate outside the local file system (i.e., they are not integrated). A user must invoke a special-purpose client program to transfer files. When invoking the client, the user specifies a remote computer on which the desired file resides and, possibly, an authorization needed to obtain access (e.g., an account or password). The client contacts a server on the remote machine and requests a copy of the file. Once the transfer is complete, the user terminates the client and uses application programs on the local system to read or modify the local copy. One advantage of whole-file copying lies in the efficiency of operations – once a program has obtained a copy of a remote file, it can manipulate the copy efficiently. Thus, many computations run faster with whole-file copying than with remote file access.

As with on-line sharing, whole-file transfer between heterogeneous machines can be difficult. The client and server must agree on authorization, notions of file ownership and access protections, and data formats. The latter is especially important because it may make inverse translations impossible. To see why, consider copying between two machines, *A* and *B*, that use different representations for floating point numbers as well as different representations for text files. As most programmers realize, it may be impossible to convert from one machine's floating point format to another's without losing precision. The same can happen with text files. Suppose system *A* stores text files as variable-length lines and system *B* pads text lines to a fixed length. Transferring a file from *A* to *B* and back can add padding to every line, making the final copy different from the original. However, automatically removing padding from the ends of lines during the transfer back to *A* will also make the copy different from the original for any files that had padding on some lines.

The exact details of differences in representation and the techniques to handle them depend on the computer systems involved. Furthermore, we have seen that not all representational differences can be accommodated – information can be lost when data must be translated from one representation to another. While it is not essential to learn about all possible representational differences, remembering that TCP/IP is designed for a heterogeneous environment will help explain some of the features of the TCP/IP file transfer protocols.

24.5 FTP: The Major TCP/IP File Transfer Protocol

File transfer is among the most frequently used TCP/IP applications, and it accounts for much network traffic. Standard file transfer protocols existed for the ARPANET before TCP/IP became operational. These early versions of file transfer software evolved into a current standard known as the *File Transfer Protocol* (*FTP*).

24.6 FTP Features

Given a reliable end-to-end transport protocol like TCP, file transfer might seem trivial. However, as the previous sections pointed out, the details of authorization, naming, and representation among heterogeneous machines make the protocol complex. In addition, FTP offers many facilities beyond the transfer function itself.

 • *Interactive Access.* Although FTP is designed to be used by programs, most implementations provide an interactive interface that allows humans to easily interact with remote servers. For example, a user can ask for a listing of all files in a directory on a remote machine. Also, the client usually responds to the input ''help'' by showing the user information about possible commands that can be invoked.

 • *Format (representation) Specification.* FTP allows the client to specify the type and format of stored data. For example, the user can specify whether a file contains text or binary integers and whether text files use the ASCII or EBCDIC character sets.

 • *Authentication Control.* FTP requires clients to authorize themselves by sending a login name and password to the server before requesting file transfers. The server refuses access to clients that cannot supply a valid login and password.

24.7 FTP Process Model

Like other servers, most FTP server implementations allow concurrent access by multiple clients. Clients use TCP to connect to a server. As described in Chapter 19, a single master server process awaits connections and creates a slave process to handle each connection. Unlike most servers, however, the slave process does not perform all the necessary computation. Instead, the slave accepts and handles the *control connection* from the client, but uses an additional process or processes to handle a separate *data transfer connection*. The control connection carries commands that tell the server which file to transfer. The data transfer connection, which also uses TCP as the transport protocol, carries all data transfers.

Usually, both the client and server create a separate process to handle the data transfer. While the exact details of the process architecture depend on the operating systems used, Figure 24.1 illustrates the concept:

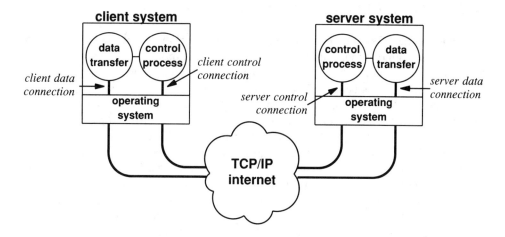

Figure 24.1 An FTP client and server with a TCP control connection between them and a separate TCP connection between their associated data transfer processes.

As the figure shows, the client control process connects to the server control process using one TCP connection, while the associated data transfer processes use their own TCP connection. In general, the control processes and the control connection remain alive as long as the user keeps the FTP session going. However, FTP establishes a new data transfer connection for each file transfer. In fact, many implementations create a new pair of data transfer processes, as well as a new TCP connection, whenever the server needs to send information to the client. The idea can be summarized:

> *Data transfer connections and the data transfer processes that use them can be created dynamically when needed, but the control connection persists throughout a session. Once the control connection disappears, the session is terminated and the software at both ends terminates all data transfer processes.*

Of course, client implementations that execute on a computer without operating system support for multiple processes may have a less complex structure. Such implementations often sacrifice generality by using a single application program to perform both the data transfer and control functions. However, the protocol requires that such clients still use multiple TCP connections, one for control and the other(s) for data transfer.

24.8 TCP Port Number Assignment

When a client forms an initial connection to a server, the client uses a random, locally assigned, protocol port number, but contacts the server at a well-known port (*21*). As Chapter 19 points out, a server that uses only one protocol port can accept connections from many clients because TCP uses both endpoints to identify a connection. The question arises, ''When the control processes create a new TCP connection for a given data transfer, what protocol port numbers do they use?'' Obviously, they cannot use the same pair of port numbers used in the control connection. Instead, the client obtains an unused port on its machine, and uses the port to contact the data transfer process on the server's machine. The data transfer process on the server machine can use the well-known port reserved for FTP data transfer (*20*). To ensure that a data transfer process on the server connects to the correct data transfer process on the client machine, the server side must not accept connections from an arbitrary process. Instead, when it issues the TCP passive open request, a server specifies the port that will be used on the client machine as well as the local port.

Finding a remote port might seem difficult, but now we can see why the protocol uses two connections: the client control process can obtain a random local port to be used in the file transfer, communicate the port number to the server over the control connection, wait for the server to establish a data transfer process accepting a connection from that port, and then start a transfer process on the client machine to make the connection. In general:

> *In addition to passing user commands to the server, FTP uses the control connection to allow client and server control processes to coordinate their use of dynamically assigned TCP protocol ports and the creation of data transfer processes that use those ports.*

What format should FTP use for data passing across the control connection? Although they could have invented a new specification, the designers of FTP did not. Instead, they allow FTP to use the TELNET network virtual terminal protocol described in Chapter 23. Unlike the full TELNET protocol, FTP does not allow option negotiation; it uses only the basic NVT definition. Thus, management of an FTP control connection is much simpler than management of a standard TELNET connection. Despite its limitations, using the TELNET definition instead of inventing a new one helps simplify FTP considerably.

24.9 The User's View Of FTP

Users view FTP as an interactive system. Once invoked, the client performs the following operations repeatedly: read a line of input, parse the line to extract a command and its arguments, and execute the command with the specified arguments. For example, to initiate the version of FTP available under BSD UNIX, the user invokes the *ftp* command:

```
% ftp
```

The local FTP client program begins and issues a prompt to the user. Following the prompt, the user can issue commands like *help*.

```
ftp> help
Commands may be abbreviated.  Commands are:
```

!	cr	macdef	proxy	send
$	delete	mdelete	sendport	status
account	debug	mdir	put	struct
append	dir	mget	pwd	sunique
ascii	disconnect	mkdir	quit	tenex
bell	form	mls	quote	trace
binary	get	mode	recv	type
bye	glob	mput	remotehelp	user
case	hash	nmap	rename	verbose
cd	help	ntrans	reset	?
cdup	lcd	open	rmdir	
close	ls	prompt	runique	

To obtain more information about a given command the user types *help command* as in the following examples (output is shown in the format *ftp* produces):

```
ftp> help ls
ls              list contents of remote directory
ftp> help cdup
cdup            change remote working directory to parent directory
ftp> help glob
glob            toggle metacharacter expansion of local file names
ftp> help bell
bell            beep when command completed
```

To execute a command, the user types the command name:

```
ftp> bell
Bell mode on.
```

24.10 An Example Anonymous FTP Session

While the access authorization facilities in FTP make it more secure, strict enforce-
ment prohibits an arbitrary client from accessing any file until they obtain a login and
password for the computer on which the server operates. To provide access to public
files, many TCP/IP sites allow *anonymous FTP*. Anonymous FTP access means a
client does not need an account or password. Instead, the user specifies login name
anonymous and password *guest*. The server allows anonymous logins, but restricts access to only publicly available files†.

Usually, users execute only a few FTP commands to establish a connection and obtain a file; few users have ever tried most commands. For example, suppose someone
has placed an on-line copy of a text in file *tcpbook.tar* in the subdirectory *pub/comer* on
machine *arthur.cs.purdue.edu*. A user logged in at another site as *usera* could obtain a
copy of the file by executing the following:

```
% ftp ftp.cs.purdue.edu
Connected to arthur.cs.purdue.edu.
220 arthur.cs.purdue.edu FTP server (Version 6.8) ready.
Name (ftp.cs.purdue.edu:usera): anonymous
331 Guest login ok, send e-mail address as password.
Password: guest
230 Guest login ok, access restrictions apply.
ftp> get pub/comer/tcpbook.tar bookfile
200 PORT command okay.
150 Opening ASCII mode data connection for tcpbook.tar (9895469 bytes).
226 Transfer complete.
9895469 bytes received in 22.76 seconds (4.3e+02 Kbytes/s)
ftp> close
221 Goodbye.
ftp> quit
```

In this example, the user specifies machine *arthur.cs.purdue.edu* as an argument to
the FTP command, so the client automatically opens a connection and prompts for authorization. The user invokes anonymous FTP by specifying login *anonymous* and
password *guest*‡ (although our example shows the password that the user types, the ftp
program does not display it on the user's screen).

After typing a login and password, the user requests a copy of a file using the *get*
command. In the example, the *get* command is followed by two arguments that specify
the remote file name and a name for the local copy. The remote file name is
pub/comer/tcpbook.tar and the local copy will be placed in *bookfile*. Once the transfer
completes, the user types *close* to break the connection with the server, and types *quit* to
leave the client.

---

†In many UNIX systems, the server restricts anonymous FTP by changing the file system root to a small,
restricted directory (e.g., */usr/ftp*).

‡In practice, the server emits additional messages that request the user to use an e-mail address instead of
guest.

Intermingled with the commands the user types are informational messages. FTP messages always begin with a 3-digit number followed by text. Most come from the server; other output comes from the local client. For example, the message that begins *220* comes from the server and contains the domain name of the machine on which the server executes. The statistics that report the number of bytes received and the rate of transfer come from the client. In general:

> *Control and error messages between the FTP client and server begin with a 3-digit number followed by text. The software interprets the number; the text is meant for humans.*

The example session also illustrates a feature of FTP described earlier: the creation of new TCP connections for data transfer. Notice the *PORT* command in the output. The client *PORT* command reports that a new TCP port number has been obtained for use as a data connection. The client sends the port information to the server over the control connection; data transfer processes at both ends use the new port number when forming a connection. After the transfer completes, the data transfer processes at each end close the connection.

24.11 TFTP

Although FTP is the most general file transfer protocol in the TCP/IP suite, it is also the most complex and difficult to program. Many applications do not need the full functionality FTP offers, nor can they afford the complexity. For example, FTP requires clients and servers to manage multiple concurrent TCP connections, something that may be difficult or impossible on personal computers that do not have sophisticated operating systems.

The TCP/IP suite contains a second file transfer protocol that provides inexpensive, unsophisticated service. Known as the *Trivial File Transfer Protocol*, or *(TFTP)*, it is intended for applications that do not need complex interactions between the client and server. TFTP restricts operations to simple file transfers and does not provide authentication. Because it is more restrictive, TFTP software is much smaller than FTP.

Small size is important in many applications. For example, manufacturers of diskless devices can encode TFTP in read-only memory (ROM) and use it to obtain an initial memory image when the machine is powered on. The program in ROM is called the system *bootstrap*. The advantage of using TFTP is that it allows bootstrapping code to use the same underlying TCP/IP protocols that the operating system uses once it begins execution. Thus, it is possible for a computer to bootstrap from a server on another physical network.

Unlike FTP, TFTP does not need a reliable stream transport service. It runs on top of UDP or any other unreliable packet delivery system, using timeout and retransmission to ensure that data arrives. The sending side transmits a file in fixed size (*512* byte) blocks and awaits an acknowledgement for each block before sending the next. The receiver acknowledges each block upon receipt.

The rules for TFTP are simple. The first packet sent requests a file transfer and establishes the interaction between client and server – the packet specifies a file name and whether the file will be read (transferred to the client) or written (transferred to the server). Blocks of the file are numbered consecutively starting at *1*. Each data packet contains a header that specifies the number of the block it carries, and each acknowledgement contains the number of the block being acknowledged. A block of less than *512* bytes signals the end of file. It is possible to send an error message either in the place of data or an acknowledgement; errors terminate the transfer.

Figure 24.2 shows the format of the five TFTP packet types. The initial packet must use operation codes *1* or *2*, specifying either a *read request* or a *write request*. The initial packet contains the name of the file as well as the access mode the client requests (*read* access or *write* access).

2-octet opcode	n octets	1 octet	n octets	1 octet
READ REQ. (1)	FILENAME	0	MODE	0

2-octet opcode	n octets	1 octet	n octets	1 octet
WRITE REQ. (2)	FILENAME	0	MODE	0

2-octet opcode	2 octets	up to 512 octets
DATA (3)	BLOCK #	DATA OCTETS...

2-octet opcode	2 octets
ACK (3)	BLOCK #

2-octet opcode	2 octets	n octets	1 octet
ERROR (5)	ERROR CODE	ERROR MESSAGE	0

Figure 24.2 The five TFTP message types. Fields are not shown to scale because some are variable length; an initial 2-octet operation code identifies the message format.

Once a *read* or *write* request has been made, the server uses the IP address and UDP protocol port number of the client to identify subsequent operations. Thus, neither *data* messages (the messages that carry blocks from the file) nor *ack* messages (the messages that acknowledge data blocks) need to specify the file name. The final message type illustrated in Figure 24.2 is used to report errors. Lost messages can be retransmitted after a timeout, but most other errors simply cause termination of the interaction.

TFTP retransmission is unusual because it is symmetric. Each side implements a timeout and retransmission. If the side sending data times out, it retransmits the last data block. If the side responsible for acknowledgements times out, it retransmits the last acknowledgement. Having both sides participate in retransmission helps ensure that transfer will not fail after a single packet loss.

While symmetric retransmission guarantees robustness, it can lead to excessive retransmissions. The problem, known as the *Sorcerer's Apprentice Bug*, arises when an acknowledgement for data packet k is delayed, but not lost. The sender retransmits the data packet, which the receiver acknowledges. Both acknowledgements eventually arrive, and each triggers a transmission of data packet $k+1$. The receiver will acknowledge both copies of data packet k+1, and the two acknowledgements will each cause the sender to transmit data packet $k+2$. The Sorcerer's Apprentice Bug can also start if the underlying internet duplicates packets. Once started, the cycle continues indefinitely with each data packet being transmitted exactly twice.

Although TFTP contains little except the minimum needed for transfer, it does support multiple file types. One interesting aspect of TFTP allows it to be integrated with electronic mail†. A client can specify to the server that it will send a file that should be treated as mail with the *FILENAME* field taken to be the name of a mailbox to which the server should deliver the message.

24.12 NFS

Initially developed by Sun Microsystems Incorporated, the *Network File System* (*NFS*) provides on-line shared file access that is transparent and integrated; many TCP/IP sites use NFS to interconnect their computers' file systems. From the user's perspective, NFS is almost invisible. A user can execute an arbitrary application program and use arbitrary files for input or output. The file names themselves do not show whether the files are local or remote.

24.13 NFS Implementation

Figure 24.3 illustrates how NFS is embedded in an operating system. When an application program executes, it calls the operating system to *open* a file, or to *store* and *retrieve* data in files. The file access mechanism accepts the request and automatically passes it to either the local file system software or to the NFS client, depending on whether the file is on the local disk or on a remote machine. When it receives a request, the client software uses the NFS protocol to contact the appropriate server on a remote machine and perform the requested operation. When the remote server replies, the client software returns the results to the application program.

---

†In practice, sites should not use TFTP to transport mail. Refer to Chapter 25 for details on electronic mail.

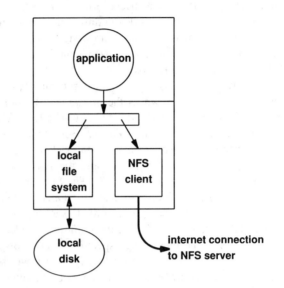

Figure 24.3 NFS code in an operating system. When an application program requests a file operation, the operating system must pass the request to the local file system or to the NFS client software.

24.14 Remote Procedure Call (RPC)

Instead of defining the NSF protocol from scratch, the designers chose to build three independent pieces: the NFS protocol itself, a general-purpose *Remote Procedure Call (RPC)* mechanism, and a general-purpose *eXternal Data Representation (XDR)*. Their intent was to separate the three to make it possible to use RPC and XDR in other software, including application programs as well as other protocols.

From the programmer's point of view, NFS itself provides no new procedures that a program can call. Instead, once a manager has configured NFS, programs access remote files using exactly the same operations as they use for local files. However, both RPC and XDR provide mechanisms that programmers can use to build distributed programs. For example, a programmer can divide a program into a client side and a server side that use RPC as the chief communication mechanism. On the client side, the programmer designates some procedures as *remote*, forcing the compiler to incorporate RPC code into those procedures. On the server side, the programmer implements the desired procedures and uses other RPC facilities to declare them to be part of a server. When the executing client program calls one of the remote procedures, RPC automatically collects values for arguments, forms a message, sends the message to the remote server, awaits a response, and stores returned values in the designated arguments. In essence, communication with the remote server occurs automatically as a side-effect of a remote procedure call. The RPC mechanism hides all the details of protocols, making it possible for programmers who know little about the underlying communication protocols to write distributed programs.

A related tool, XDR, provides a way for programmers to pass data among heterogeneous machines without writing procedures to convert among the hardware data representations. For example, not all computers represent 32-bit binary integers in the same format. Some store the most significant byte at the highest memory address, while others store the least significant byte at the highest address. Thus, if programmers use a network merely to move the bytes of an integer from one machine to another without rearranging them, the value of the integer may change. XDR solves the problem by defining a machine-independent representation. At one end of a communication channel, a program invokes XDR procedures to convert from the local hardware representation to the machine-independent representation. Once the data has been transferred to another machine, the receiving program invokes XDR routines to convert from the machine-independent representation to the machine's local representation.

The chief advantage of XDR is that it automates much of the data conversion task. Programmers do not need to type XDR procedure calls manually. Instead, they provide the XDR compiler with the declaration statements from the program for which data must be transformed, and the compiler automatically generates a program with the needed XDR library calls.

24.15 Summary

Access to data on remote files takes two forms: whole-file copying and shared on-line access. The File Transfer Protocol, FTP, is the major file transfer protocol in the TCP/IP suite. FTP uses whole-file copying and provides the ability for users to list directories on the remote machine as well as transfer files in either direction. The Trivial File Transfer Protocol, TFTP, provides a small, simple alternative to FTP for applications that need only file transfer. Because it is small enough to be contained in ROM, TFTP can be used for bootstrapping diskless machines.

The Network File System (NFS) designed by Sun Microsystems Incorporated provides on-line shared file access. It uses UDP for message transport and Sun's Remote Procedure Call (RPC) and eXternal Data Representation (XDR) mechanisms. Because RPC and XDR are defined separately from NFS, programmers can use them to build distributed applications.

FOR FURTHER STUDY

Postel [RFC 959] contains the FTP protocol standard. Over three dozen RFCs comment on FTP, propose modifications, or define new versions of the protocol. Among them, Lottor [RFC 913] describes a Simple File Transfer Protocol. DeSchon and Braden [RFC 1068] shows how to use FTP third-party transfer for background file transfer. The Trivial File Transfer Protocol described here comes from Sollins [RFC 783]; Finlayson [RFC 906] describes its use in bootstrapping computer systems.

Sun Microsystems has published three RFCs that define the Network File System and related protocols. RFC 1094 contains the standard for NFS, RFC 1057 defines RPC, and RFC 1014 specifies XDR. More details about RPC and NFS can be found in Volume 3 of this text.

EXERCISES

24.1 Why should file transport protocols compute a checksum on the file data they receive, even when using a reliable end-to-end stream transfer protocol like TCP?

24.2 Find out whether FTP computes a checksum for files it transfers.

24.3 What happens in FTP if the TCP connection being used for data transfer breaks, but the control connection does not?

24.4 What is the chief advantage of using separate TCP connections for control and data transfer? (Hint: think of abnormal conditions.)

24.5 Outline a method that uses TFTP to bootstrap a diskless machine. Be careful. Exactly what IP addresses does it use at each step?

24.6 Implement a TFTP client.

24.7 Experiment with FTP or an equivalent protocol to see how fast you can transfer a file between two reasonably large systems across a local area network. Try the experiment when the network is busy and when it is idle. Explain the result.

24.8 Try FTP from a machine to itself and then from the machine to another machine on the same local area network. Do the data transfer rates surprise you?

24.9 Compare the rates of transfer for FTP and NFS on a local area network. Can you explain the difference?

24.10 Examine the RPC definition. Does it handle datagram loss? duplication? delay? corruption?

24.11 Under what circumstances is the XDR scheme inefficient?

24.12 Consider translating floating point numbers from an internal form to an external form and back to an internal form. What are the tradeoffs in the choice of exponent and mantissa sizes in the external form?

25

Applications: Electronic Mail (822, SMTP, MIME)

25.1 Introduction

This chapter continues our exploration of internetworking by considering electronic mail service and the protocols that support it. The chapter describes how a mail system is organized, explains alias expansion, and shows how mail system software uses the client-server paradigm to transfer each message.

25.2 Electronic Mail

Many users first encounter computer networks when they send or receive electronic mail (e-mail) to or from a remote site. E-mail is the most widely used application service. Indeed, many computer users access networks only through electronic mail.

E-mail is popular because it offers a fast, convenient method of transferring information. E-mail can accommodate small notes or large voluminous memos with a single mechanism. It should not surprise you to learn that more users send files with electronic mail than with file transfer protocols.

Mail delivery is a new concept because it differs fundamentally from other uses of networks that we have discussed. In all our examples, network protocols send packets directly to destinations, using timeout and retransmission for individual segments if no acknowledgement returns. In the case of electronic mail, however, the system must provide for instances when the remote machine or the network connections have failed. A sender does not want to wait for the remote machine to become available before con-

433

tinuing work, nor does the user want the transfer to abort merely because communication with the remote machine becomes temporarily unavailable.

To handle delayed delivery, mail systems use a technique known as *spooling*. When the user sends a mail message, the system places a copy in its private storage (spool†) area along with identification of the sender, recipient, destination machine, and time of deposit. The system then initiates the transfer to the remote machine as a background activity, allowing the sender to proceed with other computational activities. Figure 25.1 illustrates the idea.

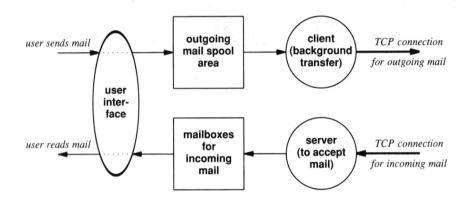

Figure 25.1 Conceptual components of an electronic mail system. The user invokes a user interface to deposit or retrieve mail; all transfers occur in the background.

The background mail transfer process becomes a client. The process first uses the domain name system to map the destination machine name to an IP address, and then attempts to form a TCP connection to the mail server on the destination machine. If it succeeds, the transfer process passes a copy of the message to the remote server, which stores the copy in the remote system's spool area. Once the client and server agree that the copy has been accepted and stored, the client removes the local copy. If it cannot form a TCP connection or if the connection fails, the transfer process records the time delivery was attempted and terminates. The background transfer process sweeps through the spool area periodically, typically once every 30 minutes, checking for undelivered mail. Whenever it finds a message or whenever a user deposits new outgoing mail, the background process attempts delivery again. If it finds that a mail message cannot be delivered after an extended time (e.g., 3 days), the mail software returns the message to the sender.

---

†Mail spool areas are sometimes called *mail queue* areas even though the term is technically inaccurate.

25.3 Mailbox Names And Aliases

There are three important ideas hidden in our simplistic description of mail delivery. First, users specify recipients by giving pairs of strings that identify the *mail destination machine name* and a *mailbox address* on that machine. Second, the names used in such specifications are independent of other names assigned to machines. Usually, a mailbox address is the same as a user's login id, and a destination machine name is the same as a machine's domain name, but that is not necessary. It is possible to assign a mailbox to a position of employment (e.g., the mailbox identifier *department-head* can refer to whoever currently chairs the department). Also, because the domain name system includes a separate query type for mail destinations, it is possible to decouple mail destination names from the usual domain names assigned to machines. Thus, mail sent to a user at *machine.com* may go to a different machine than a telnet connection to the same machine name. Third, our simplistic diagram fails to account for *mail processing* and *mail forwarding*, which include mail sent from one user to another on the same machine, and mail that arrives on a machine but which should be forwarded to another machine.

25.4 Alias Expansion And Mail Forwarding

Most systems provide *mail forwarding* software that includes a *mail alias expansion* mechanism. A mail forwarder allows the local site to map identifiers used in mail addresses to a set of one or more new mail addresses. Usually, after a user composes a message and names a recipient, the mail interface program consults the local aliases to replace the recipient with the mapped version before passing the message to the delivery system. Recipients for which no mapping has been specified remain unchanged. Similarly, the underlying mail system uses the mail aliases to map incoming recipient addresses.

Aliases increase mail system functionality and convenience substantially. In mathematical terms, alias mappings can be many-one or one-many. For example, the alias system allows a single user to have multiple mail identifiers, including nicknames and positions, by mapping a set of identifiers to a single person. The system also allows a site to associate groups of recipients with a single identifier. Using aliases that map an identifier to a list of identifiers makes it possible to establish a mail *exploder* that accepts one incoming message and sends it to a large set of recipients. The set of recipients associated with an identifier is called an *electronic mailing list*. Not all the recipients on a list need to be local. Although it is uncommon, it is possible to have a mailing list at site, *Q*, with none of the recipients from the list located at *Q*. Expanding a mail alias into a large set of recipients is a popular technique used widely. Figure 25.2 illustrates the components of a mail system that supports mail aliases and list expansion.

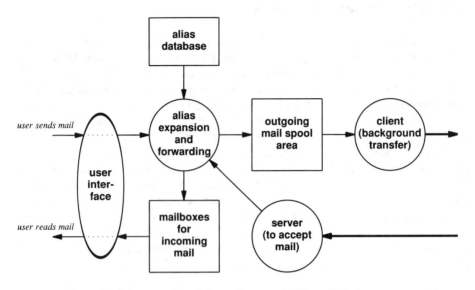

Figure 25.2 An extension of the mail system in Figure 25.1 that supports mail
aliases and forwarding. Both incoming and outgoing mail
passes through the alias expansion mechanism.

As Figure 25.2 shows, incoming and outgoing mail passes through the mail forwarder that expands aliases. Thus, if the alias database specifies that mail address x
maps to replacement y, alias expansion will rewrite destination address x, changing it to
y. The alias expansion program then determines whether y specifies a local or remote
address, so it knows whether to place the message in the incoming mail queue or outgoing mail queue.

Mail alias expansion can be dangerous. Suppose two sites establish conflicting
aliases. For example, assume site A maps mail address x into mail address y at site B,
while site B maps mail address y into address x at site A. A mail message sent to address x at site A could bounce forever between the two sites†. Similarly, if the manager
at site A accidentally maps a user's login name at that site to an address at another site,
the user will be unable to receive mail. The mail may go to another user or, if the alias
specifies an illegal address, senders will receive error messages.

25.5 The Relationship Of Internetworking And Mail

Many commercial computer systems can forward electronic mail from sites that do
not connect to the Internet. How do such systems differ from the mail system described
here? There are two crucial differences. First, a TCP/IP internet makes possible
universal delivery service. Second, electronic mail systems built on TCP/IP are in-

---

†In practice, most mail forwarders terminate messages after the number of exchanges reaches a predetermined threshold.

herently more reliable than those built from arbitrary networks. The first idea is easy to understand. TCP/IP makes possible universal mail delivery because it provides universal interconnection among machines. In essence, all machines attached to an internet behave as if attached to a single, vendor independent network. With the basic network services in place, devising a standard mail exchange protocol becomes easier.

The second claim, that using TCP/IP makes mail delivery more reliable than other mechanisms, needs explanation. The key idea here is that TCP provides end-to-end connectivity. That is, mail software on the sending machine acts as a client, contacting a server on the ultimate destination. Only after the client successfully transfers a mail message to the server does it remove the message from the local machine. Thus, direct, end-to-end delivery enforces the following principle:

> Mail systems that use end-to-end delivery can guarantee that each mail message remains in the sender's machine until it has been successfully copied to the recipient's machine.

With such systems, the sender can always determine the exact status of a message by checking the local mail spool area.

The alternative form of electronic mail delivery uses *mail gateways*†, sometimes called *mail bridges*, *mail relays*, or *intermediate mail stops* to transfer messages. In such systems, the sender's machine does not contact the recipient's machine directly, but sends mail across one or more intermediate machines that forward it on.

The main disadvantage of using mail gateways is that they introduce unreliability. Once the sender's machine transfers a message to the first intermediate machine, it discards the local copy. Thus, while the message is in transit, neither the sender nor the recipient have a copy. Failures at intermediate machines may result in message loss without informing either the sender or recipient. Message loss can also result if the mail gateways route mail incorrectly. Another disadvantage of mail gateways is that they introduce delay. A mail gateway can hold messages for minutes, hours, or even days if it cannot forward them on to the next machine. Neither the sender nor receiver can determine where a message has been delayed, why it has not arrived, or how long the delay will last. The important point is that the sender and recipient must depend on machines over which they may have no control.

If mail gateways are less reliable than end-to-end delivery, why are they used? The chief advantage of mail gateways is interoperability. Mail gateways provide connections among standard TCP/IP mail systems and other mail systems, as well as between TCP/IP internets and networks that do not support Internet protocols. Suppose, for example, that company *X* has a large internal network and that employees use electronic mail, but that the network software does not support TCP/IP. Although it may be infeasible to make the company's network part of the connected Internet, it might be easy to place a mail gateway between the company's private network and the Internet, and to devise software that accepts mail messages from the local network and forwards them to the Internet.

---

†Readers should not confuse the term *mail gateway* with the term *IP gateway*, discussed earlier.

While the idea of mail gateways may seem somewhat awkward, electronic mail has turned into such an important tool that users who do not have Internet access depend on them. Thus, although gateways service is not as reliable or convenient as end-to-end delivery, it can still be useful.

25.6 TCP/IP Standards For Electronic Mail Service

Recall that the goal of the TCP/IP protocol effort is to provide for interoperability across the widest range of computer systems and networks. To extend the interoperability of electronic mail, TCP/IP divides its mail standards into two sets. One standard specifies the format for mail messages†. The other specifies the details of electronic mail exchange between two computers. Keeping the two standards for electronic mail separate makes it possible to build mail gateways that connect TCP/IP internets to some other vendor's mail delivery system, while still using the same message format for both.

As anyone who has used electronic mail knows, each memo is divided into two parts: a header and a body, separated by a blank line. The TCP/IP standard for mail messages specifies the exact format of mail headers as well as the semantic interpretation of each header field; it leaves the format of the body up to the sender. In particular, the standard specifies that headers contain readable text, divided into lines that consist of a keyword followed by a colon followed by a value. Some keywords are required, others are optional, and the rest are uninterpreted. For example, the header must contain a line that specifies the destination. The line begins *To:* and contains the electronic mail address of the intended recipient on the remainder of the line. A line that begins *From:* contains the electronic mail address of the sender. Optionally, the sender may specify an address to which replies should be sent (i.e., to allow the sender to specify that replies should be sent to an address other than the sender's mailbox). If present, a line that begins *Reply-to:* specifies the address for replies. If no such line exists, the recipient will use information on the *From:* line as the return address.

The mail message format is chosen to make it easy to process and transport across heterogeneous machines. Keeping the mail header format straightforward allows it to be used on a wide range of systems. Restricting messages to readable text avoids the problems of selecting a standard binary representation and translating between the standard representation and the local machine's representation.

25.7 Electronic Mail Addresses

A user familiar with electronic mail knows that mail address formats vary among e-mail systems. Thus, it can be difficult to determine a correct electronic mail address, or even to understand the sender's intentions. Within the global Internet, addresses have a simple, easy to remember form:

local-part @ domain-name

---

†Mail system experts often refer to the mail message format as ''822'' because RFC 822 contains the standard (RFC 733 is a former standard no longer used).

where *domain-name* is the domain name of a mail destination† to which the mail should be delivered, and *local-part* is the address of a mailbox on that machine. For example, within the Internet, the author's electronic mail address is:

comer @ purdue . edu

However, mail gateways make addresses complex. Someone outside the Internet must either address the mail to the nearest mail gateway or have software that automatically does so. For example, when CSNET operated a mail gateway that connected between outside networks and the Internet, someone with access to the gateway might have used the following address to reach the author:

comer % purdue . edu @ relay . cs . net

Once the mail reached machine *relay.cs.net*, the mail gateway software extracted *local-part*, changed the percent sign (%) into an at sign (@), and used the result as a destination address to forward the mail.

The reason addresses become complex when they include non-Internet sites is that the electronic mail address mapping function is local to each machine. Thus, some mail gateways require the local part to contain addresses of the form:

user % domain-name

while others require:

user : domain-name

and still others use completely different forms. More important, electronic mail systems do not usually agree on conventions for precedence or quoting, making it impossible for a user to guarantee how addresses will be treated. For example, consider the electronic mail address:

comer % purdue . edu @ relay . cs . net

mentioned earlier. A site using the TCP/IP standard for mail would interpret the address to mean, "send the message to mail exchanger *relay.cs.net* and let that mail exchanger decide how to interpret *comer % purdue . edu*" (the local part). In essence, the sites act as if the address were parenthesized:

(comer % purdue . edu) @ (relay . cs . net)

At sites that use % to separate user names from destination machines, the same address might mean, "send the mail to user *comer* at the site given by the remainder of the address." That is, such sites act as if the address were parenthesized:

(comer) % (purdue . edu @ relay . cs . net)

---

†Technically, the domain name specifies a *mail exchanger*, not a machine name.

We can summarize the problem:

Because each mail gateway determines the exact details of how it in-
terprets and maps electronic mail addresses, there is no standard for
addresses that cross mail gateway boundaries to networks outside the
Internet.

25.8 Pseudo Domain Addresses

To help solve the problem of multiple mail systems, each with its own e-mail address format, a site can use domain-style names for all e-mail addresses, even if the site
does not use the domain name system. For example, a site that uses UUCP can implement a pseudo-domain, *uucp*, that allows users to specify mail addresses of the form:

uucp-style address @ uucp

or a related form:

user @ uucp-site . uucp

The local mail forwarding software recognizes the special addresses and translates them
to the address syntax required by the UUCP network software. From the user's perspective, the advantage is clear: all electronic addresses have the same general format
independent of the underlying communication network used to reach the recipient. Of
course, such addresses only work where local mailers have been instructed to map them
into appropriate forms and only when the appropriate transport mechanisms are available. Furthermore, even though pseudo-domain mail addresses have the same form as
domain names, they can only be used with electronic mail – one cannot find IP addresses or mail exchanger addresses for them using the domain name system.

25.9 Simple Mail Transfer Protocol (SMTP)

In addition to message formats, the TCP/IP protocol suite specifies a standard for
the exchange of mail between machines. That is, the standard specifies the exact format
of messages a client on one machine uses to transfer mail to a server on another. The
standard transfer protocol is known as *SMTP*, the *Simple Mail Transfer Protocol*. As
you might guess, SMTP is simpler than an earlier *Mail Transfer Protocol, MTP*. The
SMTP protocol focuses specifically on how the underlying mail delivery system passes
messages across a link from one machine to another. It does not specify how the mail
system accepts mail from a user or how the user interface presents the user with incoming mail. Also, SMTP does not specify how mail is stored or how frequently the mail
system attempts to send messages.

SMTP is surprisingly straightforward. Communication between a client and server consists of readable ASCII text. Although SMTP rigidly defines the command format, humans can easily read a transcript of interactions between a client and server. Initially, the client establishes a reliable stream connection to the server and waits for the server to send a *220 READY FOR MAIL* message. (If the server is overloaded, it may delay sending the *220* message temporarily.) Upon receipt of the *220* message, the client sends a *HELO*† command. The end of a line marks the end of a command. The server responds by identifying itself. Once communication has been established, the sender can transmit one or more mail messages, terminate the connection, or request the server to exchange the roles of sender and receiver so messages can flow in the opposite direction. The receiver must acknowledge each message. It can also abort the entire connection or abort the current message transfer.

Mail transactions begin with a *MAIL* command that gives the sender identification as well as a *FROM:* field that contains the address to which errors should be reported. A recipient prepares its data structures to receive a new mail message, and replies to a *MAIL* command by sending the response *250*. Response *250* means that all is well. The full response consists of the text *250 OK*. As with other application protocols, programs read the abbreviated commands and 3-digit numbers at the beginning of lines; the remaining text is intended to help humans debug mail software.

After a successful *MAIL* command, the sender issues a series of *RCPT* commands that identify recipients of the mail message. The receiver must acknowledge each *RCPT* command by sending *250 OK* or by sending the error message *550 No such user here*.

After all *RCPT* commands have been acknowledged, the sender issues a *DATA* command. In essence, a *DATA* command informs the receiver that the sender is ready to transfer a complete mail message. The receiver responds with message *354 Start mail input* and specifies the sequence of characters used to terminate the mail message. The termination sequence consists of 5 characters: carriage return, line feed, period, carriage return, and line feed‡.

An example will clarify the SMTP exchange. Suppose user *Smith* at host *Alpha.EDU* sends a message to users *Jones*, *Green*, and *Brown* at host *Beta.GOV*. The SMTP client software on host *Alpha.EDU* contacts the SMTP server software on host *Beta.GOV* and begins the exchange shown in Figure 25.3.

---

†*HELO* is an abbreviation for ''hello.''
‡SMTP uses *CR LF* to terminate a line, and forbids the body of a mail message to have a period on a line by itself.

```
S: 220 Beta.GOV Simple Mail Transfer Service Ready
C: HELO Alpha.EDU
S: 250 Beta.GOV

C: MAIL FROM:<Smith@Alpha.EDU>
S: 250 OK

C: RCPT TO:<Jones@Beta.GOV>
S: 250 OK

C: RCPT TO:<Green@Beta.GOV>
S: 550 No such user here

C: RCPT TO:<Brown@Beta.GOV>
S: 250 OK

C: DATA
S: 354 Start mail input; end with <CR><LF>.<CR><LF>
C: ...sends body of mail message...
C: ...continues for as many lines as message contains
C: <CR><LF>.<CR><LF>
S: 250 OK

C: QUIT
S: 221 Beta.GOV Service closing transmission channel
```

Figure 25.3 Example of SMTP transfer from Alpha.EDU to Beta.GOV.
Lines that begin with "C:" are transmitted by the client (Alpha), while lines that begin "S:" are transmitted by the server.
In the example, machine Beta.GOV does not recognize the intended recipient Green.

In the example, the server rejects recipient *Green* because it does not recognize the
name as a valid mail destination (i.e., it is neither a user nor a mailing list). The SMTP
protocol does not specify the details of how a client handles such errors – the client
must decide. Although clients can abort the delivery completely if an error occurs,
most clients do not. Instead, they continue delivery to all valid recipients and then report problems to the original sender. Usually, the client reports errors using electronic
mail. The error message contains a summary of the error as well as the header of the
mail message that caused the problem.

Once a client has finished sending all the mail messages it has for a particular destination, the client may issue the *TURN*† command to turn the connection around. If it
does, the receiver responds *250 OK* and assumes control of the connection. With the
roles reversed, the side that was originally a server sends back any waiting mail mes-

---

†In practice, few mail servers use the *TURN* command.

sages. Whichever side controls the interaction can choose to terminate the session. To do so, it issues a *QUIT* command. The other side responds with command *221*, which means it agrees to terminate. Both sides then close the TCP connection gracefully.

SMTP is much more complex than we have outlined here. For example, if a user has moved, the server may know the user's new mailbox address. SMTP allows the server to choose to inform the client about the new address so the client can use it in the future. When informing the client about a new address, the server may choose to forward the mail that triggered the message, or it may request that the client take the responsibility for forwarding.

25.10 The MIME Extension For Non-ASCII Data

To allow transmission of non-ASCII data through e-mail, the IETF defined the *Multipurpose Internet Mail Extensions* (*MIME*). MIME does not change SMTP or replace it. Instead, MIME allows arbitrary data to be encoded in ASCII and then transmitted in a standard e-mail message. To accommodate arbitrary data types and representations, each MIME message includes information that tells the recipient the type of the data and the encoding used. MIME information resides in the 822 mail header – the MIME header lines specify the version of MIME used, the type of the data being sent, and the encoding used to convert the data to ASCII. For example, Figure 25.4 illustrates a MIME message that contains a photograph in standard *GIF*† representation. The GIF image has been converted to a 7-bit ASCII representation using the *base64* encoding.

```
From: bill@acollege.edu
To: john@somewhere.com
MIME-Version: 1.0
Content-Type: image/gif
Content-Transfer-Encoding: base64

...data for the image...
```

Figure 25.4 An example MIME message. Lines in the header identify the type of the data as well as the encoding used.

In the figure, the header line *MIME-Version:* declares that the message was composed using version *1.0* of the MIME protocol. The *Content-Type:* declaration specifies that the data is a GIF image, and the *Content-Transfer-Encoding:* header declares that *base64* encoding was used to convert the image to ASCII. To view the image, a receiver's mail system must first convert from *base64* encoding back to binary, and then run an application that displays a GIF image on the user's screen.

The MIME standard specifies that a *Content-Type* declaration must contain two identifiers, a *content type* and a *subtype*, separated by a slash. In the example, *image* is the content type, and *gif* is the subtype.

---

†GIF is the Graphics Interchange Format.

The standard defines seven basic content types, the valid subtypes for each, and transfer encodings. For example, although an *image* must be of subtype *jpeg* or *gif*, *text* cannot use either subtype. In addition to the standard types and subtypes, MIME permits a sender and receiver to define private content types†. Figure 25.5 lists the seven basic content types.

Content Type	Used When Data In the Message Is
text	Textual (e.g. a document).
image	A still photograph or computer-generated image
audio	A sound recording
video	A video recording that includes motion
application	Raw data for a program
multipart	Multiple messages that each have a separate content type and encoding
message	An entire e-mail message (e.g., a memo that has been forwarded) or an external reference to a message (e.g., an FTP server and file name)

Figure 25.5 The seven basic types that can appear in a MIME *Content-Type* declaration and their meanings.

25.11 MIME Multipart Messages

The MIME multipart content type is useful because it adds considerable flexibility. The standard defines four possible subtypes for a multipart message; each provides important functionality. Subtype *mixed* allows a single message to contain multiple, independent submessages that each can have an independent type and encoding. Mixed multipart messages make it possible to include text, graphics, and audio in a single message, or to send a memo with additional data segments attached, similar to *enclosures* included with a business letter. Subtype *alternative* allows a single message to include multiple representations of the same data. Alternative multipart messages are useful when sending a memo to many recipients who do not all use the same hardware and software system. For example, one can send a document as both plain ASCII text and in formatted form, allowing recipients who have computers with graphic capabilities to select the formatted form for viewing. Subtype *parallel* permits a single message to include subparts that should be viewed together (e.g., video and audio subparts that must be played simultaneously). Finally, subtype *digest* permits a single message to contain a set of other messages (e.g., a collection of the e-mail messages from a discussion).

Figure 25.6 illustrates one of the prime uses for multipart messages: an e-mail message can contain both a short text that explains the purpose of the message and other parts that contain nontextual information. In the figure, a note in the first part of the message explains that the second part contains a photographic image.

---

†To avoid potential name conflicts, the standard requires that names chosen for private content types each begin with the string *X-* .

```
From: bill@acollege.edu
To: john@somewhere.com
MIME-Version: 1.0
Content-Type: Multipart/Mixed; Boundary=StartOfNextPart

--StartOfNextPart
John,
    Here is the photo of our research lab that I promised
to send you.  You can see the equipment you donated.

Thanks again,
Bill

--StartOfNextPart
Content-Type: image/gif
Content-Transfer-Encoding: base64
    ...data for the image...
```

Figure 25.6 An example of a MIME mixed multipart message. Each part of
the message can have an independent content type.

The figure also illustrates a few details of MIME. For example, each header line can contain parameters of the form $X = Y$ after basic declarations. The keyword *Boundary=* following the multipart content type declaration in the header defines the string used to separate parts of the message. In the example, the sender has selected the string *StartOfNextPart* to serve as the boundary. Declarations of the content type and transfer encoding for a submessage, if included, immediately follow the boundary line. In the example, the second submessage is declared to be a GIF image.

25.12 Summary

Electronic mail is among the most widely available application services. Like most TCP/IP services, it uses the client-server paradigm. The mail system buffers outgoing and incoming messages, allowing the transfer from client and server to occur in background.

The TCP/IP protocol suite provides separate standards for mail message format and mail transfer. The mail message format, called *822*, uses a blank line to separate a message header and the body. The Simple Mail Transfer Protocol (SMTP) defines how a mail system on one machine transfers mail to a server on another.

The Multipurpose Internet Mail Extensions (MIME) provides a mechanism that allows arbitrary data to be transferred using SMTP. MIME adds lines to the header of an e-mail message to define the type of the data and the encoding used. MIME's mixed multipart type permits a single message to contain multiple data types.

FOR FURTHER STUDY

The protocols described in this chapter are all specified in Internet RFCs. Postel [RFC 821] describes the Simple Mail Transfer Protocol and gives many examples. The exact format of mail messages is given by Crocker [RFC 822]. Borenstein and Freed [RFC 1521] specifies the standard for MIME, including the syntax of header declarations, the interpretation of content types, and the *base64* encoding mentioned in this chapter. Moore [RFC 1522] defines MIME header extensions for non-ASCII text, and Postel [RFC 1590] describes the procedure for registration of new content and encoding types. Partridge [RFC 974] discusses the relationship between mail routing and the domain name system. Horton [RFC 976] proposes a standard for the UNIX UUCP mail system.

EXERCISES

25.1   Some mail systems force the user to specify a sequence of machines through which the message should travel to reach its destination. The mail protocol in each machine merely passes the message on to the next machine. List three disadvantages of such a scheme.

25.2   Find out if your computing system allows you to invoke SMTP directly.

25.3   Build an SMTP client and use it to deliver a mail message.

25.4   See if you can send mail through a mail gateway and back to yourself.

25.5   Make a list of mail address forms that your site handles and write a set of rules for parsing them.

25.6   Find out how the UNIX *sendmail* program can be used to implement a mail gateway.

25.7   Find out how often your local mail system attempts delivery and how long it will continue before giving up.

25.8   Many mail systems allow users to direct incoming mail to a program instead of storing it in a mailbox. Build a program that accepts your incoming mail, places your mail in a file, and then sends a reply to tell the sender you are on vacation.

25.9   Read the SMTP standard carefully. Then use TELNET to connect to the SMTP port on a remote machine and ask the remote SMTP server to expand a mail alias.

25.10 A user receives mail in which the *To* field specifies the string *important-people*. The mail was sent from a computer on which the alias *important-people* includes no valid mailbox identifiers. Read the SMTP specification carefully to see how such a situation is possible.

25.11 Read the MIME standard carefully. What servers can be specified in a MIME external reference?

26

Applications: Internet Management (SNMP, SNMPv2)

26.1 Introduction

In addition to protocols that provide network level services and application programs that use those services, an internet needs software that allows managers to debug problems, control routing, and find computers that violate protocol standards. We refer to such activities as *internet management*. This chapter considers the ideas behind TCP/IP internet management software, and describes an internet management protocol.

26.2 The Level Of Management Protocols

Originally, many wide area networks included management protocols as part of their link level protocols. If a packet switch began misbehaving, the network manager could instruct a neighboring packet switch to send it a special *control packet*. Control packets caused the receiver to suspend normal operation and respond to commands from the manager. The manager could interrogate the packet switch to identify problems, examine or change routes, test one of the communication interfaces, or reboot the switch. Once managers repaired the problem, they could instruct the switch to resume normal operations. Because management tools were part of the lowest level protocol, managers were often able to control switches even if higher level protocols failed.

Unlike a homogeneous wide area network, a TCP/IP internet does not have a single link level protocol. Instead, the internet consists of multiple physical networks interconnected by IP routers. As a result, internet management differs from network management. First, a single manager can control heterogeneous routers†. Second, the controlled entities may not share a common link level protocol. Third, the set of machines a manager controls may lie at arbitrary points in an internet. In particular, a manager may need to control one or more machines that do not attach to the same physical network as the manager's computer. Thus, it may not be possible for a manager to communicate with machines being controlled unless the management software uses protocols that provide end-to-end connectivity across an internet. As a consequence, the internet management protocol used with TCP/IP operates above the transport level:

> *In a TCP/IP internet, IP routers form the active switches that managers need to examine and control. Because routers attach to heterogeneous networks, protocols for internet management operate at the application level and communicate using TCP/IP transport-level protocols.*

Designing internet management software to operate at the application level has several advantages. Because the protocols can be designed without regard to the underlying network hardware, one set of protocols can be used for all networks. Because the protocols can be designed without regard to the hardware on the managed machine, the same protocols can be used for all managed devices. From a manager's point of view, having a single set of management protocols means uniformity – all routers respond to exactly the same set of commands. Furthermore, because the management software uses IP for communication, a manager can control the routers across an entire TCP/IP internet without having direct attachment to every physical network or router.

Of course, building management software at the application level also has disadvantages. Unless the operating system, IP software, and transport protocol software work correctly, the manager may not be able to contact the router. For example, if the router's routing table becomes damaged, it may be impossible to correct the table or reboot the machine from a remote site. If the operating system on a router crashes, it will be impossible to reach the application program that implements the internet management protocols even if the router can still field hardware interrupts and route packets.

26.3 Architectural Model

Despite the potential disadvantages, having TCP/IP management software operate at the application level has worked well in practice. The most significant advantage of placing network management protocols at a high level becomes apparent when one considers a large internet, where a manager's computer does not need to attach directly to all physical networks that contain managed entities. Figure 26.1 shows an example of the architecture.

---

†Although managers can control both routers and hosts, we will focus on control of routers because they present the most complexity.

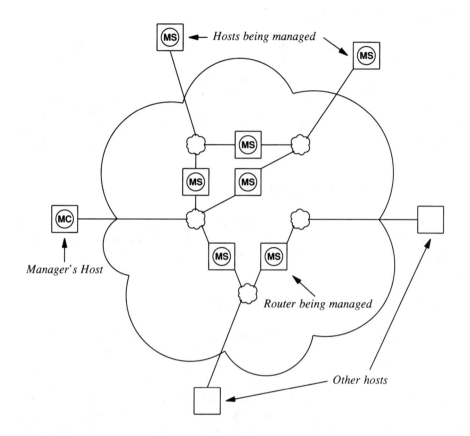

Figure 26.1 Example of network management. A manager invokes management client (MC) software that contacts management server
(MS) software on routers throughout the internet.

As the figure shows, each participating host or router runs a server program.
Technically, the server is called a *management agent*. A manager invokes client
software on the local host computer and specifies an agent with which it communicates.
After the client contacts the agent, it sends queries to obtain information or it sends
commands to change conditions in the router. Of course, not all routers in a large internet fall under a single manager. Most managers only control a few routers at their local
sites.

Internet management software uses an authentication mechanism to ensure only authorized managers can access or control a particular router. Some management protocols support multiple levels of authorization, allowing a manager specific privileges on
each router. For example, a specific router could be configured to allow several
managers to obtain information while only allowing a select subset of them to change
information or control the router.

26.4 Protocol Architecture

TCP/IP network† management protocols divide the management problem into two parts and specify separate standards for each part. The first part concerns communication of information. A protocol specifies how client software running on a manager's host communicates with an agent. The protocol defines the format and meaning of messages clients and servers exchange as well as the form of names and addresses. The second part concerns the data being managed. A protocol specifies which data items a router must keep as well as the name of each data item and the syntax used to express the name.

26.4.1 A Standard Network Management Protocol

The current standard TCP/IP network management protocol is the *Simple Network Management Protocol* (*SNMP*). A second version has been approved, but is not widely in use at the time this is being written. Known as *SNMPv2*, the new version adds new capabilities, including stronger security.

26.4.2 A Standard For Managed Information

A router being managed must keep control and status information that the manager can access. For example, a router keeps statistics on the status of its network interfaces, incoming and outgoing traffic, dropped datagrams, and error messages generated. Although it allows a manager to access these statistics, SNMP does not specify exactly which data can be accessed. Instead, a separate standard specifies the details. Known as a *Management Information Base* (*MIB*), the standard specifies the data items a host or router must keep and the operations allowed on each. For example, the MIB specifies that IP software must keep a count of all octets that arrive over each network interface, and it specifies that network management software can only read those values.

The MIB for TCP/IP divides management information into eight categories as Figure 26.2 shows. The choice of categories is important because identifiers used to specify items include a code for the category.

---

†Technically, there is a distinction between internet management protocols and network management protocols. Historically, however, TCP/IP internet management protocols are known as *network management* protocols; we will follow the accepted terminology.

MIB category	Includes Information About
system	The host or router operating system
interfaces	Individual network interfaces
addr. trans.	Address translation (e.g., ARP mappings)
ip	Internet Protocol software
icmp	Internet Control Message Protocol software
tcp	Transmission Control Protocol software
udp	User Datagram Protocol software
egp	Exterior Gateway Protocol software

Figure 26.2 Categories of information in the MIB. The category is encoded in the identifier used to specify an object.

Keeping the MIB definition independent of the network management protocol has advantages for both vendors and users. A vendor can include SNMP agent software in a product such as a router, with the guarantee that the software will continue to adhere to the standard after new MIB items are defined. A customer can use the same network management client software to manage multiple routers that have different versions of a MIB. Of course, a router that does not have new MIB items cannot provide the information in those items. However, because all routers use the same language for communication, they can all parse a query and either provide the requested information or send an error message explaining that they do not have the requested item.

26.5 Examples of MIB Variables

In addition to the standard TCP/IP MIB, which is known as *MIB-II*, many RFCs document MIB variables for specific devices. Examining a few of the data items the standard MIB includes will help clarify the contents. Figure 26.3 lists example MIB variables along with their categories.

MIB Variable	Category	Meaning
sysUpTime	system	Time since last reboot
ifNumber	interfaces	Number of network interfaces
ifMtu	interfaces	MTU for a particular interface
ipDefaultTTL	ip	Value IP uses in time-to-live field
ipInReceives	ip	Number of datagrams received
ipForwDatagrams	ip	Number of datagrams forwarded
ipOutNoRoutes	ip	Number of routing failures
ipReasmOKs	ip	Number of datagrams reassembled
ipFragOKs	ip	Number of datagrams fragmented
ipRoutingTable	ip	IP Routing table
icmpInEchos	icmp	Number of ICMP Echo Requests received
tcpRtoMin	tcp	Minimum retransmission time TCP allows
tcpMaxConn	tcp	Maximum TCP connections allowed
tcpInSegs	tcp	Number of segments TCP has received
udpInDatagrams	udp	Number of UDP datagrams received
egpInMsgs	egp	Number of EGP messages received

Figure 26.3 Examples of MIB variables along with their categories.

Values for most of the items listed in Figure 26.3 can be stored in a single integer. However, the MIB also defines more complex structures. For example, the MIB variable *ipRoutingTable* refers to a router's routing table. Additional MIB variables define the contents of a routing table entry, and allow the network management protocols to reference the data for individual entries. Of course, MIB variables present only a logical definition of each data item – the internal data structures a router uses may differ from the MIB definition. When a query arrives, software in the agent on the router is responsible for mapping between the MIB variable and the data structure the router uses to store the information.

26.6 The Structure Of Management Information

In addition to the MIB standard, which specifies network management variables and their meanings, a separate standard specifies a set of rules used to define and identify MIB variables. The rules are known as the *Structure of Management Information* (*SMI*) specification. To keep network management protocols simple, the SMI places restrictions on the types of variables allowed in the MIB, specifies the rules for naming those variables, and creates rules for defining variable types. For example, the SMI standard includes definitions of terms like *IpAddress* (defining it to be a 4-octet string) and *Counter* (defining it to be an integer in the range of 0 to 2^{32}-1), and specifies that they are the terms used to define MIB variables. More important, the rules in the SMI describe how the MIB refers to tables of values (e.g., the IP routing table).

26.7 Formal Definitions Using ASN.1

The SMI standard specifies that all MIB variables must be defined and referenced using ISO's *Abstract Syntax Notation 1 (ASN.1†)*. ASN.1 is a formal language that has two main features: a notation used in documents that humans read, and a compact encoded representation of the same information used in communication protocols. In both cases, the precise, formal notation removes any possible ambiguities from both the representation and meaning. For example, instead of saying that a variable contains an integer value, a protocol designer who uses ASN.1 must state the exact form and range of numeric values. Such precision is especially important when implementations include heterogeneous computers that do not all use the same representations for data items.

Besides keeping standards documents unambiguous, ASN.1 also helps simplify the implementation of network management protocols and guarantees interoperability. It defines precisely how to encode both names and data items in a message. Thus, once the documentation of a MIB has been expressed using ASN.1, the human readable form can be translated directly and mechanically into the encoded form used in messages. In summary:

> *The TCP/IP network management protocols use a formal notation called ASN.1 to define names and types for variables in the management information base. The precise notation makes the form and contents of variables unambiguous.*

26.8 Structure And Representation Of MIB Object Names

We said that ASN.1 specifies how to represent both data items and names. However, understanding the names used for MIB variables requires us to know about the underlying namespace. Names used for MIB variables are taken from the *object identifier* namespace administered by ISO and ITU. The key idea behind the object identifier namespace is that it provides a namespace in which all possible objects can be named. The namespace is not restricted to variables used in network management – it includes names for arbitrary objects (e.g., each international protocol standard document has a name).

The object identifier namespace is *absolute (global)*, meaning that names are structured to make them globally unique. Like most namespaces that are large and absolute, the object identifier namespace is hierarchical. Authority for parts of the namespace is subdivided at each level, allowing individual groups to obtain authority to assign some of the names without consulting a central authority for each assignment‡.

The root of the object identifier hierarchy is unnamed, but has three direct descendants managed by: ISO, ITU, and jointly by ISO and ITU. The descendants are assigned both short text strings and integers to identify them (the text strings are used

---

†ASN.1 is usually pronounced by reading the dot: 'A-S-N dot 1'.

‡Readers should recall from the Domain Name System discussion in Chapter 22 how authority for a hierarchical namespace is subdivided.

when humans need to understand object names; computer software uses the integers to form compact, encoded representations of the names). ISO has allocated one subtree for use by other national or international standards organizations (including U.S. standards organizations), and the U.S. National Institute for Standards and Technology† has allocated a subtree for the U.S. Department of Defense. Finally, the IAB has petitioned the Department of Defense to allocate it a subtree in the namespace.

Figure 26.4 illustrates pertinent parts of the object identifier hierarchy and shows the position of the node used by TCP/IP network management protocols.

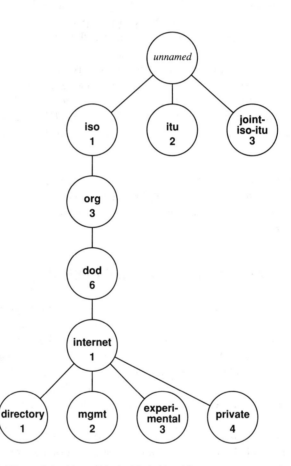

Figure 26.4 Part of the hierarchical object identifier namespace used to name MIB variables. An object's name consists of the numeric labels along a path from the root to the object.

---

†NIST was formerly the National Bureau of Standards.

The name of an object in the hierarchy is the sequence of numeric labels on the nodes along a path from the root to the object. The sequence is written with periods separating the individual components. For example, the name *1.3.6.1.1* denotes the node labeled *directory*. The MIB has been assigned a node under the *internet mgmt* subtree with label *mib* and numeric value *1*. Because all MIB variables fall under that node, they all have names beginning with the prefix *1.3.6.1.2.1*.

Earlier we said that the MIB groups all variables into eight categories. The exact meaning of the categories can now be explained: they are the eight subtrees of the *mib* node of the object identifier namespace. Figure 26.5 illustrates the idea by showing part of the naming subtree under the *mib* node.

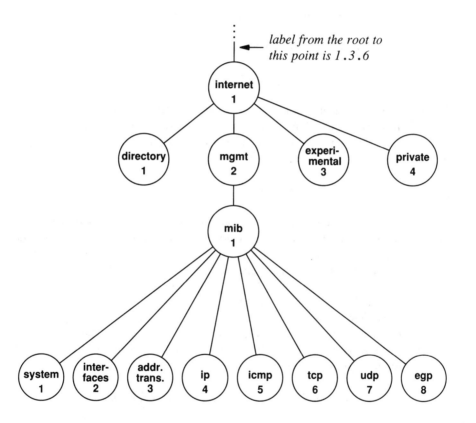

Figure 26.5 The object identifier namespace under the IAB *mib* node. Each subtree corresponds to one of the eight categories of MIB variables.

Two examples will make the naming syntax clear. Figure 26.5 shows that the category labeled *ip* has been assigned the numeric value *4*. Thus, the names of all MIB variables corresponding to IP have an identifier that begins with the prefix *1.3.6.1.2.1.4*. If one wanted to write out the textual labels instead of the numeric representation, the name would be:

iso.org.dod.internet.mgmt.mib.ip

A MIB variable named *ipInReceives* has been assigned numeric identifier *3* under the *ip* node in the namespace, so its name is:

iso.org.dod.internet.mgmt.mib.ip.ipInReceives

and the corresponding numeric representation is:

1.3.6.1.2.1.4.3

When network management protocols use names of MIB variables in messages, each name has a suffix appended. For simple variables, the suffix *0* refers to the instance of the variable with that name. So, when it appears in a message sent to a router, the numeric representation of *ipInReceives* is:

1.3.6.1.2.1.4.3.0

which refers to the instance of *ipInReceives* on that router. Note that there is no way to guess the numeric value or suffix assigned to a variable. One must consult the published standards to find which numeric values have been assigned to each object type. Thus, programs that provide mappings between the textual form and underlying numeric values do so entirely by consulting tables of equivalences – there is no closed-form computation that performs the transformation.

As a second, more complex example, consider the MIB variable *ipAddrTable*, which contains a list of the IP addresses for each network interface. The variable exists in the namespace as a subtree under *ip*, and has been assigned the numeric value *20*. Therefore, a reference to it has the prefix:

iso.org.dod.internet.mgmt.mib.ip.ipAddrTable

with a numeric equivalent:

1.3.6.1.2.1.4.20

In programming language terms, we think of the IP address table as a one-dimensional array, where each element of the array consists of a structure (record) that contains five items: an IP address, the integer index of an interface corresponding to the entry, an IP subnet mask, an IP broadcast address, and an integer that specifies the maximum datagram size that the router will reassemble. Of course, not all routers have such an array in memory. The router may keep this information in many variables or may need to follow pointers to find it. However, the MIB provides a name for the array as if it existed, and allows network management software on individual routers to map table references into appropriate internal variables.

Using ASN.1 style notation, we can define *ipAddrTable*:

$$\text{ipAddrTable ::= SEQUENCE OF IpAddrEntry}$$

where *SEQUENCE* and *OF* are keywords that define an ipAddrTable to be a one-dimensional array of *IpAddrEntry*s. Each entry in the array is defined to consist of five fields (the definition assumes that *IpAddress* has already been defined).

$$
\begin{array}{l}
\text{IpAddrEntry ::= SEQUENCE \{} \\
\quad \text{ipAdEntAddr} \\
\qquad \text{IpAddress,} \\
\quad \text{ipAdEntIfIndex} \\
\qquad \text{INTEGER,} \\
\quad \text{ipAdEntNetMask} \\
\qquad \text{IpAddress,} \\
\quad \text{ipAdEntBcastAddr} \\
\qquad \text{IpAddress,} \\
\quad \text{ipAdEntReasmMaxSize} \\
\qquad \text{INTEGER (0..65535)} \\
\text{\}}
\end{array}
$$

Further definitions must be given to assign numeric values to *ipAddrEntry* and to each item in the *IpAddrEntry* sequence. For example, the definition:

$$\text{ipAddrEntry \{ ipAddrTable 1 \}}$$

specifies that *ipAddrEntry* falls under *ipAddrTable* and has numeric value *1*. Similarly, the definition:

$$\text{ipAdEntNetMask \{ ipAddrEntry 3 \}}$$

assigns *ipAdEntNetMask* numeric value *3* under *ipAddrEntry*.

We said that *ipAddrTable* was like a one-dimensional array. However, there is a significant difference in the way programmers use arrays and the way network management software uses tables in the MIB. Programmers think of an array as a set of elements that have an index used to select a specific element. For example, the programmer might write *xyz[3]* to select the third element from array *xyz*. ASN.1 syntax does not use integer indices. Instead, MIB tables append a suffix onto the name to select a specific element in the table. For our example of an IP address table, the standard specifies that the suffix used to select an item consists of an IP address. Syntactically, the IP address (in dotted decimal notation) is concatenated onto the end of the object name to form the reference. Thus, to specify the network mask field in the IP address table entry corresponding to address 128.10.2.3, one uses the name:

iso.org.dod.internet.mgmt.mib.ip.ipAddrTable.ipAddrEntry.ipAdEntNetMask.128.10.2.3

which, in numeric form, becomes:

1.3.6.1.2.1.4.20.1.3.128.10.2.3

Although concatenating an index to the end of a name may seem awkward, it provides a powerful tool that allows clients to search tables without knowing the number of items or the type of data used as an index. The next section shows how network management protocols use this feature to step through a table one element at a time.

26.9 Simple Network Management Protocol

Network management protocols specify communication between the network management client program a manager invokes and a network management server program executing on a host or router. In addition to defining the form and meaning of messages exchanged and the representation of names and values in those messages, network management protocols also define administrative relationships among routers being managed. That is, they provide for authentication of managers.

One might expect network management protocols to contain a large number of commands. Some early protocols, for example, supported commands that allowed the manager to: *reboot* the system, *add* or *delete* routes, *disable* or *enable* a particular network interface, or *remove cached address bindings*. The main disadvantage of building management protocols around commands arises from the resulting complexity. The protocol requires a separate command for each operation on a data item. For example, the command to delete a routing table entry differs from the command to disable an interface. As a result, the protocol must change to accommodate new data items.

SNMP takes an interesting alternative approach to network management. Instead of defining a large set of commands, SNMP casts all operations in a *fetch-store paradigm†*. Conceptually, SNMP contains only two commands that allow a manager to fetch a value from a data item or store a value into a data item. All other operations are defined as side-effects of these two operations. For example, although SNMP does not have an explicit *reboot* operation, an equivalent operation can be defined by declaring a data item that gives the time until the next reboot and allowing the manager to assign the item a value (including zero).

The chief advantages of using a fetch-store paradigm are stability, simplicity, and flexibility. SNMP is especially stable because its definition remains fixed, even though new data items are added to the MIB and new operations are defined as side-effects of storing into those items. SNMP is simple to implement, understand, and debug because

---

†The fetch-store paradigm comes from a management protocol system known as HEMS. See Partridge and Trewitt [RFCs 1021, 1022, 1023, and 1024] for details.

it avoids the complexity of having special cases for each command. Finally, SNMP is especially flexible because it can accommodate arbitrary commands in an elegant framework.

From a manager's point of view, of course, SNMP remains hidden. The user interface to network management software can phrase operations as imperative commands (e.g., *reboot*). Thus, there is little visible difference between the way a manager uses SNMP and other network management protocols. In fact, vendors have begun to sell network management software that offers a graphical user interface. Such software displays diagrams of network connectivity, and uses a point-and-click style of interaction.

As Figure 26.6 shows, SNMP offers more than the two operations we have described.

Command	Meaning
get-request	Fetch a value from a specific variable
get-next-request	Fetch a value without knowing its exact name
get-response	Reply to a fetch operation
set-request	Store a value in a specific variable
trap	Reply triggered by an event

Figure 26.6 The set of possible SNMP operations†. *Get-next-request* allows the manager to iterate through a table of items.

Operations *get-request*, *get-response*, and *set-request* provide the basic fetch and store operations (as well as replies to those operations). SNMP specifies that operations must be *atomic*, meaning that if a single SNMP message specifies operations on multiple variables, the server either performs all operations or none of them. In particular, no assignments will be made if any of them are in error. The *trap* operation allows managers to program servers to send information when an event occurs. For example, an SNMP server can be programmed to send a manager a *trap* message whenever one of the attached networks becomes unusable (i.e., an interface goes down).

26.9.1 Searching Tables Using Names

We said that ASN.1 does not provide mechanisms for declaring arrays or indexing them in the usual sense. However, it is possible to denote individual elements of a table by appending a suffix to the object identifier for the table. Unfortunately, a client program may wish to examine entries in a table for which it does not know all valid suffixes. The *get-next-request* operation allows a client to iterate through a table without knowing how many items the table contains. The rules are quite simple. When sending a *get-next-request*, the client supplies a prefix of a valid object identifier, *P*. The server examines the set of object identifiers for all variables it controls, and responds by sending a *get-response* command for the one that has an object identifier lexicographically

---

†SNMPv2 adds a *get-bulk* operation that permits a manager to fetch multiple values with a single request.

greater than *P*. Because the MIB uses suffixes to index tables, a client can send the prefix of an object identifier corresponding to a table and receive the first element in the table. The client can send the name of the first element in a table and receive the second, and so on.

Consider an example search. Recall that the *ipAddrTable* uses IP addresses to identify entries in the table. A client that does not know which IP addresses are in the table on a given router cannot form a complete object identifier. However, the client can still use the *get-next-request* operation to search the table by sending the prefix:

iso . org . dod . internet . mgmt . mib . ip . ipAddrTable . ipAddrEntry . ipAdEntNetMask

which, in numeric form, is:

$$1 . 3 . 6 . 1 . 2 . 1 . 4 . 20 . 1 . 3$$

The server returns the network mask field of the first entry in *ipAddrTable*. The client uses the full object identifier returned by the server to request the next item in the table.

26.10 SNMP Message Format

Unlike most TCP/IP protocols, SNMP messages do not have fixed fields. Instead, they use the standard ASN.1 encoding. Thus, they can be difficult for humans to decode and understand. After examining the SNMP message definition in ASN.1 notation, we will review the ASN.1 encoding scheme briefly, and see an example of an encoded SNMP message.

An SNMP message consists of three main parts: a protocol *version*, an SNMP *community* identifier (used to group together the routers managed by a given manager), and a *data* area. The data area is divided into *protocol data units* (*PDUs*). Each PDU consists of a request (sent by client) or a response (sent by server). Figure 26.7 shows how the message can be described in ASN.1 notation.

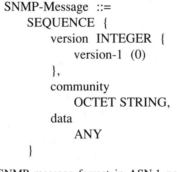

```
SNMP-Message  ::=
    SEQUENCE {
        version  INTEGER {
            version-1  (0)
        },
        community
            OCTET STRING,
        data
            ANY
    }
```

Figure 26.7 The SNMP message format in ASN.1 notation. The *data* area contains one or more protocol data units.

The five types of protocol data units are further described in ASN.1 notation in Figure 26.8.

<pre>
                  SNMP-PDUs ::=
                     CHOICE {
                        get-request
                           GetRequest-PDU,
                        get-next-request-PDU
                           GetNextRequest-PDU,
                        get-response
                           GetResponse-PDU,
                        set-request
                           SetRequest-PDU,
                        trap
                           Trap-PDU,
                     }
</pre>

Figure 26.8 The ASN.1 definitions of an SNMP PDU. The syntax for each request type must be specified further.

The definition specifies that each protocol data unit consists of one of the five request or response types. To complete the definition of an SNMP message, we must further specify the syntax of the five individual types. For example, Figure 26.9 shows the definition of a *get-request*.

<pre>
                  GetRequest-PDU ::= [0]
                     IMPLICIT SEQUENCE {
                        request-id
                           RequestID,
                        error-status
                           ErrorStatus,
                        error-index
                           ErrorIndex,
                        variable-bindings
                           VarBindList
                     }
</pre>

Figure 26.9 The ASN.1 definition of a *get-request* message. Formally, the message is defined to be a *GetRequest-PDU*.

Further definitions in the standard specify the remaining undefined terms. *Request-ID* is defined to be a 4-octet integer (used to match responses to queries). Both *Error-Status* and *ErrorIndex* are single octet integers which contain the value zero in a re-

quest. Finally, *VarBindList* contains a list of object identifiers for which the client
seeks values. In ASN.1 terms, the definitions specify that *VarBindList* is a sequence of
pairs of object name and value. ASN.1 represents the pairs as a sequence of two items.
Thus, in the simplest possible request, *VarBindList* is a sequence of two items: a name
and a *null*.

26.11 Example Encoded SNMP Message

The encoded form of ASN.1 uses variable-length fields to represent items. In general, each field begins with a header that specifies the type of object and its length in
bytes. For example, Figure 26.10 shows the string of encoded octets in a *get-request*
message for data item *sysDescr* (numeric object identifier *1.3.6.1.2.1.1.1*).

```
  30       29       02       01       00
SEQUENCE len=41 INTEGER  len=1   vers=0

  04       06       70       75       62       6C       69       63
string   len=6     p        u        b        l        i        c

  A0       1C       02       04       05       AE       56       02
getreq.  len=28 INTEGER  len=4   ------- request ID -------

  02       01       00       02       01       00
INTEGER  len=1    status  INTEGER  len=1 error index

  30       0E       30       0C       06       08
SEQUENCE len=14 SEQUENCE len=12 objectid len=8

  2B       06       01       02       01       01       01       00
  1.3   .   6   .   1   .   2   .   1   .   1   .   1   .   0

  05       00
null    len=0
```

Figure 26.10 The encoded form of a *get-request* for data item *sysDescr* with
octets shown in hexadecimal and their meanings below. Relat-
ed octets have been grouped onto lines; they are contiguous in
the message.

As Figure 26.10 shows, the message starts with a code for *SEQUENCE* which has
a length of 41 octets. The first item in the sequence is a 1-octet integer that specifies
the protocol *version*. The *community* field is stored in a character string, which in the
example, is a 6-octet string that contains the word *public*.

The *GetRequest-PDU* occupies the remainder of the message. The initial code specifies a *get-Request* operation. Because the high-order bit is turned on, the interpretation is *context specific*. That is, the hexadecimal value *A0* only specifies a *GetRequest-PDU* when used in an SNMP message; it is not a universally reserved value. Following the request octet, the length octet specifies the request is *28* octets long. The request ID is *4* octets, but each of the error status and error index are one octet. Finally, the sequence of pairs contains one binding, a single object identifier bound to a *null* value. The identifier is encoded as expected except that the first two numeric labels are combined into a single octet.

26.12 Summary

Network management protocols allow a manager to monitor and control routers and hosts. A network management client program executing on the manager's workstation contacts one or more servers, called agents, running on the computers to be controlled. Because an internet consists of heterogeneous machines and networks, TCP/IP management software executes as application programs and uses internet transport protocols (e.g., UDP) for communication between clients and servers.

The standard TCP/IP network management protocol is SNMP, the Simple Network Management Protocol. SNMP defines a low-level management protocol that provides two basic operations: fetch a value from a variable or store a value into a variable. In SNMP, all operations occur as side-effects of storing values into variables. SNMP defines the format of messages that travel between a manager's computer and a managed entity.

A companion standard to SNMP defines the set of variables that a managed entity maintains. The standard is known as a Management Information Base, or MIB. MIB variables are described using ASN.1, a formal language that provides a concise encoded form as well as a precise human-readable notation for names and objects. ASN.1 uses a hierarchical namespace to guarantee that all MIB names are globally unique while still allowing subgroups to assign parts of the namespace.

FOR FURTHER STUDY

Schoffstall, Fedor, Davin, and Case [RFC 1157] contains the standard for SNMP. ISO [May 87a] and [May 87b] contain the standard for ASN.1 and specify the encoding. McCloghrie and Rose [RFC 1213] defines the variables that comprise MIB-II, while McCloghrie and Rose [RFC 1211] contains the SMI rules for naming MIB variables.

A series of RFCs defines SNMPv2, which is a proposed standard at the time of this writing. Case, McCloghrie, Rose, Waldbusser [RFC 1441] contains an introduction to SNMPv2. Case, McCloghrie, Rose, and Waldbusser [RFC 1450] defines the

SNMPv2 MIB. Galvin and McCloghrie [RFC 1446] discusses SNMPv2 security protocols. Case, McCloghrie, Rose, Waldbusser [RFC 1448] specifies protocol operations.

An older proposal for a network management protocol called HEMS can be found
in Trewitt and Partridge [RFCs 1021, 1022, 1023, and 1024]. Davin, Case, Fedor, and
Schoffstall [RFC 1028] specifies a predecessor to SNMP known as the Simple Gateway
Monitoring Protocol (SGMP).

EXERCISES

26.1 Capture an SNMP packet with a network analyzer and decode the fields.

26.2 Read the standard to find out how ASN.1 encodes the first two numeric values from an
object identifier in a single octet. Why does it do so?

26.3 Read the specification for CMIP. How many commands does it support?

26.4 Suppose the MIB designers needed to define a variable that corresponded to a two-
dimensional array. How can ASN.1 notation accommodate references to such a variable?

26.5 What are the advantages and disadvantages of defining globally unique ASN.1 names for
MIB variables?

26.6 If you have SNMP client code available, try using it to read MIB variables in a local
router. What is the advantage of allowing arbitrary managers to read variables in all
routers?

26.7 Read the MIB specification to find the definition of variable *ipRoutingTable* that
corresponds to an IP routing table. Design a program that will use SNMP to contact
multiple routers, and see if any entries in their routing tables cause a routing loop. Exactly what ASN.1 names should such a program generate?

27

Summary Of Protocol Dependencies

27.1 Introduction

TCP/IP has spawned more protocols than we can discuss in a single text. For example, well-known distributed information systems like *gopher* and the *World Wide Web*, which provide the ability to browse and access information remotely, and remote graphic interfaces like the X-window system which allow client programs to paint text and graphics on bit-mapped displays, all use TCP/IP protocols. In general, each of these systems defines its own application protocol and relies on TCP or UDP for end-to-end transport. In fact, any programmer who builds a distributed application using TCP/IP defines yet another application-level protocol.

Although it is not important to understand the details of all protocols, it is important to know which protocols exist and how they can be used. This chapter provides a brief summary of the relationships among the major protocols we have discussed, and shows which ones are available for use by application programs.

27.2 Protocol Dependencies

The chart in Figure 27.1 shows dependencies among the major protocols we have discussed. Each enclosed polygon corresponds to one protocol, and resides directly above protocols that it uses. For example, the mail protocol, SMTP, depends on TCP, which depends on IP.

Users

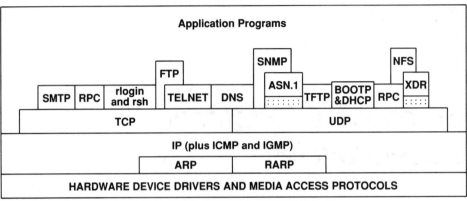

Hardware

Figure 27.1 Dependencies among major higher level TCP/IP protocols. A protocol uses those protocols that lie directly below it. Application programs can use all protocols above IP.

Several parts of the diagram need further explanation. The bottom layer represents all protocols that the hardware provides. This level includes all hardware control protocols, and ranges from media access to logical link allocation. As we have throughout the text, we will assume that any packet transfer system can be included in this layer as long as IP can use it to transfer datagrams. Thus, if a system is configured to send datagrams through a tunnel, the entry to the tunnel is treated like a hardware interface, despite its software implementation.

The second layer from the bottom lists ARP and RARP. Of course, not all machines or network technologies use them. ARP is most often used on Ethernets; RARP is seldom used except for diskless machines. Other address binding protocols can occur here, but none are currently in widespread use.

The third layer from the bottom contains IP. It includes the required error and control message protocol, ICMP, and the optional multicast group management protocol IGMP. Note that IP is the only protocol that spans an entire layer. All lower-level protocols deliver incoming information to IP, and all higher-level protocols must use IP to send outgoing datagrams. IP is shown with a direct dependency on the hardware layer because it needs to use the hardware link or access protocols to transmit datagrams after it uses ARP to bind addresses.

TCP and UDP comprise the transport layer. Of course, new transport protocols have been suggested, but none has been widely adopted yet.

The application layer illustrates the complex dependencies among the various application protocols. Recall, for example, that FTP uses the network virtual terminal definitions from TELNET to define communication on its control connection and TCP to form data connections. Thus, the diagram shows FTP depending on both TELNET and TCP. The domain name system (DNS) uses both UDP and TCP for communication, so the diagram shows both dependencies. Sun's NFS depends on the external data representation (XDR) and remote procedure call (RPC) protocols. RPC appears twice because, like the domain name system, it can use either UDP or TCP.

SNMP depends on *Abstract Syntax Notation* (ASN.1) and also uses UDP to send datagrams. Because XDR and ASN.1 simply describe syntactic conventions and data representations, they do not use either TCP or UDP. Thus, although it shows that both SNMP and NFS depend on UDP, the diagram contains a dotted area below ASN.1 and XDR because neither of them depends on UDP. In fact, many details have been omitted in our diagram. For example, it could be argued that IP depends on BOOTP/DHCP or that many protocols depend on DNS because software that implements such protocols requires name binding.

27.3 Application Program Access

Most systems restrict application programs from accessing lower-level protocols. Usually, an application program can use TCP or UDP, or it can implement higher level protocols that use them (e.g., FTP). An application may need special privilege to open specific ports, but that is different from restricting access completely. Some systems do not have mechanisms that allow an application program to access IP directly; almost none allow application programs to access protocols like ARP. Despite the usual limitations, our diagram suggests that applications can access IP (one of the exercises explores this further).

Some systems provide special purpose mechanisms that permit an application program to interact with lower protocol layers. For example, a mechanism known as the *packet filter* allows privileged programs to affect frame demultiplexing. Using the packet filter primitives, an application program establishes the criteria used to capture packets (e.g., the application program specifies that it wishes to capture all packets with a given value in the *type* field of the frame). Once the operating system accepts the filter command, it places all packets that match the specified type on a queue. The application program uses another part of the packet filter mechanism to extract packets from the queue. For such systems, the diagram should be changed to show application access at all levels.

27.4 Summary

Much of the rich functionality associated with the TCP/IP protocol suite results from a variety of high-level services supplied by application programs. The high-level protocols these programs use build on the basic services: unreliable datagram delivery and reliable stream transport. They usually follow the client-server model in which servers operate at known protocols ports so clients know how to contact them.

The highest level of protocols provides user services like file and mail transfer and remote login. The chief advantages of having an internet on which to build such services are that it provides universal connectivity and simplifies the application protocols. In particular, when used by two machines that attach to an internet, end-to-end transport protocols can guarantee that a client program on the source machine communicates directly with a server on the destination machine. Because services like electronic mail use the end-to-end transport connection, they do not need to rely on intermediate machines to forward (whole) messages.

We have seen a variety of application level protocols and the complex dependencies among them. Although many application protocols have been defined, electronic mail remains the most widely used, and file transfer accounts for most packets on the Internet.

FOR FURTHER STUDY

One of the issues underlying protocol layering revolves around the optimal location of protocol functionality. Edge [1979] compares end-to-end protocols with the hop-by-hop approach. Saltzer, Reed, and Clark [1984] argues for having the highest level protocols perform end-to-end acknowledgement and error detection. In a series of papers, Mills proposes application protocols for clock synchronization and reports on experiments [RFCs 956, 957, and 958].

EXERCISES

27.1 It is possible to translate some application protocols into others. For example, it might be possible to build a program that accepts an FTP request, translates it to a TFTP request, passes the result to a TFTP server to obtain a file, and translates the reply back to FTP form for transmission to the original source. What are the advantages and disadvantages of such protocol translation?

27.2 Consider the translation described in the previous question. Which pairs of protocols in Figure 27.1 are amenable to such translations?

27.3 Figure 27.1 suggests that some application programs invoked by users may need access to IP without using TCP or UDP. Find examples of such programs. (Hint: think of ICMP.)

27.4   Where does EGP fit into the diagram in Figure 27.1?

27.5   DNS allows access by both TCP and UDP. Find out whether your local operating system allows a single process to accept both TCP connections and UDP requests.

27.6   Choose a complex application like the *X window system* and find out which protocols it uses.

27.7   Where does RIP fit into the diagram in Figure 27.1?

27.8   The diagram in Figure 27.1 shows that FTP depends on TELNET. Does your local FTP client invoke the TELNET program, or does the FTP client contain a separate implementation of the TELNET protocol?

27.9   Read about the *Mosaic* program that uses multiple application protocols. How does a program like *Mosaic* fit into Figure 27.1?

28

Internet Security And
Firewall Design

28.1 Introduction

Like the locks used to help keep tangible property secure, computers and data networks need provisions that help keep information secure. Security in an internet environment is both important and difficult. It is important because information has significant value – information can be bought and sold directly or used indirectly to create new products and services that yield high profits. Security in an internet is difficult because security involves understanding when and how participating users, computers, services, and networks can trust one another, as well as understanding the technical details of network hardware and protocols. The security of an entire network can be compromised by a single computer. More important, because TCP/IP supports a wide diversity of users, services, and networks, and because an internet can span many political and organizational boundaries, participating individuals and organizations may not agree on a level of trust or policies for handling data.

This chapter considers a fundamental technique often used to provide inter-organization security. The technique is general because it permits each organization to determine the services and networks it will make available to outsiders and the extent to which outsiders can use resources. We begin by reviewing a few basic concepts and terminology.

28.2 Protecting Resources

The terms *network security* and *information security* refer in a broad sense to confidence that information and services available on a network cannot be accessed by unauthorized users. Security implies safety, including assurance of data integrity, freedom from unauthorized access of computational resources, freedom from snooping or wiretapping, and freedom from disruption of service. Of course, just as no physical property is absolutely secure against crime, no network is absolutely secure. Organizations make an effort to secure networks for the same reason they make an effort to secure buildings and offices: although an organization cannot completely prevent crime, basic security measures can discourage crime by making it significantly more difficult.

Providing security for information requires protecting both physical and abstract resources. Physical resources include passive storage devices such as magnetic tapes and disks as well as active devices such as users' computers. In a network environment, physical security extends to the cables, bridges, and routers that comprise the network infrastructure. Indeed, although physical security is seldom mentioned, it often plays an important role in an overall security plan. Obviously, physical security can prevent wiretapping. Good physical security can also eliminate attacks that require sabotage (e.g., disabling a router to cause packets to be routed through an alternative, less secure path).

Protecting an abstract resource such as information is usually more difficult than providing physical security because information is elusive. *Data integrity* (i.e., protecting information from unauthorized change) is crucial; so is *data availability* (i.e., guaranteeing that outsiders cannot prevent legitimate data access by saturating a network with traffic). Because information can be copied as it passes across a network, protection must also prevent unauthorized listening. That is, network security must include a guarantee of *privacy*. Because information can be accessed and transferred at high speed, it can be difficult to discern the difference between a legitimate and illegitimate access while a transfer is in progress. More important, while physical security often classifies people and resources into broad categories, (e.g., all nonemployees are forbidden from using a particular hallway), security for information usually needs to be more restrictive (e.g., some parts of an employee's record are available only to the personnel office, others are available only to the employee's boss, and others are available to the payroll office).

28.3 The Need For An Information Policy

Before an organization can enforce network security, the organization must assess risks and develop a clear policy regarding information access and protection. The policy needs to specify who will be granted access to each piece of information, the rules an individual must follow in disseminating the information to others, and a statement of how the organization will react to violations.

Although the need for a policy seems obvious, many organizations attempt to make their network secure without first deciding what security means. In organizations that have adopted a general information policy, employees may be unaware of the policy, the motivations for adopting the policy, or the consequences of violating the policy. Establishing an information policy and educating employees is crucial because:

> *Humans are usually the most susceptible point in any security scheme.*
> *A worker who is malicious, careless, or unaware of an organization's*
> *information policy can compromise the best security.*

Consequently, each employee should know the organization's information policy, and should be able to answer basic questions such as:

- How important is information to your organization? For example, do you work for a company that uses trade secrets to gain an advantage over competitors?

- What does copyright mean, and what is your organization's policy on photocopying such information? How does the policy differ if you use a computer to make copies of information on floppy disks?

- How much of the information to which you have access may you discuss with other employees? With outsiders? For example, may you pass out the organization's telephone directory?

- Do you or your organization work with information that belongs to other organizations? May you discuss such information with others? For example, are you encouraged or discouraged from discussing clients who place orders for goods or services? What details about a client's orders or business affairs are you permitted to tell to another client?

- What information may you import to the company? For example, if a friend from a competing company happens to hand you a confidential description of their plan for a new product, should you show the document to your boss?

- May you use a personal computer and modem at work to access information from a computer bulletin board service? If so, does your organization place any restrictions on the use of data obtained in such a manner?

- What are intellectual property rights, and how do they affect what you do at work?

As the questions imply, an information policy should be broad enough to cover information represented on paper as well as information stored in a computer, and should address such issues as information "entering" the organization as well as information "leaving" the organization. Furthermore, a policy should address details such as information entrusted to the organization by clients in the normal course of conducting business, and information that can be deduced or derived about clients from their orders for goods or services.

After an information policy has been established, achieving the desired level of security can be complex because doing so means enforcing the policy throughout the organization. Difficulties arise when dealing with external organizations, and internetworking makes such interaction convenient and frequent. In particular, because an internet can span multiple organizations, policies can conflict. For example, consider three organizations, A, B, and C. Suppose the policy at A allows information to be exported to B, but not to C. If the policy at B permits export to C, information can flow from A to C through B. More important, although the end effect might compromise security, no employee at any organization would violate their organization's policy.

28.4 Communication, Cooperation, And Mutual Mistrust

The example above shows that a single organization cannot guarantee an arbitrary global information policy in isolation. Indeed, when an organization communicates information to another, the ultimate disposition of information depends on the policies of the two organizations and the policies of other organizations to which the information may be passed. The mathematical term *transitivity* has been used to describe the situation: we say that when three organizations exchange information, the security security policy is the *transitive closure* of their individual security policies. As a result,

> *An organization cannot know the effect of communicating and interacting with another unless the two organizations agree on a level of* mutual trust.

Thus, the central problem of network security arises from a fundamental conflict: although communication requires a degree of mutual trust among the communicating parties, a computer network can make possible communication between groups that mistrust one another. Internetworking exacerbates the problem of trust because it can introduce third parties. In particular, as it travels across an internet from a source to a distant destination, a datagram may pass through routers and across networks owned and operated by organizations that are neither associated with the source of the datagram nor with its destination. More important, neither the sending nor receiving sites can control how the datagram is processed or routed as it travels through the part of the internet between their organizations.

28.5 Mechanisms For Internet Security

Internet security problems and the software mechanisms that help make internet communication secure can be divided into three broad sets. The first set focuses on the problems of *authorization*, *authentication*, and *integrity*. The second focuses on the problem of *privacy*, and the third set focuses on the problem of *availability* by controlling access. Because the first two sets apply to general computer security and have been studied in more detail, we will consider them briefly and concentrate on the third.

28.5.1 Authentication Mechanisms

Authentication mechanisms solve the problem of verifying identification. Many servers, for example, are configured to reject a request unless the request originates from an authorized client. When a client first makes contact, the server must verify that the client is authorized before granting service. To validate authorization, a server must know the identity of a client. For example, a weak form of internet authentication uses IP addresses. When using IP address authentication, a manager configures a server with a list of valid IP source addresses. The server examines the source IP address on each incoming request, and only accepts requests from client computers on the authorized list.

IP source authentication is *weak* because it can be broken easily. On an internet, where datagrams pass across intermediate networks and routers, source authentication can be attacked on one of the intermediate machines. For example, suppose an imposter gains control of a router, *R* that lies between a valid client and a server. To access the server, the imposter first alters routes in *R* to direct return traffic to the imposter. The imposter then generates a request using the address of the authorized client as a source address. The server will accept the request, and send the reply to the authorized client. When it reaches the compromised router, *R*, the reply will be forwarded along the incorrect route to the imposter, where it can be intercepted. If the imposter forwards all traffic except replies to illegitimate requests, neither the client nor server will detect the intrusion. The point is:

> *An authorization scheme that uses a remote machine's IP address to authenticate its identity does not prevent attacks by imposters across an unsecure internet because an imposter who gains control of an intermediate router can impersonate an authorized client.*

Interestingly, clients face the same problem as servers because an imposter can also impersonate a server. For example, we saw that a client program is responsible for sending electronic mail to a remote e-mail server. If the mail contains sensitive information, the client may need to verify that it is not communicating with an imposter.

How can client and server programs know that they are not communicating with imposters? The answer lies in providing a trusted service. For example, one form of trusted service uses a *public key encryption* system. To use a public key system, each participant must be assigned two *keys* that are used to encode and decode messages. Each key is a large integer†. A participant publishes one key, called the *public key*, in a public database, and keeps the other key secret. A message encoded using one key can be decoded using the other. For example, if a sender uses a secret key to encode a message, a receiver can use the sender's public key to decode the message. Furthermore, knowing the public key does not make it easy to guess or calculate the secret key. Thus, if a message decodes correctly using a given owner's public key, it must have been encoded using that owner's private key. A client and server that use public key encryption can each be reasonably sure that the other communicant is authentic, even if datagrams transferred between them pass across an unsecure internet.

28.5.2 Privacy Mechanisms

Encryption can also handle the problem of *privacy*. For example, if a sender and receiver both use a public key encryption scheme, the sender can guarantee that only the intended receiver can read a message. To do so, the sender uses the receiver's public key to encode the message, and the receiver uses it's private key to decode the message. Because only the intended receiver has the necessary private key, no other party can decode the message. Thus, privacy can be enforced even if a third party obtains a copy of datagrams as they pass between the sender and receiver.

Messages can be encoded twice to authenticate the sender as well as to enforce privacy. After a sender encodes the message using the sender's private key, the sender encodes the result again using the receiver's public key. The receiver first applies its own private key to get back to the first level of encryption, and then applies the sender's public key to decode the original message. To summarize:

> *Mechanisms such as public key encryption can be used to help solve the problems of authentication, authorization, and privacy. Both client and server software must be modified to use such mechanisms.*

28.6 Firewalls And Internet Access

Mechanisms that control *internet access* handle the problem of screening a particular network or an organization from unwanted communication. Such mechanisms can help prevent outsiders from: obtaining information, changing information, or disrupting communication on an organization's internal internet. Unlike authentication and privacy mechanisms, which can be added to application programs, internet access control usually requires changes to basic components of the internet infrastructure. In particular, successful access control requires a careful combination of restrictions on network topology, intermediate information staging, and packet filters.

A single technique has emerged as the basis for internet access control. The technique places a block known as an *internet firewall*‡ at the entrance to the part of the internet to be protected. For example, an organization can place a firewall at its connec-

---

†To make encryption difficult to break, each key must contain many digits; for example, some schemes require each key to contain 50 digits or more.

‡The term *firewall* is derived from building architecture in which a firewall is a thick, fireproof partition that makes a section of a building impenetrable to fire.

tion to the global Internet to protect it from unwanted access. A firewall partitions an internet into two regions, referred to informally as the *inside* and *outside*. Figure 28.1 illustrates the concept.

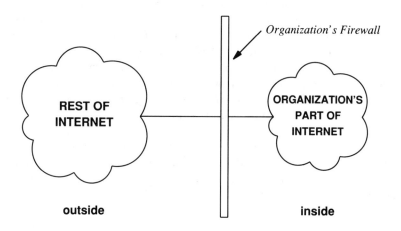

Figure 28.1 The conceptual placement of an internet firewall that protects an organization's internal networks, routers, computers, and data against unwanted communication from outsiders.

28.7 Multiple Connections And Weakest Links

Although the conceptual picture in Figure 28.1 seems simple, details can complicate firewall construction. In particular, an organization's internet can have multiple external connections. For example, if a company has a corporate wide area backbone that connects corporate sites in several cities or countries, the network manager at a given site may choose to connect the site directly to a local business or university. Multiple external connections pose a special problem for security. The organization must form a *security perimeter* by installing a firewall at each external connection. More important, to guarantee that the perimeter is effective, the organization must coordinate all firewalls to use exactly the same access restrictions. Otherwise, it may be possible to circumvent the restrictions imposed by one firewall by entering the organization's internet through another.

Circumventing a firewall can be malicious or inadvertent. Of course, someone intent on gaining access will choose to attack at the weakest point – if the organization has an unguarded external connection, an intruder will find it easier to locate and use the unguarded connection than to subvert the security mechanism on a guarded connection. In fact, the idea that a security system is only as strong as its weakest part is well-known, and has been termed the *weakest link axiom*†.

---

†The name arises from the adage that says a chain is only as strong as its weakest link.

The weakest link axiom helps explain how security of an internet in a large organization can be compromised inadvertently. Consider a corporate internet that connects computers at all the corporation's sites. If the network manager at a branch office provides an outsider with access to a computer at that office, the computer may also contain software that permits access to other computers in the organization. Even if the outsider does not intend to be malicious, he or she may request and obtain information that should be restricted to employees. Thus, a small oversight in the firewall configuration and a curious outsider can leave the entire company vulnerable.

Unfortunately, coordinating multiple firewalls can be difficult. Restrictions needed at one site do not seem important at others. Consequently, those responsible for an organization's internet firewalls must coordinate their efforts carefully. We can summarize the importance of a uniform security perimeter:

> *An organization that has multiple external connections must install a firewall on each external connection and must coordinate all firewalls. Failure to restrict access identically on all firewalls can leave the organization vulnerable.*

28.8 Firewall Implementation And High-Speed Hardware

How should a firewall be implemented? In theory, a firewall simply blocks all unauthorized communication between computers in the organization and computers outside the organization. In practice, the details depend on the network technology, the capacity of the connection, the traffic load, and the organization's policies. Thus, no single solution works for all organizations; building an effective, customized firewall can be difficult.

One of the difficulties in firewall construction arises from the processing power required. A firewall needs sufficient computational power to examine all incoming and outgoing messages. To understand why the processing power required can be significant, think of the connection between a corporation and the global internet. Although a small company can use a slow-speed link to the Internet, the connection for a medium or large corporation must operate at high speed to provide an adequate level of service. Because it needs to examine each datagram that goes between the internal and external parts of the internet, the organization's firewall must handle datagrams at the same speed as the connection. Furthermore, if a firewall delays datagrams in a buffer while it decides whether to permit transfer, the firewall will be overwhelmed with retransmissions, and the buffer will be overrun.

To operate at network speeds, a firewall must have hardware and software optimized for the task. Fortunately, most commercial routers include a high-speed filtering mechanism that can be used to perform much of the necessary work. A manager can configure the filter in a router to request that the router block specified datagrams. As we discuss the details of filter mechanisms, we will see how filters form the basic building blocks of a firewall. Later we will see how filters can be used in conjunction with another mechanism to provide communication that is safe, but flexible.

28.9 Packet-Level Filters

Many commercial routers offer a mechanism that augments normal routing and permits a manager to further control packet processing. Informally called a *packet filter*, the mechanism requires the manager to specify how the router should dispose of each datagram. For example, the manager might choose to *filter* (i.e. block) all datagrams that come from a particular source or those used by a particular application, while choosing to route other datagrams to their destination.

The term *packet filter* arises because the filtering mechanism does not keep a record of interaction or a history of previous datagrams. Instead, the filter considers each datagram separately. When a datagram first arrives, the router passes the datagram through its packet filter before performing any other processing. If the filter rejects the datagram, the router drops it immediately.

Because TCP/IP does not dictate a standard for packet filters, each router vendor is free to choose the capabilities of their packet filter as well as the interface a manager uses to configure the filter. Some routers permit a manager to configure separate filter actions for each interface, while others have a single configuration for all interfaces. Usually, when specifying datagrams that the filter should block, a manager can list any combination of source IP address, destination IP address, protocol, source protocol port number, and destination protocol port number. For example, Figure 28.2 illustrates a filter specification.

ARRIVES ON INTERFACE	IP SOURCE	IP DEST.	PROTOCOL	SOURCE PORT	DEST. PORT
2	*	*	TCP	*	21
2	*	*	TCP	*	23
1	128.5.*.*	*	TCP	*	25
2	*	*	UDP	*	43
2	*	*	UDP	*	69
2	*	*	TCP	*	79

Figure 28.2 A router with two interfaces and an example datagram filter specification. A router that includes a packet filter forms the basic building block of a firewall.

In the example, the manager has chosen to block incoming datagrams destined for a few well-known services and to block one case of outgoing datagrams. The filter blocks all outgoing datagrams that originate from any host on the class B network *128.5.0.0* that are destined for a remote e-mail server (TCP port *25*). The filter also blocks incoming datagrams destined for FTP (TCP port *21*), TELNET (TCP port *23*), WHOIS (UDP port *43*), TFTP (UDP port *69*), or FINGER (TCP port *79*).

28.10 Security And Packet Filter Specification

Although the example filter configuration in Figure 28.2 specifies a small list of services that should be blocked, such an approach does not work well for an effective firewall. There are three reasons. First, the number of well-known ports is large and growing. Thus, a manager would need to update such a list continually because a simple error of omission could leave the firewall vulnerable. Second, much of the traffic on an internet does not travel to or from a well-known port. In addition to programmers who can choose port numbers for their private client-server applications, services like *Remote Procedure Call* (*RPC*) assign ports dynamically. Third, listing ports of well-known services leaves the firewall vulnerable to *tunneling*, a technique in which one datagram is temporarily encapsulated in another for transfer across part of an internet. Tunneling is used to circumvent security by arranging for a host or router on the inside to accept encapsulated datagrams from an outsider, remove one layer of encapsulation, and forward the datagram on to the service that would otherwise be restricted by the firewall.

How can a firewall use a packet filter effectively? The answer lies in reversing the idea of a filter: instead of specifying the datagrams that should be filtered, a firewall should be configured to block all datagrams except those destined for specific networks, hosts, and protocol ports for which external communication has been approved. Thus, a manager begins with the assumption that communication is not allowed, and then must examine the organization's information policy carefully before enabling any port. In fact, many packet filters allow a manager to specify a set of datagrams to admit instead of a set of datagrams to block. We can summarize:

> To be effective, a firewall that uses datagram filtering should restrict access to all IP sources, IP destinations, protocols, and protocol ports except those computers, networks, and services the organization explicitly decides to make available externally. A packet filter that allows a manager to specify which datagrams to admit instead of which datagrams to block can make such restrictions easy to specify.

28.11 The Consequence Of Restricted Access For Clients

A blanket prohibition on datagrams arriving for an unknown protocol port seems to solve many potential security problems by preventing outsiders from accessing arbitrary servers in the organization. Such a firewall has an interesting consequence: it also prevents an arbitrary computer inside the firewall from becoming a client that accesses a service outside the firewall. To understand why, recall that although each server operates at a well-known port, a client does not. When a client program begins execution, it requests the operating system to select a protocol port number that is neither among the well-known ports nor currently in use on the client's computer. When it attempts to communicate with a server outside the organization, a client will generate one or more datagrams and send them to the server. Each outgoing datagram has the client's protocol port as the source port and the server's well-known protocol port as the destination port. The firewall will not block such datagrams as they leave. When it generates a response, the server reverses the protocol ports. The client's port becomes the destination port and the server's port becomes the source port. When the datagram carrying the response reaches the firewall, however, it will be blocked because the destination port is not approved. Thus, we can see an important idea:

> *If an organization's firewall restricts incoming datagrams except for ports that correspond to services the organization makes available externally, an arbitrary application inside the organization cannot become a client of a server outside the organization.*

28.12 Accessing Services Through A Firewall

Of course, not all organizations configure their firewalls to block all datagrams destined for unknown protocol ports (in fact, not all organizations have a firewall to protect their networks). In cases where a secure firewall is needed to prevent unwanted access, however, users on the inside need a safe mechanism that provides access to services outside. That mechanism forms the second major piece of firewall architecture.

In general, an organization can only provide safe access to outside services through a secure computer. Instead of trying to make all computer systems in the organization secure (a daunting task), an organization usually associates one secure computer with each firewall. Because a computer must be strongly fortified to serve as a secure communication channel, it is often called a *bastion host*. Figure 28.3 illustrates the concept.

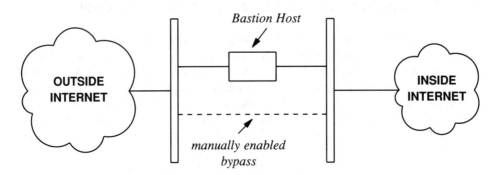

Figure 28.3 The conceptual organization of a bastion host embedded in a firewall. The bastion host provides secure access to outside services without requiring an organization to admit datagrams with arbitrary destinations.

To permit safe access, the firewall has two conceptual barriers. The outer barrier blocks all incoming traffic except (1) datagrams destined for services on the bastion host that the organization chooses to make available externally, and (2) datagrams destined for clients on the bastion host. The inner barrier blocks incoming traffic except datagrams that originate on the bastion host. Most firewalls also include a *manual bypass* that enables managers to temporarily pass some or all traffic between a host inside the organization and a host outside (e.g., for testing or debugging the network). In general, organizations that desire maximum security, never enable such a bypass.

To understand how a bastion host operates, consider the FTP service. Suppose a user in the organization needs to access an external FTP server to obtain a copy of a file. Because the firewall prevents the user's computer from receiving incoming datagrams, the user cannot run FTP client software directly. Instead, the user must run the FTP client on the bastion host. After the file has been copied to the bastion host, the user can run a file transfer between the bastion host and their local computer.

How can a user in an organization run client software on a bastion host? Organizations usually follow one of two basic schemes. Some organizations require users to use a remote login service (e.g., TELNET) to contact the bastion host. The user then invokes client software from the command interpreter. Other organizations provide users with modified client programs that run on their computer, but automatically contact the bastion host as needed. The advantages of the first approach lie in generality, economy, and security – only the bastion host needs a copy of a client program for each Internet service, and only that copy needs to be made secure. Because remote login provides access to all commands on the bastion host, a user on an arbitrary computer in the organization only needs remote login software to enable access to any service on the Internet. The chief disadvantage of the first approach arises because additional mechanisms may be needed to transfer information from the bastion host to the user's computer.

The advantage of the second approach lies in convenience – a user does not need an account on the bastion host, does not need to log in before accessing a remote server, and does not need to learn the syntax of the bastion host's command interpreter. The chief disadvantage of the second approach lies in cost and overhead – each computer in the organization needs a special client program for each service, and the bastion host needs special software that can communicate with hosts in the organization as well as with a server on the Internet.

28.13 The Details Of Firewall Architecture

Now that we understand the basic firewall concept, the implementation should appear straightforward. Each of the barriers shown in Figure 28.3 requires a router that has a packet filter. Networks interconnect the routers and a bastion host. For example, an organization that connects to the global Internet over a serial line might choose to implement a firewall as Figure 28.4 shows.

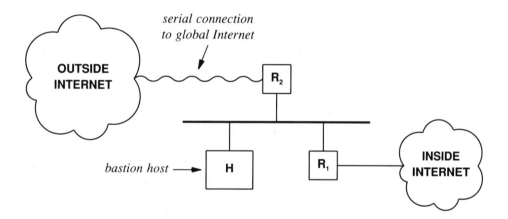

Figure 28.4 A firewall implemented with two routers and a bastion host. A serial line connects the organization to the rest of the Internet.

As the figure shows, router R_2 implements the outer barrier; it filters all traffic except datagrams destined for the bastion host, H. Router R_1 implements the inner barrier that isolates the rest of the corporate internet from outsiders; it blocks all incoming datagrams except those that originate on the bastion host.

Of course, the safety of an entire firewall depends on the safety of the bastion host. If an intruder can gain access to the computer system running on the bastion host, they will gain access to the entire inside internet. Moreover, an intruder can exploit security flaws in either the operating system on the bastion host or the network applications it runs. Thus, managers must be particularly careful when choosing and configuring software for a bastion host. In summary:

> *Although a bastion host is essential for communication through a firewall, the security of the firewall depends on the safety of the bastion host. An intruder who exploits a security flaw in the bastion host operating system can gain access to hosts inside the firewall.*

28.14 Stub Network

It may seem that Figure 28.4 contains a superfluous network that connects the two routers and the bastion host. Such a network is often called a *stub network* because it consists of a short (i.e., stubby) wire to which only three computers connect. The question arises, ''Is the stub network necessary or could a site place the bastion host on one of its production networks?'' The answer depends on the traffic expected from the outside. The stub network isolates the organization from incoming datagram traffic. In particular, because router R_2 admits all datagrams destined for the bastion host, an outsider can send an arbitrary number of such datagrams across the stub network. If an external connection is slow relative to the capacity of a stub network, a separate physical wire may be unnecessary. However, a stub network is usually an inexpensive way for an organization to protect itself against disruption of service on an internal production network.

28.15 An Alternative Firewall Implementation

The firewall implementation in Figure 28.4 works well for an organization that has a single serial connection to the rest of the global Internet. Some sites have a different interconnection topology. For example, suppose a company has three or four large customers who each need to deposit or extract large volumes of information. The company wishes to have a single firewall, but allow connections to multiple sites†. Figure 28.5 illustrates one possible firewall architecture that accommodates multiple external connections.

---

†A single firewall can be less expensive and easier to administrate than a separate firewall per connection.

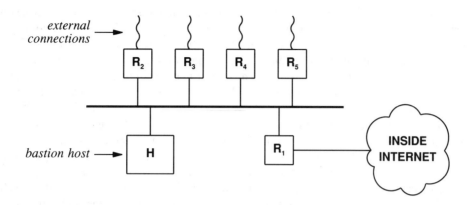

Figure 28.5 An alternative firewall architecture that permits multiple external
connections through a single firewall. Using one firewall for
multiple connections can reduce the cost.

As the figure shows, the alternative architecture extends a firewall by providing an
outer network at which external connections terminate. Router R_1 acts as in Figure 28.4
to protect the site by restricting incoming datagrams to those sent from the bastion host.
Routers R_2 through R_5 each connect one external site to the firewall.

To understand why firewalls with multiple connections often use a router per connection, recall that all sites mistrust one another. That is, the organization running the
firewall does not trust any of the external organizations completely, and none of the
external organizations trust one another completely. The packet filter in a router on a
given external connection can be configured to restrict traffic on that particular connection. As a result, the owner of the firewall can guarantee that although all external connections share a single, common network, no datagram from one external connection
will pass to another. Thus, the organization running the firewall can assure customers
that it is safe to connect.

To summarize:

> *When multiple external sites connect through a single firewall, an ar-*
> *chitecture that has a router per external connection can prevent*
> *unwanted packet flow from one external site to another.*

28.16 Monitoring And Logging

Monitoring is one of the most important aspects of a firewall design. The network
manager responsible for a firewall needs to be aware of attempts to bypass security.
Unless a firewall reports incidents, a manager may be unaware of problems.

Monitoring can be *active* or *passive*. In active monitoring, a firewall notifies a manager whenever an incident occurs. The chief advantage of active monitoring is speed – a manager finds out about a potential problem immediately. The chief disadvantage is that active monitors often produce so much information that a manager cannot comprehend it or notice problems. Thus, most managers prefer passive monitoring, or a combination of passive monitoring with a few high-risk incidents also reported by an active monitor.

In passive monitoring, a firewall logs a record of each incident in a file on disk. A passive monitor usually records information about normal traffic (e.g., simple statistics) as well as datagrams that are filtered. A manager can access the log at any time; most managers use a computer program. The chief advantage of passive monitoring arises from its record of events – a manager can consult the log to observe trends and, when a security problem does occur, review the history of events that led to the problem. More important, a manager can analyze the log periodically (e.g., daily) to determine whether attempts to access the organization increase or decrease over time.

28.17 Summary

Security problems arise because an internet can connect organizations that do not have mutual trust. Several techniques are available to help ensure that information remains secure when being sent across an internet. A client and a server can use encryption to guarantee their identities; servers need such authentication to determine whether a client is authorized to access a service. Encryption can also solve the problem of privacy because it means a sender and receiver can communicate across an unsecure channel without fear of the communication being overheard. Before an organization can choose mechanisms to enforce security, it needs to establish an information policy.

The firewall mechanism is used to control internet access. An organization places a firewall at each external connection to guarantee that the organization's internal networks remain free from unauthorized traffic. A firewall consists of two barriers and a secure computer called a bastion host. Each barrier uses a filter to restrict datagram traffic. The bastion host offers externally-visible servers, and runs clients that access outside servers. The organization uses its information and internet access policies to determine how to configure the filter. Usually, a firewall blocks all datagrams arriving from external sources except those datagrams destined for the bastion host.

A firewall can be implemented in one of several ways; the choice depends on details such as the number of external connections. In many cases, each barrier in a firewall is implemented with a router that contains a packet filter. A firewall can also use a stub network to keep external traffic off an organization's production networks.

FOR FURTHER STUDY

Many RFCs address issues of internet security and propose policies, procedures, and mechanisms. Crocker, Fraser, and Pethia [RFC 1281] discusses the secure operation of the Internet, while Holbrook and Reynolds [RFC 1244] discusses site security. Galvin and McCloghrie [RFC 1446] presents the security introduced in SNMPv2. Cheswick and Bellovin [1994] discusses firewalls and other topics related to the secure operation of TCP/IP internets.

A protocol that guarantees the privacy of electronic mail messages has been considered many times. Four related RFCs by Linn [RFC 1421], Kent [RFC 1422], Balenson [RFC 1423], and Kaliski [RFC 1424] present a protocol for *Privacy Enchanced Mail* (*PEM*). Kohl and Neuman [RFC 1510] describes the *kerberos* authentication service, and Borman [RFC 1411] discusses how *kerberos* can be used to authenticate TELNET.

The COAST security project at Purdue University has assembled an extensive archive of information related to computer and network security. The archive can be accessed through gopher, ftp, or the World Wide Web:

> *gopher://coast.cs.purdue.edu*
> *ftp://coast.cs.purdue.edu/pub*
> *http://www.cs.purdue.edu/coast/coast.html*

EXERCISES

28.1   Many sites that require all file transfers to go through a bastion host arrange for the file transfer software to scan the file before admitting it to the organization. Why do organizations scan files? (Hint: think of importing programs that run on a personal computer.)

28.2   Read the description of a packet filter for a commercially available router. What features does it offer?

28.3   Collect a log of traffic entering your site that has one entry per datagram. Analyze the log to determine the percentage of traffic that arrives from or is destined to a well-known protocol port. Do the results surprise you?

28.4   If encryption software is available on your computer, measure the time required to encrypt a 10 Mbyte file, transfer it to another computer, and decrypt it. Compare to the time required for the transfer if no encryption is used.

28.5   Survey users at your site to determine if they send sensitive information in e-mail. Do users understand that SMTP transfers messages in ASCII, and that anyone watching network traffic can see the contents of an e-mail message?

28.6   Survey employees at your site to find out how many use modems and personal computers to import or export information. Ask if they understand the organization's information policy.

28.7   Can a firewall be used with other protocol suites such as Appletalk or Netware? Why or why not?

28.8   The military only releases information to those who "need to know." Will such a scheme work for all information in your organization? Why or why not?

28.9   Give two reasons why the group of people who administer an organization's security policies should be separate from the group of people who administer the organization's computer and network systems.

28.10   Some organizations use firewalls to isolate groups of users internally. Give examples of ways that internal firewalls can improve network performance, and examples of ways internal firewalls can degrade network performance.

29

The Future Of TCP/IP
(IPng, IPv6)

29.1 Introduction

Evolution of TCP/IP technology is intertwined with evolution of the global Internet for several reasons. First, the Internet is the largest installed TCP/IP internet, so many problems related to scale arise in the Internet before they surface in other TCP/IP internets. Second, funding for TCP/IP research and engineering comes from companies and government agencies that use the operational Internet, so they tend to fund projects that impact the Internet. Third, most researchers engaged in TCP/IP work have connections to the Internet and use it daily. Thus, they have immediate motivation to solve problems that will improve service and extend functionality.

With millions of users at tens of thousands of sites around the world depending on the global Internet as part of their daily work environment, it might seem that the Internet is a completely stable production facility. We have passed the early stage of development in which every user was also an expert, and entered a stage in which few users understand the technology. Despite appearances, however, neither the Internet nor the TCP/IP protocol suite is static. New groups interconnect their networks and discover new ways to use the technology. Researchers solve new networking problems, and engineers improve the underlying mechanisms. In short, the technology continues to evolve.

The purpose of this chapter is to consider the ongoing evolutionary process and examine one of the most important engineering efforts underway. In particular, we will examine a proposed revision of IP. If the proposal is both approved as a standard and adopted by vendors, it will have a major impact on TCP/IP and the Internet. Whether

489

the new protocol becomes part of TCP/IP in the next months, years, or decades is unimportant; the goal is to give the reader an understanding of the effort. The reader should be aware that the proposal we will consider is not a final standard, and that details may change.

29.2 Why Change TCP/IP And The Internet?

The basic TCP/IP technology has worked well for over a decade. Why should it change? In a broad sense, developments that stimulate the evolution of TCP/IP and the Internet architecture fall into four categories. After describing each category, we will examine a proposed new version of IP, and see how each category has affected the design.

29.2.1 New Computer And Communication Technologies

Like most technically oriented groups, researchers and engineers working on TCP/IP protocols maintain a keen interest in new technologies. As higher-speed computer systems become available, they are used as hosts and routers. As new network technologies emerge, they are used to carry IP datagrams. For example, in addition to LANs and conventional leased serial communication lines, TCP/IP researchers have studied point-to-point satellite communication, multiple station synchronized satellites, packet radio, and ATM. More recently, researchers have studied wireless networks that use infrared or spread-spectrum radio frequency technologies.

29.2.2 New Applications

One of the most exciting frontiers of research and development in the Internet, new applications often create a demand for facilities or services that the current protocols cannot provide. For example, a surge of interest in multimedia has created a demand for protocols that can transfer sound and images efficiently. Similarly, interest in real-time audio and video communication has created a demand for protocols that can guarantee to deliver information within a fixed delay, and protocols that can synchronize video and audio data streams.

29.2.3 Increases In Size And Load

The global Internet has experienced many years of sustained exponential growth, doubling in size every nine months or faster. By early 1994, on the average, a new host appeared on the Internet every 30 seconds, and the rate was increasing dramatically. Surprisingly, Internet traffic load has increased faster than the number of networks. The increases in traffic can be attributed to several causes. First, the Internet population is shifting from academicians and scientists to the general public. Consequently, people now use the Internet after business hours for activities such as shopping and entertainment. Second, new applications that transfer images and real-time video generate more traffic than applications that transfer text. Third, automated search tools generate a substantial amount of traffic as they relentlessly probe Internet sites to find data.

29.2.4 New Policies

As it expands into new industries and new countries, the Internet changes in a fundamental way: it gains new administrative authorities. Changes in authority produce changes in administrative policies, and mandate new mechanisms to enforce those policies. As we have seen, both the architecture of the connected Internet and the protocols it uses are evolving away from a centralized core model. Evolution continues as more national backbone networks attach, producing increasingly complex policies regulating interaction. When multiple corporations interconnect private TCP/IP internets, they face similar problems as they try to define policies for interaction and then find mechanisms to enforce those policies. Thus, many of the research and engineering efforts surrounding TCP/IP continue to focus on finding ways to accommodate new administrative groups.

29.3 Motivation For Changing IPv4

Version *4* of the Internet Protocol (*IPv4*) provides the basic communication mechanism of the TCP/IP suite and the global Internet; it has remained almost unchanged since its inception in the late 1970s†. The longevity of version *4* shows that the design is flexible and powerful. Since the time IPv4 was designed, processor performance has increased over two orders of magnitude, typical memory sizes have increased by a factor of 32, network bandwidth of the Internet backbone has risen by a factor of 800, LAN technologies have emerged, and the number of hosts on the Internet has risen from a handful to 4 million. Furthermore, the changes did not occur simultaneously – IP has accommodated changes in one technology, before changes in others.

Despite its sound design, IPv4 must be replaced soon. Chapter 10 describes the main motivation for updating IP: the imminent address space exhaustion. When IP was designed, a 32-bit address space was more than sufficient. Only a handful of organizations used a LAN; fewer had a corporate WAN. Now, however, most medium-sized corporations have multiple LANs, and most large corporations have a corporate WAN. Consequently, the current 32-bit IP address space cannot accommodate projected growth of the global Internet.

Although the need for a larger address space is forcing an immediate change in IP, other factors are contributing to the design as well. In particular, much thought has been given to support for new applications. For example, because real-time audio and video need guaranteed bounds on delay, a new version of IP should provide a mechanism that makes it possible to associate a datagram with a preassigned resource reservation. Furthermore, because many new Internet applications need secure communication, a new version of IP should include facilities that make it possible to authenticate the sender.

---

†Versions *1* through *3* were never formally assigned, and version number *5* was assigned to the *ST* protocol.

29.4 The Road To A New Version Of IP

Groups in the IETF have been working to formulate a new version of IP for several years. Because they strive to produce *open* standards, the IETF has invited the entire community to participate in the standardization process. Consequently, researchers, computer manufacturers, network hardware and software vendors, programmers, managers, users, telephone companies, and the cable television industry have all specified their requirements for the next IP, and have all commented on specific proposals.

Many designs have been proposed to serve a particular purpose or a particular community. One of the proposed designs would have made IP more sophisticated at the cost of increased complexity and processing overhead. Another design proposed using a modification of the OSI CLNS protocol. A third major design proposed retaining most of the ideas in IP, but making simple extensions to accommodate larger addresses. The design, known as *SIP (Simple IP)*, became the basis for an extended proposal that included ideas from other proposals. The extended version of SIP was named *Simple IP Plus (SIPP)*, and eventually emerged as the design selected as a basis for the next IP.

Choosing a new version of IP has not been easy. The popularity of the Internet means that the market for IP products around the world is staggering. Many groups see the economic opportunity, and hope that the new version of IP will help them gain an edge over the competition. In addition, personalities have been involved – some individuals hold strong technical opinions; others see active participation as a path to a promotion. Consequently, the discussions have generated heated arguments.

29.5 The Name Of The Next IP

Early in the discussion about changing IP, the IAB published a policy statement that referred to the next version as *IP version 7*. The statement caused widespread confusion. People asked, "What happened to versions *5* and *6*?" Did the IAB mean to say *version 5*, or did the IAB mean to set a policy for the long-term future? Evidently, the error occurred because the ST protocol was assigned version number *5*, and one of the documents available to the IAB mistakenly reported the current version of IP as *6*.

To avoid confusion, the IETF chose a new name. Following the name of a popular television show, the IETF chose "IP – The Next Generation," and the effort became known by its acronym *IPng*.

Formally, it has been decided that the next version of IP will be assigned version number *6*. Thus, to distinguish it from the current version of IP (*IPv4*), the next version will be named *IPv6*. In the past, the term *IPng* has been used in a broad context to refer to all the discussions and proposals for a next version of IP, while the term *IPv6†* has been used to refer to the specific proposal emerging from the IETF. Current literature often treats the two terms as synonyms and uses them interchangeably. To help distinguish general discussion from the current proposal, we will use the term *IPv6* to refer to the specific protocol being proposed, and *IPng* to refer to all efforts related to developing a next generation of IP.

---

†Some authors use the abbreviation *IP6*.

29.6 Features Of IPv6

The proposed IPv6 protocol retains many of the features that contributed to the success of IPv4. In fact, the designers have characterized IPv6 as being basically the same as IPv4 with a few modifications. For example, IPv6 still supports connectionless delivery (i.e., allows each datagram to be routed independently), allows the sender to choose the size of a datagram, and requires the sender to specify the maximum number of hops a datagram can make before being terminated. As we will see, IPv6 also retains most of the concepts provided by IPv4 options, including facilities for fragmentation and source routing.

Despite many conceptual similarities, IPv6 changes most of the protocol details. For example, IPv6 uses larger addresses, and adds a few new features. More important, IPv6 completely revises the datagram format by replacing IPv4's variable-length options field by a series of fixed-format headers. We will examine details after considering major changes and the underlying motivation for each.

The changes introduced by IPv6 can be grouped into five categories:

- *Larger Addresses.* The new address size is the most noticeable change. IPv6 quadruples the size of an IPv4 address from 32 bits to 128 bits. The IPv6 address space is so large that it cannot be exhausted in the foreseeable future.

- *Flexible Header Format.* IPv6 uses an entirely new and incompatible datagram format. Unlike IPv4, which uses a fixed-format datagram header where all fields except options occupy a fixed number of octets at a fixed offset, IPv6 uses a set of optional headers.

- *Improved Options.* Like IPv4, IPv6 allows a datagram to include optional control information. IPv6 includes new options that provide additional facilities not available in IPv4.

- *Support For Resource Allocation.* IPv6 replaces IPv4's type-of-service specification with a mechanism that permits preallocation of network resources. In particular, the new mechanism supports applications such as real-time video that require guarantees on bandwidth and delay.

- *Provision for protocol extension.* Perhaps the most significant change in IPv6 is a move away from a protocol that fully specifies all details to a protocol that can permit additional features. The extension capability has the potential to allow the IETF to adapt the protocol to changes in underlying network hardware or to new applications.

29.7 General Form Of An IPv6 Datagram

IPv6 completely changes the datagram format. As Figure 29.1 shows, an IPv6 datagram has a fixed-size *base header* followed by zero or more *extension headers*, followed by data.

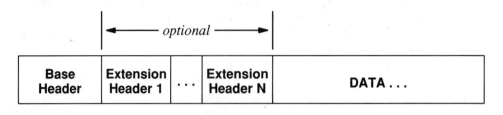

Figure 29.1 The general form of an IPv6 datagram with multiple headers. Only the base header is required; extension headers are optional.

29.8 IPv6 Base Header Format

Interestingly, although it must accommodate larger addresses, an IPv6 base header contains less information than an IPv4 datagram header. Options and some of the fixed fields that appear in an IPv4 datagram header have been moved to extension headers in IPv6. In general, the changes in the datagram header reflect changes in the protocol:

- Alignment has been changed from 32-bit multiples to 64-bit multiples.

- The header length field has been eliminated, and the datagram length field has been replaced by a *PAYLOAD LENGTH* field.

- The size of source and destination address fields has been increased to 16 octets each.

- Fragmentation information has been moved out of fixed fields in the base header into an extension header.

- The *TIME-TO-LIVE* field has been replaced by a *HOP LIMIT* field.

- The *SERVICE TYPE* field has been replaced by a *FLOW LABEL* field.

- The *PROTOCOL* field has been replaced by a field that specifies the type of the next header.

Figure 29.2 shows the contents and format of an IPv6 base header. Several fields in an IPv6 base header correspond directly to fields in an IPv4 header. As in IPv4, the initial 4-bit *VERS* field specifies the version of the protocol; *VERS* always contains *6* in an IPv6 datagram. As in IPv4, the *SOURCE ADDRESS* and *DESTINATION ADDRESS* fields specify the addresses of the sender and intended recipient. In IPv6, however, each address requires 16 octets. The *HOP LIMIT* field corresponds to the IPv4 *TIME-TO-LIVE* field. Unlike IPv4, which interprets a time-to-live as a combination of hop-count and maximum time, IPv6 interprets the value as giving a strict bound on the maximum number of hops a datagram can make before being discarded.

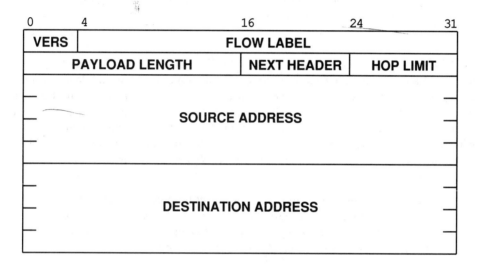

Figure 29.2 The format of the 40-octet IPv6 base header. Each IPv6 datagram begins with a base header.

IPv6 handles datagram length specifications in a new way. First, because the size of the base header is fixed at 40 octets, the base header does not include a field for the header length. Second, IPv6 replaces IPv4's datagram length field by a 16-bit *PAY-LOAD LENGTH* field that specifies the number of octets carried in the datagram excluding the header itself. Thus, an IPv6 datagram can contain 64K octets of data.

A new mechanism in IPv6 supports resource reservation and allows a router to associate each datagram with a given resource allocation. The underlying abstraction, a *flow*, consists of a path through an internet along which intermediate routers guarantee a specific quality of service. For example, two applications that need to send video can establish a flow on which the delay and bandwidth is guaranteed. Alternatively, a network provider may require a subscriber to specify the quality of service desired, and then use a flow to limit the traffic a specific computer or a specific application sends. Note that flows can also be used within a given organization to manage network resources and ensure that all applications receive a fair share.

Field *FLOW LABEL* in the base header contains information that routers use to associate a datagram with a specific flow and priority. The field is divided into two subfields as Figure 29.3 shows.

4 bits	24 bits
TCLASS	FLOW IDENTIFIER

Figure 29.3 The two subfields of a flow label. Each IPv6 datagram carries a flow label, which can be used to associate the datagram with a specific quality of service.

Within the flow label, the 4-bit field *TCLASS* specifies the traffic class for the datagram. Values *0* through *7* are used to specify the time-sensitivity of flow-controlled traffic; values *8* through *15* are used to specify a priority for non-flow traffic. The remaining 24-bit field contains a *FLOW IDENTIFIER*. The source chooses a flow identifier when establishing the flow (e.g., at random). There is no potential conflict between computers because a router uses the combination of datagram source address and flow identifier when associating a datagram with a specific flow. To summarize:

> *Each IPv6 datagram begins with a 40-octet base header that includes fields for the source and destination addresses, the maximum hop limit, the flow label, and the type of the next header. Thus, an IPv6 datagram must contain at least 40 octets in addition to the data.*

29.9 IPv6 Extension Headers

The paradigm of a fixed base header followed by a set of optional extension headers was chosen as a compromise between generality and efficiency. To be totally general, IPv6 needs to include mechanisms to support functions such as fragmentation, source routing, and authentication. However, choosing to allocate fixed fields in the datagram header for all mechanisms is inefficient because most datagrams do not use all mechanisms; the large IPv6 address size exacerbates the inefficiency. For example, when sending a datagram across a single local area network, a header that contains empty address fields can occupy a substantial fraction of each frame. More important, the designers realize that no one can predict which facilities will be needed.

The IPv6 extension header paradigm works similar to IPv4 options – a sender can choose which extension headers to include in a given datagram and which to omit. Thus, extension headers provide maximum flexibility. We can summarize:

IPv6 extension headers are similar to IPv4 options. Each datagram includes extension headers for only those facilities that the datagram uses.

29.10 Parsing An IPv6 Datagram

Each of the base and extension headers contains a *NEXT HEADER* field. Software on intermediate routers and at the final destination that need to process the datagram must use the value in the *NEXT HEADER* field of each header to parse the datagram. Extracting all header information from an IPv6 datagram requires a sequential search through the headers. For example, Figure 29.4 shows the *NEXT HEADER* fields of three datagrams that contain zero, one, and two extension headers.

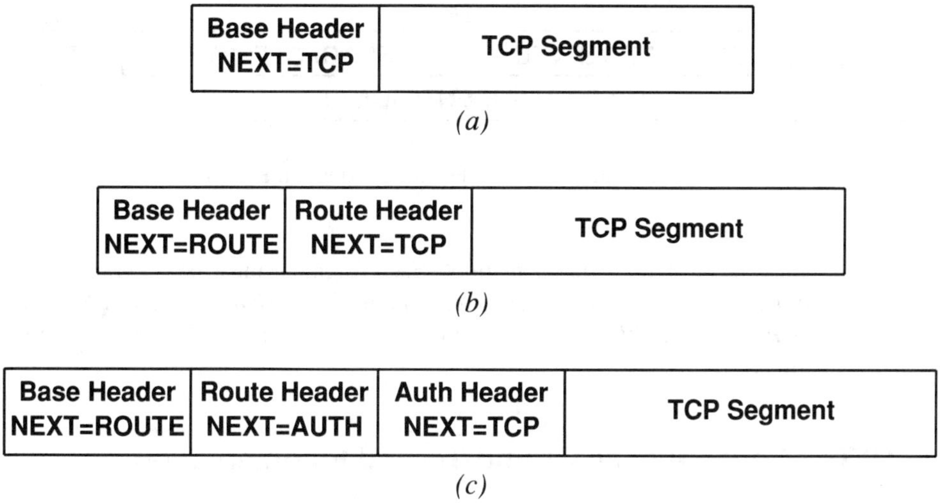

Base Header NEXT=TCP	TCP Segment

(a)

Base Header NEXT=ROUTE	Route Header NEXT=TCP	TCP Segment

(b)

Base Header NEXT=ROUTE	Route Header NEXT=AUTH	Auth Header NEXT=TCP	TCP Segment

(c)

Figure 29.4 Three datagrams with (a) only a base header, (b) a base header and one extension, and (c) a base header plus two extensions. The *NEXT HEADER* field in each header specifies the type of the following header.

Of course, parsing an IPv6 datagram that only has a base header and data is as efficient as parsing an IPv4 datagram. Furthermore, we will see that intermediate routers seldom need to process all extension headers.

29.11 IPv6 Fragmentation And Reassembly

As in IPv4, IPv6 arranges for the ultimate destination to perform datagram reassembly. However, the designers made an unusual decision about fragmentation. Recall that IPv4 requires an intermediate router to fragment any datagram that is too large for the MTU of the network over which it must travel. In IPv6, fragmentation is restricted to the original source. Before sending traffic, a source must perform a *Path MTU Discovery* technique to identify the minimum MTU along the path to the destination. Before sending a datagram, the source fragments the datagram so that each fragment is less than the Path MTU. Thus, fragmentation is end-to-end; no fragmentation needs to occur in intermediate routers.

The IPv6 base header does not contain fields analogous to the fields used for fragmentation in an IPv4 header. Instead, when fragmentation is needed, the source inserts a small extension header after the base header in each fragment. Figure 29.5 shows the contents of a *Fragment Extension Header*.

0	8	16	29 31
NEXT HEADER	RESERVED	FRAG. OFFSET	MF
DATAGRAM IDENTIFICATION			

Figure 29.5 The format of a Fragment Extension Header.

IPv6 retains much of IPv4 fragmentation. Each fragment must be a multiple of *8* octets, a bit in field *MF* marks the last fragment like the IPv4 *MORE FRAGMENTS* bit, and the *DATAGRAM IDENTIFICATION* field carries a unique ID that the receiver uses to group fragments†.

29.12 The Consequence Of End-To-End Fragmentation

The motivation for using end-to-end fragmentation lies in its ability to reduce overhead in routers and permit each router to handle more datagrams per unit time. Indeed, the CPU overhead required for IPv4 fragmentation can be significant – in a conventional router, the CPU can reach 100% utilization if the router fragments many or all of the datagrams it receives. However, end-to-end fragmentation has an important consequence: it changes a fundamental assumption about the Internet.

To understand the consequence of end-to-end fragmentation, recall that IPv4 is designed to permit routes to change at any time. For example, if a network or router fails, traffic can be rerouted along a different path. The chief advantage of such a system is flexibility – traffic can be routed along an alternate path without disrupting service and without informing the source or destination. In IPv6, however, routes cannot be changed as easily because a change in a route can also change the Path MTU. If the Path MTU along a new route is less than the Path MTU along the original route, either

---

†IPv6 expands the IPv4 *IDENTIFICATION* field to 32 bits to accommodate higher speed networks.

an intermediate router must fragment the datagram or the original source must be in-formed. The problem can be summarized:

> *An internet protocol that uses end-to-end fragmentation requires a sender to discover the Path MTU to each destination, and to fragment any outgoing datagram that is larger than the Path MTU. End-to-end fragmentation does not accommodate route changes.*

To solve the problem of route changes that affect the Path MTU, IPv6 allows inter-mediate routers to tunnel IPv6 through IPv6. When an intermediate router needs to fragment a datagram, the router does not insert a fragment extension header, nor does it change fields in the base header. Instead, the intermediate router creates an entirely new datagram that encapsulates the original datagram as data. The router divides the new datagram into fragments by replicating the base header and inserting a fragment ex-tension header in each. Finally the router sends each fragment to the final destination. At the final destination, the original datagram can be formed by collecting incoming fragments into a datagram, and then extracting the data portion. Figure 25.6 illustrates the encapsulation.

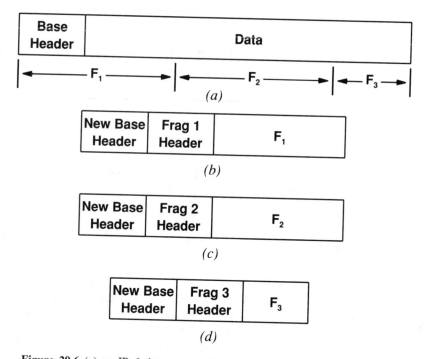

Figure 29.6 (a) an IPv6 datagram, and (b) through (d) three fragments that result when a router encapsulates and fragments the datagram. The destination will reassemble the original datagram including the header.

29.13 IPv6 Source Routing

IPv6 retains the ability for a sender to specify a loose source route. Unlike IPv4, in which source routing is provided by options, IPv6 uses a separate extension header. As Figure 29.7 shows, fields of the Routing Header correspond to fields of an IPv4 source route option. The header contains a list of addresses that specify intermediate routers through which the datagram must pass. Field *NUM ADDRS* specifies the total number of addresses in the list, and field *NEXT ADDRESS* specifies the next address to which the datagram should be sent.

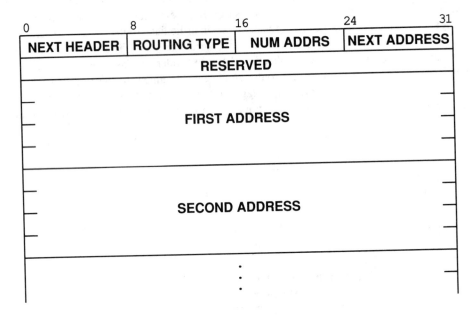

Figure 29.7 The format of an IPv6 Routing Header. Fields correspond to those of an IPv4 source route option.

29.14 IPv6 Options

It may seem that IPv6 extension headers completely replace IPv4 options. However, the designers propose two additional extension headers to accommodate any miscellaneous information not included in other extension headers. The additional headers consist of a *Hop By Hop Extension Header* and an *End To End Extension Header*. As the names imply, the two option headers separate the set of options that should be examined at each hop from the set that are only interpreted at the destination.

Although each of the two option headers has a unique type code, both headers use the format that Figure 29.8 illustrates.

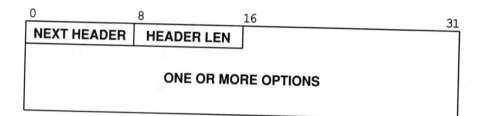

Figure 29.8 The format of an IPv6 option extension header. Both the *hop-by-hop* and *end-to-end* option headers use the same format; the *NEXT HEADER* field of the previous header distinguishes between the two types.

As usual, field *NEXT HEADER* gives the type of the header that follows. Because an option header does not have fixed size, the field labeled *HEADER LEN* specifies the total length of the header. The area labeled *ONE OR MORE OPTIONS* represents a sequence of individual options. Figure 29.9 illustrates how each individual option is encoded with a type, length, and value†; options are not aligned or padded.

```
0                8                16 . . . . . . . . . . . . . . . . . . . . . . . . . . . .
   TYPE           LENGTH                      VALUE
. . . . . . . . . . . . . . . . . . . . . . . . . . . .
```

Figure 29.9 Encoding of an individual option in the IPv6 option extension header. Each option consists of a one-octet type and a one-octet length followed by zero or more octets of data for the option.

As the figure shows, IPv6 options follow the same form as IPv4 options. Each option begins with a one-octet *TYPE* field followed by a one-octet *LENGTH* field. If the option requires additional data, octets that comprise the *VALUE* follow the *LENGTH*.

The two high-order bits of each option *TYPE* field specify how a host or router should dispose of the datagram if it does not understand the option:

Bits In Type	Meaning
00	Skip this option
01	Discard datagram; do not send ICMP message
10	Discard datagram; send ICMP message to source
11	Discard datagram; send ICMP for non-multicast

---

†In the literature, an encoding of type, length, and value is sometimes called a *TLV encoding*.

29.15 Size Of The IPv6 Address Space

In IPv6, each address occupies 16 octets, four times the size of an IPv4 address. The large address space guarantees that IPv6 can tolerate any reasonable address assignment scheme. In fact, if the designers decide to change the addressing scheme later, the address space is sufficiently large to accommodate a reassignment.

It is difficult to comprehend the size of the IPv6 address space. One way to look at it relates the magnitude to the size of the population: the address space is so large that every person on the planet can have sufficient addresses to have their own internet as large as the current Internet. Another way to understand the size relates it to address exhaustion. For example, consider how long it would take to assign all possible addresses. A 16-octet integer can hold 2^{128} values. Thus, the address space is greater than 3.4×10^{38}. If addresses are assigned at the rate of one million addresses every microsecond, it would take over twenty years to assign all possible addresses.

29.16 IPv6 Colon Hexadecimal Notation

Although it solves the problem of having insufficient capacity, the large address size poses an interesting new problem: humans who maintain internets must read, enter, and manipulate such addresses. Obviously, binary notation is untenable. However, the dotted decimal notation used for IPv4 does not make such addresses sufficiently compact either. To understand why, consider an example 128-bit number expressed in dotted decimal notation:

$$104.230.140.100.255.255.255.255.0.0.17.128.150.10.255.255$$

To help make address slightly more compact and easier to enter, the IPv6 designers propose using *colon hexadecimal notation* (abbreviated *colon hex*) in which the value of each 16-bit quantity is represented in hexadecimal separated by colons. For example, when the value shown above in dotted decimal notation has been translated to colon hex notation and printed using the same spacing, it becomes:

$$68E6:8C64:FFFF:FFFF:0:1180:96A:FFFF$$

Colon hex notation has the obvious advantage of requiring fewer digits and fewer separator characters than dotted decimal. In addition, colon hex notation includes two techniques that make it extremely useful. First, colon hex notation allows *zero compression* in which a string of repeated zeros is replaced by a pair of colons. For example, the address:

$$FF05:0:0:0:0:0:0:B3$$

can be written:

$$FF05::B3$$

To ensure that zero compression produces an unambiguous interpretation, the proposal specifies that it can be applied only once in any address. Zero compression is especially useful when used with the proposed address assignment scheme because many addresses will contain contiguous strings of zeros. Second, colon hex notation incorporates dotted decimal suffixes; we will see that such combinations are intended to be used during the transition from IPv4 to IPv6. For example, the following string is valid colon hex notation:

$$0:0:0:0:0:0:128.10.2.1$$

Note that although the numbers separated by colons each specify the value of a 16-bit quantity, numbers in the dotted decimal portion each specify the value of one octet. Of course, zero compression can be used with the number above to produce an equivalent colon hex string that looks quite similar to an IPv4 address:

$$::128.10.2.1$$

29.17 Three Basic IPv6 Address Types

Like IPv4, IPv6 associates an address with a specific network connection, not with a specific computer. Thus, address assignments are similar to IPv4: an IPv6 router has two or more addresses, and an IPv6 host with one network connection needs only one address. IPv6 also retains (and extends) the IPv4 address hierarchy in which a physical network is assigned a prefix. However, to make address assignment and modification easier, IPv6 permits multiple prefixes to be assigned to a given network, and allows a computer to have multiple, simultaneous addresses assigned to a given interface.

In addition to permitting multiple, simultaneous addresses per network connection, IPv6 expands, and in some cases unifies, IPv4 special addresses. In general, a destination address on a datagram falls into one of three categories:

Unicast   The destination address specifies a single computer (host or router); the datagram should be routed to the destination along a shortest path.

Cluster   The destination is a set of computers that all share a single address prefix (e.g., attach to the same physical network); the datagram should be routed to the group along a shortest path, and then delivered to exactly one member of the group (e.g., the closest member).

Multicast   The destination is a set of computers, possibly at multiple locations. One copy of the datagram will be delivered to each member of the group using hardware multicast or broadcast if viable.

29.18 The Duality Of Broadcast And Multicast

IPv6 does not use the terms *broadcast* or *directed broadcast* to refer to delivery to all computers on a physical network or a logical IP subnet. Instead, it uses the term *multicast*, and treats broadcast as a special form of multicast. The choice may seem odd to anyone who understands network hardware because more hardware technologies support broadcast than support multicast. In fact, a hardware engineer is likely to view multicasting as a restricted form of broadcasting – the hardware sends a multicast packet to all computers on the network exactly like a broadcast packet, and the interface hardware on each computer filters all multicast packets except those that software has instructed the interface hardware to accept.

In theory, the choice between multicast and limited forms of broadcast is irrelevant because one can be simulated with the other. That is, broadcasting and multicasting are duals of one another that provide the same functionality. To understand why, consider how to simulate one with the other. If broadcast is available, a packet can be delivered to a group by sending it to all machines and arranging for software on each computer to decide whether to accept or discard the incoming packet. If multicast is available, a packet can be delivered to all machines by arranging for all machines to listen to one multicast group similar to the *all hosts* group discussed in Chapter 17.

29.19 An Engineering Choice And Simulated Broadcast

Knowing that broadcasting and multicasting are theoretical duals of one another does not help choose between them. To see why the designers of IPv6 chose multicasting as the central abstraction instead of broadcasting, consider applications instead of looking at the underlying hardware. An application either needs to communicate with a single other application or with a group of applications. Direct communication is handled best via unicast; group communication is handled best by multicast or broadcast. To provide the most flexibility, group membership should not be determined by network connections, because group members can reside at arbitrary locations. Using broadcast for all group communication does not scale to handle an internet as large as the global Internet.

Not surprisingly, the designers pre-define multicast addresses that correspond to IPv4's network and subnet broadcast addresses. Thus, in addition to its own unicast address, each host is required to accept packets addressed to the *All Nodes* multicast group and to the *All Hosts* multicast group for its local environment; an *All Routers* address also exists.

29.20 Proposed IPv6 Address Space Assignment

The question of how to partition the address space has generated much discussion. There are two central issues: how to manage address assignment and how to map an address to a route. The first issue focuses on the practical problem of devising a hierarchy of authority. Unlike the current Internet, which uses a two-level hierarchy of network prefix (assigned by the Internet authority) and host suffix (assigned by the organization), the large address space in IPv6 permits a multi-level hierarchy or multiple hierarchies. The second issue focuses on computational efficiency. Independent of the hierarchy of authority that assigns addresses, a router must examine each datagram and choose a path to the destination. To keep the cost of high-speed routers low, the processing time required to choose a path must be kept small.

As Figure 29.10 shows, the designers of IPv6 propose assigning address classes in a way similar to the scheme used for IPv4. Although the first eight bits of an address is sufficient to identify its type, the address space is not partitioned into sections of equal size.

Binary Prefix	Type Of Address	Part Of Address Space
0000 0000	Reserved (IPv4 compatible)	1/256
0000 0001	Reserved	1/256
0000 001	NSAP Addresses	1/128
0000 010	IPX Addresses	1/128
0000 011	Reserved	1/128
0000 100	Reserved	1/128
0000 101	Reserved	1/128
0000 110	Reserved	1/128
0000 111	Reserved	1/128
0001	Reserved	1/16
001	Reserved	1/8
010	Provider-Assigned Unicast	1/8
011	Reserved	1/8
100	Reserved for Geographic	1/8
101	Reserved	1/8
110	Reserved	1/8
1110	Reserved	1/16
1111 0	Reserved	1/32
1111 10	Reserved	1/64
1111 110	Reserved	1/128
1111 1110	Available for Local Use	1/256
1111 1111	Used For Multicast	1/256

Figure 29.10 The proposed division of IPv6 addresses into types, which are analogous to IPv4 classes. As in IPv4, the prefix of an address determines its address type.

29.21 IPv4 Address Encoding And Transition

Observe from Figure 29.10 that over *72%* of the address space has been reserved for future use, not including the section reserved for geographic addresses. Although the prefix *0000 0000* is labeled *Reserved* in the figure, the designers plan to use a small fraction of addresses in that section to encode IPv4 addresses. In particular, any address that begins with 80 zero bits followed by 16 bits of all ones or 16 bits of all zeros contains an IPv4 address in the low-order 32 bits. The encoding will be needed during a transition from IPv4 to IPv6 for two reasons. First, a computer may choose to upgrade from IPv4 to IPv6 software before it has been assigned a valid IPv6 address. Second, a computer running IPv6 software may need to communicate with a computer that runs only IPv4 software.

Having a way to encode an IPv4 address in an IPv6 address does not solve the problem of making the two version interoperate. In addition to address encoding, translation is needed. To use a translator, an IPv6 computer generates a datagram that contains the IPv6 encoding of the IPv4 destination address. The IPv6 computer sends the datagram to a translator, which uses IPv4 to communicate with the destination. When the translator receives a reply from the destination, it translates the IPv4 datagram to IPv6 and sends it back to the IPv6 source.

It may seem that translating protocol addresses could fail because higher layer protocols verify address integrity. In particular, TCP and UDP, use a *pseudo header* in their checksum computation. The pseudo header includes both the source and destination protocol addresses, so changing such addresses could affect the computation. However, the designers planned carefully to allow TCP or UDP on an IPv4 machine to communicate with the corresponding transport protocol on an IPv6 machine. To avoid checksum mismatch, the IPv6 encoding of an IPv4 address has been chosen so that the 16-bit 1's complement checksum for both an IPv4 address and the IPv6 encoding of the address are identical. The point is:

> In addition to choosing technical details of a new Internet Protocol, the IETF work on IPng has focused on finding a way to transition from the current protocol to the new protocol. In particular, the current proposal for IPv6 allows one to encode an IPv4 address inside an IPv6 address such that address translation does not change the pseudo header checksum.

29.22 Providers, Subscribers, And Address Hierarchy

An example will help clarify how the designers envision IPv6 addresses being used. Consider a *Network Access Provider (NAP)*. Such a company offers Internet connectivity to customers, whom we will call *subscribers*. To permit such providers to allocate addresses, the Internet authority assigns each provider a unique identifier. The provider can then assign each subscriber a unique identifier, and use both identifiers when assigning a block of addresses. The subscriber then assigns a unique ID to each physical network, and assigns each computer on a network a unique node ID. Figure 29.11 illustrates one possible division of an address into subfields.

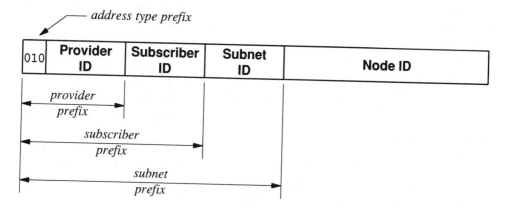

Figure 29.11 The IPv6 address hierarchy for an address assigned by a network access provider. The Internet authority assigns each provider a unique ID, the provider assigns each subscriber a unique ID, and the subscriber assigns a unique ID to each subnet and each node.

As Figure 29.11 shows, each successively larger prefix has a name. The initial string *010* identifies the address as the Provider-Assigned Type. For such addresses, the *provider prefix* includes the address type plus the provider's ID. The *subscriber prefix* covers the provider prefix plus the subscriber's ID. Finally, the *subnet prefix* includes the subscriber prefix plus subnet information.

Fields in Figure 29.11 are not drawn to scale. For example, although the address prefix appears large in the figure, it occupies only 3 of 128 bits. The designers recommend that the *Node ID* field contain at least 48 bits to permit IEEE 802-style addresses to be used. Thus, it will be possible for an IPv6 node to use its Ethernet address as its node ID.

29.23 Additional Hierarchy

Although the address format shown above implies a 4-level hierarchy, an organization can introduce additional levels by dividing the *Subnet ID* field into multiple fields. For example, an organization could choose to divide its subnet into areas, and assign subnets within the area. Doing so is similar to the IPv4 subnet addressing scheme in which the host portion of an address is partitioned into two pieces. The large IPv6 address space permits division into many pieces.

29.24 Summary

Neither the global Internet nor the TCP/IP protocols are static. Through its Internet Engineering Task Force, the Internet Architecture Board fosters active, ongoing efforts that keep the technology stretching and evolving. The stimulus for change occurs as increases in load and size force improvements needed to maintain service, as new applications demand more from the underlying technology, and as new technologies make it possible to provide new services.

An effort to define the next generation of the Internet Protocol (IPng) has produced much discussion and several proposals. A consensus is emerging from the IETF to adopt a proposal known as *Simple IP Plus* as the standard for IPng. Because it will be assigned version number 6, the proposed protocol is often labeled IPv6 to distinguish it from the current protocol, IPv4.

IPv6 retains many of the basic concepts from IPv4, but changes most details. Like IPv4, IPv6 provides a connectionless, best-effort datagram delivery service. However, the IPv6 datagram format is completely different than the IPv4 format, and IPv6 provides new features such as authentication, a mechanism for flow-controlled streams of datagrams, and support for security.

IPv6 organizes each datagram as a series of headers followed by data. A datagram always begins with a 40-octet base header, which contains source and destination addresses and a flow identifier. The base header may be followed by zero or more extension headers, followed by data. Extension headers are optional – IPv6 uses them to hold much of the information IPv4 encodes in options.

An IPv6 address is 128 bits long, making the address space so large that each person on the planet could have an internet as large as the current Internet. IPv6 divides addresses into types analogous to the way IPv4 divides addresses into classes. A prefix of the address determines the location and interpretation of remaining address fields. Many IPv6 addresses will be assigned by authorized network service providers; such addresses have fields that contain a provider ID, subscriber ID, subnet ID, and node ID.

FOR FURTHER STUDY

Many RFCs have appeared that contain information pertinent to IPng, including discussions of requirements, procedures, and specific proposals. Bradner and Mankin [RFC 1550] calls for discussion and proposals, and many later RFCs respond. For example, Britton and Tavs [RFC 1678] and Fleischman [RFC 1687] both comment on IPng in large corporate networks. Gross [RFC 1719] discusses a general direction, Partridge and Kastenholz [RFC 1726] discusses technical criteria for choosing IPng technology, and Brazdziunas [RFC 1680] comments on IPng support for ATM. Bellovin [RFC 1675] comments on security in IPng.

Bradner and Mankin [RFC 1752] summarizes proposals, and contains the recommendation of IETF area managers for IPng. Readers should be aware that the proposal for IPv6 is not yet a thoroughly-tested standard, and at least some details are likely to change.

EXERCISES

29.1   The proposed IPv6 has no header checksum. What are the advantages and disadvantages of this approach?

29.2   How should extension headers be ordered to minimize processing time?

29.3   Although IPv6 addresses are assigned hierarchically, a router does not need to parse an address completely to select a route. Devise an algorithm and data structure for efficient routing. (Hint: consider a longest-match approach.)

29.4   Argue that 128-bit addresses are larger than needed, and that 96 bits provides sufficient capacity.

29.5   Assume your organization intends to adopt IPv6. Devise an address scheme the organization will use to assign each host an address. Did you choose a hierarchical assignment within your organization? Why or why not?

29.6   What is the chief advantage of encoding an Ethernet address in an IPv6 address? The chief disadvantage?

29.7   If you had to choose sizes for the provider, subscriber, and subnet ID fields of an IPv6 address, how large would you make each? Why?

29.8   Read about the IPv6 authentication and security headers. Why are two headers proposed?

Appendix 1

A Guide To RFCs

Introduction

Most of the written information about TCP/IP and the connected Internet, including its architecture, protocols, and history, can be found in a series of reports known as *Request For Comments* or *RFCs*. An informal, loosely coordinated set of notes, RFCs are unusually rich in information and color. Before we consider the more serious aspects of RFCs, it is fitting that we take a few minutes to pay attention to the colorful side. A good place to begin is with Cerf's poem *'Twas the Night Before Start-up* (RFC 968), a humorous parody that describes some of the problems encountered when starting a new network. Knowing not to take itself too seriously has pervaded the Internet effort. Anyone who can remember both their first Internet meeting, filled with networking jargon, and Lewis Carroll's *Jabberwocky*, filled with strangely twisted English, will know exactly why D. L. Covill put them together in *ARPAWOCKY* (RFC 527). Anyone that has read Knuth's *The Art Of Computer Programming* may chuckle over RFC 473 asking where on the ARPANET one could execute MIX programs. We can imagine Pickens filled with pride when responding with RFC 485, *MIX and MIXAL at UCSB*. The University of California at Santa Barbara wasn't alone in offering MIX to the world. In RFC 494, Walden provides a list of all hosts on the network that supported MIX programming.

Other RFCs seem equally frivolous. Interspersed amid the descriptions of ideas that would turn out to dramatically change networking, we find notes like RFC 416, written in early November, 1972: *The ARC System will be Unavailable for Use During Thanksgiving Week.* It says exactly what you think it says. Or consider Crispin's tongue-in-cheek humor found in RFC 748, which describes the *TELNET Randomly-Lose Option* (a proposed option for TELNET that makes it randomly drop characters). If notes like that do not seem insignificant, think about the sixty seven RFCs listed as *never issued.* They were all assigned a number and had an author, but none ever saw the light of day. All that remains are the holes in the numbering scheme, preserved as little reminders of ideas that vaporized or work that remains incomplete.

Even after the silly, lighthearted, and useless RFCs have been removed, the remaining documents do not conform to most standards for scientific writing. Unlike scholarly scientific journals that concentrate on identifying papers of important archival interest, screening them carefully, and filing them for posterity, RFCs provide a record of ongoing conversations among the principals involved in designing, building, measuring, and using the global Internet. The reader understands at once that RFCs include the thoughts of researchers on the leading edge of technological innovation, not the studied opinions of scholars who have completely mastered a subject. The authors are not always sure of the consequences of their proposals, or even of the contents, but they clearly realize the issues are too complex to understand without community discussion.

Despite the inconsistencies in RFCs that sometimes make them difficult for beginners to understand, the RFC mechanism has evolved and now works extremely well. Because RFCs are available electronically, information is propagated to the community quickly. Because they span a broad range of interests, practitioners as well as designers contribute. Because they record informal conversations, RFCs capture discussions and not merely final conclusions. Even the disagreements and contradictory proposals are useful in showing what the designers considered before settling on a given protocol (and readers interested in the history of a particular idea or protocol can use RFCs to follow it from its inception to its current state).

Importance Of Host And Gateway Requirements Documents

Unlike most RFCs, which concentrate on a single idea or protocol, three special RFCs cover a broad range of protocols. The special documents are entitled *Requirements for Internet Gateways* and *Requirements for Internet Hosts* (parts 1 and 2).

The requirements documents were published in the late 1980s, after many years of experience with the TCP/IP protocols, and are considered a major revision to the protocol standards. In essence, requirement documents each review many protocols. They point out known weaknesses or ambiguities in the RFCs that define the protocols, state conventions that have been adopted by vendors, document problems that occur in practice, and list solutions to those problems that have been accumulated through experience. The RFCs for individual protocols have *not* been updated to include changes and updates from the requirements documents. Thus, readers must be careful to always consult the requirements documents when studying a particular protocol.

How To Obtain An RFC Over The Internet

RFCs are available electronically from many repositories around the world. Check with your local network administrator to find the site nearest you. If you cannot find a site, use the instructions given below to access the INTERnet Network Information Center (INTERNIC).

The Internet domain name for the host that provides the archive is:

$$ds.internic.net$$

To obtain a copy of the text file for an RFC directly from the archive, use the File Transfer Protocol (FTP) on a computer attached to the Internet. After invoking an FTP client, supply retrieval commands. First, issue the *user* command to identify yourself to the remote server. Supply the user name *anonymous* and the password *guest* when prompted. Once the server acknowledges your name and password, use the *get* command to retrieve a file named:

$$\text{get rfc/rfc}N\text{.txt} \quad LocalFile$$

where N is the number of the RFC desired†, and *LocalFile* is the name of a file into which the *ftp* program should place a copy. For example, to obtain a copy of RFC 822, issue the command:

$$\text{get rfc/rfc822.txt} \quad LocalFile$$

The retrieved file will contain ASCII text with a form feed character separating each page and a newline (line feed) character separating each line. Except for the newline and form feed characters, the entire file contains printable text that can be rendered with a conventional line printer. No line drawings or other special graphics are included.

The following UNIX command script illustrates how one might build a program that uses FTP to retrieve an RFC:

---

†A few RFCs are only available in postscript; their names end in *.ps*

```
#! /bin/sh
#
# rfc - UNIX (Bourne) shell script to obtain a copy of one or more RFCs,
#        keeping a local cache for subsequent requests.
#
# use: rfc number [number...]
#
PATH=/bin:/usr/bin:/usr/ucb
PUB=/usr/pub/RFC
INTERNIC=ds.internic.net
for i in $*
do      if test ! -r $PUB/RFC.$i -o $i = "-index"
        then echo Retrieving RFC $i from $INTERNIC >&2
#
# invoke FTP under UNIX and feed it retrieval commands as input.
#
                ftp -n $INTERNIC  >/dev/null 2>&1 <<!
user anonymous guest
get rfc/rfc$i.txt $PUB/RFC.$i
quit
!
    fi
#
# Have obtained file; give copy to user if retrieval was successful.
#
        if test -r $PUB/RFC.$i
        then cat $PUB/RFC.$i
        else echo Could not retrieve RFC $i 1>&2
        fi
done
```

The script shown above does more than use FTP to retrieve an RFC. It leaves a copy of the RFC in directory *lusr/publ/RFC*. The advantage of keeping a local copy of an RFC is that subsequent requests are much faster than the first because they do not use FTP nor do they pass information across the Internet. If the script finds one of the requested RFCs in the cache, it merely presents the user with a copy. Note that the script does not look in the cache when retrieving the special file *-index*, because the index contains a list of all RFCs and will change as new RFCs appear.

How To Obtain An RFC Through Electronic Mail

The INTERNIC and many other sites operate information servers that respond to electronic mail messages. That is, one sends an electronic mail message to a special e-mail address, a computer program reads the incoming mail, consults its database of information, and returns an answer using e-mail. The e-mail address of the information server at the INTERNIC is:

mailserv @ ds . internic . net

The database contains text documents for RFCs along with other information. To obtain an RFC, an e-mail message must include the line:

send rfc$N$.txt

where N is the number of an RFC. For more information, send a message that contains the single line:

help

How To Obtain A Paper Copy Of An RFC

People without access to electronic networks can still obtain copies of RFCs. In North America, the toll-free number to call is 1-800-444-4345. Before calling, use this appendix to make a list of the RFCs needed.

Browsing Through RFCs

There are several indexes that can help one browse through RFCs. First, the file *rfc/rfc-index.txt* contains an accurate list of all RFCs listed in reverse chronological order. It is kept at the archive along with text files for the RFCs. Anyone can obtain the index file using FTP or e-mail; users who plan to browse through RFCs usually obtain the index first to verify that they know about the latest RFCs. Second, many RFCs contain summaries or index other RFCs. For example, RFC 899 contains an index of all RFCs numbered 800 through 899, in reverse chronological order. Third, readers often need to know which RFC contains the latest version of an official Internet protocol or which protocols are official and which are unofficial. To accommodate such needs, the IAB periodically publishes an RFC entitled *INTERNET OFFICIAL PROTOCOL STANDARDS*, which provides a list of all protocols that have been adopted as TCP/IP standards, along with the number of the most recent RFC or RFCs describing each protocol. In addition RFC 1602, *The Internet Standards Process – Revision 2,* describes the Internet standardization process and defines the meaning of the terms *proposed standard*, *draft standard*, *Internet standard*, *required*, *recommended*, and *historic*.

The *Internet Assigned Numbers Authority* (*IANA*) at The University of Southern California's Information Sciences Institute publishes information about protocol constants in RFCs entitled *Internet Numbers*. The Internet Numbers RFCs contain values used in various fields of the official protocols (e.g., the Internet Numbers RFC specifies that the *protocol* field in an IP datagram header must contain the value 6 when the datagram contains a TCP segment).

Despite the available indexes, browsing through RFCs can be difficult, especially when the reader is searching for information pertinent to a given topic. Reading a chronological list of all RFCs becomes tedious, but there is no mechanism that allows one to find related groups of RFCs. To exacerbate the problem, information on a given topic may be spread across many years. Browsing through a chronological index of RFCs is particularly difficult because titles do not provide sufficient identification of the information in an RFC. (How could one guess from the title *Leaving Well Enough Alone* that the RFC pertains to FTP?) Finally, having multiple RFCs with a single title (e.g., Internet Numbers) can be confusing because the reader cannot easily tell whether a document is out-of-date without checking the archive.

RFCs Arranged By Topic

The final section of this appendix provides help in finding information in RFCs because it contains a list of the first 1750 RFCs arranged by topic. Readers can find an earlier topical index in RFC 1000, which also includes an annotated chronological listing of the first 1000 RFCs. Although long, RFC 1000 is highly recommended as a source of authoritative and valuable critique – its introduction is especially fascinating. Recalling the origin of RFCs along with the origin of the ARPANET, the introduction captures the spirit of adventure and energy that still characterizes the Internet.

RFCs Organized By Major Category And Subtopic
(Also see RFC 1000 for an earlier version)

1. Administrative

1a. Assigned Internet Numbers (official values used by protocols)

1700, 1340, 1117, 1062, 1060, 1020, 1010, 997, 990, 960, 943, 923, 900, 870, 820, 790, 776, 770, 762, 758, 755, 750, 739, 717, 604, 503, 433, 349, 322, 317, 204, 179, 175, 167.

1b. Official IAB Standards and Other Lists of Protocols

1720, 1610, 1600, 1540, 1500, 1410, 1360, 1280, 1250, 1200, 1140, 1130, 1100, 1083, 1011, 991, 961, 944, 924, 901, 880, 840, 694, 661, 617, 582, 580, 552.

774, 766 - Internet Protocol Handbook Table of Contents

1c. Meeting Notes and Minutes

1636 - Report of IAB Workshop on Security in the Internet Architecture - February 8-10, 1994

1210 - Network and Infrastructure User Requirements for Transatlantic Research Collaboration - Brussels, July 16-18, and Washington July 24-25, 1990

1152 - Workshop report: Internet research steering group workshop on very-high-speed networks

1077 - Critical issues in high bandwidth networking

1019 - Report of the Workshop on Environments for Computational Mathematics

1017 - Network requirements for scientific research: Internet task force on scientific computing

898 - Gateway Special Interest Group Meeting Notes

808, 805, 469 - Computer Mail Meeting Notes

910, 807 - Multimedia Mail Meeting Notes

585 - ARPANET Users Interest Working Group Meeting

549, 396, 282, 253 - Graphics Meeting Notes

371 - International Computer Communications Conference

327 - Data and File Transfer Workshop Notes

316 - Data Management Working Group Meeting Report

164, 131, 108, 101, 082, 077, 063, 037, 021 - Network Working Group Meeting

1d. Meeting Announcements and Group Overviews

1588 - WHITE PAGES MEETING REPORT

1160, 1120 - Internet Activities Board

828 - Data Communications: IFIP's International "Network" of Experts

631 - Call for Papers: International Meeting on Minicomputers and Data Communication

584 - Charter for ARPANET Users Interest Working Group

537 - Announcement of NGG Meeting

526 - Technical Meeting - Digital Image Processing Software Systems

504 - Workshop Announcement

483 - Cancellation of the Resource Notebook Framework Meeting

474, 314, 246, 232, 134 - Network Graphics Working Group

471 - Announcement of a (Tentative) Workshop on Multi-Site Executive Programs

461 - Telnet Meeting Announcement

457 - TIPUG

456 - Memorandum

454 - File Transfer Protocol Meeting Announcement

453 - Meeting Announcement to Discuss a Network Mail System

374 - IMP System Announcement

359 - The Status of the Release of the New IMP System (2600)

343, 331 - IMP System Change Notification

324 - RJE Protocol Meeting

323 - Formation of Network Measurement Group (NMG)

320 - Workshop on Hard Copy Line Graphics

309 - Data and File Transfer Workshop Announcement

299 - Information Management System

295 - Report of the Protocol Workshop

291, 188, 173 - Data Management Meetings

245, 234, 207, 140, 116, 099, 087, 085, 075, 043, 035 - Network Working Group Meetings

222 - System Programmer's Workshop

212 - NWG Meeting on Network Usage

157 - Invitation to the Second Symposium on Problems in the Optimization of Data Communication Systems

149 - The Best Laid Plans...

130 - Response to RFC 111: Pressure from the chairman

111 - Pressure from the Chairman

048 - A Possible Protocol Plateau

046 - ARPA Network Protocol Notes

1e. Distribution Lists

402, 363, 329, 303, 300, 211, 168, 155 - ARPA Network Mailing Lists
069 - Distribution List Change for MIT
052 - Updated Distribution List

1f. Policies Documents

1603 - IETF Working Group Guidelines and Procedures
1371 - Choosing a "Common IGP" for the IP Internet (The IESG's
       Recommendation to the IAB)
1124 - Policy issues in interconnecting networks
1087 - Ethics and the Internet
1052 - IAB recommendations for the development of Internet network
       management standards
1039 - DoD statement on Open Systems Interconnection protocols
980 - Protocol Document Order Information
952, 810, 608 - Host Table Specification
945 - A DoD Statement on the NRC Report
902 - ARPA-Internet Protocol Policy
849 - Suggestions for Improved Host Table Distribution
678 - Standard file formats
602 - The Stockings Were Hung by the Chimney With Care
115 - Some Network Information Center Policies on Handling Documents
053 - An Official Protocol Mechanism

1g. Request for Comments Administrative

1543, 1111 - Instructions to RFC Authors
1150 - F.Y.I. on F.Y.I.: Introduction to the F.Y.I. notes
1000 - Request For Comments reference guide
999, 899, 800, 699 - Requests for Comments Summary
825 - Request for Comments on Requests for Comments
629 - Scenario for Using the Network Journal
628 - Status of RFC Numbers and a Note on Pre-assigned Journal Numbers
598, 200, 170, 160, 100, 084 - RFC Index

1h. Other

1718, 1539, 1391 - The Tao of IETF: A Guide for New Attendees of the
       Internet Engineering Task Force
1690 - Introducing the Internet Engineering and Planning Group (IEPG)
1689 - A Status Report on Networked Information Retrieval: Tools and Groups
1640 - The Process for Organization of Internet Standards Working Group
       (POISED)

1602, 1310 - The Internet Standards Process

1601, 1358 - I. Architecture Board (IAB)

1527 - What Should We Plan Given the Dilemma of the Network?

1481 - IAB Recommendation for an Intermediate Strategy to Address the Issue
       of Scaling

1438 - Internet Engineering Task Force Statements Of Boredom (SOBs)

1435 - IESG Advice from Experience with Path MTU Discovery

1401 - Correspondence between the IAB and DISA on the use of DNS
       throughout the Internet

1396 - The Process for Organization of Internet Standards Working Group
       (POISED)

1380 - IESG Deliberations on Routing and Addressing

1311 - Introduction to the STD Notes

1297 - NOC Internal Integrated Trouble Ticket System Functional
       Specification Wishlist ("NOC TT REQUIREMENTS")

1287 - Towards the Future Internet Architecture

1272 - Internet Accounting: Background

1261 - Transition of NIC Services

1174 - IAB Recommended Policy on Distributing Internet Identifier
       Assignment and IAB Recommended Policy Change to Internet
       "Connected" Status

1166 - Internet Numbers

637 - Change of Network Address for SU-DSL

634 - Change in Network Address for Haskins Lab

616 - Latest Network Maps

609 - Statement of Upcoming Move of NIC/NLS Service

590 - MULTICS Address Change

588 - London Node is Now Up

551 - NYU, ANL, and LBL Joining the Net

544 - Locating On-Line Documentation at SRI-ARC

543 - Network Journal Submission and Delivery

518 - ARPANET Accounts

511 - Enterprise Phone Service to NIC From ARPANET Sites

510 - Request for Network Mailbox Addresses

440 - Scheduled network software maintenance

432 - Network Logical Map

423, 389 - UCLA Campus Computing Network Liaison Staff for ARPA
       Network

421 - A Software Consulting Service for Network Users

419 - MIT-DMS on Vacation

416 - The ARC System will be Unavailable for Use During Thanksgiving
       Week

405 - Correction to RFC 404

404 - Host Address Changes Involving Rand and ISI

403 - Desirability of a Network 1108 Service

386 - Letter to TIP Users - 2

384 - Official Site IDENTS for Organizations in the ARPA Networks

381 - Three Aids to Improved Network Operation

365 - Letter to all TIP users

356 - ARPA Network Control Center

334 - Network Use on May 8

305 - Unknown Host Numbers

301 - BBN IMP No. 5 and NCC Schedule for March 4, 1972

289 - What we hope is an official list of host names

276 - NIC Course

249 - Coordination of Equipment and Supplies Purchase

223 - Network Information Center Schedule for Network Users

185 - NIC Distribution of Manuals and Handbooks

154 - Exposition Style

136 - Host Accounting and Administrative Procedures

118 - Information Required for Each Service Available to the Network

095 - Distribution of NWG/RFC's Through the NIC

016 - MIT

2. Requirements Documents And Major Protocol Revisions

2a. Host requirements

1127 - Perspective on the Host Requirements RFCs

1123 - Requirements for Internet hosts - application and support

1122 - Requirements for Internet hosts - communication layers

2b. Gateway requirements

1009 - Requirements for Internet gateways

3. Network Interface Level (Also see Section 8)

3a. Address Binding (ARP, RARP)

1735 - NBMA Address Resolution Protocol (NARP)

1433 - Directed ARP

1329 - Thoughts on Address Resolution for Dual MAC FDDI Networks

1293 - Inverse Address Resolution Protocol

1027 - Using ARP to implement transparent subnet gateways

925 - Multi-LAN Address Resolution Protocol

903 - A Reverse Address Resolution Protocol

826 - Address Resolution Protocol

3b. Internet Protocol over another network (encapsulation)

1626 - Default IP MTU for use over ATM AAL5

1577 - Classical IP and ARP over ATM

1490, 1294 - Multiprotocol Interconnect over Frame Relay

1483 - Multiprotocol Encapsulation over ATM Adaptation Layer 5

1390, 1188, 1103 - Transmission of IP and ARP over FDDI Networks

1374 - IP and ARP on HIPPI

1241 - A Scheme for an Internet Encapsulation Protocol: Version 1

1226 - Internet Protocol Encapsulation of AX.25 Frames

1221, 907 - Host Access Protocol (HAP) Specification

1209 - The Transmission of IP Datagrams over the SMDS Service

1201, 1051 - Transmitting IP Traffic over ARCNET Networks

1149 - Standard for the transmission of IP datagrams on avian carriers

1088 - Standard for the transmission of IP datagrams over NetBIOS networks

1055 - Nonstandard for transmission of IP datagrams over serial lines: SLIP

1044 - Internet Protocol on Network System's HYPERchannel: Protocol specification

1042 - Standard for the transmission of IP datagrams over IEEE 802 networks

948 - Two Methods for the Transmission of IP Datagrams Over IEEE 802.3 Networks

895 - A Standard for the Transmission of IP Datagrams over Experimental Ethernet Networks

894 - A Standard for the Transmission of IP Datagrams over Ethernet Networks

893 - Trailer Encapsulations

877 - A Standard for the Transmission of IP Datagrams Over Public Data Networks

3c. Other

1326 - Mutual Encapsulation Considered Dangerous

4. Internet Level

4a. Internet Protocol (IP)

1624, 1141 - Computation of the Internet Checksum via Incremental Update

1191 - Path MTU Discovery

1190 - Experimental Internet Stream Protocol, Version 2 (ST-II)

1071 - Computing the Internet checksum

1063 - IP MTU discovery options

1025 - TCP and IP bake off

815 - IP Datagram Reassembly Algorithms

791, 760 - Internet Protocol (IP)

781 -   A Specification of the Internet Protocol IP Timestamp Option

4b. Internet Control Message Protocol (ICMP)

1256 - ICMP Router Discovery Messages

1018 - Some comments on SQuID

1016 - Something a host could do with source quench: The Source Quench
Introduced Delay (SQuID)

792, 777 - Internet Control Message Protocol (ICMP)

4c. Internet Group Management Protocol (IGMP)

1112, 1054, 988 - Host extensions for IP multicasting

4d. Routing and Gateway Algorithms (BGP, GGP, RIP, OSPF)

1745 - BGP4/IDRP for IP---OSPF Interaction

1723, 1388 - RIP Version 2 Carrying Additional Information

1722 - RIP Version 2 Protocol Applicability Statement

1721, 1387 - RIP Version 2 Protocol Analysis

1702 - Generic Routing Encapsulation over IPv4 networks

1701 - Generic Routing Encapsulation (GRE)

1656 - BGP-4 Protocol Document Roadmap and Implementation Experience

1655, 1268, 1164 - Application of the Border Gateway Protocol in the Internet

1654 - A Border Gateway Protocol 4 (BGP-4)

1587 - The OSPF NSSA Option

1586 - Guidelines for Running OSPF Over Frame Relay Networks

1585 - MOSPF: Analysis and Experience

1584 - Multicast Extensions to OSPF

1583, 1247, 1131 - OSPF Version 2

1582 - Extensions to RIP to Support Demand Circuits

1581 - Protocol Analysis for Extensions to RIP to Support Demand Circuits

1520 - Exchanging Routing Information Across Provider Boundaries in the
CIDR Environment

1519, 1338 - Classless Inter-Domain Routing (CIDR): an Address Assignment
and Aggregation Strategy

1517 - Applicability Statement for the Implementation of Classless Inter-
Domain Routing (CIDR)

1504 - Appletalk Update-Based Routing Protocol: Enhanced Appletalk Routing

1482 - Aggregation Support in the NSFNET Policy Routing Database

1479 - Inter-Domain Policy Routing Protocol Specification: Version 1

1478 - An Architecture for Inter-Domain Policy Routing

1477 - IDPR as a Proposed Standard

1465 - Routing coordination for X.400 MHS services within a multi protocol / multi network environment Table Format V3 for static routing

1403, 1364 - BGP OSPF Interaction

1397 - Default Route Advertisement In BGP2 And BGP3 Versions Of The Border Gateway Protocol

1383 - An Experiment in DNS Based IP Routing

1370 - Applicability Statement for OSPF

1322 - A Unified Approach to Inter-Domain Routing

1267, 1163 - A Border Gateway Protocol 3 (BGP-3)

1266 - Experience with the BGP Protocol

1265 - BGP Protocol Analysis

1264 - Internet Routing Protocol Standardization Criteria

1254 - Gateway Congestion Control Survey

1246 - Experience with the OSPF Protocol

1245 - OSPF Protocol Analysis

1222 - Advancing the NSFNET Routing Architecture

1195 - Use of OSI IS-IS for Routing in TCP/IP and Dual Environments

1142 - OSI IS-IS Intra-domain Routing Protocol

1136 - Administrative Domains and Routing Domains: A model for routing in the Internet

1133 - Routing between the NSFNET and the DDN

1126 - Goals and functional requirements for inter-autonomous system routing

1125 - Policy requirements for inter Administrative Domain routing

1105 - Border Gateway Protocol (BGP)

1104 - Models of policy based routing

1102 - Policy routing in Internet protocols

1093 - NSFNET routing architecture

1092 - EGP and policy based routing in the new NSFNET backbone

1075 - Distance Vector Multicast Routing Protocol

1074 - NSFNET backbone SPF based Interior Gateway Protocol

1058 - Routing Information Protocol

1046 - Queuing algorithm to provide type-of-service for IP links

985 -   Requirements for Internet Gateways

975 -   Autonomous Confederations

970 -   On Packet Switches With Infinite Storage

911 -   EGP Gateway under Berkeley Unix

904, 890, 888, 827 - Exterior Gateway Protocol

875 -   Gateways, Architectures, and Heffalumps

823 -   Gateway Gateway Protocol

4e. IP: The Next Generation (IPng)

1753 - IPng Technical Requirements Of the Nimrod Routing and Addressing
    Architecture

1752 - The Recommendation for the IP Next Generation Protocol

1726 - Technical Criteria for Choosing IP:The Next Generation (IPng)

1710 - Simple Internet Protocol Plus White Paper

1707 - CATNIP: Common Architecture for the Internet

1705 - Six Virtual Inches to the Left: The Problem with IPng

1688 - IPng Mobility Considerations

1687 - A Large Corporate User's View of IPng

1686 - IPng Requirements: A Cable Television Industry Viewpoint

1683 - Multiprotocol Interoperability In IPng

1682 - IPng BSD Host Implementation Analysis

1680 - IPng Support for ATM Services

1679 - PN Working Group Input to the IPng Requirements Solicitation

1678 - IPng Requirements of Large Corporate Networks

1677 - Tactical Radio Frequency Communication Requirments for IPng

1676 - INFN Requirements for an IPng

1675 - Security Concerns for IPng

1674 - A Cellular Industry View of IPng

1673 - Electric Power Research Institute Comments on IPng

1672 - Accounting Requirements for IPng

1671 - IPng White Paper on Transition and Other Considerations

1670 - Input to IPng Engineering Considerations

1669 - Market Viability as a IPng Criteria

1668 - Unified Routing Requirements for IPng

1667 - Modeling and Simulation Requirements for IPng

1622 - Pip Header Processing

1621 - Pip Near-term Architecture

1606 - A Historical Perspective On The Usage Of IP Version 9

1550 - IP: Next Generation (IPng) White Paper Solicitation

1526 - Assignment of System Identifiers for TUBA/CLNP Hosts

1475 - TP/IX: The Next Internet

1454 - Comparison of Proposals for Next Version of IP

1385 - EIP: The Extended Internet Protocol A Framework for Maintaining
    Backward Compatibility

1375 - Suggestion for New Classes of IP Addresses

1365 - An IP Address Extension Proposal

1347 - TCP and UDP with Bigger Addresses (TUBA), A Simple Proposal for
    Internet Addressing and Routing

1335 - A Two-Tier Address Structure for the Internet: A Solution to the
    Problem of Address Space Exhaustion

4f. Other

1744 - Observations on the Management of the Internet Address Space

1716 - Towards Requirements for IP Routers

1715 - The H Ratio for Address Assignment Efficiency

1631 - The IP Network Address Translator (Nat)

1620 - Internet Architecture Extensions for Shared Media

1597 - Address Allocation for Private Internets

1560 - The MultiProtocol Internet

1518 - An Architecture for IP Address Allocation with CIDR

1476 - RAP: Internet Route Access Protocol

1467, 1367 - Schedule for IP Address Space Management Guidelines

1466, 1366 - Guidelines for Management of IP Address Space

1393 - Traceroute Using an IP Option

1363 - A Proposed Flow Specification

1349 - Type of Service in the Internet Protocol Suite

1219 - On the Assignment of Subnet Number

986 - Working Draft - Guidelines for the Use of Internet-IP Addressing in the ISO Connectionless-Mode Network

981 - An Experimental Multiple-Path Routing Algorithm

963 - Some Problems with the Specification of the Military Standard Internet Protocol

950 - Internet Standard Subnetting Procedure

947 - Multi-Network Broadcasting Within the Internet

940, 917, 932, 936 - Internet Subnets Protocol

922, 919 - Broadcasting Internet datagrams in the presence of subnets

871 - A Perspective on the ARPANET Reference Model

831 - Backup Access to the European Side of SATNET

817 - Modularity and Efficiency in Protocol Implementation

816 - Fault Isolation and Recovery

814 - Name, Addresses, Ports, and Routes

796 - Address Mapping

795 - Service Mappings

730 - Extensible Field Addressing

5. Host Level

5a. User Datagram Protocol (UDP)

768 - User Datagram Protocol

5b. Transmission Control Protocol (TCP)

1644 - T/TCP -- TCP Extensions for Transactions Functional Specification

1379 - Extending TCP for Transactions -- Concepts

1337 - TIME-WAIT Assassination Hazards in TCP

1323, 1185 - TCP Extensions for High Performance

1263 - TCP Extensions Considered Harmful

1146, 1145 - TCP alternate checksum options

1144 - Compressing TCP/IP headers for low-speed serial links

1110 - Problem with the TCP big window option

1106 - TCP big window and NAK options

1078 - TCP port service Multiplexer (TCPMUX)

1072 - TCP extensions for long-delay paths

983 - ISO Transport Services on Top of the TCP

964 - Some Problems with the Specification of the Military Standard
       Transmission Control Protocol

962 - TCP-4 prime

896 - Congestion Control in IP/TCP Internetworks

889 - Internet Delay Experiments

879 - The TCP Maximum Segment Size and Related Topics

872 - TCP-ON-A-LAN

813 - Window and acknowlegement strategy in TCP

794 - Pre-Emption

793, 761, 675 - Transmission Control Protocol

721 - Out of Band Control Signals in a Host to Host Protocol

700 - A Protocol Experiment

5c. Point-To-Point Protocols

1717 - The PPP Multilink Protocol (MP)

1663 - PPP Reliable Transmission

1662, 1549 - PPP in HDLC Framing

1661, 1548 - The Point-to-Point Protocol (PPP)

1638, 1220 - Point-to-Point Protocol Extensions for Bridging

1619 - PPP over SONET/SDH

1618 - PPP over ISDN

1598 - PPP in X.25

1570 - PPP LCP Extensions

1552 - The PPP Internetwork Packet Exchange Control Protocol (IPXCP)

1547 - Requirements for an Internet Standard Point-to-Point Protocol

1378 - The PPP AppleTalk Control Protocol (ATCP)

1377 - The PPP OSI Network Layer Control Protocol (OSINLCP)

1376 - The PPP DECnet Phase IV Control Protocol (DNCP)

1334 - PPP Authentication Protocols

1333 - PPP Link Quality Monitoring

1332, 1172 - The Point-to-Point Protocol (PPP) Initial Configuration Options

1331, 1171, 1134 - The Point-to-Point Protocol for the Transmission of Multi-Protocol Datagrams Over Point-to-Point Links

5d. Reliable Datagram Protocols (RDP, VMTP)

1151, 908 - Reliable Data Protocol (RDP)

1045 - VMTP: Versatile Message Transaction Protocol: Protocol specification

5e. Transaction Protocols and Distributed Operating Systems

955 - Towards a Transport Service for Transaction Processing Applications

938 - Internet Reliable Transaction Protocol Functional and Interface Specification

722 - Thoughts on Interactions in Distributed Services

713 - MSDTP -- Message Services Data Transmission Protocol

712 - A Distributed Capability Computing System DCCS

708 - Elements of a Distributed Programming System

707 - A High-Level Framework for Network-Based Resource Sharing

684 - A Commentary on Procedure Calling as A Network Protocol

677 - The Maintenance of Duplicate Databases

674 - Procedure Call Documents--Version 2

672 - A Multi-Site Data Collection Facility

671 - A Note on Reconnection Protocol

645 - Network Standard Data Specification Syntax

615 - Proposed Network Standard Data Pathname Syntax

610 - Further Datalanguage Design Concepts

592 - Some Thoughts on System Design to Facilitate Resource Sharing

578 - Using MIT-MATHLAB MACSYMA From MIT-DMS Muddle - An Experiment in Automated Resource Sharing

515 - Specifications for Datalanguage, Version 0/9

500 - The Integration of Data Management Systems on a Computer Network

441 - Inter-Entity Communication - An Experiment

437 - Data Reconfiguration Service at UCSB

203 - Achieving Reliable Communication

076 - Connection-by-Name: User-Oriented Protocol

062 - A System for Interprocess Communication in a Resource Sharing Computer Network

061 - A Note on Interprocess Communication in a Resource Sharing Computer Network

051 - Proposal for a Network Interchange Language

031 - Binary Message Forms in Computer Networks

5f. Protocols For Personal Computers (NETBIOS)

1002 - Protocol standard for a NetBIOS service on a TCP/UDP transport:
Detailed specifications

1001 - Protocol standard for a NetBIOS service on a TCP/UDP transport:
Concepts and methods

5g. Other

1469 - IP Multicast over Token-Ring Local Area Networks

1458 - Requirements for Multicast Protocols

1312, 1159 - Message Send Protocol

1301 - Multicast Transport Protocol

998, 969 - NETBLT: A Bulk Data Transfer Protocol

979 -   PSN End-to-End Functional Specification

966 -   A Multicast Extension to the Internet Protocol

869 -   Host Monitoring Protocol

741 -   Specifications for the Network Voice Protocol NVP

643 -   Cross Net Debugger

162 -   NETBUGGER3

6. Application Level

6a. Telnet Protocol (TELNET)

1647 - TN3270 Enhancements

1646 - TN3270 Extensions for LUname and Printer Selection

1576 - TN3270 Current Practices

1205 - 5250 Telnet Interface

1184 - Telnet Linemode Option

854, 764 - Telnet Protocol Specification

818 -   The Remote User Telnet Service

782 -   A Virtual Terminal Management Model

728 -   A Minor Pitfall in the Telnet Protocol

703, 702, 701, 679, 669 - Survey of New-Protocol Telnet Servers

688 -   Tentative Schedule for the New Telnet Implementation for the TIP

681 -   Network Unix

600 -   Interfacing an Illinois Plasma Terminal to the ARPANET

596 -   Second Thoughts on Telnet Go-Ahead

595 -   Some Thoughts in Defense of the Telnet Go-Ahead

593 -   Telnet and FTP Implementation Schedule Change

576 -   Proposal for Modifying Linking

570 -   Experimental Input Mapping Between NVT ASCII and UCSB Online
System

562 - Modifications to the Telnet Specification

559 - Comments on the New Telnet Protocol and Its Implementation

529 - A Note on Protocol Synch Sequences

513 - Comments on the New Telnet Specifications

495 - Telnet Protocol Specification

466 - Telnet Logger/Server for Host LL-67

452 - Telnet Command at Host LL

435 - Telnet Issues

426 - Reconnection Protocol

393 - Comments on Telnet Protocol Changes

377 - Using TSO Via ARPA Network Virtual Terminal

357 - An Echoing Strategy for Satellite Links

355, 346 - Satellite Considerations

340 - Proposed Telnet Changes

339 - MLTNET - A "Multi-Telnet" Subsystem for TENEX

328 - Suggested Telnet Protocol Changes

318 - Ad Hoc Telnet Protocol

216 - Telnet Access to UCSB's On-Line System

215 - NCP, ICP, and Telnet: The Terminal IMP Implementation

206 - A User Telnet Description of an Initial Implementation

205 - NETCRT - A Character Display Protocol

190 - DEC PDP-10 - IMLAC Communication System

158 - Proposed Telnet Protocol

139 - Discussion of Telnet Protocol

137 - Telnet Protocol - A Proposed Document

135, 110 - Conventions for Using an IBM 2741 Terminal as a User Console
            for Access to Network Server Hosts

103 - Implementation of Interrupt Keys

097 - A First Cut at a Proposed Telnet Protocol

091 - A Proposed User-User Protocol

6b. Telnet Options

1572, 1408 - Telnet Environment Option

1571 - Telnet Environment Option Interoperability Issues

1416, 1409 - Telnet Authentication Option

1412 - Telnet Authentication : SPX

1411 - Telnet Authentication: Kerberos Version 4

1372, 1080 - Telnet remote flow control option

1143 - Q method of implementing Telnet option negotiation

1116 - Telnet Linemode option

1097 - Telnet subliminal-message option

1096 - Telnet X display location option

1091 - Telnet terminal-type option

1079 - Telnet terminal speed option

1073 - Telnet window size option

1053 - Telnet X.3 PAD option

1043 - Telnet Data Entry Terminal option: DODIIS implementation

1041 - Telnet 3270 regime option

946 -   Telnet Terminal Location Number Option

933 -   Output Marking Telnet Option

930 -   Telnet Terminal Type Option

927 -   TACACS User Identification Telnet Option

885 -   Telnet End of Record Option

884 -   Telnet Terminal Type Option

861 -   Telnet Extended Options - List Option

860 -   Telnet Timing Mark Option

859 -   Telnet Status Option

858 -   Telnet Suppress Go Ahead Option

857 -   Telnet Echo Option

856 -   Telnet Binary Transmission

855 -   Telnet Option Specifications

779 -   Telnet Send-Location Option

749 -   Telnet SUPDUP-OUTPUT Option

748 -   Telnet Randomly-Lose Option

736 -   Telnet SUPDUP Option

735 -   Revised Telnet Byte Macro Option

747 -   Recent Extensions to the SUPDUP Protocol

746 -   The SUPDUP Graphics Extension

732 -   Telnet Data Entry Terminal Option

731 -   Telnet Data Entry Terminal Option

729 -   Telnet Byte Macro Option

727 -   Telnet Logout Option

726 -   Remote Controlled Transmission and Echoing Telnet Option

719 -   Discussion on RCTE

718 -   Comments on RCTE from the Tenex Implementation Experience

698 -   Telnet Extended ASCII Option

659 -   Announcing Additional Telnet Options

658 -   Telnet Output Line Feed Disposition

657 -   Telnet Output Vertical Tab Disposition Option

656 -   Telnet Output Vertical Tab Stops Option

655 -   Telnet Output Form Feed Disposition Option

654 -   Telnet Output Horizontal Tab Disposition Option

653 -   Telnet Output Horizontal Tab Stops Option

652 -   Telnet Output Carriage Return Disposition Option

651 -   Revised Telnet Status Option

587 -   Announcing New Telnet Options

581 -   Corrections to RFC 560 - Remote Controlled Transmission and Echoing
        Telnet Option

563 -   Comments on the RCTE Telnet Option

560 -   Remote Controlled Transmission and Echoing Telnet Option

6c. File Transfer and Access Protocols (FTP, TFTP, SFTP, NFS)

1639, 1545 - FTP Operation Over Big Address Records (FOOBAR)

1635 - How to Use Anonymous FTP

1579 - Firewall-Friendly FTP

1440 - SIFT/UFT: Sender-Initiated/Unsolicited File Transfer

1415 - FTP-FTAM Gateway Specification

1350, 783 - The TFTP Protocol Revision 2

1282, 1258 - BSD Rlogin

1235 - The Coherent File Distribution Protocol

1094 - NFS: Network File System Protocol specification

1068 - Background File Transfer Program (BFTP)

1037 - NFILE - a file access protocol

959, 765, 542, 354, 265, 172, 114 - The File Transfer Protocol

949 -   FTP Unique-Named Store Command

913 -   Simple File Transfer Protocol

906 -   Bootstrap Loading Using TFTP

775 -   Directory Oriented FTP Commands

743 -   FTP Extension: XRSQ/XRCP

737 -   FTP Extension: XSEN

697 -   CWD Command of FTP

691 -   One More Try on the FTP

686 -   Leaving Well Enough Alone

683 -   FTPSRV -- Tenex Extension for Paged Files

662 -   Performance Improvement in ARPANET File Transfers from Multics

640 -   Revised FTP Reply Codes

630 -   FTP Error Code Usage for More Reliable Mail Service

624 -   Comments on the File Transfer Protocol

614 -   Response to RFC 607 - Comments on the FTP

607 -   NIC-21255 Comments on the File Transfer Protocol

571 -   Tenex FTP Problem

535 -   Comments on File Access Protocol

532 -   The UCSD-CC Server-FTP Facility

520 - Memo to FTP Group (Proposal for File Access Protocol)

506 - An FTP Command Naming Problem

505 - Two Solutions to a File Transfer Access Problem

501 - Un-Muddling "Free File Transfer"

487 - Host-Dependent FTP Parameters

486 - Data Transfer Revisited

480 - Host-Dependent FTP Parameters

479 - Use of FTP by the NIC Journal

478 - FTP Server-Server Interaction - II

468 - FTP Data Compression

463 - FTP Comments and Response to RFC 430

448 - Print Files in FTP

438 - FTP Server-Server Interaction

430 - Comments on File Transfer Protocol

418 - Server File Transfer Under TSS/360 at NASA/Ames Research Center

414 - File Transfer Protocols (FTP): Status and Further Comments

412 - User FTP Documentation

385 - Comments on the File Transfer Protocol (RFC 354) 310 - Another
        Look at Data and File Transfer Protocols

294 - The Use of "Set Data Type" Transaction in the File Transfer Protocol

281 - A Suggested Addition to File Transfer Protocol

269 - Some Experience with File Transfer

264, 171 - The Data Transfer Protocol

250 - Some Thoughts on File Transfer

242 - Data Descriptive Language for Shared Data

238 - Comments on DTP and FTP Protocols

163 - Data Transfer Protocols

141 - Comments on RFC 114 (A File Transfer Protocol)

133 - File Transfer and Error Recovery

6d. Domain Name System (DNS)

1713 - Tools for DNS debugging

1712 - DNS Encoding of Geographical Location

1706, 1637, 1348 - DNS NSAP Resource Records

1591 - Domain Name System Structure and Delegation

1537 - Common DNS Data File Configuration Error

1536 - Common DNS Implementation Errors and Suggested Fixes

1535 - A Security Problem and Proposed Correction With Widely Deployed
        DNS Software

1480, 1386 - The US Domain

1464 - Using the Domain Name System To Store Arbitrary String Attributes

1394 - Relationship of Telex Answerback Codes to Internet Domains

1183 - New DNS RR Definitions

1101 - DNS encoding of network names and other types

1035 - Domain names - implementation and specification

1034 - Domain names - concepts and facilities

1033 - Domain administrators operations guide

1032 - Domain administrators guide

1031 - MILNET name domain transition

973 -   Domain System Changes and Observations

953, 811 - Hostname Server

921, 897 - Domain Name System Implementation Schedule

920 -   Domain Requirements

883 -   Domain Names - Implementation and Specification

882 -   Domain Names - Concepts and Facilities

881 -   The Domain Names Plan and Schedule

830 -   A Distributed System for Internet Name Service

819 -   The Domain Naming Convention for Internet User Applications

799 -   Internet Name Domains

756 -   The NIC Name Server -- A Datagram-Based Information Utility

752 -   A Universal Host Table

6e. Mail and Message Systems (SMTP, MIME, X.400)

1741 - MIME Content Type for BinHex Encoded Files

1740 - MIME Encapsulation of Macintosh files - MacMIME

1734 - POP3 AUTHentication command

1733 - DISTRIBUTED ELECTRONIC MAIL MODELS IN IMAP4

1732 - IMAP4 COMPATIBILITY WITH IMAP2 AND IMAP2BIS

1731 - IMAP4 Authentication mechanisms

1730 - INTERNET MESSAGE ACCESS PROTOCOL (IMAP) - VERSION 4

1725, 1460, 1225, 1082, 1081 - Post Office Protocol - version 3

1711 - Classifications in E-mail Routing

1685 - Writing X.400 O/R Names

1664 - Using the Internet DNS to Distribute RFC1327 Mail Address Mapping
         Tables

1653, 1427 - SMTP Service Extension for Message Size Declaration

1652, 1426 - SMTP Service Extension for 8bit-MIMEtransport

1651, 1425 - SMTP Service Extensions

1649 - Operational Requirements for X.400 Management Domains in the GO-
         MHS Community

1648 - Postmaster Convention for X.400 Operations

1642 - UTF-7 - A Mail-Safe Transformation Format of Unicode

1641 - Using Unicode with MIME

1616 - X.400(1988) for the Academic and Research Community in Europe

1615 - Migrating from X.400(84) to X.400(88)

1590 - Media Type Registration Procedure

1563, 1523 - The text/enriched MIME Content-type

1557 - Korean Character Encoding for Internet Messages

1556 - Handling of Bi-directional Texts in MIME

1555 - Hebrew Character Encoding for Internet Messages

1544 - The Content-MD5 Header Field

1524 - A User Agent Configuration Mechanism For Multimedia Mail Format Information

1522, 1342 - Representation of Non-ASCII Text in Internet Message Headers

1521, 1341 - MIME (Multipurpose Internet Mail Extensions): Mechanisms for Specifying and Describing the Format of Internet Message Bodies

1506 - A tutorial on gatewaying between X.400 and Internet mail

1505, 1154 - Encoding Header Field for Internet Messages

1502 - X.400 Use of Extended Character Sets

1496 - Rules for downgrading messages from X.400/88 to X.400/84 when MIME content-types are present in the messages

1495, 1327, 1148, 1138 - Mapping between X.400(1988) / ISO 10021 and RFC 822

1494 - Equivalences between 1988 X.400 and RFC-822 Message Bodies

1437 - The Extension of MIME Content-Types to a New Medium

1428 - Transition of Internet Mail from Just-Send-8 to 8Bit-SMTP/MIME

1405 - Mapping between X.400(1984/1988) and Mail-11 (DECnet mail)

1357 - A Format for E-mailing Bibliographic Records

1344 - Implications of MIME for Internet Mail Gateways

1343 - A User Agent Configuration Mechanism For Multimedia Mail Format Information

1339 - Remote Mail Checking Protocol

1328 - X.400 1988 to 1984 downgrading

1211 - Problems with the Maintenance of Large Mailing Lists

1204 - Message Posting Protocol (MPP)

1203, 1176, 1064 - Interactive Mail Access Protocol: Version 2

1168 - Intermail and Commercial Mail Relay Services

1153 - Digest message format

1137 - Mapping between full RFC 822 and RFC 822 with restricted encoding

1090 - SMTP on X.25

1056, 993, 984 - PCMAIL: A distributed mail system for personal computers

1049 - Content-type header field for Internet messages

1047 - Duplicate messages and SMTP

1026 - Addendum to RFC 987: (Mapping between X.400 and RFC-822)

987 - Mapping Between X.400 and RFC 822

977 - Network News Transfer Protocol

976 - UUCP Mail Interchange Format Standard

974 - Mail Routing and the Domain System

934 - Proposed Standard for Message Encapsulation

915 - Network Mail Path Service

886 - Proposed Standard for Message Header Munging

850 - Standard for Interchange of USENET Messages

841 - Specification for Message Format for Computer Based Message
       Systems

822 - Standard for the Format of ARPA Internet Text Messages

821, 788 - Simple Mail Transfer Protocol

806 - Specification for Message Format for Computer Based Message
       Systems

780, 772 - Mail Transfer Protocol

786 - Mail Transfer Protocol - ISI TOPS-20 MTP-NIMAIL Interface

785 - Mail Transfer Protocol - ISI TOPS-20 File Definitions

784 - Mail Transfer Protocol - ISI TOPS-20 Implementation

771 - Mail Transition Plan

763 - Role Mailboxes

757 - A Suggested Solution to the Naming, Addressing, and Delivery Problem
       for ARPANET Message Systems

754 - Out-of-Net Host Addresses for Mail

753 - Internet Message Protocol

751 - Survey of FTP Mail and MLFL

744 - MARS - a Message Archiving and Retrieval Service

733 - Standard for the Format of ARPA Network Text Messages

724 - Proposed Official Standard for the Format of ARPA Network Messages

720 - Address Specification Syntax for Network Mail

706 - On the Junk Mail Problem

680 - Message Transmission Protocol

644 - On the Problem of Signature Authentication for Network Mail

577 - Mail Priority

574 - Announcement of a Mail Facility at UCSB

561 - Standardizing Network Mail Headers

555 - Responses to Critiques of the Proposed Mail Protocol

539, 524 - A Proposed Mail Protocol

498 - On Mail Service to CCN

491 - What is "Free"?

475 - FTP and the Network Mail System

458 - Mail Retrieval via FTP

333 - A Proposed Experiment with a Message Switching Protocol

278, 224, 221, 196 - A Mail Box Protocol

6f. Facsimile and Bitmaps

809 - UCL Facsimile System

804 - Facsimile Formats

803 - Dacom 450/500 Facsimile Date Transcoding

798 - Decoding Facsimile Data From the Rapicom 450

797 - Bitmap Formats

769 - Rapicom 450 Facsimile File Format

6g. Graphics and Window Systems

1198 - FYI on the X Window System

1013 - X Window System Protocol, version 11: Alpha update April 1987

965 - A Format for a Graphical Communication Protocol

553 - Draft Design for a Text/Graphics Protocol

493 - Graphics Protocol

401 - Conversion of NGP-0 Coordinates to Device Specific Coordinates

398 - UCSB Online Graphics

387 - Some Experiences in Implementing Network Graphics Protocol Level 0

351 - Information Form for the ARPANET Graphics Resources Notebook

336 - Level 0 Graphics Input Protocol

296 - DS-1 Display System

292 - Graphics Protocol - Level 0 only

285 - Network Graphics

268 - Graphics Facilities Information

199 - Suggestions for a Network Data-Telnet Graphics Protocol

192 - Some Factors Which a Network Graphics Protocol Must Consider

191 - Graphics Implementation and Conceptualization at ARC

186 - A Network Graphics Loader

184 - Proposed Graphic Display Modes

181, 177 - A Device Independent Graphical Display Description

178 - Network Graphics Attention Handling

125, 086 - Proposal for a Network Standard Format for a Data Stream to
        · Control Graphics Display

094 - Some Thoughts on Network Graphics

6h. Data Management

304 - A Data Management System Proposal for the ARPA Network

195 - Data Computers - Data Descriptions and Access Language

194 - The Data Reconfiguration Service - Compiler/Interpreter
      Implementation Notes
166 - Data Reconfiguration Service - An Implementation Specification
144 - Data Sharing on Computer Networks
138 - Status Report on Proposed Data Reconfiguration Service
083 - Language-Machine for Data Reconfiguration

6i. Remote Job Entry (NETRJE, NETRJS)

740, 599, 589, 325, 189, 088 - CCN Network Remote Job Entry Program -
      NETRJS
725 - An RJE Protocol for a Resource Sharing Network
499 - Harvard's Network RJE
490 - Surrogate RJS for UCLA-CCN
477, 436 - Remote Job Service at UCSB
407 - Remote Job Entry
368 - Comments on "Proposed Remote Job Entry Protocol"
360 - Proposed Remote Job Entry Protocol
338 - EBCDIC/ASCII Mapping for Network RJE
307 - Using Network Remote Job Entry
283 - NETRJT - Remote Job Service Protocol for TIPS
105 - Network Specification for Remote Job Entry and Remote Job Output
      Retrieval at UCSB

6j. Remote Procedure Call (RPC)

1057 - RPC: Remote Procedure Call Protocol specification version 2
1050 - RPC: Remote Procedure Call Protocol specification

6k. Time And Date (NTP)

1708 - NTP PICS PROFORMA For the Network Time Protocol Version 3
1589 - A Kernel Model for Precision Timekeeping
1361 - Simple Network Time Protocol (SNTP)
1305, 1119 - Network Time Protocol
1165 - Network Time Protocol (NTP) over the OSI Remote Operations Service
1129 - Internet time synchronization: The Network Time Protocol
1128 - Measured performance of the Network Time Protocol in the Internet
       system
1059 - Network Time Protocol (version 1) specification and implementation
958, 957, 956 - Network Time Protocol
868 - Time Server Protocol
867 - Daytime Protocol
778 - DCNET Time Server Protocol

738 - Time Server

685 - Response Time in Cross-network Debugging

034 - Some Brief Preliminary Notes on the ARC Clock

032 - Some Thoughts on SRI's Proposed Real Time Clock

028 - Time Standards

6l. Presentation and Representation (XDR)

1489 - Registration of a Cyrillic Character Set

1468 - Japanese Character Encoding for Internet Messages

1456 - Conventions for Encoding the Vietnamese Language VISCII:
        VIetnamese Standard Code for Information Interchange VIQR:
        VIetnamese Quoted-Readable Specification

1314 - A File Format for the Exchange of Images in the Internet

1278 - A String Encoding of Presentation Address

1197 - Using ODA for Translating Multimedia Information

1014 - XDR: External Data Representation standard

1003 - Issues in defining an equations representation standard

6m. Network Management (SNMP, CMOT, MIB)

1749 - IEEE 802.5 Station Source Routing MIB using SMIv2

1748, 1743, 1231 - IEEE 802.5 MIB using SMIv2

1742, 1243 - AppleTalk Management Information Base II

1724, 1389 - RIP Version 2 MIB Extension

1697 - Relational Database Management System (RDBMS) Management
        Information Base (MIB) using SMIv2

1696 - Modem Management Information Base (MIB) using SMIv2

1695 - Definitions of Managed Objects for ATM Management Version 8.0
        using SMIv2

1694, 1304 - Definitions of Managed Objects for the SIP Interface Type

1666 - Definitions of Managed Objects for SNA NAUs using SMIv2

1665 - Definitions of Managed Objects for SNA NAUs using SMIv2

1660, 1318 - Definitions of Managed Objects for Parallel-printer-like Hardware
        Devices

1659, 1317 - Definitions of Managed Objects for RS-232-like Hardware
        Devices

1658, 1316 - Definitions of Managed Objects for Character Stream Devices

1657 - Definitions of Managed Objects for the Fourth Version of the Border
        Gateway Protocol (BGP-4) using SMIv2

1650 - Definitions of Managed Objects for the Ethernet-like Interface Types
        using SMIv2

1643, 1623, 1398, 1284 - Definitions of Managed Objects for the Ethernet-like
        Interface Types

1628 - UPS Management Information Base

1612 - DNS Resolver MIB Extensions

1611 - DNS Server MIB Extensions

1604, 1596 - Definitions of Managed Objects for Frame Relay Service

1595 - Definitions of Managed Objects for the SONET/SDH Interface Type

1592, 1228 - SNMP-DPI - Simple Network Management Protocol Distributed
     Program Interface

1593 - SNA APPN Node MIB

1573, 1229 - Extensions to the Generic-Interface MIB

1567 - X.500 Directory Monitoring MIB

1566 - Mail Monitoring MIB

1565 - Network Services Monitoring MIB

1559, 1289 - DECnet Phase IV MIB Extensions

1525, 1493, 1286 - Definitions of Managed Objects for Bridges

1516, 1368 - Definitions of Managed Objects for IEEE 802.3 Repeater Devices

1515 - Definitions of Managed Objects for IEEE 802.3 Medium Attachment
     Units (MAUs)

1514 - Host Resources MIB

1513 - Token Ring Extensions to the Remote Network Monitoring MIB

1512, 1285 - FDDI Management Information Base

1503 - Algorithms for Automating Administration in SNMPv2 Managers

1474 - The Definitions of Managed Objects for the Bridge Network Control
     Protocol of the Point-to-Point Protocol

1473 - The Definitions of Managed Objects for the IP Network Control
     Protocol of the Point-to-Point Protocol

1472 - The Definitions of Managed Objects for the Security Protocols of the
     Point-to-Point Protocol

1471 - The Definitions of Managed Objects for the Link Control Protocol of
     the Point-to-Point Protocol

1461 - SNMP MIB extension for MultiProtocol Interconnect over X.25

1452 - Coexistence between version 1 and version 2 of the Internet-standard
     Network Management Framework

1451 - Manager to Manager Management Information Base

1450 - Management Information Base for version 2 of the Simple Network
     Management Protocol (SNMPv2)

1449 - Transport Mappings for version 2 of the Simple Network Management
     Protocol (SNMPv2)

1448 - Protocol Operations for version 2 of the Simple Network Management
     Protocol (SNMPv2)

1447 - Party MIB for version 2 of the Simple Network Management Protocol
     (SNMPv2)

1446 - Security Protocols for version 2 of the Simple Network Management
    Protocol (SNMPv2)

1445 - Administrative Model for version 2 of the Simple Network Management
    Protocol (SNMPv2)

1444 - Conformance Statements for version 2 of the Simple Network
    Management Protocol (SNMPv2)

1443 - Textual Conventions for version 2 of the Simple Network Management
    Protocol (SNMPv2)

1442 - Structure of Management Information for version 2 of the Simple
    Network Management Protocol (SNMPv2)

1441 - Introduction to version 2 of the Internet-standard Network Management
    Framework

1420, 1298 - SNMP over IPX

1419 - SNMP over AppleTalk

1414 - Ident MIB

1407, 1233 - Definitions of Managed Objects for the DS3/E3 Interface Type

1406, 1232 - Definitions of Managed Objects for the DS1 Interface Type

1382 - SNMP MIB Extension for the X.25 Packet Layer

1381 - SNMP MIB Extension for X.25 LAPB

1369 - Implementation Notes and Experience for The Internet Ethernet MIB

1354 - IP Forwarding Table MIB

1353 - Definitions of Managed Objects for Administration of SNMP Parties

1352 - SNMP Security Protocols

1351 - SNMP Administrative Model

1346 - Resource Allocation, Control, and Accounting for the Use of Network
    Resources

1315 - Management Information Base for Frame Relay DTEs

1303 - A Convention for Describing SNMP-based Agents

1271 - Remote Network Monitoring Management Information Base

1270 - SNMP Communications Services

1269 - Definitions of Managed Objects for the Border Gateway Protocol
    (Version 3)

1253, 1252, 1248 - OSPF Version 2 Management Information Base

1239 - Reassignment of Experimental MIBs to Standard MIBs

1230 - IEEE 802.4 Token Bus MIB

1227 - SNMP MUX Protocol and MIB

1224 - Techniques for Managing Asynchronously Generated Alerts

1215 - A Convention for Defining Traps for use with the SNMP

1214 - OSI Internet Management: Management Information Base

1213, 1158, 1156, 1066 - Management Information Base for network
    management of TCP/IP-based internets

1212 - Concise MIB Definitions

1189, 1095 - Common Management Information Services and Protocol over
        TCP/IP (CMOT)

1187 - Bulk Table Retrieval with the SNMP

1418, 1283, 1161 - SNMP over OSI

1157, 1098, 1067 - Simple Network Management Protocol (SNMP)

1109 - Report of the second Ad Hoc Network Management Review Group

1089 - SNMP over Ethernet

1076 - HEMS monitoring and control language

1155, 1065 - Structure and identification of management information for
        TCP/IP-based internets

1028 - Simple Gateway Monitoring Protocol

1024 - HEMS variable definitions

1023 - HEMS monitoring and control language

1022 - High-level Entity Management Protocol (HEMP)

1021 - High-level Entity Management System (HEMS)

6n. Directory Services (X.500)

1684 - Introduction to White Pages services based on X.500

1632, 1292 - A Catalog of Available X.500 Implementations

1617 - Naming and Structuring Guidelines for X.500 Directory Pilots

1609 - Charting Networks in the X.500 Directory

1608 - Representing IP Information in the X.500 Directory

1564 - DSA Metrics (OSI-DS 34 (v3))

1562 - Naming Guidelines for the AARNet X.500 Directory Service

1558 - A String Representation of LDAP Search Filters

1491 - A Survey of Advanced Usages of X.500

1488 - The X.500 String Representation of Standard Attribute Syntaxes

1487 - X.500 Lightweight Directory Access Protocol

1485 - A String Representation of Distinguished Names (OSI-DS 23 (v5))

1484 - Using the OSI Directory to achieve User Friendly Naming (OSI-DS 24
        (v1.2))

1431 - DUA Metrics

1430 - A Strategic Plan for Deploying an Internet X.500 Directory Service

1384 - Naming Guidelines for Directory Pilots

1373 - PORTABLE DUAs

1309 - Technical Overview of Directory Services Using the X.500 Protocol

1308 - Executive Introduction to Directory Services Using the X.500 Protocol

1279 - X.500 and Domains

1277 - Encoding Network Addresses to Support Operation Over Non-OSI
        Lower Layers

1276 - Replication and Distributed Operations extensions to provide an Internet
       Directory using X.500

1275 - Replication Requirements to provide an Internet Directory using X.500

1274 - The COSINE and Internet X.500 Schema

1255, 1218 - A Naming Scheme for c=US

1249 - DIXIE Protocol Specification

1202 - Directory Assistance Service

1107 - Plan for Internet directory services

6o. Information services (WWW, Gopher, WAIS)

1738 - Uniform Resource Locators (URL)

1737 - Functional Requirements for Uniform Resource Names

1729 - Using the Z39.50 Information Retrieval Protocol in the Internet
       Environment

1728 - Resource Transponders

1727 - A Vision of an Integrated Internet Information Service

1714 - Referral Whois Protocol (RWhois)

1630 - Universal Resource Identifiers in WWW: A Unifying Syntax for the
       Expression of Names and Addresses of Objects on the Network as used
       in the World-Wide Web

1625 - WAIS over Z39.50-1988

1614 - Network Access to Multimedia Information

1436 - The Internet Gopher Protocol (a distributed document search and
       retrieval protocol)

954, 812 - Whois Protocol

6p. Bootstrap And Configuration Protocols (BOOTP, DHCP)

1542, 1532 - Clarifications and Extensions for the Bootstrap Protocol

1541, 1531 - Dynamic Host Configuration Protocol

1534 - Interoperation Between DHCP and BOOTP

1533, 1497, 1395, 1084, 1048 - DHCP Options and BOOTP Vendor
       Extensions

951 -   Bootstrap Protocol

6q. Other

1703, 1569 - Principles of Operation for the TPC.INT Subdomain: Radio
       Paging -- Technical Procedures"

1692 - Transport Multiplexing Protocol (TMux)

1645, 1568 - Simple Network Paging Protocol - Version 2

1530 - Principles of Operation for the TPC.INT Subdomain: General Principles
       and Policy

1529 - Principles of Operation for the TPC.INT Subdomain: Remote Printing --
       Administrative Policies

1528 - Principles of Operation for the TPC.INT Subdomain: Remote Printing --
       Technical Procedures

1546 - Host Anycasting Service

1492 - An Access Control Protocol, Sometimes Called TACACS

1486 - An Experiment in Remote Printing

1459 - Internet Relay Chat Protocol

1429 - Listserv Distribute Protocol

1413, 931, 912 - Identification Protocol

1307 - Dynamically Switched Link Control Protocol

1288, 1196, 1194, 742 - The Finger User Information Protocol

1193 - Client Requirements for Real-Time Communication Services

1179 - Line Printer Daemon Protocol

978 - Voice File Interchange Protocol (VFIP)

972 - Password Generator Protocol

937, 918 - Post Office Protocol

909 - Loader Debugger Protocol

891 - DCN Local Net Protocol

887 - Resource Location Protocol

866 - Active Users Protocol

865 - Quote of the Day Protocol

864 - Character Generator Protocol

863, 348 - Discard Protocol

862, 347 - Echo Protocol

767 - Document Formats

759 - Internet Message Protocol

734 - SUPDUP Protocol

666 - Specification of the Unified User-Level Protocol

621 - NIC User Directories at SRI-ARC

569 - Network Standard Text Editor

470 - Change in Socket for TIP News Facility

451 - Tentative Proposal for a Unified User Level Protocol

109 - Level III Server Protocol for the Lincoln Laboratory NIC 360/67 Host

098, 079 - Logger Protocol

029 - Note in Response to Bill English's Request for Comments

7. Program Documentation

496 - A TNLS Quick Reference Card is Available

494 - Availability of MIX and MIXAL in the Network

488 - NLS Classes at Network Sites

485 - MIS and MIXAL at UCSB

431 - Update on SMFS Login and Logout

411 - New Multics Network Software Features

409 - TENEX Interface to UCSB's Simple-Minded File System

399 - SMFS Login and Logout

390 - TSO Scenario Batch Compilation and Foreground Execution

382 - Mathematical Software on the ARPA Network

379 - Using TSO at CCN

373 - Arbitrary Character Sets

350 - User Accounts for UCSB On-Line System

345 - Interest Mixed Integer Programming (MPSX on 360/91 at CCN)

321 - CBI Networking Activity at MITRE

311 - New Console Attachments to the UCSB Host

251 - Weather Data

217 - Specification Changes for OLS, RJE/RJOR, and SMFS

174 - UCLA-Computer Science Graphics Overview

122 - Network Specifications for UCSB's Simple-Minded File System

121 - Network On-Line Operators

120 - Network PL1 Subprograms

119 - Network FORTRAN Subprograms

074 - Specifications for Network Use of the UCSB On-Line System

8. Network Specific (also see section 3)

8a. ARPANET

1005, 878, 851, 802 - The ARPANET 1822L Host Access Protocol

852 - The ARPANET Short Blocking Feature

789 - Vulnerabilities of Network Control Protocols: An Example

745 - JANUS interface specifications

716 - Interim Revision to Appendix F of BBN 1822

704 - IMP/Host and Host/IMP Protocol Change

696 - Comments on the IMP/HOST and HOST/IMP Protocol Changes

695 - Official Change in Host-Host Protocol

692 - Comments on IMP/Host Protocol Changes

690 - Comments on the Proposed Host/IMP Protocol Changes

687 - IMP/Host and Host/IMP Protocol

667 - BBN Host Ports

660 -   Some Changes to the IMP and the IMP/Host Interface

642 -   Ready Line Philosophy and Implementation

638, 633 - IMP/TIP Preventive Maintenance Schedule

632 -   Throughput Degradation for Single Packet Message

627 -   ASCII Text File of Hostnames

626 -   On a possible Lockup Condition in IMP Subnet due to Message
        Sequencing

625 -   On Line Hostnames Service

623 -   Comments on On-line Host Name Service

622 -   Scheduling IMP/TIP Down Time

620 -   Request for Monitor Host Table Updates

619 -   Mean Round-Trip Times in the ARPANET

613 -   Network Connectivity: A Response to RFC 603

611 -   Two Changes to the IMP/Host Protocol

606 -   Host Names On-Line

594 -   Speedup of Host-IMP Interface

591 -   Addition to the Very Distant Host Specification

568, 567 - Cross-Country Network Bandwidth

548 -   Hosts Using the IMP Going Down Message Specification

547 -   Change to the Very Distant Host Specification

533 -   Message-ID Numbers

528 -   Software Checksumming in the IMP and Network Reliability

521 -   Restricted Use of IMP DDT

508 -   Real-Time Data Transmission on the ARPANET

476, 434 - IMP/TIP Memory Retrofit Schedules

449, 442 - The Current Flow-Control Scheme for IMPSYS

447, 445 - IMP/TIP Preventive Maintenance Schedule

417 -   LINK Usage Violation

410 -   Removal of the 30-second Delay When Hosts Come Up

406 -   Scheduled IMP Software Releases

395 -   Switch Settings on IMPs and TIPs

394 -   Two Proposed Changes to the IMP-HOST Protocol

369 -   Evaluation of ARPANET Services (January through March, 1972)

335 -   New Interface-IMP/360

312 -   Proposed Change in IMP-to-Host Protocol

297 -   TIP Message Buffers

280 -   A Draft Set of Host Names

274 -   Establishing a Local Guide for Network Usage

273, 237 - The NIC's View of Standard Host Names

271 -   IMP System Change Notification

270 -   Correction to the BBN Report No. 1822

263 - "Very Distant" Host Interface

254 - Scenarios for Using ARPANET Computers

247 - Proffered Set of Standard Host Names

241 - Connecting Computers to NLC Ports

239 - Host Mnemonics Proposed in RFC 226

236 - Standard Host Names

233 - Standardization of Host Call Letters

230 - Toward Reliable Operation of Minicomputer-based Terminals on a TIP

229 - Standard Host Names

228 - Clarification

226 - Standardization of Host Mnemonics

218 - Changing the IMP Status Reporting

213 - IMP System Change Notification

209 - Host/IMP Interface Documentation

208 - Address Tables

073, 067 - Proposed Change to Host/IMP Spec to Eliminate Marking

071 - Reallocation in Case of Input Error

070 - A Note On Padding

064 - Getting Rid of Marking

041 - IMP/IMP Teletype Communication

025 - No High Link Numbers

019 - Two Protocol Suggestions to Reduce Congestion at Swap-Bound Nodes

017 - Some Questions Re: HOST-IMP Protocol

012 - IMP-HOST Interface Flow Diagrams

007 - HOST-IMP Interface

006 - Conversation with Bob Kahn

8b. Host Front End Protocols

929, 928, 705, 647 - Host-Front End Protocol

8c. ARPANET NCP (Obsolete predecessor of TCP/IP)

801 - NCP/TCP Transition Plan

773 - Comments on NCP/TCP Mail Service Transition Strategy

714 - A Host/Host Protocol for an ARPANET-type Network

689 - Tenex NCP Finite State Machine for Connections

663 - A Lost Message Detection and Recovery Protocol

636 - TIP/TENEX Reliability Improvements

635 - An Assessment of ARPANET Protocols

534, 516, 512 - Lost Message Detection

492, 467 - Proposed Change to Host-Host Protocol Resynchronization of
        Connection Status

489 - Comment on Resynchronization of Connection Status Proposal

425 - "But my NCP Costs $500 a day..."

210 - Improvement of Flow Control

176 - Comments on Byte Size for Connections

165 - A Proferred Official Initial Connection Protocol

147 - The Definition of a Socket

142 - Time-out Mechanism in the Host-Host Protocol

132, 124, 107, 102 - Output of the Host-Host Protocol Glitch Cleaning
      Committee

129 - A Request for Comments on Socket Name Structure

128 - Bytes

117 - Some Comments on the Official Protocol

072 - Proposed Moratorium on Changes to Network Protocol

068 - Comments on Memory Allocation Control Commands (CEASE, ALL,
      GVB, RET) and RFNM

065 - Comments on Host-Host Protocol Document Number 1

060 - A Simplified NCP Protocol

059 - Flow Control-Fixed Versus Demand Allocation

058 - Logical Message Synchronization

057, 054 - An Official Protocol Proffering

056 - Third Level Protocol

055 - A Prototypical Implementation of the NCP

050, 049, 047, 045, 044, 040, 039, 038, 036, 033 - New Host-Host Protocol

042 - Message Data Types

023 - Transmission of Multiple Control Messages

022 - Host-Host Control Message Formats

018 - Comments Re: Host-Host control link

015 - Network Subsystem for Time Sharing Hosts

011 - Implementation of the Host-Host Software Procedures in GORDO

009, 001 - Host Software

008 - ARPA Network Functional Specifications

005 - DEL

002 - Links

8d. ARPANET Initial Connection Protocol

202 - Possible Deadlock in ICP

197 - Initial Connection Protocol - Revised

161 - A Solution to the Race Condition in the ICP

151, 148, 143, 127, 123 - A Proferred Official ICP

150 - The Use of IPC Facilities

145 - Initial Connection Protocol Control Commands

093 -   Initial Connection Protocol
080 -   Protocol and Data Formats
066 -   3rd Level Ideas and Other Noise

8e. USENET

1036 - Standard for interchange of USENET messages

8f. Other

1553 - Compressing IPX Headers Over WAN Media (CIPX)
1132 - Standard for the transmission of 802.2 packets over IPX networks
935 -   Reliable Link Layer Protocols
916 -   Reliable Asynchronous Transfer Protocol
914 -   Thinwire Protocol
824 -   The Cronus Virtual Local Network

9. Measurement

9a. General

1404 - A Model for Common Operational Statistics
1273 - A Measurement Study of Changes in Service-Level Reachability in the
       Global TCP/IP Internet: Goals, Experimental Design, Implementation,
       and Policy Considerations
1262 - Guidelines for Internet Measurement Activities
557 -   Revelations in Network Host Measurements
546 -   Tenex Load Averages for July 1973
415 -   TENEX Bandwidth
392 -   Measurement of Host Costs for Transmitting Network Data
352 -   TIP Site Information Form
308 -   ARPANET Host Availability Data
286 -   Network Library Information System
214, 193 - Network Checkout
198 -   Site Certification - Lincoln Labs
182 -   Compilation of List of Relevant Site Reports
180 -   File System Questionnaire
156 -   Status of the Illinois Site (Response to RFC 116)
153 -   SRI ARC-NIC Status
152 -   SRI Artificial Intelligence Status Report
126 -   Ames Graphics Facilities at Ames Research Center
112 -   User/Server Site Protocol Network HOST Questionnaire
104 -   Link 191
106 -   USER/SERVER Site Protocol Network Host Questionnaire

9b. Surveys

971 - A Survey of Data Representation Standards

876 - Survey of SMTP Implementations

848 - Who Provides the "Little" TCP Services?

847 - Summary of Smallberg Surveys

844 - Who Talks ICMP, too? Survey of 18 February 1983

846, 845, 843, 842, 839, 838, 837, 836, 835, 834, 833, 832 - Who Talks TCP?

787 - Connectionless Data Transmission Survey/Tutorial

565 - Storing Network Survey Data at the Datacomputer

545 - Of What Quality be the UCSB Resource Evaluators?

530 - A Report on the SURVEY Project

523 - SURVEY is in Operation Again

519 - Resource Evaluation

514 - Network Make-Work

464 - Resource Notebook Framework

460 - NCP Survey

459 - Network Questionnaire

450 - Multics Sampling Timeout Change

446 - Proposal to Consider a Network Program Resource Notebook

096 - An Interactive Network Experiment to Study Modes of Access to the Network Information Center

090 - CCN as a Network Service Center

081 - Request for Reference Information

078 - NCP Status Report: UCSB/Rand

9c. Statistics

1030 - On testing the NETBLT Protocol over divers networks

996 - Statistics Server

618 - A Few Observations on NCP Statistics

612, 601, 586, 579, 566, 556, 538, 522, 509, 497, 482, 455, 443, 422, 413, 400, 391, 378 - Traffic Statistics

603, 597, 376, 370, 367, 366, 362, 353, 344, 342, 332, 330, 326, 319, 315, 306, 298, 293, 288, 287, 267, 266 - Network Host Status

550 - NIC NCP Experiment

388 - NCP Statistics

255, 252, 240, 235 - Site Status

10. Privacy, Security, And Authentication

10a. General

1751 - A Convention for Human-Readable 128-bit Keys

1750 - Randomness Recommendations for Security

1704 - On Internet Authentication

1511 - Common Authentication Technology Overview

1510 - The Kerberos Network Authentication Service (V5)

1509 - Generic Security Service API : C-bindings

1508 - Generic Security Service Application Program Interface

1507 - DASS - Distributed Authentication Security Service

1457 - Security Label Framework for the Internet

1455 - Physical Link Security Type of Service

1424 - Privacy Enhancement for Internet Electronic Mail: Part IV: Key
       Certification and Related Services

1423, 1115 - Privacy Enhancement for Internet Electronic Mail: Part III:
       Algorithms, Modes, and Identifiers

1422, 1114 - Privacy Enhancement for Internet Electronic Mail: Part II:
       Certificate-Based Key Management

1421, 1113, 989 - Privacy Enhancement for Internet Electronic Mail: Part I:
       Message Encryption and Authentication Procedures

1355 - Privacy and Accuracy Issues in Network Information Center Databases

1281 - Guidelines for the Secure Operation of the Internet

1244 - Site Security Handbook

1170 - Public Key Standards and Licenses

1135 - Helminthiasis of the Internet

1040 - Privacy enhancement for Internet electronic mail: Part I: Message
       encipherment and authentication procedures

1038 - Draft revised IP security option

1108 - U.S. Department of Defense Security Options for the Internet Protocol

1004 - Distributed-protocol authentication scheme

10b. Message Digest Algorithms

1321 - The MD5 Message-Digest Algorithm

1320, 1186 - The MD4 Message Digest Algorithm

1319 - The MD2 Message-Digest Algorithm

11. Network Experience and Demonstrations

1306 - Experiences Supporting By-Request Circuit-Switched T3 Networks

968 - 'Twas the Night Before Start-up

967 - All Victims Together

573 - Data and File Transfer - Some Measurement Results

527 - ARPAWOCKY

525 -   MIT-Mathlab Meets UCSB-OLS
439 -   PARRY Encounters the Doctor
420 -   CCA ICC Weather Demo
372 -   Notes on a Conversation with Bob Kahn on the ICCC
364 -   Serving Remote Users on the ARPANET
302 -   Exercising the ARPANET
231 -   Service Center Standards for Remote Usage - A User's View
227 -   Data Transfer Rates (RAND/UCLA)
113 -   Network Activity Report: UCSB and Rand
089 -   Some Historic Moments in Networking
004 -   Network Timetable

12. Site Documentation

30, 27, 24, 10, 3 - Documentation Conventions

13. Protocol Standards By Other Groups Of Interest To The Internet

13a. ANSI

183 -   The EBCDIC Codes and Their Mapping to ASCII
020 -   ASCII Format for Network Interchange

13b. NRC

942 -   Transport Protocols for Department of Defense Data Networks
939 -   Executive Summary of the NRC Report on Transport Protocols for
        Department of Defense Data Networks

13c. ISO

1698 - Octet Sequences for Upper-Layer OSI to Support Basic
       Communications Applications
1629, 1237 - Guidelines for OSI NSAP Allocation in the Internet
1575, 1139 - An Echo Function for CLNP (ISO 8473)
1574 - Essential Tools for the OSI Internet
1561 - Use of ISO CLNP in TUBA Environments
1554 - ISO-2022-JP-2: Multilingual Extension of ISO-2022-JP
1330 - Recommendations for the Phase I Deployment of OSI Directory
       Services (X.500) and OSI Message Handling Services (X.400) within
       the ESnet Community
1238, 1162 - CLNS MIB - for use with Connectionless Network Protocol (ISO
       8473) and End System to Intermediate System (ISO 9542)
1223 - OSI CLNS and LLC1 Protocols on Network Systems HYPERchannel
1008 - Implementation guide for the ISO Transport Protocol

1007 - Military supplement to the ISO Transport Protocol
995 - End System to Intermediate System Routing Exchange Protocol for Use
       in Conjunction with ISO 8473
994 - Final Text of DIS 8473, Protocol for Providing the Connectionless
       Mode Network Service
982 - Guidelines for the Specification of the Structure of the Domain Specific
       Part (DSP) of the ISO Standard NSAP Address
941 - Addendum to the Network Service Definition Covering Network Layer
       Addressing
926 - Protocol for Providing the Connectionless-Mode Network Services
905 - ISO Transport Protocol Specification (ISO DP 8073)
892 - ISO Transport Protocol
873 - The Illusion of Vendor Support

14. Interoperability With Other Applications And Protocols

14a. Protocol Translation And Bridges

1086 - ISO-TP0 bridge between TCP and X.25
1029 - More fault tolerant approach to address resolution for a Multi-LAN
       system of Ethernets

14b. Tunneling And Layering

1634, 1551, 1362 - Novell IPX Over Various WAN Media (IPXWAN)
1613 - cisco Systems X.25 over TCP (XOT)
1538 - Advanced SNA/IP : A Simple SNA Transport Protocol
1434 - Data Link Switching: Switch-to-Switch Protocol
1356 - Multiprotocol Interconnect on X.25 and ISDN in the Packet Mode
1240 - OSI Connectionless Transport Services on top of UDP - Version: 1
1234 - Tunneling IPX Traffic through IP Networks
1085 - ISO presentation services on top of TCP/IP based internets
1070 - Use of the Internet as a subnetwork for experimentation with the OSI
       network layer
1006 - ISO transport services on top of the TCP: Version: 3

14c. Mapping of Names, Addresses and Identifiers

1439 - The Uniqueness of Unique Identifiers
1236 - IP to X.121 Address Mapping for DDN
1069 - Guidelines for the use of Internet-IP addresses in the ISO
       Connectionless-Mode Network Protocol

15. Miscellaneous

15a. General

1746 - Ways to Define User Expectations

1739 - A Primer On Internet and TCP/IP Tools

1709 - K-12 Internetworking Guidelines

1681 - On Many Addresses per Host

1627 - Network 10 Considered Harmful (Some Practices Shouldn't be
     Codified)

1691 - The Document Architecture for the Cornell Digital Library

1633 - Integrated Services in the Internet Architecture: an Overview

1607 - A VIEW FROM THE 21ST CENTURY

1605 - SONET to Sonnet Translation

1580 - Guide to Network Resource Tools

1578 - FYI on Questions and Answers: Answers to Commonly Asked
     ''Primary and Secondary School Internet User'' Questions

1501 - OS/2 User Group

1498 - On the Naming and Binding of Network Destinations

1462 - FYI on ''What is the Internet?''

1594, 1325, 1206, 1177 - FYI on Questions and Answers - Answers to
     Commonly Asked "New Internet User" Questions

1470, 1147 - FYI on a Network Management Tool Catalog: Tools for
     Monitoring and Debugging TCP/IP Internets and Interconnected
     Devices

1453 - A Comment on Packet Video Remote Conferencing and the
     Transport/Network Layers

1432 - Recent Internet Books

1417, 1295 - NADF Standing Documents: A Brief Overview

1402, 1290 - There's Gold in them thar Networks! Searching for Treasure in
     all the Wrong Places

1400 - Transition and Modernization of the Internet Registration Service

1392 - Internet Users' Glossary

1359 - Connecting to the Internet What Connecting Institutions Should
     Anticipate

1345 - Character Mnemonics & Character Sets

1336, 1251 - Who's Who in the Internet: Biographies of IAB, IESG and IRSG
     Members

1324 - A Discussion on Computer Network Conferencing

1313 - Today's Programming for KRFC AM 1313 Internet Talk Radio

1302 - Building a Network Information Services Infrastructure

1300 - Remembrances of Things Past

1296 - Internet Growth (1981-1991)

1291 - Mid-Level Networks: Potential Technical Services

1259 - Building The Open Road: The NREN As Test-Bed For The National Public Network

1257 - Isochronous Applications Do Not Require Jitter-Controlled Networks

1242 - Benchmarking Terminology for Network Interconnection Devices

1217 - Memo from the Consortium for Slow Commotion Research (CSCR)

1216 - Gigabit Network Economics and Paradigm Shifts

1208 - A Glossary of Networking Terms

1207 - Answers to Commonly asked "Experienced Internet User" Questions

1199, 1099 - Request for Comments Summary RFC Numbers 1100-1199

1192 - Commercialization of the Internet Summary Report

1181 - RIPE Terms of Reference

1180 - A TCP/IP Tutorial

1178 - Choosing a Name for Your Computer

1173 - Responsibilities of Host and Network Managers A Summary of the "Oral Tradition" of the Internet

1169 - Explaining the Role of GOSIP

1167 - Thoughts on the National Research and Education Network

1121 - Act one - the poems

1118 - Hitchhikers guide to the Internet

1015 - Implementation plan for interagency research Internet

992 - On communication support for fault tolerant process groups

874 - A Critique of X.25

531 - Feast or famine? A response to two recent RFC's about network information

473 - MIX and MIXAL?

472 - Illinois' reply to Maxwell's request for graphics information NIC 14925

429 - Character generator process

408 - NETBANK

361 - Deamon processes on host 106

313 - Computer based instruction

256 - IMPSYS change notification

225 - Rand/UCSB network graphics experiment

219 - User's view of the datacomputer

187 - Network/440 protocol concept

169 - Computer networks

146 - Views on issues relevant to data sharing on computer networks

013 - No Title

15b. Bibliographies

1463 - FYI on Introducing the Internet--A Short Bibliography of Introductory
       Internetworking Readings for the Network Novice
1175 - FYI on Where to Start - A Bibliography of Internetworking Information
1012 - Bibliography of Request For Comments 1 through 999
829 -   Packet Satellite Technology Reference Sources
290 -   Computer Network and Data Sharing: A Bibliography
243 -   Network and Data Sharing Bibliography

16 Unissued.

16a Never Issued.

1061, 853, 723, 715, 711, 710, 709, 693, 682, 676, 673, 670, 668, 665, 664,
650, 649, 648, 646, 641, 639, 605, 583, 575, 572, 564, 558, 554, 541, 540,
536, 517, 507, 502, 484, 481, 465, 444, 428, 427, 424, 397, 383, 380, 375,
358, 341, 337, 284, 279, 277, 275, 272, 262, 261, 260, 259, 258, 257, 248,
244, 220, 201, 159, 092, 026, 014

16b Not yet Issued.

1752, 1747, 1736, 1719, 1699, 1693, 1599, 1499, 1399, 1299, 1260, 1182

Appendix 2

Glossary Of Internetworking Terms And Abbreviations

TCP/IP Terminology

Like most large enterprises, TCP/IP has a language all its own. A curious blend of networking jargon, protocol names, project names, and names of government agencies, the language is both difficult to learn and difficult to remember. To outsiders, discussions among the cognoscenti sound like meaningless babble laced with acronyms at every possible opportunity. Even after a moderate amount of exposure, readers may find that specific terms are difficult to understand. The problem is compounded because some terminology is loosely defined and because the sheer volume is overwhelming.

This glossary helps solve the problem by providing short definitions for terms used throughout the Internet. It is not intended as a tutorial for beginners. Instead, we focus on providing a concise reference to make it easy for those who are generally knowledgeable about networking to look up the meaning of specific terms or acronyms quickly. Readers will find it substantially more useful as a reference after they have studied the text than before.

A Glossary of Terms and Abbreviations
In Alphabetical Order

10Base-T
The technical name for twisted pair Ethernet.

576
The minimum datagram size all hosts and routers must handle.

802.3
The IEEE standard for Ethernet.

822
The TCP/IP standard format for electronic mail messages. Mail experts often refer to ''822 messages.'' The name comes from RFC 822 that contains the specification. 822 format was previously known as 733 format.

AAL
Abbreviation for *ATM Adaptation Layer*.

ACK
Abbreviation for *acknowledgement*.

acknowledgement
A response sent by a receiver to indicate successful reception of information. Acknowledgements may be implemented at any level including the physical level (using voltage on one or more wires to coordinate transfer), at the link level (to indicate successful transmission across a single hardware link), or at higher levels (e.g., to allow an application program at the final destination to respond to an application program at the source).

active open
The operation that a client performs to establish a TCP connection with a server at a known address.

address mask
A bit mask used to select bits from an IP address for subnet addressing. The mask is 32 bits long, and selects the network portion of the IP address and one or more bits of the local portion.

address resolution

Conversion of a protocol address into a corresponding physical address (e.g., conversion of an IP address into an Ethernet address). Depending on the underlying network, resolution may require broadcasting on a local network. See ARP.

Advanced Networks and Services

The company that owns and operates the Internet backbone in 1995.

agent

In network management, an agent is the server software that runs on a host or router being managed.

ANSI

(*American National Standards Institute*) A group that defines U.S. standards for the information processing industry. ANSI participates in defining network protocol standards.

anonymous FTP

An FTP session that uses login name *anonymous* to access public files. A server that permits anonymous FTP often allows the password *guest*.

ANS

Abbreviation for *Advanced Networks and Services*.

ANSNET

The Wide Area Network that forms the Internet backbone in 1995.

ARP

(*Address Resolution Protocol*) The TCP/IP protocol used to dynamically bind a high-level IP Address to a low-level physical hardware address. ARP is used across a single physical network and is limited to networks that support hardware broadcast.

ARPA

(*Advanced Research Projects Agency*) The government agency that funded the AR-PANET, and later, the global Internet. The group within ARPA with responsibility for the ARPANET was IPTO (*Information Processing Techniques Office*), later called ISTO (*Information Systems Technology Office*). ARPA was named *DARPA* for many years.

ARPANET

A pioneering long haul network funded by ARPA (later DARPA) and built by BBN. It served from 1969 through 1990 as the basis for early networking research and as a central backbone during development of the Internet. The ARPANET consisted of individual packet switching nodes interconnected by leased lines.

ARQ

(Automatic Repeat reQuest) Any protocol that uses positive and negative acknowledgements with retransmission techniques to ensure reliability. The sender automatically repeats the request if it does not receive an answer.

ASN.1

(Abstract Syntax Notation.1) The ISO presentation standard protocol used by SNMP to represent messages.

Assigned Numbers

The RFC document that specifies (usually numeric) values used by TCP/IP protocols.

ATM

(Asynchronous Transfer Mode) A connection-oriented network technology that uses small, fixed-size cells at the lowest layer. ATM has the potential advantage of being able to support voice, video, and data with a single underlying technology.

ATM Adaptation Layer (AAL)

One of several protocols defined for ATM that specifies how an application sends and receives information over an ATM network. Data transmissions use AAL5.

ATMARP

The protocol a host uses for address resolution when sending IP over an ATM network.

AUI

Abbreviation for *Attachment Unit Interface*, the connector used for thick-wire Ethernet.

authority zone

A part of the domain name hierarchy in which a single name server is the authority.

autonomous system

A collection of routers and networks that fall under one administrative entity and cooperate closely to propagate network reachability (and routing) information among themselves using an interior gateway protocol of their choice. Routers within an autonomous system have a high degree of trust. Before two autonomous systems can communicate, one router in each system sends reachability information to a router in the other.

backbone network

Any network that forms the central interconnect for an internet. A national backbone is a WAN; a corporate backbone can be a LAN.

base header

In the proposed IPng, the required header found at the beginning of each datagram.

baseband

Characteristic of any network technology like Ethernet that uses a single carrier frequency and requires all stations attached to the network to participate in every transmission. Compare to broadband.

bastion host

A secure computer that forms part of a security firewall and runs applications that communicate with computers outside an organization.

baud

Literally, the number of times per second the signal can change on a transmission line. Commonly, the transmission line uses only two signal states (e.g., two voltages), making the baud rate equal to the number of bits per second that can be transferred. The underlying transmission technique may use some of the bandwidth, so it may not be the case that users experience data transfers at the line's specified bit rate. For example, because asynchronous lines require 10 bit-times to send an 8-bit character, a 9600 baud asynchronous transmission line can only send 960 characters per second.

Berkeley broadcast

A reference to a nonstandard IP broadcast address that uses all zeros in the host portion instead of all ones. The name arises because the technique was introduced and propagated in Berkeley's BSD UNIX.

best-effort delivery

Characteristic of network technologies that do not provide reliability at link levels. IP works well over best-effort delivery hardware because IP does not assume that the underlying network provides reliability. The UDP protocol provides best-effort delivery service to application programs.

BGP

Abbreviation for the *Border Gateway Protocol*.

big endian

A format for storage or transmission of binary data in which the most-significant byte (bit) comes first. The TCP/IP standard network byte order is big endian. Compare to *little endian*.

BISYNC

(*BInary SYNchronous Communication*) An early, low-level protocol developed by IBM and used to transmit data across a synchronous communication link. Unlike most modern link level protocols, BISYNC is byte-oriented, meaning that it uses special characters to mark the beginning and end of frames. BISYNC is often called BSC, especially in commercial products.

BNC

The style of connector used with thin-wire Ethernet.

BOOTP

Abbreviation for *BOOTstrap Protocol*, a protocol a host uses to obtain startup information, including its IP address, from a server.

Border Gateway Protocol (BGP)

An exterior gateway protocol used in NSFnet. Four major versions of BGP have appeared.

bps

(*bits per second*) A measure of the rate of data transmission.

bridge

A computer that connects two or more networks and forwards packets among them. Bridges operate at the physical network level. For example, an Ethernet bridge connects two physical Ethernet cables, and forwards from one cable to the other exactly those packets that are not local. Bridges differs from repeaters because bridges store and forward complete packets, while repeaters forward all electrical signals. Bridges differ from routers because bridges use physical addresses, while routers use IP addresses.

broadband

Characteristic of any network technology that multiplexes multiple, independent network carriers onto a single cable (usually using frequency division multiplexing). For example, a single 50 Mbps broadband cable can be divided into five 10 Mbps carriers, with each treated as an independent Ethernet. The advantage of broadband is less cable; the disadvantage is higher cost for equipment at connections. See baseband.

broadcast

A packet delivery system that delivers a copy of a given packet to all hosts that attach to it is said to broadcast the packet. Broadcast may be implemented with hardware (e.g., as in Ethernet) or with software (e.g., as in Cypress).

brouter

(*Bridging ROUTER*) A device that operates as a bridge for some protocols and as a router for others (e.g., a brouter can bridge DECNET protocols and router IP).

BSC

(*Binary Synchronous Communication*) See BISYNC.

BSD UNIX

(*Berkeley Software Distribution UNIX*) The version of UNIX released by U.C. Berkeley or one of the commercial systems derived from it. BSD UNIX was the first to include TCP/IP protocols.

Chernobylgram

(*Chernobyl datagram*) A packet so malformed that it causes the receiving system to "meltdown" (i.e. crash).

CCIRN

(*Coordinating Committee for Intercontinental Research Networking*) An international group that helps coordinate international cooperation on internetworking research and development.

CCITT

(*Consultative Committee on International Telephony and Telegraphy*) Now named the International Telecommunications Union.

cell

A small, fixed-size frame used on ATM networks. Each ATM cell contains 48 octets of data and 5 octets of header.

checksum

A small, integer value computed from a sequence of octets by treating them as integers and computing the sum. A checksum is used to detect errors that result when the sequence of octets is transmitted from one machine to another. Typically, protocol software computes a checksum and appends it to a packet when transmitting. Upon reception, the protocol software verifies the contents of the packet by recomputing the checksum and comparing to the value sent. Many TCP/IP protocols use a 16-bit checksum computed with one's complement arithmetic, with all integer fields in the packet stored in network byte order.

CIDR

Abbreviation for *Classless Inter-Domain Routing*.

class of address

The category of an IP address. The class of an address determines the location of the boundary between network prefix and host suffix.

Classless Inter-Domain Routing (CIDR)

An addressing and routing scheme that uses a group of contiguous class C addresses in place of a class B address. CIDR was adopted as a temporary solution to the problem of class B address space exhaustion.

client-server

The model of interaction in a distributed system in which a program at one site sends a request to a program at another site and awaits a response. The requesting program is called a client; the program satisfying the request is called the server. It is usually easier to build client software than server software.

connection

An abstraction provided by protocol software. TCP provides a connection from an application on one computer to an application on another.

connectionless service

Characteristic of the packet delivery service offered by most hardware and by the Internet Protocol (IP). A connectionless service treats each packet or datagram as a separate entity that contains the source and destination address.

core gateway

One of a set of routers with explicit routes to all destinations in an internet. The Internet core system participates in a single routing protocol; all core routers exchange routing updates periodically to ensure that their routing tables remain consistent.

CRC

(*Cyclic Redundancy Code*) A small, integer value computed from a sequence of octets used to detect errors that result when the sequence of octets is transmitted from one machine to another. Typically, packet switching network hardware computes a CRC and appends it to a packet when transmitting. Upon reception, the hardware verifies the contents of the packet by recomputing the CRC and comparing to the value sent. Although more expensive to compute, a CRC detects more errors than a checksum that uses additive methods.

CSMA/CD

A characteristic of network hardware that operates by allowing multiple stations to contend for access to a transmission medium by listening to see if the medium is idle, and a mechanism that allows the hardware to detect when two stations simultaneously attempt transmission. Ethernet uses CSMA/CD.

DARPA

(*Defense Advanced Research Projects Agency*) Former name of ARPA.

datagram

See IP datagram.

DCE

(*Data Communications Equipment*) Term ITU-TS protocol standards apply to switching equipment that forms a packet switched network to distinguish it from the computers or terminals that connect to the network. Also see DTE.

DDCMP

(*Digital Data Communication Message Protocol*) The link level protocol used in the original NSFNET backbone.

DDN

(*Defense Data Network*) The part of the Internet associated with U.S. military sites.

demultiplex

To separate from a common input into several outputs. Demultiplexing occurs at many levels. Hardware demultiplexes signals from a transmission line based on time or carrier frequency to allow multiple, simultaneous transmissions across a single physical cable. IP software demultiplexes incoming datagrams, sending each to the appropriate high-level protocol module or application program.

DHCP

(*Dynamic Host Configuration Protocol*) A protocol that a host uses to obtain all necessary configuration information including an IP address.

directed broadcast address

An IP address that specifies ''all hosts'' on a specific network. A single copy of a directed broadcast is routed to the specified network where it is broadcast to all machines on that network.

DNS

(*Domain Name System*) The on-line distributed database system used to map human-readable machine names into IP addresses. DNS servers throughout the connected Internet implement a hierarchical namespace that allows sites freedom in assigning machine names and addresses. DNS also supports separate mappings between mail destinations and IP addresses.

domain

A part of the DNS naming hierarchy. Syntactically, a domain name consists of a sequence of names (labels) separated by periods (dots).

dotted decimal notation

The syntactic representation for a 32-bit integer that consists of four 8-bit numbers written in base 10 with periods (dots) separating them. Many TCP/IP application programs accept dotted decimal notation in place of destination machine names.

DS3

A telephony classification of speed for leased lines equivalent to approximately 45 Mbps.

DTE

(*Data Terminal Equipment*) Term ITU-TS protocol standards apply to computers and/or terminals to distinguish them from the packet switching network to which they connect. Also see DCE.

DVMRP

(*Distance Vector Multicast Routing Protocol*) A protocol used to propagate multicast routes.

E.164

An address format specified by ITU-TS and used with ATM.

EACK

(*Extended ACKnowledgement*) Synonym for SACK.

Ethernet meltdown

An event that causes saturation or near saturation on an Ethernet. It usually results from illegal or misrouted packets, and typically lasts only a short time.

EGP

(*Exterior Gateway Protocol*) The protocol used by a router in one autonomous system to advertise the IP addresses of networks in that autonomous system to a router in another autonomous system.

EIA

(*Electronics Industry Association*) A standards organization for the electronics industry. Known for RS232C and RS422 standards that specify the electrical characteristics of interconnections between terminals and computers or between two computers.

encapsulation

The technique used by layered protocols in which a lower level protocol accepts a message from a higher level protocol and places it in the data portion of the low-level frame. Encapsulation means that datagrams traveling across a physical network have a sequence of headers in which the first header comes from the physical network frame, the next from the Internet Protocol (IP), the next from the transport protocol, and so on.

epoch date

A point in history chosen as the date from which time is measured. TCP/IP uses January 1, 1900, Universal Time (formerly called Greenwich Mean Time) as its epoch date. When TCP/IP programs exchange date or time of day they express time as the number of seconds past the epoch date.

Ethernet

A popular local area network technology invented at the Xerox Corporation Palo Alto Research Center. An Ethernet itself is a passive coaxial cable; the interconnections contain all active components. Ethernet is a best-effort delivery system that uses CSMA/CD technology. Xerox Corporation, Digital Equipment Corporation, and Intel Corporation developed and published the standard for 10 Mbps Ethernet. Originally, Ethernet used a coaxial cable. Later versions use a smaller coaxial cable (*thinnet*) or twisted pair cable (10Base-T).

eXternal Data Representation

See XDR.

fair queueing

A well-known technique for controlling congestion in routers. Called "fair" because it restricts every host to an equal share of router bandwidth. Fair queueing is not completely satisfactory because it does not distinguish between small and large hosts or between hosts with a few active connections and those with many.

FCCSET

(*Federal Coordinating Council for Science, Engineering, and Technology*) A government group noted for its report that called for high-speed computing and high-speed networking research.

FDDI

(*Fiber Distribution Data Interface*) A token ring network technology based on fiber optics. FDDI specifies a 100 Mbps data rate using 1300 nanometer light wavelength and limits networks to approximately 200 km in length, with repeaters every 2 km or less.

FDM

(*Frequency Division Multiplexing*) The method of passing multiple, independent signals across a single medium by assigning each a unique carrier frequency. Hardware to combine signals is called a multiplexor; hardware to separate them is called a demultiplexor. Also see TDM.

file server

A process running on a computer that provides access to files on that computer to programs running on remote machines. The term is often applied loosely to computers that run file server programs.

firewall

A configuration of routers and networks placed between an organization's internal internet and a connection to an external internet to provide security.

flat namespace

Characteristic of any naming in which object names are selected from a single set of strings (e.g., street names in a typical city). Flat naming contrasts with hierarchical naming in which names are divided into subsections that correspond to the hierarchy of authority that administers them.

flow control

Control of the rate at which hosts or routers inject packets into a network or internet, usually to avoid congestion.

fragmentation

The process of dividing an IP datagram into smaller pieces when they must travel across a network that cannot handle the original datagram size. Each fragment has the same format as a datagram; fields in the IP header specify whether a datagram is a fragment, and if so, the offset of the fragment in the original datagram. IP software at the receiving end must reassemble fragments to produce the original datagram.

frame

Literally, a packet as it is transmitted across a serial line. The term derives from character oriented protocols that added special start-of-frame and end-of-frame characters when transmitting packets. We use the term throughout this book to refer to the objects that physical networks transmit.

FTP

(*File Transfer Protocol*) The TCP/IP standard, high-level protocol for transferring files from one machine to another. FTP uses TCP.

FYI

(*For Your Information*) A subset of the RFCs that are not technical standards or descriptions of protocols. FYIs convey general information about topics related to TCP/IP or the connected Internet.

gated

(*GATEway Daemon*) A program run on a router that uses an IGP to collect routing information from within one autonomous system and EGP to advertise the information to another autonomous system.

gateway

Originally, researchers used the term *IP gateway* for dedicated computers that route packets; vendors have adopted the term *IP router*. Gateway now refers to an application program that interconnects two services (e.g., an e-mail gateway).

gateway requirements

A document that specifies requirements for an IP router.

GGP

(*Gateway to Gateway Protocol*) The protocol originally used by core gateways to exchange routing information. GGP is now obsolete.

gopher

An information service used throughout the Internet.

GOSIP

(*Government Open Systems Interconnection Profile*) A U.S. government procurement document that specifies agencies may use OSI protocols in new networks after August 1991. Although GOSIP was originally thought to eliminate the use of TCP/IP on government internets, clarifications have specified that government agencies can continue to use TCP/IP.

hardware address

The low-level addresses used by physical networks. Each type of network hardware has its own addressing scheme (e.g., an Ethernet address is 48 bits).

HELLO

The protocol used on the original NSFNET backbone. Hello is interesting because it chooses the route with minimum delay.

HELO

The command on the initial exchange of the SMTP protocol.

hierarchical routing

Routing that is based on a hierarchical addressing scheme. Most TCP/IP routing is based on a two-level hierarchy in which an IP address is divided into a network portion and a host portion. Routers use only the network portion until the datagram reaches a router that can deliver it directly. Subnetting introduces additional levels of hierarchical routing.

hop count

A measure of distance between two points in an internet. A hop count of n means that n routers separate the source and destination.

host

Any end-user computer system that connects to a network. Hosts range in size from personal computers to supercomputers. Compare to router.

host requirements

A long document that contains a revision and update of many TCP/IP protocols. The host requirements document is published in a pair of RFCs.

hub

An electronic device to which multiple computers attach, usually using twisted pair wiring. A hub simulates a network that interconnects the attached computers. Hub technology is popular for Ethernets.

IAB

(*Internet Architecture Board*) A small group of people who set policy and direction for TCP/IP and the global Internet. See IETF.

IANA

(*Internet Assigned Number Authority*) The group responsible for assigning constants used in TCP/IP protocols. Most constants are numbers.

ICCB

(*Internet Control and Configuration Board*) A predecessor to the IAB.

ICMP

(*Internet Control Message Protocol*) An integral part of the Internet Protocol (IP) that handles error and control messages. Specifically, routers and hosts use ICMP to send reports of problems about datagrams back to the original source that sent the datagram. ICMP also includes an echo request/reply used to test whether a destination is reachable and responding.

IEN

(*Internet Engineering Notes*) A series of notes developed in parallel to RFCs. Although the series is obsolete, some IENs contain early discussion of TCP/IP and the Internet not found in RFCs.

IETF

(*Internet Engineering Task Force*) A group of people closely connected to the IAB who work on the design and engineering of TCP/IP and the global Internet. The IETF is divided into areas, which each has an independent manager. Areas are further divided into working groups.

IESG

(*Internet Engineering Steering Group*) A committee consisting of the IETF chairperson and the area managers. The IESG coordinates activities among the IETF working groups.

IGP

(*Interior Gateway Protocol*) The generic term applied to any protocol used to propagate network reachability and routing information within an autonomous system. Although there is no single standard IGP, RIP is among the most popular.

IGMP

(*Internet Group Management Protocol*) A protocol that hosts use to keep local routers apprised of their membership in multicast groups. When all hosts leave a group, routers no longer forward datagrams that arrive for the group.

INOC

(*Internet Network Operations Center*) Originally, a group of people at BBN that monitored and controlled the Internet core gateway system. Now applied to any group that monitors an internet.

International Organization for Standardization

See ISO.

International Telecommunications Union (ITU)

An international organization that sets standards for interconnection of telephone equipment. It defined the standards for X.25 network protocols. (Note: in Europe, PTTs offer both voice telephone services and X.25 network services).

internet

Physically, a collection of packet switching networks interconnected by routers along with TCP/IP protocols that allow them to function logically as a single, large, virtual network. When written in upper case, Internet refers specifically to the global Internet.

Internet

The collection of networks and routers that spans 61 countries, and uses TCP/IP protocols to form a single, cooperative virtual network. The Internet connects more than four million computers.

Internet address

See IP address.

Internet Protocol

See IP.

Internet Society

The non-profit organization established to foster interest in the Internet. The Internet Society is the host organization of the IAB.

Internet worm

A program designed to travel across the Internet and replicate itself endlessly. When a student released the Internet worm, it made the Internet and many attached computers useless for hours.

INTERNIC

(*INTERnet Network Information Center*) An organization that provides information about Internet services and protocol documents. In addition, the INTERNIC handles registration of IP addresses and domain names.

interoperability

The ability of software and hardware on multiple machines from multiple vendors to communicate meaningfully. This term best describes the goal of internetworking, namely, to define an abstract, hardware independent networking environment that makes it possible to build distributed computations that interact at the network transport level without knowing the details of underlying technologies.

IP

(*Internet Protocol*) The TCP/IP standard protocol that defines the IP datagram as the unit of information passed across an internet and provides the basis for connectionless, best-effort packet delivery service. IP includes the ICMP control and error message protocol as an integral part. The entire protocol suite is often referred to as TCP/IP because TCP and IP are the two fundamental protocols.

IP address

A 32-bit address assigned to each host that participates in a TCP/IP internet. IP addresses are the abstraction of physical hardware addresses just as an internet is an abstraction of physical networks. To make routing efficient, each IP address is divided into a network portion and a host portion.

IP datagram

The basic unit of information passed across a TCP/IP internet. An IP datagram is to an internet as a hardware packet is to a physical network. It contains a source and destination address along with data.

IPng

(*Internet Protocol – the Next Generation*) A term applied to all the activities surrounding the specification and standardization of the next version of IP. Also see IPv6.

IPv4

Synonym for the current version of IP.

IPv6

The official name of the next version of IP. Also see IPng.

IRTF

(*Internet Research Task Force*) A group of people working on research problems related to TCP/IP and the connected Internet.

ISDN

(*Integrated Services Digital Network*) The name of the digital network service that telephone carriers intend to provide.

ISO

(*International Organization for Standardization*) An international body that drafts, discusses, proposes, and specifies standards for network protocols. ISO is best know for its 7-layer reference model that describes the conceptual organization of protocols. Although it has proposed a suite of protocols for Open System Interconnection, the OSI protocols have not been widely accepted in the commercial market.

ISOC

Abbreviation for *Internet SOCiety*.

ISODE

(*ISO Development Environment*) Software that provides an ISO transport level protocol interface on top of TCP/IP. ISODE was designed to allow researchers to experiment with ISO's higher-level OSI protocols without requiring an internet that supports the lower levels of the OSI suite.

ITU-TS

Abbreviation for *Telecommunication Section* of the *International Telecommunication Union*.

Karn's Algorithm

An algorithm that allows transport protocols to distinguish between good and bad round-trip time samples and thus improve round-trip estimations.

Kbps

(*Kilo Bits Per Second*) A measure of the rate of data transmission. Also see Mbps and baud.

Kramer

Humorous term applied to an odd-looking packet; the term is taken from a television show.

LAN

(*Local Area Network*) Any physical network technology designed to span short distances (up to a few thousand meters). Usually, LANs operate at tens of megabits per second through several gigabits per second. Examples include Ethernet and FDDI. See MAN and WAN.

level 1

A reference to the hardware interface level of communication. The name is derived from the ISO 7-layer reference model. Level 1 specifications refer to physical connections, including connector configuration and voltages on wires.

level 2

A reference to link level communication (e.g., frame formats) or link level connections derived from the ISO 7-layer reference model. For local area networks, level 2 refers to physical frame format and addressing. Thus, a level 2 address is a physical frame address (e.g., an Ethernet address).

level 3

A reference to transport level communication derived from the ISO 7-layer reference model. For TCP/IP internets, level 3 refers to IP and the IP datagram format. Thus, a level 3 address is an IP address.

LIS

(*Logical IP Subnet*) A group of computers connected via ATM that use ATM as an isolated local network. A computer in one LIS cannot send a datagram directly to a computer in another LIS.

little endian

A format for storage or transmission of binary data in which the least-significant byte (bit) comes first. See *big endian*.

LLC

(*Logical Link Control*) One of the fields in an NSAP header.

MAC

(*Media Access Control*) A general reference to the low-level hardware protocols used to access a particular network. The term *MAC address* is often used as a synonym for *physical address*.

mail bridge

Informal term used as a synonym for a mail gateway.

mail exchanger

A computer that accepts e-mail; some mail exchangers forward the mail to other computers. DNS has a separate address type for mail exchangers.

mail exploder

Part of an electronic mail system that accepts a piece of mail and a list of addresses as input and sends a copy of the message to each address on the list. Most electronic mail systems incorporate a mail exploder to allow users to define mailing lists locally.

mail gateway

A machine that connects to two or more electronic mail systems (especially dissimilar mail systems on two different networks) and transfers mail messages among them. Mail gateways usually capture an entire mail message, reformat it according to the rules of the destination mail system, and then forward the message.

MAN

(*Metropolitan Area Network*) Any of several new physical network technologies that operate at high speeds (usually hundreds of megabits per second through several gigabits per second) over distances sufficient for a metropolitan area. See LAN and WAN.

Management Information Base

See MIB

martians

Humorous term applied to packets that turn up unexpectedly on the wrong network, often because of incorrect routing tables.

maximum segment lifetime

The longest time a datagram can survive in the Internet. Protocols use the MSL to guarantee a bound on the time duplicate packets can survive.

maximum segment size

A term used with TCP. The MSS is the largest amount of data that can be transmitted in one segment. Sender and receiver negotiate maximum segment size at connection startup.

maximum transfer unit

See MTU.

MBONE

(*Multicast BackBONE*). A cooperative agreement among sites to forward multicast datagrams across the Internet by the use of IP tunneling.

Mbps

(*Millions of Bits Per Second*) A measure of the rate of data transmission.

MIB

(Management Information Base) The set of variables (database) that a router running SNMP maintains. Managers can fetch or store into these variables. MIB-II is the current standard.

MILNET

(MILitary NETwork) Originally part of the ARPANET, MILNET was partitioned in 1984.

MIME

(Multipurpose Internet Mail Extensions) A standard used to encode data such as images as printable ASCII text for transmission through e-mail.

Mosaic

A program that provides users with a graphical interface for FTP, gopher, and WWW.

mrouted

(Multicast ROUTE Daemon) A program used with a multicast kernel to establish multicast routing.

MSS

Abbreviation for *Maximum Segment Size*.

MTU

(Maximum Transfer Unit) The largest amount of data that can be transferred across a given physical network. The MTU is determined by the network hardware.

multi-homed host

A host using TCP/IP that has connections to two or more physical networks.

multicast

A technique that allows copies of a single packet to be passed to a selected subset of all possible destinations. Some hardware (e.g., Ethernet) supports multicast by allowing a network interface to belong to one or more multicast groups. IP supports an internet multicast facility.

Nagle algorithm

A self-clocking heuristic that clumps outgoing data to improve throughput and avoid silly window syndrome.

NAK

(*Negative Acknowledgement*) A response from the recipient of data to the sender of that data to indicate that the transmission was unsuccessful (e.g., that the data was corrupted by transmission errors). Usually, a NAK triggers retransmission of the lost data.

NAP

(*Network Access Provider*) A company that provides Internet connectivity.

name resolution

The process of mapping a name into a corresponding address. The domain name system provides a mechanism for naming computers in which programs use remote name servers to resolve a machine name into an IP address.

NetBIOS

(*Network Basic Input Output System*) NetBIOS is the standard interface to networks on IBM PC and compatible personal computers. TCP/IP includes guidelines that describe how to map NetBIOS operations into equivalent TCP/IP operations.

network byte order

The TCP/IP standard for transmission of integers that specifies the most significant byte appears first (big endian). Sending machines are required to translate from the local integer representation to network byte order, and receiving machines are required to translate from network byte order to the local machine representation.

network management

See MIB and SNMP.

NFS

(*Network File System*) A protocol developed by SUN Microsystems, Incorporated that uses IP to allow a set of cooperating computers to access each other's file systems as if they were local.

NIC

(*Network Information Center*) A predecessor of the INTERNIC.

NIST

(*National Institute of Standards and Technology*) Formerly, the National Bureau of Standards. NIST is one standards organization within the US that establishes standards for network protocols.

NOC

(*Network Operations Center*) Originally, the organization at BBN that monitored and controlled several networks that formed part of the global Internet. Now, used for any organization that manages a network.

NSAP

(*Network Service Access Point*) An address format that can be encoded in 20 octets. The ATM Forum recommends using NSAP addresses.

NSF

(*National Science Foundation*) A U.S. government agency that funded some of the research and development of the Internet.

NSFNET

(*National Science Foundation NETwork*) Used to describe the Internet backbone in the U.S., which is supported by NSF.

OC3

A bit rate of approximately 155 million bits per second used over fiber optic connections.

OSI

(*Open Systems Interconnection*) A reference to protocols, specifically ISO standards, for the interconnection of cooperative computer systems.

OSPF

(*Open Shortest Path First*) A routing protocol design by the IETF.

packet

Used loosely to refer to any small block of data sent across a packet switching network.

PDN

(*Public Data Network*) A network service offered by a common carrier. Typically, PDNs use X.25 protocols.

PEM

(*Privacy Enchanced Mail*) A protocol for encrypting e-mail to prevent others from reading messages as they travel across an internet.

PING

(*Packet InterNet Groper*) The name of a program used with TCP/IP internets to test reachability of destinations by sending them an ICMP echo request and waiting for a reply. The term is now used like a verb as in, ''please ping host *A* to see if it is alive.''

port

See protocol port.

positive acknowledgement

See ACK.

PPP

(*Point to Point Protocol*) A protocol for framing IP when sending across a serial line. Also see SLIP.

promiscuous ARP

See proxy ARP.

protocol

A formal description of message formats and the rules two or more machines must follow to exchange those messages. Protocols can describe low-level details of machine to machine interfaces (e.g., the order in which the bits from a byte are sent across a wire), or high-level exchanges between application programs (e.g., the way in which two programs transfer a file across an internet). Most protocols include both intuitive descriptions of the expected interactions as well as more formal specifications using finite state machine models.

protocol port

The abstraction that TCP/IP transport protocols use to distinguish among multiple destinations within a given host computer. TCP/IP protocols identify ports using small positive integers. Usually, the operating system allows an application program to specify which port it wants to use. Some ports are reserved for standard services (e.g., electronic mail).

proxy ARP

The technique in which one machine, usually a router, answers ARP requests intended for another by supplying its own physical address. By pretending to be another machine, the router accepts responsibility for forwarding packets. The purpose of proxy ARP is to allow a site to use a single IP network address with multiple physical networks.

pseudo header

Source and destination IP address information sent in the IP header, but included in a TCP or UDP checksum.

public key encryption

An encryption technique that generates encryption keys in pairs. One of the pair must be kept secret, and one is published.

PUP

(*Parc Universal Packet*) In the internet system developed by Xerox Corporation, a PUP is the fundamental unit of transfer, like an IP datagram is in a TCP/IP internet. The name was derived from the name of the laboratory at which the Xerox internet was developed, the Palo Alto Research Center (PARC).

push

The operation an application performs on a TCP connection to force data to be sent immediately. A bit in the segment header marks pushed data.

RARP

(*Reverse Address Resolution Protocol*) The TCP/IP protocol a diskless machine uses at startup to find its IP address. The machine broadcasts a request that contains its physical hardware address and a server responds by sending the machine its IP address. RARP takes its name and message format from another IP address resolution protocol, ARP.

RDP

(*Reliable Datagram Protocol*) A protocol that provides reliable datagram service on top of the standard unreliable datagram service that IP provides. RDP is not among the most widely implemented TCP/IP protocols.

reassembly

The process of collecting all the fragments of an IP datagram and using them to create a copy of the original datagram. The ultimate destination performs reassembly.

redirect

An ICMP message sent from a router to a host on a local network to instruct the host to change a route.

repeater

A hardware device that extends a LAN. A repeater copies electrical signals from one physical network to another. No longer popular.

reverse path forwarding

A technique used to propagate broadcast packets. IP uses reverse path forwarding to propagate subnet broadcasts.

RFC

(*Request For Comments*) The name of a series of notes that contain surveys, measurements, ideas, techniques, and observations, as well as proposed and accepted TCP/IP protocol standards. RFCs are available on-line.

RIP

(*Routing Information Protocol*) A protocol used to propagate routing information inside an autonomous system. RIP derives from an earlier protocol of the same name developed at Xerox.

RJE

(*Remote Job Entry*) A service that allows submission of a (batch) job from a remote site.

rlogin

(Remote LOGIN) The remote login protocol developed for UNIX by Berkeley. Rlogin offers essentially the same service as TELNET.

ROADS

(*Running Out of ADdress Space*) A reference to imminent exhaustion of the class B addresses.

route

In general, a route is the path that network traffic takes from its source to its destination. In a TCP/IP internet, each IP datagram is routed independently; routes can change dynamically.

routed

(*Route Daemon*) A program devised for UNIX that implements the RIP protocol. Pronounced ''route-d.''

router

A special purpose, dedicated computer that attaches to two or more networks and forwards packets from one to the other. In particular, an IP router forwards IP datagrams among the networks to which it connects. A router uses the destination address on a datagram to choose a next-hop to which it forwards the datagram. Researchers originally used the term *IP gateway*.

RPC

(*Remote Procedure Call*) A technology in which a program invokes services across a network by making modified procedure calls. The NFS protocol uses a specific type of RPC.

RS232

A standard by EIA that specifies the electrical characteristics of slow speed interconnections between terminals and computers or between two computers. Although the standard commonly used is RS232C, most people refer to it as RS232.

RTO

(*Round Trip time-Out*) The delay used before retransmission. TCP computes RTO as a function of the current round trip time and variance.

RTT

(*Round Trip Time*) A measure of delay between two hosts. The round trip time consists of the total time taken for a single packet or datagram to leave one machine, reach the other, and return. In most packet switching networks, delays vary as a result of congestion. Thus, a measure of round trip time is an average, which may have high standard deviation.

SACK

(*Selective ACKnowledgement*) An acknowledgement mechanism used with sliding window protocols that allows the receiver to acknowledge packets received out of order, but within the current sliding window. Also called extended acknowledgement. Compare to the cumulative acknowledgement scheme used by TCP.

segment

The unit of transfer sent from TCP on one machine to TCP on another. Each segment contains part of a stream of bytes being sent between the machines as well as additional fields that identify the current position in the stream and a checksum to ensure validity of received data.

selective acknowledgement

See SACK.

self-identifying frame

Any network frame or packet that includes a field to identify the type of the data being carried. Ethernet uses self-identifying frames, but ATM does not.

SGMP

(*Simple Gateway Monitoring Protocol*) A predecessor of SNMP.

signaling

A telephony term that refers to protocols that establish a circuit.

silly window syndrome

A condition that can arise in TCP in which the receiver repeatedly advertises a small window and the sender repeatedly sends a small segment to fill it. The resulting transmission of small segments makes inefficient use of network bandwidth.

SIP

(*Simple IP*) An early proposal that formed the basis for IPng.

SIPP

(*SIP Plus*) An extension of SIP that has been proposed as IPng. The IETF is expected to endorse SIPP. See IPv6.

sliding window

Characteristic of protocols that allow a sender to transmit more than one packet of data before receiving an acknowledgement. After receiving an acknowledgement for the first packet sent, the sender "slides" the packet window and sends another. The number of outstanding packets or bytes is known as the *window size*; increasing the window size improves throughput.

SLIP

(*Serial Line IP*) A framing protocol used to send IP across a serial line. SLIP is popular when sending IP over dialup phone lines. See PPP.

slow-start

A congestion avoidance scheme in TCP in which TCP increases its window size as ACKs arrive. The term is a slight misnomer because slow-start achieves high throughput by using exponential increases.

SMDS

(*Switched Multimegabit Data Service*) A connectionless packet service developed by regional telephone companies.

SMTP

(*Simple Mail Transfer Protocol*) The TCP/IP standard protocol for transferring electronic mail messages from one machine to another. SMTP specifies how two mail systems interact and the format of control messages they exchange to transfer mail.

SNA

(*System Network Architecture*) The name applied to an architecture and a class of network products offered by IBM Corporation. SNA does not interoperate with TCP/IP.

SNAP

(*SubNetwork Attachment Point*) A small header added to data when sending across a network that does not have self-identifying frames. The SNAP header specifies the type of the data.

SNMP

(*Simple Network Monitoring Protocol*) A standard protocol used to monitor hosts, routers, and the networks to which they attach. The second version of the protocol is named SNMPv2. Also see MIB.

SOA

(*Start Of Authority*) A keyword used with DNS to denote the beginning of those records for which a particular server is the authority. Other records in the server are reported as non-authoritative answers.

socket

The abstraction provided by the UNIX operating system that allows an application program to access the TCP/IP protocols.

source quench

A congestion control technique in which a machine experiencing congestion sends a message back to the source of the packets requesting that the source stop transmitting. In a TCP/IP internet, routers use ICMP source quench to stop or reduce the transmission of IP datagrams.

source route

A route that is determined by the source. In IP, a source route consists of a list of routers a datagram should visit; the route is specified as an IP option. Source routing is most often used for debugging.

SPF

(*Shortest Path First*) A class of routing update protocols that uses Dijkstra's algorithm to compute shortest paths.

STD

(*STanDard*) The designation used to classify a particular RFC as describing a standard protocol.

subnet addressing

An extension of the IP addressing scheme that allows a site to use a single IP network address for multiple physical networks. Outside of the site using subnet addressing, routing continues as usual by dividing the destination address into a network portion and local portion. Routers and hosts inside a site using subnet addressing interpret the local portion of the address by dividing it into a physical network portion and host portion.

SubNetwork Attachment Point

See SNAP.

supernet addressing

Another name for Classless Inter-Domain routing.

SWS

See *Silly Window Syndrome*.

SYN

(*SYNchronizing segment*) The first segment sent by the TCP protocol, it is used to synchronize the two ends of a connection in preparation for opening a connection.

T3

The telephony designation for a protocol used over DS3-speed lines. The term is often used (incorrectly) as a synonym for DS3.

TCP

(*Transmission Control Protocol*) The TCP/IP standard transport level protocol that provides the reliable, full duplex, stream service on which many application protocols depend. TCP allows a process on one machine to send a stream of data to a process on another. TCP is connection-oriented in the sense that before transmitting data, participants must establish a connection. All data travels in TCP segments, which each travel across the Internet in an IP datagram. The entire protocol suite is often referred to as TCP/IP because TCP and IP are the two fundamental protocols.

TCP/IP Internet Protocol Suite

The official name of the TCP/IP protocols.

TDM

(*Time Division Multiplexing*) A technique used to multiplex multiple signals onto a single hardware transmission channel by allowing each signal to use the channel for a short time before going on to the next one. Also see FDM.

TDMA

(*Time Division Multiple Access*) A method of network access in which time is divided into slots and each node on the network is assigned one of the slots. Because all nodes using TDMA must synchronize exactly (even though the network introduces propagation delays between them), TDMA technologies are difficult to design and the equipment is expensive.

TELNET

The TCP/IP standard protocol for remote terminal service. TELNET allows a user at one site to interact with a remote timesharing system at another site as if the user's keyboard and display connected directly to the remote machine.

TFTP

(*Trivial File Transfer Protocol*) The TCP/IP standard protocol for file transfer with minimal capability and minimal overhead. TFTP depends only on the unreliable, connectionless datagram delivery service (UDP), so it can be used on machines like diskless workstations that keep such software in ROM and use it to bootstrap themselves.

thicknet

Used to refer to the original thick coaxial cable used with Ethernet. See thinnet and 10Base-T.

thinnet

Used to refer to the thinner, more flexible coaxial cable used with Ethernet. See thicknet and 10Base-T.

TLI

(*Transport Layer Interface*) An alternative to the socket interface defined for System V UNIX.

TLV encoding

Any representation format that encodes each item with a type field followed by a length field followed by a value. IP options often use TLV encoding.

tn3270

A version of TELNET for use with IBM 3270 terminals.

token ring

When used in the generic sense, a type of network technology that controls media access by passing a distinguished packet, called a token, from machine to machine. A computer can only transmit a packet when holding the token. When used in a specific sense, it refers to the token ring network hardware produced by IBM.

TOS

(*Type Of Service*) Each IP datagram header includes a field that allows the sender to specify the type of service desired. In practice, few routers use TOS when choosing a route.

TP-4

A protocol designed by ISO to be similar to TCP.

traceroute

A program that prints the path to a destination. Traceroute sends a sequence of datagrams with the Time-To-Live set to 1, 2, etc., and uses ICMP TIME EXCEEDED messages that come back to determine routers along the path.

trailers

A nonconventional method of encapsulating IP datagrams for transmission in which the "header" information is placed at the end of the packet. Trailers have been used with Ethernet to aid in aligning data on page boundaries. ATM's AAL5 uses trailers.

transceiver

A device that connects a host interface to a local area network (e.g., Ethernet). Ethernet transceivers contain analog electronics that apply signals to the cable and sense collisions.

TRPB

(*Truncated Reverse Path Broadcast*) A technique used to propagate multicast datagrams.

TTL

(*Time To Live*) A technique used in best-effort delivery systems to avoid endlessly looping packets. For example, each IP datagram is assigned an integer time to live when it is created. Each router decrements the time to live field when the datagram arrives, and a router discards any datagram if the time to live counter reaches zero.

tunneling

A technique in which a packet is encapsulated in a high-level protocol and passed across a transport system. The MBONE tunnels each IP multicast datagram inside a conventional IP datagram.

twisted pair Ethernet

An Ethernet wiring scheme that uses twisted pair wires from each computer to a hub. See thicknet and thinnet.

type of service routing

A routing scheme in which the choice of path depends on the characteristics of the underlying network technology as well as the shortest path to the destination. In principle, the Internet Protocol (IP) accommodates type of service routing because datagrams contain a type of service request field. In practice, few routers honor type of service requests.

UART

(*Universal Asynchronous Receiver and Transmitter*) An electronic device consisting of a single chip that can send or receive characters on asynchronous serial communication lines that use RS232. UARTs are flexible because they have control lines that allow the designer to select parameters like transmission speed, parity, number of stop bits, and modem control. UARTs appear in terminals, modems, and on the I/O boards in computers that connect the computer to terminal(s).

UCBCAST

See Berkeley broadcast.

UDP

(*User Datagram Protocol*) The TCP/IP standard protocol that allows an application program on one machine to send a datagram to an application program on another. UDP uses the Internet Protocol (IP) to deliver datagrams. Conceptually, the important difference between UDP datagrams and IP datagrams is that UDP includes a protocol port number, allowing the sender to distinguish among multiple application programs on a given remote machine. In practice, UDP also includes an optional checksum over the data being sent.

unicast

The method by which a packet is sent to a single destination. Most IP datagrams are sent via unicast. See multicast.

universal time

The international standard time reference that was formerly called Greenwich Mean Time. It is also called universal coordinated time.

urgent data

The method used in TCP to send data out of band. A receiver processes urgent data immediately upon receipt.

URL

(*Uniform Resource Locator*) A string that gives the location of a piece of information. The string begins with a protocol type (e.g., FTP) followed by the identification of specific information (e.g., the domain name of a server and the path name to a file on that server).

UUCP

(*Unix to Unix Copy Program*) An application program developed in the mid 1970s for version 7 UNIX that allows one UNIX timesharing system to copy files to or from another UNIX timesharing system over a single (usually dialup) link. Because UUCP is the basis for electronic mail transfer in UNIX, the term is often used loosely to refer to UNIX mail transfer.

vBNS

The 155 Mbps Internet backbone scheduled to be deployed in the U.S. during 1995.

VPI/VCI

(*Virtual Path Identifier and Virtual Circuit Identifier*) The two fields of an ATM connection identifier; each connection a host opens has a unique VPI/VCI pair.

vector-distance

A class of routing update protocols that use a distributed shortest path algorithm in which each participating router sends its neighbors a list of networks it can reach and the distance to each network. Compare to SPF.

very high speed Backbone Network Service

See vBNS.

virtual circuit

The basic abstraction provided by a connection-oriented protocol like TCP. Once a virtual circuit has been created, it stays in effect until explicitly shut down.

WAN

(*Wide Area Network*) Any physical network technology that spans large geographic distances. Also called long-haul networks, WANs usually operate at slower speeds and have significantly higher delays than networks that operate over shorter distances. See LAN and MAN.

well-known port

Any of a set of protocol port numbers preassigned for specific uses by transport level protocols (i.e., TCP and UDP). Each server listens at a well-known port, so clients can locate it.

window

See sliding window.

Winsock

An application program interface that permits a program using socket calls to run on Microsoft Windows.

working group

The term applied to a committee of the IETF. Each working group is responsible for a particular protocol or design issue.

World Wide Web

The large-scale information service that allows a user to browse information. WWW offers a hypermedia system that can store information as text, graphics, audio, etc.

WWW

See *World Wide Web*.

X

See X-Window System.

X.25

The ITU-TS standard protocol for transport level network service. It is possible to tunnel IP through X.25. X.25 is most popular in Europe.

X25NET

(*X.25 NETwork*) A service offered by CSNET that passed IP traffic between a subscriber site and the Internet using X.25.

X.400

The ITU-TS protocol for electronic mail.

XDR

(*eXternal Data Representation*) The standard for a machine-independent data representation. To use XDR, a sender translates from the local machine representation to the standard external representation and a receiver translates from the external representation to the local machine representation.

X-Window System

A software system developed at MIT for presenting and managing output on bit-mapped displays. Each window consists of a rectangular region of the display that contains textual or graphical output from one remote program. A special program called a window manager allows the user to create, move, overlap, and destroy windows.

zone of authority

Term used in the domain name system to refer to the group of names for which a given name server is an authority. Each zone must be supplied by two name servers that have no common point of failure.

Bibliography

ABRAMSON, N. [1970], The ALOHA System – Another Alternative for Computer Communications, *Proceedings of the Fall Joint Computer Conference.*

ABRAMSON, N. and F. KUO (EDS.) [1973], *Computer Communication Networks,* Prentice Hall, Englewood Cliffs, New Jersey.

ANDREWS, D. W., and G. D. SHULTZ [1982], A Token-Ring Architecture for Local Area Networks: An Update, *Proceedings of Fall 82 COMPCON,* IEEE.

BALL, J. E., E. J. BURKE, I. GERTNER, K. A. LANTZ, and R. F. RASHID [1979], Perspectives on Message-Based Distributed Computing, *IEEE Computing Networking Symposium,* 46-51.

BBN [1981], A History of the ARPANET: The First Decade, *Technical Report* Bolt, Beranek, and Newman, Inc.

BBN [December 1981], Specification for the Interconnection of a Host and an IMP (revised), *Technical Report 1822*, Bolt, Beranek, and Newman, Inc.

BIAGIONI E., E. COOPER, and R. SANSOM [March 1993], Designing a Practical ATM LAN, *IEEE Network*, 32-39.

BERTSEKAS D. and R. GALLAGER [1987], *Data Networks,* Prentice-Hall, Englewood Cliffs, New Jersey.

BIRRELL, A., and B. NELSON [February 1984], Implementing Remote Procedure Calls, *ACM Transactions on Computer Systems*, 2(1), 39-59.

BOGGS, D., J. SHOCH, E. TAFT, and R. METCALFE [April 1980], Pup: An Internetwork Architecture, *IEEE Transactions on Communications.*

BORMAN, D., [April 1989], Implementing TCP/IP on a Cray Computer, *Computer Communication Review,* 19(2), 11-15.

BROWN, M., K. KOLLING, and E. TAFT [November 1985], The Alpine File System, *ACM Transactions on Computer Systems,* 3(4), 261-293.

BROWNBRIDGE, D., L. MARSHALL, and B. RANDELL [December 1982], The Newcastle Connections or UNIXes of the World Unite!, *Software – Practice and Experience*, 12(12), 1147-1162.

CASNER, S., and S. DEERING [July 1992], First IETF Internet Audiocast, *Computer Communications Review*, 22(3), 92-97.

CERF, V., and E. CAIN [October 1983], The DOD Internet Architecture Model, *Computer Networks*.

CERF, V., and R. KAHN [May 1974], A Protocol for Packet Network Interconnection, *IEEE Transactions of Communications*, Com-22(5).

CERF, V. [October 1989], A History of the ARPANET, *ConneXions, The Interoperability Report*, 480 San Antonio Rd, Suite 100, Mountain View, California.

CHERITON, D. R. [1983], Local Networking and Internetworking in the V-System, *Proceedings of the Eighth Data Communications Symposium*.

CHERITON, D. R. [April 1984], The V Kernel: A Software Base for Distributed Systems, *IEEE Software*, 1(2), 19-42.

CHERITON, D. [August 1986], VMTP: A Transport Protocol for the Next Generation of Communication Systems, *Proceedings of ACM SIGCOMM '86*, 406-415.

CHERITON, D., and T. MANN [May 1984], Uniform Access to Distributed Name Interpretation in the V-System, *Proceedings IEEE Fourth International Conference on Distributed Computing Systems*, 290-297.

CHESSON, G. [June 1987], Protocol Engine Design, *Proceedings of the 1987 Summer USENIX Conference*, Phoenix, AZ.

CLARK, D. [December 1985], The structure of Systems Using Upcalls, *Proceedings of the Tenth ACM Symposium on Operating Systems Principles*, 171-180.

CLARK, D., M. LAMBERT, and L. ZHANG [August 1987], NETBLT: A High Throughput Transport Protocol, *Proceedings of ACM SIGCOMM '87*.

CLARK, D., V. JACOBSON, J. ROMKEY, and H. SALWEN [June 1989], An Analysis of TCP Processing Overhead, *IEEE Communications*, 23-29.

COHEN, D., [1981], On Holy Wars and a Plea for Peace, *IEEE Computer*, 48-54.

COMER, D. E. and J. T. KORB [1983], CSNET Protocol Software: The IP-to-X25 Interface, *Computer Communications Review*, 13(2).

COMER, D. E. [1984], *Operating System Design – The XINU Approach*, Prentice-Hall, Englewood Cliffs, New Jersey.

COMER, D. E. [1987], *Operating System Design Vol II. – Internetworking With XINU*, Prentice-Hall, Englewood Cliffs, New Jersey.

COMER, D. E. and D. L. STEVENS [1994] *Internetworking With TCP/IP Volume II – Design, Implementation, and Internals*, 2nd edition, Prentice-Hall, Englewood Cliffs, New Jersey.

COMER, D. E. and D. L. STEVENS [1993] *Internetworking With TCP/IP Volume III – Client-Server Programming And Applications, BSD socket version*, Prentice-Hall, Englewood Cliffs, New Jersey.

COMER, D. E. and D. L. STEVENS [1994] *Internetworking With TCP/IP Volume III – Client-Server Programming And Applications, AT&T TLI version*, Prentice-Hall, Englewood Cliffs, New Jersey.

COMER, D. E., T. NARTEN, and R. YAVATKAR [April 1987], The Cypress Network: A Low-Cost Internet Connection Technology, *Technical Report TR-653,* Purdue University, West Lafayette, IN.

COMER, D. E., T. NARTEN, and R. YAVATKAR [1987], The Cypress Coaxial Packet Switch, *Computer Networks and ISDN Systems,* vol. 14:2-5, 383-388.

COTTON, I. [1979], Technologies for Local Area Computer Networks, *Proceedings of the Local Area Communications Network Symposium.*

CROWLEY, T., H, FORSDICK, M. LANDAU, and V. TRAVERS [June 1987], The Diamond Multimedia Editor, *Proceedings of the 1987 Summer USENIX Conference,* Phoenix, AZ.

DALAL Y. K., and R. S. PRINTIS [1981], 48-Bit Absolute Internet and Ethernet Host Numbers, *Proceedings of the Seventh Data Communications Symposium.*

DEERING S. E., and D. R. CHERITON [May 1990], Multicast Routing in Datagram Internetworks and Extended LANs, *ACM Transactions on Computer Systems,* 8(2), 85-110.

DEERING, S., D. ESTRIN, D. FARINACCI, V. JACOBSON, C-G LIU, and L. WEI [August 1994], An Architecture for Wide-Area Multicasting Routing, *Proceedings of ACM SIGCOMM '94,* 126-135.

DENNING P. J., [September-October 1989], *The Science of Computing: Worldnet,* in American Scientist, 432-434.

DENNING P. J., [November-December 1989], *The Science of Computing: The ARPANET After Twenty Years,* in American Scientist, 530-534.

DE PRYCKER, M. [1993] *Asynchronous Transfer Mode Solution for Broadband ISDN,* 2nd edition, Ellis Horwood, UK.

DIGITAL EQUIPMENT CORPORATION., INTEL CORPORATION, and XEROX CORPORATION [September 1980], *The Ethernet: A Local Area Network Data Link Layer and Physical Layer Specification.*

DION, J. [Oct. 1980], The Cambridge File Server, *Operating Systems Review,* 14(4), 26-35.

DRIVER, H., H. HOPEWELL, and J. IAQUINTO [September 1979], How the Gateway Regulates Information Control, *Data Communications.*

EDGE, S. W. [1979], Comparison of the Hop-by-Hop and Endpoint Approaches to Network Interconnection, in *Flow Control in Computer Networks,* J-L. GRANGE and M. GIEN (EDS.), North-Holland, Amsterdam, 359-373.

EDGE, S. [1983], An Adaptive Timeout Algorithm for Retransmission Across a Packet Switching Network, *Proceedings of ACM SIGCOMM '83.*

ENSLOW, P. [January 1978], What is a 'Distributed' Data Processing System? *Computer,* 13-21.

ERIKSSON, H. [August 1994] MBONE: The Multicast Backbone, *Communications of the ACM,* 37(8), 54-60.

FALK, G. [1983], The Structure and Function of Network Protocols, in *Computer Communications, Volume 1: Principles,* CHOU, W. (ED.), Prentice-Hall, Englewood Cliffs, New Jersey.

FARMER, W. D., and E. E. NEWHALL [1969], An Experimental Distributed Switching System to Handle Bursty Computer Traffic, *Proceedings of the ACM Symposium on Probabilistic Optimization of Data Communication Systems,* 1-33.

FCCSET [November 1987], A Research and Development Strategy for High Performance Computing, *Report from the Executive Office of the President and Office of Science and Technology Policy.*

FEDOR, M. [June 1988], GATED: A Multi-Routing Protocol Daemon for UNIX, *Proceedings of the 1988 Summer USENIX conference*, San Francisco, California.

FEINLER, J., O. J. JACOBSEN, and M. STAHL [December 1985], *DDN Protocol Handbook Volume Two, DARPA Internet Protocols,* DDN Network Information Center, SRI International, 333 Ravenswood Avenue, Room EJ291, Menlo Park, California.

FLOYD, S. and V. JACOBSON [August 1993], Random Early Detection Gateways for Congestion Avoidance, *IEEE/ACM Transactions on Networking*, 1(4).

FRANK, H., and W. CHOU [1971], Routing in Computer Networks, *Networks,* 1(1), 99-112.

FRANK, H., and J. FRISCH [1971], *Communication, Transmission, and Transportation Networks,* Addison-Wesley, Reading, Massachusetts.

FRANTA, W. R., and I. CHLAMTAC [1981], *Local Networks,* Lexington Books, Lexington, Massachusetts.

FRICC [May 1989], *Program Plan for the National Research and Education Network*, Federal Research Internet Coordinating Committee, US Department of Energy, Office of Scientific Computing report ER-7.

FRIDRICH, M., and W. OLDER [December 1981], The Felix File Server, *Proceedings of the Eighth Symposium on Operating Systems Principles,* 37-46.

FULTZ, G. L., and L. KLEINROCK, [June 14-16, 1971], Adaptive Routing Techniques for Store-and-Forward Computer Communication Networks, presented at *IEEE International Conference on Communications,* Montreal, Canada.

GERLA, M., and L. KLEINROCK [April 1980], Flow Control: A Comparative Survey, *IEEE Transactions on Communications.*

GOSIP [April 1989], U.S. Government Open Systems Interconnection Profile (GOSIP) version 2.0, GOSIP Advanced Requirements Group, National Institute of Standards and Technology (NIST).

GRANGE, J-L., and M. GIEN (EDS.) [1979], *Flow Control in Computer Networks,* North-Holland, Amsterdam.

GREEN, P. E. (ED.) [1982], *Computer Network Architectures and Protocols,* Plenum Press, New York.

HINDEN, R., J. HAVERTY, and A. SHELTZER [September 1983], The DARPA Internet: Interconnecting Heterogeneous Computer Networks with Gateways, *Computer.*

INTERNATIONAL ORGANIZATION FOR STANDARDIZATION [June 1986a], Information processing systems — Open Systems Interconnection — *Transport Service Definition,* International Standard number 8072, ISO, Switzerland.

INTERNATIONAL ORGANIZATION FOR STANDARDIZATION [July 1986b], Information processing systems — Open Systems Interconnection — *Connection Oriented Transport Protocol Specification,* International Standard number 8073, ISO, Switzerland.

INTERNATIONAL ORGANIZATION FOR STANDARDIZATION [May 1987a], Information processing systems — Open Systems Interconnection — *Specification of Basic Specification of Abstract Syntax Notation One (ASN.1)*, International Standard number 8824, ISO, Switzerland.

INTERNATIONAL ORGANIZATION FOR STANDARDIZATION [May 1987b], Information processing systems — Open Systems Interconnection — *Specification of Basic Encoding Rules for Abstract Syntax Notation One (ASN.1)*, International Standard number 8825, ISO, Switzerland.

INTERNATIONAL ORGANIZATION FOR STANDARDIZATION [May 1988a], Information processing systems — Open Systems Interconnection — *Management Information Service Definition, Part 2: Common Management Information Service*, Draft International Standard number 9595-2, ISO, Switzerland.

INTERNATIONAL ORGANIZATION FOR STANDARDIZATION [May 1988a], Information processing systems — Open Systems Interconnection — *Management Information Protocol Definition, Part 2: Common Management Information Protocol*, Draft International Standard number 9596-2.

JACOBSEN, O. J. (PUBLISHER) [1987-], ConneXions, The Interoperability Report, *Interop Company*, a division of Softbank Exposition and Conference Company, Foster City, California.

JACOBSON, V. [August 1988], Congestion Avoidance and Control, *Proceedings ACM SIGCOMM '88*.

JAIN, R. [January 1985], On Caching Out-of-Order Packets in Window Flow Controlled Networks, *Technical Report*, DEC-TR-342, Digital Equipment Corporation.

JAIN, R. [March 1986], Divergence of Timeout Algorithms for Packet Retransmissions, *Proceedings Fifth Annual International Phoenix Conference on Computers and Communications*, Scottsdale, AZ.

JAIN, R. [October 1986], A Timeout-Based Congestion Control Scheme for Window Flow-Controlled Networks, *IEEE Journal on Selected Areas in Communications*, Vol. SAC-4, no. 7.

JAIN, R. [May 1992], Myths About Congestion Management in High-speed Networks, *Internetworking: Research and Experience*, 3(3), 101-113.

JENNINGS, D. M., L. H. LANDWEBER, and I. H. FUCHS [February 28, 1986], Computer Networking for Scientists and Engineers, *Science* vol 231, 941-950.

JUBIN, J. and J. TORNOW [January 1987], The DARPA Packet Radio Network Protocols, *IEEE Proceedings*.

KAHN, R. [November 1972], Resource-Sharing Computer Communications Networks, *Proceedings of the IEEE*, 60(11), 1397-1407.

KARN, P., H. PRICE, and R. DIERSING [May 1985], Packet Radio in the Amateur Service, *IEEE Journal on Selected Areas in Communications*,

KARN, P., and C. PARTRIDGE [August 1987], Improving Round-Trip Time Estimates in Reliable Transport Protocols, *Proceedings of ACM SIGCOMM '87*.

KENT, C., and J. MOGUL [August 1987], Fragmentation Considered Harmful, *Proceedings of ACM SIGCOMM '87*.

KLINE, C. [August 1987], Supercomputers on the Internet: A Case Study, *Proceedings of ACM SIGCOMM '87*.

KOCHAN, S. G., and P. H. WOODS [1989], *UNIX Networking*, Hayden Books, Indianapolis, IN.

LABARRE, L. (ED.) [December 1989], OSI Internet Management: Management Information Base, *Internet Draft <IETF.DRAFTS>DRAFT-IETF-SNMP-MIB2-01.TXT*, DDN Network Information Center, SRI International, Ravenswood, CA.

LAMPSON, B. W., M. PAUL, and H. J. SIEGERT (EDS.) [1981], *Distributed Systems - Architecture and Implementation (An Advanced Course)*, Springer-Verlag, Berlin.

LANZILLO, A. L., and C. PARTRIDGE [January 1989], Implementation of Dial-up IP for UNIX Systems, *Proceedings 1989 Winter USENIX Technical Conference*, San Diego, CA.

LAQUEY, T. L., [July 1989], *User's Directory of Computer Networks*, Digital Press, Bedford, MA.

LAZAR, A. [November 1983], Optimal Flow Control of a Class of Queuing Networks in Equilibrium. *IEEE Transactions on Automatic Control*, Vol. AC-28:11.

LEFFLER, S., M. McKUSICK, M. KARELS, and J. QUARTERMAN [1989], *The Design and Implementation of the 4.3BSD UNIX Operating System*, Addison-Wesley, Reading, Massachusetts.

LYNCH, D. C., (FOUNDER) [1987-], The NETWORLD+INTEROP Conference, *Interop Company*, a division of Softbank Exposition and Conference Company, Foster City, California.

MCNAMARA, J. [1982], *Technical Aspects of Data Communications*, Digital Press, Digital Equipment Corporation, Bedford, Massachusetts.

MCQUILLAN, J. M., I. RICHER, and E. ROSEN [May 1980], The New Routing Algorithm for the ARPANET, *IEEE Transactions on Communications*, (COM-28), 711-719.

MERIT [November 1987], Management and Operation of the NSFNET Backbone Network: A Proposal Funded by the National Science Foundation and the State of Michigan, *MERIT Incorporated*, Ann Arbor, Michigan.

METCALFE, R. M., and D. R. BOGGS [July 1976], Ethernet: Distributed Packet Switching for Local Computer Networks, *Communications of the ACM*, 19(7), 395-404.

MILLER, C. K., and D. M. THOMPSON [March 1982], Making a Case for Token Passing in Local Networks, *Data Communications*.

MILLS, D., and H-W. BRAUN [August 1987], The NSFNET Backbone Network, *Proceedings of ACM SIGCOMM '87*.

MITCHELL, J., and J. DION [April 1982], A Comparison of Two Network-Based File Servers, *Communications of the ACM*, 25(4), 233-245.

MORRIS, R. [1979], Fixing Timeout Intervals for Lost Packet Detection in Computer Communication Networks, *Proceedings AFIPS National Computer Conference*, AFIPS Press, Montvale, New Jersey.

NAGLE, J. [April 1987], On Packet Switches With Infinite Storage, *IEEE Transactions on Communications*, Vol. COM-35:4.

NARTEN, T. [Sept. 1989], Internet Routing, *Proceedings ACM SIGCOMM '89.*

NEEDHAM, R. M. [1979], System Aspects of the Cambridge Ring, *Proceedings of the ACM Seventh Symposium on Operating System Principles,* 82-85.

NELSON, J. [September 1983], 802: A Progress Report, *Datamation.*

OPPEN, D., and Y. DALAL [October 1981], The Clearinghouse: A Decentralized Agent for Locating Named Objects, Office Products Division, XEROX Corporation.

PARTRIDGE, C. [June 1986], Mail Routing Using Domain Names: An Informal Tour, *Proceedings of the 1986 Summer USENIX Conference,* Atlanta, GA.

PARTRIDGE, C. [June 1987], Implementing the Reliable Data Protocol (RDP), *Proceedings of the 1987 Summer USENIX Conference,* Phoenix, Arizona.

PARTRIDGE, C. [1994], *Gigabit Networking,* Addison-Wesley, Reading, Massachusetts.

PETERSON, L. [1985], *Defining and Naming the Fundamental Objects in a Distributed Message System,* Ph.D. Dissertation, Purdue University, West Lafayette, Indiana.

PIERCE, J. R. [1972], Networks for Block Switching of Data, *Bell System Technical Journal,* 51.

POSTEL, J. B. [April 1980], Internetwork Protocol Approaches, *IEEE Transactions on Communications,* COM-28, 604-611.

POSTEL, J. B., C. A. SUNSHINE, and D. CHEN [1981], The ARPA Internet Protocol, *Computer Networks.*

QUARTERMAN, J. S. [1990], *The Matrix: Computer Networks and Conferencing Systems Worldwide,* Digital Press, Digital Equipment Corporation, Maynard, MA.

QUARTERMAN, J. S., and J. C. HOSKINS [October 1986], Notable Computer Networks, *Communications of the ACM,* 29(10).

RAMAKRISHNAN, K. and R. JAIN [May 1990], A Binary Feedback Scheme For Congestion Avoidance In Computer Networks, *ACM Transactions on Computer Systems,* 8(2), 158-181.

REYNOLDS, J., J. POSTEL, A. R. KATZ, G. G. FINN, and A. L. DESCHON [October 1985], The DARPA Experimental Multimedia Mail System, *IEEE Computer.*

RITCHIE, D. M., and K. THOMPSON [July 1974], The UNIX Time-Sharing System, *Communications of the ACM,* 17(7), 365-375; revised and reprinted in *Bell System Technical Journal,* 57(6), [July-August 1978], 1905-1929.

ROSE, M. (ED.) [October 1989], Management Information Base for Network Management of TCP/IP-based Internets, *Internet Draft <IETF.DRAFTS>DRAFT-IETF-OIM-MIB2-00.TXT,* DDN Network Information Center, SRI International, Ravenswood, CA.

ROSENTHAL, R. (ED.) [November 1982], *The Selection of Local Area Computer Networks,* National Bureau of Standards Special Publication 500-96.

SALTZER, J. [1978], Naming and Binding of Objects, *Operating Systems, An Advanced Course,* Springer-Verlag, 99-208.

SALTZER, J. [April 1982], Naming and Binding of Network Destinations, *International Symposium on Local Computer Networks,* IFIP/T.C.6, 311-317.

SALTZER, J., D. REED, and D. CLARK [November 1984], End-to-End Arguments in System Design, *ACM Transactions on Computer Systems,* 2(4), 277-288.

SCHWARTZ, M., and T. STERN [April 1980], *IEEE Transactions on Communications,* COM-28(4), 539-552.

SHOCH, J. F. [1978], Internetwork Naming, Addressing, and Routing, *Proceedings of COMPCON.*

SHOCH, J. F., Y. DALAL, and D. REDELL [August 1982], Evolution of the Ethernet Local Computer Network, *Computer.*

SNA [1975], *IBM System Network Architecture – General Information,* IBM System Development Division, Publications Center, Department E01, P.O. Box 12195, Research Triangle Park, North Carolina, 27709.

SOLOMON, M., L. LANDWEBER, and D. NEUHEGEN [1982], The CSNET Name Server, *Computer Networks* (6), 161-172.

STALLINGS, W. [1984], *Local Networks: An Introduction,* Macmillan Publishing Company, New York.

STALLINGS, W. [1985], *Data and Computer Communications,* Macmillan Publishing Company, New York.

SWINEHART, D., G. MCDANIEL, and D. R. BOGGS [December 1979], WFS: A Simple Shared File System for a Distributed Environment, *Proceedings of the Seventh Symposium on Operating System Principles,* 9-17.

TANENBAUM, A. [1981], *Computer Networks: Toward Distributed Processing Systems,* Prentice-Hall, Englewood Cliffs, New Jersey.

TICHY, W., and Z. RUAN [June 1984], Towards a Distributed File System, *Proceedings of Summer 84 USENIX Conference,* Salt Lake City, Utah, 87-97.

TOMLINSON. R. S. [1975], Selecting Sequence Numbers, *Proceedings ACM SIGOPS/SIGCOMM Interprocess Communication Workshop*, 11-23, 1975.

WARD, A. A. [1980], TRIX: A Network-Oriented Operating System, *Proceedings of COMPCON,* 344-349.

WATSON, R. [1981], Timer-Based Mechanisms in Reliable Transport Protocol Connection Management, *Computer Networks*, North-Holland Publishing Company.

WEINBERGER, P. J. [1985], The UNIX Eighth Edition Network File System, *Proceedings 1985 ACM Computer Science Conference,* 299-301.

WELCH, B., and J. OSTERHAUT [May 1986], Prefix Tables: A Simple Mechanism for Locating Files in a Distributed System, *Proceedings IEEE Sixth International Conference on Distributed Computing Systems,* 1845-189.

WILKES, M. V., and D. J. WHEELER [May 1979], The Cambridge Digital Communication Ring, *Proceedings Local Area Computer Network Symposium.*

XEROX [1981], Internet Transport Protocols, *Report XSIS 028112,* Xerox Corporation, Office Products Division, Network Systems Administration Office, 3333 Coyote Hill Road, Palo Alto, California.

ZHANG, L. [August 1986], Why TCP Timers Don't Work Well, *Proceedings of ACM SIGCOMM '86.*

Index

Constants and numeric items

10Base-T 25, 558
1822 38
220 441
221 443
250 441
576 96, 558
802.3 20, 558
822 438, 446, 513, 558
9180 312

A

AAL 558
AAL1 310
AAL5 310
abort 205
absolute name 453
Abstract Syntax Notation 1 165, 453
accept system call 346
access control 475, 476
ACK 193, 558
acknowledgement 193, 208, 558
    ambiguity 211
    cumulative 208
    delayed 225
active 271
active monitoring 486
active open 201, 558
adapter 21, 26
adaptive bridge 31
adaptive retransmission algorithm 209

address 5, 51, 59, 384
    ARPANET 39
    Ethernet 28
    IP 60
    X.121 45
    X.25 45
    broadcast 29
    class 60
    class D 291
    hardware 20, 28
    internet 60, 73, 83
    mail 435, 438
    multicast 29
    network 20
    physical 28
    resolution 73, 74
    supernet 153
    unicast 29
address boundary 118
address lease 373
address mask 136, 558
address resolution 559
address resolution problem 74
Address Resolution Protocol 75
address-to-name translation 383
Advanced Networks and Services 44, 559
advertise routes 242
agent 449, 559
algorithm
    routing 116
    shortest path 246

alias
    mail 435
all hosts group 292
all hosts multicast 504
all nodes multicast 504
all routers multicast 504
alternative subtype (MIME) 444
ambiguity of acknowledgements 211
anonymous FTP 426, 559
ANS 44, 559
ANSI 559
ANSNET 44, 559
application program 179
area 280
ARP 75, 559
    encapsulation 79
    hack 142
    implementation 77
    protocol 73
ARPA 2, 37, 559
ARPA/NSF Internet 2
ARPANET 37, 559
ARPANET address 39
ARPANET port 38
ARQ 560
ASN.1 453, 467, 560
Assigned Numbers 560
Asynchronous Transfer Mode 36, 303
ATM 36, 303, 560
    NNI 304
    UNI 304
ATM Adaptation Layer 308, 560
ATMARP 316, 560
atomic assignment 459
attachment unit interface 21
AUI 21, 560
authentication 280, 475
authority zone 403, 560
authorization 475
automatic configuration 372
autonomous confederation 265
autonomous system 252, 560
autonomous system number 253
availability 475

B

backbone network 39, 560
backoff 27
base header 494, 561
base64 443
baseband 561
bastion host 481, 561
baud 561
BBN 37
Bellman 240
Bellman-Ford 240
Berkeley broadcast 561
Berkeley Software Distribution 6
Berkeley UNIX 6
best-effort delivery 27, 91, 291, 561
BGP 266, 561
big endian 69, 561
bind system call 339
BISYNC 562
block 479
BNC 562
BNC connector 24
BOOTP 136, 365, 366, 562
BOOTP protocol 365
bootstrap 365, 427
BOOTstrap Protocol 366
Border Gateway Protocol 562
bps 562
bridge 109, 562
    mail 437
broadband 562
broadcast 26, 152, 504, 562
broadcast address 62, 289
broadcasting 289
brouter 563
BSC 563
BSD UNIX 6, 563
buffer 180
bus 26
Butterfly 246
byte 29
byte order 69

C

capacity 28
carriage control 410
carrier sense 27
CCIRN 563
CCITT 39, 45, 164, 563
CDDI 32
cell 36, 308, 563
checksum 100, 126, 563
Chernobylgram 563
CIDR 154, 563
circuit switching 18
class A address 61
class B address 61
class C address 61
class D address 291
class of address 60, 563
class of name 390
Classless Inter-Domain Routing 154, 564
client 325, 326, 368
    example 357
client-server 325, 564
    see Volume III
CLNS 492
close 217
closing connections 217
clumping 226
cluster 503
coaxial cable 20
collision 27
colon hexadecimal notation 502
community 460
congestion 130, 214
congestion avoidance 215
congestion collapse 214
congestion control 203
congestion window 214
congestion window limit 214
connect system call 340
connected socket 340
connection 5, 192, 216, 306, 564
    closing 217
    reset 219
connection abstraction 199

connection endpoint 200
connection oriented 18, 36
connectionless 18, 91
connectionless service 91, 564
content type 443
context specific 463
control connection 422
control message 123
control packet 447
convergence 311
Copper Distributed Data Interface 32
core gateway 564
core router 235
cosmic significance 418
count to infinity 272
counter rotating 33
CRC 29, 564
CSMA 27
CSMA/CD 27, 564
CSNET 44
cumulative acknowledgement 208

D

DARPA 564
data availability 472
data field 29
data mark 414
data stream 201
data transfer connection 422
datagram 5, 91, 92, 564
    MTU 95
    UDP 181
    fragmentation control 98
    size 95
    time to live 99
    type of service 93
datagram format 92
datagram options 100
date service 328
DCA 37
DCE 565
DDCMP 565
DDN 37, 565
default route 233, 276

default router 115
Defense Communication Agency 6
delay 19
delayed acknowledgement 225
demultiplex 174, 565
designated router 280
destination port 180
destination unreachable 128
DHCP 365, 366, 372, 565
DHCP lease 373
DHCP protocol 365
dial-up IP 46
digest subtype (MIME) 444
Dijkstra shortest path algorithm 246
direct delivery 111
directed broadcast address 62, 565
distance metric 242
Distance Vector Multicast Routing Proto-
    col 297
DNS 8, 387, 467, 565
dn_comp procedure 354
dn_expand procedure 353
DO (TELNET) 415
do not fragment 98, 367
DOD 2
DOE 2
domain 565
domain class 390
domain name 383, 387
    pointer query 400
    recursive resolution 393
    server 391
    zone 403
Domain Name System 8, 383
domain name system 387
domain suffix list 400
domain type 390
DON'T (TELNET) 415
dotted decimal notation 65, 565
dotted hexadecimal 290
dotted quad notation 65
draft standard 516
dropping packets 129
DS3 44, 566

DTE 566
DVMRP 297, 566
dynamic configuration 372
Dynamic Host Configuration Proto-
    col 366, 372

E

e-mail
    see electronic mail
E.164 316, 566
EACK 566
echo
    GGP request/reply 245
    ICMP request/reply 127
    UDP request/reply 326
    UDP server 326
echo port 326
echo service 326
EGP 176, 254, 566
    message header 255
    neighbor 255
    neighbor acquisition 256
    neighbor reachability 257
    peer 255
    poll request 258
    protocol 249
    routing update 255, 259
    third party restriction 259
EGP2 264
EGP3 264
EIA 566
electronic mail 4, 433
    destination 435
    list 435
    spool 434
encapsulation 94, 566
    ICMP 125
    IP 94
    IP datagram 95
    RARP 85
enclosures 444
encoding type 443
encryption 475
end-of-packet bit 311

end-to-end   166, 168
endhostent procedure   355
endnetent procedure   355
endpoint   200
endprotoent procedure   356
endservent procedure   356
entension header   494
epoch date   328, 567
error reporting mechanism   124
escape   408
escape sequence   413
establishing a connection   216
ether   20
Ethernet   20, 567
    AUI   21
    CRC   29
    address   28
    broadcast   26
    collision   27
    data field   29
    frame   29
    host adapter   21
    host interface   21
    hub   25
    preamble   29
    repeater   30
    transceiver   21
    type   95
    type field   29
Ethernet meltdown   566
Ethernet multicast   290
exchanger (e-mail)   439
exec system call   338
exploder   435
exponential backoff   27
Exterior Gateway Protocol   254
exterior neighbor   254
exterior router   254
eXternal Data Representation   430, 567
extra hop problem   251

F

fair queueing   567
FCCSET   15, 567

FDDI   32, 567
    frame   35
    symbol   35
FDM   567
fetch-store paradigm   458
file descriptor   336
file server   326, 419, 567
file transfer   4, 421
File Transfer Protocol   421
filter   479
fingerd   330
finite state machine   219
firewall   471, 568
flat namespace   384, 568
flow   495
flow control   130, 201, 568
FLOW LABEL   494
Ford Fulkerson   240
fork system call   338
forwarding
    mail   435
fragment bit   98
Fragment Extension Header   498
fragmentation   95, 498, 568
fragmentation control   98
fragmentation needed   129
frame   29, 35, 164, 568
    self-identifying   30
FTP   65, 421, 467, 568
full duplex   193
Fuzzball   41
FYI   568

G

gated   279, 568
gateway   52, 109, 242, 254, 569
    VAN   45
    designated   280
    mail   437
gateway requirements   569
gateway-to-gateway protocol   242
Gbps   36
getdomainname system call   349
gethostbyaddr procedure   355

gethostbyname procedure 354
gethostent procedure 355
gethostname system call 348
getnetbyaddr procedure 355
getnetbyname procedure 355
getnetent procedure 355
getpeername system call 344
getprotobyname procedure 355
getprotobynumber procedure 356
getprotoent procedure 356
getservbyname procedure 356
getservbyport procedure 356
getservent procedure 356
getsockname system call 345
GGP 242, 569
GIF 443
gif 444
global Internet 2
global name 453
gopher 12, 465, 569
GOSIP 569
graceful shutdown 217

H

half duplex 193
hardware address 20, 28, 74, 569
HDLC 39, 164
header length field 93
HELLO 267, 569
hello (OSPF) 281
hello interval (EGP) 256
HELO 441, 569
HHS 2
hidden network 251
hierarchical addressing 145
hierarchical routing 145, 569
high-level name 384
historic 516
history 6
hold down 273
hop count 133, 242, 271, 569
hop count metric 271
HOP LIMIT 494
host 38, 570

host adapter 21
host interface 21
host requirements 570
host table 71
htonl procedure 351
htons procedure 351
hub 25, 570

I

IAB 8, 570
IANA 66, 516, 570
IBM token ring 46
ICCB 6, 570
ICMP 123, 124, 176, 570
    address mask 136
    checksum 126
    code 126
    destination unreachable 128
    echo request/reply 127
    encapsulation 126
    information request/reply 136
    message format 125
    message types 127
    parameter problem 134
    protocol 123
    redirect 131
    redirect message 131
    source quench 130
    subnet mask 136
    time exceeded 133
    timestamp 134
    type 126
IEEE 28
IEN 11, 570
IESG 10, 571
IETF 10, 570
    area manager 10
    working group 10
IGMP 289, 294, 571
IGP 269, 571
IMP 37
implementation
    see Volume II
InATMARP 319

indirect delivery 111
inet_addr procedure 351
inet_inaof procedure 352
inet_makeaddr procedure 352
inet_netof procedure 352
inet_network procedure 351
inet_ntoa procedure 352
infinity 373
infinity (small) 272
information request 136
information security 472
INOC 571
inside 477
integrated 420
integrity 475
interface 21
Interface Message Processor 37
interior
    router or gateway 267
interior gateway protocol 269
interior neighbor 254
internals
    see Volume II
International Organization for Standardiza-
    tion 571
International Telecommunications Un-
    ion 571
Internet 571
internet 50, 51, 89, 571
    address 60, 73, 83
    control message 123
    properties 51
    router 52
    routing table 113
internet access 476
Internet Activities Board 8
Internet address 571
internet address 74
    dotted decimal notation 65
Internet Architect 9
Internet Architecture Board 8
Internet Assigned Number Authority 66
Internet Assigned Numbers Authori-
    ty 516

Internet Control Message Protocol 124
Internet datagram 91
Internet draft 11, 12
Internet Engineering Notes 11
Internet Engineering Steering Group 10
Internet Engineering Task Force 10
internet firewall 476
internet gateway 52
Internet Group Management Proto-
    col 294
internet layer 167
internet management 447
Internet Network Information Center 66
Internet Protocol 89, 91, 571
    version 4 491
Internet Research Group 11
Internet Research Steering Group 11
Internet Research Task Force 10
internet router 52
internet routing 110
internet security 472
internet services 3
Internet Society 11, 572
Internet standard 516
Internet Task Force 8
Internet worm 37, 330, 572
internetwork
    see internet
internetworking 1
INTERNIC 11, 66, 384, 513, 572
interoperability 3, 572
interpret as command 413
interrupt 205
Inverse ARP 87
Inverse ATMARP 319
inverse query 400
IP 572
    address 60
    checksum 100
    data 100
    destination address 100
    dial-up 46
    encapsulation 94, 95
    header length 93

option code 100
precedence 93
protocol field 494
purpose 91
reassembly 96
record route 102
router 52
source address 100
source route 103
time to live 99
timestamp 104
type of service 93
version 93
IP address 60, 91, 572
    dotted decimal notation 65
IP datagram 92, 572
IP forwarding 110
IP gateway 242, 254
IP multicasting 291
IP next generation 492
IP options 100
IP router 109
IP routing 110
IP switching 110
IP-based technology 91
IP6 492
ipAddrTable 456
ipInReceives 456
IPng 492, 572
    see IPv6
IPv4 491, 492, 573
IPv6 492, 573
    broadcast 504
    cluster 503
    destination 495
    end-to-end header 500
    fragmentation 498
    hop limit 495
    hop-by-hop header 500
    multicast 503, 504
    path MTU 498
    payload length 495
    provider prefix 507
    source route 500

subnet prefix 507
subscriber prefix 507
unicast 503
version 495
IRSG 11
IRTF 10, 573
ISDN 573
ISO 163, 573
ISO model 163
ISOC 573
ISODE 573
iterative name resolution 393
ITU-TS 45, 164, 573

J

jpeg 444

K

k-out-of-n rule 246, 257
Karn's Algorithm 212, 573
Kbps 573
kerberos 487
Kramer 573

L

label 387
LAN 19, 574
LAPA 164
LAPB 39, 164
layering 159, 166
    ISO 163
    TCP/IP 165
layering principle 169
learning bridge 31
lease 373
level 1 574
level 2 574
level 3 574
limited broadcast address 62
linefeed 410
link-state 245
LIS 314, 574
listen system call 346

little endian 69, 574
LLC 312, 574
load balancing 280
local area network 19
local network broadcast address 62
logging 485
Logical IP Subnet 314
Logical Link Control 312
long haul network 19
longest-match 155
loopback 65
loose source routing 104
low-level name 384

M

MAC 574
machine status
    see ruptime
magic cookie 370
mail alias expansion 435
mail bridge 437, 574
mail destination 435
mail exchanger 390, 439, 574
mail exploder 435, 575
mail forwarding 435
mail gateway 437, 575
mail processing 435
mail queue 434
mail relay 437
mail spool area 434
mailbox address 435
mailing list 435
MAN 575
management agent 449
Management Information Base 450, 575
manual bypass 482
manual configuration 372
martians 575
maximum segment lifetime 219, 575
maximum segment size 206, 575
maximum transfer unit 95, 575
MBONE 300, 575
Mbps 575
metric transformation 265

MIB 450, 576
MIB-II 451
mid-level network 39
military network 6
MILNET 6, 37, 576
MIME 576
mixed subtype (MIME) 444
monitoring 485
Mosaic 469, 576
MOTIS 165
mrouted 298, 576
MSS 206, 576
MTP 440
MTU 95, 576
    datagram 95
multi-homed host 61, 576
multicast 289, 503, 504, 576
    all hosts 504
    all nodes 504
    all routers 504
multicast address 29
Multicast Backbone 300
multicast group 29
multicast kernel 298
multicast routers 291
multicasting 63, 290
multimode 304
multipart type (MIME) 444
multiplex 174
multiplicative decrease 214
Multipurpose Internet Mail Exten-
    sions 443
mutual trust 474

N

Nagle algorithm 226, 576
NAK 577
name 51, 59, 384
    abbreviation 399
    domain 383, 387
    recursive resolution 393
    resolver 391
name caching 395
name resolution 393, 577

name server 8
name-to-address translation 383
namespace partition 386
NAP 506, 577
NASA 2
National Institute for Standards and Tech-
    nology 454
National Science Foundation 39
NBS 454
neighbor 242
neighbor acquisition 255
neighbor router 254
NetBIOS 577
netstat 65, 333
network 18
    address 20, 59
    capacity 28
Network Access Provider 506
network byte order 577
Network File System 429
network information center 11
network interface 166, 167
network management 450, 577
network MTU 95
network security 472
Network Service Access Point 316
Network Service Provider 154
network services 4
network standard byte order 69
Network to Network Interface 304
network virtual terminal 408, 410, 424
next generation 492
NEXT HEADER 497
next hop 113, 117, 150
NFS 429, 577
NIC 577
NIST 577
NNI 304
NOC 37, 577
non-selfreferential 608
nonauthoritative 395
noncore router 235
nonrouting router 235
NSAP 578

NSAP address 317
NSF 2, 39, 578
NSFNET 7, 40, 578
nslookup 404
ntohl procedure 351
ntohs procedure 351
null 463
number of hops 242, 271
NVT 410

O

object identifier 453
OC3 578
octet 29
on-line access 420
Open SPF protocol 279
open standard 492
open system interconnection 1
open-read-write-close 336
Option Overload 379
options 100
Organizationally Unique Identifier 313
OSI 578
OSPF 267, 279, 578
OUI 313
out of band 205, 414
outside 477
overlapping segment problem 229

P

packet 18, 578
packet filter 467, 479
packet radio 47
packet switch 19
packet switching 18
Packet Switching Node 37
PAD 165
parallel subtype (MIME) 444
parameter problem 134
parent domain 394
passive 271
passive monitoring 486
passive open 201

Path MTU   498
PDN   45, 578
PDU   460
peer backbone networks   238
PEM   487, 578
permanent virtual circuit   306
PF_INET   337, 340
physical address   28, 74
piggybacking   193
PING   127, 138, 578
pipe   338
Point to Point Protocol   171
pointer query   400, 401
poison reverse   274
polling interval (EGP)   256
port   129, 326, 578
    ARPANET   38
PORT command (FTP)   427
port unreachable   186
positive acknowledgement   193, 578
PPP   171, 579
preamble   29
primary server   86
privacy   472, 475, 476
privacy enhanced mail   487
process   179, 326
promiscuous ARP   142, 579
proNET   46
proposed standard   516
protocol   3, 579
    ARP   73
    BOOTP   365
    DHCP   365
    EGP   249, 254
    GGP   242
    HELLO   267, 276
    ICMP   123
    IGMP   289
    IGP   269
    IP   89
    IPng   492
    IPv4   492
    IPv6   492
    Internet   89

    MTP   440
    OSPF   267, 279
    RARP   83, 84
    RIP   267, 270
    SMTP   440
    SNMP   450
    ST   492
    TCP   191, 198
    TELNET   408
    UDP   179, 180
    application   166
    data link   166
    datagram   179
    internet   166
    layering   159, 166
    network management   450
    port   180
    standards   12
    stream   191
protocol data unit   460
protocol family   159
protocol port   199, 221, 326, 579
protocol standards   8
protocol suite   159
provider prefix   507
proxy ARP   142, 579
pseudo header   182, 207, 506, 579
pseudo terminal   410
PSN   37
Public Data Networks   45
public key encryption   475, 579
PUP   579
purpose of IP   91
push   193, 221, 580
PVC   306

R

RARP   83, 84, 136, 580
RARP server   85
rcp   7
RDP   580
reachability   262
Read Only Memory   83
read request   428

read system call   343
readv system call   343
reassembly   96, 97, 311, 498, 580
reassembly timer   97
receiver SWS avoidance   224
recommended   516
record route option   102
recursive name resolution   393
recvfrom system call   344
recvmsg system call   344
redirect   131, 580
redirect message   131
reference model   163
regional network   39
relay
    mail   437
relay agent   373
reliable stream service   90
reliable transfer   193
remote login   4, 408
Remote Procedure Call   430, 480
repeater   30, 580
Request For Comments   11, 511
required   516
reset   219
resolving addresses   74
resolving names   393
resource records   398
res_init procedure   353
res_mkquery procedure   353
res_send   353
retransmission   193, 208, 209
retransmit   194, 208
Reverse Address Resolution Protocol   84
reverse path forwarding   152, 580
RFC   11, 511, 580
RFNM   38
ring   33
RIP   270, 580
RIP protocol   267
RJE   581
rlogin   416, 581
ROADS   153, 581
ROM   83

round trip sample   209
route   53, 59, 131, 581
route advertisement   242
routed   270, 298, 581
router   52, 109, 112, 131, 581
    designated   280
    exterior   254
    interior   254
    nonrouting   235
    stub   235
router hops   242
routing   91, 109
routing cycle   133
routing hierarchically   145
Routing Information Protocol   270
routing loops   239
routing table   113
routing update   243, 255, 259
RPC   430, 467, 581
RS232   581
rsh   416
RTO   581
RTT   582
ruptime   331

S

SACK   582
sample round trip time   209
SAR (ATM)   311
security   115, 471, 472
security perimeter   477
segment   201, 203, 582
segmentation   311
selective acknowledgement   582
self clocking   226
self-healing   33
self-identifying frame   30, 38, 312, 582
send system call   342
sender SWS avoidance   225
sendmsg system call   342
sendto system call   342
Serial Line IP   171
server   84, 325, 368
    RARP   85

example 359
file 326
primary 86
time of day 326
service
connectionless service 5
reliable stream service 5
reliable stream transport 191
unreliable packet delivery 91
SERVICE TYPE 494
setdomainname system call 349
sethostent procedure 355
sethostname system call 348
setnetent procedure 355
setprotoent procedure 356
setservent procedure 356
SGMP 464, 582
shortest path algorithm 246
Shortest Path First 245
signaling 306, 582
silly window syndrome 224, 582
Simple IP 492
Simple IP Plus 492
Simple Network Management Protocol 450
SIP 492, 582
SIPP 492, 582
size
datagram 95
sliding window 195, 583
SLIP 171, 583
slow convergence 272
slow-start 214, 215, 583
small infinity 272
SMDS 312, 583
SMTP 440, 583
SNA 583
SNAP 313, 583
SNMP 450, 467, 583
SNMPv2 450
SOA 583
sockaddr 340
sockaddr_in 340
socket 7, 337, 584

socket library 363
socket system call 337
soft-start 215
Sorcerer's Apprentice Bug 429
source port 180
source quench 130, 584
source route 103, 129, 500, 584
source route option 103
SPF 245, 584
split horizon update 273
spoofing 143
spooling 434
SPREAD 246
ST protocol 492
standard byte order 69
standard error 417
standard input 417
standard output 417
standardization 12
STD 584
stream 192
strict source routing 104
Structure of Management Information 452
stub network 484
stub router 235
subnet address 143
subnet addressing 584
subnet broadcast 152
subnet mask 136, 147, 150
subnet prefix 507
subnet route 143
subnet routing 149
subnet rule 149
subnetting 143
SubNetwork Attachment Point 313, 584
subscriber 506
subscriber prefix 507
subtype 443
supernet addressing 153, 584
supernetting 153
SVC 306
Switched Multimegabit Data Service 312

switched virtual circuit 306
SWS 584
SWS avoidance 224
symbol 35
symmetric 415
SYN 584
SYNCH 414
system call 336

T

T3 44, 585
tap 21
task 179
TCP 176, 191, 198, 585
    protocol port 221
TCP header 204
TCP protocol 191
TCP/IP 2
TCP/IP Internet 2
TCP/IP Internet Protocol Suite 585
TDM 585
TDMA 585
technology independence 5
telephone system 386
TELNET 65, 408, 424, 467, 585
TFTP 427, 585
thick Ethernet 24
thicknet 24, 585
thin-wire Ethernet 23, 24
thinnet 23, 24, 586
time exceeded message 133
time service 328
time to live 99, 133, 171, 291, 298, 395,
    494
time-of-day server 326
timeout 208, 209
timeout and retransmission 367
timer backoff 212
timestamp option 104
timestamp reply 135
timestamp request 135
TLI 363, 586
TLV encoding 501, 586
tn3270 418, 586

token 33
token ring 33, 46, 586
TOS 93, 586
TP-4 586
traceroute 138, 586
traffic class 496
trailers 586
transceiver 21, 586
transceiver cable 21
transient multicast groups 291
Transmission Control Protocol 191, 198
transparent access 420
transparent router 141
transparent service 408
transport layer 166
Transport Layer Interface 363
triggered updates 274
Trivial File Transfer Protocol 427
TRPB 298, 587
truncated reverse path broadcast 298
trust 474
trusted hosts 408
TTL 99, 298, 587
tunnel 298, 299
tunneling 45, 480, 587
twisted pair Ethernet 25, 587
two-stage oscillation 277
type field 29
type of name 390
Type Of Service 93
type of service routing 280, 587

U

UART 587
UCBCAST 587
UDP 176, 180, 587
    echo server 326
    encapsulation 183
    message format 181
    port 180
    protocol 179
    pseudo header 182
unacknowledged packet 196
unconnected socket 340

UNI 304
unicast 29, 503, 588
unicast address 290
universal assignment 186
universal communication service 59
universal interconnection 5, 50
universal time 105, 328, 588
unreachable destination 128
unreliable 91
unreliable packet delivery 90, 91
urgent data 205, 414, 418, 588
URL 588
user datagram 179, 181, 365
User Datagram Protocol 180
user level process 179
user process 326
User to Network Interface 304
UUCP 440, 588

V

VAN gateway 45
vBNS 44, 588
VCI 307
vector-distance 240, 588
very high speed Backbone Network Service 44, 588
virtual circuit 45, 192, 588
virtual circuit identifier 307
virtual path identifier 307
VPI 307
VPI/VCI 307, 588

W

WAN 19, 589
weak authentication 475
weakest link axiom 477
well-known address 291
well-known port 186, 221, 589
whole-file copying 420
wide area network 19
wildcard 346
WILL (TELNET) 415
window 196, 589

congestion 214
window advertisement 202
window size 196, 582
Winsock 335, 363, 589
wireless network 47
wiring 26
WON'T (TELNET) 415
working group 10, 589
World Wide Web 12, 465, 589
worm 37, 330
write 226
write request 428
write system call 341
writev system call 341
WWW 589

X

X 589
X-Window System 590
X.25 39, 45, 589
X.400 165, 589
X25NET 44, 589
XDR 430, 467, 590
XNS 107

Z

zero compression 502
zone of authority 403, 590

The Series Of Internetworking Books
from Douglas Comer and Prentice Hall

Internetworking With TCP/IP Volume I: Principles, Protocols, and Architecture   3rd ed., 1995, ISBN 0-13-216987-8

The classic reference in the field for anyone who wants to understand Internet technology, Volume I surveys the TCP/IP and describes each component. The highly accessible text presents the scientific principles used in the construction of TCP/IP, and shows how the components were designed to work together. It covers details of each protocol, including ARP, RARP, IP, TCP, UDP, RIP, OSPF and others.

Internetworking With TCP/IP Volume II: Design, Implementation, and Internals (with D. Stevens)   2nd ed: 1994, ISBN 0-13-125527-4

Ideal for implementors, Volume II continues the discussion of Volume I by using code from a running implementation of TCP/IP to illustrate all the details. The text shows, for example, how TCP's slow start algorithm interacts with the Partridge-Karn exponential retransmission backoff, and how routing updates interact with datagram forwarding.

Internetworking With TCP/IP Volume III: Client-Server Programming and Applications (with D. Stevens)
BSD Socket Version: 1992, ISBN 0-13-474222-2
AT&T TLI Version: 1993, ISBN 0-13-474230-3

Volume III describes the fundamental concept of client-server computing used to build all distributed computing systems. The text discusses various server designs as well as the tools and techniques used to build clients and servers, including Remote Procedure Call (RPC). It contains examples of running programs that illustrate each of the designs and tools. Two versions of volume III are available for the widely used BSD socket and AT&T TLI interfaces.

The Internet Book: Everything you need to know about computer networking and how the Internet works
Paperback: 1995, ISBN 0-13-151565-9
Study Guide: 1995, ISBN 0-13-188012-8
Book plus Study Guide: 1995, ISBN 0-13-400029-3

A gentle introduction to networking and the Internet, *The Internet Book* does not assume the reader has a technical background. It explains the Internet, how it works, and services available in general terms, without focusing on a particular computer or a particular brand of software. Ideal for someone who wants to become Internet and computer networking literate, *The Internet Book* explains the terminology as well as the concepts; an extensive glossary of terms and abbreviations is included. A separate *Study Guide* provides suggestions for readers, review questions, and exercises).

**To order from North America, contact your local bookstore,
call 1-515-284-6751 or send a FAX 1-515-284-2607
Outside North America, contact your Prentice Hall representative**